Arbitration Beyond Borders

Arbitration Beyond Borders

Essays in Memory of Guillermo Aguilar Álvarez

Edited by

Nigel Blackaby KC
W. Michael Reisman

Wolters Kluwer

Published by:
Kluwer Law International B.V.
PO Box 316
2400 AH Alphen aan den Rijn
The Netherlands
E-mail: lrs-sales@wolterskluwer.com
Website: www.wolterskluwer.com/en/solutions/kluwerlawinternational

Sold and distributed by:
Wolters Kluwer Legal & Regulatory U.S.
920 Links Avenue
Landisville, PA 17538
United States of America
E-mail: customer.service@wolterskluwer.com

ISBN 978-94-035-2380-4

e-Book: ISBN 978-94-035-2381-1
web-PDF: ISBN 978-94-035-2382-8

Editors

Nigel Blackaby KC is a partner in the international arbitration group of Freshfields Bruckhaus Deringer, which he led for eight years (2014-2022) in addition to his continued coleadership of the firm's Latin America practice. He was admitted as King's Counsel in 2020. He is Adjunct Professor of International Investment Law at the Washington College of Law, American University in Washington, D.C. and coauthor of the last four editions of *Redfern and Hunter on International Arbitration* (Oxford University Press 7th ed., 2022) and member of the editorial board of *Arbitration International*. He is a member of the Court of the Singapore International Arbitration Centre (SIAC) and formerly led the IBA subcommittee on investment arbitration. Nigel has appeared as counsel or arbitrator in over 100 international arbitration proceedings in English, Spanish, French and Portuguese under the auspices of the ICC, ICSID, LCIA, the AAA-ICDR and the Stockholm Chamber of Commerce with a particular focus on energy and natural resources (including as counsel in over fifty investment arbitrations).

W. Michael Reisman is Myres McDougal Professor Emeritus of Law at the Yale Law School (Connecticut) and has been Visiting Professor in Tokyo, Hong Kong, Berlin, Basel, Paris, Tel Aviv and Geneva. He has been elected to the Institut de Droit International and is a fellow of the World Academy of Art and Science and a board member of the Foreign Policy Association. He was President of the Arbitration Tribunal of the Bank for International Settlements, President of the Inter-American Commission on Human Rights of the Organization of American States, Honorary President of the American Society of International Law and Editor-in-Chief of the *American Journal of International Law*. He has served as arbitrator and counsel in many international cases and was presiding arbitrator in the OSPAR arbitration (*Ireland v. UK*) and arbitrator in the Eritrea/Ethiopia Boundary Dispute and in the Abyei (Sudan) Boundary Dispute.

Contributors

David Arias is a partner at Arias SLP. He was Chair of the IBA Arbitration Committee in 2016-2017 and, previously, chaired the Subcommittee on Conflicts of Interest that published the 2014 IBA Guidelines on Conflicts of Interest in International Arbitration. He was also President of the Spanish Arbitration Club in 2013-2017 and is currently Honorary President. David is a Professor of Procedural Law and Arbitration. He obtained his B.A. in Law, with Honors, and his Ph.D., also with Honors, from Universidad Complutense de Madrid (Spain).

Julien Cantegreil, Ph.D., a graduate of the Ecole normale supérieure, Yale Law School (Connecticut) and Sorbonne, is an educator, lawyer and entrepreneur. He is a former member of the Cabinet of the French Minister of Economics and Finance and Deputy General Counsel of KERING. He founded and manages the Space Situational Awareness company, SpaceAble, to help promote sustainability and efficiency in Low Earth Orbit operations.

Oliver Cojo is a partner at Arias SLP. He was Cochair of the young practitioners' group of the Spanish Arbitration Club in 2019-2020. Oliver is an Associate Professor of Arbitration at IE University (Spain). He holds a B.A. in Law and Business Management from Universidad de Valladolid (Spain) and an LL.M. from Maastricht University (the Netherlands).

María Inés Corrá is Cohead of the International Arbitration, Administrative Law and Economic Regulation areas at Bomchil, Argentina. She acts as counsel and international arbitrator. She is the President of the Arbitration & ADR Commission of ICC Argentina, member of the board of the Latin American Arbitration Association (ALArb), cofounder and leader of Women Way in Arbitration LatAm (WWA). She has an LL.M. in Administrative Law and is Professor of Arbitration and Mediation at the Universidad Torcuato Di Tella (Argentina) of Administrative Law at the Universidad de Buenos Aires and of Economic Regulation at the Argentine Catholic University (Argentina).

Yves Derains is a founding partner of Derains & Gharavi. He is the former secretary-general of the ICC Court, and honorary Chairman of the ICC Institute of World Business Law. He is coauthor of the celebrated work, *A Guide to the ICC Rules of Arbitration*, with Eric Schwartz, published by Kluwer Law International.

Rocío Digón is a legal consultant at White & Case LLP and holds a J.D. from Yale Law School (Connecticut) and an LL.M. from Leiden University (the Netherlands) in Public International Law. She has served as counsel in commercial and investment treaty arbitration under the rules of leading arbitral institutions, including ICSID, ICC and ICDR/AAA and has acted as sole arbitrator under the rules of the CAM.

Georgios Dimitropoulos is Associate Professor of Law and Associate Dean for Academic Affairs at HBKU College of Law. He holds an LL.M. and J.S.D. from Yale Law School (Connecticut), and has previously held positions at the University of Heidelberg (Germany), New York University School of Law and the Max Planck Institute Luxembourg. His publications have appeared, among others, in the *University of Pennsylvania Journal of International Law*, the *Washington Law Review*, the *Journal of International Economic Law*, and the *Journal of International Dispute Settlement*.

Juan Fernández-Armesto is a professional arbitrator. He was formerly Chairman of the Spanish SEC, Professor of Commercial Law at ICADE University (Spain) and partner of the law firm Uría Menéndez.

Horacio A. Grigera Naón is an independent international arbitrator and consultant on arbitration, business and international law matters. He is a former secretary-general of the International Court of Arbitration of the International Chamber of Commerce and the Director of the International Commercial Arbitration Center of the Washington College of Law, American University, Washington, D.C.

Juan Pablo Hugues is an international associate at Foley Hoag LLP, focused on litigious and advisory work on public international law matters for States. He also serves as Officer of the IBA. He holds a law degree from Mexico's CIDE and an LL.M. from Harvard Law School (Massachusetts).

Brian Jacobi is a lecturer in U.S. law at Université Clermont Auvergne. He was previously an associate in King & Spalding's International Arbitration team in the Houston office. Brian's practice focuses on complex investment disputes and commercial matters worldwide. He holds a law degree from Columbia University (New York) and a B.A. in Russian and Eastern European Studies from the University of Texas (Austin).

Nartnirun Junngam is Associate Professor of Law at the Faculty of Law, Thammasat University (Thailand), where he served as the Director of the International Law Centre from 2014 to 2016. He received his LL.B. (Hons) from Thammasat University (Thailand), and received his LL.M. and J.S.D. from Yale Law School (Connecticut). He has been a member of the Executive Council of the Asian Society of International Law and is also a reviewer of the *Asian Journal of International Law*. In 2019, Professor

Junngam was a visiting fellow at the Lauterpacht Centre for International Law at the University of Cambridge (England).

Edward G. Kehoe is the Managing Partner of King & Spalding's New York office, specializing in business arbitration and litigation. He is Cohead of its International Arbitration practice, and a member of the firm's ten-person management committee. Since 2007, Edward has been recognized in *Chambers USA* as one of the top lawyers in the field. A frequent writer and lecturer on international arbitration issues, Edward is a member of the Board of Editors of *Global Arbitration Review* and the Advisory Board of the Institute for Transnational Arbitration.

Aloysius (Louie) Llamzon is a partner at King & Spalding's international arbitration practice in Washington, D.C. and New York. He is Research Professor of Law at the Ateneo de Manila University School of Law (the Philippines), and was formerly Senior Legal Counsel at the Permanent Court of Arbitration in The Hague. He obtained A.B. and J.D. degrees from the Ateneo de Manila University (the Philippines), and LL.M. and J.S.D. degrees from Yale Law School (Connecticut). Guillermo Aguilar Álvarez was Louie's professor at Yale and colleague at K&S.

Fernando Mantilla-Serrano is a partner at Latham & Watkins. He is a member of the commission created by the Spanish Minister of Justice to draft Spain's arbitration act (Law 60 of 2003). He is a Fellow of the Chartered Institute of Arbitrators (CIArb) and member of the International Law Association (ILA), the Court of Arbitration of SIAC and the Governing Board of ICCA. He is admitted to the bars of Colombia, New York, Paris and Madrid. He holds a J.D. in Law and Economics—Pontificia Universidad Javeriana (Bogota); MCJ (LL.M.)—New York University (Fulbright Scholar); DEA in International Private Law and International Trade and DSU in EU Law—Université de Paris II.

Sara McBrearty is a senior associate on King & Spalding's International Arbitration team in the Houston office. She has acted as counsel in international and domestic arbitration proceedings held under the auspices of ICSID, ICC, AAA/ICDR, SIAC, HKIAC, ECT, CRCICA, JAMS and ad hoc cases under the Permanent Court of Arbitration and UNCITRAL Rules. Sara holds a law degree from the University of Texas School of Law.

Santiago Montt is CEO of Los Andes Copper Ltd and President of Minera Vizcachitas. He worked for BHP (2011-2021) as Vice President of Corporate Affairs for the Americas, VP Litigation (Global), VP Legal Brazil, and VP Legal Copper. He is Assistant Professor at Universidad de Chile Law School. He obtained his B.A.A. (Law) from Universidad de Chile, LL.M. and J.S.D. from Yale University (Connecticut), and M.P.P. from Princeton University (New Jersey).

Alexis Mourre is a member of the Paris Bar and an international arbitrator. He has served in more than 300 international arbitrations, both ad hoc and before most international arbitral institutions. Alexis is a past president of the ICC International

Court of Arbitration and the author of numerous books and publications in the field of international business law, private international law and arbitration law.

Jaime Olaiz-González is Professor of International Law, Constitutional Theory and American Jurisprudence at Universidad Panamericana Law School in Mexico City. Professor Olaiz received his law degree from Universidad Panamericana and his J.S.D.'15 and LL.M.'09 from Yale Law School (Connecticut). He was a Fulbright-García Robles Grantee. Professor Olaiz was Dean for the J.D. program at Universidad Panamericana (México) where he currently serves as Vice Dean for International Programs. He teaches, researches, and publishes on constitutional change, political transformations, international law, human rights, legal education, transitional justice, and constitutional adjudication.

Dirk Pulkowski is the Deputy Legal Adviser and Deputy Director of the Office of Legal Affairs at NATO Headquarters in Brussels. He previously acted as Senior Legal Counsel of the Permanent Court of Arbitration in The Hague. He holds a Doctorate in Law from Ludwig-Maximilians-Universität (Munich) and an LL.M. degree from Yale Law School (Connecticut). He has published widely in the fields of public international law, trade and investment law, and legal theory.

Brian M. Richardson is an assistant professor and the Jia Jonathan Zhu & Ruyin Ruby Ye Sesquicentennial Faculty Fellow at Cornell Law School (New York). At Cornell, Professor Richardson teaches Public International Law, Conflicts of Law, and Constitutional Law. His research concerns public and private international law and American public law.

Mikaël Schinazi is an associate at Gaillard Banifatemi Shelbaya Disputes and a visiting lecturer at Sciences Po Law School (Paris). A member of the New York Bar, he holds a B.A. *magna cum laude* with highest honors from Harvard University (Massachusetts), an LL.B. from the University of Cambridge (England), an LL.M. from Columbia Law School (New York), and a Ph.D. in Law from the Institut d'Études Politiques de Paris (Sciences Po). His book, *The Three Ages of International Commercial Arbitration*, was published by Cambridge University Press in 2022.

Eduardo Silva Romero is Professor Emeritus at Rosario University (Bogotá) and Professor of International Arbitration at Panthéon-Assas, Sciences Po, MIDS and Paris-Dauphine. He is the Chairman of the ICC Institute of World Business Law. He is an International Arbitration Partner at Dechert LLP.

Chan Leng Sun is Chartered Arbitrator and Senior Counsel at Duxton Hill Chambers, Member of SIAC Court of Arbitration and Member of ICC Commission on Arbitration and ADR.

Amnart Tangkiriphimarn is a faculty member at the Faculty of Law, Thammasat University (Thailand), where he teaches Arbitration Law and International Investment Law. He was a teaching assistant for the International Investment Law course co-taught by Professor Guillermo Aguilar Álvarez and Professor W. Michael Reisman at Yale Law

School (Connecticut) in 2016. Amnart was awarded the YLS Permanent Court of Arbitration Fellowship in 2017.

Albert Jan van den Berg is a partner at Hanotiau & van den Berg, Brussels. He also serves as Visiting Professor at Georgetown University Law Center (Washington, D.C.), and Tsinghua University School of Law (DPR China); Emeritus Professor, Erasmus University (the Netherlands); former President, International Council for Commercial Arbitration (ICCA) and Netherlands Arbitration Institute (NAI).

Scott Vesel is a partner at Three Crowns LLP, where he practices international commercial and investment arbitration. He is an adjunct professor at Georgetown University Law Center (Washington, D.C.) and previously served as an Attorney-Adviser at the U.S. Department of State.

Matteo M. Winkler is Associate Professor of Law at HEC Paris. He obtained a Ph.D. from Bocconi University (Italy) and an LL.M. from Yale Law School (Connecticut). Before joining HEC, he worked as a lawyer in Milan (Italy), specializing in international business transactions, litigation and arbitration. He has published, *inter alia*, in the *Business Law Review*; the *Journal of Law, Medicine and Ethics*; the *International & Comparative Law Quarterly*; and the *International Lawyer*. At HEC, he acts as Academic Director of CEMS and Cochair of the Diversity Committee.

Karim A. Youssef is the Founder, Chairman, and CEO of Youssef & Partners Attorneys, a prominent GAR 100 firm and a regional MENA leader in dispute resolution and international arbitration. He leads the international arbitration and international law practices at the firm. He has been ranked as a Star Individual in *Chambers & Partners* since 2016 and recognized as a Thought Leader in arbitration by *Who's Who Legal*. Karim is a prolific writer and speaker about contemporary issues in arbitration. Karim was educated at Yale Law School (Connecticut), Paris 1 (Sorbonne) and Cairo University Law School (Egypt).

Romain Zamour is a senior associate at Debevoise & Plimpton LLP, based in New York. His practice focuses on the resolution of international disputes, including through international commercial and investment arbitration, international litigation, and public international law processes. He is admitted to practice in New York and Paris.

Eduardo Zuleta is an independent arbitrator who has served as an arbitrator in commercial and investment treaty cases under the rules of the ICC, ICSID, UNCITRAL, LCIA, and ICDR, among others. He is Adjunct Professor of International Arbitration at Georgetown Law (Washington, D.C.), codirector of the ICC Alumni Group and member of the World Bank Sanctions Board. Mr. Zuleta formerly served as Vice President of the ICC Court of Arbitration and Copresident of the Arbitration Committee of the International Bar Association.

Summary of Contents

Table of Contents

Preface

All those who knew Guillermo (or Memo as his friends would call him) were immediately struck by his humanity, his patience and his sense of humor. He had a hunger for life, a deep love for his family and a passion for his work as a professor at Yale and as an arbitrator and practitioner. This passion caused him to push the boundaries of accepted wisdom and become a trailblazer both in his work at the ICC and later in the new world of investment arbitration.

At the ICC, he led the first Spanish-speaking team from the mid-1980s before becoming General Counsel, no doubt resulting in the domination of the ICC as a dispute resolution mechanism in Latin America. He can also rightly consider himself a founding father of investment arbitration through his work negotiating NAFTA Chapter 11 for Mexico from 1990 and later as counsel in many cases such as *GAMI v. Mexico, South American Silver v. Bolivia* or *Teinver v. Argentina*. His work in this field was not limited to acting as counsel, and he was an early arbitrator in seminal cases such as *Lanco v. Argentina* and *BG Group v. Argentina*, as well as being a constant contributor to the academic literature on the topic.

Each of us has our own special memories of Guillermo and how he impacted our lives. Associates remember his mentorship, his guidance as to how to find their place in the legal field, when to speak up and when not to do so. He taught them to value structure and well-drafted documents, and if there was anything that needed to be done, it had to be done to the best of one's ability. Each day had its daily challenge with tough questioning and debate. Others recall his ability to break down complex ideas into easily understandable concepts. All recall the generosity with which he gave his time to develop the next generation of international dispute lawyers.

As an arbitrator, he was known for valuing evidence over advocacy, always recalling that evidence had to be considered as a whole—hallmarks of a well-organized and probing adjudicator. If you appeared before Guillermo, you had to be well prepared and know the record. As counsel, he was a fierce opponent in the best sense of the word—always on top of the issues with novel arguments that kept the other party up well into the night looking for responses. But he was always ready to agree to sensible procedural accommodations and was scrupulously ethical in his approach at all times.

Guillermo was a man of many parts, but there was only one Guillermo. He did not have a separate teaching *persona*. As in his interactions in all his roles, his students were his peers. He liked and respected them, and they appreciated that they were in a collaborative learning process. His unique experience as a lawmaker let him see legal rules as artifacts designed to secure social and economic consequences. Thus, learning "the law" with Guillermo was only the beginning of his legal inquiry. As important were the effects of their practical application and whether alternative rules were called for. His experience as arbitrator let him appreciate and convey the critical importance of mastering the idiosyncratic facts of each case to identify the shared normative universe of the parties.

To continue his tradition of helping his students, the editors have agreed with Kluwer that any student who wishes to access a chapter of this book may do so free of charge by following a simple process. His legacy to students also persists through the ICCA-Guillermo Aguilar Alvarez Memorial Prize which is awarded biennially by ICCA to an individual under 40 who has written the best-published work on international dispute settlement over the preceding two years. In Mexico, a prize has also been established by the Arbitration Center of Mexico (CAM) in memory of Guillermo for works on arbitration published in Spanish.

In fond memory of his inspirational legacy, many of his friends and colleagues have generously contributed pieces to this work which pursue ideas dear to Guillermo and which he would have greatly enjoyed debating. Many of them reflect Guillermo as an "internationalist" as much at home in Paris and New York as in Mexico City. For that reason, this book permitted authors to submit in any of Guillermo's languages of Spanish, English or French. However, being a citizen of the world did not loosen Guillermo's links to his beloved Mexico – he was a true patriot who represented the very best of his country and its important contribution to international law.

Each of us impacted by Guillermo agrees that we should honor his life by practicing law ethically to the highest standards and upholding the rule of law while not forgetting to place family and friends above all.

Thank you, Guillermo, for your friendship and wisdom and all you taught us. You are sorely missed but your spirit lives on. This book is dedicated to your legacy and memory and to your beloved family Andrea, Claudio and Patricio.

General Editors:
W. Michael Reisman and Nigel Blackaby KC
Editorial Committee:
Cecilia Azar
Luis Alberto Aziz
Carlos Dávalos

CHAPTER 1

International Commercial Arbitration and National Courts: Reflections on a Complex but Indispensable Relationship

W. Michael Reisman & Brian M. Richardson

The key reason why national courts cannot serve as reliable international commercial fora derives from a failure of public international law: It has been unable to prescribe and effectively implement a clear allocation of judicial jurisdiction among the many territorial communities of the international system. In 1927, in the *Lotus* case, France and Turkey were unable to agree as to which of them should have jurisdiction to make and apply law to a collision at sea between their respective flag vessels. Their dispute was referred to the Permanent Court of International Justice, which held that:

> Far from laying down a general prohibition to the effect that States may not extend the application of their laws and the jurisdiction of their courts to persons, property and acts outside their territory, [international law] leaves them in this respect a wide measure of discretion, which is only limited in certain cases by prohibitive rules; as regards other cases, every State remains free to adopt the principles which it regards as best and most suitable.[1]

Public international law has not advanced much beyond this theory of "concurrent jurisdiction." In the International Court's *Arrest Warrant* case in 2002, only the joint Separate Opinion of Judges Higgins, Kooijmans and Buergenthal detected some tendencies *away* from what they called the *Lotus'* "laissez-faire" conception of jurisdiction. But even these judges still concluded that "the only prohibitive rule [on national courts' exercising their jurisdiction] is that *criminal* jurisdiction should not be

1. 1927 P.C.I.J. (Ser. A) No. 10, at 19.

exercised, without permission, within the territory of another State (emphasis added)."[2]

What does this mean for the resolution of international commercial disputes? Because international law has not resolved the allocation of judicial jurisdiction, either party to an international commercial transaction can—in the absence of a binding and effective agreement to the contrary—turn to that national court which it believes will be partial to it or whose law is believed to work to its advantage in a specific case. This jurisdictional co-archy actually militates *against* amicable settlement: in a situation of jurisdictional uncertainty, each party to a transaction has an incentive to hurry to its preferred courthouse before its counterparty gets to its own. The ethical principle is "do unto others *before* they do unto you (emphasis added)."

Happily, businesses operating transnationally can turn to international commercial arbitration, thanks to an intricately designed treaty-based system incorporating substantial and predictable governmental and intergovernmental support. So parties to a commercial transaction can agree, as part of their contract, to insert a clause committing them in the event of a dispute not to go to any court but to repair only to arbitration. And this arbitral clause will be enforced by national courts. Thanks to the treaty-based system, award enforcement, the ultimate test of international arbitration, is able to engage a number of different jurisdictions simultaneously or sequentially.

But no treaty arrangement is self-sustaining. It requires that the national institutions discharge their assigned roles appropriately. And that is one of the questions which this chapter addresses.

I WHEN NATIONAL COURTS PLAY A ROLE

In any arbitral system, states, through their courts, can play a role *before* the arbitration commences, *during* the arbitration, or *after* an award has been rendered. An arbitration clause between parties from different jurisdictions will only be effective if the courts in *all* relevant jurisdictions faithfully play appropriate supportive roles at each of these phases. At the outset, courts must predictably refuse to exercise judicial jurisdiction over the merits of the case—other than to compel the reluctant party to repair to arbitration. When this is performed properly, neither party will be able to jump the arbitration clause by shunting the dispute to a national court it believes will favor it. In the course of an arbitration—the middle phase—orders that a tribunal may issue, but which it cannot, on its own, enforce, may require the assistance of national courts—either at the place of arbitration or elsewhere. At the other end of the arbitral process, parties are unlikely to invest the time and money necessary to prosecute an arbitration if, upon award, either the loser cannot be compelled to comply where it has assets or courts in other jurisdictions do not honor the validity and finality of the arbitral decision.

An effective international system thus requires the coordination of many governments with different ideologies and different internal factions, constituencies, positions

2. Arrest Warrant of April 11, 2000 (*De. Rep. Congo v. Belg.*) 2002, ¶ 51.

in the international capital system, and agendas for addressing problems that are urgent but unique to themselves. The designers of the international system have had to adapt and channel the cooperation of the only agencies within those states which are readily available and to which private parties have ready access: *national* courts. Yet, these courts are the very entities which international arbitration seeks to avert. The working assumption in international arbitral design is that if national courts are able to delve too far into the substance of the disputes in the "before," "middle," or "after" phases of an arbitration, they may be prone to favor their own nationals over the invariably foreign counterparty.

The Convention on the Recognition and Enforcement of Foreign Arbitral Awards, signed in New York in 1958 ("New York Convention"), is the most comprehensive and successful effort to create the necessary coordination.[3] The Convention accomplishes this by locating its control mechanism in the very national courts of its states-parties while assigning to those courts distinctive roles.

The New York Convention is an avowed compromise. The Convention of 1958 was sparked by a more radical proposal, five years earlier, by the International Chamber of Commerce to create a new regime that would recognize "the idea of an international award, i.e. an award completely independent of national laws." Embracing, finally, the idea of party autonomy, the International Chamber of Commerce (ICC) sought a new international arbitration system that would see to it that such awards are "enforced in all ... countries in the same way."[4] Stated so starkly, the idea of an "award completely independent of national laws" was resisted. The United States delegation to the New York Convention, for example, characterized the ICC proposal as "the idea of a supranational law of arbitration which would free arbitral awards entirely from control by national laws."[5]

In the process of negotiating the New York Convention, the states-parties significantly moderated the ICC's proposed reform. In the end, the international system required a more attentive solution to the problem, as the Secretary-General phrased it, of defining "the conditions under which the competent authorities of a country where the recognition and enforcement of an arbitral award is sought may refuse to grant such a request." The system must account for the interdependent nodes of "judicial control." The system must attend, on the one hand, to the imperative national courts will feel to "refuse the enforcement of a foreign arbitral award if such action should be necessary to safeguard the basic rights of the losing party or if the award would impose obligations clearly incompatible with the public policy of the country of enforcement." And, on the other hand, the system must address the persistent worry that too much

3. Convention on the Recognition and Enforcement of Foreign Arbitral Awards, 21 U.S.T. 2517, T.I.A.S. No. 6997, 330 U.N.T.S. 38 [hereinafter "New York Convention"].
4. International Chamber of Commerce, Report and Preliminary Draft Convention adopted by the Committee on International Commercial Arbitration at its meeting of March 13, 1953, *reprinted in* 9 ICC Int'l Court of Arb. Bull. 32 (1998).
5. *Report of the U.S. Delegation to the United Nations Conference on International Commercial Arbitration*, 19 AM. REV. INT'L ARB. 91, 94 (2008).

"re-examination" by domestic courts would lead to a "full judicial examination of the award" that would defeat the principal purpose of the arbitration system.[6]

The New York Convention has now been adopted by more than 160 states[7] to the point that, for all intents and purposes, that part of the world which is most actively engaged in international commercial arbitration operates under its regime.[8] We will briefly review the structure of the New York Convention and then turn to several recent decisions by United States' courts which involve adjustments, for better or for worse, in our application of the Convention.

Under Article II of the Convention, the courts of any contracting state are obliged to compel arbitration if a party to a written agreement to arbitrate seeks to ignore arbitration by initiating ordinary litigation in its territory. But the national court is not obliged to compel arbitration if it finds that the arbitration agreement does not meet the personal and material requirements of the Convention, or if it finds the agreement "null and void, inoperative, or incapable of being performed."

The Supreme Court most recently addressed Article II in the *GE Power* case,[9] with mixed implications for international arbitration. Faced with a split in appellate authority about whether Article II's text (as implemented by Chapter 2 of the Federal Arbitration Act) displaces domestic contract-law doctrines, the court intervened to decide that the Convention does *not* displace state law on whether non-signatories may be bound by arbitration clauses. So, for example, the domestic doctrine of equitable estoppel can bind a non-signatory to an arbitration clause in an international agreement even though that third party has not expressly agreed "in writing" to the arbitration agreement. While Article II of the Convention, in the court's view, sets a "baseline"[10] definition of whose agreements to arbitrate must be enforced by domestic courts, it "does not prevent the application of domestic laws that are more generous in enforcing arbitration agreements."[11]

Because the court's analysis, and the Solicitor General's analysis as *amicus*, properly focused on the text and *travaux preparatoires* of the treaty, the *GE Power* decision can be squared with Article II. That article is generally opaque about "which non-signatories may be held to be parties to … an arbitration agreement,"[12] and, indeed, the preparatory work suggests that more elaborate treatments of Article II's "in-writing requirement" were considered and rejected.[13] One state-party went so far

6. Note by the Secretary-General, General observations and presentation of the objective of the Conference, E/Conf.26/2, ¶¶ 8-9 (March 6, 1958).
7. Status, 1958 Convention in the Recognition and Enforcement of Foreign Arbitral Awards, *available at* http://www.uncitral.org/uncitral/en/uncitral_texts/arbitration/NYConvention_status.html.
8. For early experiments, *see* Geneva Protocol on Arbitration Clauses (1923); Geneva Protocol for the Pacific Settlement of International Disputes (1924); Geneva Convention on the Execution of Foreign Arbitral Awards (1927).
9. *GE Energy Power Conversion France SAS Corp. v. Outokumpu Stainless USA, LLC*, 140 S.Ct. 1637 (2020).
10. *Ibid.*, at 1646.
11. *Ibid.*, at 1645.
12. 1 Gary Born, *International Commercial Arbitration* § 10.01, at 1406 (2014).
13. *See, e.g.*, Statement of Mr. Pscolka (Czechoslovakia), E/Conf.26/SR.12 at p. 6 (discussing various proposals regarding the "agreement in writing" provisions).

as to express the preference that "the question should be determined under the law of the State in which enforcement of the award was sought."[14] Because the Supreme Court was careful to ensure that the treaty was silent before too readily reaching for state law, *GE Power* properly situated domestic law in its interpretation of the architecture of the international arbitration system.

At the back end of the international arbitration process, the Convention provides in Article III for the recognition and enforcement of awards that qualify under its terms. The technical requirements referred to in Article III are set out in Article IV.[15] Some of the Convention's other technical conditions, which have the potential for allowing the national legal values of the enforcement forum to intrude into the decision of the arbitrator, do not exclude the application of national law altogether; instead, they insulate the foreign award from discrimination by requiring that whatever procedural conditions the national court imposes be no more onerous than those set out in the Convention.[16]

The most complex contribution of the Convention—the place where the rubber hits the road—is its intricate system of controlling against excesses in arbitration while, at the same time, controlling the control-agents themselves from exercising their powers overzealously. At this point, we must digress and consider a distinction that is central to international commercial arbitration.

There are two types of institutional control mechanisms. *Review* confines itself to an examination of the *extrinsic* features of the decision *process*: whether it was appropriately constituted, and whether it operated neutrally and within the limits of the powers which were assigned to it. By contrast, *appeal* examines the *intrinsic* quality of the decision: whether it was consistent with its governing law or policy. The question of whether a mode of review is sufficiently "summary" or "de novo" does not quite capture the relevant distinction. In a word, review asks if the *process* was right; appeal asks if the *decision* was right.

---

14. *Ibid.*
15. Article IV states:

> 1. To obtain the recognition and enforcement mentioned in the preceding article, the party applying for recognition and enforcement shall, at the time of the application, supply:
>   (a) The duly authenticated original award or a duly certified copy thereof;
>   (b) The original agreement referred to in Article 11 or a duly certified copy thereof.
> 2. If the said award or agreement is not made in an official language of the country in which the award is relied upon, the party applying for recognition and enforcement of the award shall produce a translation of these documents into such language. The translation shall be certified by an official or sworn translator or by a diplomatic or consular agent.

16. *See* New York Convention, Article III (providing that "[t]here shall not be imposed substantially more onerous conditions or higher fees or charges on the recognition or enforcement of arbitral awards to which this Convention applies than are imposed on the recognition or enforcement of domestic arbitral awards"). Similarly, section 208 of the United States Federal Arbitration Act provides that the law for domestic arbitration, in Chapter 1, "applies to actions and proceedings brought under this chapter to the extent that chapter is not in conflict with this chapter or the Convention as ratified by the United States." 9 U.S.C. § 208.

With respect to the architecture of the international commercial arbitration system, the proper locations of review and appeal must be allocated across the many domestic courts that might claim such competence. As control mechanisms, neither appeal nor review is superior to the other but, in different contexts, each registers a different legitimacy quotient. In a well-organized domestic legal system, the presence of reliable judicial hierarchies allows a *domestic* arbitral system designer to select either appeal or review as the control mechanism—a domestic policy favoring arbitration can elect a degree of judicial review based on its own policy preferences and legitimacy norms. Because comparable reliable judicial hierarchies are spotty and even largely absent in international and transnational settings, however, designers of international arbitral procedures have, until now, opted for review as a control mechanism, and, even then, they try to insulate their arbitral awards from overcontrol by *ipsos custodes*, the guards themselves.

As part of its review and enforcement system, the New York Convention establishes the grounds on which a national court may deny a request for recognition or enforcement: to be precise, under the Convention, a court "may ... only" deny the request for recognition or enforcement if specific conditions are met. The first paragraph of Article V[17] provides, in our paraphrase:

(1) Recognition and enforcement may only be refused:
  (a) if the agreement to arbitrate was invalid under the applicable law;
  (b) if the loser was not given proper notice of the appointment of the arbitrator or of the proceeding;
  (c) if the award exceeds the scope of the submission to arbitration;
  (d) if the composition of the tribunal or the procedure was not in accordance with the agreement or the law of the place of arbitration;

17. "1. Recognition and enforcement of the award may be refused, at the request of the party against whom it is invoked, only if that party furnishes to the competent authority where the recognition and enforcement is sought, proof that:

    (a) the parties to the agreement referred to in Article II were, under the law applicable to them, under some incapacity, or the said agreement is not valid under the law to which the parties have subjected it or, failing any indication thereon, under the law of the country where the award was made; or
    (b) The party against whom the award is invoked was not given proper notice of the appointment of the arbitrator or of the arbitration proceedings or was otherwise unable to present his case; or
    (c) The award deals with a difference not contemplated by or not falling within the terms of the submission to arbitration, or it contains decisions on matters beyond the scope of the submission to arbitration, provided that, if the decisions on matters submitted to arbitration can be separated from those not so submitted, that part of the award which contains decisions on matters submitted to arbitration may be recognized and enforced; or
    (d) The composition of the arbitral authority or the arbitral procedure was not in accordance with the agreement of the parties, or, failing such agreement, was not in accordance with the law of the country where the arbitration took place; or
    (e) The award has not yet become binding on the parties, or has been set aside or suspended by a competent authority of the country in which, or under the law of which, that award was made."

(e) if the award has not yet become binding on the parties, or has been set aside or suspended by a competent authority of the country in which, or under the law of which, that award was made.

In addition to these grounds, Article V(2) authorizes domestic courts to refuse to enforce awards for two additional reasons:

(2) Recognition and enforcement of an arbitral award may also be refused if the competent authority in the country where recognition and enforcement are sought finds that:
   (a) the subject matter of the difference is not capable of settlement by arbitration under the law of that country; or
   (b) the recognition or enforcement of the award would be contrary to the public policy of that country.

These two additional grounds contemplate that a national court petitioned to enforce an award may refuse to do so—even when the award does not run afoul of the procedural standards of the Convention—because enforcing the award would offend the court's views of its country's public policy. Notably, section 2(b) does not state the converse: it does *not* authorize a court to refuse enforcement because it appraises the *nonrecognition* or *nonenforcement* of an award to be the public policy of that country. Because, by definition, states that have signed and implemented the New York Convention have expressed a public policy favoring, in the abstract, a predictably functioning arbitration regime, the Convention's structure frames reviewing courts' discretion in an important way: courts that are parsing Article V(2)'s exceptions must decide, in the face of an award that is presumptively enforceable, that a public policy favoring enforcement of awards is overcome by contrary public-policy interests.

Understood in this way, the two additional grounds of Article V(2) function as safety valves. By anticipating what national courts would probably be pressed to do anyway under endogamous political-cultural pressures, the valves make adherence to the Convention more palatable and may actually increase the likelihood of enforceability. They accommodate, in the words of a participant in the drafting Conference, the "jurisdictional prerogatives of States," and the fact that "for psychological reasons the [national] courts could hardly be expected to have confidence in an award which had not been made within the framework of a legal system and whose form or substance did not respect the mandatory provisions of the law."[18] To be precise, the safety valves are not grounds for an appellate nullification of the award but rather grounds for discretionary nonenforcement upon *review*—a distinction which acquires importance in reference to the differences between primary and secondary forums in the scheme of the Convention. We will turn to this difference between fora, and its fascinating case law, in a moment.

---

18. Statement of Mr. Matteucci, United Nations Conference on International Commercial Arbitration, Meeting of May 21, 1958, E/Conf.26/SR.2 at p. 7.

The regime in Article V is both: (i) an enforcement mechanism; and (ii) an agreed policy statement about the proper scope and division of control by national courts over international commercial arbitration. Incorporating, as it must, the courts of many coarchical national jurisdictions for commercial disputes, it fills the gap left by international law's theory of "concurrent" jurisdictions.

For arbitration to be both an effective and a credible method of dispute resolution in an international context, a fine balance must be struck between arbitral autonomy on the one hand, and national judicial review, on the other. Too much arbitrator autonomy creates a situation ripe for moral hazard. If abuses occur—and the theory of moral hazard holds that some will in the absence of credible controls—national courts will become increasingly reluctant to lend the state power which they wield to a preferred, fast-track enforcement of privately rendered awards. But too extensive and searching a national judicial review—review that begins to slide into appeal—will transfer real decision power from the arbitration tribunal, selected by the parties in order to be nonnational and neutral, to a national court of one of the parties whose neutrality may appear to be—and may actually be—less reliable.

To navigate between these extremes, the Convention establishes two tiers of review competence, making a distinction between so-called primary or venue jurisdictions and "secondary" or "enforcement" jurisdictions. "Primary" jurisdictions are those in which the arbitration took place, "the arbitration state," or the state whose law governed the arbitration, the "law state." Both of these are selected by the parties directly or by a backup appointment authority, itself selected by the parties. "Secondary" or "enforcement" jurisdictions are any other jurisdiction subject to the Convention, in which recognition and enforcement of the award may be sought.

Parties to an arbitration agreement bargain over the designation of a primary forum, in part because the legal effects which the Convention assigns to the national judicial acts of the primary and secondary jurisdictions differ significantly. The secondary jurisdiction may only decide whether or not to *enforce* the award. There are not to be any "nullificatory" consequences for the decisions of secondary jurisdictions: they are limited to reviewing the question of enforcement, and only for their own forum; their decisions are to have no wider radial effects. By limiting the grounds for reviewing an award and its consequences, the Convention restrains secondary jurisdictions which a hypothetical loser of a valid award could search out in an effort to undo the award's intended effect, or to which an unscrupulous winner of a defective award could turn in order to win enforcement against the other party's assets. By contrast, the nullificatory (as opposed to nonenforcement) consequences of decisions in primary jurisdictions are designed to have a *universal* effect. That is why Article V(1)(e) sweepingly permits any court to refuse to enforce an award that has "been set aside or suspended by a competent authority of the country in which, or under the law of which, that award was made"—even if that award otherwise adheres to the Convention's other requirements. In terms of the dynamic of the Convention, once an award has been set aside in a primary jurisdiction, it is not, as we understand the architecture of the Convention, supposed to be enforceable anywhere else.

To put this more concretely, once a venue (or a governing law) is selected by the parties or by their designated backup authority, the Convention assigns to these jurisdictions a primacy with regard to the ultimate validity of the award. If an award is rendered, let us say, in Switzerland and is nullified under Swiss law, it is not supposed to be enforceable in any other jurisdiction. Otherwise, there would be no difference between primary and secondary fora, and, instead of finality, there would be an incentive to flout it. However, if the award is rendered in Switzerland but *enforcement* is refused in France, where the award debtor has property, the French judgment should have no effect outside of France. This limited nullificatory effect holds even if the French judgment explicitly based itself on a ground of nullity which would have nullified the award everywhere had it been applied by a primary jurisdiction. The award creditor is still free to seek enforcement in any other state party to the Convention. Given that the world economy is highly integrated and capital fluid, the ability to enforce an award worldwide is indispensable. The critical difference between primary and secondary fora, then, is the radius of effects of their respective decisions. As opposed to the nullification of the hypothetical award in Switzerland, which should have a universal effect, a putative "nullification" in France, while refusing enforcement, should have no effect beyond France.[19]

A coherent control theory and a proper interpretation of the texts *require* the national jurisdictions implicated in an arbitration to perform, as the case may be, a primary or secondary control function, in accordance with Article V. While that obligation is subject to local interpretation and, inevitably, some variation, the Convention's function as a common matrix for a shared control system would be defeated if there were no such core obligations. Indeed, assurances of the performance of primary control functions permit responsible agencies in the secondary states to lend their state power to the summary review of decisions that are privately effected in

19. A comparable primacy is given to the *law* under which the award was made. This means that if the award were rendered in Switzerland but under, let us say, Indian law (a mix of venue and law available to the parties), and the award were subsequently nullified by an Indian court, that nullification, like nullification in Switzerland, would terminate the validity of the award in all other jurisdictions.

This, while theoretically cogent, may be anachronistic in practice. In terms of the logic and dynamics of a control system, the assignment of primacy to a legal system whose law the parties had chosen but which has no other connection with the arbitration is puzzling. Control under the New York Convention essentially involves policing procedure and not substance. Thus, a United States federal district court in the Southern District of New York (SDNY) ruled, in interpreting the New York Convention, that "the competent authority of the country under the law of which, [the] award was made refers exclusively to procedural and not substantive law, and more precisely, to the regimen or scheme or arbitral procedural law under which the arbitration was conducted, and not the substantive law of contract which was applied in the case." *International Standard Electric Corporation v. Bridas Sociedad Anonima Petrolera Industrial y Comercial*, 745 F. Supp. 172, 178 (S.D.N.Y. 1990). The court explained its view as follows: "Any suggestion that a Court has jurisdiction to set aside a foreign award based upon the use of its domestic, substantive law in the foreign arbitration defies the logic both of the Convention debates and of the final text, and ignores the nature of the international arbitral system." *Ibid.*, at 177.

The SDNY's judgment appears to be a clarification, if not a refinement, of the control system, and the court's approach has been accepted by the Second Circuit Court of Appeals as well as district courts in other jurisdictions. *See, e.g.*, *Yusuf Ahmed Alghanim & Sons, W.L.L. v. Toys "R" Us, Inc.*, 126 F.3d 15, 20 (2d Cir. 1997); *Four Seasons Hotels & Resorts v. Consorcio Barr, S.A.*, 267 F. Supp. 2d 1335, 1346 (S.D. Fla. 2003), *Steel Corp. v. Int'l Steel Servs.*, 2006 354 F. App'x 689 (3d Cir. 2009).

another jurisdiction: the primary forum remains open should either party seek nullification.

The genius of the New York Convention is its adroit enlisting of national courts in the service of the arbitral system while, at the same time, confining the scope of their exercise of judicial power. Parties initially agree to a primary jurisdiction for their arbitration in order to avoid the potential bias of a particular national court which might have a predilection for its own national or affiliate. Limiting the radial effects of decisions in secondary jurisdictions provides an important protection for the arbitration "winner" (whether claimant or respondent), and thus vindicates one of the key reasons for going to international arbitration.

But arbitration is not an autonomous system, as we stated at the outset; its functioning is inextricably linked to the tolerance and active support of national courts. Because there is no international arbitral sheriff to enforce an award, those same national courts that can be skirted by the earlier phases of the arbitration process must then be recruited for enforcement once an award is rendered. And because the loser's national courts may be called on to enforce an award, and because one of the common purposes of arbitration is to allow the parties to stay out of each other's courts insofar as possible, it is necessary to design a system which confines the radial effects of the res judicata of these secondary enforcers to their own territory in order to avoid the possibility of the frustration of the entire arbitration. The winner will often bring an award to the loser's forum if, as is often the case, the loser holds substantial assets there, but because it is usually a secondary forum, the arbitration winner does not risk universal nullification in the loser's courts. Otherwise, there would be an ever-present danger that the loser might retreat to its own national courts, either to try to secure the nullification of an award it loathes or to revive an award it loves after it has been annulled by a primary forum.

But this control system must also allocate a primary jurisdiction to some domestic jurisdiction in order to anticipate the converse peril. If no forum enjoyed the nullificatory power with universal effect accorded to primary jurisdictions under the Convention, the winner of a defective award could fail to enforce the award in one forum yet move on to others in a serial effort to find a forum that will come to a different judgment. Such a process would predictably harass the other party and force it either to settle for a nuisance value factored by the number of jurisdictions in which it could be pursued or to expend great amounts of time and effort to block, and block, and block yet again enforcement efforts without ever securing a terminal annulment. Such undesirable effects are limited if only one primary jurisdiction has the capacity to nullify an award with effect *erga omnes*.

II UNITED STATES COURTS' STRUGGLE WITH ABUSE BY FOREIGN COURTS

A treaty depends, for its vigor, on its faithful application by the parties to it. United States courts have been supportive of international commercial arbitration, and the decisions have for the most part reflected an understanding of the theory of the New

York Convention and the role which its architecture assigns to national courts. That has not always been easy. The intricate control system in Article V of the Convention presupposes not only that the primary forum will be respected by secondary fora but that the primary forum will not abuse the power with which it has been entrusted by virtue of it being the venue of the arbitration. Alas, cases of abuse began to occur as the number of states available for selection as the arbitral venue expanded and more and more countries were selected as venues by the contracting parties. United States courts, finding themselves functioning as secondary jurisdictions under the Convention, began to wrestle with the consequences.

In *Chromalloy Aeroservices, Inc. v. Egypt*, a dispute between the American service provider, Chromalloy, and the Egyptian Air Force led to the cancelation by Egypt of the contract. Chromalloy exercised its right to arbitration in the contract, and both parties proceeded to appoint arbitrators. A lengthy arbitration ensued in Egypt. The tribunal awarded in favor of Chromalloy, which then applied to the District Court of the District of Columbia for enforcement of the award. Several weeks later, Egypt appealed to the Egyptian Court of Appeal seeking nullification of the award; ultimately, the Court of Appeal issued an order annulling the award.

Back in Washington, Judge Green observed that "there are no reported cases in which a court of the United States has faced a situation, under the Convention, in which the court of a foreign nation has nullified an otherwise valid arbitral award." Having found that, as a matter of U.S. law, the arbitration agreement precluded an appeal to Egyptian courts and that the Egyptian court, on the initiative of the Egyptian government, had nonetheless acted, she concluded that to recognize the decision of the Egyptian court "would violate this clear U.S. public policy." So the court, finding that the tribunal's award was valid as a matter of U.S. law, and that the United States court need not grant res judicata effect to the decision of the Egyptian court, recognized and enforced the nullified award. But as it was deciding in the posture of a reviewing court, it departed from Article V of the New York Convention.

Three years later, the Second Circuit Court of Appeal expressed more fidelity to Article V of the Convention in *Baker Marine v. Chevron*, holding "recognition of the Nigerian [annulment of the arbitral award] in this case does not conflict with United States public policy," even though the misbehavior of the Nigerian court was not unlike that of the Egyptian court in *Chromalloy*. And, in 2007, the D.C. Circuit adopted the *Baker Marine* holding in *TermoRio v. Elantra*. As the panel explained, "[t]he Convention does not endorse a regime in which secondary States (in determining whether to enforce an award) routinely second-guess the judgment of a court in a primary State, when the court in the primary State has lawfully acted pursuant to 'competent authority' to 'set aside' an arbitration award made in its country."[20]

As we have explained, a nullificatory decision by a competent court sitting in the primary forum *should* ordinarily have universal effect under one of the New York Convention's exceptions to the presumptive enforceability of arbitral awards. That is because some national court must be allocated the competence to arrest an unlawful

20. *TermoRio S.A. E.S.P. v. Electranta S.P.*, 487 F.3d 928, 937 (D.C. Cir. 2007).

award and to head off a vexatious game of whack-a-mole across potential enforcement jurisdictions. And, as we have explained, it is reasonable to vest such power in the primary jurisdiction(s) because, among other reasons, no party, who understood the Convention, would ordinarily agree to a venue that it feels would unreasonably discriminate against it. But where that assumption does not hold, and the government of the primary forum or its privies is also a party to an arbitration, one reasonably entertains considerably less confidence that the primary forum will comport itself neutrally. And, at the extremes, it is conceivable in such a scenario that the primary forum might breach other fundamental requirements of the Convention system—such as its obligations to recognize and enforce its own arbitration agreements in its domestic courts—to the prejudice of its adversary in arbitration. In such circumstances, the difficult question is whether courts in secondary fora should take account of such improper behavior by the primary forum, or whether, instead, an annulment decision by the primary forum must entail nullification in all secondary fora. The Convention's text—which speaks in mandatory language when describing the duty to enforce awards ("shall recognize arbitral awards as binding and enforce them") in Article III, but permissive language in describing the Article V exceptions ("[r]ecognition and enforcement of the award may be refused")—does not disclose an obvious answer.

One important recent case from the Second Circuit Court of Appeals, *Commissa v. Pemex*,[21] illustrates this dilemma. In *Pemex*, the Second Circuit was asked to review a lower court's decision to enforce an arbitration award that was adverse to a state-owned Mexican enterprise. The award had been rendered pursuant to an arbitration agreement that denominated Mexico as the situs of arbitration and Mexican law as the applicable law (Mexico was thus the "primary forum," and, in accordance with our analysis of primary fora, only Mexican courts' judgments concerning validity and nonenforcement should have a radiative effect on enforcement decisions by courts in other states). But Mexico misbehaved. While the arbitration was proceeding, the Mexican legislature passed a statute making the Commisa-Pemex dispute nonarbitrable and drastically shortening the relevant statute of limitations from ten years to forty-five days. The state-owned enterprise then procured a domestic judgment annulling the arbitrators' award in light of the new domestic legislation, and brought that judgment to an American court to argue that the award was unenforceable under Article V(1)(e).

Strictly with respect to Article V's distinction between primary and secondary fora, Mexico's actions conformed to the understanding of the Convention that the Second Circuit explained in *Baker Marine*: a judgment in the primary forum annulling the award based on the nonarbitrability of the dispute under local law falls within Article V(1)(e). But the *Pemex* courts nevertheless conducted a stepwise New York Convention inquiry that escaped the primary forum's annulment.[22] First, pursuant to

21. 832 F.3d 92 (2d Cir. 2016).
22. The case also implicated the Inter-American Convention on International Commercial Arbitration ("Panama Convention"), which is materially identical to the New York Convention in all relevant respects.

Article III, the American court considered itself bound to presumptively "recognize arbitral awards as binding and enforce them." Second, only then "may" the court, pursuant to Article V, refuse enforcement if Mexico proved it had "been set aside or suspended by a competent authority" in the primary forum. In the Second Circuit's view, the New York Convention established that courts "*must* enforce an arbitral award rendered abroad unless a litigant satisfies one of the seven enumerated defenses; if one of the defenses is established, [courts] may choose to refuse recognition of the award (emphasis added)."[23] The special radiative effect that Article V(1)(e) ordinarily accords to decisions by the primary forum is diminished: the language of the Convention, which provides that enforcement "*may* be refused (emphasis added)" if an award is annulled by the primary forum, is ultimately permissive.

You will notice a certain question-begging *petitio principii* here, for by starting with Article III rather than Article V, the court presumed that the award was presumptively enforceable, and that it was the validity of the annulment by the primary forum that should be questioned. Faced with what American courts viewed as an effort by the primary forum to "violate[] basic notions of justice" by "appl[ying] a law that was not in existence at the time,"[24] the Second Circuit looked beyond the New York Convention to its own domestic law of judgments. That is to say, in lieu of the New York Convention inquiry, the court asked whether the primary forum's annulment decision should be treated as "conclusive" under its generic domestic choice-of-law principles regarding the effect of foreign judgments.[25] The domestic law of judgments provided, in turn, that foreign judgments are not conclusive where their enforcement would "offend the public policy of the state in which enforcement is sought."[26]

In sum, after postulating the presumptive validity of the award, the *Pemex* court engrafted onto Article V(1)(e)'s set-aside provision an exception to the exception: recognition may be refused only if the award has been set aside by a court of competent authority *and* that decision by the primary forum does not violate the public policy of the secondary forum. There is, of course, a public-policy exception in the New York Convention, but as we have explained, it appears as one of Article V(2)'s safety valves that allow courts to refuse recognition or enforcement of *an otherwise valid award* where enforcement "would be contrary to the public policy of that country." The Convention thus includes an express domestic-public-policy exception for award enforcement, but contains no such express exception regarding nullification judgments by the primary forum.

It is difficult to read a domestic-public-policy exception into the language of Article V without placing the distinction between primary and secondary fora at risk. Both the District Court and the Court of Appeals in *Pemex* were plainly sensitive to the departure from a strict reading of Article V. In an effort to unify prior case law, the District Court went so far as to say "*Chromalloy* remains alive, for both *Baker Marine* and *TermoRio* recognized that a district court should hesitate to defer to a judgment of

23. 832 F.3d at 106.
24. 832 F.3d at 100.
25. 832 F.3d at 106.
26. *Ibid.*

nullification that conflicts with fundamental notions of fairness." But recall the nightmare scenario evoked by the Second Circuit in *Baker Marine*: "if a party whose arbitration award has been vacated at the site of the award" could nonetheless "obtain enforcement of the award under the domestic laws of other nations, a losing party will have every reason to pursue its adversary with enforcement actions from country to country until a court is found, if any, which grants the enforcement."[27] *Pemex* poses the converse nightmare scenario, for here, it was a tainted *judgment* by a domestic court that was, thanks to Article V, claiming the right to enjoy worldwide effect.

As a matter of the New York Convention's architecture, the Second Circuit's public-policy exception mixed metaphors in reading the domestic law of judgments into the Convention's enforcement exceptions: the domestic law of judgments might be relevant if Mexico offered the judgment as conclusive proof of the legal question decided by the Mexican court (e.g., that the dispute was nonarbitrable under Mexican law or that the statute of limitations had run). But, under the Convention, that complex choice-of-law question is replaced instead with the question of whether the judgment *exists* and whether it was rendered by the right authority—that is, whether the "award ... has been set aside or suspended by a competent authority." Having offered duly authenticated proof that the judgment was issued by a competent court in the primary forum, Mexico satisfied the proof requirements of Article V(1)(e).

The D.C. Circuit, for its part, also transplants a public-policy exception from domestic conflicts-of-law precedents, but it sees its approach as requiring an especially strong showing: "[we] cannot enforce an annulled award on a mere showing that the annulment is erroneous or conflicts with the United States's public policy. Instead, we will set aside an annulment only if it violates this country's 'most basic notions of morality and justice.'"[28] Though the reference to "basic notions of morality and justice," and comity concerns typical of choice-of-law analyses, may make this public-policy review more exacting, the courts' doctrine is, in the end, a "narrow public policy gloss on Article V(1)(e)."[29]

The harder question for Mexico, and for our theory of the primary-secondary architecture of the New York Convention, is whether the Convention's repose of *some* margin of enforcement discretion in secondary fora (e.g., by using the word "may" or "may ... only" in framing Article V(1)'s exceptions to enforcement) is—or should be—wide enough to allow secondary fora to consider their *domestic* public policy in

27. *Baker Marine (Nig.) Ltd. v. Chevron (Nig.) Ltd.*, 191 F.3d 194, 197 n.2 (2d Cir. 1999) (quoting Albert Jan van den Berg, *The New York Arbitration Convention of 1958: Towards a Uniform Judicial Interpretation* 355 (1981)).
28. *Getma Int'l v. Republic of Guinea*, 862 F. 3d 45, 48-49 (D.C. Cir. 2017).
29. *See TermoRio S.A. v. Electranta S.P.*, 487 F.3d 928, 937 (D.C. Cir. 2007). *See also Thai-Lao Lignite (Thailand) Co. v. Gov't of Lao People's Democratic Republic*, 864 F.3d 172, 184 (2d Cir. 2017) ("In *Pemex*, we adopted this view of the scope of our courts' discretion under Article V(1)(e), concluding that refusal to recognize a foreign judgment nullifying an award is 'appropriate only to vindicate "fundamental notions of what is decent and just" in the United States.' Pemex, of course, found that in the 'rare circumstances' of that case it would not be an abuse of discretion to reject the demands of comity in favor of honoring public policy. *Ibid.*, at 111. But it nonetheless recognized a strong presumption in favor of following the primary jurisdiction's ruling") (internal citations omitted).

refusing to accord conclusive effect to a nullificatory decision by the primary forum. Can Articles III through V be read so that courts must enforce awards that are set aside by a competent primary forum if they decide that *non*enforcement of a nullified award would conflict with public policy? And how could this be done without bringing the structure of Article V toppling down?

In our thinking, the discretion reposed in secondary fora by Article V mimics a public-policy exception of a highly disciplined kind. Where, as in *Pemex*, a primary forum's annulment or nonenforcement decisions give a secondary forum reason to think that the primary forum's actions departed from the Convention's overarching norms, secondary fora will have increased discretion to depart from the primary forum's decision in their Article V analysis. As relevant here, the Convention's overarching norms include the allocation of competence between primary and secondary fora; the duty to recognize arbitration agreements; the duty to compel parties to arbitration; the duty of nondiscrimination against foreign awards during recognition and enforcement; and the presumption of enforceability. Each of these norms is found in the text, and represents a complex compromise between states-parties with quite different normative priorities.

Because the facts of *Pemex* disproved the assumption that parties to international arbitration agreements will ordinarily avoid primary fora that are likely to prejudice only one of them, it thus gives us occasion to observe a case in which a primary forum may have breached its duty of nondiscrimination and duty to refer disputes to arbitration. On this view, the Second Circuit can be said to have preserved the Convention's cogency by allocating to the secondary forum the discretion to consider whether Article V(1)(e)'s set-aside exception requires nonenforcement on the facts of that case.

Some commentators, with the most recent draft of the Restatement of the United States Law of International Arbitration chief among them, have taken a different tack in response to the *Pemex* problem. Instead of casting the problem posed by Mexico's set-aside judgment as a problem to be solved within the Convention's normative system, the Restatement instead fashions *Pemex*'s recourse to domestic choice-of-law principles into a "judgment-centric" approach. To that end, the Restatement proposes that courts should follow the typical Article V(1)(e) rule when called upon to enforce a set-aside judgment,[30] but subject to a critical exception: "[e]ven if a Convention award has been set aside by a competent authority, a court of the United States may recognize or enforce the award if the judgment setting it aside is not entitled to recognition under the principles governing the recognition of judgments in the court, or in other extraordinary circumstances."[31] The Restatement explains that "[c]onsistent with the approach taken in some federal appeals decisions, the Restatement view focuses on the foreign judgment of set-aside, testing it against the law of judgments of

30. Proposed Final Draft, Restatement (Third) U.S. Law of Int'l Comm. Arb. § 4.14(a) (2019) ("Upon request, a court may deny recognition or enforcement of a Convention award to the extent that the award has been set aside by a competent authority of the country in which, or under the arbitration law of which, the award was made").

31. *Ibid.* § 4.14(b).

the court where recognition or enforcement is sought. That jurisprudence alone will address many troubling fact patterns."[32]

While a domestic law-of-judgments approach to the *Pemex* problem is indeed generally applicable, the Restatement's "judgment-oriented" approach does not maintain the necessarily circumspect standards of review that underpin the Convention's distinction between primary and secondary fora. The Restatement instead contemplates that a country's domestic law of judgments will allow a court to overlook a set-aside in many circumstances: an annulment can be overlooked if, for example, it was rendered by a "judicial system that does not provide impartial tribunals or procedures compatible with the requirements of due process of law, or when the court did not have subject matter or personal jurisdiction. Additionally, nonrecognition is permitted but not required when the defendant in the proceeding did not receive notice of the proceeding in sufficient time to enable it to defend, when the judgment was obtained by fraud that deprived the losing party of an adequate opportunity to present its case, or when the cause of action ... on which the judgment was based was repugnant to the public policy of the enacting state or of the United States."[33] Stated so broadly, the Restatement's approach to primary forum competence comes close to embracing a public-policy exception of such great breadth that it may swallow the rule of the primary forum's set-aside competence.

When an international regime, such as international commercial arbitration, depends for its implementation on national courts for whom it provides controlling guidance and those national courts encounter a practice which the guidance had not foreseen, national courts should fashion a response by reference to the policies of the international regime that are implicit in its structure. They should not, instead, declare a lacuna and fill them by turning to national law. Especially for international commercial arbitration, which depends for its success on national courts respecting assigned limited functions, one state's noncompliance, as in *Pemex*, should not be repaired by states' "remedial" *renvoi* to their own conflicts-of-law jurisprudence or other analogous modes of domestic judicial review.

The difficulty in the Courts of Appeals' and the Restatement's approach is perhaps best illustrated in the less exotic cases that have come in the wake of *Pemex*. In a case called *Getma v. Republic of Guinea*, the District of Columbia Circuit faced the more typical scenario foreseen by the primary-secondary architecture of the Convention: an arbitration "loser" successfully annulled an award in the primary forum. The primary forum's vacatur followed repeated orders denying the arbitrators' requests for fee awards, and the arbitrators' eventual "'breach[of] their duty by deliberately ignoring the mandatory provisions' governing fees."[34] Although the primary forum's decision was without prejudice to the parties starting the arbitration anew, the

32. *Ibid.*, reporter's note d.
33. *Ibid.*
34. *Getma Int'l v. Republic of Guinea*, 862 F.3d 45, 48 (D.C. Cir. 2017) (internal quotation marks omitted).

"winner" instead shopped the now-vacated award around among enforcement jurisdictions in search of assets—the very mischief for which the Convention gives the primary forum special competence to act with universal effect.

Within the terms of the New York Convention, the D.C. courts' review of the *Getma* claimant's petition to enforce the now-vacated award could have been summary. On the facts of *Getma*, it is utterly consistent with the system's architecture for a "competent authority" to annul an award rendered by arbitrators who evaded the authority's supervision of fee arrangements, and for secondary fora to cite merely that fact in declining to enforce the award pursuant to Article V(1)(e). Basic notions of morality and justice, even those drawn from a jurisdiction's highly refined law of judgments, are immaterial to the New York Convention assessment. The District Court and the Court of Appeals were thus right to decline to enforce an annulled award—not, as the panel said, because the annulment failed to offend the "country's most basic notions of morality and justice"—but rather because the primary jurisdiction's nullification did not offend the New York Convention's normative architecture.

Unless a primary forum's nonenforcement or nullification decision offends the architecture of the Convention system itself, the Convention makes that forum's decision conclusive as to all secondary fora in the ordinary case. The alternative, taken to its extreme—i.e., that each secondary forum's public policy permits it to second-guess a nullification decision by the primary forum—undoes the Convention's necessary allocation of competences to the ruin of the system's functioning. It is a fine distinction, but one on which the effectiveness of the New York Convention may stand or fall.

CHAPTER 2

Anatomy of a Case Dealing with (Negative and Positive) Recognition Claims of Awards: Some Considerations on Legitimate Interest and Linked Awards

David Arias & Oliver Cojo

I INTRODUCTION

Guillermo Aguilar Álvarez was one of the leading exponents of international arbitration. He greatly contributed to the development of the institution in Latin America and elsewhere. This book is an expression of the arbitration community's gratitude for his contribution to our field, and it is therefore a privilege to be a part of it.

In this chapter, we discuss a litigation case connected to arbitration in which we participated as counsel for the respondent. The case was somewhat unconventional as it involved negative and positive recognition claims of awards. In particular, the claimants first sought a declaration from the Spanish courts that an award on jurisdiction issued in an arbitration seated in France could not be recognized in Spain. This was opposed by the respondent. Later, the claimants sought an identical declaration in relation to an award on costs issued in the same arbitration. The respondent not only opposed this latter negative recognition claim but also filed a positive recognition claim (as a counterclaim) seeking to have part of the relief of the award on costs recognized in Spain.

Negative recognition claims of awards give rise to a variety of issues. There are a handful of judicial decisions, books and articles that have discussed, for instance, whether these claims are possible under the New York Convention or under the applicable *lex fori*.[1] Our focus here is, however, on a more specific issue: the requirement of legitimate interest to bring negative recognition claims against awards. This issue, which we discuss in light of the aforesaid case, is the first focal point of the chapter. Although negative recognition claims of awards are rather unusual, the possibility that they become more common in the future is not to be ruled out due to the influence of legal instruments that explicitly allow for negative recognition claims of foreign judicial decisions, such as the Brussels I Regulation Recast or the Spanish Act on International Legal Cooperation in Civil Matters.[2]

The second focal point of the chapter is the counterclaim seeking to have recognized part of the relief of the award on costs and the Spanish Court's decision denying it. The basis of this denial was that the award on jurisdiction issued in the same arbitration was a premise to the award on costs, and, therefore, the latter award could not be given legal effect if the former had not been recognized. In our opinion, the decision is at odds with the New York Convention and deserves to be denounced in the hope of preventing similar rulings in the future. This is another reason to discuss the case in the present chapter.

Regarding the structure of the chapter, first, we provide a detailed summary of the case (II). Then, we illustrate how the lack of a legitimate interest may be a basis to oppose negative recognition claims (III). Finally, we explain why the absence of recognition of a prior linked award is not a ground to deny a positive recognition claim under the New York Convention (IV).

II PRESENTATION OF THE CASE

The case concerns a 2003 contract between a Spanish company and an African company (the 'ACo') for the development of a project in Africa (the 'Contract'). In 2012, the ACo initiated an arbitration against the Spanish company and its three shareholders (the 'Shareholders') based on the arbitration agreement included in the Contract.

The Shareholders raised objections to the jurisdiction of the arbitral tribunal, but the arbitral tribunal rejected them in a partial award issued in September 2015 (the 'Award on Jurisdiction'). The arbitral tribunal based its decision on French law because the seat of the arbitration was Paris, and the parties had always referred to that

1. Kronke, H., Nacimiento, P., Otto, D. & Port, N.C. (2010). *Recognition and Enforcement of Foreign Arbitral Awards: A Global Commentary on the New York Convention*. Alphen aan den Rijn: Kluwer Law International, pp. 133-135. Hussain, R. (2015). Abdullah v. M/S CNAN Group SpA: Negative Declaration Preventing the Recognition and Enforcement of Foreign Arbitral Awards. *TDM 12*(2). Retrieved from https://www.transnational-dispute-management.com/article.asp?key=2213. Gaillard, E. & Savage, J. (1999). *Fouchard Gaillard Goldman on International Commercial Arbitration*. Alphen aan den Rijn, The Netherlands: Wolters Kluwer/Kluwer Law International, pp. 921-922. Van den Berg, A.J. (1991). France No. 16, Acteurs Auteurs Associés – AAA SA v. Hemdale Film Corporation, Tribunal de Grande Instance [Court of First Instance], Paris, Not Indicated, 22 November 1989. *Yearbook Commercial Arbitration 16*, 543-545, pp. 543-545.
2. Brussels I Regulation Recast, 2012, Article 45. Act on International Legal Cooperation in Civil Matters, 2015, Article 42(2).

law when discussing competence. In particular, the arbitral tribunal applied the French doctrine known as 'critère de l'implication'. This doctrine, developed through case law, allows for the extension of an arbitration agreement to a third party if that third party was aware of the arbitration agreement and was directly involved in the execution of the contract containing it. The arbitral tribunal considered that these two requirements had been met in respect of the Shareholders and that they were, therefore, bound by the arbitration agreement contained in the Contract.

In mid-2016, the Shareholders submitted to the Spanish courts a negative recognition claim against the Award on Jurisdiction in which they sought a declaration that the award could not be recognized in Spain. They argued that the application of the French doctrine breached Spanish public policy since the Award on Jurisdiction declared that the arbitral tribunal had competence over the Shareholders, even though they allegedly never consented to be bound by the arbitration agreement unequivocally.

The claim was notified to the ACo in October 2017, which opposed it by raising various arguments. In particular, the ACo argued that, even under the hypothesis that awards could be the subject of negative recognition claims in Spain, the Shareholders lacked a legitimate interest to submit this kind of claim against the Award on Jurisdiction.

It is important to note that the arbitration continued while the negative recognition claim was pending to be notified to the ACo. In October 2016, the arbitral tribunal issued an award that released the Shareholders from any liability in relation to the subject matter of the dispute (the 'Award on Liability'). In April 2017, it issued another award on costs allocating the costs of the phase on jurisdiction to the Shareholders and the costs of the phase on liability to the ACo (the 'Award on Costs').

The Shareholders submitted another negative recognition claim against the Award on Costs, which was also based on the supposed absence of unequivocal consent by them to be bound by the arbitration. Further, the Shareholders argued that the Award on Costs was manifestly unreasonable considering that the Award on Liability had released them from liability. The ACo presented a submission in which it opposed this new negative recognition claim and counterclaimed seeking to have recognized in Spain part of the relief of the Award on Costs.

Both negative recognition claims and the counterclaim seeking recognition of the Award on Costs were ultimately decided together.[3] In particular, the negative recognition claims were denied because neither the Award on Jurisdiction nor the Award on Costs breached Spanish public policy. The counterclaim was also rejected on the basis that the Award on Costs could not be recognized without the prior recognition of the Award on Jurisdiction, which had not been requested.

3. ATSJ PV 277/2018.

III LACK OF LEGITIMATE INTEREST AS A BASIS TO OPPOSE A NEGATIVE RECOGNITION CLAIM

As explained above, the first point that this chapter intends to address is legitimate interest in light of the aforesaid case, where the lack of it was one of the arguments raised by the ACo to oppose the Shareholders' negative recognition claim against the Award on Jurisdiction.

In the following paragraphs, we first provide some clarifications about the nature of negative recognition claims (A) and about the meaning of legitimate interest (B). After that, we move on to explain the particularities of the argument raised by the ACo in the Spanish proceedings (C) and what the Spanish Court decided in this respect (D).

A Nature of Negative Recognition Claims: Merely Declaratory Claims

The term 'negative recognition claims' refers to claims seeking a declaration from a State's court that a foreign award cannot be recognized in that State. Therefore, they are neither performance claims nor constitutive claims, but merely declaratory claims.

Although it may be obvious to the reader, performance claims are those aimed at obtaining a ruling from the court ordering performance of some kind to the respondent (e.g., payment of an amount of money), and constitutive claims are those seeking a ruling that creates, transforms or terminates a right or legal relationship (e.g., termination of a contract). However, the goal of declaratory claims is less ambitious, as the relief sought is merely a court declaration.

This declaration may sometimes be a direct logical antecedent for ulterior relief, such as when a court is requested to declare that a contract has been breached by the respondent and, consequently, to order the respondent to pay damages to the claimant for any harm suffered due to the breach. However, the declaration does not always serve as antecedent for another relief; sometimes it is an end in itself. Claims seeking this type of declaration (e.g., negative recognition claims) are labelled as merely declaratory claims.

The aim of merely declaratory claims is essentially to create legal certainty as to a legal or factual situation. The benefit for the party seeking this kind of relief is therefore not as evident as when it comes, for instance, to a request for damages. This may raise doubts as to whether it is justified to entertain the courts and have public resources spent in cases where this relief is sought.

Furthermore, the declarations that may be made in relation to a legal relationship are virtually limitless. Consider, for instance, a contract for the delivery of certain materials. The potential declarations that could be sought in relation to this contract might include: that the materials have been delivered on a certain date; that they were supposed to be delivered by a prior date; that the materials have therefore been delivered late; that the seller has breached the contract; that the buyer was obliged to deliver the materials to a third party on a certain date as per a different contract; that it could not do so because of the breach; that, as a result, the buyer had to buy the same materials from another seller; that the price of this transaction was higher than that of the original contract; the list goes on.

This has traditionally raised concerns that declaratory claims could be submitted indiscriminately and end up flooding the court system with unnecessary proceedings.[4] That is why the introduction of this kind of claims has been accompanied by restrictions in various jurisdictions.[5]

In particular, proving legal interest was established as a prerequisite for a claimant to be entitled to seek declaratory relief from the courts in the codes passed in the middle of the nineteenth century in some territories of Germany and in the German Code of Civil Procedure of 1877.[6] This inspired equivalent provisions in Austria or Switzerland, although a more liberal approach has ultimately prevailed in the latter, where the prerequisite has moved from proving a legal interest to proving a legitimate interest, which encompasses not only legal but also factual interest.[7]

A claimant's entitlement to seek merely declaratory relief has also been limited to the showing of a legitimate interest in Spain, where the Constitutional Court has ruled that 'the admissibility of merely declaratory claims is conditional to the existence of an interest worthy of [judicial] protection'.[8] This notion (i.e., interest worthy of judicial protection) has to be understood as having the same meaning than the term 'legitimate interest', which is indeed used by the Spanish Constitution when establishing the fundamental right to access to court. It is also used in various provisions of the Spanish Act on Civil Procedure and in the Act on International Legal Cooperation in Civil Matters, which establishes that any claimant bringing a declaratory claim of exequatur must prove a legitimate interest.[9]

Common law countries have also established some restrictions in relation to declaratory claims once they started to be developed. In particular, the discretion of English judges to grant merely declaratory relief has been limited by case law, which generally accepts that kind of relief unless there is no real interest in terms of justice and utility.[10]

Although not strictly identical, the restrictions to declaratory relief in these jurisdictions are to a certain extent comparable.[11] Nonetheless, the case that is being dissected in this chapter was dealt with by the Spanish courts, where the restrictions imposed on merely declaration claims are based on the existence of a legitimate interest, as explained above. Furthermore, the scholars that have studied negative recognition claims of awards suggest that they should only be permitted when the

4. Kalisz, B. G.-K. vel. (2019). *The Legal, Real and Converged Interest in Declaratory Relief*. Alphen aan den Rijn, The Netherlands: Wolters Kluwer/Kluwer Law International, p. 13.
5. Leimgruber, S. (2014). Declaratory Relief in International Commercial Arbitration. *ASA Bulletin 32*, 469-473.
6. Kalisz, 2019, pp. 12-13.
7. Kalisz, 2019, pp. 13-15 and 35.
8. STC 210/1992 (*'la admisibilidad de las acciones meramente declarativas está condicionada a la existencia de un interés digno de tutela'*).
9. Act on International Legal Cooperation in Civil Matters, 2015, Article 54(1).
10. Kalisz, 2019, p. 71.
11. Leimgruber, 2014, pp. 472-473.

claimant 'shows a legitimate interest or need'.[12] That is why we focus on the concept of legitimate interest in the following section.

B The Concept of Legitimate Interest

Statutory law in the jurisdictions that establish legitimate interest as a prerequisite for the submission of declaratory claims does not define this notion. The concept has been developed casuistically by national courts over the years. The Swiss Federal Tribunal is the court that has possibly approached this issue in the most methodical manner by developing a three-pronged test that seeks to confirm that:

(i) there is an uncertainty stemming from a disagreement between the parties in relation to a right or relationship, which is generally evidenced by their assertions or protests;[13]
(ii) the uncertainty is no longer bearable by the claimant because its effect is such that it inhibits its economic freedom of choice, and it is not expected to be resolved in the near future;[14]
(iii) there is no other proper remedy to obtain equivalent relief (i.e., to settle the disagreement and put an end to the uncertainty).[15]

If these three steps are confirmed, then the claimant is considered to have a legitimate interest to bring a declaratory claim in Switzerland. Nonetheless, if the declaration sought is of a negative kind, courts, when assessing the existence of a legitimate interest, also consider the respondent's position by having to conduct proceedings at a time that may be inopportune.[16] Let us point out that the respondent in proceedings dealing with negative declaratory claims is supposed to be in the position of creditor, and, therefore, it generally bears the burden of proving that it indeed has a credit against its counterparty.

The Swiss Federal Tribunal test probably serves to adequately conceptualize legitimate interest, as it sets out its constitutive elements in a succinct and clear manner. Nonetheless, as the case analysed here concerns a negative recognition claim of an award brought before the Spanish courts, we should also explain what the Spanish courts and scholars understand by legitimate interest in this context. As we will see, the statements shaping their understanding resemble the Swiss test to a certain extent.

In particular, the Spanish Constitutional Court has identified legitimate interest as an 'interest in having the courts put an end to the lack of clarity about a legal relationship'.[17] In this regard, the Spanish Supreme Court has further specified that there needs to be a 'real controversy', so the existence of a legitimate interest is to be

12. Kronke, Nacimiento, Otto, & Port, 2010, p. 134.
13. Kalisz, 2019, pp. 19-20.
14. Kalisz, 2019, pp. 19 and 21-22.
15. Kalisz, 2019, pp. 19 and 22-24.
16. Kalisz, 2019, pp. 19 and 26-27.
17. STC 210/1992 (*'La acción meramente declarativa como modalidad de tutela jurisdiccional que se agota en la declaración de la existencia, inexistencia o modo de ser de una relación jurídica, no*

ruled out when the declaration simply seeks 'a mere opinion or advice' from the courts or when it concerns matters that are 'neither current nor effective' or 'future or hypothetical'.[18] This requirement is analogous to the first step of the aforesaid test establishing the need for an uncertainty as a result of a disagreement between the parties in relation to a right or relationship.

The Spanish Supreme Court has also asserted that there must be 'a dissatisfied right that aims to be protected by means of the claim'.[19] As for the Spanish Constitutional Court, it has declared that, for a legitimate interest to exist, issuing the declaration must produce 'a benefit or the elimination of a detriment that does not necessarily need to have an economic content'.[20] In a similar vein, scholars dealing with negative recognition claims of awards have associated the finding of a legitimate interest with the requirement 'to show an existing adverse impact of the arbitration award, such as a denial of rights or other use of the award by the award-holder'.[21] This requirement somehow relates to the second step of the Swiss test, although it possibly covers a broader range of situations because the positive effect derived from the declaration does not need to be of an economic nature, as seems to be the case in Switzerland.

C Grounds of the Argument Based on the Lack of Legitimate Interest of the Shareholders

Having clarified what legitimate interest means, we move on to explain the argument raised in our case by the ACo to oppose the negative recognition claim against the Award on Jurisdiction, based on the Shareholders' lack of a legitimate interest. For obvious reasons, this argument was essentially based on the understanding as to the meaning of legitimate interest developed by Spanish courts and scholars.

As explained above, according to this understanding, the declaratory relief sought must be aimed at putting an end to the lack of clarity about a legal relationship and must produce a positive effect for the claimant for a legitimate interest to exist. The existence of a lack of clarity or the fact that the declaration would put an end to it was not questioned by the ACo. The debate revolved around the second element: the positive effect for the Shareholders as a result of the declaration.

---

existe como tal si no se da una verdadera necesidad de tutela jurisdiccional cifrable en el interés en que los órganos judiciales pongan fin a una falta de certidumbre en torno a la relación jurídica de que se trate').

18. STS 2470/2010 (*'tal ejercicio se halla condicionado a que la acción esté justificada por: a) La existencia de una verdadera controversia: "Por ello, se entiende que no pueden plantearse «cuestiones no actuales ni efectivas, futuras o hipotéticas, o cuya decisión no tenga incidencia alguna en la esfera de derechos e intereses del actor; se requiere que exista un caso o controversia, una verdadera «litis», pero no cabe solicitar del Juez una mera opinión o un consejo»"'*).
19. STS 2470/2010 (*'Se precisa de la "existencia de un derecho insatisfecho, al que se trata de tutelar mediante el ejercicio de la acción"'*).
20. STC 164/2003 (*'relación material unívoca entre el sujeto y el objeto de la pretensión de suerte que, de estimarse ésta, se produzca un beneficio o la eliminación de un perjuicio que no necesariamente ha de revestir un contenido patrimonial'*).
21. Kronke, Nacimiento, Otto, & Port, 2010, p. 134.

The Shareholders attempted to argue that this was the case because the arbitration seated in Paris was still ongoing, with them as parties, and this circumstance was causing them serious harm since they were facing considerable legal expenses and devoting human and economic resources to the arbitration.

However, the ACo replied that the Spanish Court issuing the declaration sought by the Shareholders would have neither impeded the continuance of the arbitration nor released them from being a party to it. This could only be achieved with the annulment of the Award on Jurisdiction by the French courts. Applying the Swiss standard, it could be said that not only was there an alternative remedy but also the alternative remedy available was indeed the appropriate one for obtaining the sought purpose.

It is also important to note that, as explained above, the Award on Liability and the Award on Costs had already been rendered when the ACo opposed the negative recognition claim. Consequently, the arbitration had ended for the Shareholders at that time, and the argument that they raised to support the existence of a legitimate interest could no longer have any basis.

According to the ACo, the only positive effect that the negative declaration claim could have for the Shareholders was to avoid the recognition of the Award on Jurisdiction in the future. However, as ACo reminded the court, the Award on Jurisdiction was a declaratory award on jurisdiction that did not require the State's executive force to have its content enforced, so the ACo had no intention to try to have it recognized in Spain.[22] Further, using the negative recognition claim against the Award on Jurisdiction to torpedo the ACo's potential future attempts to enforce subsequent awards issued in the arbitration proceedings was unjustifiable. Therefore, the ACo argued that the Shareholders lacked legitimate interest.

D Decision of the Spanish Court on Legitimate Interest

Despite the above, in its decision, the Spanish Court rejected the allegation that the Shareholders lacked a legitimate interest to submit the negative recognition claim.[23]

As already explained, this ruling decided not only on the negative recognition claim submitted by the Shareholders against the Award on Jurisdiction but also on the negative recognition claim submitted later against the Award on Costs. The ruling analyses legitimate interest without detailing to which of the claims it is referring. Nonetheless, the lack of a legitimate interest was not an argument raised by the ACo to oppose the negative recognition claim against the Award on Costs, as the ruling itself points out. It is, therefore, to be understood that the analysis made by the Spanish Court in the ruling is in relation to the negative recognition claim against the Award on Jurisdiction.

---

22. Dunand, P. & Kostyska, M. (2012). Declaratory Relief in International Arbitration. *Journal of International Arbitration 29*(1), 2.
23. ATSJ PV 277/2018.

In particular, the ruling asserts that the claim is based on:

> a substantial, concrete and defined interest (legitimate interest) because it is unquestionable that the arbitral tribunal's decision affects them [the Shareholders] in a real and effective manner.[24]

The ruling further states that:

> the legal burden upon the claimants (legitimate interest) deserves protection and justifies the request for ex ante protection of a right that is understood to have been violated, by means of a direct formulation based on the causes to deny recognition, as merely resisting or opposing the request for recognition would not guarantee the protection of certain interests that, being legitimate, would not be sufficiently protected if their defense depended exclusively on the conduct of the counterparty.[25]

These statements seem to be based on the following ideas: (i) it is prejudicial for the Shareholders to be dragged into an arbitration if they have not given their consent to submit disputes to arbitration; (ii) this situation may result in a violation of their right to liberty based on party autonomy (Article 10 of the Spanish Constitution); and (iii) legal expenses and the human and economic resources used to defend themselves are the most notorious prejudices that may be caused by the situation.

The foregoing ideas are accurate, but it is difficult to infer from them how exactly the Shareholders would be affected by the Award on Jurisdiction and, most importantly, why the negative declaration sought by the Shareholders would end that impact. As explained above, the arbitration had already ended for the Shareholders when the Spanish Court issued its ruling and, in any case, the negative declaration would not have impeded the continuance of the arbitration nor released the Shareholders from being a party to it.

There are scenarios where there may be a legitimate interest in bringing a negative recognition claim against certain awards within the confines of Article V of the New York Convention. Nonetheless, it would seem difficult to argue that a legitimate interest exists when that kind of claim is addressed against an award on jurisdiction, as in this case. That is why we consider that the court should have explained more precisely why it considered that the Shareholders had a legitimate interest. Perhaps, a deeper analysis in this regard would have resulted in a different judgment. In any case, we fully respect the decision rendered by this Spanish Court, which is actually praised for its well-known pro-arbitration stance over the years.

---

24. ATSJ PV 277/2018 (*'un interés sustancial, concreto y definido (interés legítimo), al ser indudable que la decisión del Tribunal arbitral les afecta de forma real y efectiva'*).
25. ATSJ PV 277/2018 (*'la situación jurídica de gravamen en que se encuentran las demandantes (interés legítimo) es digna de protección y justifica la iniciativa de solicitar una protección anticipada de un derecho que se cree conculcado, mediante una formulación directa apoyándose en las causales de denegación, pues la postura de mera resistencia u oposición a la demanda de reconocimiento, no garantizaría la protección de unos intereses que, por ser legítimos, no estarían suficientemente tutelados si se hiciera depender su defensa, únicamente, de la conducta adoptada por la contraparte'*).

IV LACK OF RECOGNITION OF A PRIOR LINKED AWARD AS A BASIS TO OPPOSE A POSITIVE RECOGNITION CLAIM

We now move on to the second focal point of this chapter, where we aim to denounce that the Spanish Court's decision in relation to the counterclaim contravenes the New York Convention. The reason is that the Convention does not establish that the absence of recognition of a prior linked award issued in the same arbitration constitutes a ground to deny the positive recognition claim of an award, as the Spanish Court seems to understand.

For that purpose, we first explain the counterclaim brought by the ACo (A) and then scrutinize the decision ultimately rendered by the Spanish Court in that respect (B).

A ACo's Counterclaim Seeking Recognition of the Award on Costs

As a matter of introduction, the ACo made two preliminary observations in its submission that may be of interest to the reader: (i) the counterclaim had been filed to avoid a potential risk of preclusion given that some Spanish scholars suggest that the respondent has the burden to counterclaim if it has the chance to do so to avoid preclusion;[26] and (ii) it is perfectly possible to have only part of the relief of an award recognized.[27]

Having clarified those points, the ACo moved on to explain that the New York Convention only allows a contracting State to deny recognition of a foreign award if the party against whom recognition is invoked proves any of the grounds established in Article V.1 or if the competent court finds that the subject matter of the dispute is non-arbitrable or the award is contrary to public policy.

In that vein, the ACo indicated that none of the grounds of Article V.1 had even been alleged by the Shareholders in their negative recognition claim against the Award on Costs and that the subject matter of the dispute was clearly arbitrable. It further explained that, contrary to the Shareholders' assertion, the Award on Costs was not contrary to public policy. Let us remember here that the two arguments raised by the Shareholders to contend that the Award on Cost breached Spanish public policy were: (i) the supposed absence of unequivocal consent on the part of the Shareholders to be bound by arbitration; and (ii) the manifest unreasonableness of the Award on Costs in light of the Award on Liability.

On the one hand, the ACo explained that consent does not need to be explicit to be unequivocal and that, in this case, the arbitral tribunal had considered, by applying the French doctrine known as 'critère de l'implication', that the Shareholders were

26. De la Oliva Santos, A. & Díez-Picazo Giménez, I. (2001). *Derecho Procesal Civil. El proceso de declaración*. Madrid: Editorial Centro de Estudios Ramón Areces, p. 271. Méndez González, F.P. & Palao Moreno, G. (2017). *Comentarios a la Ley de Cooperación Jurídica Internacional*. Valencia: Tirant lo Blanch, p. 490.

27. Poudret, J.F. & Besson, S. (2008). *Comparative Law of International Arbitration*. London: Sweet & Maxwell, para. 955. Virgós Soriano, M. & Garcimartín Alférez, F.J. (2007). *Derecho Procesal Civil Internacional*. Litigación Internacional. Pamplona: Aranzadi, p. 568.

bound by the arbitration agreement contained in the contract because they had implicitly consented to it. The ACo also pointed out that the Spanish legal system extends arbitration agreements to non-signatories under circumstances that are very similar (and in some instances more exceptional) to those in the case at hand.[28]

On the other hand, the ACo clarified that the Award on Liability released the Shareholders from any liability in relation to the subject matter of the dispute, but this did not prevent them from having to bear part of the costs of the arbitration. It further indicated that the Award on Costs was perfectly reasoned, and it had simply applied the costs-follow-the-event rule and taken into account the conduct of the parties to allocate the costs of the phase on jurisdiction and the phase on liability to the losing party in each of them (i.e., the Shareholders and the ACo, respectively).

Therefore, the ACo concluded that the counterclaim seeking positive recognition of the Award on Costs had to be granted.

B Decision on the Counterclaim

In its decision, the Spanish Court found that it was indeed possible to have only part of the relief of an award recognized and that the Award on Costs was not contrary to Spanish public policy. However, it surprisingly accepted the Shareholder's thesis based on the idea that the Award on Jurisdiction needed to have been previously recognized for the Award on Costs to obtain recognition. In this regard, the court stated the following:

> [The ACo] cannot expect to be successful in the recognition of an award (No. 4) [Award on Costs] that derives from the former (No. 2) [Award on Jurisdiction] which has not been recognized by the court when rejecting the negative recognition claim nor is the subject of a positive recognition claim.[29]

The rationale seems to be that the Award on Costs 'is inseparably linked to' the Award on Jurisdiction, given that the payment of costs ordered in the former is based on the findings made in the latter. As a result, the Spanish Court could not 'give legal effect' to the Award on Costs 'if no legal effect has been given to its underlying premise', i.e., the Award on Jurisdiction.[30]

28. STS 3403/2005. STSJ CV 10330/2014. STSJ CV 3413/2015.
29. ATSJ PV 277/2018 ('*ADO no puede pretender tener éxito instando el reconocimiento del laudo (No.4) que deriva de aquél (No.2) que ni ha sido reconocido al desestimar este Tribunal la demanda de no reconocimiento, ni se ha instado su reconocimiento*').
30. ATSJ PV 277/2018 ('*para que el Tribunal arbitral pueda cumplir con su deber de liquidar gastos entre las partes (Laudo No.4), necesariamente debe conocer el resultado de las solicitudes respectivas de las partes y valorar la conducta de las mismas en el procedimiento arbitral (Laudo No.2), de suerte que la base y conexión del Laudo No.4 con el 2, no es tanto la declaración de competencia o incompetencia arbitral, pues tiene facultades para ello, es decir, para laudar, sino el éxito y/o fracaso de las respectivas pretensiones de las partes en el desarrollo del mismo, por lo que el Laudo No.4 está indisolublemente unido al Laudo No.2, no pudiendo otorgar efectos jurídicos al Laudo No.4 sin haber otorgado efectos jurídicos a su premisa, esto es, al Laudo No.2, respecto del cual, insistimos, ni se ha declarado su reconocimiento ni se ha instado el mismo*').

Considering the foregoing, the Spanish Court rejected the counterclaim and, therefore, denied recognition of the Award on Costs.

The Spanish Court did not mention in its ruling which ground of the New York Convention justified its decision. Consequently, the ACo submitted a request for clarification in this regard, which was, however, rejected by the court.[31] The foregoing is indicative of the lack of correspondence between the circumstance leading to the denial of recognition and any of the grounds contemplated in Article V of the New York Convention.

In fact, our opinion is that such correspondence does not exist. None of the grounds of Article V requires that, for an award to be recognized, a prior linked award issued in the same arbitration be previously recognized. Indeed, it would be odd to request recognition of such a prior linked award when that award rules on jurisdiction because, as explained above, these kinds of awards do not require the State's executive force to have their content enforced. Therefore, we respectfully consider that the decision on this point contravenes the New York Convention, and it is denounced here in the hope of preventing similar rulings in the future.

REFERENCES

Books and Articles

De la Oliva Santos, A. & Díez-Picazo Giménez, I. (2001). *Derecho Procesal Civil. El proceso de declaración*. Madrid: Editorial Centro de Estudios Ramón Areces.

Dunand, P. & Kostyska, M. (2012). Declaratory Relief in International Arbitration. *Journal of International Arbitration 29*(1), 1-18.

Gaillard, E. & Savage, J. (1999). *Fouchard Gaillard Goldman on International Commercial Arbitration*. Alphen aan den Rijn, The Netherlands: Wolters Kluwer/Kluwer Law International.

Hussain, R. (2015). Abdullah v. M/S CNAN Group SpA: Negative Declaration Preventing the Recognition and Enforcement of Foreign Arbitral Awards. *TDM 12*(2). Retrieved from https://www.transnational-dispute-management.com/article.asp?key=2213.

Kalisz, B. G.-K. vel. (2019). *The Legal, Real and Converged Interest in Declaratory Relief*. Alphen aan den Rijn, The Netherlands: Wolters Kluwer/Kluwer Law International.

Kronke, H., Nacimiento, P., Otto, D. & Port, N.C. (2010). *Recognition and Enforcement of Foreign Arbitral Awards: A Global Commentary on the New York Convention*. Alphen aan den Rijn: Kluwer Law International.

Leimgruber, S. (2014). Declaratory Relief in International Commercial Arbitration. *ASA Bulletin 32*, 467-489.

Méndez González, F.P. & Palao Moreno, G. (2017). *Comentarios a la Ley de Cooperación Jurídica Internacional*. Valencia: Tirant lo Blanch.

31. AATSJ PV 368/2018.

Poudret, J.F. & Besson, S. (2008). *Comparative Law of International Arbitration.* London: Sweet & Maxwell.

Van den Berg, A.J. (1991). France No. 16, Acteurs Auteurs Associés - AAA SA v. Hemdale Film Corporation, Tribunal de Grande Instance [Court of First Instance], Paris, Not Indicated, 22 November 1989. *Yearbook Commercial Arbitration 16*, 543-545.

Virgós Soriano, M. & Garcimartín Alférez, F.J. (2007). *Derecho Procesal Civil Internacional.* Litigación Internacional. Pamplona: Aranzadi.

Legislation

Act on International Legal Cooperation in Civil Matters. (2015). *Act 29/2015, of 30 July, on international judicial cooperation in civil matters.* Retrieved from https://www.boe.es/boe/dias/2015/07/31/pdfs/BOE-A-2015-8564.pdf

Brussels I Regulation Recast. (2012). *Regulation (EU) No 1215/2012 of the European Parliament and of the Council of 12 December 2012 on jurisdiction and the recognition and enforcement of judgments in civil and commercial matters.* Retrieved from https://eur-lex.europa.eu/legal-content/EN/TXT/PDF/?uri=CELEX:32012R1215&from=EN.

Case Law

Ruling of Basque Country High Court of Justice, 29 November 2018 (Roj: AATSJ PV 368/2018).

Ruling of Basque Country High Court of Justice, 7 November 2018 (Roj: ATSJ PV 277/2018).

Ruling of Valencia High Court of Justice, 5 May 2015 (Roj: STSJ CV 3413/2015).

Ruling of Valencia High Court of Justice, 19 November 2014 (Roj: STSJ CV 10330/2014).

Ruling of Spanish Supreme Court, 26 April 2010 (Roj: STS 2470/2010).

Ruling of Spanish Supreme Court, 26 May 2005 (Roj: STS 3403/2005).

Ruling of Spanish Constitutional Court, 29 September 2003 (STC 164/2003).

Ruling of Spanish Constitutional Court, 30 November 1992 (STC 210/1992).

CHAPTER 3

The Evolution of the Illegality Defense in Investor-State Arbitration: An Interpretation

Romain Zamour[*]

I INTRODUCTION

In recent years, the illegality defense has taken center stage in investor-State arbitration. This is perhaps unsurprising, given its potentially outcome-determinative character, and the examples of high-profile decisions fully dismissing claims on the basis of investor illegality. Numerous tribunals address the defense in detail, sometimes in separate decisions. Parties and tribunals can dedicate entire distinct phases of arbitrations to debate whether illegality occurred and if so what the consequences are. The law has also been in flux, and making sense of it is rendered more complex by the relative terminological ambiguity of the decided cases, and the difficulty in translating the holding of treaty cases into contract arbitrations, and vice versa. This chapter is an attempt at interpreting the evolution of the law governing the illegality defense in investor-State arbitration. The proposed interpretation delineates three phases in the history of the defense.

* It is a privilege to have known Guillermo Aguilar Álvarez, and to have been taught by him. He was a wonderful educator and mentor—benevolent, approachable, and generous and always the most perfect gentleman. I would like to thank him and Professor W. Michael Reisman, who together first taught me international investment law, and taught me to consider not just legal rules and principles, but also the policies underlying them; Dr. Aloysius (Louie) Llamzon, who through his verve and writings prompted my interest in the law governing the illegality defense, and continues to educate me on this subject; and Donald Francis Donovan and Natalie L. Reid, for the long conversations, sometimes debates, that we have had talking through this thorny issue, and for showing me how to be both rigorous and creative in crafting legal arguments. The views expressed in this chapter are mine alone. In particular, they do not represent the views of my firm, Debevoise & Plimpton LLP, or of any of its clients.

In the first phase, from about 2006 to 2013, the decided cases developed along two distinct axes: a chronological axis and a "cause of action" axis. Under the chronological axis, developed in treaty cases, tribunals dismissed claims on the basis of explicit legality requirements contained in bilateral investment treaties. The central proposition in this line of cases is that illegality at the time of the "making" of the investment leads to dismissal of claims for lack of jurisdiction; and illegality postdating the making of the investment and occurring during its operation or performance is a merits issue. Under the "cause of action" axis, developed principally in contract cases, but also present in certain treaty cases, tribunals dismissed claims as inadmissible when the claim or cause of action was itself based or founded on an illegal act. The tribunals used various notions to justify this result: international public policy (or transnational public policy), unclean hands, or various Latin maxims. But the principle was the same. In the contract cases, its application was straightforward, as the source of the claim or cause of action was the contract. In treaty cases, application of the principle was more ambiguous: the source of the cause of action did not necessarily need to be the original, initial investment, but it could be.

The second phase began with the issuance of the *Yukos v. Russia* award in 2014.[1] This decision reframed the illegality defense and merged the two separate axes under which it had developed to date, subsuming the "cause of action" axis under the chronological axis. First, the *Yukos* tribunal reinforced the chronological axis by finding, as a number of other arbitral tribunals had done in dicta before, that legality requirements, even if not explicitly included in an investment treaty, must be implied. Thus, the fundamental distinction between the making and the performance of the investment becomes universal, in treaty cases at least. Second, *Yukos* fully subsumed the "cause of action" axis under the chronological axis: it declared that there is no doctrine of "unclean hands" at international law, and interpreted the "unclean hands" treaty cases as implicit legality requirement cases. Thus, the law was simplified: illegality at the making of the investment prevents the exercise of jurisdiction; illegality during the performance of the investment goes to the merits; there is no separate doctrine of unclean hands. Following this landmark decision, tribunals designed legal tools to nuance this rather rigid chronological framework. This chapter discusses three of them: (*i*) the notion of the "making" of the investment was diluted and stretched into the past and into the future; (*ii*) the scope of international public policy, on which *Yukos* was silent, has been expanding; and (*iii*) tribunals have developed tools to address illegality on the merits without having to pass on unclean hands or international public policy issues.

Finally, this chapter discusses what might be seen as the premises of a third phase, characterized by a potential reemergence of the "cause of action" principle and the injection of proportionality considerations, enabling tribunals to reach more nuanced results through more nuanced reasoning. The premises of such a potential

1. *Yukos Universal Limited (Isle of Man) v. The Russian Federation*, PCA Case No. AA 227, UNCITRAL (1976), Award dated July 18, 2014 ("*Yukos* Award").

new phase are visible in the recent decision on jurisdiction in *Kim v. Uzbekistan.*[2] As of the time of writing, the final decision on the merits remains pending. Only time will tell if these premises will remain premises or will grow to become authoritative, controlling, principles governing the illegality defense.

II FIRST PHASE: THE DEVELOPMENT OF THE ILLEGALITY DEFENSE ALONG TWO AXES

A The Temporal Jurisdictional Axis: From *Fraport I* (2007) to *Metal-Tech* (2013)

In the investor-State dispute resolution provision of bilateral investment treaties ("BITs"), the State parties typically give open offers to arbitrate investment disputes with yet unspecified investors of the other State party. Upon commencement of the arbitration, the investor purports to accept one of these offers to arbitrate. To determine whether it has jurisdiction, the tribunal must determine whether the State's offer could indeed be accepted by the investor. In the treaty, the State parties limit their open offer to arbitrate, relying on various criteria: they only agree to arbitrate certain disputes with certain investors. Thus, among other things, the investor must demonstrate that it is a qualifying "investor" within the meaning of the treaty. It must also demonstrate that the kind of dispute it seeks to arbitrate is the kind of dispute the State party consented to arbitrate. Bilateral investment treaties typically refer to "investment disputes," or disputes relating to or concerning an "investment," as defined in the treaty. Thus, if there is no qualifying "investment" within the meaning of the treaty, there can be no "investment dispute," and the tribunal lacks jurisdiction.

Many bilateral investment treaties contain so-called legality requirements. They are phrased in different ways and can appear in different parts of the treaty. Typically, they appear in the definition of "investment," and provide in essence that the investment must be made "in accordance with the laws and regulations" of the host State.

It has been argued, with force, that this reference to the host State's laws "is surely nothing more and nothing less than recognition of the *lex situs* rule for the acquisition of ... tangible and intangible property rights," that is, the principle according to which "[t]he foreign national must have acquired an asset that is recognized by the host State's laws in a manner that is effective under such laws."[3] But that is not how the decided cases have interpreted such provision, finding instead that the "in accordance with the laws" clause implies that investments that are made in violation of the law of the host State are not "investments" within the meaning of the treaty.

2. *Vladislav Kim v. Republic of Uzbekistan*, ICSID Case No. ARB/13/6, Decision on Jurisdiction dated March 8, 2017 ("*Kim* Jurisdiction Decision").
3. Zachary Douglas, The Plea of Illegality in Investment Treaty Arbitration, *ICSID Review*, Vol. 29(1) (2014), pp. 155-186, at p. 173.

The first decision to pass on a "legality requirement" did so very briefly and in a dictum. In 2001, the *Salini v. Morocco* tribunal stated that the legality requirement in the Italy-Morocco BIT "refers to the validity of the investment and not to its definition" and added that the requirement "seeks to prevent the Bilateral Treaty from protecting investments that should not be protected, because they would be illegal."[4] The dictum was repeated in subsequent cases.[5] But the decision that perhaps did the most to inform the early jurisprudence on the interpretation of legality requirements came in 2007: the *Fraport v. Philippines* (*Fraport I*) decision.[6]

In that case, the relevant bilateral investment treaty—the Germany-Philippines BIT—provided that "[t]he term 'investment' shall mean any kind of asset accepted in accordance with the respective laws and regulations of either Contracting State."[7] The tribunal found that this and other provisions "are manifestly limitations *ratione materiae*."[8] According to the tribunal, "economic transactions undertaken by a national of one of the parties to the BIT had to meet certain legal requirements of the host state in order to qualify as an 'investment' and fall under the Treaty."[9] The requirement was said to be one of "compliance with the law of the host state."[10]

Having found that the investor had violated Philippine law by entering into a secret shareholding agreement at the time of the making of the investment, in order to circumvent the requirements of the foreign ownership and control legislation known as the Anti-Dummy Law, the *Fraport I* tribunal concluded that "[b]ecause there is no 'investment in accordance with law,' the Tribunal lacks jurisdiction *ratione materiae*."[11]

In dicta, the tribunal also addressed the argument that this requirement of compliance with the law of the host State applied throughout the life of the investment. It emphasized the special status of the "initiation" of the investment, opposing it to "the course of the investment":

> The language of both Articles 1 and 2 of the BIT emphasizes the *initiation* of the investment. Moreover the effective operation of the BIT regime would appear to require that jurisdictional compliance be limited to the initiation of the investment. If, at the time of the initiation of the investment, there has been compliance with the law of the host state, allegations by the host state of violations of its law in the

4. *Salini Costruttori S.P.A. v. Kingdom of Morocco*, ICSID Case No. ARB/00/4, Decision on Jurisdiction dated July 23, 2001, ¶ 46.
5. *See Tokios Tokeles v. Ukraine*, ICSID Case No. ARB/02/18, Decision on Jurisdiction dated April 29, 2004, ¶ 84.
6. *Fraport AG Frankfurt Airport Services Worldwide v. The Republic of the Philippines*, ICSID Case No. ARB/03/25, Award dated August 16, 2007 ("*Fraport I* Award"). This decision was annulled in 2010. *See Fraport AG Frankfurt Airport Services Worldwide v. Republic of the Philippines*, ICSID Case No. ARB/03/25, Decision on the Application for Annulment of Fraport AG Frankfurt Airport Services Worldwide dated December 23, 2010. Following annulment, the claimant resubmitted a claim, leading to a second award in 2014. *Fraport AG Frankfurt Airport Services Worldwide v. Republic of the Philippines*, ICSID Case No. ARB/11/12, Award dated December 10, 2014.
7. *See Fraport I* Award ¶ 335 (quoting Article 1(1) of the BIT).
8. *Fraport I* Award ¶ 339.
9. *Fraport I* Award ¶ 340.
10. *Fraport I* Award ¶ 345.
11. *Fraport I* Award ¶ 401.

> course of the investment, as a justification for state action with respect to the investment, might be a defense to claimed *substantive* violations of the BIT, but could not deprive a tribunal acting under the authority of the BIT of its jurisdiction.[12]

Finally, while emphasizing that "the Tribunal's decision in this matter does not rest on policy," the *Fraport I* tribunal also articulated the policy argument for its interpretation of the "legality requirement," underlining "[r]espect for the integrity of the law of the host state" as a critical concern of the investment protection regime:

> As for policy, BITs oblige governments to conduct their relations with foreign investors in a transparent fashion. Some reciprocal if not identical obligations lie on the foreign investor. One of those is the obligation to make the investment in accordance with the host state's law. It is arguable that even an investment which is not made in accordance with host state law may import economic value to the host state. But that is not the only goal of this sector of international law. Respect for the integrity of the law of the host state is also a critical part of development and a concern of international investment law.[13]

The *Fraport I* decision was a majority decision, over a dissent by Bernardo Cremades. Mr. Cremades defended the ownership interpretation mentioned above: "It is clear from the context of Article 1(1) that the word 'asset' is qualified by 'accepted in accordance with the respective laws and regulations of either Contracting States' because certain assets by law cannot be owned by foreign investors."[14] In other words, "[t]he inquiry at the jurisdictional phase required by the phrase 'in accordance with the laws and regulations of the Host State' is limited to determining whether the type of asset is legal in domestic law."[15] He also advanced a policy argument against the majority's interpretation, underlining the systematic imbalance it fostered: "If the legality of the Claimant's conduct is a jurisdictional issue, and the legality of the Respondent's conduct a merits issue, then the Respondent Host State is placed in a powerful situation. In the Biblical phrase, the Tribunal must first examine the speck in the eye of the investor and defer, and maybe never address, a beam in the eye of the Host State."[16]

In sum, the *Fraport I* tribunal was the first to advance in clear terms three key propositions, central in the development of the illegality defense. First, an "in accordance with the law" provision is a jurisdictional requirement demanding compliance with the host State's law, not an ownership rule. Second, the requirement only concerns the initiation or making of the investment, not its performance and the subsequent conduct of the investor. Third, as a matter of policy, the requirement makes good policy sense, and "[r]espect for the integrity of the law of the host state" is a critical concern of the international investment regime.

12. *Fraport I* Award ¶ 345 (emphasis in the original).
13. *Fraport I* Award ¶ 402.
14. *Fraport AG Frankfurt Airport Services Worldwide v. The Republic of the Philippines*, ICSID Case No. ARB/03/25, Dissenting Opinion of Mr. Bernardo M. Cremades dated July 19, 2007, ¶ 12 ("*Fraport I* Cremades Dissent").
15. *Fraport I* Cremades Dissent ¶ 38.
16. *Fraport I* Cremades Dissent ¶ 37.

Subsequent cases reaffirmed these propositions. The 2013 decision in *Metal-Tech v. Uzbekistan* is illustrative.[17] The case is famous for being the first treaty case in which a tribunal found that it lacked jurisdiction because of corruption, and for the way in which the tribunal found that corruption did occur, relying on inferences and red flags. But the focus here is on the legal framework that the tribunal adopted to justify its decision.

The relevant treaty—the Israel-Uzbekistan BIT—defined investments as "any kind of assets, implemented in accordance with the laws and regulations of the Contracting Party in whose territory the investment is made."[18] The claimant accepted that this provision consisted in a "compliance with the law" requirement. The tribunal found that the "subject-matter scope of the legality requirement" covered: "(i) non-trivial violations of the host State's legal order ..., (ii) violations of the host State's foreign investment regime ..., and (iii) fraud."[19] The provisions of Uzbek law prohibiting corruption fell within such subject-matter scope.

As to the time at which the legality requirement applies, the tribunal rejected the State's argument that the legality requirement covered both the establishment and the operation of the investment: "the term 'assets implemented' refers to the time when the investment was made. In other words, the Treaty requires that the investment must be legal when it is initially established. Article 1 simply does not address whether or not the investment must be operated lawfully after it is in place."[20]

Having found that the investor engaged in corruption at the time of the establishment of the investment in Uzbekistan, the tribunal concluded that it lacked jurisdiction.[21]

Under the trend initiated by *Fraport I*, legality requirements in BITs operate at a jurisdictional level, along a temporal axis: if illegality occurs at the time of the making, initiation, or establishment of the investment, the tribunal has no jurisdiction; but subsequent illegality, occurring during the performance, operation, or course of the investment, has no jurisdictional consequences. Separately, the law has also developed under a separate, parallel trend.

B The Claim Admissibility Axis

The law governing the illegality defense has developed along a second axis: the "cause of action" or "claim" axis. In this context, the legal consequence of the illegality is not the tribunal's lack of jurisdiction, but the inadmissibility of the claimant's claims. The question is not *when* the illegality occurred, but whether the illegality vitiates or taints the investor's *claims*.

17. *Metal-Tech Ltd. v. The Republic of Uzbekistan*, ICSID Case No. ARB/10/3, Award dated October 4, 2013 ("*Metal-Tech* Award").
18. *Metal-Tech* Award ¶ 164 (quoting Article 1(1) of the BIT).
19. *Metal-Tech* Award ¶ 165.
20. *Metal-Tech* Award ¶ 193.
21. *Metal-Tech* Award ¶¶ 372-373.

1 *Contract Cases: From* World Duty Free *(2006) to the* Niko *Jurisdiction Decision (2013)*

Cases in this context are contract cases, not treaty cases. The 2006 decision in *World Duty Free v. Kenya* is famous for being the first ICSID decision to dismiss a claim on the basis of a finding of corruption.[22] But, again, the focus of this chapter is on the legal framework adopted by the tribunal.

In *World Duty Free*, the tribunal's jurisdiction and the claimant's causes of action were based on a contract, in which the arbitration agreement called for English law and the choice-of-law clause for Kenyan law.[23] The tribunal generally "consider[ed] the two legal systems to have the same material effect as applied to th[at] case."[24] After the claimant's CEO submitted a witness statement describing a USD 2 million "donation" he had made to then-President Moi,[25] Kenya filed an application seeking dismissal of the claims on the ground that a contract procured by bribery was unenforceable,[26] and shortly afterward declared the contract avoided.[27]

After reviewing the evidence, the tribunal concluded that the payment "must be regarded as a bribe made in order to obtain the conclusion of the [contract],"[28] and dismissed the claims. The tribunal identified three distinct grounds for this result: (*i*) the contract-law doctrine of avoidance in English and Kenyan law, under which Kenya "was legally entitled to avoid and did avoid legally" the contract;[29] (*ii*) "public policy both under English law and Kenyan law," which compelled the conclusion that "the Claimant is not legally entitled to maintain any of its pleaded claims in these proceedings";[30] and (*iii*) "transnational public policy."[31]

As to the second ground, the tribunal concluded that the claimant was "not legally entitled to maintain any of its pleaded claims in these proceedings on the ground of *ex turpi causa non oritur actio*."[32] The tribunal quoted Lord Mansfield in *Holman v. Johnson*: "The principle of public policy is this: *ex dolo malo non oritur actio*. No court will lend its aid to a man who founds his cause of action upon an immoral or illegal act. If, from the plaintiff's own stating or otherwise, the cause of action appears to arise *ex turpi causa*, or the transgression of a positive law of this country, there the court says he has no right to be assisted."[33]

As to the third ground, the tribunal surveyed a number of authorities over the course of twenty paragraphs to arrive at the conclusion that "bribery is contrary to the

22. *World Duty Free Company Limited v. The Republic of Kenya*, ICSID Case No. ARB/00/7, Award dated October 4, 2006 ("*World Duty Free* Award").
23. *World Duty Free* Award ¶¶ 6, 158.
24. *World Duty Free* Award ¶ 159.
25. *World Duty Free* Award ¶ 130.
26. *World Duty Free* Award ¶¶ 41, 105.
27. *World Duty Free* Award ¶ 109.
28. *World Duty Free* Award ¶ 136.
29. *World Duty Free* Award ¶¶ 183, 188.
30. *World Duty Free* Award ¶ 179.
31. *World Duty Free* Award ¶ 157.
32. *World Duty Free* Award ¶ 179.
33. *World Duty Free* Award ¶ 181 (quoting *Holman v. Johnson* (1775) 1 Cowp. 341, 343 (Lord Mansfield)).

international public policy of most, if not all, States or, to use another formula, to transnational public policy."[34] In the very next sentence, the tribunal then stated: "Thus, *claims based* on contracts of corruption or *on contracts obtained by corruption cannot be upheld* by this Arbitral Tribunal."[35]

A very different logic is at play here than in the legality requirement context. The illegality does not affect the tribunal's jurisdiction: it affects the viability of the "claims"—specifically, though the *World Duty Free* tribunal was not explicit on this point, their admissibility. And the question is not when the illegality occurred (at the time of the making of the investment, or subsequently) but whether the claims are "based" on an illegal act (here, a contract obtained by corruption), whether the cause of action is founded on an illegal act.

The same kind of reasoning is to be found in another important contract case, the 2013 decision on jurisdiction in *Niko v. Bangladesh*.[36] In *Niko*, the claims were based on two contracts, a joint venture agreement (JVA) dated October 2003 and a Gas Purchase and Sale Agreement (GPSA) dated December 2006. In that case, it was uncontested that the investor had engaged in certain acts of corruption. Specifically, the investor had admitted having given Bangladesh's Minister of Energy an expensive automobile and several thousand dollars' worth of nonbusiness-related travel.[37] The respondents advanced an illegality defense.

In rejecting the defense, the tribunal averred that "[t]he case of bribery which has been established in the present case *did not procure the contracts on which the claims in this arbitration are based*."[38] The issue was whether *the basis for the claims* was vitiated by the corruption: it was not, as there was "no link of causation between the established acts of corruption and the conclusion of the agreements."[39]

The tribunal also examined the respondents' purported reliance on the "clean hands" doctrine.[40] While noting that "[t]he principle of clean hands is known as part of equity in common law countries," the tribunal emphasized the uncertain status of the doctrine at international law: "The question whether the principle forms part of international law remains controversial and its precise content is ill defined."[41] Indeed, the pedigree of the "clean hands" doctrine is multifaceted—its roots include the Roman law principles discussed by the *World Duty Free* tribunal, *ex dolo non oritur actio* and *ex turpi causa*.[42] While refraining from deciding whether the "clean hands" doctrine formed part of international law, the *Niko* tribunal reasoned that, in any event,

34. *World Duty Free* Award ¶¶ 138-157 (quotation at ¶ 157).
35. *World Duty Free* Award ¶ 157 (emphasis added).
36. *Niko Resources (Bangladesh) Ltd. v. People's Republic of Bangladesh, BAPEX, & PETROBANGLA*, ICSID Cases Nos. ARB/10/11 & ARB/10/18, Decision on Jurisdiction dated August 19, 2013 ("*Niko* Jurisdiction Decision").
37. *Niko* Jurisdiction Decision ¶¶ 384-385.
38. *Niko* Jurisdiction Decision ¶ 454 (emphasis added).
39. *Niko* Jurisdiction Decision ¶ 455.
40. *See Niko* Jurisdiction Decision ¶¶ 476-485.
41. *Niko* Jurisdiction Decision ¶ 477.
42. Aloysius Llamzon, Case Comment: *Yukos Universal Limited (Isle of Man) v. The Russian Federation*—The State of the "Unclean Hands" Doctrine in International Investment Law: *Yukos* as both Omega and Alpha, *ICSID Review*, Vol. 30(2) (2015), pp. 315-325, at p. 316 ("The doctrine has deep roots, stemming from various Roman law principles, which, while not exactly the

necessary requirements for the application of the doctrine were not satisfied here. In particular, like the *World Duty Free* tribunal did, the *Niko* tribunal emphasized the need for a connection between the claim or cause of action and the alleged illegality: because there was "no relation of reciprocity between the relief which the Claimant now seeks in this arbitration and the acts in the past which the Respondents characterise as involving unclean hands," the defense had to fail.[43]

Thus, whether it is called public policy, international public policy, "unclean hands," or a Latin maxim such as *ex turpi causa* or *ex dolo malo non oritur actio*, a legal principle was said to bar claims or causes of actions founded on an illegal act. As such, the claims should not be heard and are inadmissible.

The identification of the basis or source of the claims and causes of action is easy in contract cases. The basis for the claim is the contract. The contract also normally contains the agreement to arbitrate, and often constitutes the investment itself. The situation is more complex in treaty cases.

2 Treaty Cases: **Inceysa** *(2006) and* **Plama** *(2008)*

While, in contract cases, the instrument constituting the making of the investment and the instrument supporting the claim or cause of action tend to coincide in the investment contract, this will not necessarily be the case in treaty cases.

In treaty cases, the claim most often is one of violation of the substantive protections afforded by the BIT. But, of course, the question is not whether the conclusion of the BIT itself was tainted by illegality. Alternatively, one could say that BITs typically protect the investment, so that a potential cause of action arises as soon as an investor has made an investment. But this would fail to account for the fact that, in many situations, the investment considerably expands during its operation, so that the original initiation of the investment may well have very little to do with the claims subsequently asserted in a treaty arbitration. The key would appear to be the source of the rights and expectations relied on by the investor in advancing its treaty claim. Often, the investor will rely on expectations or rights originating long after the original initiation of the investment.

Suppose that an investment is made at a certain point in time: the incorporation of a local subsidiary to conduct mining exploration activities. Suppose that after years of exploration and the identification of a significant mineral resource, the investor concludes a mining agreement with the State. In subsequent treaty arbitration, the investor could rely on certain provisions of the mining agreement as part of its treaty claims, for instance, to advance a fair and equitable treatment claim or an expropriation claim. Suppose further that the mining agreement was obtained by unlawful means. Such illegality affecting the conclusion of the agreement would not have occurred at the time of the initiation of the investment, but years after, yet it might be

same, bear aspects of the unclean hands doctrine—the *ex turpi causa* defense has been given near equivalence by some scholars of international arbitration, for example") (internal footnotes omitted).

43. *Niko* Jurisdiction Decision ¶ 483; *see* Llamzon, *Yukos* as both Omega and Alpha, at p. 318.

said to vitiate or taint a treaty claim relying on the provisions of the convention to frame its treaty causes of action. But it is also possible that the original initiation of the investment and the time when the rights and expectations relied on by the investor in advancing its treaty claim crystalize coincide. This would be the case if the relevant expectations and rights originate at the time of the initiation of the investment.

As should be apparent, translating the reasoning of contract cases such as *World Duty Free* or *Niko* on the illegality defense and the admissibility of claims to the treaty context is far from easy. And indeed, decisions in treaty cases adopting the same kind of reasoning have been ambiguous.

In the 2006 award in *Inceysa v. El Salvador*,[44] the tribunal dismissed the claimant's claim for lack of jurisdiction, on the basis of what the tribunal read as an explicit legality requirement in the El Salvador-Spain BIT,[45] and a finding of illegality at the time of the initiation of the investment. Thus, *Inceysa* could be categorized as a typical explicit "legality requirement" case, such as *Fraport I* or *Metal-Tech*. But the tribunal went on to analyze the legality of Inceysa's investment "in light of the general principles of law" and to make much broader pronouncements.[46] It found the investment to be in violation of the principle of good faith,[47] the principle *nemo auditur propriam turpitudinem allegans*,[48] international public policy,[49] and the prohibition of unjust enrichment.[50] The tribunal also referred to the maxim "[*e*]*x dolo malo non oritur actio*,"[51] and asserted that "above any claim of an investor, there is a meta-positive provision that prohibits attributing effects to an act done illegally."[52] And further: "No legal system based on rational grounds allows the party that committed a chain of clearly illegal acts to benefit from them."[53]

Thus, even though the tribunal expressly relied on what it found to be a legality requirement in the El Salvador-Spain BIT, and thus dismissed the claims on jurisdictional grounds, it made general pronouncements similar to those in *World Duty Free*, averring that claims based on illegal acts cannot prosper.

The tribunal's 2008 decision in *Plama v. Bulgaria* was even closer to the admissibility holding in *World Duty Free*.[54] There, the tribunal found that the claimant "[was] not entitled to any of the substantive protections afforded by the ECT."[55] The claimant brought its claims under the Energy Charter Treaty ("ECT"), which does not contain an explicit legality requirement. The tribunal made clear that the alleged

44. *Inceysa Vallisoletana, S.L. v. Republic of El Salvador*, ICSID Case No. ARB/03/26, Award dated August 2, 2006 ("*Inceysa* Award").
45. *Inceysa* Award ¶¶ 203, 207, 264.
46. *Inceysa* Award ¶ 229.
47. *Inceysa* Award ¶¶ 230-239.
48. *Inceysa* Award ¶¶ 240-244.
49. *Inceysa* Award ¶¶ 245-252.
50. *Inceysa* Award ¶¶ 253-257.
51. *Inceysa* Award ¶ 240.
52. *Inceysa* Award ¶ 248.
53. *Inceysa* Award ¶ 244.
54. *Plama Consortium Limited v. Republic of Bulgaria*, ICSID Case No. ARB/03/24, Award dated August 27, 2008 ("*Plama* Award").
55. *Plama* Award ¶ 325(3).

illegality on the part of the claimant "[did] not pertain to the Tribunal's jurisdiction."[56] The tribunal characterized the investment as "the result of a deliberate concealment amounting to fraud."[57] The tribunal found the claimant's behavior in making the investment contrary to Bulgarian law "and to international law."[58] Placing particular reliance on *Inceysa* and *World Duty Free*,[59] the tribunal found that "granting the ECT's protections to Claimant's investment would be contrary to the principle *nemo auditur propriam turpitudinem allegans*" and "contrary to the basic notion of international public policy—that a contract obtained by wrongful means (fraudulent misrepresentation) should not be enforced by a tribunal."[60] This latter quote, referring to the enforcement of a contract when the claimant was primarily advancing treaty claims, is revealing the difficulty in translating the contract holding of *World Duty Free* to the treaty context. The *Plama* tribunal concluded with reference to yet another Latin maxim associated with the unclean hands doctrine: "in light of the *ex turpi causa* defence, this Tribunal cannot lend its support to Claimant's request and cannot, therefore, grant the substantive protections of the ECT."[61] This clearly was an admissibility holding. Yet in *Plama*, it so happened that the fraudulent misrepresentation occurred when the investor made its investment, a fact which the tribunal also emphasized.[62]

Thus, as of 2013, the illegality defense had developed along two axes. First, a temporal jurisdictional axis, the "legality requirement" principle: tribunals dismissed claims on jurisdictional grounds when illegality occurred at the time of the making of the investment and the relevant treaty contained an "in accordance with the law" clause. Second, a claim admissibility axis, the "unclean hands" principle: tribunals dismissed claims on admissibility grounds when illegality vitiated the claims themselves. While the principle was easy to apply in contract cases, where the source of the claim is the contract, it was ambiguous in treaty cases. In both *Inceysa* and *Plama*, the two leading treaty cases purporting to apply this principle, it so happened that the alleged illegality had occurred at the time of the initiation of the investment, leading to a coincidental overlap between the two axes. But that overlap was merely coincidental. In 2014, the *Yukos v. Russia* decision reframed the issue.

III SECOND PHASE: *YUKOS* (2014) AS "OMEGA AND ALPHA"[63]

Rendered in 2014, the *Yukos* award reorganized and reframed the law on the illegality defense. In a profound and prescient case comment published shortly after the issuance of the award, Dr. Llamzon characterized the award as "both Omega and

56. *Plama* Award ¶ 112.
57. *Plama* Award ¶ 135.
58. *Plama* Award ¶ 135.
59. *See Plama* Award ¶¶ 141-142 (quoting *Inceysa* Award and *World Duty Free* Award).
60. *Plama* Award ¶ 143.
61. *Plama* Award ¶ 146.
62. *See Plama* Award ¶¶ 139, 144.
63. *See generally* Llamzon, *Yukos* as both Omega and Alpha.

Alpha."[64] As "Omega," the *Yukos* award reframed and reinterpreted the two parallel trends discussed in the previous section, making them intersect and merge. As "Alpha," *Yukos* foreshadowed new developments in the illegality defense, which Dr. Llamzon could only predict at the time he published his case comment, and which we can now observe and describe.

A *Yukos* as Omega: The Intersection and Merger of the Two Axes

In *Yukos*, Russia advanced a wide-ranging illegality defense. The claimant brought its claims under the ECT, which, as noted above, does not contain an explicit legality requirement. The *Yukos* tribunal made two fundamental findings on the illegality defense, one for each axis.

First, the tribunal reaffirmed and expanded the temporal jurisdictional axis. It confirmed that the illegality defense rests on a fundamental temporal distinction between the making and the performance of the investment:

> There is no compelling reason to deny altogether the right to invoke the ECT to any investor who has breached the law of the host State in the course of its investment. If the investor acts illegally, the host state can request it to correct its behavior and impose upon it sanctions available under domestic law, as the Russian Federation indeed purports to have done by reassessing taxes and imposing fines. However, if the investor believes these sanctions to be unjustified (as Claimants do in the present case), it must have the possibility of challenging their validity in accordance with the applicable investment treaty.[65]

Following the dicta of prior tribunals,[66] the *Yukos* tribunal also expanded the reach of the temporal jurisdictional axis, by making it independent of an explicit legality requirement. Even though the ECT does not contain an explicit legality requirement, the *Yukos* tribunal applied the typical legality requirement framing: "An investor who has *obtained an investment* in the host State only by acting in bad faith or in violation of the laws of the host state, has brought itself within the scope of application of the ECT through wrongful acts. Such an investor should not be allowed to benefit from the Treaty."[67]

Thus, the *Yukos* decision marks the culmination of a trend initiated with the *Fraport I* decision. Illegality prevents the exercise of jurisdiction if it occurs chronologically at the time of the making of the investment. Whether the relevant treaty contains an explicit "in accordance with the law" clause or not and what precisely the clause provides is irrelevant: illegality in the making of the investment defeats or at least prevents the exercise of jurisdiction as a matter of policy and principle.

64. *See generally* Llamzon, *Yukos* as both Omega and Alpha.
65. *Yukos* Award ¶ 1355. The tribunal took into account illegalities in the performance of the investment, in the form of a quantum reduction based on the doctrine of contributory fault. *See Yukos* Award ¶¶ 1633-1637.
66. *See Yukos* Award ¶ 1351.
67. *Yukos* Award ¶ 1352 (emphasis added).

Second, the *Yukos* tribunal seriously weakened the claim admissibility, "unclean hands" axis, by declaring that "'unclean hands' does not exist as a general principle of international law which would bar a claim by an investor."[68] The magnitude of the compensation awarded, the detailed reasoning provided to support the conclusions, the unanimity among the tribunal members, and their identity (including Judge Stephen Schwebel who in his dissenting opinion in *Nicaragua v. United States* had written one of the strongest statements supporting the existence of the unclean hands doctrine at international law),[69] all implied that *Yukos* was likely to be "the leading case on the unclean hands doctrine that all succeeding international tribunals (investment treaty or not) will have to contend with."[70] And while the award was annulled at the seat at first instance on unrelated grounds, the award was reinstated on appeal.[71]

The tribunal noted that "Respondent has been unable to cite a single majority decision where an international court or arbitral tribunal has applied the principle of 'unclean hands' in an inter-State or investor-State dispute and concluded that, as a principle of international law, it operated as a bar to a claim."[72] The tribunal could make such a statement because it read *Plama* as a pure "legality requirement" case, concerned exclusively with illegality at the time of the making of the investment.[73] The tribunal also did not mention *World Duty Free*.

In other words, *Yukos* subsumed the "claim" axis under the "chronological" axis. As Dr. Llamzon puts it: this was "a significant development of the law, effectively slotting the unclean hands doctrine within the framework of an emerging 'legality requirement.'"[74] This could only be done by treating as identical the two distinct issues of when the investment occurred and what the source of the investor's cause of action is. Or, as Dr. Llamzon puts it: "Only by considering the facts that attended the securing of the investment, rather than the facts related to the claimant's strict cause of action ... as the juridical link between investor claim and host State defence, can the legality doctrine truly be said to be of sufficient identity with the unclean hands doctrine."[75]

Thus, in treaty cases at least,[76] the law was simplified, and the two axes unified or merged. The main issue was the timing of the illegality: if made at the time of the

68. *Yukos* Award ¶ 1363.
69. *Military and Paramilitary Activities in and against Nicaragua (Nicaragua v. United States of America)*, Merits, Judgment, June 27, 1986, Dissenting Opinion of Judge Schwebel, [1986] ICJ Reports 259, at 392-394.
70. Llamzon, *Yukos* as both Omega and Alpha, at pp. 315-316.
71. *See generally* Court of Appeal in The Hague, The Netherlands, *Veteran Petroleum Limited, Yukos Universal Limited & Hulley Enterprises Limited v. The Russian Federation*, Case Number 200.197.079/01, Decision of February 18, 2020 (overruling District Court of The Hague, The Netherlands, *The Russian Federation v. Veteran Petroleum Limited, Yukos Universal Limited & Hulley Enterprises Limited* (C/09/477160 / HA ZA 15-1, C/09/477162 / HA ZA 15-2 and C/09/481619 / HA ZA 15-112), Decision of April 20, 2016). A further appeal is pending in the Dutch Supreme Court.
72. *Yukos* Award ¶ 1362.
73. *See Yukos* Award ¶ 1350 (discussing *Plama* Award).
74. Llamzon, *Yukos* as both Omega and Alpha, at p. 321.
75. Llamzon, *Yukos* as both Omega and Alpha, at p. 323.
76. *See* Llamzon, *Yukos* as both Omega and Alpha, at p. 321 (noting that "*Yukos*' extension to contract-based arbitrations that do not automatically involve public international law" is a "more open question").

making of the investment, the claim was barred; if made during the performance of the investment, the illegality defense went to the merits. No "unclean hands" doctrine could automatically sanction claims founded on illegal acts post-making of the investment. Note that the *Yukos* tribunal remained essentially silent on transnational public policy. Thus, this concept could be used to nuance the framework established by the *Yukos* tribunal. And indeed, as discussed below, it was so used.

B *Yukos* as Alpha: The Emergence of Transitional Legal Tools

In his case comment published shortly after the *Yukos* award was issued, Dr. Llamzon predicted that "future tribunals may yet consider the [*Yukos*] case as a starting point for deliberating difficult questions of investor wrongdoing rather than its terminus."[77] In other words, *Yukos* was not just an "Omega" but also an "Alpha." The prediction has turned out to be correct. Following the *Yukos* tribunal's landmark reordering of the legality defense, the decided cases started to evolve and develop along new axes.

In the immediate aftermath of *Yukos*, the law evolved in a peculiar way through reliance on legal tools meant to nuance and subtly amend the framework *Yukos* had established. Such tools may be expected to appear when the demands of reality and authoritative legal decisions collide. If existing legal principles yield unsatisfactory results, then it is expected that these legal principles will evolve. But authoritative decisions have strong inertia. It is often impossible to alter or overrule them suddenly and firmly. Instead, subsequent decisions purport to adopt the same legal framework, while they, in fact, undermine this framework, as needed to reach satisfactory results: the means to achieve such ends are legal constructs that serve to alter a legal framework while paying lip service to it.

Such process occurred in the aftermath of *Yukos*. As noted, at the time when it was rendered at least, the *Yukos* award was considered highly authoritative, and it would have been quite hard for a subsequent tribunal openly to criticize its conclusions. On the other hand, the consecration of the temporal dividing line in the illegality defense to the apparent exclusion of other considerations, and the burial of the "unclean hands" doctrine, led to practical problems, demanding concrete resolution. Indeed, the "temporal dividing line" has been subject to firm criticism. According to one commentator, such dividing line "has no sound basis in principle" and "leads to artificial results."[78] The argument is that if "the essence of the illegality would be identical," it should not matter precisely when the illegality happened to take place.[79] As a matter of principle, whether the illegality took place exactly when the investment was initiated, a few weeks afterward, or after a couple of years, should not matter. At the same time, "the moral impetus that first led to the appropriation of the unclean

77. Llamzon Case Comment *Yukos* 325.
78. Douglas, The Plea of Illegality in Investment Treaty Arbitration, at p. 175.
79. Douglas, The Plea of Illegality in Investment Treaty Arbitration, at p. 175; *see also* Llamzon, *Yukos* as both Omega and Alpha, at p. 322 ("one may legitimately argue whether the legality doctrine is calibrated appropriately, given that a dividing line based on temporality can sometimes lead to problematic results").

hands doctrine in investment arbitration ... has not dissipated."[80] Thus, the law evolved in small, silent steps. While apparently respecting the *Yukos* framework, subsequent decisions nuanced it. Three such steps are addressed below.

The first practical and pressing question that parties and tribunals needed to confront was the following: what if an illegality is so grave that it should vitiate the claim in its entirety, but the illegality did not occur at the time of the initiation of the investment?

1 *The Dilution of the Notion of "Making" of the Investment*

The first legal tool used tacitly to assail the omnipotence of the temporal dividing line was the dissolution of the notion of "making" of investment. The temporal dividing line is based on the premise that a discrete moment can be identified as the moment when the investment is made. Before that moment, there was no investment. After that moment, the investment is not "made," but "performed" or "operated."

If one wants to weaken the importance of that dividing line, one need only make the notion of "making" more flexible and malleable, so that there is greater discretion in determining whether a given illegality occurred at the time of the making of the investment or not. This would enable a tribunal to dismiss a claim based on a serious illegality even if the illegality did not happen to occur at the time of the initiation of the investment *stricto sensu*, but before or even afterward.

This very possibility was anticipated by the *Yukos* tribunal. The tribunal stated that "an examination of the legality of an investment should not be limited to verifying whether the last in a series of transactions leading up to the investment was in conformity with the law."[81] Instead, "[t]he making of the investment will often consist of several consecutive acts and all of these must be legal and *bona fide*."[82]

The *Yukos* tribunal made this statement in the course of addressing Russia's argument that illegality predating the formal acquisition of the investment by the claimant was relevant.[83] On the facts of the case, the *Yukos* tribunal rejected Russia's argument, finding that "Respondent has failed to demonstrate that the alleged illegalities to which it refers are sufficiently connected with the final transaction by which the investment was made by Claimants."[84] But it did not categorically reject the possibility that illegality predating the formal initiation of the investment could trigger the legality requirement. The same kind of reasoning could be applied to alleged illegality postdating the formal initiation of the investment. If, a few years after the initiation of the investment, the investor receives a permit or enters into a contract with the host State that fundamentally transforms the scope and nature of the investment, could it be said that this is a new, decisive "step" in the making or expansion of the same

80. Llamzon, *Yukos* as both Omega and Alpha, at p. 316.
81. *Yukos* Award ¶ 1369.
82. *Yukos* Award ¶ 1369.
83. *See Yukos* Award ¶¶ 1370-1372; *see generally Alasdair Ross Anderson v. Republic of Costa Rica*, ICSID Case No. ARB(AF)/07/3, Award of May 19, 2010.
84. *Yukos* Award ¶ 1370.

investment? Or is this perhaps an entirely new investment, deserving distinct treatment? Or is this merely the "performance" of the original investment? Depending on how these questions are answered, one could effectively dissolve the temporal dividing line while purporting to apply it.

2 The Expansion of the Scope of Transnational Public Policy

As noted, the *Yukos* tribunal remained essentially silent on transnational public policy, and completely silent on *World Duty Free*. Thus, the notion of transnational public policy can be used to circumvent the *Yukos* tribunal's burial of the "unclean hands" doctrine. Even though "'unclean hands' does not exist as a general principle of international law which would bar a claim by an investor,"[85] transnational public policy does. In this sense, transnational public policy becomes a "very unclean hands" doctrine: the issue is not whether illegality vitiates the claim, but whether a very serious illegality, serious enough to trigger the transnational public policy doctrine, does. And if it does, then transnational public policy only serves to justify an inadmissibility finding.

Further, in assessing the seriousness of the illegality, transnational public policy does not consider the specifics of the alleged wrong. Instead, it considers *categories* of wrongs: certain kinds of wrongs are said to trigger the doctrine. As a result, tribunals relying on the doctrine are forced to make very broad pronouncements, going much beyond the circumstances of the specific case they must decide.

Such result-oriented expansion of the doctrine is not how transnational public policy is meant to be utilized. As Professor Reisman has presciently warned, the abuse of transnational public policy leads to conceptual confusion and deleterious consequences:

> [P]ublic policy in domestic law is a legal concept with a verifiable judicial history. Not so in international law. When an alleged international public policy is given the force of law by an international commercial arbitral tribunal, it is not subjected to the discipline of customary international law analysis which requires that the state practice justifying the inference that a customary rule has been produced must be shown to be wide and extensive and to be accompanied by *opinio juris*. Without this discipline, the invocation of "transnational public policy" becomes an easy way for those claiming to have an insight into the heart and the soul of international law to effect their own preferences without having to prove that they have become customary international law.[86]

But if a tribunal accepts the legal premise that "unclean hands" does not exist in international law, that only illegality going to the making of the investment triggers the legality requirement, and that the illegality in front of it occurred after the making of the

85. *Yukos* Award ¶ 1363.
86. W. Michael Reisman, Law, International Public Policy (So-Called) and Arbitral Choice in International Commercial Arbitration, in *International Arbitration 2006: Back to Basics?, ICCA Congress Series Vol. 13* (van den Berg ed. 2007), pp. 849-856, at pp. 855-856.

investment, then to dismiss the claim in its entirety (and not engage in a merits analysis), the tribunal has to rely on transnational public policy.

This is what happened in *Churchill Mining & Planet Mining v. Indonesia* (2016), apparently the first decision categorically to dismiss a claim on the basis of illegality that admittedly took place during the performance of the investment.[87]

The East Kutai Coal Project (EKCP) was a mining project developed by the claimants jointly with various Indonesian companies in the Regency of East Kutai (the Regency) in Indonesia. Following the Regent's issuance of certain revocation decrees in May 2010, the claimants commenced arbitration in May 2012 on the basis of the UK-Indonesia BIT and the Australia-Indonesia BIT, claiming that the revocation decrees were in breach of Indonesia's treaty obligations. On September 25, 2014, Indonesia filed an Application for Dismissal of Claimants' Claims, on the ground that the mining licenses and related approvals companies were forged. The tribunal rendered an award on December 6, 2016, finding all of the claimants' claims inadmissible.

Having found that the licenses were forgeries and fraud (without identifying the authors of such forgeries and fraud), the tribunal turned to the legal consequences of such finding. It emphasized that "[n]either the ICSID Convention nor the BITs contain substantive provisions addressing the consequences of unlawful conduct by a claimant or its business associate during the performance of an investment."[88] Thus, under the *Yukos* framework, the tribunal would normally address the consequences of the illegality as a merits issue.

After making broad pronouncements and referring to rather vague principles, such as "the general principle that one does not benefit from treaty protection when underlying conduct is deemed improper,"[89] the tribunal noted that "particularly serious cases of fraudulent conduct, such as corruption, have been held to be contrary to international or transnational public policy."[90] Immediately after, it also referred to the unclean hands doctrine, though, perhaps surprisingly, it failed explicitly to acknowledge the findings of the *Yukos* tribunal: "The common law doctrine of unclean hands barring claims based on illegal conduct has also found expression at the international level, although its status and exact contours are subject to debate and have been approached differently by international tribunals."[91]

After this series of references, without much precise explanation, the tribunal asserted that it viewed the question of the consequences of the fraud "as a matter of admissibility,"[92] and then in the immediately following paragraph concluded, without more, that "[t]he Tribunal agrees with the Respondent that claims arising from rights based on fraud or forgery which a claimant deliberately or unreasonably ignored are

87. *Churchill Mining PLC & Planet Mining Pty Ltd v. Republic of Indonesia*, ICSID Cases Nos. ARB/12/14 & ARB/12/40, Award dated December 6, 2016 ("*Churchill Mining* Award").
88. *Churchill Mining* Award ¶ 488.
89. *Churchill Mining* Award ¶ 492.
90. *Churchill Mining* Award ¶ 493.
91. *Churchill Mining* Award ¶ 493 & n. 779 (no reference to *Yukos* Award).
92. *Churchill Mining* Award ¶ 507.

inadmissible as a matter of international public policy."[93] The tribunal said no more on international public policy in the rest of the award, did not use the term again in the summary of its conclusions, nor in the *dispositif*.

In fact, the tribunal essentially applied the unclean hands doctrine. But it did so without explicitly confronting the *Yukos* tribunal's pronouncement that the unclean hands doctrine does not exist in international law, and instead formally based its decision on international public policy. The result is the same, but the conceptual baggage is much heavier and far-reaching.

3 *The Development of Tools to Address Illegality as a Merits Issue*

The first two legal tools addressed immediately above enable tribunals categorically to dismiss claims even though, under the *Yukos* framework strictly construed, the alleged illegality does not trigger the legality requirement. But there might also be situations where the tribunal considers that the appropriate response is to treat the illegality as parts of the merits analysis, and needs a legal tool to *avoid* the conclusion that the claims must be categorically dismissed.

One such tool was devised by the tribunal in *Copper Mesa v. Ecuador* (2016).[94] The tribunal rejected an attempt by Ecuador to invoke alleged "flagrant breaches of Ecuadorian and international human rights law and international public policy"[95] as the basis for preliminary objections, when Ecuador had failed to complain of the alleged conduct before the arbitration. The tribunal observed that even though "[a]ll, or almost all, of [the] alleged conduct took place ... openly and in view of the Respondent's governmental authorities," when it came to "international law, international public policy and human rights, not a single complaint was made by the Respondent against the Claimant at the time."[96] In fact, the tribunal emphasized, "[s]uch a complaint surfaced for the first time after the commencement of this arbitration."[97] After taking into consideration "the Respondent's obligation of good faith under the Treaty in regard to arbitration," the tribunal concluded that it was simply "far too late for the Respondent to raise such objections to the Tribunal's exercise of jurisdiction in this arbitration," and held Ecuador "precluded from raising this objection as to admissibility."[98]

This enabled the tribunal to avoid having to decide whether the alleged illegality constituted a violation of international public policy, as Ecuador contended, and to avoid having to pass on the status of the unclean hands doctrine. Instead, the tribunal went on to treat the illegality as parts of its merits analysis. It took care to distinguish the *World Duty Free* decision, noting that in that case "the claim, as a cause of action,

93. *Churchill Mining* Award ¶ 508.
94. *Copper Mesa Mining Corporation v. Republic of Ecuador*, Award dated March 15, 2016 ("*Copper Mesa* Award").
95. *Copper Mesa* Award ¶ 5.42 (quoting the respondent).
96. *Copper Mesa* Award ¶ 5.63.
97. *Copper Mesa* Award ¶ 5.63.
98. *Copper Mesa* Award ¶ 5.64.

was directly based from the beginning upon the claimant's own illegal act."[99] Thus, the tribunal explicitly associated the unclean hands doctrine with the requirement that "the claim, as a cause of action" be "directly based" on the illegality.

The tribunal categorized the illegality as a contributory fault issue: "the Tribunal there prefers to take into account the Claimant's case not in the form of the doctrine of unclean hands as such, but rather under analogous doctrines of causation and contributory fault applying to the merits of the Claimants' claims arising from events subsequent to the acquisition of its investment."[100] It reduced relevant damages by 30% on the basis of such contributory fault.[101]

By relying on the "Respondent's obligation of good faith under the Treaty," the tribunal was able to avoid having to decide on the status of the unclean hands doctrine and the scope of international public policy. It could treat the illegality in the performance of the investment as a merits issue, and take it into account when quantifying damages, very much like what the *Yukos* tribunal did.

IV THIRD PHASE: THE EMERGENCE OF A PROPORTIONALITY FRAMEWORK?

One would expect legal tools developed in the aftermath of *Yukos* to be no more than transitional. If established legal principles do not yield acceptable results, and need to be nuanced and even tacitly amended by reliance on such legal tools, one would expect these established legal principles ultimately to be amended, and openly so. As the pressure for change increases, so legal tools designed to alter the authoritative framework at the margins multiply. The accumulation of such tools and the intrinsic pressure created by the unsatisfactory nature of the results yielded by a mechanical application of the established principles, eventually lead to a reformulation or reframing of the law, a new paradigm.

In the case of the illegality defense, such comprehensive reframing has not yet occurred. But we may be witnessing the emergence of such a new paradigm, de-emphasizing the temporal divide between making and performance of the investment, re-emphasizing the relationship between the alleged illegality and the specific claim said to be vitiated, and introducing considerations of proportionality enabling tribunals to reach nuanced results through nuanced reasoning. While the injection of proportionality considerations has long been recommended by eminent commentators,[102] it is now explicitly featured in decided cases.

99. *Copper Mesa* Award ¶ 5.66.
100. *Copper Mesa* Award ¶ 5.65.
101. *Copper Mesa* Award ¶ 6.133.
102. *See, e.g.*, Aloysius P. Llamzon, 2014, *Corruption in International Investment Arbitration*, at p. 221 ("[C]orruption is illegal and must be sanctioned; but the *degree* of sanction should be subject to the particular facts of the case, and any wrongful investor conduct must at least be capable of being weighed against the complicity or negligence of public officials and the host State itself. The idea that the application of anti-corruption norms are an almost peremptory 'trump' that can drown out every other policy consideration (including the minimum protection of investors from egregious host State conduct) seems incompatible with a discourse of

The key decision that may be read to herald such new paradigm is the 2017 Decision on Jurisdiction in *Kim v. Uzbekistan*.[103] Following the untimely passing of the tribunal's president, the tribunal was reconstituted, and, as of the time of writing, a decision on the merits is pending.

The claim was brought under the Kazakhstan-Uzbekistan BIT and related to the claimants' interest in two cement plants. The respondent made four objections as to jurisdiction and admissibility, including that the claimants' investment was not made in compliance with the law; and that the claimants procured their investment through corruption, and the claims were therefore inadmissible. As to corruption, the respondent alleged that the claimants made a USD 8 million "overpayment" to Ms. Karimova, the daughter of the president, and a USD 3 million payment to a consultant, Mr. Bizakov, who served as a "conduit" between the claimants and Ms. Karimova. As to illegality, the respondent alleged that the claimants' investment was made in violation of Uzbek securities laws and regulations. The tribunal rejected all such objections. In the course of reaching this decision, it made important pronouncements on the legality defense.

The treaty had an explicit legality requirement. The disagreement between the parties turned on the scope of that legality requirement. The tribunal started by endorsing the standard temporal divide. The tribunal found that "the legality requirement has a temporal dimension."[104] "[T]he test applies at the time the investment is established. It is not a requirement subsequent to the making of the investment."[105] An "additional consideration" is "whether the illegal action was related to Claimants' making of the investment."[106]

The tribunal noted that the legality requirement had been analyzed by many tribunals and that "[t]he dominant tendency within these awards is (1) to state that the substantive scope of the legality requirement is limited to violations of fundamental laws of the Host State and (2) to state a variety of rule-like statements whereby the first proposition may be applied."[107] The tribunal did not find such analysis satisfactory.[108] It articulated instead a potentially revolutionary analysis of the legality requirement, based on a proportionality framework. "The denial of the protections of the BIT is a harsh consequence that is a proportional response only when its application is triggered by *noncompliance with a law that results in a compromise of a correspondingly significant interest of the Host State*."[109]

The tribunal explained:

> The phrase "noncompliance with a law that results in a compromise of a correspondingly significant interest of the Host State" is chosen so as to focus more

fairness, as no space is left for the accommodation of other important interests within the system") (emphasis in the original).

103. *Kim* Jurisdiction Decision.
104. *Kim* Jurisdiction Decision ¶ 374.
105. *Kim* Jurisdiction Decision ¶ 374.
106. *Kim* Jurisdiction Decision ¶ 376.
107. *Kim* Jurisdiction Decision ¶ 384.
108. *Kim* Jurisdiction Decision ¶ 385.
109. *Kim* Jurisdiction Decision ¶ 396 (emphasis in the original).

> sharply the substantive scope of the legality requirement *not on whether the law is fundamental but rather on the significance of the violation. The Tribunal believes that the gravity of the law itself is a central part of the examination but not the sole focal point. It is not only the law, but the act of noncompliance (or in some wordings, the violation) that is key.* The seriousness of the act is a combination of both the importance of the requirements in the law and the flagrancy of the investor's noncompliance. The text or standing of the law—although central—does not in and of itself determine whether the legality requirement is triggered. Rather, the law must be considered in concert with the particulars of the investor's violation. An investor may violate a law of some import egregiously or it may violate a law of fundamental importance in only a trivial or accidental way. Seriousness to the Host State is to be determined by the overall outcome, which will depend on the seriousness of the law viewed in concert with the seriousness of the violation.[110]

The tribunal explained that the application of proportionality involved three steps. First, the tribunal "must assess the significance of the obligation with which the investor is alleged to not comply."[111] The tribunal provided the following nonexhaustive list of relevant factors: What does the level of sanction provided in the law suggest as to the significance of the obligation to the State? What does a general nonenforcement of an obligation by the host State suggest as to the significance to the state of that obligation? What does the specific decision of the host State not to investigate or prosecute the particular alleged act of noncompliance suggest as to the significance to the state of the obligation in the specific context? What does the evidence of widespread noncompliance suggest as to the significance of the obligation to the State?[112]

Second, the tribunal "must assess the seriousness of the investor's conduct."[113] Again, the tribunal provided a nonexhaustive list of relevant factors: was there a violation? What was the investor's intent? Was the law unclear or evolving? Did the investor exercise due diligence? What does a failure of the State to investigate or prosecute the alleged particular act of noncompliance suggest as to the seriousness of the investor's conduct? What does the subsequent conduct of the investor suggest as to the seriousness of the alleged act of noncompliance?[114]

Third, the tribunal "must evaluate whether the combination of the investor's conduct and the law involved results in a compromise of a significant interest of the Host State to such an extent that the harshness of the sanction of placing the investment outside of the protections of the BIT is a proportionate consequence for the violation examined."[115] One may wonder whether it is possible to evaluate in a given case "the harshness of the sanction of placing the investment outside of the protections of the BIT" without considering the merits of the claims.

After a detailed analysis of the laws allegedly breached and of the relevant facts in each case, the tribunal concluded: "The Tribunal, by a majority, finds that

110. *Kim* Jurisdiction Decision ¶ 398 (emphasis added).
111. *Kim* Jurisdiction Decision ¶ 406.
112. *Kim* Jurisdiction Decision ¶ 406.
113. *Kim* Jurisdiction Decision ¶ 407.
114. *Kim* Jurisdiction Decision ¶ 407.
115. *Kim* Jurisdiction Decision ¶ 408.

Respondent either has failed to establish that Claimants acted in noncompliance with various laws or that such acts of noncompliance do not result in a compromise of an interest that justifies, as a proportionate response, the harshness of denying application of the BIT."[116] In other words, one arbitrator found that there was no illegality, and another found that there was but that the illegality was not serious enough to justify dismissal of the claims. Strikingly, the minority did not seem to disagree with the proportionality framework: "The minority view is that Respondent has established the intent required to conclude that Claimants acted in noncompliance with various laws and that such acts of noncompliance ... result in the compromise of a correspondingly significant interest of Uzbekistan that renders proportionate the exclusion of the investment from the protections of the BIT."[117]

Whether the proportionality framework also applied to corruption allegations was unclear. The tribunal rejected the allegations of corruption relating to the making of the investment on the facts. It reserved its decision on corruption allegations pertaining to the performance of the investment: "[T]he Tribunal notes that its focus, at this stage of these proceedings, is on jurisdictional matters and therefore on bribery or corruption only that pertains to Claimants' initial investment. Any matters as regards bribery or corruption that arose later are more appropriately addressed at the merits stage."[118] In passing, the tribunal asserted that not all instances of corruption would vitiate a claim: "[t]he Tribunal does not foreclose that there may exist a set of circumstances that does not trigger the illegality requirement: for example, the provision of an item with trivial value that an Uzbek court might find deserving of only a minimal fine."[119]

Of course, the jurisdiction decision in *Kim* is not the tribunal's final word. It remains to be seen how the tribunal, reconstituted, will rule on the remaining allegations of illegality at the merits stage, and what legal framework it will adopt. That said, the decision has already received explicit support from at least two investment tribunals, explicitly endorsing the same proportionality framework.[120] As the *Cortec* tribunal put it: "The Tribunal endorses the application of the *Kim* principle of proportionality to an assessment of the impact of alleged illegalities."[121]

The U.K. Supreme Court also recently issued a landmark decision in *Patel v. Mirza*, reframing the illegality defense in English law and adopting a proportionality framework.[122] English courts shall now apply a "range of factors approach" in assessing an illegality defense:

> [I]t is necessary a) to consider the underlying purpose of the prohibition which has been transgressed and whether that purpose will be enhanced by denial of the

116. *Kim* Jurisdiction Decision ¶ 541.
117. *Kim* Jurisdiction Decision ¶ 541.
118. *Kim* Jurisdiction Decision ¶ 553.
119. *Kim* Jurisdiction Decision ¶ 556.
120. *Cortec Mining Kenya Limited v. Republic of Kenya*, ICSID Case No. ARB/15/29, Award of October 22, 2018, ¶ 320 ("*Cortec* Award"); *Álvarez y Marín Corporación S.A. v. Republic of Panama*, ICSID Case No. ARB/15/14, Award of October 12, 2018 (Spanish), ¶ 153.
121. *Cortec* Award ¶ 320.
122. *Patel (Respondent) v. Mirza (Appellant)*, [2016] UKSC 42 ("*Patel v. Mirza* Decision").

> claim, b) to consider any other relevant public policy on which the denial of the claim may have an impact and c) to consider *whether denial of the claim would be a proportionate response to the illegality*, bearing in mind that punishment is a matter for the criminal courts.[123]

In delivering the principal opinion in *Patel*, Lord Toulson stated that "[t]he integrity and harmony of the law permit—and I would say require—such flexibility," explaining that "[r]espect for the integrity of the justice system is not enhanced if it appears to produce results which are arbitrary, unjust or disproportionate."[124] On the need to consider proportionality, Lord Toulson quoted Lord Bingham:

> Where issues of illegality are raised, the courts have (as it seems to me) to steer a middle course between two unacceptable positions. On the one hand it is unacceptable that any court of law should aid or lend its authority to a party seeking to pursue or enforce an object or agreement which the law prohibits. On the other hand, it is unacceptable that the court should, on the first indication of unlawfulness affecting any aspect of a transaction, draw up its skirts and refuse all assistance to the plaintiff, no matter how serious his loss nor how disproportionate his loss to the unlawfulness of his conduct.[125]

As Lord Toulson concluded, "[t]he public interest is best served by a principled and transparent assessment of the considerations identified, rather by than [*sic*] the application of a formal approach capable of producing results which may appear arbitrary, unjust or disproportionate."[126]

In these decisions, the premises of a new paradigm may be emerging. The *Kim* tribunal, in its decision on jurisdiction, adopted a proportionality framework to interpret an explicit legality requirement in the treaty and focused on alleged illegalities relating to the making of the investment only. It remains to be seen how the reconstituted *Kim* tribunal will address the remaining alleged illegalities at the merits stage, and whether, following the lead of *Patel v. Mirza*, it will also apply a proportionality framework at that stage, allowing for more graduated results than the binary alternative of fully dismissing the claims or fully rejecting the defense. The *Kim* decision also suggests, if only in passing, that not all instances of corruption vitiate a claim, and that even an act understood to be contrary to international public policy (a corrupt transaction) may be subject to proportionality analysis at the legality requirement stage.[127] Again, it remains to be seen how the *Kim* tribunal will treat any remaining international public policy defense at the merits stage.

In sum, there is now substantial authority for the application of a proportionality framework at the "making" of the investment stage. This proportionality framework allows for consideration of numerous factors so that the occurrence of illegality does not automatically lead to full dismissal of claims. If a similar proportionality framework is used at the performance of the investment stage, allowing for nuanced reasoning and

123. *Patel v. Mirza* Decision ¶¶ 83, 120 (emphasis added).
124. *Patel v. Mirza* Decision ¶ 108.
125. *Saunders v. Edwards* [1987] 1 WLR 1116, 1134 (quoted at *Patel v. Mirza* Decision ¶ 106).
126. *Patel v. Mirza* Decision ¶ 120.
127. *See Kim* Jurisdiction Decision ¶ 556.

nuanced outcomes, the temporal divide will have effectively lost its importance. In each case, no matter when the illegality occurs, the questions will be whether the illegality is serious enough to vitiate the claim, whether full dismissal of the claims is proportionate; and if the answer is negative, what a proportionate remedy for the illegality would be.

V CONCLUSION

This chapter offers an interpretation of the evolution of the law governing the illegality defense in investor-State arbitration, delineating three phases. In a first phase, the decided cases developed along two distinct axes. Under a chronological axis, developed in treaty cases, tribunals dismissed claims on the basis of explicit legality requirements contained in BITs. Under a "cause of action" axis, developed principally in contract cases, tribunals dismissed claims as inadmissible when the claim was itself based on an illegal act. The second phase began with the issuance of the *Yukos* award in 2014, which reframed and simplified the defense: illegality at the making of the investment prevents the exercise of jurisdiction; illegality during the performance of the investment goes to the merits; there is no separate doctrine of unclean hands. Following this landmark decision, tribunals designed tools to nuance this rather rigid chronological framework: the notion of the "making" of the investment was diluted; the scope of international public policy has been expanding; and tribunals found ways to address illegality on the merits. Finally, we may be currently seeing the premises of a third phase: a potential reemergence of the "cause of action" principle and the injection of proportionality considerations, enabling tribunals to reach more nuanced results through more nuanced reasoning. Only time will tell if these premises will remain premises or will grow to become authoritative, controlling, principles governing the illegality defense.

CHAPTER 4

Defining and Enforcing Ethical Standards for Party-Representatives in International Arbitration

Chan Leng Sun SC[*]

I WHEN DIVERSITY IS NOT ALWAYS GOOD

The subject of ethics for party-representatives in international arbitration has been around for as long as there has been international arbitration.

Its cousin, ethics for arbitrators, is equally and some might say even more important. Arbitration as an institution depends on trust in its central component – the arbitral tribunal. As a consequence, arbitration institutions often have codes of ethics for their arbitrators. Soft instruments such as the IBA Guidelines on Conflicts of Interest in International Arbitration supplement significant volumes of case law on the arbitrator's twin duties of independence and impartiality. There remain challenges in policing the conduct and harmonizing the behaviour of arbitrators. Yet, the task of identifying ethical rules for arbitrators and enforcing them has not faced the same daunting doctrinal and practical challenges as that of ethical rules for party-representatives. Instruments regulating the conduct of party-representatives are scant. There is virtually no law applicable to the subject.

In this chapter, the term 'party-representatives' is used because it is wide enough to cover not only licensed legal practitioners but also all others who represent a party in arbitration proceedings.

At its root, the main problem is not that party-representatives are unethical – most are. It is that their idea of what is or is not ethical behaviour varies depending on where they come from. International arbitration is a melting pot of legal traditions. It is

[*] Views expressed are the author's personal views.

often seen as an amalgamation and occasional clash of common law and civil law practices. This is an oversimplification, especially when it comes to civil law. There is such diversity among civil law systems that one cannot simply say that one particular practice represents them all.

When it comes to how counsel should conduct themselves in arbitration, there are even more points of departure. It is true that there are some core values that inform all systems. The problem is that in international arbitration, these core values are not often articulated. Every legal profession in every jurisdiction is guided by the ethical rules of their profession, be it in statutory form or a code of conduct. These rules vary from place to place. Even where there are core values, how these are interpreted and practised can vary. Hence, there can be misunderstandings when one descends into specific ethical issues in international arbitration.

Much conference time has been spent and much ink has been spilled on whether this is enough of a problem to warrant well-intentioned but overreaching regulation.

There is one view that ethical divergences in party-representatives have not been a significant enough problem in international arbitration. A counsel who gets witnesses to lie, hides documents or engages in other dubious behaviour will often be exposed and will not last long in the arbitration community. Some experienced arbitrators opine that they have not seen many cases where unethical behaviour actually affected the fairness or outcome of the proceedings.

Another view is that, leaving aside egregious behaviour such as outright deceit, misunderstandings over the parameters of permissible behaviour can be disruptive to international arbitration. They can even undermine its fairness if one party behaves according to the more restrictive rules of its counsel's home jurisdiction while the other takes a more liberal approach. It can lead to challenges to the process and, potentially, even to the award. At a Singapore Institute of Arbitrators (SIArb) seminar in 2019, a straw poll revealed strong support from the packed hall that something ought to be done to move the needle towards common standards of ethical behaviour.[1]

In his recent paper, *Counsel Conduct in International Arbitration: An Ethical 'No-Man's Land'*, Margie Jaime argues that 'there exists a need for a uniform enforceable global code of ethical conduct for counsel in international arbitration because there is, indeed, no longer a place for an 'ethical no man's land' in international arbitration.'[2] Jaime duly gives credit to leading Ethics Exponent Professor Catherine Rogers who first described the ethical gap in international arbitration as 'no man's land' fifteen years ago.[3] On the other side of the fence, Gary Born famously said

1. SIArb Seminar on 24 January 2019 titled, 'Party-Representative Ethics: Time to Move the Needle?' featuring panelists Gary Born, Michael Hwang SC, VK Rajah SC, Lucy Reed and moderated by Chan Leng Sun SC. A detailed report dated 14 March 2019 by rapporteur Adriana Uson can be found on the SIArb website: https://siarb.org.sg/events/past-events/355-party-representative-ethics-time-to-move-the-needle-24-january-2019.
2. (2019) 85(3) Arbitration at 209.
3. Catherine A. Rogers, *Fit and Function in Legal Ethics: Developing a Code of Attorney Conduct for International Arbitration* (2002) 23 Mich. J. Intl. 348.

that the proliferation of instruments on the subject has made the no-man's land as cluttered as a teenager's bedroom.[4]

II IDENTIFYING ETHICAL STANDARDS

A The Importance of Identifying Ethical Standards

Sceptics say that there is no point uttering pious aspirations if they cannot be enforced. But before questions of enforcement can be addressed, standards need to be identified and articulated. If they are not, no concrete breach can be alleged by a complainant and no sanction can be placed by the tribunal on the offending party.

But not every system needs an enforcer to be effective. If we take the example of public international law, there are few mandatory rules enforceable with the sanction of a binding enforcing authority. In particular, the International Court of Justice does not have overarching and mandatory jurisdiction over disputes. The Security Council that can decide on sanctions is bogged down by politics. Nonetheless, few actually question that public international law is indeed law. States consider it in their self-interest to be perceived as law-abiding members of the international community. When they do something that appears shocking, even apparently illegal, they do not say that the rules of public international law (be they treaty rules or customary international law) are not law. Rather, they seek to justify their actions under that very system.[5]

Identifying ethical standards has benefits, whether or not enforcement is achievable.

First, as mentioned above, they can help parties get through the first threshold: was there a breach of ethical standards in the first place? Expressly stated parameters of permissible behaviour minimize arguments on whether a line has been crossed.

Second, widely publicized rules can inform behaviour. Eventually, they help to shape norms that, over time, become widely accepted and harmonize conduct across different jurisdictions. The IBA Guidelines on Conflicts of Interest in International Arbitration, for example, are neither law nor arbitration rules. They do not bind arbitration institutions, parties or arbitrators. Nonetheless, experience shows that they are indeed used as a point of reference when questions arise as to whether a scenario definitively gives rise to a conflict, or should at least be disclosed, or raises no concern at all (i.e., whether it falls within a red, orange or green list).

Third, ethical rules can become binding if parties adopt them in a particular arbitration. For example, parties commonly agree to be bound by, or agree that the tribunal can have reference to, the IBA Rules on the Taking of Evidence in International Arbitration. However, the IBA Guidelines on Party Representation in International

---

4. Born first used this metaphor at the inaugural conference on 11 September 2014 of the Queen Mary Institute for Regulation and Ethics, on *The Arguments For and Against Further Regulation of Arbitration Counsel*. He repeated it at SIArb seminars in 2017 and 2019.
5. Robert F. Turner, *International Law Is Really Law*, (Spring 1998) 2(1) Intl. & Natl. Security L. Practice Group Newsletter 2-3.

Arbitration are not widely referred to or adopted in the same way. The caveat here is that if ethical standards are expressed merely as contractual options to be adopted, they lose their moral and normative force. That was one of the criticisms of the IBA Guidelines on Party Representation. Michael Hwang equates the voluntary approach with asking turkeys to vote for Thanksgiving.[6]

B Existing Instruments

As Born alluded to, there are already a number of instruments setting out certain standards of conduct for party-representatives.

Margrete Stevens and Doak Bishop presented a draft International Code of Ethics for Lawyers Practising before International Arbitral Tribunals for the ICCA Congress in 2010.[7] Known as 'The Rio Code', it never developed beyond its draft form.

In the same year, the International Law Association Study Group on the Practice and Procedure of International Courts and Tribunals 'proposed' a list of principles on ethical standards called the Hague Principles on Ethical Standards for Counsel Appearing before International Courts and Tribunals.[8]

In 2013, the International Bar Association (IBA) released its Guidelines on Party Representation in International Arbitration.[9] This is not the place for a commentary on the IBA Guidelines. As an explanation might be due as to why they do not suffice for the purpose proposed in this chapter, a short answer might be that reception to them has been lukewarm, with some notable criticisms being made by respectable commentators and organizations, such as the *Association Suisse de l'Arbitrage* (ASA).[10]

In 2014, the London Court of International Arbitration (LCIA) incorporated the General Guidelines for the Parties' Legal Representatives in its arbitration rules.[11] This takes a different approach altogether from the IBA or other aspirational declarations. Although called 'Guidelines', LCIA has given them teeth by requiring in Article 18.5 of the Rules that:

> Each party shall ensure that all its legal representatives appearing by name before the Arbitral Tribunal have agreed to comply with the general guidelines contained in the Annex to the LCIA Rules, as a condition of such representation. In permitting

6. Michael Hwang and Adriana Uson, *Continuing the Discourse on Party-Representative Ethics in International Arbitration* (2019) 1 SIArb J 37 at 40. *See also* Felix Dasser, *A Critical Analysis of the IBA Guidelines on Party Representation*, from *The Sense and Non-Sense of Guidelines, Rules and other Para-regulatory Texts in International Arbitration* – ASA Special Series No. 37, at p. 37.
7. *See* draft of the Code of Ethics at: https://www.arbitration-icca.org/media/0/12763302939400/stevens_bishop_draft_code_of_ethics_in_ia.pdf.
8. *See* Hague Principles on Ethical Standards for Counsel Appearing before International Courts and Tribunals at: https://www.ucl.ac.uk/international-courts/sites/international-courts/files/hague_sept2010.pdf.
9. *See* International Bar Association at: https://www.ibanet.org/.
10. For an in-depth commentary, *see* Felix Dasser, *A Critical Analysis of the IBA Guidelines on Party Representation*, from *The Sense and Non-Sense of Guidelines, Rules and other Para-regulatory Texts in International Arbitration* – ASA Special Series No. 37, at p. 33.
11. *See* Annex to the LCIA Rules, General Guidelines for the Parties' Legal Representatives at: https://www.lcia.org/Dispute_Resolution_Services/lcia-arbitration-rules-2014.aspx.

> any legal representative so to appear, a party shall thereby represent that the legal representative has agreed to such compliance.

Article 18.6 leaves the sanctions to the arbitral tribunal, which can be any or all of the following: (i) a written reprimand; (ii) a written caution as to future conduct in the arbitration; and (iii) any other measure necessary to fulfil the tribunal's general duties to act fairly and impartially and to provide a fair, efficient and expeditious means to finally resolve the dispute.

C The SIArb Guidelines on Party-Representative Ethics

Having surveyed the landscape and after deliberating on the form that its work on the subject should take, SIArb launched its Guidelines on Party-Representative Ethics in 2018.[12] This was preceded by a period of public consultation in 2017 when a Consultation Paper on the SIArb Guidelines was published. This explains the rationale for a set of guidelines rather than a prescriptive set of mandatory rules.

The Working Group avoided an overly ambitious set of prescriptions that might be based on the peculiarities of just one system which could cause discomfort and appear too idiosyncratic to gain widespread acceptance. In that case, the Working Group was careful not to blindly follow the 2015 Singapore Legal Profession (Professional Conduct) Rules or the 2014 Singapore Legal Profession (Foreign Representation in Singapore International Commercial Court) Rules, though these were considered, along with professional conduct regulations from other countries.

As the Consultation Paper explained, the Working Group drafted the Guidelines to reflect the minimum standard for ethical conduct recognized between all or the majority of the different jurisdictions under study. The Working Group also included certain rules which are reflective of common sense and that would add value to the arbitral process. The Guidelines apply to all party-representatives, whether they are qualified lawyers, in-house counsel or other disputes professionals who represent disputants in arbitral proceedings.

The SIArb Guidelines set out three primary principles for ethical conduct, followed by more detailed guidance on each of those principles.

Principle 1: Integrity of the Arbitration Proceedings

Principle 1 states that:

> A Party Representative should respect the integrity of arbitration proceedings, including the independence of the Tribunal, the Tribunal's members, and any Potential Arbitrator(s).

This Principle is followed by two specific Guidelines, the first limiting *ex parte* communications between the tribunal and each of the parties and the second proscribing a party-representative from abusing the arbitral process. Some may wonder if

12. *See* Singapore Institute of Arbitrators, Guidelines on Party-Representative Ethics at: https://www.siarb.org.sg/images/SIARB_Party-Rep-Ethics_Guidelines_Aprl18.pdf.

'abuse of process' is too vague to be applied. The Working Group believes that it provides tribunals with sufficient flexibility effectively to police proceedings. Indeed, it exists as a term of art in some court procedures (including those of Singapore). It is broad enough to cover guerrilla tactics or any moves calculated to undermine the fair and orderly resolution of disputes.

Principle 2: Honesty

Principle 2 states that:

> A Party Representative should act honestly and with integrity in all of his or her dealings with the Tribunal and parties involved in the arbitration proceedings.

All party-representatives will protest that they always act with honesty and integrity, so one might think this clause is superfluous. However, it gains more purpose when reinforced by the three specific Guidelines under this Principle.

The first Guideline prohibits a party-representative from knowingly deceiving or misleading the tribunal. They shall also not knowingly assist in falsifying documentary or witness evidence, destroy evidence or submit any documentary or witness evidence knowing that it is false. The Consultation Paper points out that the degree to which witness preparation is permitted varies from country to country, but at a minimum, party-representatives cannot falsify or assist in falsifying witness evidence.

The second Guideline prohibits a knowingly false submission of law to the tribunal. The Working Group found that many jurisdictions recognize the fundamental duty of counsel not to knowingly submit false legal statements and authorities to mislead a tribunal on the law.

The third Guideline states that where a party-representative becomes aware that their client or a witness for their client has given false evidence to the tribunal, the party-representative must advise the client to take remedial measures. The party-representative must conduct the case in a manner that does not perpetuate the falsehood if they continue to act, or if they cannot do so, they should cease to act for the client.

Principle 3: Respect and Professionalism

Principle 3 states as follows:

> A Party Representative should treat the tribunal and other parties with respect and act with the highest degree of professionalism.

There are three Guidelines to demonstrate the practical application of this Principle.

First, a party-representative should not engage in threatening or abusive conduct and should conduct itself with courtesy towards all involved in the arbitration.

Second, a party-representative shall communicate with the other party's party-representative and avoid communicating directly with the opposing party or any expert engaged by the other party. This reflects the rule in some, but not all, jurisdictions which considers it improper for counsel to communicate with the opposing party when the opposing party already has counsel. This may unduly influence the opposing party without their counsel's knowledge.

Third, a party-representative shall not speak to a witness called by its party from the time that cross-examination of that witness has started. This reflects a common practice, and many tribunals will include such a rule in their procedural order for the hearing and give a similar reminder to the witness to avoid speaking to anyone until released at the end of his or her testimony. The SIArb Guideline refers to the start of cross-examination because direct examination is usually excluded or brief and limited to the content of the witness' written statement (i.e., no new issues can arise which could be the subject of influence by the party-representative). Witness statements are taken to be evidence-in-chief, so cross-examination is usually where the substantive testimony begins.

III MAKING ETHICAL STANDARDS WORK

The main reason that ethical standards for party-representatives have not become common is the vexing problem of enforcement. Unlike arbitrators, who can be removed by either the arbitral institution who administers the arbitration or by the supervisory court at the seat of arbitration, party-representatives are not obvious subjects of supervision by either.

In 2014, ASA proposed a Global Arbitration Ethics Council (GAEC) to enforce ethical standards and impose sanctions. That idea immediately ran into obstacles. Parties or their representatives are unlikely to voluntarily submit to the GAEC. Disclosure to the GAEC will run afoul of the confidentiality of arbitration. There is also the mundane but practical question of funding the GAEC. In 2016, ASA acknowledged that the time for the GAEC 'has not yet come'.[13]

An arbitral institution can incorporate rules that give it the power to police counsel conduct or impose sanctions. That is currently an unattractive burden to most institutions. Alternatively, it can empower the tribunal, as the LCIA has done. The incorporation of regulations on party-representatives into its rules has not adversely affected the LCIA. There is no indication that parties or their lawyers find the LCIA any less attractive because of this feature.

The LCIA approach is understandably cautious regarding the extent to which it empowers the tribunal to act. Even then, some say it is too little or too much. On the one hand, the Guidelines are said to be too brief and vague. On the other hand, there is concern that the tribunal should not be saddled with the burden of judging counsel. Doing so distracts it from its primary task of deciding the dispute. It creates an unhealthy tension between the tribunal and at least one party's representatives. That might even expose it later to the accusation that it has formed a bias against one party's representatives, opening the door to a collateral attack on the award. It is true that judges in court can penalize counsel and even hold counsel in contempt. It is equally

13. ASA News, ASA Working Group on Counsel Ethics Releases latest Findings (3 October 2016).

true, however, that judges can do a lot of things that arbitrators cannot do without exposing the award to challenge.

The tribunal faces a further restriction - given that arbitration proceedings are confidential, a tribunal may not be able to lodge a complaint with the regulator or professional body that supervises the party-representative in their home jurisdiction.

At the SIArb Seminar in 2019, Michael Hwang SC identified three types of sanctions that a tribunal might impose at three stages of the arbitral proceedings:

- At the early stages of the arbitral proceedings - when the arbitral tribunal has been constituted but the hearing has not yet commenced - the arbitral tribunal has the power to impose preventive sanctions or take pre-emptive actions to prevent a breach of ethical conduct by counsel. For instance, arbitral tribunals dealing with a challenge to counsel due to a conflict of interest can exercise their power to disqualify that counsel from representing a party in the arbitration to avoid disruption. From a practical standpoint, this power is not controversial as it is done at the very early stage and does not disrupt the arbitral proceedings.
- The second stage occurs when the proceedings have started. The arbitral tribunal can theoretically impose remedial sanctions, that is, to control, stop and even punish objectionable conduct by counsel to preserve the integrity of the proceedings. An extreme example would be when counsel makes trouble at the actual hearing. In such a case, the arbitral tribunal may exercise immediate action by either admonishing or imposing penalties on counsel. Although theoretically this form of sanction can be justified, in practice it is quite difficult.
- The third stage would be after the hearing but before the award is issued. During this period, the arbitral tribunal may choose to retroactively impose punitive sanctions on 'non-disruptive' but nonetheless unethical behaviour that was committed during the hearing. Arbitral tribunals, however, would find it difficult to discipline counsel at this stage without putting their own positions in peril. Dr Hwang noted that there is a risk that the offending counsel would use this as an excuse to challenge the arbitral tribunal on the grounds of bias, thereby delaying the release of the award. On the other hand, if punitive sanctions are imposed after the award is issued, arguments might be raised that the arbitral tribunal is *functus officio*.[14]

Subsequently, he developed his ideas further with co-author Adriana Uson (a member of the SIArb Working Group on Guidelines on Party-Representative Ethics) in a paper, *Continuing the Discourse on Party-Representative Ethics in International Arbitration*.[15] With regard to egregious behaviour that will in all likelihood be

14. The Report dated 14 March 2019 by rapporteur Adriana Uson can be found on the SIArb website: https://siarb.org.sg/events/past-events/355-party-representative-ethics-time-to-move-the-needle-24-january-2019.
15. (2019) 1 SIArb J. 37, at 48-49.

proscribed by national professional rules, the authors proposed a greater role for national bar associations. First, to update their professional rules to apply to international arbitration and misconduct committed outside their home jurisdiction. Second, to amend arbitration rules to permit a tribunal to make a complaint to the offending counsel's bar association. With regard to levelling the playing field in international arbitration, they believe that a global standard of ethics will still have a role to play in harmonizing the conduct of party-representatives in fundamental areas. These may not involve issues of dishonesty as much as discrepancies in practices, such as *ex parte* communications, document disclosure, witness preparation and the duty of a party-representative when making submissions to a tribunal.

IV CONCLUSION

There is good reason why the subject of ethical standards for party-representatives in international arbitration has not gone away. In fact, there is increasing support for the policing of the conduct of party-representatives. Having touched on arbitrator and counsel ethics at his speech at the ICCA Congress in 2012, the Chief Justice of Singapore Sundaresh Menon re-focused his attention on counsel ethics in international arbitration in his keynote address at the 2018 SIAC Congress.

At the SIArb Seminar in 2019, VK Rajah SC (former Attorney General and Judge of Appeal) said that this is not a subject that can be left to self-regulation. He acknowledged not only the practical and complex issues surrounding the topic but also that the first giant step forward is to agree on common ethical standards.

The IBA Guidelines had not been well received for a myriad of reasons. The SIArb Guidelines are a first in Asia and do not yet have the cachet of an international instrument. Yet, there is no reason for them to be limited to any geographical region. To adopt VK Rajah SC's application of the Deng Xiaoping maxim, it does not matter if a cat is black or white so long as it catches mice. Whether or not it is the SIArb Guidelines, an improved iteration of the same or another instrument altogether, what matters is that stakeholders recognize that something ought to be done, and throw their support behind a set of standards for the sake of harmonization. If altruism does not work, one may recall another International Council for Commercial Arbitration (ICCA) keynote address by Doak Bishop in 2010:

> The lack of clarity as to which ethical rules apply, the existence of conflicting rules and obligations, the non-transparency and the increased size of many proceedings, combined with greater public scrutiny, creates a certain instability in the system that could result in a future crisis of confidence. It only takes one highly visible, public spectacle to shake confidence in the entire system. There are already critics of arbitration in various countries, and if a public spectacle does occur involving counsel, what easier target than to point to the fact that international arbitration does not even have a Code of Ethics for counsel.

Having a widely accepted set of standards is therefore a first step. Given the difficulty of agreeing even on content, it is probably better not to combine the set of standards with the thorny issues of sanctions and enforcement.

It is not that sanctions and enforcement are unimportant. They have to be addressed. There is sense in the view expressed by Hwang and Uson that arbitration rules ought to be amended to permit a tribunal to lodge complaints of egregious conduct with national bar associations. This is only a small step. For one, that would not catch party-representatives who are not subject to any professional regulation. However, these are a minority. Furthermore, it would not be appropriate to refer to a bar association's breaches of standards that are specific to international arbitration but may not be viewed as unethical under local bar rules.

In any case, there has to be, in time, a broader mechanism that applies during the course of the arbitration itself. Hwang had previously suggested that the task of administering sanctions be left to the arbitral institution administering the arbitration, which should set up a disciplinary committee. This has the advantage of distancing the tribunal from distracting collateral disciplinary proceedings. Hwang now thinks that arbitral institutions will not have the incentive or appetite to take on this task.

Hwang's idea should not be discarded even if the current climate does not favour it. Climates change. The LCIA has already taken a step, albeit a small step, which no arbitral institution has taken before. In time, perhaps more arbitral institutions will find that it does not hurt to take more assertive steps to deal with party-representative ethics. This is part of the process of preserving the integrity and fairness of the arbitral process. As the straw poll at the SIArb Seminar of 2019 shows, the wider community does want something to be done.

CHAPTER 5

The Reasons Requirement in State-State, Commercial and Investment Treaty Arbitration

Rocío Digón & Juan Pablo Hugues[*]

I INTRODUCTION

Before I had even met Guillermo Aguilar Álvarez, I had already agreed to assist him and Professor Michael Reisman with *The Reasons Requirement in International Arbitration*. In that book, I contributed a chapter on the reasoning in the *LG&E v. Argentina* award.[1] Now, more than a decade later, alongside Juan Pablo, I take up again the topic of reasons, focusing not only on the International Centre for Settlement of Investment Disputes (ICSID) system and annulment for a failure to state reasons, but looking more broadly at the reasons requirements (or the lack thereof) in state-state, commercial, and investment arbitration. We consider questions such as: what obligation do arbitrators have to provide reasons in international arbitration? At what point do poor reasons warrant setting aside or annulling an award? Has there been an increase or decrease of reasons, and what latitude, if any, do arbitrators have to provide their own reasons when those provided by the parties are inaccurate?

* Any views expressed in this publication are strictly those of the authors and should not be attributed in any way to White & Case LLP. White & Case means the international legal practice comprising White & Case LLP, a New York State registered limited liability partnership, White & Case LLP, a limited liability partnership incorporated under English law and all other affiliated partnerships, companies and entities. This chapter is prepared for the general information of interested persons. It is not, and does not attempt to be, comprehensive in nature. Due to the general nature of its content, it should not be regarded as legal advice. The authors wish to extend their utmost gratitude to Chloe Do, Law Clerk at White & Case LLP (New York), for her support while drafting this chapter.

1. Rocío Digón, *The Decision on Liability in LG&E v. Argentina*, *in* THE REASONS REQUIREMENT IN INTERNATIONAL INVESTMENT ARBITRATION 117-148 (Alvarez & Reisman eds., 2008).

This chapter is organized as follows: Section I addresses the reasons requirement in state-state, international commercial, and investment treaty arbitration. Section II addresses how awards may be set aside or annulled due to a problem of reasons. Section III analyzes the decisions to annul for a failure to state reasons in two jurisdictions, the United States and Mexico, and in the ICSID system. Section IV analyzes arbitrators reasoning beyond what the parties argued. Finally, we offer conclusions.

II THE REASONS REQUIREMENT IN INTERNATIONAL ARBITRATION

It is generally accepted that providing reasons for decisions is an important aspect of an arbitral process[2] and it has been identified as "one of the central duties of arbitral tribunals."[3] As the International Court of Justice ("ICJ" or "World Court") explained in the *Arbitral Award* case between Honduras and Nicaragua, an award must "deal[] in logical order and in some detail with all relevant considerations and ... contain[] ample reasoning and explanation in support of the conclusions arrived at by the arbitrator."[4] The tribunal's duty is to "identify, and ... let the parties know, the factual and legal premises leading the [t]ribunal to its decision."[5]

Reasons serve many functions: they provide legitimacy to the arbitral process,[6] they satisfy winning and losing parties of the substantive outcome of the dispute,[7] they guarantee (or not) the repeat appointment of arbitrators,[8] and they facilitate the enforcement (rather than the annulment or setting aside) of the award.[9] As will be

2. Most national arbitration laws and arbitration rules require that an award be reasoned unless the parties agree that no reasons are to be given. *See* G. BORN, INTERNATIONAL COMMERCIAL ARBITRATION 3022 (2d ed. 2014); E. GAILLARD & J. SAVAGE, FOUCHARD, GAILLARD, AND GOLDMAN ON INTERNATIONAL COMMERCIAL ARBITRATION 761 (1999).
3. *Tidewater Investment SRL and Tidewater Caribe, C.A. v. Bolivarian Republic of Venezuela*, ICSID Case No. ARB/10/5, Decision on Annulment, ¶ 163 (December 27, 2016).
4. *Arbitral Award made by the King of Spain on 23 December 1906 (Hond. v. Nicar.)*, Judgment, 1960 I.C.J. 192, at 216 (November 18).
5. *Wena Hotels Ltd. v. Arab Republic of Egypt*, ICSID Case No. ARB/98/4, Decision on the Application by the Arab Republic of Egypt for Annulment of the Arbitral Award dated December 8, 2000, ¶ 79 (February 5, 2002).
6. *See, e.g.*, *Bolivarian Republic of Venezuela v. Tenaris S.A. & Talta*, ICSID Case No. ARB/12/23, Decision on Annulment, ¶ 109 (December 28, 2018) (discussing the importance of reasons in international arbitration, the tribunal held that "the 'legitimacy of the process depends on its intelligibility and transparency'").
7. *See, e.g.*, Toby Thomas Landau, *Reasons for Reasons: The Tribunal's Duty in Investor-State Arbitration*, *in* 50 YEARS OF THE NEW YORK CONVENTION: ICCA INTERNATIONAL ARBITRATION CONFERENCE 190 (Albert Jan Van den Berg ed., 2009).
8. *See* Marta Infantino, *International Arbitral Awards' Reasons: Surveying the State-of-the-Art in Commercial and Investment International Dispute Settlements*, 5(1) J. INT'L DISP. SETTLEMENT 175 (2014).
9. *See, e.g.*, *The Government of Sudan v. The Sudan People's Liberation Movement/Army*, PCA 30 R.I.A.A., Award, ¶ 531 (July 22, 2009) ("[A]wards may be set aside for failure to state reasons where conclusions are not supported by any reasons at all, where the reasoning is incoherent or where the reasons provided are obviously contradictory or frivolous").

further discussed below, in state-state and investment treaty arbitration, these functions become heightened as there is a sovereign involved who is accountable to a broader populace,[10] the awards develop international treaty standards even without any system of *stare decisis*,[11] and a state's failure to comply with an award may have consequences on the world stage and before international institutions.[12]

Furthermore, deficient reasons in any arbitral award may trigger a series of problems: the losing party may seek to set aside or annul the award,[13] or simply fail to comply with its (unconvincing) findings.[14] If it is a partial rather than a final award, it may affect the likelihood of a settlement between the parties.[15] A deficiently reasoned award may undermine the perception of arbitration as an effective form of dispute settlement.[16]

A The Reasons Requirement in State-State Arbitration

The reasons requirement in state-state arbitration is "all the more stringent."[17] Not only has a reasoned arbitral award for centuries been an expectation and command in arbitration between sovereigns, but it may be advanced that, under general principles of international law,[18] a failure to state reasons in these sorts of proceedings calls for the nullity of the award rendered.[19]

10. *See* Marta Infantino, *International Arbitral Awards' Reasons: Surveying the State-of-the-Art in Commercial and Investment International Dispute Settlements*, 5(1) J. Int'l Disp. Settlement 175 (2014).
11. *See, e.g.*, *Wintershall Aktiengesellschaft v. Argentine Republic*, ICSID Case No. ARB/04/14, Award, ¶ 194 (December 8, 2008) ("*[S]tare decisis* has no application to decisions of ICSID tribunals . . . ."); Alexandra Diehl, *Part I: The Framework of Protection, Chapter 1: Sources of the FET Standard*, *in* The Core Standard of International Investment Protection 120 (2012) ("[T]here is no doctrine of *stare decisis* in international arbitration . . . .").
12. *See, e.g.*, *Recognition and Enforcement–ICSID Convention Arbitration*, International Centre for Settlement of Investment Disputes, https://icsid.worldbank.org/en/Pages/process/Recognition-and-Enforcement-Convention-Arbitration.aspx (last visited December 4, 2019).
13. *See* Marta Infantino, *International Arbitral Awards' Reasons: Surveying the State-of-the-Art in Commercial and Investment International Dispute Settlements*, 5(1) J. Int'l Disp. Settlement 175 (2014).
14. Convention on the Settlement of Investment Disputes Between States and Nationals of Other States Article 53(1), International Centre for Settlement of Investment Disputes, April 2006 [hereinafter "ICSID Convention"].
15. Marta Infantino, *International Arbitral Awards' Reasons: Surveying the State-of-the-Art in Commercial and Investment International Dispute Settlements*, 5(1) J. Int'l Disp. Settlement 175 (2014) (citing *Saluka Investment BC (The Netherlands) v. the Czech Republic*, UNCITRAL, Partial Award (March 17, 2006)).
16. *See* Marta Infantino, *International Arbitral Awards' Reasons: Surveying the State-of-the-Art in Commercial and Investment International Dispute Settlements*, 5(1) J. Int'l Disp. Settlement 175 (2014) (citing Rocío Digón, *The Decision on Liability in LG&E v. Argentina*, *in* The Reasons Requirement 148 n. 5 (Alvarez & Reisman eds., 2008)).
17. Giovanni Distefano, Fundamentals of Public International Law, A Sketch of the International Legal Order, 866 (2019).
18. Statute of the International Court of Justice Article 36(1)(c), June 26, 1945, 59 Stat. 1055, 33 U.N.T.S. 933.
19. International Law Commission, Model Rules on Arbitration Procedure, Article 35(c); *see also* International Law Commission, Commentary on the Draft Convention on Arbitral Procedure adopted by the ILC at its Fifth Session, document A/CN.4/92 (1955), Article 30, Commentary.

The above considerations are closely linked to the foundations of public international law. Arbitration has been the premier means of peaceful settlement of disputes between sovereigns.[20] However, arbitral awards dating back to medieval times—that is, those dictated by the Pope or the Holy Roman Emperor as sole arbitrators—had no reasoning, leading to no legal consequences.[21] Those arbitrators saw no commitment to articulate the reasons for their decisions, and did not wish for such articulation to be known, or scrutinized.[22] This tendency to avoid scrutiny has historically pervaded almost all forms of awards rendered without reasons, whether in civil or common law jurisdictions.[23]

The birth of sovereign equality—and, arguably of modern public international law—with the 1648 Peace of Westphalia brought a change in that sovereigns would no longer consent to third parties settling their disputes, and much less doing so with no articulated reasons.[24] This signified the demise of the peaceful settlement of disputes and particularly of state-state arbitration.[25] Nevertheless, the General Treaty of Friendship, Commerce and Navigation between the United States and Great Britain, famously known as the 1794 Jay Treaty, which established arbitration as the means to settle disputes between the US and the UK stemming from the former's War of Independence, brought arbitration's second air and served as a stepping stone for the duty of reasoned awards in state-state dispute settlement.[26]

Indeed, at the start of the second half of the twentieth century, the International Law Commission, entrusted with the codification of customary international law and its progressive development,[27] considered the duty to provide reasons in international arbitration as a "fundamental rule of procedure" and its absence thereof as a "serious departure" from such rule, amounting to the decision's nullity.[28]

20. *See* U.N. Charter Article 33, ¶ 1.
21. Antonio Sanchez De Bustamante, The World Court 3 (Elizabeth F. Read trans., 1925). *See also* Charles N. Brower II, *The Functions and Limits of Arbitration and Judicial Settlement under Private and Public International Law,* 18:259 Duke J. Comp. & Int'l. L., 269-270 (2008). This situation also applied to court judgments. *See, for instance,* Accursius, Gloss on Digests, D. 11.6.1; P. Taxier, *Jalons pour une histoire de la motivation des sentences, in* La motivation, Travaux de l'Association H. Capitant 5, 8 (1998).
22. Charles N. Brower II, *The Functions and Limits of Arbitration and Judicial Settlement under Private and Public International Law,* 18 Duke J. Comp. & Int'l. L. 259, 270 n. 83 (2008).
23. *Id.* (citing J.G. Merrills, International Dispute Settlement 89 (3d ed. 1998); Jackson H. Ralston, The Law And Procedure Of International Tribunals 55, 91-92 (rev. ed. 1926); Georges Abi-Saab, *Fragmentation or Unification: Some Concluding Remarks,* 31 N.Y.U. J. Int'l L. & Pol. 919, 921-922 (1999)).
24. Georges Abi-Saab, *Fragmentation or Unification: Some Concluding Remarks,* 31 N.Y.U. J. Int'l L. & Pol. 919, 922 (1999).
25. Geoffrey Best, *Peace Conferences and the Century of Total War: The 1899 Hague Conference and What Came After,* 75 Int'l Aff. 619, 628 (1999).
26. *See* Charles N. Brower II, *The Functions and Limits of Arbitration and Judicial Settlement under Private and Public International Law,* 18:259 Duke J. Comp. & Int'l. L. 265, 266-270 (2008) ("Virtually all writers trace the modern history of international tribunals to the General Treaty of Friendship, Commerce and Navigation between the United States and Great Britain, commonly known as the Jay Treaty of November 19, 1794").
27. *Object of the Commission,* International Law Commission, https://legal.un.org/ilc/work.shtml (last visited December 5, 2019).
28. International Law Commission, Commentary on the Draft Convention on Arbitral Procedure adopted by the ILC at its Fifth Session, U.N. Doc. A/CN.4/92 (1955), Art. 30, Commentary.

This perception on the significance of reasons in state-state arbitration was soon shared by renowned scholars[29] and states. As referenced by Judge Weeramantry, as early as 1843, prominent publicists have criticized the lack of reasons in the King of Prussia's award over a France-United Kingdom dispute and President Grover Cleveland's award on the *Cerruti* dispute between Colombia and Italy of the late nineteenth century.[30] This duty is confirmed more than a century later in ongoing state practice. An (allegedly) unreasoned decision affecting sovereigns was disputed before the ICJ in the *ICAO Council Jurisdiction* case between Bahrain et al. and Qatar.[31] Whereas the court did not rule on the challenge presented against the relevant award for its lack of reasoning, it neither decided that there was no need to provide reasons in arbitral awards, under international law.[32] Similarly, one of the criticisms against the controversial 2016 *South China Sea Arbitration* between the Philippines and China was the tribunal's (supposed) failure to state reasons in one of its decisions.[33]

Notwithstanding, the particular standard of arbitral reasoning demanded by public international law is unclear. In both its decisions on the *Arbitral Award* cases between Honduras and Nicaragua, on the one hand, and Guinea-Bissau and Senegal, on the other hand, the World Court upheld a one-sentence arbitral reasoning on the issue in dispute. Also, although it held in the Honduras and Nicaragua case that the

29. H. Lauterpacht, The Development of International Law by the International Court 39-40 (reprinted ed., 1982) ("A tribunal which fails to give full reasons for its decision invites the reproach that it lays down new law Absence of reasons—or of adequate reasons—unavoidably creates the impression of arbitrariness . . . When a tribunal, by failing to base a decision on articulate grounds, makes it difficult to scrutinise the law underlying the decision, it leaves the door wide"). *See also* J. L. Simpson and H. Fox, International Arbitration—Law and Practice 224, 255 (1959) ("Failure to state reasons is now generally regarded as a ground for treating the award as a nullity . . . [O]nly a comprehensive exposition of the considerations upon which the award is based . . . can suffice, and failure to support part of the award with reasons will vitiate the award as a whole . . . .").
30. *Arbitral Award of 31 July 1989 (Guinea-Bissau v. Sen.)*, I.C.J. Rep. 1991, Dissenting Opinion of Judge Weeramantry, at 115-16.
31. The necessity to state reasons in international dispute settlement between sovereigns has been espoused by Claimant in such case. The case is currently pending before the ICJ. *See*, for instance, *Appeal Relating to the Jurisdiction of the ICAO Council under Article 84 of the Convention on International Civil Aviation (Bahrain, Egypt, Saudi Arabia and United Arab Emirates v. Qatar)*, Memorial of the Kingdom of Bahrain, the Arab Republic of Egypt, the Kingdom of Saudi Arabia and the United Arab Emirates, Volume I of VII, December 27, 2018, 82-85; *Appeal Relating to the Jurisdiction of the ICAO Council under Article 84 of the Convention on International Civil Aviation (Bahrain, Egypt, Saudi Arabia and United Arab Emirates v. Qatar)*, Memorial of the Kingdom of Bahrain, the Arab Republic of Egypt, the Kingdom of Saudi Arabia and the United Arab Emirates, Volume I of VII, May 27, 2019, 57-59.
32. *Appeal Relating to the Jurisdiction of the ICAO Council under Article 84 of the Convention on International Civil Aviation (Bahrain, Egypt, Saudi Arabia and United Arab Emirates v. Qatar)*, I.C.J. Report 2020, Judgment, ¶¶ 116-124.
33. *See, for instance,* The Chinese Society of International Law, *The South China Sea Arbitration Awards: A Critical Study*, 17 Ch. J. Int'l. L. 2, 785-802 (2018). For an overall critic to this study, *see, for instance,* Douglas Guilfoyle, *A new twist in the South China Sea Arbitration: The Chinese Society of International Law's Critical Study*, EJIL: Talk!, May 25, 2018, https://www.ejiltalk.org/a-new-twist-in-the-south-china-sea-arbitration-the-chinese-society-of-international-laws-critical-study/.

reasoning must contain "ample reasoning and explanation,"[34] in the Guinea-Bissau and Senegal case, the court espoused that a reasoning that was "brief, and could doubtless have been developed further," still sufficed.[35]

In 2009, the Permanent Court of Arbitration (PCA) also had the opportunity to clarify the standard of reasoning under public international law in the *Abyei* case between the Government of Sudan—a sovereign—and the Sudan People's Liberation Movement—a political party in South Sudan.[36] Although the arbitration did not involve a dispute between two states, nor the examination of an arbitral award between two sovereigns, the tribunal traced the rule of reasoning under public international law governing sovereigns and other subjects of international law.[37] It concluded that:

> An award should contain sufficient ratiocination to allow the reader to understand how the tribunal reached its binding conclusions (regardless of whether the ratiocination might persuade a disengaged third party that the award is substantively correct). As to the substantive issue, awards may be set aside for failure to state reasons where conclusions are not supported by any reasons at all, where the reasoning is incoherent or where the reasons provided are obviously contradictory or frivolous.[38]

The *Abyei* tribunal put an important weight on ICSID annulment proceedings to reach the above standard.[39] It must be borne in mind that: (i) these proceedings follow the ICSID Convention's particular rules on the duty of reasoning, explained in Section 1(b) *infra*; and (ii) investor-state arbitration, although also governed by international treaties, generally does not deal with disputes between equal sovereigns in the international legal field. Even if reasons in international arbitration serve various purposes—such as legitimacy or enforceability, among others—that are applicable to any type of arbitration, the duty of reasons in state-state dispute settlement is aimed at justifying the imposition of a legal duty over an entity that has no superior in the international legal order (a sovereign) against another equal entity (another sovereign). It is not difficult to see that, in part, the peaceful settlement of disputes between sovereigns, the paradigm and cornerstone of modern international law,[40] rests a great deal on this consideration. Hence, while the tribunal did not explain in detail the reasons behind the weight given to ICSID case law on the matter, it can be assumed that it followed the fact that it is the most comprehensive international case law on reasons in international arbitration that comprises sovereigns.

---

34. *Arbitral Award made by the King of Spain on 23 December 1906 (Hond. v. Nicar.)*, Judgment, 1960 I.C.J. 192, at 216 (November 18).
35. *Id.* ¶ 43.
36. *The Government of Sudan v. The Sudan People's Liberation Movement/Army*, PCA 30 R.I.A.A., Award, ¶ 531 (July 22, 2009).
37. *Id.* ¶¶ 527-31.
38. *Id.*
39. *Id.* ¶ 528. After analyzing certain annulment decisions within the ICSID system, the tribunal found the following trends in reasoning concerning failure to state reasons: (i) committees may not impose what they consider "correct" or "ideal" argumentation; (ii) they should not deal with whether the ICSID tribunal dealt with all parties' arguments; (iii) arguments for every decision, not of the full award, are assessed; (iv) annulment committees are not appeal bodies.
40. *See* U.N. Charter Article 33(1).

Hence, international law obliges arbitral awards settling disputes between sovereigns to be reasoned.[41] Otherwise, the award may be set aside. Whereas the particular standard of reasoning is yet unclear, it may be advanced that extensive argumentation is unnecessary, as long as the reasoning is not contradictory or frivolous and articulates in a clear manner the decision, its basis, and its relation to the parties' arguments.

B The Reasons Requirement in Investment Treaty Arbitration

The requirement of reasons likewise exists under the institutional rules that apply to investment treaty arbitration. While in the case of the Stockholm Chamber of Commerce (SCC) and the International Chamber of Commerce (ICC), the rules that apply to these proceedings are the same as those that apply to commercial arbitrations, certain institutions have specialized rules that may apply in the case of investment treaty arbitration, as in the case of the Singapore International Arbitration Centre (SIAC).[42]

In this vein, the most frequently used institution for investment treaty arbitration—ICSID—has rules specifically tailored to disputes arising between investors and states. Article 48(3) of the ICSID Convention provides that "[t]he award shall deal with every question submitted to the Tribunal, and shall state the reasons upon which it is based."[43] Identical language is repeated in the ICSID Arbitration Rules.[44] In this sense, Professor Schreuer explains that the "purpose of a statement of reasons is to explain to the reader of the award, especially to the parties, how and why the tribunal came to its decision in the light of the facts and applicable law."[45]

In investment treaty arbitration, the reasons requirement is "so fundamental that it cannot be waived."[46] Resonating with the discussion on state-state arbitration above, the importance of reasons is heightened by the presence of a state in these proceedings, as a tribunal is called upon to scrutinize sovereign conduct. State measures may be based on specific policy decisions and influenced by domestic or global political

41. *See* Permanent Court of Arbitration Optional Rules for Arbitrating Disputes between Two States, Article 32(3) ("[t]he arbitral tribunal shall state the reasons upon which the award is based, unless the parties have agreed that no reasons are to be given"). Other means of settlement of international disputes provide the same direction. *See* Statute of the International Court of Justice, Article 56(1); Statute of the International Tribunal for the Law of the Sea, Article 30(1), establishing that "[t]he judgment shall state the reasons on which it is based." *See also* Rome Statute of the International Criminal Court, Article 74(5); Model Rules on Arbitral Procedure 1958 of the International Law Commission, Article 29.
42. The SIAC Investment Arbitration Rules came into effect on January 1, 2017, and apply to any arbitration under those rules that is commenced on or after that date. Given the recent adoption of these rules, it is too early to determine their impact on the market. It bears mention that these rules apply not only to investor-state arbitrations, but may also be applied to commercial disputes involving state entities or intergovernmental organizations. *SIAC Investment Arbitration Rules* (2017)-an overview, LexisNexis, https://www.wilmerhale.com/-/media/897896fb7a8f4dc6903e099764dc0d80.pdf.
43. ICSID Arbitration Rules Article 48(3).
44. *Id.*
45. Christoph Schreuer *et al.*, The ICSID Convention: A Commentary 1003 (2009).
46. *Malicorp Limited v. Arab Republic of Egypt*, ICSID Case No. ARB/08/18, Decision on Annulment, ¶ 38 (July 3, 2013).

developments, and states themselves have governmental responsibility to their citizens. The impact of an arbitral award, assuming the state loses, can have serious socioeconomic effects on a country—both in terms of paying an arbitral award and also on future foreign investments.[47]

The importance of reasons in investment treaty arbitration also lies in the fact that investment awards are essential to the development of an international rule of law—they establish a threshold for the scrutiny of sovereign conduct, and contribute to the development of case law and international treaty standards, having an impact that goes beyond the particular state.[48] Even though there is no system of *stare decisis*, tribunals have emphasized their role in developing the rule of law. As the *Churchill Mining* tribunal explained:

> In its judgment [the tribunal] must pay due consideration to earlier decisions of international tribunals. Specifically, it believes that, subject to compelling grounds to the contrary, it has a duty to adopt principles established in a series of consistent cases. It further believes that, subject always to the text of the BITs and the circumstances of each particular case, it has a duty to contribute to the harmonious development of international investment law, with a view to meeting the legitimate expectations of the community of States and investors towards legal certainty and the rule of law.[49]

States and investors alike rely on this consistency in existing awards, and have some expectation that reasoning will be provided, particularly when there is a deviation or alteration of a standard or its application.[50] However, as in the case of state-state and commercial arbitration, discussed below, neither the ICSID Convention nor the Arbitration Rules explain what constitutes "sufficient reasons" for an award rendered to comply with the ICSID Rules.

Hence, reasons are mandatory in investment arbitration, to the point that a failure to state such reasons can entail annulment of the award in the ICSID system. The annulment or ad hoc committee decisions discussed below shed some light on

47. The socioeconomic toll of investment arbitration has been most recently evident in Spain, where the government approved a law that would end USD 7.3 billion in pending treaty claims over renewable energy reform. Investors would be offered economic incentives in exchange for abandoning their treaty claims. The law has not yet come into effect, as it first has to be passed by the Congress. Cosmo Sanderson, *Spain offers incentives to end renewables claims*, GLOBAL ARBITRATION REVIEW (November 22, 2019), https://globalarbitrationreview.com/article/1211227/spain-offers-incentives-to-end-renewables-claims.
48. *See* Marta Infantino, *International Arbitral Awards' Reasons: Surveying the State-of-the-Art in Commercial and Investment International Dispute Settlements*, 5(1) J. INT'L DISP. SETTLEMENT 175 (2014).
49. *Churchill Mining Plc v. Republic of Indonesia*, ICSID Case No. ARB/12/14 and 12/40, Award, ¶ 253 (December 6, 2016).
50. Stephen Hunter, *A Duty to Give Reasons, But Only Just*, KLUWER ARBITRATION BLOG (November 1, 2016), http://arbitrationblog.kluwerarbitration.com/2016/11/01/a-duty-to-give-reasons-but-only-just/?doing_wp_cron=1591281938.9439361095428466796875 ('arbitrating parties typically expect reasons' in the respective award). *See also, for instance*, The Chinese Society of International Law, *The South China Sea Arbitration Awards: A Critical Study*, 17 CH. J. INT'L. L. 2, 785-802 (2018) (as mentioned above, criticizing the arbitral award for, supposedly, failing to state reasons).

what the standard is. However, the line between sufficient and insufficient reasons remains a point of controversy.

C The Reasons Requirement in International Commercial Arbitration

Akin to the other two arbitration systems analyzed here, international commercial arbitration also calls for reasoned awards. Indeed, the rules of international arbitral institutions almost unanimously provide that unless the parties agree otherwise, an arbitral award should provide the reasons upon which it is based.[51]

However, also in line with the subsections above, institutional rules do not provide any guidance on how much—or how little—reasoning is sufficient; nor do the existing commentaries to institutional rules.[52] For example, the commentary to the 2014 LCIA Rules simply provides that "[LCIA Rules] state[] that an award must be reasoned ... but [do] not set a standard regarding the extent to which the reasons must be detailed or convincing. The relevant standard thus depends on the law governing the arbitration and possibly the law on the place of enforcement."[53]

As a result, there is ongoing discussion about how far a tribunal has to go in order to satisfy the reasons requirement found in most institutional arbitration rules. This question has taken on increased importance in commercial arbitration recently, where institutions have started taking steps to increase accountability and transparency. For instance, the ICC announced in January 2019 that, due to its commitment to publicize and disseminate information about arbitration to facilitate the development of international trade, it would publish awards no less than two years after the conclusion of a case.[54] The awards may be anonymized, the parties may object to their publication, and in the case of a confidentiality agreement, publication will be subject to the parties'

51. UNCITRAL Arbitration Rules Article 34(3), United Nations Commission on International Trade Law (2010); LCIA Arbitration Rules Article 26(2), London Court of International Arbitration (2014); ICC Rules of Arbitration Article 31(2), International Chamber of Commerce (2017); WIPO Arbitration Rules Article 64(c), World Intellectual Property Organization (2014); CIETAC Arbitration Rules Article 49(3), China International Economic and Trade Arbitration Commission (2015); International Dispute Resolution Procedures Article 30(1), International Centre for Dispute Resolution (2016). *See also* Anja Ipp, *Show, Don't Tell: Creative Writing for Arbitrators*, Speech at the 39th ICC Institute Annual Conference: Explaining why you lost (December 17, 2019). In fact, the ICC conducts a scrutiny of the draft award. "The objective is, therefore, twofold: make sure that the award is intelligible for the parties and that there are no irregularities affecting the validity of the award." Charles Jarrosson, *Reasoning in Arbitration*, Keynote Speech at the 39th ICC Institute Annual Conference: Explaining why you lost ¶ 30 (December 17, 2019).
52. *See, e.g.*, Phillip Landolt & Alejandro García, *Commentary on WIPO Arbitration Rules* ¶¶ 64.9-64.13, WIPO ARBITRATION AND MEDIATION CENTER (2017); Helen Tang, Celine Wang & Briana Young, *A guide to the CIETAC Arbitration Rules*, HERBERT SMITH FREEHILLS (2015); Vanessa Naisha, Hannah Ambrose & Rebecca Warder, *LCIA arbitration (2014 Rules): a step-by-step guide*, HERBERT SMITH FREEHILLS.
53. MAXI SCHERER, ARBITRATING UNDER THE 2014 LCIA RULES, A USER'S GUIDE, 335 (2015).
54. ICC Note to Parties and Arbitral Tribunals on the Conduct of the Arbitration ¶¶ 40-46. For the influence of this trend in reasoning of awards, *see* Charles Jarrosson, *Reasoning in Arbitration*, Keynote Speech at the 39th ICC Institute Annual Conference: Explaining why you lost ¶¶ 20-21 (December 17, 2019).

specific consent. Also, since 2016, the ICC began publishing names of arbitrators,[55] the LCIA has published decisions on challenges,[56] and the International Centre for Dispute Resolution has published redacted excerpts of certain awards and decisions in a single volume.[57]

One exception, or divergence, from the requirement of reasons in arbitral awards may be found in the expedited rules provisions that institutions have adopted with some frequency in recent years.[58] On the one hand, the ICC Note to Parties and Arbitral Tribunals on the Conduct of the Arbitration provides that awards under the expedited rules must be reasoned, providing also that "[a]rbitral tribunals may limit the factual and/or procedural sections of the award, and state the reasons of the award in as concise a fashion as possible."[59] On the other hand, under the SCC Expedited Rules, and also the American Arbitration Association's Expedited Procedures, reasons are not required unless requested by one of the parties. For instance, Article 42(1) of the SCC Expedited Rules provides that "[t]he Arbitrator shall make the award in writing and sign the award. A party may request a reasoned award no later than at the closing statement." Further, the SIAC and the Rules of the Hong Kong International Arbitration Centre (HKIAC) fast-track rules provide that an award may be rendered "based in summary form."[60]

Hence, in general, international commercial awards must also be reasoned. Arbitral innovations such as expedited procedures may provide one unique exception to this duty. However, be as it may, there is no clear guideline as to the extent of the

55. Michael McIlwrath, *ICC To Name Sitting Arbitrators And Penalize Delay In Issuing Awards*, Kluwer Arbitration Blog (January 6, 2016), http://arbitrationblog.kluwerarbitration.com/2016/01/06/icc-to-name-sitting-arbitrators-and-penalize-delay-in-issuing-awards/?_ga=2.121999951.599014802.1575388167-1483886718.1574441010; *ICC Arbitral Tribunals*, International Chamber of Commerce, https://iccwbo.org/dispute-resolution-services/arbitration/icc-arbitral-tribunals/ (last visited December 6, 2019); *ICC Note to Parties and Arbitral Tribunals on the Conduct of Arbitration* ¶¶ 40-46, International Chamber of Commerce (January 1, 2019), https://cdn.iccwbo.org/content/uploads/sites/3/2017/03/icc-note-to-parties-and-arbitral-tribunals-on-the-conduct-of-arbitration.pdf.
56. *Challenge Decision Database*, The London Court of International Arbitration, https://www.lcia.org/challenge-decision-database.aspx (last visited December 6, 2019).
57. International Centre for Dispute Resolution, ICDR Awards and Commentaries (Grant Hanessian ed., 2012).
58. *See Expedited Procedure Provisions*, International Chamber of Commerce, https://iccwbo.org/dispute-resolution-services/arbitration/expedited-procedure-provisions/ (last visited December 3, 2019); P. Jean Baker, *AAA Unveils Enhanced International Arbitration Rules*, American Bar Association (September 3, 2014), https://www.adr.org/sites/default/files/ICDR%20Rules_0.pdf; *The emergency arbitrator and expedited procedure in SIAC: a new direction for arbitration in Asia*, Singapore International Arbitration Centre, http://www.siac.org.sg/2013-09-18-01-57-20/2013-09-22-00-27-02/articles/420-the-emergency-arbitrator-and-expedited-procedure-in-siac-a-new-direction-for-arbitration-in-asia (last visited December 3, 2019); *Expedited HKIAC Arbitration*, Hong Kong International Arbitration Centre, https://www.hkiac.org/arbitration/process/expedited-hkiac-arbitration (last visited December 3, 2019).
59. *ICC Note to Parties and Arbitral Tribunals on the Conduct of the Arbitration* ¶ 78, International Chamber of Commerce (January 1, 2019), https://iccwbo.org/content/uploads/sites/3/2017/03/icc-note-to-parties-and-arbitral-tribunals-on-the-conduct-of-arbitration.pdf.
60. SIAC Rules 2016 Rule 5.2, Singapore International Arbitration Centre, http://www.siac.org.sg/our-rules/rules/siac-rules-2016.

required reasoning from the institutions; accordingly, it is appropriate to look to the place of eventual enforcement for guidance.

III ANNULLING AWARDS ON THE BASIS OF DEFICIENT OR ABSENT REASONS

The international arbitral system is set up in such a way that the grounds for set-aside or annulment are limited, the threshold for a successful set-aside or annulment is high, and considerable deference is given to the arbitral award when it is reviewed. These three features may be considered relevant to an award being challenged in domestic courts, as well as to requests for annulments before ICSID or the ICJ. Furthermore, there will probably never be a case where there is a total absence of reasons for the award. However, "even short of a total failure, some defects in the statement of reasons could give rise to annulment" or to setting aside the relevant award.[61] We hereby describe the primary systems under which a failure to state reasons could affect the validity of an arbitral award.

A The New York Convention

The 1958 Convention on the Recognition and Enforcement of Foreign Arbitral Awards (the New York Convention) establishes, among other things, the rules for the international recognition and enforcement of arbitral awards by national courts. Given the relevance of this exercise, the Convention has been recognized as one of the most influential for the rule of law internationally.[62]

Particularly, Article V of the New York Convention provides the grounds upon which recognition and enforcement of an arbitral award may be refused. Article V(1) provides that the following are grounds to refuse recognition and enforcement of an award: (i) invalidity or non-existence of the arbitration agreement upon which the award rests; (ii) violation of arbitral due process; (iii) excess of the tribunal's authority; (iv) departure from the parties' agreement or the law of the seat in the constitution of the tribunal or the conduct of the arbitral proceeding; and (v) set-aside or suspension of the award by a competent authority of the country in which, or under the law of which, it was rendered.[63]

---

61. *Hussein Nuaman Soufraki v. United Arab Emirates*, ICSID Case No. ARB/02/7, Decision of the Ad Hoc Committee on the Application for Annulment of Mr. Soufraki, ¶ 122 (June 5, 2007). *See also Bolivarian Republic of Venezuela v. Tenaris S.A. & Talta*, Decision on Annulment, ICSID Case No. ARB/12/23, ¶ 112 (December 28, 2018) ("[A] total absence of reasons is so improbable that an appropriate interpretation, taking into consideration the mandate of VCLT Article 31, must extend the meaning of 'failure' to practically relevant insufficiencies such as total incoherence or genuine contradiction in order to give an effet utile to the term and to satisfy the purpose of the provision, i.e. the intelligibility of the award for the parties and the public").
62. *See, e.g.*, Reinmar Wolff, New York Convention on the Recognition and Enforcement of Foreign Arbitral Awards Commentary (Wolff ed. 2012).
63. Convention on the Recognition and Enforcement of Foreign Arbitral Awards Article V, United Nations Conference on International Commercial Arbitration, 1958 [hereinafter "the New York Convention"].

Article V(2) of the Convention lists two additional defenses to enforcement, which can either be raised by a party or invoked by the court sua sponte: (i) subject matter non-arbitrability; and (ii) incompatibility with public policy. Both Articles V(1) and V(2) permit, rather than require, a court to refuse enforcement when one of the conditions is satisfied.

As evident from the list of grounds under which an award may be refused recognition or enforcement under the New York Convention, an absence—or insufficiency—of reasons is not one of the enumerated grounds.[64] Parties have tried to fit an absence of reasons into the grounds of departure from the parties' agreement (where the parties have expressly agreed on a reasoned award), or the grounds of public policy.[65] However, this line of argument has had limited success. National courts have recognized awards that fail to provide a persuasive argumentation or to analyze every single piece of evidence submitted by the parties.[66] Conversely, trying to link the failure to state reasons to a heightened concern, such as the violation of a party's due process rights (that is, the right to be heard), has led contradictory awards or awards with short and concise reasons to be set aside.[67] Nevertheless, the demonstration that a failure to state reasons can indeed trigger indirectly one of the grounds for non-recognition or enforcement of an arbitral award is highly casuistic.[68] As

64. Charles Jarrosson, *Reasoning in Arbitration*, Keynote Speech at the 39th ICC Institute Annual Conference: Explaining why you lost ¶ 36 (December 17, 2019) ("The French Cour de Cassation has consistently taken this approach in its jurisprudence since the *Elmassian* case in 1960, and this rule has now found its way into art. 1483 of the Code of Civil Procedure according to which the failure to state reasons only constitutes a ground for annulment in relation to domestic arbitral awards").
65. Marta Infantino, *International Arbitral Awards' Reasons: Surveying the State-of-the-Art in Commercial and Investment International Dispute Settlements*, 5(1) J. INT'L DISP. SETTLEMENT 175 (2014) (citing WL Craig, *The Arbitrator's Mission and the Application of Law in International Commercial Arbitration*, 21 AM. REV. INT'L ARB. 243, 284 (2010); GA Berman, *Writing the Award–An Arbitrator's Perspective, in* INTERNATIONAL ARBITRATION CHECKLISTS 175 (2d ed. 2009)).
66. *See, e.g.*, Cour d'appel [court of appeal] Paris, December 16, 2004, 2005 Rev. Arb. 217.
67. *See, e.g.*, *Mut. Shipping Corp. v. Bayshore Shipping Co., The Montan* [1985] 1 Lloyd's Rep. 189 (English Ct. App.) (an unreasoned award is contrary to English public policy); *Domotique Secant Inc. v. Smart Sys. Tech. Inc.* [2005] Can. LII 36874 (Can. Qué. S. Ct.) (refusing to recognize unreasoned U.S. award); Corte di cassazione (Cass.), 3 Aprile 1987, XVII Y.B. Comm. Arb. 529 (It.) (public policy requires non-recognition of awards with insufficient and illogical reasons); *Société Havas et autre v société DentsuInc*, Cour de Cassation [Cass.] [Court of Cassation], January 13, 2011, REV. ARB., 2011/4, p. 1.042 (Belg.); Tribunal fédérale [TF], May 16, 2011, Case 4A_46/2011, ASA Bull. 3/2011, p. 643 (Switz.) (an award which does not take into account evidence presented by the parties and which are decisive for its decisions is contrary to the parties' right to be heard).
68. Charles Jarrosson, *Reasoning in Arbitration*, Keynote Speech at the 39th ICC Institute Annual Conference: Explaining why you lost ¶ 36 (December 17, 2019) ("[A] very recent decision by the Paris Court of Appeal dated 2 April 2019 which took the opposite view; holding that 'the obligation for *judicial decisions to state their reasons is an element of the right to a fair trial. Arbitrators who fail to state reasons for their decisions disregard the scope of their mission and recognition of an award devoid of legal reasons goes against the French conception of International Public Policy*'"). For instance, in 2016, the Austrian Supreme Court changed a line of reasoning with respect to setting aside award with insufficient reasoning, stating that an insufficient reasoning of an interim award was indeed a basis to setting aside such award in Austria, under the country's Civil Code of Procedure. *See* Sebastian Lukic and Anne-Karin Grill, *Austrian Supreme Court Establishes New Standards as Regards the Decisive Underlying Reasoning of Arbitral Awards*, KLUWER ARBITRATION BLOG (December 24, 2016), *available at* http://

espoused by the Supreme Court of Sweden, "only a total lack of reasons, or reasons that are so lacking that they can be equated to a total lack of reasons, can constitute a procedural error."[69]

The grounds for non-recognition and/or enforcement codified in the New York Convention have greatly influenced those codified by national jurisdictions, rendering it the quasi-universal standard of very limited grounds for not recognizing or enforcing an arbitral award.[70] This is also confirmed by the grounds for annulment available in the United Nation's Commission on International Trade Law's (UNCITRAL) Model Law—which has been the template for *lex arbitri* across jurisdictions in the world.

B ICSID

Unlike in commercial arbitration or other investment treaty arbitration, annulment of an ICSID award is not sought before a domestic court, but instead within its own international control mechanism, which is described in Article 52 of the ICSID Convention. Specifically, Article 52(1)(e) provides that either party may request annulment of an award where "the award has failed to state the reasons on which it is based."[71]

Professor Schreuer has identified three generations of annulment committee decisions on a failure to state reasons.[72] The first generation is represented by *Klockner I* and *AMCO I,* in which reasons had to be "sufficiently relevant."[73] The second generation is represented by *Klockner II, AMCO II* and *MINE v. Guinea*, in which the reasons requirement is satisfied "as long as the award enables one to follow how the tribunal proceeded from Point A to Point B and eventually to its conclusion."[74] The third generation is represented by *Wena* and *Vivendi I*, in which annulment committees were urged to consider the "significance of the error relative to the legal rights of

---

arbitrationblog.kluwerarbitration.com/2016/12/24/austrian-supreme-court-establishes-new-standards-as-regards-the-decisive-underlying-reasoning-of-arbitral-awards/.

69. Supreme Court of Sweden, March 31, 2019, Decision of the Supreme Court of Sweden, Case No. T 4387-07/NJA 2009 s. 128, https://www.arbitration.sccinstitute.com/Swedish-Arbitration-Portal/Supreme-Court/The-Supreme-Court2/The-Supreme-Court/d_1023208-decision-of-the-supreme-court-of-sweden-31-march-2009-case-no.-t-4387-07nja-2009-s.-128?search = hochtieff.
70. *See UNCITRAL Secretariat Guide on the Convention on the Recognition and Enforcement of Foreign Arbitral Awards–2016 Edition*, UNITED NATIONS COMMISSION ON INTERNATIONAL TRADE LAW (2016), http://newyorkconvention1958.org/pdf/guide/2016_Guide_on_the_NY_Convention.pdf; Miguel de Serpa Soares, Under-Secretary-General for Legal Affairs and United Nations Legal Counsel, Convention on the Recognition and Enforcement of Foreign Arbitral Awards (New York, 1958) (the "New York Convention"): a beacon for international trade (June 28, 2018).
71. ICSID Convention Article 52(1)(e).
72. Christoph Schreuer, *Three Generations of ICSID Annulment Proceedings, in* ANNULMENT OF ICSID AWARDS–IAI SERIES NO. 1 (Gaillard and Banifatemi eds., 2004).
73. *Klöckner Industrie-Anlagen GmbH and others v. United Republic of Cameroon and Société Camerounaise des Engrais*, ICSID Case No. ARB/81/2, Decision for Annulment (May 3, 1985) ¶ 120.
74. *Maritime International Nominees Establishment v. Republic of Guinea*, ICSID Case No. ARB/84/4, Decision of the Ad Hoc Annulment Committee (December 22, 1989) ¶ 5.09.

the parties"[75] when determining whether there had been a failure to state reasons. It has been argued that a fourth generation may exist, which emerges following the annulment decisions in *Sempra, Enron, Helnan* and *Vivendi II*. Nevertheless, this fourth generation has not been necessarily characterized by a particular interpretation of the failure to state reasons in ICSID arbitration, as in the case of the past three generations.[76]

Be that as it may, the failure to state reasons remains a fundamental ground of annulment. As of June 30, 2019, ICSID Annulment Committees have rendered seventy-six decisions: fifty-eight rejecting the application for annulment and eighteen annulling the award in part or in full.[77] In the eighteen successful applications for annulment, seven were annulled, at least in part, for a failure to state reasons.[78]

C State-State Arbitration

The means to challenge the failure to state reasons in international commercial and investment arbitration have been referred to as "compulsory control" systems.[79] They are not applicable to state-state arbitration. First, these awards are not rendered under the ICSID Convention or its Arbitration Rules. Second, national courts have little say on the validity of such awards. State-state awards establish international law obligations for sovereigns. It has been advanced that sovereign immunity from jurisdiction and/or enforcement would prevent national courts from ruling on the validity of such obligations.[80] In any case, it would be highly impractical for national courts to attempt to enforce state-state awards; for instance, there would be no means for any such court to enforce a maritime or territorial delimitation established by a state-state award.

75. *Compañiá de Aguas del Aconquija S.A. and Vivendi Universal S.A. (formerly Compagnie Générale Des Eaux) v. Argentine Republic*, ICSID Case No. ARB/97/3, Decision on Annulment (July 3, 2002) ¶ 63. *See also* Irmgard Marboe, *ICSID Annulment Decisions: Three Generations Revisited, in* International Investment Law for the 21st Century: Essays in Honor of Christoph Schreuer (Binder, Kriebaum, Reinisch, and Wittich eds., 2009).
76. *ICSID annulment awards: the fourth generation?*, 5 Gl. Arb. Rev. (October 28, 2010).
77. *The ICSID Caseload—Statistics Issue 2019-2*, International Centre for Settlement of Investment Disputes (2019), https://icsid.worldbank.org/en/Documents/ICSID_Web_Stats_2019-2_(English).pdf.
78. *Decisions on Annulment*, International Centre for Settlement of Investment Disputes, https://icsid.worldbank.org/en/Pages/Process/Decisions-on-Annulment.aspx.
79. Peter Tzeng, *The Annulment of Interstate awards*, Kluwer Arbitration Blog (July 1, 2017), *available at* http://arbitrationblog.kluwerarbitration.com/2017/07/01/the-annulment-of-interstate-arbitral-awards/.
80. *See id.*; *Chagos Marine Protected Area (Mauritius v. United Kingdom)*, Reasoned Decision on Challenge, ITLOS Annex VII, ¶ 117 (November 30, 2017) ("The United Kingdom argues that a Dutch court would have no basis to intervene and that if it did, the Netherlands would be in breach of international law pursuant to the European Convention on State Immunity, Articles 12(2) and 17 of the 2004 United Nations Convention on the Jurisdictional Immunities of States and Their Property, according to which, a State may claim immunity from the jurisdiction of a domestic court in a proceeding relating to an arbitration between States").

This does not mean that state-state awards are not subject to control or even that they should not be subject to control. Quite the contrary.[81] In fact, the failure to state reasons has been one of the principal grounds tested in the few instances of control of state-state awards. In 1984, Nicaragua asked the ICJ to annul an arbitral award rendered by the King of Spain on the maritime delimitation with Honduras, due to the King of Spain's failure to state the reasons for his decision.[82] In 1989, Guinea-Bissau invoked a similar ground before the ICJ for the nullity of an arbitral award establishing a maritime boundary with Senegal.[83] Although these arbitral awards were not nullified by the World Court, the ICJ did not miss the opportunity to state the significance of reasons in state-state arbitration and the fact that it could nullify an award containing insufficient reasoning.[84] The court has expressed this principle even in cases not necessarily related to state-state arbitration.[85]

Therefore, state-state awards are subject to different systems of control for the failure to state reasons. This is particularly relevant given the heightened importance of reasons in these decisions, as previously discussed.

IV ABSENT OR DEFICIENT REASONS: A JURISDICTIONAL COMPARISON

Notwithstanding institutional or international rules on the recognition and/or enforcement of arbitral awards, *lex arbitri* plays an important role in the determination of the duty to state reasons in an arbitral award sited in any given state, and the consequences for failing to state such reasons.[86] To illustrate how these systems interact with the

81. For arguments on the establishment of clear control of State-State awards, *see* Peter Tzeng, *The Annulment of Interstate awards*, KLUWER ARBITRATION BLOG (July 1, 2017), http://arbitrationblog.kluwerarbitration.com/2017/07/01/the-annulment-of-interstate-arbitral-awards/.
82. *Arbitral Award made by the King of Spain on 23 December 1906 (Hond. v. Nicar.)*, Judgment, 1960 I.C.J. 192 (November 18).
83. *Id.*
84. *Id.* ¶ 532 (an award must "dea[l] in logical order and in some detail with all relevant considerations and ... contain[n] ample reasoning and explanation in support of the conclusions arrived at by the arbitrator"); *Arbitral Award of 31 July 1989 (Guinea-Bissau v. Senegal)*, I.C.J. Rep. 1991, ¶¶ 43, 63; *see particularly* Dissenting Opinion of Judge Weeramantry, at 115-16, reasoning, among other things, that the "necessity for reasons in an arbitral award is of course obvious as it removes any appearance of arbitrariness in the Tribunal's decision. It is a long-established and well-respected rule... it is to be hoped, in the interests of proper arbitral practice, that... inadequate statements of reasons will not be looked upon in the future as adequate foundations on which to rest important portions of an award".
85. *See, for instance, Application for Review of Judgment No. 158 of the United Nations Administrative Tribunal*, Advisory Opinion, I.C.J. Reports 1973, at 210, ¶ 94 (July 12, 2973) ("The fact that failure to state reasons was not expressly mentioned in the list of grounds for review does not exclude the possibility that failure to state reasons may constitute one of the errors in procedure comprised in Article 11[185]. Not only is it of the essence of judicial decisions that they should be reasoned, but Article 10, paragraph 3, of the Tribunal's Statute, which this Court has found to be a provision 'of an essentially judicial character' (I.C.J. Reports 1954, at 52), requires that: 'the judgements shall state the reasons on which they are based'").
86. *See* Giuditta Cordero Moss, *Reasoning in arbitration: what do users want or need?*, Speech at the 39th ICC Institute Annual Conference: Explaining why you lost (December 17, 2019). One of the few jurisdictions that includes a failure to state reasons as an express ground for setting aside an

international and institutional rules previously introduced, the following sections explore the duty to state reasons, and the legal consequences for failing to do so, in arbitrations seated in the United States and Mexico, which were also the closest legal systems to Guillermo's legal practice. Further, the ICSID jurisprudence on annulment of awards for failure to state reasons is outlined. This jurisprudence gains great relevance as it is the only international "compulsory control" system of awards that incorporates failure to state reasons as a ground for annulling an arbitral award.

A Failure to State Reasons in United States Courts

As a threshold matter, the United States has a strong policy toward arbitration that recognizes the finality of an arbitral award. The highest state and federal courts have confirmed this over the past several decades. For example, the Supreme Court in its 2008 *Hall Street* decision provided that the Federal Arbitration Act (FAA), which incorporates as its Chapter 2 the New York Convention, "substantiat[es] a national policy favoring arbitration with just the limited review needed to maintain arbitration's essential virtue of resolving disputes straightaway. Any other reading opens the door to the full-bore legal and evidentiary appeals that can 'rende[r] informal arbitration merely a prelude to a more cumbersome and time-consuming judicial review process'."[87] Moreover, the FAA does not set out a specific duty to reason awards in any of its chapters. This further reinforces the conclusion that United States case law does not require reasoned awards.[88]

Nevertheless, the FAA sets out that *vacatur* is in place "where the arbitrators exceeded their powers, or so imperfectly executed them that a mutual, final and

arbitral award is Belgium, which it has preserved even following a reform to its arbitration law in 2013. However, the insufficiency of reasoning may not bar enforcement of an arbitral award if the award was "rendered in a country where the reasoning of an arbitral award is not mandatory." The reform to Belgium's arbitration law had the purpose of aligning it to the UNCITRAL Model Law, with a few notable exceptions, e.g., that an arbitral award may be set aside if the tribunal is found to have exceeded its powers, and if the award is found to have been obtained by fraud. *See* Gautier Matray, *Belgium Adopts a New Law on Arbitration*, KLUWER ARBITRATION BLOG (July 4, 2013), http://arbitrationblog.kluwerarbitration.com/2013/07/04/belgium-adopts-a-new-law-on-arbitration/. *See* Code Civil [C.Civ.] Article 1721(1) (Belg.).

87. *Hall St. Assocs., L.L.C. v. Mattel, Inc.*, 552 U.S. 576, 588 (2008).
88. *United Steelworkers of Am. v. Enter. Wheel & Car Corp.*, 363 U.S. 593, 598 (1960) ("Arbitrators have no obligation to the court to give their reasons for an award"); *Eljer Mfg Inc. v. Kowin Dev. Corp.*, 14 F.3d 1250 (7th Cir. 1994) ("[A]n arbitrator is simply not required to state the reasons for his decision"); *Virgin Islands Nursing Ass'n v. Schneider*, 668 F.2d 221 (3d Cir. 1981) (rejecting argument that court should "exercise [its] supervisory power to enunciate a new requirement that arbitrators file written opinions, or, at least, findings of fact"); *D.H. Blair & Co. v. Gottdiener*, 462 F.3d 95, 110 (2d Cir. 2006) ("[A]rbitrator's rationale for an award need not be explained"); MARTIN DOMKE, DOMKE ON COMMERCIAL ARBITRATION § 34:7 (2008) ("Arbitrators are not required to state the reasons for their award … . Of course, the written and signed award is a general requirement under the law in all jurisdictions in the United States, but it need not be accompanied by an opinion setting forth the arbitrator's reasoning"); Thomas E. Carbonneau, *Rendering Arbitral Awards with Reasons: The Elaboration of A Common Law of International Transactions*, 23 COLUM. J. TRANSNAT'L L. 579, 581 (1985) ("The prevalent practice has been to render international arbitral awards without explaining the reasons by which the decision was reached").

definite award upon the subject matter was not made."[89] Hence, in cases where the parties to an arbitration seated in the United States have agreed in their contract or the arbitration rules for an award to be reasoned, a tribunal that fails to meet this requirement *may* be exceeding its powers.[90] In such cases, "reasoning should [then] be part of the face of the award."[91] However, a lack of reasoning in an arbitration where the parties have agreed to a reasoned decision does not necessarily entail its *vacatur*; courts have instead called for the relevant tribunal to revert with a reasoned decision, for instance.[92] As recently as March 2019, the Southern District of New York set aside an arbitral award for a failure to state reasons.[93] The underlying dispute concerned the sale of allegedly non-compliant generators, and the parties had requested a reasoned award for the dispute.[94]

Consequently, in line with one of the core foundations of arbitration in general, certain US courts would be inclined to vacate a US arbitral award for failing to state reasons, notwithstanding the FAA and case law, provided the parties consented to such reasons. In this instance, *vacatur* responds to the failure to comply with the parties' mandate.

B Failure to State Reasons in Mexican Courts

Mexican law establishes a duty for arbitral awards to be reasoned.[95] Nevertheless, Mexican positive law also allows parties to waive the reasons requirement in arbitral

89. FAA, § 9 U.S.C. § 1, § 10(a).
90. *See, e.g., Tully Construction Co. v. Canam Steel Corp.*, 2015 U.S. Dist. LEXIS 25690 (S.D.N.Y. March 2, 2015).
91. *Bankers Life & Cas. Ins. Co. v. CBRE Inc.*, 830 F.3d 729, 733 (7th Cir. 2016) (internal quotation marks omitted).
92. *Smarter Tools, Inc. v. Chongqing SENCI Import & Export Trade Co.*, 2019 U.S. Dist. LEXIS 50633, at *13-14 (S.D.N.Y. March 26, 2019); *Tully Construction Co. v. Canam Steel Corp.*, 2015 U.S. Dist. LEXIS 25690 (S.D.N.Y. March 2, 2015).
93. *Smarter Tools, Inc. v. Chongqing SENCI Import & Export Trade Co.*, 2019 U.S. Dist. LEXIS 50633 (S.D.N.Y. March 26, 2019).
94. *Id.*
95. *See, e.g.*, José Massas Farrell, *Motivación del Laudo: una primera reflexión del Artículo 1448 del Código de Comerico en vigor*, 84 ICC México Pauta 116, 123 (2017) (citing Ignacio Gómez Placio, *El laudo arbitral no motivado. Vía de solución poco explorada en México*, UNAM: IIJ, https://archivos.juridicas.unam.mx/www/bjv/libros/6/2552/16.pdf). In particular, Mexico's Code of Commerce, the country's *lex arbitri*, determines that arbitral awards must be "motivated" (*motivados*) (Código de Comercio [CCom], Article 1448, Diario Oficial de la Federación [DOF] 13-12-1889, últimas reformas DOF 28-03-2018 (Mex.) ("[E]l laudo del tribunal arbitral deberá ser motivado, a menos que las partes hayan convenido otra cosa")). "Motivation" (*motivación*) is a term of art in Mexican constitutional law. *Grosso modo*, it obliges the decision maker to state the reasons why, given a particular set of facts and an applicable law, a particular outcome is provided. Hence, it may be argued that Mexican law requires arbitral awards to be reasoned. *Motivación* is also commonly used in Latin traditions "the etymology is interesting: it comes from *motus:* movement, and *movere:* to move. *Motivation* or *motivazione* or *motivación* (which means 'justification' in French or Italian or Spanish) is what encourages you to go in that direction, it is the expression of what leads your opinion in this direction rather than any other." Charles Jarrosson, Reasoning in Arbitration, Keynote Speech at the 39th ICC Institute Annual Conference: Explaining why you lost ¶ 13 (December 17, 2019).

awards.[96] This formula follows the UNCITRAL Model Law template,[97] and renders the duty to state reasons in arbitral awards in Mexico as a non-fundamental requirement. To some extent, this supports the fact that, even absent parties' waiver for a reasoned award, a failure to state reasons in Mexico would not lead to major legal consequences against an award, in principle.[98] Indeed, echoing UNCITRAL's Model Law and the New York Convention explained *supra*, failure to state reasons is not one of the limited issues for which Mexican courts may decline to recognize and/or enforce an arbitral award.[99]

However, presented with an "ill-reasoned" arbitral award, a party may request denial of its recognition and/or enforcement on other grounds. For instance, it may be advanced that such failure amounts to a disregard of the applicable law (such as Mexican *lex arbitri* requiring an award to be *motivated* (reasoned), or an institutional rule in this same direction).[100] There is no known case discussing this possibility, and publicists have likewise left this particular query open.[101]

A heightened degree of complexity is added to "ill-reasoned" arbitral awards in Mexico. Per Mexico's Constitution, an act from an authority may only affect an individual's rights if such act is "founded" and "motivated" (*fundado y motivado*)—that is, if it duly establishes the legal rules applicable to the decision, and the reasons why a particular result is provided, respectively.[102] In principle, this proviso does not extend to arbitral awards, given that arbitrators are not authorities under Mexican law.[103] Nevertheless, in 2013, a legal reform in Mexico opened the door for private entities affecting individuals' rights to be considered authorities, per

96. Código de Comercio [CCom], Article 1448, Diario Oficial de la Federación [DOF] 13-12-1889, últimas reformas DOF 28-03-2018 (Mex.) ("[E]l laudo del tribunal arbitral deberá ser motivado, a menos que las partes hayan convenido otra cosa").
97. *See* UNCITRAL Model Law, Article 31 ("... 2) El laudo del tribunal arbitral deberá ser motivado, a menos que las partes hayan convenido en otra cosa o que se trate de un laudo pronunciado en los términos convenidos por las partes conforme al artículo 30....").
98. *See* in support of this opinion José Massas Farrell, *Motivación del Laudo: una primera reflexión del Artículo 1448 del Código de Comerico en vigor*, 84 ICC México Pauta 116, 120-121 (2017) ("La complicación surge cuando se formula la interrogante natural de cuál sería la consecuencia del incumplimiento de dicho deber [de motivar un laudo] por parte de los árbitros. La respuesta intuitiva es que al violarse un deber consagrado en ley, un laudo carente de motivación es ilegal; sin embargo, ello no es acertado y si aun cuando lo fuera, tampoco es suficiente ni tan grave para repercutir en la validez del laudo"); Ignacio Gómez Placio, *El laudo arbitral no motivado. Vía de solución poco explorada en México*, UNAM: IIJ, available at https://archivos.juridicas.unam.mx/www/bjv/libros/6/2552/16.pdf.
99. *See* Código de Comercio, Article 1457.
100. Francisco González de Cossío, Arbitraje 712 (2011).
101. *Id.*; José Massas Farrell, *Motivación del Laudo: una primera reflexión del Artículo 1448 del Código de Comerico en vigor*, 84 ICC México Pauta 116, 123-124 (2017).
102. Constitución Política de los Estados Unidos Mexicanos Article 16, February 5, 1917 ("Nadie puede ser molestado en su persona, familia, domicilio, papeles o posesiones, sino en virtud de mandamiento escrito de la autoridad competente, que funde y motive la causa legal del procedimiento").
103. *See, e.g.*, Amparo en Revisión 2160/2009, Primer Sala, Suprema Corte de Justicia de la Nación [SCJN], 8 de septiembre de 2010, Páginas 35-38 (Mex.). For a detailed argumentation in this respect, *see* Francisco González de Cossío, Arbitraje 1106-1125 (2014).

functions established in a legal rule of general character.[104] Per this reasoning, given that arbitrators adjudicate over individuals' rights and obligations, as authorized by Mexican law (namely, Mexico's Constitution and Mexico's Code of Commerce), it can be argued that they should be equated to a Mexican authority. Hence, according to this argument, arbitrators should always reason and motivate their decisions. However, even after the 2013 legal amendment, Mexican courts have continued to hold that arbitrators are not "authorities" under Mexican law, and hence, the constitutional duties of *fundamentación* and *motivación* are not applicable to arbitral awards in Mexico, notwithstanding the "motivation" requirement in Mexico's *lex arbitri*.[105]

Given the above, Mexican law does require arbitral awards to be reasoned. However, this is not a fundamental requirement, in the sense that a failure to comply with it would not necessarily lead Mexican courts to deny recognition and/or enforcement of such an award.

C Failure to State Reasons at ICSID

As previously explained, Article 52(1)(e) of the ICSID Convention provides that an award may be annulled when it fails to state reasons on which it is based.[106] "Failure to state reasons" ordinarily means absence of reasons in respect of all or part of the award and/or providing "unintelligible" reasons which amount to "a lack of reasons."[107] Based on case law, a reasoned award allows one to understand: (i) the

104. Ley De Amparo, Reglamentaria De Los Artículos 103 Y 107 De La Constitución Política De Los Estados Unidos Mexicanos [LARACPEUM], Article 5.II, Diario Oficial de la Federación [DOF] 02-04-2013, últimas reformas DOF 15-06-2018 (Mex.) Article 5.II ("... [L]os particulares tendrán la calidad de autoridad ... cuando realicen actos equivalentes a los de autoridad, que afecten derechos en los términos de esta fracción, y cuyas funciones estén determinadas por una norma general"). *See also Postura del Instituto Mexicano de Arbitraje sobre el árbitro como posible autoridad responsable*, Instituto Mexicano de Arbitraje (2013), https://www.iccmex.mx/uploads/arbitraje/arbitro/Postura%20sobre%20improcedencia%20de%20amparo%20contra%20arbitro%20(IMA).pdf.
105. Laudo Emitido Por Árbitro Particular, Es Incompetente El Tribunal Colegiado De Circuitio Para Conocer De Él En El Amparo Directo, 1.5°.C.76 C (10ª.), 2007320, I.5o.C.76 C (10a.). Tribunales Colegiados de Circuito [TCC], Gaceta del Semanario Judicial de la Federación, Décima Época, Libro 9, Agosto de 2014, Pagina 1841 (Mex.). Arbitraje Comercial. Los Artículos 1415 A 1463 Del Código De Comercio No Violan La Garantía De Seguridad Jurídica. 166509. 1a. CLXXIV/2009. Primera Sala, Semanario Judicial de la Federación y su Gaceta, Novena Época, Tomo XXX, Septiembre de 2009, Página 428 (Mex.).
106. ICSID Convention, Article 52(1)(e).
107. *AES Summit Generation Limited and AES-Tisza Erömü Kft. v. Republic of Hungary*, ICSID Case No. ARB/07/22, Decision of the Ad Hoc Committee on the Application for Annulment, ¶ 17 (June 29, 2012). *See also Compañía de Aguas del Aconquija S.A. and Vivendi Universal (formerly Compagnie Générale des Eaux) v. Argentine Republic*, ICSID Case No. ARB/97/3, Decision on Annulment, ¶ 64 (July 3, 2002) (stating that "failure to state reasons" concerns a "failure to state *any* reasons with respect to all or part of the award" (emphasis in the original)); *Joseph C. Lemire v. Ukraine*, ICSID Case No. ARB/06/18, Excerpts of Decision on Annulment, ¶ 278 (July 8, 2013); *Víctor Pey Casado and President Allende Foundation v. Republic of Chile*, ICSID Case No. ARB/98/2, Decision on the Application for Annulment of the Republic of Chile, ¶ 86 (December 18, 2012) (stating that "as long as there is no express rationale for the conclusions with respect to a pivotal or outcome-determinative point, an annulment must

reasons upon which the award is based;[108] (ii) the facts and law, as applied by the tribunal;[109] and (iii) how and why the tribunal reached its conclusions that were determinative for its decisions.[110] Inadequate, frivolous, or contradictory explanations offered by the tribunal for its conclusions may thus warrant an annulment of the relevant award.[111] Also, certain committees have suggested that they have discretion to further explain, clarify, or infer the reasoning of the tribunal rather than annul the award.[112] In this sense, the *Tulip v. Turkey* Annulment Committee mentioned that "an

follow, whether the lack of rationale is due to a complete absence of reasons or the result of frivolous or contradictory explanations").

108. *Rumeli Telekom A.S. and Telsim Mobil Telekomunikasyon Hizmetleri A.S. v. Republic of Kazakhstan*, ICSID Case No. ARB/05/16, Decision of the Ad Hoc Committee of March 25, 2010 ("*Rumeli v. Kazakhstan*, Decision on Annulment") ¶ 104; *see also MTD Equity Sdn Bhd. v Republic of Chile*, ICSID Case No. ARB/01/7, Decision on Annulment, March 21, 2007 ¶ 92; *SGS Société Générale de Surveillance S.A. v. Republic of Paraguay*, ICSID Case No. ARB/07/29, Decision on Annulment, May 19, 2014 ¶ 140 (citing *MTD Equity Sdn Bhd. v Republic of Chile*).
109. *Joseph C. Lemire v. Ukraine*, ICSID Case No. ARB/06/18, Excerpts of Decision on Annulment, July 8, 2013 ¶ 277 (stating that "[f]ailure to state reasons as a ground for annulment is intended to ensure that parties can understand the reasoning of the Tribunal, meaning that parties can understand the facts and law applied by the Tribunal in coming to its conclusion").
110. *Poštová banka, a.s. and ISTROKAPITAL SE v. Hellenic Republic*, ICSID Case No. ARB/13/8, Decision on Annulment, ¶ 136 (September 29, 2016) (stating that it is upon committees' consideration "whether the reasons are sufficient to allow a reader to understand how the tribunal's conclusion was reached. In other words, the standard relates to the existence of reasons and not the validity of the reasons"). *See also SAUR International S.A. v. Argentine Republic*, ICSID Case No. ARB/04/4, Decision on Annulment, ¶¶ 185-189 (December 19, 2016); *Suez, Sociedad General de Aguas de Barcelona S.A. and Vivendi Universal S.A v. Argentine Republic*, ICSID Case No. ARB/03/19, Decision on Annulment, ¶ 154 (May 5, 2017).
111. *See, e.g., Maritime Int'l Nominees Establishment (MINE) v. Government of Guinea*, ICSID Case No. ARB/84/4, Decision on Annulment, ¶ 5.09 (December 14, 1989) (stating that: "minimum requirement is in particular not satisfied by either contradictory or frivolous reasons"); *Víctor Pey Casado and President Allende Foundation v. Republic of Chile*, ICSID Case No. ARB/98/2, Decision on the Application for Annulment of the Republic of Chile, ¶ 86 (December 18, 2012) (stating that "as long as there is no express rationale for the conclusions with respect to a pivotal or outcome-determinative point, an annulment must follow, whether the lack of rationale is due to a complete absence of reasons or the result of frivolous or contradictory explanations"); *Tidewater Investment SRL and Tidewater Caribe, C.A. v. Bolivarian Republic of Venezuela*, ICSID Case No. ARB/10/5, Decision on Annulment, ¶ 196 (December 27, 2016) (where the committee annulled the award in part because award was internally inconsistent and the tribunal had applied a "contradictory reasoning on the amount of compensation" that "canceled out another reasoning with respect to the same compensation"); *MTD Equity Sdn Bhd. v Republic of Chile*, ICSID Case No. ARB/01/7, Decision on Annulment, ¶ 92 (March 21, 2007) (noting that "[i]n the end the question is whether an informed reader of the Award would understand the reasons given by the Tribunal and would discern no material contradiction in them").
112. *Suez, Sociedad General de Aguas de Barcelona, S.A. and Vivendi Universal, S.A. (formerly Aguas Argentinas, S.A., Suez, Sociedad General de Aguas de Barcelona, S.A. and Vivendi Universal, S.A.) v. Argentine Republic (II)*, ICSID Case No. ARB/03/19, Decision on Argentina's Application for Annulment, ¶ 292 (May 5, 2017); *Wena Hotels Ltd. v. Arab Republic of Egypt*, ICSID Case No. ARB/98/4, Decision (Annulment Proceeding), ¶ 83 (February 5, 2002); *Hussein Nuaman Soufraki v. The United Arab Emirates*, ICSID Case No. ARB/02/7, Decision of the Ad Hoc Committee on the Application for Annulment of Mr. Soufraki ¶ 24 (June 5, 2007); *CMS Gas Transmission Company v. The Republic of Argentina*, ICSID Case No. ARB/01/8, Decision of the Ad Hoc Committee on the Application for Annulment of the Argentine Republic, ¶ 127 (September 25, 2007); *Rumeli Telekom A.S. and Telsim Mobil Telekomunikasyon Hizmetleri A.S. v. Republic of Kazakhstan*, ICSID Case No. ARB/05/16, Decision of the Ad Hoc Committee,

award is not subject to annulment if the reasons for a decision, though not stated explicitly, are readily apparent ... Implicit reasoning is sufficient as long as the committee can infer them reasonably from the terms and conclusions of the award as well as from the record before the tribunal."[113] Furthermore, the reasoning duty spans beyond the tribunal's internal analysis and applies, to some extent, to the consideration of the parties' arguments and evidence.[114]

First, ICSID Arbitration Rule 47(1)(i) requires that the award include "the decision of the Tribunal on every question submitted to it, together with the reasons upon which the decision is based."[115] Additionally, Article 48(3) of the ICSID Convention provides that the award "shall deal with every question submitted to the Tribunal."[116]

Second, as stated by the *TECO v. Guatemala* Annulment Committee, "A tribunal is duty bound to the parties to at least address those pieces of evidence that the parties deem to be highly relevant to their case and, if it finds them to be of no assistance, to set out the reasons for this conclusion."[117] In fact, the Committee partially annulled that award because the tribunal "failed to address" expert reports on damages in which the parties heavily relied on, and evidence "which at least appeared to be relevant" in the case.[118] Similarly, the *MINE v. Guinea* Annulment Committee partially annulled the underlying award because the tribunal "disregarded or implicitly rejected" one of Respondent's arguments on damages without a detailed explanation.[119]

The above clarifies different approaches to the failure to state reasons, concerning both what is considered a failure to state reasons and the particular consequences of such a finding. Whereas the ICSID system of annulment may present a more institutional and advanced system (given also its international scope) than the US or Mexican approach, the fact remains that reasons play an increasingly important role in international arbitration.

¶ 83 (March 25, 2010) (with the caveat that if non-stated reasons "do not necessarily follow or flow from the award's reasoning, an *ad hoc* committee should not construct reasons in order to justify the decision of the tribunal").

113. *Tulip Real Estate and Development Netherlands B.V. v. Republic of Turkey*, ICSID Case No. ARB/11/28, Decision on Annulment, ¶ 108 (December 30, 2015).

114. *TECO Guatemala Holdings, LLC v. Republic of Guatemala*, ICSID Case No. ARB/10/23, Decision on Annulment, ¶ 131 (April 5, 2016) ("[A] tribunal cannot be required to address within its award each and every piece of evidence in the record, that cannot be construed to mean that a tribunal can simply gloss over evidence upon which the Parties have placed significant emphasis, without any analysis and without explaining why it found that evidence insufficient, unpersuasive or otherwise unsatisfactory").

115. ICSID Arbitration Rule, Rule 47(1)(i).

116. ICSID Convention, Article 48(3).

117. *TECO Guatemala Holdings, LLC v. Republic of Guatemala*, ICSID Case No. ARB/10/23, Decision on Annulment, ¶ 131 (April 5, 2016).

118. *TECO Guatemala Holdings, LLC v. Republic of Guatemala*, ICSID Case No. ARB/10/23, Decision on Annulment, ¶ 138 (April 5, 2016).

119. *Maritime Int'l Nominees Establishment (MINE) v. Government of Guinea*, ICSID Case No. ARB/84/4, Decision on Annulment, ¶¶ 6.84, 6.101 (December 14, 1989). The tribunal explained that the fact that Respondent's argument could not prevail "did not free the Tribunal from its duty to give reasons for its rejection as an indispensable component of the statement of reasons on which its conclusion was based."

V SUPPLYING OR SUPPLANTING REASONS: CAN IT BE DONE?

Having determined that reasons are necessary for all types of arbitration procedures analyzed here, it is important to determine whether the reasons provided for a particular outcome must derive from the parties' arguments, or can go beyond them, and what the consequences would be of this exercise.

It is accepted that arbitrators have the power, but not the *duty*, to rely on rules and authorities beyond those presented by the parties.[120] Certain arbitral rules and *lex arbitri* provide for this power, at least implicitly.[121] Whereas there has been criticism of the adoption of the civil law *iura novit curia* principle to arbitration,[122] there are many decisions sustaining its application in arbitration—principally, investor-state—as *iura novit arbiter.*[123]

Nevertheless, the fact that arbitrators' legal decisions may rely on rules, authorities, or arguments beyond those presented by the parties does not mean they can supplant the reasoning of the parties. This distinction has had divergent results in practice. On the one hand, in a ruling cited as a basis for *iura novit arbiter*, the ad hoc ICSID Committee of *Compañia de Aguas del Aconquija v. Argentina* ruled that a decision of the tribunal based on a theory that "surprised" Respondent did not amount to a "serious departure of a rule of procedure" that called for the annulment of the relevant award.[124] In partial contrast, the tribunal of *Magyar Farming v. Hungary* noted, in the latest publicly known decision on this principle, that it could rely on rules

120. *See* Phillip Landolt, *Arbitrators' Initiatives to Obtain Factual and Legal Evidence*, 28:2 ARB. INT'L 180-190 (2002).

121. Section 34 of the English *Arbitration Act*; Art. 22.1(c) of the LCIA Rules of Arbitration (tribunals have the power "to conduct such enquiries as may appear to the Arbitral Tribunal to be necessary or expedient, including whether and to what extent the Arbitral Tribunal should itself take the initiative in identifying the issues and ascertaining the relevant facts and the law(s) or rules of law applicable to the arbitration, the merits of the parties' dispute and the Arbitration Agreement"); *but see* Phillip Landolt, *Arbitrators' Initiatives to Obtain Factual and Legal Evidence*, 28:2 Arb. Int'l (2002), 189.

122. Phillip Landolt, *Arbitrators' Initiatives to Obtain Factual and Legal Evidence*, 28:2 ARB. INT'L 184 (2002).

123. *See*, among others, *Daimler Financial Services A.G. v. Argentine Republic*, ICSID Case No. ARB/05/1, Decision on Annulment, ¶ 295 (January 7, 2015) ("[...] an arbitral tribunal is not limited to referring to or relying upon only the authorities cited by the parties. It can, sua sponte, rely on other publicly available authorities, even if they have not been cited by the parties, provided that the issue has been raised before the tribunal and the parties were provided an opportunity to address it"); *Oostergetel v. The Slovak Republic*, UNCITRAL, Final Award, ¶ 414 (April 23, 2012); *Bosch International, Inc. and B&P L td Foreign Investments Enterprise v. Ukraine*, ICSID Case No. ARB/08/11, Award, ¶ 30 (October 25, 2012).

124. *Compañía de Aguas del Aconquija S.A. and Vivendi Universal (formerly Compagnie Générale des Eaux)*, ICSID Case No. ARB/97/3, Decision on Annulment, ¶ 84 (July 3, 2002) ("Claimants contend the Tribunal's decision came unannounced, and that they had no opportunity to present arguments on the decision to dismiss their claim on the merits on grounds related to Article 16(4) of the Concession Contract. It may be true that the particular approach adopted by the Tribunal in attempting to reconcile the various conflicting elements of the case before it came as a surprise to the parties, or at least to some of them. But even if true, this would by no means be unprecedented in judicial decision-making, either international or domestic, and it has nothing to do with the ground for annulment contemplated by Article 52(1)(d) of the ICSID Convention").

and authorities outside those presented by the parties, provided they were debated by the parties *and* did not surprise them.[125] At least in investment arbitration, this approach is closer to the most recent developments on the issue[126] and works against the argument that arbitrators may espouse reasons unrelated to the presentations of the parties.

On the other hand, the Annulment Committee in *Enron v. Argentina* advanced additional arguments and Article 52 grounds not relied on by Argentina. Specifically, it decided that the tribunal's acceptance of the late submission of an expert report was a departure from a fundamental rule of procedure—party autonomy—as the parties themselves had agreed on the submission deadlines.[127] The committee again invoked departure from a fundamental rule of procedure in regard to an alleged lack of impartiality, a ground on which Argentina did not rely for its argument.[128] Notwithstanding such a conclusion, it is important to recognize that ICSID Annulment Committees are "not ... court[s] of appeal. [They're] not authorized to qualify a tribunal's reasoning as superficial, substandard, deficient, wrong or otherwise faulty, and thus, substitute its judgment for that of the tribunal."[129] This principle applies *mutatis mutandis* to all adjudicative organs analyzing the failure to state reasons in either commercial or investment treaty arbitration.[130]

Given the above, even if *iura novit arbiter* is applicable in arbitration, it is unlikely that tribunals will provide a reasoning completely detached from what was argued or debated by the parties. It is unlikely that an award that failed to set out a relevant argument not advanced by the parties would run the risk of annulment or a refusal of recognition or enforcement. *Enron v. Argentina* therefore appears to be an exception.

Interestingly, if the same tribunal had decided to rely on a relevant argument that the parties had not presented under the theory of *iura novit arbiter* then the award would also likely survive challenge provided the tribunal has applied the legal system applicable to the dispute.[131] Such application of a new argument does not fall into one

125. *Magyar Farming Company Ltd, Kintyre Kft and Inicia Zrt v. Hungary*, ICSID Case No. ARB/17/27, Award, ¶ 27 (November 13, 2019) ("When applying the law, whether municipal or international, the Tribunal is not bound by the arguments and sources invoked by the Parties. The principle of iura novit arbiter allows the Tribunal to form its own opinion of the meaning of the law, provided that it does not surprise the Parties with a legal theory that was not subject to debate and that the Parties could not anticipate").

126. *Vestey Group Ltd v. Bolivarian Republic of Venezuela*, ICSID Case No. ARB/06/4, Award, ¶ 118 (April 15, 2016) ("When applying the law (whether national or international), the Tribunal is of the view that it is not bound by the arguments and sources invoked by the Parties. The principle iura novit curia-or better, iura novit arbiter-allows the Tribunal to form its own opinion of the meaning of the law, provided that it does not surprise the Parties with a legal theory that was not subject to debate and that the Parties could not anticipate").

127. *Enron Creditors Recovery Corp. & Ponderosa Assets, L.P. v. The Argentine Republic*, Decision on the Application for Annulment of the Argentine Republic ¶ 197 (July 30, 2010).

128. *Id.* ¶ 278.

129. *Bolivarian Republic of Venezuela v. Tenaris S.A. & Talta*, ICSID Case No. ARB/12/23, Decision on Annulment, ¶ 110 (December 28, 2018).

130. *Updated Background Paper on Annulment for the Administrative Council of ICSID*, International Centre for Settlement of Investment Disputes, ¶ 74 (May 5, 2016).

131. Phillip Landolt, *Arbitrators' Initiatives to Obtain Factual and Legal Evidence*, 28:2 Arb. Int'l 192 (2002) ("The predominant tendency in arbitration is to treat as *ultra petita* only those awards which decide beyond the relief sought by the parties, and not those in which the reasoning goes

of the limited grounds for annulling an interstate, an investor-state or a commercial arbitration award.

It must be borne in mind that the reasons brought by the tribunal to an award sua sponte are not isolated; they coexist with the duty to uphold basic principles of due process, such as procedural equality and the duty not to exceed powers or go beyond the parties' consent.[132] Whereas novel or additional reasoning may not per se raise a ground for annulment, it could be utilized to argue the breach of another ground such as due process where the parties were not provided an opportunity to comment on the tribunal's new reasons. For instance, it may be argued that certain sources utilized by the tribunal, and not by the parties, favored one particular party, breaching a duty of procedural equality.

VI CONCLUSIONS

Reasons have a critical role in state-state, investor-state and international commercial arbitration. While it is difficult to prescribe what form reasons should take in an award, or how exhaustive they should be, it is our position that arbitrators should use the following signposts as guides:

- Regardless of the type of arbitration, arbitrators should consider the parties' arguments and facts, and allow the reader to follow the tribunal's path in reaching a particular decision.
- In arbitrations involving state parties and sovereign interests, tribunals should render awards that recognize the sovereign interests at stake, and the implications of a particular decision in the system within which it is circumscribed (investment arbitration or public international law, even in the absence of *stare decisis*).
- Tribunals in any type of arbitration should be mindful of control systems available, where failure to state reasons can cause annulment of the award and, in the long term, negatively affect rather than settle the dispute submitted to it.
- Whenever analyzing the reasons in international arbitration, finality of arbitral awards should be respected. No body that controls arbitral awards for failure to state reasons, or for any other reason, should be an appeal instance of the award, unless clearly provided by the parties.
- Whereas arbitrators have the power to undertake their own investigation into the laws relevant to the settlement of the dispute, they should avoid deciding cases upon points not raised by the parties without first giving them an opportunity to comment.

---

beyond the parties' submissions, if in fact the result of this is an award within the relief sought by the parties. By consequence, arbitrators need not usually fear interference with their award on the basis of a challenge of *ultra petita*").

132. Phillip Landolt, *Arbitrators' Initiatives to Obtain Factual and Legal Evidence*, 28:2 ARB. INT'L 191-194 (2002).

It is no surprise that reasons in international arbitration caught Guillermo Aguilar Álvarez's attention. Guillermo was a brave advocate of international arbitration as a means to settle international disputes. As demonstrated, reasons are an element sitting at the core of this mechanism, making and preserving it as—possibly—the most attractive means to settle international disputes. We hope that these guidelines will support arbitrators in their quest to provide effective, well-written and well-reasoned awards.

CHAPTER 6

The Viability of the Alternatives to International Investment Law and Arbitration: International and Domestic Perspectives

Georgios Dimitropoulos[*]

I INTRODUCTION

There is a burgeoning discussion on the role of international investment law and arbitration (IILA), as well as its reform, currently taking place in academic circles, international organizations, and national governments.[1] Several proposals have been put forward for reform of the international investment regime.[2] Most proposals concern reform of the system of investor-State arbitration—commonly referred to as Investor-State Dispute Settlement (ISDS).[3] The international community seems to have placed all its reform hopes on an aspired Multilateral Investment Court (MIC).[4] The

* I would like to thank Professors W. Michael Reisman, Julien Chaisse and Lauge Poulsen for very insightful comments. All errors remain mine.

1. For an early discussion of this topic, *see* Guillermo Aguilar Álvarez & William W. Park, "The New Face of Investment Arbitration: NAFTA Chapter 11" (2003) 28 *Yale Journal of International Law* 365.
2. *See, e.g.*, Georgios Dimitropoulos, "Investor-State Dispute Settlement Reform and Theory of Institutional Design" (2018) 9 *JIDS* 535 (proposing a theory of institutional design for international dispute settlement and ISDS more specifically).
3. But *see, e.g.*, Catharine Titi, "The Evolution of Substantive Investment Protections in Recent Trade and Investment Treaties," *RTA Exchange* (Geneva: International Centre for Trade and Sustainable Development and the Inter-American Development Bank, 2018), available at http://www.ictsd.org/sites/default/files/research/ictsd_-_the_evolution_of_substantive_investment_protections_in_recent_trade_and_investment_treaties_-_titi.pdf accessed September 15, 2019 (discussing reform of substantive standards of protection).
4. *See* section II.E below.

chapter suggests that investment law has an expanding domestic life, which remains largely understudied.[5] A complementary and sometimes alternative approach States have been developing to promote foreign investment away from international law has been to focus on the development of new domestic legislative frameworks such as investment laws, arbitration laws, and new regimes of Special Economic Zones (SEZs). The domestic side of investment law and its role in investment law reform deserve a closer look.

International investment law was only developed as a separate field of international law in the 1960s. Before the advent of the Bilateral Investment Treaty (BIT) system, overseas investors relied mostly on the domestic law of the territory in which they were investing, and domestic law was the main body of law regulating investment.[6] The domestic and the international level of protection of investors and investments are thus to some extent functionally equivalent. The present chapter aims to bring this layer of the international investment regime to the forefront of the debates on international investment law and its reform.[7] In accordance with the overall focus of the book, which is dedicated to the memory of Guillermo Aguilar Álvarez, examples will be drawn from Latin America. Some Latin American governments have been leading the backlash movement against international investment arbitration—and substantive international investment law.[8] Bolivia and Ecuador have terminated many of their BITs. Some South American States have also denounced the ICSID Convention in accordance with Article 71 of the same treaty, namely Bolivia on May 2, 2007,

5. But *see* Georgios Dimitropoulos, "National Sovereignty and International Investment Law: Sovereignty Reassertion and Prospects of Reform" (2020) 21 *Journal of World Investment & Trade* 71. *See also* Sergio Puig & Gregory Shaffer, "Imperfect Alternatives: Institutional Choice and the Reform of Investment Law" (2018) 112 *American Journal of International Law* 361.
6. International investment law as a separate field of international law may be viewed as being established with the 1959 Germany-Pakistan BIT, available at https://investmentpolicy.unctad.org/international-investment-agreements/treaties/bilateral-investment-treaties/1732/germany---pakistan-bit-1959-). Investment clauses were previously included in Friendship, Commerce, and Navigation (FCN) Treaties that were mostly signed between Western States. Investment protection has otherwise been part of general international law in the form of the MST. For an excellent historical account, *see* Thomas Johnson Jr. and Jonathan Gimblett, "From Gunboats To Bits: The Evolution of Modern International Investment Law," in Karl P. Sauvant ed., *Yearbook on International Investment Law & Policy* (Oxford University Press 2010-2011) 649; *see also* generally Stephan W. Schill, Christian J. Tams & Rainer Hofmann, International Investment Law and History (Edward Elgar 2018); Taylor St. John, *The Rise of Investor-State Arbitration: Politics, Law, and Unintended Consequences* (OUP 2018).
7. *See generally* on the interplay between domestic and international law Hege Elisabeth Kjos, *Applicable Law in Investor-State Arbitration: The Interplay Between National and International Law* (OUP 2013).
8. Professor Reisman suggests that in large part the reaction against the "Great Compact" of the contemporary international investment system has been spearheaded by the originally capital-exporting countries that have now found themselves also at the capital-importing end; *see* W. Michael Reisman, "The Empire Strikes Back: The Struggle to Reshape ISDS," *White & Case International Arbitration Lecture (The Lamm Lecture)* (February 16, 2017), available at SSRN: https://ssrn.com/abstract=2943514, at 12-16; on the broader socioeconomic reasons for the reaction against the Great Compact, *see ibid.*, at 16-21. On backlash in IILA, *see* generally Michael Waibel, Asha Kaushal, Kyo-Hwa Chung and Claire Balchin (eds.), *The Backlash Against Investment Arbitration. Perceptions and Reality* (Wolters Kluwer 2012); Malcolm Langford, Daniel Behn and Ole Kristian Fauchald, "Backlash and State Strategies in International Investment Law," in Tanja Aalberts and Thomas Gammeltoft-Hansen (eds.), *The Changing Practices of*

Ecuador on July 16, 2009, and Venezuela on January 24, 2012. Latin America has also been the testing ground for most of the reform initiatives at the international and domestic levels of governance.[9] Brazil, for example, has started developing a new model of bilateral investment agreement that focuses on investment facilitation. The move to domestic law in investor protection shows that the backlash against IILA does not signify a new era of economic isolation for States. It is rather an effort to achieve similar ends under the BIT system, using different means, of attracting foreign investors, by exercising at the same time more control over foreign investment.

The chapter makes moreover an effort to develop standards to measure the viability of the alternatives to IILA as it currently stands. The alternatives can be measured against international law and domestic law standards; both international and domestic law standards are considered, with the suggestion that there are two ways ahead regarding the future of IILA: either strengthening the existing market system in international arbitration and addressing concerns of States by providing a larger and more diverse pool of arbitrators or increasing reliance on domestic law and institutions. Domestic law and institutions have started operating as signals of good investment environment to attract foreign investors when they make investment decisions in the same way that BITs operated during the era of BIT proliferation.

The chapter proceeds as follows: Section II discusses the international law alternatives to the current system of IILA, focusing on dispute resolution alternatives. Section III turns to alternatives from the domestic law of the host State of the investment. It discusses aspects of domestic law that have been developed to manage specifically foreign investment flows and also other aspects of a domestic legislative framework that may have an influence on foreign investment. Section IV presents normative standards for the assessment of the alternatives to the current system of IILA. The standards are drawn from the normative framework of both international and domestic laws and help identify what reform alternatives should be preferred over others. Section V draws conclusions.

II INTERNATIONAL LAW ALTERNATIVES TO THE CURRENT SYSTEM OF IILA

IILA has been subject to various criticisms as it has been argued that investment tribunals reflect the values of the private system of commercial arbitration.[10] As a result, there is a failure to provide consistent and coherent case law for the field of international investment law; the costs of proceedings have become excessive, the

International Law (CUP 2018), 70; Georgios Dimitropoulos, "The Conditions for Reform: A Typology of 'Backlash' and Lessons for Reform in International Investment Law and Arbitration" (2020) 18 *LPICT* 416.

9. *See also* Catharine Titi, "Investment Arbitration in Latin America: The Uncertain Veracity of Preconceived Ideas" (2014) 30 *Arbitration International* 357; Mélida N. Hodgson, "Reform and Adaptation: The Experience of the Americas with International Investment Law" (2020) 21 *JWIT* 140.
10. *See generally* Thomas Schultz, "The Ethos of Arbitration," in Thomas Schultz and Federico Ortino (eds), *Oxford Handbook of International Arbitration* (OUP 2020) 235.

duration is overlong, and decisions are incorrect. In addition, it has been said that the arbitrator network is not sufficiently diverse, while arbitrators may be perceived as dependent, partial, and non-neutral. More broadly, IILA has been criticized for lacking the legitimacy of permanent dispute resolution bodies.[11]

As a reaction, a series of institutional reform alternatives have been proposed. International organizations like the United Nations Conference on Trade and Development (UNCTAD) and the United Nations Commission on International Trade Law (UNCITRAL) have been heavily involved in the debate,[12] alongside legal academics.[13] One can imagine two areas of reform of IILA: one is to improve the substantive provisions of international investment law included in BIT and multilateral investment treaties, such as the standards of protection and expropriation; another is the reform of ISDS. Most proposals have focused on the latter. The present chapter discusses some of the proposals with a focus on ISDS reform.[14]

A Institutional Selection of Arbitrators

International investment arbitration draws on international commercial arbitration, where party autonomy is largely prevalent; party autonomy finds its utmost expression as the right of the parties to appoint arbitrators of their choice. Given the lack of

11. *See* Malcolm Langford, Daniel Behn and Laura Letourneau-Tremblay, "Investment Arbitration and its Discontents: An Empirical Assessment," *EJIL:Talk* (April 5, 2019) (drawing on the work of the Academic Forum of the UNCITRAL WG III); *see also* Julien Chaisse and Rahul Donde, "The State of Investor-State Arbitration: A Reality Check of the Issues, Trends, and Directions in Asia-Pacific" (2018) 51(1) *The International Lawyer* 47.
12. *See* UNCTAD, "Reform of Investor-State Dispute Settlement: In Search of a Roadmap," *IIA Issues Note No 2* (June 2013). The ISDS reform discussion process is currently taking place within Working Group III (WGIII): Investor-State Dispute Settlement Reform of the United Nations Commission on International Trade Law (UNCITRAL), the workings of which are made available online at: http://www.uncitral.org/uncitral/en/commission/working_groups/3 Investor_State.html accessed September 15, 2019; *see generally* Malcolm Langford, Michele Potestà, Gabrielle Kaufmann-Kohler and Daniel Behn, "Special Issue: UNCITRAL and Investment Arbitration Reform: Matching Concerns and Solutions – An Introduction" (2020) 21 *Journal of World Investment & Trade* 167 (*see also* the other contributions in the same special issue); *see also* Chiara Giorgetti, Laura Létourneau-Tremblay, Daniel Behn and Malcolm Langford, "Reforming International Investment Arbitration: an Introduction" (2019) 18 *The Law and Practice of International Courts and Tribunals* 303 (*see also* the other contributions in the same special issue).
13. The Academic Forum on ISDS has the purpose of providing a venue for academics to exchange views, explore issues and options, test ideas and solutions, and make a constructive contribution to the ongoing discussions on possible reform of ISDS, in particular to discussions in the context of UNCITRAL's WGIII; *see* Academic Forum on ISDS, Statement of Purpose (CIDS—Geneva Center for International Dispute Settlement, March 12, 2018), available at https://www.cids.ch /images/Documents/ISDS-AcademicForum/Academic_Forum_ISDS_Statement_of_Purpose.pd f accessed September 15, 2019; *see also* Georgios Dimitropoulos, "Comparative and International Investment Law: Prospects for Reform—An Introduction" (2020) 21 *Journal World Investment & Trade* 1 (*see also* the other contributions in the same special issue).
14. This section is largely based on Dimitropoulos, "Constructing the Independence of International Investment Arbitrators: Past, Present and Future" (2016) 36 Northwestern Journal of International Law and Business 371, and Dimitropoulos, *supra* n. 2.

court-like institutional independence guarantees in international investment arbitration,[15] it has been suggested that all members of an arbitral tribunal should be appointed by arbitral institutions.[16] The abolition of party appointment and the institutional selection of arbitrators would allow for more transparency in the appointment process, better control of the quality of the appointed arbitrators, and possibly more diversity of the selected arbitrators.

B Appeals Facility

One of the main criticisms of the current system of ISDS is the limited control of the arbitral awards by another instance of review.[17] The annulment proceeding available under International Centre for Settlement of Investment Disputes (ICSID) only allows a rejection of the claim or annulment of the decision of the tribunal for a limited set of reasons.[18] Introducing an appeals facility as a second instance of review similar to the World Trade Organization Appellate Body (WTO AB) has attracted considerable attention as a reform option.[19] Standing appellate bodies could correct erroneous decisions of first-instance ad hoc tribunals, enhance consistency, and thus contribute to greater accountability of the system.[20]

This reform alternative is possible independent of whether the future of ISDS remains in the format of arbitration tribunals or ISDS is replaced by an investment court. Some international treaties have already included a second instance of review. Article 28(10) of the US Model BIT of 2012 as well as recent treaties concluded by the United States have the possibility of establishing an appeals panel.[21] The Comprehensive Economic and Trade Agreement (CETA) between Canada and the EU includes a

15. Dimitropoulos, *supra* n. 14.
16. Jan Paulsson, "Moral Hazard in International Dispute Resolution" (2010) 25 *ICSID Review* 339; Albert Jan van den Berg, "Dissenting Opinions by Party-Appointed Arbitrators in Investment Arbitration," in Mahnoush Arsanjani et al. (eds.), *Looking to the Future: Essays on International Law in Honor of W. Michael Reisman* (Brill 2011) 821.
17. UNCTAD, *Investor-State Dispute Settlement A Sequel: Series on Issues in International Investment Agreements* (UN 2014) 27.
18. Articles 52 and 53 ICSID Convention.
19. Johanna Kalb, "Creating an ICSID Appellate Body" (2005) 10 UCLA Journal of International Law and Foreign Affairs 179; Andrea K. Bjorklund, "The Continuing Appeal of Annulment: Lessons from Amco Asia and CME," in Todd Weiler (ed.), *International Investment Law and Arbitration: Leading Cases from the ICSID, NAFTA, Bilateral Treaties And Customary International Law* (Cameron May 2005) 471, 479; Christian J. Tams, "An Appealing Option? The Debate about an ICSID Appellate Structure," *Essays in Transnational Economic Law No. 57* (June 2006); David A. Gantz, "An Appellate Mechanism for Review of Arbitral Decisions in Investor-State Disputes: Prospects and Challenges" (2006) 39 *Vanderbilt Journal of Transnational Law* 39; Karl P. Sauvant (eds.), *Appeals Mechanism in International Investment Disputes* (OUP 2008).
20. UNCTAD, *World Investment Report 2015: Reforming International Investment Governance* (UN 2015) 150.
21. Article 28(10) US Model BIT (2012); Article 10.20(10) and Annex 10-F of the United States-Central American Dominican Republic Free Trade Agreement (CAFTA-DR).

"Tribunal" and an "Appellate Tribunal,"[22] and the EU-Singapore Free Trade Agreement (FTA) sets up a "Tribunal of First Instance" and an "Appeal Tribunal."[23]

C Codes of Conduct

International investment agreements (IIAs) also increasingly include ethical requirements for adjudicators in the form of codes of conduct.[24] The EU and its partners, for example, have drafted codes of conduct with specific obligations that will be applicable to all adjudicators in all instances operating within the framework of the agreements.[25] The codes include provisions on conflicts of interests, as well as on broader questions concerning the ethics and conduct of adjudicators.[26] The Secretariats of ICSID and UNCITRAL also released a first draft of the Code of Conduct for Adjudicators in ISDS.[27] These codes can coexist with any system of dispute settlement in investment law.

D List System

Article 23 of the Convention for the Pacific Settlement of Disputes of 1899 that established the Permanent Court of Arbitration (PCA) introduced the "list system" in the selection of arbitrators. According to the Convention, the PCA drafts a list of eligible arbitrators from which the parties can select their preferred arbitrators—this is offered as an option, not as an obligation.[28] The ICSID Convention also uses a list for arbitrator selection.[29] The list consists of designations by the Chairman of the Administrative Council of ICSID—the President of the World Bank Group—[30] and designations by contracting States.[31] The list is not closed, and the parties to disputes are free to appoint arbitrators not included in the list.

A closed list arrangement would limit the choice of arbitrators to a narrow number of individuals so as to avoid the "double hat" practice.[32] The current Article 8.27(17) CETA, for example, provides for a closed list of arbitrators binding on an appointing authority if the parties fail to constitute a tribunal within the prescribed

22. Articles 8.27 and 8.28 respectively of Section F Chapter Eight of CETA (all references in the present Article to CETA refer to Section F of Chapter Eight; final version).
23. Article 3.9 and 3.10 respectively of Section A Chapter Three of the EU-Singapore FTA.
24. *See generally* Chiara Giorgetti and Mohammed Wahab, "A Code of Conduct for Arbitrators and Judges," *Academic Forum on ISDS Concept Paper 2019/12* (October 13, 2019).
25. Annex 29B CETA.
26. *See also European Commission, Investment Protection and Investor-to-State Dispute Settlement in EU Agreements* (November 2013) 9.
27. ICSID and UNCITRAL, Draft Code of Conduct for Adjudicators in Investor-State Dispute Settlement, available at https://icsid.worldbank.org/en/Documents/Draft_Code_Conduct_Adjudicators_ISDS.pdf accessed July 1, 2020.
28. Article 23 of the Convention for the Pacific Settlement of Disputes of 1899.
29. Article 3 ICSID Convention.
30. *See* Article 13(2) ICSID Convention.
31. *See* Article 13(1) ICSID Convention
32. *See* Malcolm Langford, Daniel Behn and Runar Hilleren Lie, "The Revolving Door in International Investment Arbitration" (2017) 20 Journal of International Economic Law 301.

timeframe. This system does not abandon the idea of party appointment but tries at the same time to increase the safeguards of independence and impartiality of adjudicators.

E Diplomacy and ADR

The traditional public international law means of resolving disputes involving foreign nationals has been through diplomacy.[33] Some recent reform proposals include a return to diplomatic protection in international investment law.[34] UNCTAD, for example, has developed a toolkit for dispute resolution using the means of classical international law, or what is called in contemporary parlance Alternative Dispute Resolution (ADR)—negotiation, conciliation, and mediation or other managed conflict prevention measures like good offices and inquiry—but in a more structured way within investment treaties.[35] Means of resolving disputes through ADR have been included in some recent IIAs.[36]

Since 2015, Brazil has adopted a modified version of this approach in its recently signed Agreements on Cooperation and Facilitation of Investments (ACFIs) with countries in Latin America and Africa. The focus of the agreements is on dispute prevention rather than dispute resolution. Facilitation of dialogue and coordination between States and investors are achieved through a joint committee and an ombudsperson appointed by the two parties to the ACFIs.[37] The ACFIs provide progressive steps for the settlement of investment disputes: the Ombudsperson shall act as a mediator to settle any dispute amicably; if amicable settlement fails, one of the governments may bring the dispute before the Joint Committee; if the dispute is not settled by the Joint Committee, the two governments may decide to resort to interstate arbitration.

F Standing International Investment Court(s)

The most radical solution for the revamping of ISDS has been the idea of creating standing courts in place of the system of ad hoc tribunals.[38] The idea for a standing

33. *See* Johnson Jr. and Gimblett, *supra* n. 6.
34. M. Sornarajah, "Starting Anew in International Investment Law," *Columbia FDI Perspectives no. 74* (July 16, 2012).
35. UNCTAD, *Investor-State Disputes: Prevention and Alternatives to Arbitration* (United Nations 2010).
36. *See, e.g.*, Article 3 (Amicable Resolution), Article 4 (Consultations), Article 5 (Mediation), as well as Annex III (Mediation Mechanism for Investment Disputes) of the EU-Vietnam FTA.
37. Nitish Monebhurrun, "Novelty in International Investment Law: The Brazilian Agreement on Cooperation and Facilitation of Investments as a Different International Investment Agreement Model" (2017) 8 *JIDS* 79; Michelle Ratton Sanchez Badin and Fabio Morosini, "Navigating between Resistance and Conformity with the International Investment Regime: the Brazilian Agreements on Cooperation and Facilitation of Investments (ACFIs)" in Fabio Morosini and Michelle Ratton Sanchez Badin (eds.), *Reconceptualizing International Investment Law from the Global South* (Cambridge University Press 2017) 188.
38. *See, e.g.*, Gabrielle Kaufmann-Kohler and Michele Potestà, *Can the Mauritius Convention Serve as a Model for the Reform of Investor-State Arbitration in Connection with the Introduction of a Permanent Investment Tribunal or An Appeal Mechanism? Analysis and Roadmap* (CIDS 2016);

investment court was expressed in UNCTAD's World Investment Report of 2015,[39] and the UNCTAD Investment Policy Framework for Sustainable Development (IPFSD).[40] UNCITRAL started discussing possible multilateral approaches in ISDS in 2017.[41]

The EU has become the strongest advocate for this approach and has envisaged two types of standing investment courts: (1) bilateral or plurilateral investment courts operating within the framework of a BIT or an FTA—referred to as the Investment Court System (ICS),[42] an idea that has become a reality in treaties that the EU has signed such as CETA and the EU-Vietnam Free Trade Agreement (EVFTA); (2) a multilateral investment court (MIC), namely an international court with the power to hear disputes over investments between an investor and a State that accepts its jurisdiction.[43] The goal of the EU is to finally merge all bilateral and potentially plurilateral courts into a multilateral court system.[44]

The main source of inspiration for these proposals has been the WTO AB. Permanent investment courts could help avoid potential appearances of bias party-appointed arbitrators are potentially exposed to. The tenured position of judges on a permanent court would lead to increasing independence and impartiality of adjudicators since tenured judges would not need to be concerned about future appointments as arbitrators arguably do. At the same time, a permanent court would help remedy the problem of inconsistency of arbitral awards.

III DOMESTIC LAW ALTERNATIVES

International investment law developed as a separate field of international law during the period of decolonization of the South and East.[45] There was previously a limited need for an international law for the protection of investors overseas, as they operated under a domestic law they were familiar with. International investment law started thus operating as a functional equivalent to domestic-level protection previously

Marc Bungenberg and August Reinisch (eds.), "From Bilateral Arbitral Tribunals and Investment Courts to a Multilateral Investment Court: Options Regarding the Institutionalization of Investor-State Dispute Settlement," *European Yearbook of International Economic Law* (2020).

39. UNCTAD, *World Investment Report 2015: Reforming International Investment Governance* (UN 2015) 152.
40. UNCTAD, *Investment Policy Framework for Sustainable Development* (UN 2015), available at http://investmentpolicyhub.unctad.org/Upload/Documents/POLICY_FRAMEWORK_2015.pdf accessed September 15, 2019.
41. *See* "UNCITRAL Deliberates Possible Reform of Investor-State Dispute Settlement," *UNIS/L/257* (December 8, 2017), available at http://www.unis.unvienna.org/unis/en/pressrels/2017/unisl257.html accessed September 15, 2019.
42. *See also* European Commission, *Trade for all: Towards a More Responsible Trade and Investment Policy* (October 14, 2015) 21.
43. Speech of Cecilia Malmström, EU Commissioner for Trade, to the European Parliament (March 18, 2015), available at http://europa.eu/rapid/press-release_SPEECH-15-4624_en.htm.
44. Cf. European Commission, "A Multilateral Investment Court," *State of the Union 2017*, available at http://trade.ec.europa.eu/doclib/docs/2017/september/tradoc_156042.pdf accessed January 15, 2018, 2.
45. *See generally* Antony Anghie, *Imperialism, Sovereignty and the Making of International Law* (CUP 2005), Chapters 4 and 5; David Schneiderman, The Coloniality of Investment Law (May 21, 2019), *available at SSRN: https://ssrn.com/*abstract = 3392034.

offered to investors. Countries around the world have started moving again the focus or developing a parallel focus from international investment law to domestic investment law—and accordingly developing robust domestic frameworks for the management of foreign investment flows. This may be interpreted as a move in the broader field of investment law from the international to the domestic. This move does not mean abandoning the values of international law, broadly speaking, or the need for some freedom of movement of capital across borders. It is rather to be interpreted as the invention of domestic means to achieve international law goals.

The present section of the chapter discusses the domestic life of investment law. It presents the variety of domestic investment laws and differentiates between investment promotion and facilitation laws (IPFLs) on the one side and investment screening laws (ISLs) on the other. It moves on to discuss statutorily delimited jurisdictions for the attraction and promotion of investment, the so-called SEZs. It further discusses domestic laws that are not specifically directed at foreign investors but play a crucial role in attracting foreign investment; public-private partnership (PPP) laws serve such a function alongside other more general laws, such as property and nationality laws.

A Domestic Investment Laws

The investment law framework of a country may be comprised of legislation that is specialized and addressed to foreign investors or of more general legislative instruments that may have an influence on foreign investment flows. With the partial retreat from international investment law, this layer of investor protection becomes more visible. For example, in the recent effort to reclaim powers that had been previously delegated to international investment treaties and tribunals, countries in Latin America, such as Bolivia and Ecuador, and beyond, have terminated a number of their BITs; other States have allowed many of their BITs to expire.[46] In the absence of a BIT, foreign investors are subject to the general legal framework of the host country—alongside the Minimum Standard of Treatment (MST) under customary international law.

When the international investment law safeguards are removed, one still has to distinguish between domestic legislative frameworks that differentiate between domestic and foreign investors, and such frameworks that do not. There are three possible alternatives:

(1) *(General) laws that do not differentiate between domestic and foreign investors.* Foreign as well as domestic investors are sometimes subject to the same sets of laws that do not differentiate between domestic and foreign investors. Hong Kong, for example, became an important trade and investment hub not

46. In March 2014, Indonesia, for example, announced that it would not renew its BIT with the Netherlands with effect from July 1, 2015. This was followed by a further announcement from Indonesia that it would allow all its BITs to expire; *see* Antony Crockett, "Indonesia's Bilateral Investment Treaties: Between Generations?" (2015) 30 *ICSID Review—Foreign Investment Law Journal* 437.

only for the British and other Europeans at the end of the nineteenth century but also for the Chinese who found the English common law system of private property rights particularly attractive.[47] Until today, Hong Kong has no general foreign investment legislation governing the admission of foreign investment.[48]

(2) *Specialized laws with similar treatment.* Other countries have developed specialized legal frameworks for the regulation of foreign investment while not differentiating between domestic and foreign investors when it comes to investment protection. Bolivia, for example, withdrew from ICSID in 2007 and started to systematically refuse to renew BITs that reached their expiration date. In 2013, the government of Bolivia denounced all its remaining BITs and replaced them with Law No. 516 of April 4, 2014, on Investment Promotion of the Plurinational State of Bolivia.[49] This statute applies to both Bolivian and foreign investments.[50] In other parts of the world, South Africa has been replacing BITs with a domestic law applicable to both national and foreign investors—the Protection of Investment Act, 2015.[51] This statute also guarantees national treatment to foreign investors.[52]

(3) *Specialized laws with different treatment.* A third alternative is to create specialized investment laws applicable only to foreign investors. Countries in the Gulf Region have followed this pathway. Qatar, the United Arab Emirates (UAE) and Kuwait, for example, have a longstanding tradition of regulating domestic and foreign investors in a different way, and placing investment restrictions on foreign nationals regarding both sectors of the economy in which they are allowed to operate, as well as mandating the involvement of their nationals in economic activity. Non-nationals are usually allowed to invest in most sectors of the economy, provided that they become shareholders in a company that is established according to national law and that they have a local partner that contributes no less than 51% of the capital of the company.[53] This has recently started changing as more countries lift some of the relevant restrictions by adopting new foreign investment laws. Qatar and

47. Tristram Hunt, "Hong Kong," in *Ten Cities That Made an Empire* (Penguin 2015) 252-253.
48. Terry Miller, Anthony B. Kim and James M Roberts, *2018 Report of Index of Economic Freedom* (The Heritage Foundation 2018) 215. At the same time, Hong Kong has only signed a limited number of FTAs and BITs; *see* Hong Kong, China SAR, on UNCTAD's Investment Policy Hub, available at https://investmentpolicy.unctad.org/international-investment-agreements/countries/93/hong-kong-sar-china.
49. Ley de Promoción de Inversiones, Ley N° 516, Ley de 4 de Abril de 2014.
50. *Ibid.*, Article 2.
51. Act No. 22 of 2015: Protection of Investment Act, 2015 (Government Gazette Vol. 606 Cape Town December 15, 2015 No. 39514).
52. *See* section 8 of PIA.
53. Foreign investors were allowed to only invest in Qatar, for example, until 2018 in accordance with the provisions of Law No. 13 of 2000 "Regulation of the Investment of Non-Qatari Capital in the Economic Activity." Foreign investment was generally limited to 49% of the capital for most business activities with Qatari partner(s) holding at least 51%. Foreign investors were not allowed to invest under Law No. 13 of 2000 in commercial agencies or, broadly speaking, real estate; *see* Investment Law No. 13 of 2000 art 2.3. No. 2.

the UAE have new laws in place allowing 100% foreign ownership in domestic companies as a default rule for almost all sectors.[54]

One may further distinguish between two different types of domestic investment laws: IPFLs and ISLs.[55] IPFLs are meant to attract foreign investment;[56] such statutes usually provide incentives for foreign investment in certain sectors. Organizationally, IPFLs may also establish Investment Promotion Agencies (IPAs) to proactively promote and facilitate foreign investment in the host jurisdiction.[57] More recently, laws that are meant to regulate and control foreign investment have started becoming popular among governments worldwide. Almost all major economies in the world have put in place mechanisms to control inward foreign investment flows. Among these mechanisms, foreign investment screening mechanisms have become widespread—often following the example of the Committee on Foreign Investment in the United States (CFIUS).[58] Investment screening mechanisms established under ISLs often block or limit the entry of foreign investors, generally or for certain sectors, and/or subject them to certain requirements.[59]

B SEZ Laws

SEZs represent one more strategy of applying domestic law instead of—or in parallel with—international investment law as a way to attract foreign investment and provide safeguards to foreign investors. The difference between this and the strategies presented in the previous section is that zones of this type carve out a "special" jurisdiction for a separate economic regime within the country—as the term SEZ indicates.[60]

54. *See, e.g.*, UAE Federal Law by Decree No 19 of 2018 "Regarding Foreign Direct Investment"; and Qatar Investment Law No. 1 of 2019 "Regulating the Investment of Non-Qatari Capital in Economic Activity."
55. Investment laws—invariably of the first sort—are to be found under "Investment Laws Navigator" of the UNCTAD's Investment Policy Hub, available at https://investmentpolicy.unctad.org/investment-laws.
56. States started adopting IPFLs in the 1960s and increasingly so in the 1990s. *See generally* Jarrod Hepburn, "Domestic Investment Statutes in International Law" (2018) 112 *American Journal of International Law* 658 (referring to them as domestic investment statutes).
57. Mariana Zanatta, "Foreign Direct Investment: Key Issues for Promotion Agencies" (2006) 10 *Policy Brief-United Nations University* 1.
58. Apart from the US, Australia, Canada, Japan as well as the Member States of the European Union (EU) have investment screening mechanisms in place. According to UNCTAD, at least eleven countries have introduced new laws for the screening of foreign investment since 2011, while forty-one significant amendments in fifteen jurisdictions have taken place during the same time, and even more are forthcoming; *see* UNCTAD, *World Investment Report: Special Economic Zones* (UN 2019), 94.
59. Usually, the relevant statutes deal with the foreign acquisition and foreign control of certain business enterprises and with foreign acquisition of infrastructure and land interests; *see generally* Georgios Dimitropoulos, "National Security: The Role of Investment Screening Mechanisms," in Julien Chaisse, Leïla Choukroune and Sufian Jusoh (eds.), *Handbook of International Investment Law and Policy* (Springer 2020).
60. *See generally* FIAS, *Special Economic Zone: Performance, Lessons Learned, and Implication for Zone Development* (World Bank 2008); Thomas Farole and Gokhan Akinci (eds.), *Special Economic Zones: Progress, Emerging Challenges, and Future Directions* (World Bank 2011).

Overall, SEZ regimes differ from domestic investment laws in geographic scope, substance, and governance mechanisms. Countries in Latin America have also experimented with SEZs.[61] The first zone of the postwar period was developed in Latin America, namely in Puerto Rico.[62]

SEZ is a generic term to describe geographic areas that are designated as zones for the promotion of trade and attraction of foreign investment. According to a definition by the World Bank, "SEZs are generally defined as geographically delimited areas administered by a single body, offering certain incentives (generally duty-free importing and streamlined customs procedures, for instance) to businesses which physically locate within the zone."[63] SEZs are usually fenced-in areas located in or near seaports or airports. The number of such zones multiplied in the 1980s and continues to rise exponentially in the twenty-first century.[64] Many different types of SEZs have been developed, such as Free Trade Zones, Export Processing Zones, Industrial Parks, and Bonded Logistics Parks. The different types of zones signify different degrees of willingness to promote foreign investment and openness in different areas of economic activity. In some parts of the world nowadays, special zones are no longer limited to trade in goods but are also used to attract foreign investment in services—prominently financial services. The Qatar Financial Centre is one such example.[65]

Zones are usually governed by specifically designated Free Zone Authorities that have broad regulatory and operational powers within the zones. Rules applied in these areas—investment and trade laws, tax laws, labor laws, customs laws, etc.—differ from the rest of the domestic jurisdiction and are specifically tailored to increase foreign investment and international trade. Financial incentives in the form of subsidies and/or tax holidays also accompany the creation of the zones. Zone laws are generally more "investor-friendly"; a trend that is starting to emerge is to develop zone laws that are based or generally inspired by the (English) common law. This strategy assumes that foreign investors are more familiar with Anglo-American common law, as it is used in major global financial and trade hubs such as London, New York, Hong Kong and Singapore.[66]

---

61. The Latin American zones are interesting in that they were developed in the absence of the semicolonial tradition of Free Ports.
62. *See generally*, as well as on the influence of the US in the development of SEZ policies, Patrick Neveling, "Export Processing Zones, Special Economic Zones and the Long March of Capitalist Development Policies during the Cold War," in Leslie James and Elisabeth Leake (eds.), *Decolonization and the Cold War: Negotiating Independence* (Bloomsbury 2015) 63. Another well-known example is the Colon Free Zone in Panama, which was established in Colon Harbour, Panama in the 1950s; *see* FIAS, *supra* n. 60, at 23 (with further examples from the Americas).
63. FIAS, *supra* n. 60, at 2.
64. UNCTAD, World Investment Report 2019—Special Economic Zones (UNCTAD 2019), 128 and passim.
65. The Qatar Financial Centre is also one of the rare cases of zones that may be characterized as "onshore," meaning that registered entities are allowed to operate and offer services everywhere in the borders of the country, not exclusively within the geographical borders of the zone.
66. Abu Dhabi, for example, established in 2013 the Abu Dhabi Global Market (ADGM) as an SEZ with the goal of attracting financial capital. The English common law is directly applicable within the SEZ; *see* ADGM, "Application of English Law Regulations 2015."

C PPP Laws

Over the last few decades, almost all States have delegated parts of their sovereignty to private actors, as well as to international actors beyond their borders. The first process is generally called "privatization," while the second one has been labeled as "globalization." Foreign investment finds itself at the intersection between privatization and globalization—and this is what makes it a sometimes sensitive topic.[67] Allowing for foreign investment flows in one country means at the same time allowing for privatization of domestic State-Owned Enterprises (SOEs) and other public assets, as well as publicly owned properties. This raises concerns about diminishing sovereignty as well as about national security, particularly when privatization is of strategic economic or political significance.[68] Traditional capital-exporting countries have been until recently in a better position to treat privatization as a question of domestic policy[69]—while the current proliferation of ISLs in the West is striking. In different parts of the world, privatization has instead sometimes been seen as transferring control of national interests to foreign parties.[70]

Public procurement and PPPs are the two main financing tools to attract private expertise for public projects.[71] Public procurement means that the government pays for products and services provided by the private sector; the government specifies the quantity and quality, and then the products and services are provided by private companies who win the contract bids through a tendering process. At the end of the process, the products are transferred to and services are provided by the government itself. By contrast, PPP is "... an agreement between the government and one or more private partners (which may include the operators and the financers) according to which the private partners deliver the service in such a manner that the service delivery objectives of the government are aligned with the profit objectives of the private partners and where the effectiveness of the alignment depends on a sufficient transfer of risk to the private partners."[72] In the case of infrastructure procurement using the PPP method, for example, the government specifies the quality and quantity of the service it requires from the private partner(s), and the private partners may be assigned different tasks to design, construct, finance, operate and manage a capital asset, delivering a service to the government or directly to end users. The private partner will

67. *See* Paul Starr, "The Meaning of Privatization" (1988) 6 *Yale Law & Policy Review* 6, 33.
68. *Ibid.*
69. *Ibid.*
70. *Ibid.*, at 32.
71. *See generally* Philippe Burger and Ian Hawkesworth, "How to Attain Value for Money: Comparing PPP and Traditional Infrastructure Public Procurement," *OECD Journal on Budgeting 2011/1*. A third alternative is the use of procurement processes for the government to buy the raw material and other inputs necessary for the construction of an asset and then to construct the asset itself.
72. OECD, *Public-Private Partnerships: In Pursuit of Risk Sharing and Value for Money* (OECD Publishing 2008) 17.

either receive a stream of payments from the government (so-called pure PPPs), or charge directly on the end users (so-called concessions), or both.[73]

The allocation of risk and the role of risk as an efficiency driver are different in public procurement and PPP. In a traditionally procured project, the risk of private parties is relatively limited—and does not usually extend beyond the construction phase. PPP contracts tend to integrate the construction and operational aspects of the project in one package; this operates as an incentive for an early delivery of the project as the private party can only start making profit after completing the project. PPPs are generally viewed as more efficient. Overall investment performance is transferred to the private investor, who would tend to avoid cost overruns and delays and may also be contractually obliged to pay fines or other penalties when performance is below the contractually agreed thresholds.[74] PPPs are of course not a panacea for all problems of public financing and public service delivery. In worst-case scenarios—such as bankruptcy—the cost of project completion will eventually come out of the public purse.

Foreign investors will have the tendency to favor PPPs over traditional procurement, as PPPs are long-term engagements with greater prospects for profit for investors. The private party involved in PPPs remains part of the project for a longer period, often twenty, twenty-five, or even thirty years. This frequently raises issues of control of domestic resources by foreign private investors, which may give rise to national security concerns—as has been showcased with the proliferation of ISLs.

Many countries have used PPP laws as a substitute or as a complement for international investment law. The government of Ecuador, for example, famously terminated a number of its BITs based on the findings of the Ecuador Investment Treaties Audit Commission (CAITISA).[75] At the same time, it introduced a new PPP law with the aim of replacing the international law protection mechanism with a domestic framework.[76] Eventually, the government presented in March 2018 a new Model BIT that draws on the conclusions of the CAITISA. The PPP served thus to enable a smooth reactivation of the engagement of Ecuador with the international investment regime.

73. The PPP definition covers mostly output-based partnerships but also input-based partnerships may be included; the latter are called Private Finance Initiatives (PFIs). The main categories of PPPs are concessions, Build-Operate-Transfer (BOT) Projects, and Design-Build-Operate (DBO) Projects. BOT and DBO Projects typically involve significant design and construction as well as long-term operations, for new build (greenfield) or projects involving significant refurbishment and extension (brownfield); *see* World Bank, Concessions, *Build-Operate-Transfer (BOT) and Design-Build-Operate (DBO) Projects*, available at https://ppp.worldbank.org/public-private-partnership/agreements/concessions-bots-dbos#Concessions/ accessed September 15, 2019.

74. *Ibid.*

75. Ecuador Investment Treaties Audit Commission (CAITISA), "Findings and Recommendations," available at https://www.tni.org/en/article/why-did-ecuador-terminate-all-its-bilateral-investment-treaties accessed September 15, 2019.

76. *See* Javier Jaramillo and Ricardo Montalvo, "The New Ecuadorian PPP Act: A New Opportunity for Foreign Investment? Some Caveats Regarding Arbitration," *Kluwer Arbitration Blog*, available at http://arbitrationblog.kluwerarbitration.com/2017/02/19/the-new-ecuadorian-ppp-act-a-new-opportunity-for-foreign-investment-some-caveats-regarding-arbitration/ accessed September 15, 2019.

Contemporary PPP laws include a series of legal and institutional arrangements for procuring PPP Projects that are deemed as attracting domestic and foreign investors.[77] While procurement through PPP was in the past done through the general procurement laws, there is nowadays a tendency for countries to develop separate PPP laws. Some countries have their PPP frameworks aligned with the general legal framework of investment laws. This encourages better PPP fiscal management as well as more consistency of PPP Projects with investment priorities. Another crucial element of a PPP regulatory framework is the existence of a PPP unit to manage the partnership and the interaction with the involved private parties. PPP laws and units serve as positive signals of a good investment environment to domestic and foreign investors and have the potential to play a similar role as IPFLs for foreign investors.

D Other Laws: The Broader Substantive and Dispute Resolution Framework

Regimes for the attraction, promotion, and protection of investment are parts of a broader governance infrastructure that includes legal variables, such as taxation, tariffs, property rights, contract enforcement, and broader human right protection, as well as non-legal variables in a country such as political stability and public and private corruption, and digitization in the public sector.[78] Investment laws do not operate in isolation from the rest of the legal order; the overall legal framework for both substantive protection and dispute resolution plays an at least equally important role in attracting foreign investment.

An often disregarded category of laws critical for foreign investment is property laws. Many jurisdictions place restrictions on real estate ownership by foreigners; for instance, countries in the Middle East and North Africa Region have traditionally had in place laws limiting the purchase of land by foreign nationals. Comparatively, Latin American countries are open to foreign investment in real estate and infrastructure sectors, making foreign ownership of land and investment in infrastructure generally possible.[79] Besides property laws, employment laws will naturally affect decisions on foreign investment as well. Nationality and residence laws are equally important. In view of this, governments have started placing a greater emphasis on these aspects of

77. World Bank, *Benchmarking Public-Private Partnerships Procurement* (World Bank 2018), available at http://pubdocs.worldbank.org/en/256451522692645967/PIP3-2018.pdf accessed September 15, 2019; *see also* Fernanda Ruiz-Nunez, "PPI Investments in IDA Countries, 2011 to 2015," *IDA PPI Update* (2016) 8; Tyler Duvall, Alastair Green and Mike Kerlin, *Making the Most of a Wealth of Infrastructure Finance* (McKinsey 2015).

78. *See* Steven Globerman and Daniel Shapiro, "Governance Infrastructure and US Foreign Direct Investment" (2003) 34 *Journal of International Business Studies* 19; *see also* Frank L. Bartels and S.A. de Crombrugghe, "FDI Policy Instruments: Advantages and Disadvantages," *Working Paper 01/2009* (UNIDO 2009).

79. *See* Global Property Guide, Property Rights Index in Latin-America, available at https://www.globalpropertyguide.com/Latin-America/property-rights-index accessed September 15, 2019.

the domestic investment framework by issuing, for example, immigrant visas for foreign investors, or adopting "golden visa" schemes to attract foreign investors.[80]

When it comes to dispute resolution, even reform proposals that use international law as their starting point consider the increased involvement of domestic courts in investment law matters - in addition to or in place of the prevalent ISDS system.[81] It has been proposed that domestic courts could be involved in the broader international dispute resolution process by, for example, making the exhaustion of local remedies a necessary prerequisite.[82] Some proposals envisage an international court with the authority to hear preliminary reference questions from domestic courts in the same way as the Court of Justice of the EU does; other proposals claim a greater role for domestic courts to hear investment law disputes and suggest an international court as a second instance of review.[83]

As already explained, there are proposals for a more radical dissociation from ISDS in the resolution of investment disputes. The basic argument in favor of domestic court involvement is that foreign and domestic investors should be granted the same treatment as foreign investors.[84] The origins of this argument are to be found in Latin America and the Calvo doctrine with its continuing influence until today.[85]

National arbitration laws are often drafted based on an international arbitration law template, the UNCITRAL Model Law.[86] Countries in Latin America have more recently started following the trend, tailoring their domestic arbitration laws to the UNCITRAL Model Law as well.[87] This is to give reassurance to foreign investors that potential disputes will be adjudicated based on arbitration laws that they are familiar with. This does raise the question, though, as to how the countries that adopt an UNCITRAL-based domestic law would differentiate themselves from other jurisdictions that also use arbitration laws drawn on the UNCITRAL Model Law. As such, the adoption of the Model Law is not really an incentive for investment but rather a removal of a potential hindrance for investment.

80. Golden visas may provide either residence—permanent or temporary—status or citizenship to their holders; *see generally* Allison Christians, "Buying In: Residence and Citizenship by Investment" (2017) 62 *Saint Louis University Law Journal* 51.
81. *See generally* Gabrielle Kaufmann-Kohler and Michele Potestà, *Investor-State Dispute Settlement and National Courts: Current Framework and Reform Options* (Springer 2020).
82. Stephan W. Schill, "The European Commission's Proposal of an 'Investment Court System' for TTIP: Stepping Stone or Stumbling Block for Multilateralizing International Investment Law?" (April 22, 2016) 20 *ASIL Insights*.
83. *See ibid.*
84. This has been one of the reasons for the reexamination of the foreign and domestic investment law policy of South Africa; *see* South Africa Department of Trade and Industry, "Bilateral Investment Treaty Policy Framework Review" (2009) www.pmg.org.za/policy-documents/2009/06/25/bilateral-investment-treatypolicy-framework-review accessed September 15, 2019.
85. *See, e.g.*, Wenhua Shan, "From North-South Divide to Private-Public Debate: Revival of the Calvo Doctrine and the Changing Landscape in International Investment Law" (2006-2007) 27 *Northwestern Journal of International Law & Business* 631.
86. One recent example is the long-awaited Arbitration Law of the United Arab Emirates, which is largely based on the UNCITRAL Model Law; *see* Federal Law No. 6 of 2018 ("Arbitration Law").
87. Nathan J. Arentsen and Matthew S. Weber, "UNCITRAL Model Law: Still a Model or Second Best?," *Kluwer Arbitration Blog* (July 1, 2014), available at http://arbitrationblog.kluwerarbitration.com/2014/07/01/uncitral-model-law-still-a-model-or-second-best/.

IV ASSESSING THE ALTERNATIVES TO INTERNATIONAL INVESTMENT LAW AND ARBITRATION

Policy reformers are presented with alternatives to the current system of IILA at the international level as well as the domestic level of governance. Also, the normative standard against which the viability of alternatives to IILA may be measured can be drawn from either international law or domestic law. The final section of the chapter presents an international law assessment of the reform proposals, showcasing how the international law standard may be drawn again from different blocks of law: international economic law or other areas of international law, such as human rights. It finally makes an assessment based on domestic law standards and shows how domestic law has the potential to play the role that international law has played so far in the contemporary investment law regime.

A An International Law Assessment

What is the appropriate measure to assess the viability of the alternatives to IILA? Robert Howse, for example, has developed a conceptual framework to assess reform proposals of IILA by matching some of the declared rationales for giving foreign investors special protections under international investment law with the substantive norms that would better match the rationale.[88] Sergio Puig and Gregory Shaffer have applied comparative institutional analysis to evaluate the various alternatives to the resolution of investment disputes.[89] These scholars recommend that reforms should stress the complementarity between domestic and international institutions. International institutions should serve the role of supporting the domestic rule of law.[90] This can be achieved by relying on domestic courts as the first instance to decide investment claims.[91]

One obvious response to the question posed at the beginning of the previous paragraph is that the standard should be drawn from international law. The international law standard may be extracted from different international law regimes, such as international economic law and international investment law, more specifically; IILA has been developed to serve certain functions, among which are the protection of foreign investors as well as the creation of a favorable environment to promote foreign investment.[92] This ought to be taken into account in the assessment of the proposed reform proposals. Another approach would be to resort to concepts, ideas, and

88. Robert Howse, "International Investment Law and Arbitration: A Conceptual Framework" in Hélène Ruiz Fabri (ed.), *International Law and Litigation* (Nomos 2019).
89. Puig and Shaffer, *supra* n. 5.
90. Cf. also *Fraport AG Frankfurt Airport Services Worldwide v. The Republic of the Philippines*, ICSID Case No. ARB/03/25, para. 402.
91. Puig and Shaffer, *supra* n. 5, 408 and passim. The selection of domestic courts or institutions has to consider the different investment environments of individual States, such as capital endowment, market size, politics and ideology, institutional development, and historical legacy; *ibid.*, 409.
92. Cf. Matthias Herdegen, *Principles of International Economic Law* (2nd ed., Oxford University Press 2016) 10.

objectives outside of the international economic law regime. Human rights law, for example, has started exercising a limited influence on international investment law—human rights are nowadays sometimes taken into account by international investment tribunals as well as in the design of international treaties.[93]

International economic law of the second half of the twentieth century was developed as a field of law that relies on the functioning of the market for the delivery of its aspired public goods. A proposal to reform IILA relying on an international law normative standard—that also moves away from the now contested normative foundations of international investment law while focusing on the ontology of the broader field of international economic law—would be to emphasize the improvement of the functioning of the investment arbitration market. The appropriate institutional design would thus be best chosen based on the existing characteristics of the ISDS system: the existence of an arbitration community and the operation of a market of arbitrators. The market would still bring its own accountability mechanisms to international investment arbitration supported by interventions that have the goal of improving its functioning. A normative standard of this sort would favor reforms that respect the basic structure of international investment arbitration, and try to find ways to enhance the propensity of the arbitration community toward self-regulation.[94] A number of the proposals presented above, such as codes of conduct for arbitrators, could help improve the market in the direction suggested here. Another proposal along these lines would be to introduce a system of certification of international arbitrators operating in the field of IILA.[95] At the same time, such a normative standard would not necessarily favor the idea of establishing a multilateral investment court.

B A Domestic Law Assessment

The preceding analysis has tried to illustrate how domestic law can operate as a functional equivalent to IILA—which is not carefully considered in the current reform discussions.[96] From a domestic law perspective, an obvious normative standard for the evaluation of the alternatives to IILA is respect for the principle of sovereignty. Concerns about excessive intrusion into national sovereignty have triggered much of the current backlash against investment law and arbitration.[97] Sovereignty is the expression of a special power for which there is only one power holder: the State. This

93. *See generally* Eric De Brabandere, "Human Rights and International Investment Law," in Markus Krajewski and Rhea Hoffmann (eds.), *Research Handbook on Foreign Direct Investment* (Edward Elgar 2019) Chapter 20.
94. *See generally* Yves Dezalay and Bryan G. Garth, *Dealing in Virtue* (University of Chicago Press 1996).
95. Dimitropoulos, *supra* n. 14.
96. But *see* Puig and Shaffer, *supra* n. 5. Applying comparative institutional analysis to various alternatives to the investment dispute resolutions, Puig and Shaffer suggest that resort to domestic courts may be the more appropriate solution for IILA reform. The authors also recommend that the reforms should stress the complementarity between domestic and international institutions. International institutions should serve the role of supporting the domestic rule of law.
97. *See generally* Dimitropoulos, *supra* n. 5.

power is territorial in nature and all-encompassing. It is a power of powers—which may be of course translated into separate powers authorizing the exercise of specific public functions. Sovereignty is at the same time a principle that mediates between domestic and international law; it is the entry point of international law into the domestic realm of the State, as well as the entry point for States into the system of international law. Sovereignty as a metric for the evaluation of reform proposals would prioritize alternatives that give way to the consideration of the national interest over the interests of foreign investors.

The discussion of domestic alternatives has also showcased that there is a much more complicated relationship between the domestic and the international than is often assumed: Moving away from international investment law does not mean abandoning the values of international law, broadly speaking, or rejecting the need for some freedom of movement of capital across borders. Most domestic law alternatives do not necessarily reject international investment law or its values; they propose different—domestic law—means of achieving similar goals as the ones that have otherwise been pursued by resorting to international investment law.

Looking into the reasons for the initial development and proliferation of BITs may be helpful in understanding this point, as well as responding to the question of which alternatives are viable reform proposals and which are not. Several theories explaining the diffusion of BITs, the main legal instrument for the protection of foreign investment over the last fifty years, have been proposed. The dominant theory is that BITs offer a credible commitment mechanism helping to reduce the perceived uncertainty of foreign investors in the host State.[98] The credible commitment strategy theory draws on rational choice theory and explains the behavior of States as rational in the face of the decision of how to increase the pie in their domestic economy.[99] Attracting foreign investment will improve the competitiveness of domestic companies and lead to a better overall economic output through increased competition between domestic and foreign competitors.[100]

Rational choice theory has been recently contested as a dominant paradigm for the explanation of individual behavior and decision-making. "Pure" rationality in decision-making is giving way to the notion of "bounded rationality" of decision-makers in theories of cognitive psychology and behavioral (law and) economics.[101] Lauge Poulsen has used the updated conceptual framework of bounded rationality to

98. *See* Kenneth J. Vandevelde, "Investment Liberalization and Economic Development: The Role of Bilateral Investment Treaties" (1998) 36 *Columbia Journal of Transnational Law* 501; *see also* Zachary Elkins, Andrew Guzman and Beth Simmons, "Competing for Capital: The Diffusion of Bilateral Investment Treaties, 1960-2000" (2006) 60 *International Organization* 811; Julien Chaisse and Christian Bellak, "Navigating the Expanding Universe of Investment Treaties: Creation and Use of Critical Index" (2015) 18 *Journal of International Economic Law* 79.

99. Vandevelde, *supra* n. 98.

100. *Ibid.*

101. *See generally* Christine Jolls, Cass R. Sunstein and Richard H. Thaler, "A Behavioral Approach to Law and Economics" (1998) 50 *Stanford Law Review* 1471; on the application of behavioral law and economics in international law, *see* Anne van Aaken, "Behavioral International Law and Economics" (2014) 55 *Harvard International Law Journal* 501; Tomer Broude, "Behavioral International Law" (2015) 163 *University of Pennsylvania Law Review* 1099.

explain the diffusion of BITs.[102] According to this approach, governments are also subject to certain heuristics and cognitive biases that may have led to the adoption of such treaties; namely, the adoption of BITs may be explained by biases such as overestimation of national economic benefits and disregard for costs, availability of the BIT model during the time of adoption, and overconfidence in the sovereign powers of the signatory States to regulate foreign direct investment (FDI).

Based again on the conceptual model of bounded rationality, Poulsen suggests a different theory explaining how the contemporary system of IILA may have diffused; according to the author, bounded rationality may also explain why the BIT system established itself in the first phases of expansion even in the absence of ISDS clauses in BITs. BITs may be understood as working as "focal points" and "coordination devices"—not necessarily as credible commitments.[103] They exercise an "expressive function" that operates as a "coordination-enhancing device" even in the absence of credible enforcement mechanisms such as investor-State tribunals.[104] Domestic law could not work as a focal point during the initial years of the development of international investment law as it was itself the source of investment disputes as well as it was enmeshed in the historical and political context of the postcolonial era.[105]

This may have been the case in the early stages of the development of BITs; given the backlash against IILA, BITs have more recently started losing their focal point nature—at least for certain governments, and even more so in parts of the world such as Latin America. Their visibility and uniqueness—important aspects for the exercise of their expressive function—operate nowadays sometimes in the opposite way: As the discussion on the domestic law alternatives to IILA highlights, BITs are today perceived by an increasing number of governments as a hindrance to economic development.

Domestic laws are designed nowadays as signals of good investment environment to attract foreign investors when they make investment decisions. There is a plethora of new—specialized or general—domestic laws regulating aspects of foreign investment as well as domestic institutions in the host States that have an expressive function in the same way that BITs had in the past. Domestic investment laws and institutions—mostly IPFLs and IPAs—in a national legal order play today the role that BITs were designed to play and operate as liaisons between foreign private investors and the domestic governance level. The same role is played *par excellence* by SEZs and the laws that apply within their boundaries. This may also explain the convergence of SEZ laws—as well as their convergence toward the most recognizable set of laws in contemporary legal practice, the common law. There is, moreover, a tendency to develop separate PPP legal frameworks that are managed by distinct PPP entities.

102. Lauge N. Skovgaard Poulsen, "Bounded Rationality and the Diffusion of Modern Investment Treaties" (2014) 58 *International Studies Quarterly* 1.
103. Lauge N. Skovgaard Poulsen, "Beyond Credible Commitments: (Investment) Treaties as Focal Points" (2020) 64 *International Studies Quarterly* 26.
104. *Ibid.*, at 28 and *passim*.
105. *Ibid.*, at 28.

These legal frameworks and institutions operate as coordination-enhancing mechanisms between investors, often foreign, and domestic governments.[106] They can thus work as viable alternatives to the institutions of IILA.

V CONCLUSION

Reform in IILA is one of the most hotly debated topics in contemporary international law. While there is abundant literature as well as reform efforts trying to rethink the role of international law in foreign investment protection, there is no systematic effort to think of the role that the domestic law of host States could play in the reform process. Reforms may be measured against two standards: an international and a domestic. The international standard would favor efforts to improve the international market for adjudicators. At the same time, domestic law alternatives have a major role to play in the reform process as they nowadays exercise the same expressive and coordination function that BITs used to in the past. This expressive function can nowadays sometimes be better played by domestic statutes and institutions. Ultimately, the two systems are complementary: a better domestic legal framework can help IILA perform their role in a better way[107] and the other way round.

106. It is worth mentioning that some of the new domestic reform efforts are again initiated or supported by international organizations. PPP laws are often inspired by World Bank and OECD standards (*see* OECD, *Recommendation of the Council on Principles for Public Governance of Public-Private Partnerships* (May 2012)); domestic arbitration laws are often drafted based on the UNCITRAL Model Law (*see* above section III.D); domestic investment laws are often developed in consultation with the World Bank (*see* Tarald Laudal Berge and Taylor St. John, "Asymmetric Diffusion: World Bank 'Best Practice' and the Spread of Arbitration in National Investment Laws" (2021) 28 *Review of International Political Economy* 584).

107. *See* Szilárd Gáspár-Szilágyi, "Foreign Investors, Domestic Courts and Investment Treaty Arbitration," in Daniel Behn, Ole Kristian Fauchald and Malcolm Langford (eds.), *The Legitimacy of Investment Arbitration: Empirical Perspectives* (Cambridge University Press, 2022).

CHAPTER 7

Is There a Latin American Arbitration?: The Myth and Beyond

Eduardo Zuleta

I INTRODUCTION

Arbitration in Latin America or Latin American Arbitration are concepts that are widely used in the arbitration world by practitioners and scholars. There are books and articles about arbitration in Latin America, specialists in Latin American Arbitration, law firms with Latin American practices, and Latin American sections or divisions in arbitral institutions. The basis to characterize a case as part of the concept of Latin American Arbitration is diverse. It could refer to arbitration based in a Latin American country or to arbitration involving Latin American parties. The focus of the analysis of arbitration in Latin America has generally referred to whether or not the different countries have adopted the UNCITRAL Model Law or modern arbitration laws, whether or not the country is a signatory of the New York Convention and on the attitude of the courts of each jurisdiction toward the recognition and enforcement of awards under the New York Convention or in general on the attitude of the courts in Latin American countries with respect to arbitration.

Latin America has been characterized as a region that has been reluctant to accept arbitration but has evolved, particularly during the second half of the twentieth century, toward a more favorable attitude to the resolution of disputes by arbitration. Carlos Calvo and the Calvo doctrine are frequently cited as an example of the doctrines that have prevailed in Latin America and that may have affected the evolution of arbitration in the region.[1] Not infrequently Brazil was mentioned as an outlier for not

1. Fernández Arroyo, D. (2019). *La Evolución del Arbitraje en América Latina: De la supuesta hostilidad a la evidente aceptación*. Biblioteca Jurídica Virtual del Instituto de Investigaciones

having ratified the 1958 New York Convention or the International Centre for Settlement of Investment Disputes (ICSID) Convention. Argentina and Uruguay have been praised for adopting the UNCITRAL Model Law. The constitutional protection remedies of *amparo* or *tutela* are described as a characteristic of Arbitration in Latin America and as one of the most relevant barriers for the development of arbitration in the region.

Generally, articles referring to arbitration in the region and to the historical attitude of the different countries toward arbitration have analyzed the history and development of arbitration, focusing mostly on arbitration of disputes involving States or State parties. The history of domestic arbitration, its development and the impact on the approach to international arbitration are usually forgotten or left for those interested in the local laws or in comparative law.

Some scholars and practitioners, however, have correctly questioned whether Latin America can be analyzed as a single entity, as a region that has a uniform approach toward arbitration.[2] One must ask first whether the differences in their approach to arbitration are sufficient so as to separate the different countries either individually or by blocks that share a view of arbitration; and second, whether the development of local arbitration and local arbitration traditions in isolation from international arbitration has impacted and still impacts international arbitration it what has been called Latin America.

This chapter reviews the origin of the concept of Latin America; some of the differences that may be considered when approaching the region; the attempts made by Latin American countries to originate international instruments in the region to foster the development of arbitration; the adoption of different arbitration law models that attempt to preserve arbitral traditions while reflecting the international instruments related to arbitration; and the impact of such combination on the future of arbitration in the region.

II WHAT IS LATIN AMERICA?

Concepts taken in the abstract seem easy to understand and use. The issue, however, is to describe and place the given concept in precise and accurate terms.[3] The concept of Latin America is generally taken for granted. But what is Latin America? Is it a group of countries and if so, which countries does it include? Is it a political concept? A perception? A discriminatory term? Moreover, is it a fixed and undisputed concept or a concept that changes depending on who is using it and for which purposes?

There is debate as to the origin of the concept of Latin America. "[M]any scholars assume that French imperialists invented 'Latin America' in order to justify their country's occupation of Mexico (1862-1867). And the idea did stem from the French

Jurídicas de la UNAM. Retrieved from https://archivos.juridicas.unam.mx/www/bjv/libros/11/5120/19.pdf, last visited December 2, 2021.

2. Jana A. (2015). International Commercial Arbitration in Latin America: Myths and Realities. *Journal of International Arbitration*. Kluwer Law International, Volume 32, Issue 4 pp. 413-446.
3. Sloman, S. and Fernbach, P. (2017). *The Knowledge Illusion. Why We Never Think Alone*. Riverhead Books, pp. 19-36.

concept of a 'Latin race,' which Latin American émigrés in Europe helped spread to the other side of the Atlantic."[4] However, "the term 'Latin America' had already been used in 1856 by Central and South Americans protesting U.S. expansion into the Southern Hemisphere. Less known is the fact that these resisting Latin Americans also feared European intervention, albeit to a lesser extent. Such fears involved not only French designs on Mexico but also Spain's efforts to regain territories it had lost with the Spanish-American wars of independence. Opposition to U.S. and European imperialism thus underpinned the idea of Latin America. This anti-imperial impulse helps explain why 'Latin America' lives on, in contrast to the concept of 'Latin Africa,' which was developed by French imperialists in the late nineteenth century but adopted by few Africans."[5]

The concept of Latin America is said to have been created by a French diplomat, Chevalier, probably to justify the French presence in Mexico, and to differentiate a region that had allegedly more links to France, in terms of language and cultural traditions ("Latin language and Latin traditions"), than to the "other America," the United States of America. "In the early nineteenth century, however, elites in the Southern Hemisphere rarely identified themselves and the continent with the Latin race. Initially, their preferred terms were *americanos* and *América*. As John Chasteen shows, these centuries-old terms became prevalent in the 1810s and 1820s, when the region waged wars of independence against Spain. With this struggle, *americano* took on an anticolonial meaning and no longer encompassed only people of European descent, but also those of indigenous, African, and mixed-race descent. As U.S. expansionists began to threaten Mexico in the 1830s, elites in Central and South America increasingly adopted the term *Hispano-América* to differentiate their societies from the United States, which was claiming 'America' all for itself."[6] Therefore, in its origins, the concept of Latin America was not substantially different from the concept used by Spain to refer to its former colonies, la *America Española*, the Spanish America.

Whether the source of the term originates in France, Spain, the United States or countries in Latin America, the concept of Latin America was not meant to encompass a group of countries as if they were one and the same, but rather to attempt to find their affinities in terms of race and culture with Europe and the United States and, from the perspective of the Latin American countries, to stress their independence from Europe and the United States. The differences among the countries of the region are significant. Various factors have historically contributed to such differences.[7]

In the precolonial period, there were immense empires (Incas, Aztecs, Mayas) and smaller and extremely primitive indigenous communities.[8] Different institutions evolved after the colonization and during the Spanish presence in the region which were largely dependent upon the type of indigenous communities and their degree of

4. Gobat, M. (2013). *The Invention of Latin America: A Transnational History of Anti-Imperialisms, Democracy and Race*. American Historical Review. Oxford University Press, pp. 1345-1375.
5. *Ibid.*
6. *Ibid.*
7. Bethell L. (1984). *The Cambridge History of Latin America, Vol. 1, Colonial Latin America*. Cambridge University Press.
8. *Ibid.*

development.[9] The territorial divisions resulting from the independence of the colonies from Spain and Portugal were, in a significant number of cases, political decisions that did not consider the affinities of the inhabitants or the natural geography of the territory.[10]

Over the years, policies on migration and origins of migrants have marked a difference in the cultures of the countries in the region. There were large European migrations, particularly Italian and German, in Argentina and Uruguay; Brazil had the largest Japanese community after Japan; Peru received sizeable migration from China and Japan; Bolivia, with one of the largest indigenous populations in the American continent, had low levels of immigration; Colombia had historically little immigration except for Lebanese migration on the Caribbean coast, although now has received huge numbers of migrants from Venezuela.[11]

As for the legal regimes, during the colonial period, the applicable law was generally the Indian law ("*derecho indiano*") dictated by Spain for its colonies.[12] But after independence, rather than seeking consolidation of the Spanish rules or the harmonization of the existing legislation, the young republics searched for independent legal systems. Even though the French Civil Code (the so-called Napoleon Code) had a great influence, it was the subject of different approaches. Chile adopted the Civil Code prepared by Andres Bello and modeled on the French Civil Code. Colombia and Venezuela adopted the Andres Bello Code. The Dominican Republic adopted the French Civil Code almost verbatim. Cuba and Puerto Rico followed the Spanish Civil Code. Panama took inspiration from the Spanish Civil Code but adopted its own version. Argentina followed the works of Velez Sarsfield and his adoption of the French Civil Code. Brazil and Mexico adopted modern codes to some extent departing from the French influence.[13]

Following the French influence, various jurisdictions developed the concepts of administrative contracts and administrative acts with a special legal regime and specialized courts, the administrative courts and the Council of State. The definition of an administrative contract was dependent either upon the subject matter or upon the type of contracting entity or both. Administrative contracts were generally governed by administrative law or special regimes for State contracts, subject to the exclusive

9. *Ibid.*
10. Bethell L. (1985). *The Cambridge History of Latin America, Vol. 3, From Independence to c. 1870.* Colonial Latin America. Cambridge University Press; Lynch J. (1986). *The Spanish American Revolutions 1808-1826.* W. W. Norton & Company. Second Edition.
11. Martínez Pizarro, J. (2008). *América Latina y el Caribe: migración internacional, derechos humanos y desarrollo.* Comisión Económica para América Latina y el Caribe (CEPAL) Santiago de Chile; Solimano, A. (Ed). *Migraciones Internacionales en America Latina. Booms, Crisis y Desarrollo.* Fondo de Cultura Económica, Chile, 2008.
12. C. Mirow, Matthew (2004) *Latin American Law A History of Private Law and Institutions in Spanish America.* University of Texas Press or (2) C. Mirow, Matthew (2004) El Código de Napoleón y los Códigos de Belo y Vélez Sarsfield. *Anuario de Derecho Privado,* Numero 33. Universidad de los Andes, Facultad de Derecho.
13. C. Mirow, Matthew (2004) *Latin American Law A History of Private Law and Institutions in Spanish America.* University of Texas Press or (2) C. Mirow, Matthew (2004) El Código de Napoleón y los Códigos de Belo y Vélez Sarsfield. *Anuario de Derecho Privado,* Numero 33. Universidad de los Andes, Facultad de Derecho.

jurisdiction of the local courts and the State and State entities reserved for themselves the so-called exorbitant powers that included the possibility to unilaterally interpret or terminate the contract and the power to declare the caducity of the contract for the reasons provided for in the law, which generally included reasons of public policy or public convenience. Decisions based on the exorbitant powers of the State were subject to the control of the domestic courts.

The development of arbitration in this diverse environment must be approached with care. Even though there are overlaps, the approach of State-to-State arbitration, arbitration involving the State or State entities, investment arbitration and arbitration involving private parties has been different. There seems to have been an openness to accept local arbitration rules and even regional treaties touching on arbitration, but a reluctance to follow international models, treaties and rules. The approach to arbitration in Latin America should be focused not only on whether the countries of the region have adopted models that were accepted and acceptable in Europe or the United States but also on whether there has been a particular culture of arbitration in the different jurisdictions and how such culture has impacted the evolution of arbitration in the diverse countries of Latin America.

Domestic arbitration between private parties is not new. Traces of arbitration provisions have been found even in the colonial period. Arbitration was recognized and regulated in Spain, and since Spanish law was applicable in the territories of Spanish America, the arbitral provisions were part of the law of the land.[14] The "birth certificate" of arbitration in Latin America is said to be the order (*pragmatica*) issued by the Emperor Charles V (Charles I of Spain) on December 10, 1532, pursuant to which the arbitration provisions of Castille shall be applied in "the Indias," i.e., in Spanish America. The order (*pragmatica*) was in turn incorporated in the *Recopilación de las Leyes de los Reynos de las Indias* (Book Fifth, Title X, Law V) published in 1680 under Charles II.[15] Provisions on arbitration were included in several procedural codes since the nineteenth-century[16] Judicial Code of Colombia, Law 105 of 1890 Article 307; Argentinian Code of Procedure of August 20, 1880; the Chilean Law on Organization of Tribunals of 1875 and even in the National Constitutions, for example, the 1830 Constitution of Venezuela which follows the formula provided for under the Spanish Constitution of 1812. Different provisions on different types of arbitration may also be found in the Constitutions of Chile (1823), Brazil (1824) and Ecuador (1878).

The purpose of arbitration in its origins seems to have been focused on allowing private parties, particularly merchants, to resolve their disputes. Over time the laws on arbitration were focused on other objectives, notably to reduce the workload of the

14. Cárdenas Mejía, JP. (2019). Introducción a la Historia del Arbitraje en Colombia. *Revista Arbitrio, Centro de Arbitraje de la Cámara de Comercio de Bogotá*. pp. 19-29.
15. Anzola, E. Nacimiento del Arbitraje en América. Retrieved from: http://eanzola.com/images/uploads/Acta_de_Nacimiento.pdf (last visited December 2, 2021); Cárdenas Mejía, JP. (2019). Introducción a la Historia del Arbitraje en Colombia. *Revista Arbitrio, Centro de Arbitraje de la Cámara de Comercio de Bogotá*. pp. 19-29.
16. Fernández Arroyo, D. (2019). *La Evolución del Arbitraje en América Latina: De la supuesta hostilidad a la evidente aceptación*. Biblioteca Jurídica Virtual del Instituto de Investigaciones Jurídicas de la UNAM. Retrieved from https://archivos.juridicas.unam.mx/www/bjv/libros/11/5120/19.pdf (last visited December 2, 2021).

courts that were clearly incapable of handling the number of cases filed with the scarce resources available. Under this latter objective, arbitration was considered an alternative method to the judicial system and a limited derogation from the jurisdiction of the courts. In case of doubt, jurisdiction of the courts was to prevail. This restrictive approach dominated and limited the evolution of arbitration for a significant period of time.

The participation of States and State entities in domestic arbitration was heavily restricted on the basis that decisions involving the so-called exorbitant powers of the State should not be submitted to scrutiny by private tribunals and, therefore, it was necessary to preserve the jurisdiction of the courts as the "natural judges" to decide State contract disputes with private parties.[17]

The rules on arbitration were initially included in the Codes of Civil Procedure, resembling the procedural rules followed by the courts, only for disputes between private parties and as an exception to the jurisdiction of the courts. It was a derogation from the natural jurisdiction of the courts that needed to be interpreted restrictively so that if there were a doubt in the interpretation of the arbitration agreement, such doubt had to be interpreted in favor of the jurisdiction of the local courts. State arbitration was generally reserved for disputes between sovereigns but not to disputes between States and private parties, much less with foreign private parties or subject to foreign arbitral tribunals.

A significant number of authors and scholars rely on the Calvo[18] and Drago[19] doctrines to support the widely spread theory that Latin America has traditionally resisted arbitration. However, the Calvo doctrine was a reaction to an abuse of diplomatic protection, and the Drago doctrine was a reaction to the use of force. They both refer to acts that involve States but did not have the impact sometimes attributed to them in the development of arbitration that does not involve States or State entities. The issues affected by these doctrines, therefore, were public interest and State contracts which could not be said to have been the cause of a reluctance to accept the concept of commercial arbitration.[20]

The causes that have slowed the development of arbitration in the region are a combination of State policies and the reluctance by practitioners, particularly experts in procedural law, to accept a mechanism outside of the "natural jurisdiction" of the courts. This resulted in a sort of compromise through a set of laws and rules that looked for more flexibility and a speedier resolution of conflicts while respecting both the rules

17. Tawil, G. (2011). *On the Internationalization of Administrative Contracts, Arbitration and the Calvo Doctrine*, in Albert Jan van den Berg (ed.), Arbitration Advocacy in Changing Times, ICCA Congress Series, 2010 Rio Volume 15, Kluwer Law International, pp. 325-347.
18. The Calvo doctrine (1903) is defined as "[t]he rule that resident aliens have the same rights to protection as citizens, but no more." *Black's Law Dictionary* (11th ed. 2019), Calvo doctrine.
19. The Drago doctrine (1906) is the principle that "no public debt should be collected from a sovereign state by force or through the occupation of American territory by a foreign power." *Black's Law Dictionary* (11th ed. 2019), Drago doctrine.
20. Fernández Arroyo, D. (2019). *La Evolución del Arbitraje en América Latina: De la supuesta hostilidad a la evidente aceptación*. Biblioteca Jurídica Virtual del Instituto de Investigaciones Jurídicas de la UNAM. Retrieved from https://archivos.juridicas.unam.mx/www/bjv/libros/11/5120/19.pdf (last visited December 2, 2021).

contained in the *lex arbitri* and rules in the codes of civil procedure that were perceived as part of the public policy of the State. The theory of the "natural judge"; the reference in local arbitration laws to rules of the codes of civil or administrative procedure; the never-ending debates as to whether arbitration is contractual or procedural; the consideration that arbitration is part of the judicial system of the State and that arbitrators are equivalent to judges and therefore have the powers, limitation and responsibilities of judges; the so-called *constitutionalization* of arbitration; the rigid and formalistic approach to the rules that must be followed in arbitration are circumstances that have maintained a particular "culture of arbitration" that departs in various respects to what are considered "acceptable standards" of arbitration in the United States and Western Europe.

III THE LATIN AMERICAN CONFERENCES AND TREATIES

The different countries in the region not only considered it necessary to issue rules on domestic arbitration but also explored the possibility of agreeing on uniform international rules related to arbitration and particularly, but not exclusively, on the transnational enforcement of awards. Such efforts at unification were made at a regional level. "The nations of Latin America have been among those championing the cause of unification of law. In the course of the 19th century the trend toward unification was reflected in the adoption of comprehensive multilateral treaties on private international law. Those comprehensive efforts toward unification were deeply rooted in the optimistic universal ideology current at the time. At a time when lawyers and governments in Europe were becoming concerned with the question of unification and harmonization of laws, Latin America made the first attempt in the world to codify rules on private international law."[21]

The First South American Congress on Private International Law that took place in Montevideo, Uruguay, between August 1888 and February 1889 gave rise to the Treaty of International Procedural Law (*Tratado de Derecho Procesal Internacional*), signed on January 11, 1889, section III of which provides, *inter alia*, for the enforcement of arbitral awards and judicial decisions. Argentina, Bolivia, Brazil, Chile, Paraguay, Peru and Uruguay signed the treaty. It was thereafter ratified by Argentina, Bolivia, Colombia, Paraguay, Perú, and Uruguay.

During the Fifth International American Conference (*Quinta Conferencia Internacional Americana*) that took place in Santiago, Chile, between March and May 1923, the participants approved a recommendation for the organization of chambers of commerce in the continent and for such chambers of commerce to enter into agreements for the extrajudicial solution of mercantile disputes. The participants also approved a recommendation for the study of mandatory arbitration as a means to decide disputes between merchants located in different jurisdictions.

21. Garro, A.M. (1992). Unification and Harmonization of Private Law in Latin America. *The American Journal of Comparative Law*. Volume 40, Issue 3, Oxford University Press. pp. 587-616.

The Convention on International Private Law signed in Havana, Cuba, on February 20, 1928 (known as the Code of International Private Law or *Codigo Bustamante*), one of the most significant efforts of unification of private law in the region, contained an entire book (Book 4) devoted to International Procedural Law. The code contained detailed rules for the international enforcement of judicial decisions, requirements of court procedures, requirements to appear in a foreign court and added that the procedure and effects provided for in the norms to regulate these issues should also apply to decisions issued by arbitrators in any of the Member States. The Bustamante Code, however, had few signatures and so many reservations that it did not have the effects that the participant countries were seeking.[22]

The Seventh American International Conference (Montevideo, Uruguay, 1933) recommended that the chambers of commerce of the different States adopt a convention on arbitration similar to the one agreed upon between the Bolsa de Comercio de Buenos Aires and the Chamber of Commerce of the United States of America in 1916. The resolution from the Conference recommended that chambers of commerce that administer arbitration adopt essential procedures and practices for the operation of an Inter-American arbitration system. Such procedures and practices included the need for the arbitration agreement to be valid and enforceable; the liberty of the parties to appoint arbitrators and provide for their replacement; the obligation of the parties or the arbitral institutions to define clear rules of procedure to be applied by the arbitrators; the obligation of the arbitrators or the arbitral institution to define clear rules of procedure; the obligation of the arbitrators to be impartial and of the institution to provide for means for rules that assure the right to challenge the arbitrators; the obligation to forbid the right of appeal, except for procedural matters or for those matters on the merits that the parties agree be subject to appeal.

The Treaty of International Procedural Law signed in Montevideo, Uruguay, on March 19, 1940, again refers to international commercial arbitration and provides that arbitral awards issued in a state party to the treaty shall have in the territories of the other State parties the same effects assigned to the given award in the State where it is issued provided that the treaty requirements are met. Two salient features of the treaty are the need for the Attorney General of the State where enforcement is sought to intervene and for the possibility of the enforcing court to issue, even ex officio, the necessary measures to ensure the effectiveness of the award in accordance with the provisions of its local law regarding attachments of assets and other preventive measures.

While such regional conferences were taking place and regional treaties were being signed, in the aftermath of the First World War, the international community was also exploring the same topics, including the international enforcement of awards. The 1923 Geneva Protocol on Arbitration Clauses, issued under the aegis of the League of Nations, provided not only for the recognition of the validity of arbitration agreements but also for their enforcement by domestic courts who, when faced with such

22. Organization of American States. Código de Derecho Internacional Privado (1928). Retrieved from: https://www.oas.org/juridico/spanish/mesicic3_ven_anexo3.pdf, last visited December 2, 2021.

agreements, would send the parties to arbitration. However, Brazil was the only country in the region to sign the protocol.

The Convention on the Enforcement of Foreign Arbitral Awards signed in Geneva on September 26, 1927, had the same lack of success in the region. It was only signed, but never ratified, by Bolivia, Nicaragua and Peru.

Even though various States of the region participated in the preparatory works of the Convention on the Recognition and Enforcement of Arbitral Awards of 1958—the New York Convention—the steps toward ratification were slow, and several jurisdictions elected to maintain either the regional treaties they had already ratified or their local rules for enforcement of judicial decisions applicable to arbitral awards. Ten years after its signature, the New York Convention had only entered into force in Ecuador, Chile and Mexico.

By 1983, twenty-five years after signature, only Colombia and Uruguay added to the list of States where the New York Convention was in force. Colombia, however, had a "limbo" of two years when the applicability of the New Convention was heavily debated. Colombia enacted the New York Convention through Law 37 of 1979. However, in 1988 the Supreme Court of Justice declared that such law was unconstitutional, as it had been signed by a Minister of Government who was temporarily replacing the President, who was traveling at the time. The Court considered that the temporary authorities of the Minister did not include the signing of international treaties.[23] As a result of the declaration of unconstitutionality, the New York Convention ceased to be incorporated into the Colombian legal system, but remained valid and enforceable for Colombia under international law. This situation remained for two years until Congress approved Law 39 of 1990, incorporating once more the New York Convention into Colombia's legal system.

The New York Convention entered into force in five additional countries during the 1980s after its 25th anniversary (Guatemala in 1984; Panama in 1985; Costa Rica and Peru in 1988; and Argentina in 1989). Four more countries in the region joined the New York Convention in the 1990s (Bolivia in 1995; Venezuela in 1995; El Salvador and Paraguay in 1998). Finally, the New York Convention entered into force in Honduras in 2000; in Brazil and the Dominican Republic in 2002 and in Nicaragua in 2003.

In addition to an international system of arbitration, the countries of the Americas discussed the possibility of adopting a uniform law on arbitration, and at the meeting of the Inter-American Council of Jurists in Mexico in 1956, a model law was recommended. However, the law was not adopted by any of the so-called Latin American countries.

But at the same time that the countries in the region were deciding whether to adopt the New York Convention, efforts were undertaken toward a uniform regional set of rules for arbitration following the lead of the Bustamante Code.

The Inter-American Council of Jurists proposed a draft Inter-American Convention on International Commercial Arbitration at its meeting in Rio de Janeiro in 1967.

23. Supreme Court of Justice of Colombia, Case No. 1805, October 6, 1988.

The final version was signed in Panama on January 30, 1975, during the First Specialized Inter-American Conference on Private International Law by Brazil, Chile, Colombia, Costa Rica, Ecuador, El Salvador, Guatemala, Honduras, Nicaragua, Panama, Uruguay and Venezuela. Currently, the Convention has been ratified by Argentina, Bolivia, Brazil, Chile, Colombia, Costa Rica, Dominican Republic, Ecuador, El Salvador, Guatemala, Honduras, Mexico, Nicaragua, Panama, Paraguay, Peru, the United States, Uruguay and Venezuela. The United States made three "reservations" in ratifying the Panama Convention: First, if the Rules of Procedure of the Inter-American Commercial Arbitration Commission (IACAC Rules) in effect as of January 1, 1980 (referred to in Article 3 of the Convention), are changed or amended, the Government of the United States reserves the right to accept or reject the amendment. Second, the United States will only enforce awards under Article 4 made in the territory of a contracting state. Third, in the event that both the Panama Convention and the New York Convention are applicable in a given case, the former would prevail if a majority of the parties to the arbitration agreement are citizens or entities of a state or States that have both ratified or acceded to the Panama Convention and are Member States of the Organization of American States.

The Panama Convention was not adopted to complement or fill gaps of the New York Convention, but rather as a separate instrument for the recognition and enforcement of awards between countries in the Americas. Since its approval, it received some criticism as to its need and usefulness in light of the New York Convention. Professor van den Berg, referring to one such criticism, commented that "A comment in 1975 on the adoption of the Panama Convention stated that 'Latin Americans, generally, are rather secluded in their world outlook' and that 'they trust global organizations less than they trust themselves.'"[24] "With respect, I dare to take issue with that comment, certainly in 1989. More Latin American countries have now adhered to the global New York Convention than to the regional Panama Convention and Latin Americans participate increasingly on a world-wide level in international arbitration. Within this perspective, the Panama Convention can be considered to constitute a bridgehead to international arbitration in general and the New York Convention in particular."[25]

The debate as to whether the two conventions—Panama and New York—are compatible or whether they may coexist, and if so how, led to a debate of great interest for U.S. courts, practitioners and scholars. However, I have found no record of courts in the Americas, outside of the U.S., that have applied the Panama Convention for the recognition and enforcement of awards instead of the New York Convention, or that have analyzed their compatibility or relative precedence in light of the local law, much less in light of the rules on treaty interpretation. The conflicts that have existed in the courts of the region as to the applicability of the New York Convention refer to the alleged incompatibility of the New York Convention with local rules of procedure, of

24. van den Berg A.J (September 1, 1989), *The New York Convention 1958 and Panama Convention 1975: Redundancy or Compatibility*? Arbitration International, Volume 5, Issue 3, pp. 214-229, citing Lliteras, J. (1975 2nd quarter), *The Panama Convention Strengthens Arbitration in the Americas*, in Inter-American Arbitration, IACAC, p. 2.
25. van den Berg A.J (September 1, 1989), *The New York Convention 1958 and Panama Convention 1975: Redundancy or Compatibility*? Arbitration International, Volume 5, Issue 3, pp. 214-229.

the prevalence of local rules on grounds of public policy or even the dual application of both local rules and the rules of the New York Convention.

The question is not, therefore, whether the Panama Convention is an instrument reflecting the tendency of Latin Americans to isolate themselves in their world outlook, but rather whether it makes sense to maintain a convention that appears to apply principally for the recognition and enforcement in the U.S. of awards issued in other countries of the Americas, given the ratification of the New York Convention by all countries in the region.

One of the key features and advantages of the Panama Convention which differentiates it from the New York Convention is the application of a modern set of arbitration rules (the IACAC Rules) to arbitrations in the region in the absence of an agreement of the parties. pursuant to Article 3. However, the adoption of the UNCITRAL model arbitration law in various jurisdictions of the region and the proliferation of regional arbitration centers that are adapting their rules to handle international cases raise serious doubts as to the relevance and influence of the Panama Convention in general and the IACAC Rules in particular.

IACAC arbitration is today administered by the International Centre for Dispute Resolution (ICDR) of the American Arbitration Association pursuant to an agreement between the two institutions. There is no information available, either on the IACAC web page or in the website of ICDR as to the number of IACAC cases administered by ICDR.[26] In his proposal for the denunciation of the Panama Convention, Claus Von Wobeser notes that "Although I hope that it is a temporary situation, when attempting to find statistics on the arbitrations administered by the institution, on its web page it simply states that this information is 'under construction', which perhaps is a reflection of the lack of solidity and resources of the institution."[27] The situation remains the same as of the publication of this chapter, without even a note indicating that the information is "in construction" or where it can be accessed.

In sum, a convention perceived by some in its origins as a Latin American instrument and as an isolation of the Latin American countries from the world of arbitration is, in today's reality, a convention applied by U.S. courts for the enforcement of awards in the U.S. Moreover, the IACAC arbitrations are administered by the ICDR, a U.S. arbitral institution. But even in the U.S., there has been debate and confusion on the application of the Panama Convention and its relationship with the New York Convention.[28]

---

26. http://www.sice.oas.org/dispute/comarb/iacac/iacac1e.asp, last visited February 10, 2023. https://www.icdr.org/, last visited February 10, 2023.
27. Von Wobeser, C. (2008). The influence of the New York Convention in Latin America and on the Inter American Convention on International Commercial Arbitration. *Dispute Resolution International*. Volume 2, Issue 1. pp. 43, 54-55.
28. Bowman, J. (2000). The Panama Convention and its implementation under the federal Arbitration Act. *The American Review of International Arbitration*, Vol. 11, Issues 1-2; Leathley, C. (2007). *Inter American Commercial Arbitration Commission (IACAC)*. In Leathley C. (Ed.) *International Dispute Resolution in Latin America: An Institutional Overview*. Kluwer Law International. pp. 79-106; Leathley, C and Villaggi, F. (2017). *The Panama Convention in the United States. Chapter 3 of the FAA*. In Shore, L., et al. (eds), *International Arbitration in the United States*. Kluwer Law International, pp. 599-615.

As a consequence, the Panama Convention has had little, if any, impact on the development of arbitration in the countries of Latin America. The evolution of arbitration has been rather, as suggested by von Wobeser,[29] the result of the adoption and application of the New York Convention, the increasing adoption of the UNCITRAL Model Law and the individual efforts of lawyers and judges in each country to learn and master the key features of arbitration. An additional factor that has influenced the development of arbitration in the region has been the creation of local chambers of commerce and the trust placed in such institutions to administer arbitrations.

One additional multilateral convention that is worth mentioning is the Inter-American Convention on the Extraterritorial Efficacy of Foreign Judicial Decisions and Arbitral Awards (*Convención Interamericana sobre Eficacia Extraterritorial de las Sentencias y Laudos Arbitrales Extranjeros*) signed in Montevideo in May 1979. Some scholars have considered this Convention as complementary to the Panama Convention.[30] However, the Montevideo Convention of 1979 refers to the enforcement of both foreign judicial decisions and foreign arbitral awards. It may thus add to the confusion that still exists in some Latin American jurisdictions as to the applicability to foreign arbitral awards of the local procedural rules applicable to the enforcement of foreign judicial decisions. It is also an instrument that has been even more irrelevant than the Panama Convention in its application and contribution to the development of arbitration in the region. Once again, the real debate and conflict as to the applicable rules for enforcement of awards in the region has been between the local rules and the New York Convention but not between the latter and the regional treaties such as the Montevideo Convention, or between the regional treaties themselves, or between the local rules and the regional treaties.

In addition to regional treaties on arbitration, there are bilateral treaties on private international law that add to the proliferation of regional legal instruments dealing with arbitration. These agreements have had little contribution to the development of arbitration and have been a further source of confusion as exemplified by the decision rendered by the Supreme Court of Colombia in the *Poligráfica C.A. v. Columbia Tecnología Ltda* case. The Supreme Court was asked to grant recognition of an award issued in an arbitration seated in Quito, Ecuador, and it decided to apply the Treaty on International Private Law entered into between Colombia and Ecuador on June 18, 1903. The Supreme Court based its decision on a particular reading of Article VII of the New York Convention pursuant to which the New York Convention had a 'residual' character with regard to other international treaties ratified by Colombia. Since there was a specific treaty signed by Colombia and Ecuador, it held that such treaty should prevail.[31]

29. Von Wobeser, C. (2008). The Influence of the New York Convention in Latin America and on the Inter American Convention on International Commercial Arbitration. *Dispute Resolution International.* Volume 2, Issue 1, pp. 43, 54-55.
30. Galán Barrera, D.R. (2007). Citation: El arbitraje comercial internacional en América Latina. *Precedente. Revista Jurídica.* pp. 185-210. Retrieved from: https://doi.org/10.18046/prec.v0.1438, last visited December 2, 2021.
31. Supreme Court of Justice of Colombia, Poligráfica C.A. v. Columbia Tecnología Ltda. Case No. 11001-0203-000-2008-00317-00, November 19, 2013.

IV THE UNCITRAL MODEL LAW: FOLLOWING THE MODEL?

The adoption of the UNCITRAL Model Law on Arbitration has been considered as one of the factors in measuring the progress of arbitration in Latin America.

According to the UNCITRAL website, Argentina, Chile, Costa Rica, Dominican Republic, Guatemala, Honduras, Mexico, Nicaragua, Paraguay, Peru, Uruguay and Venezuela have implemented legislation based on the UNCITRAL Model Law.[32]

This information, however, must be approached with caution. First, because the States enacting the legislation may have departed from the text of the UNCITRAL Model Law and therefore the "legislation of each State should be considered in order to identify the exact nature of any possible deviation from the model in the legislative text that was adopted."[33] Indeed, there may be countries that report their laws as following the UNCITRAL Model Law, but where there are substantial departures from the model. Second, because the information contained in the UNCITRAL web page is merely indicative of the laws that were reported to the UNCITRAL Secretariat, there may be countries that have adopted laws based on the UNCITRAL Model Law that are not included in the UNCITRAL report. Last, there are jurisdictions where the law does not distinguish international from domestic arbitration; or refers to arbitration in general but contains specific provisions with particular consequences for domestic arbitration; or has completely separate provisions for national and international arbitration. Based on these latter characteristics, the different laws in the region have been considered monist (same treatment) or dualist (differential treatment).[34]

Therefore, an analysis of the status of the adoption of the UNCITRAL Model Law requires an analysis of whether the relevant departures of the local law from the Model Law are so significant as to raise doubts as to whether the local law is really based on the UNCITRAL Model Law at all. With regard to those countries with a dualist regime, the question is asked whether the law follows the UNCITRAL Model Law for both domestic and international arbitration or only for international arbitration. If the latter, to what extent do the provisions of the law addressing local arbitration impact the provisions on international arbitration so as to affect the implementation of the UNCITRAL Model Law?

A detailed review of each of the features of the law of each jurisdiction that may follow or depart from the UNCITRAL Model Law would exceed the extent and scope of this chapter. However, some examples may illustrate the difficulties that have to be considered when approaching the arbitration law of each country.

32. United Nations Commission on International Trade Law (2002). Retrieved from: https://uncitral.un.org/en/texts/arbitration/modellaw/commercial_arbitration/status, last visited December 2, 2021.
33. *Ibid.*, at Disclaimer.
34. Jana, A. (2015). International Commercial Arbitration in Latin America: Myths and Realities. *Journal of International Arbitration*. Kluwer Law International, Volume 32, Issue 4 pp. 413-446; Rey Vallejo, A.P. (2014). *Los modelos regulatorios del arbitraje latinoamericano: un análisis de las normativas de arbitraje doméstico en Colombia y en el hemisferio*. Revista 128 Vniversitas. Retrieved from: http://www.scielo.org.co/pdf/vniv/n128/n128a09.pdf, last visited December 2, 2021.

Mexico is probably the country that most closely follows the UNCITRAL Model Law and is a "monist" jurisdiction where the law refers to domestic arbitration but does not assign any consequences to the distinction with international arbitration.[35] Venezuela closely follows the UNCITRAL Model Law, without distinction between domestic and international arbitration, but with special rules for the participation of public entities and a remission to the Code of Civil Procedure for the grounds to challenge an arbitrator.[36] Likewise, Peru bases its arbitration law on the UNCITRAL Model Law and has a single statute for domestic and international arbitration. However, Peruvian law provides for specific rules and consequences depending on whether the arbitration is domestic or international.[37] It also contains some particularities that seem unique in the region such as the obligation to submit to arbitration any works, service, consulting or procurement contract executed by the Peruvian State[38] and specific rules for extension of the arbitration clause to non-signatories.[39]

Chile, Costa Rica, Argentina and Uruguay have adopted, with some modifications, the UNCITRAL Model Law as a separate statute applicable to international commercial arbitration alone, while preserving the rules contained in separate statutes for domestic arbitration. Colombia in turn adopted a single statute containing both the rules on domestic and international arbitration, although in separate chapters. In the case of Colombia,[40] the commission appointed by the Government to draft a new arbitration statute—in which I participated as a member—attempted to draft a single statute following the UNCITRAL Model Law and derogating the rules that so far had applied to local arbitration. After a couple of meetings, the mission proved impossible. A monist law would imply so many additions and amendments to the UNCITRAL Model Law that the end result would be far worse than the existing provisions. The decision was therefore made to divide the commission into two groups, one that would draft the "national portion" of the law and the other that would adopt, with very few amendments, the UNCITRAL Model Law.

Considering the long tradition of local arbitration in the countries listed above, it seems that the reason for the adoption of separate statutes for international arbitration was to balance the need to have a modern law on international arbitration with the need to preserve the traditions of domestic arbitration which was (and is) widely used by local litigators with a close resemblance to judicial proceedings.

35. Mexico's Commercial Code, published in the Official Gazette of the Federation from October 7 to December 13, 1889, last amendment published on March 28, 2018, at Title IV of Book V, Articles 1415 et seq.
36. Venezuela's Commercial Arbitration Law, published in the Official Gazette No. 36.430 on April 7, 1998, at Articles 1, 4, 25 and 50.
37. Jana, A. (2015). International Commercial Arbitration in Latin America: Myths and Realities. *Journal of International Arbitration*. Kluwer Law International, Volume 32, Issue 4.
38. Law No. 30225, State Contracting Law, published in the Official Gazette El Peruano on July 11, 2014, as modified by Legislative Decree No. 1341, published in the Official Gazette El Peruano on September 16, 2018.
39. Law No. 26572, General Law of Arbitration, published in the Official Gazette El Peruano on January 5, 1996, at Article 14.
40. Law No. 1563, published in the Official Gazette No. 48.489 on July 12, 2012.

The division between domestic and international arbitration—dualism—in Latin America may result in the law and practices of local arbitration gradually adapting to the standards of international arbitration and thus allowing the passage of a single law for arbitration. Alternatively, it may result in further development and separation of the local rules to such an extent that a monist approach is simply not possible. But in the meantime, the existence of dual statutes may lead to confusion and uncertainty. In the *Gecelca* case,[41] a debate on whether the arbitration was domestic or international led to two different awards, an action to set aside and a constitutional action (acción de tutela), and the matter is still unresolved.

On December 22, 2010, Gecelca S.A E.S.P ("Gecelca") and its subsidiary Gecelca 3 S.A.S E.S.P ("Gecelca 3"), and the Consortium CUC-DTC, formed between China United Engineering Corporation and Dongfang Turbine Co. LTD. (the "Consortium"), executed an engineering, procurement and construction contract to build a thermo-electric power plant (the "Contract"). The arbitration clause provided for arbitration in Bogota under the rules of the Arbitration Center of the Bogota Chamber of Commerce. During the performance of the Contract, certain disputes arose between the parties. On December 29, 2014, the Consortium submitted a request for arbitration under the arbitration clause of the Contract. The parties disputed whether the arbitration was international, since at the time of the request, the arbitration clause and the dispute complied with the requirements of Law 1563 of 2012 for an arbitration to be considered international, or domestic because, at the time the contract containing the arbitration clause was entered into, Law 1563 of 2102 was not yet in force and the intent of the parties at the time was to submit the disputes to domestic arbitration.

The parties did not agree on the members of the Tribunal, and therefore they were appointed by the Center of Arbitration of the Bogota Chamber of Commerce. The Center of Arbitration of the Bogota Chamber of Commerce has a list of arbitrators for national arbitrations which is composed of approximately four hundred members and divided into categories A and B depending on the experience of the arbitrators, and a list of international arbitrators of approximately thirty members. The Tribunal was appointed from the list of international arbitrators. The Tribunal was constituted on March 11, 2015, and on May 8, 2015, the Tribunal issued a partial award deciding that the arbitration was international. The Tribunal considered that the requirements for an arbitration to be considered international are of a procedural nature and thus of immediate effect and that, at the time of submission of the request for arbitration, two of the three criteria set forth in Article 62 of Law 1563 of 2012 for an arbitration to be considered international had been met, namely, that the parties were domiciled in different States at the time of execution of the arbitral clause and that the dispute affected the interests of international trade.

---

41. Zuleta, E. and Rincon, M.C (2019). *Colombia's Constitutional Court Declares That Constitutional Injunctions (Tutela) Can Be Upheld Against Awards In International Arbitration.* Retrieved from: http://arbitrationblog.kluwerarbitration.com/2019/11/04/colombias-constitutional-court-declares-that-constitutional-injunctions-tutela-can-be-upheld-against-awards-in-international-arbitration, last visited December 2, 2021.

The final award was issued on December 4, 2017, and on January 11, 2018, Gecelca 3 filed an action before the Council of State to set aside because, among other reasons, it was inconsistent with Colombia's international public policy. Almost simultaneously and before the same court—the Council of State—on February 28, 2018, Gecelca and Gecelca 3 applied for a constitutional injunction (*tutela*) against the award alleging, *inter alia*, that by applying the rules of international arbitration to a national arbitration, the Tribunal had violated their fundamental rights to due process and access to justice as such principles are better protected by the provisions applicable to national arbitration.

On July 26, 2018, the Fourth Section of the Council of State—the first-level competent court—declared that the *tutela* was inadmissible since this mechanism could not be used to reopen a legal debate addressed during the arbitral proceedings. On September 12, 2018, the Fifth Section of the Council of State—the second-level competent court—confirmed the first instance decision and added that, since constitutional injunctions are subsidiary remedies, the *tutela* was not admissible because the decision to set aside the Final Award was still pending.

The *tutela* decisions were selected for review by the Constitutional Court, and on October 29, 2018, the 10th Selection Chamber of the Court selected the *tutela* for revision. In a decision dated August 6, 2019,[42] the Fifth Revision Chamber of the Constitutional Court reiterated that it is legally possible to apply for *tutela* action against awards issued in international arbitrations seated in Colombia but clarified that constitutional injunctions against awards in international arbitrations are even more exceptional ("*excepcionalísima*") than in the case of awards in national arbitration. Yet, it is a discretional matter for the competent judge to decide.

But the issue is far from being settled. First, the Constitutional Court concluded that the *tutela* was not admissible in the specific case because the annulment proceedings had not been exhausted and suggested that once the Council of State decided on the annulment, it would be possible to return to the Constitutional Court and apply for a *tutela* against the award. Second, there are several other cases before the various arbitration centers where the issue of whether the arbitration is national or international has been decided by arbitral tribunals and legal actions against such decisions are expected. Finally, this is a decision of one of the Chambers of the Court, not a decision of the plenary of the Court nor a decision to unify jurisprudence, and therefore it only applies to the specific case and may be revisited.

It is worth noting that, at the request of the Constitutional Court, the Latin American Arbitration Association (ALARB) submitted an opinion in this case in response to a specific question as to whether *tutela* actions should proceed against awards issued in international arbitrations seated in Colombia. The opinion of ALARB was in the negative considering, *inter alia*, that unlike arbitrators in national arbitrations, arbitrators in international arbitrations are not deemed to be judges and do not derive their power from the Colombian Constitution. This opinion was simply mentioned, but not fully considered, by the Constitutional Court in its decision.

42. Constitutional Court of Colombia, decision T-354/19, August 6, 2019.

In sum, several jurisdictions in Latin America claim to have adopted the UNCITRAL Model Law or to have an arbitration law based on the UNCITRAL Model Law. The UNCITRAL website lists just the countries that have reported to have adopted the UNCITRAL Model Law. In the end, however, a careful analysis is required to determine whether, although not reported as a UNCITRAL Model Law country, the given jurisdiction has a modern and competitive law (Brazil) or a law tailored to local peculiarities (Bolivia) and whether the law of a country reported as adopting the UNCITRAL Model Law has really followed that model or the model of other jurisdictions (Guatemala, Honduras). The generalization that Latin American countries have adopted modern laws based on the UNCITRAL Model Law has thus to be approached with caution.

V NEW LAWS: REFOCUSED ARBITRATION CENTERS

The adoption of laws based or inspired on the UNCITRAL Model Law and in general the adoption of modern arbitration laws resulted not only in a change in the approach of the courts to arbitration but also in an enhancement of the prestige of regional arbitration centers. Much has been said about the change of attitude of the courts in Latin America as a result of the adoption of new arbitration laws and the ratification of the New York Convention, but that has been just one effect of this trend of new laws.

Historically, local and regional arbitration centers were focused on the administration of national arbitrations, collaboration with international institutions (ICC (International Chamber of Commerce), ICDR, IACAC) and organization of conferences under the sponsorship and organization of international institutions. But in recent years, these centers have seen in the new arbitration laws an opportunity to participate and compete in the market for international arbitrations. In the beginning, the participation seemed to be limited to those international cases where at least one of the parties was a national of the jurisdiction where the arbitration center was located. But over time, those centers began to offer the services of appointing authority in regional cases or administering regional cases subject to UNCITRAL Rules. One of the goals of the international regional conferences mentioned before—the administration of international arbitrations by the local and regional chambers of commerce—seems now a reality.

It is true that there is a significant, probably excessive, number of arbitration centers in Latin America; more than 165 in 2011 according to the survey performed by Institute for Transnational Arbitration.[43] But some of them have taken a leading role not only in their own jurisdictions but in neighboring countries. Institutions like the Brazil-Canada Chamber of Commerce, and the centers of arbitration administered by the Chambers of Commerce of Bogota, Lima, Quito, and Santiago have significantly increased their international cases and have acquired relevance in recent years. Moreover, there is a significant number of cases administered by these centers that may

43. Institute for International Arbitration (2011). *The Inaugural Survey of Latin America Arbitral Institutions*. Retrieved from: http://www.cailaw.org/media/files/ITA/Publications/arbitral-institutions-guide-dec.pdf, last visited December 2, 2021.

not legally qualify as international under the law of the given jurisdiction but are international in that they have foreign elements and are administered by such centers. Arbitration between local companies and subsidiaries of multinational companies or arbitrations resulting from project finance structures that involve foreign elements are not uncommon in any of the listed arbitration centers.

The growth of these centers may be explained on various grounds. First, as mentioned above, equipped with a modern arbitration law in the given country, they now feel in a position to offer that country as the seat of arbitration. Second, because both in the countries with a monist regime and in those with a dualist regime, the courts seem to reserve for international arbitration a different and more favorable treatment, than for local arbitration. Not only do the courts seem to have a certain deference to awards in international cases when actions to set aside are filed, but have also imposed limits and restrictions on the use—and abuse—of the constitutional remedies of *amparo* and *tutela* for awards issued in international arbitrations. The horror stories of the Merck, Radio Centro and Termorio cases,[44] to mention only a few, seem to be in the past.[45] Third, the centers have issued rules that combine the provisions of well-known international rules such as ICC and UNCITRAL with particularities of the local rules and practices. For example, the Rules of Arbitration of the Chamber of Commerce of Lima contain provisions on expedited arbitration and emergency arbitrators and rules on ethics; the rules of arbitration of the centers of Bogota and Quito maintain, for international arbitration, the rule that when the center has to appoint arbitrators it will do so by means of a draw among the members of the list of arbitrators. This approach may not only generate more confidence in the foreign parties but also ease the transition of local parties from purely local rules, to which they are used, to more international standards. Fourth, for some State entities and their counsel, it seems easier to accept international arbitration if the venue is their home and they are familiar with the arbitration center, its managers and administrators and the international rules consider local practices. Moreover, local practitioners with experience in local commercial arbitration may recommend the use of local centers with which they are familiar for international cases. Fifth, and last, regional centers have seriously invested in improving their facilities and available technology for international cases.

The end result, for users and counsel, is an environment where counsel with international experience, newcomers with some experience in international arbitration and local practitioners with experience in litigation and local arbitration may find a comfort zone where everyone may have some sense of familiarity with the rules, the way in which the arbitrators conduct the hearing and a balanced combination of pure civil advocacy with the practices of those countries with a common law tradition.

44. *Merck Sharpe & Dohme (I.A.) LLC v. The Republic of Ecuador*, PCA Case No. 2012-10. *Termorio S.A. E.S.P. et al. v. Electrificadora Del Atlantico S.A. E.S.P. et al.*, ICC Case No.10346/KGA/ESR.
45. Jana A. (2015). International Commercial Arbitration in Latin America: Myths and Realities. *Journal of International Arbitration*. Kluwer Law International, Volume 32, Issue 4, pp. 413-446.

VI A LOOK AHEAD

The adoption of modern laws and the ratification of the New York Convention are no doubt giant steps for the countries in Latin America. There is a sense that courts in the region are improving in their approach to arbitration. It is for practitioners and international institutions to continue their efforts of providing the courts in Latin America with information and materials that may ease their work and improve their learning curve. The efforts undertaken by institutions like the ICC, ICCA (International Council for Commercial Arbitration), ALARB and IBA (International Bar Association) and by practitioners through conferences, meetings and publications are to be applauded and should be joined by other practitioners and institutions.

The constitutional protections of *amparo* and *tutela* may still be a matter of concern, but there are significant legal and cultural differences in the approach to these constitutional mechanisms in the different jurisdictions in Latin America, and there are even countries where the mechanism is not used or does not exist. These differences must be carefully studied to avoid generalizations.

Countries in Latin America should seriously consider whether, in light of the ratification of the New York Convention by all countries, existing conventions on arbitration in the region, including the Panama Convention, should be maintained or if the time has come for their denunciation.

It is difficult to guess whether the efforts of the Latin American centers to compete in international arbitration (both among themselves and with the institutions that have a long tradition in the region such as the ICC or ICDR) will, in the long run, result in an increase in the number of cases they administer or whether the problems that users may experience as a result of their sharp learning curve will end up favoring the traditional international institutions. In the meantime, we see the opening of opportunities in international arbitration for the regional centers through an interesting mix of rules and practices with the participation of internationally experienced counsel and newcomers, facing the inevitable growing pains that result from some lack of experience on the part of the centers. It is to be seen whether this is merely a transition toward the full adoption of international rules, institutions and practices, or whether such mixed arbitration procedures are in the region to stay.

CHAPTER 8

Arbitration and Insolvency: Important Aspects for Tribunals to Consider

Fernando Mantilla-Serrano[*]

I had the opportunity to meet Guillermo Aguilar Álvarez when he was General Counsel at the International Chamber of Commerce (ICC) International Court of Arbitration. A man of legendary generosity, Guillermo opened the doors of the ICC to me and, by the same token, introduced me to what would become my professional career —international arbitration. But Guillermo's privileged legal mind transcended dispute resolution. He was a true specialist in corporate law, which was the subject of his Juris Doctor graduation paper in Mexico. On many occasions, I benefited from his encyclopedic knowledge of comparative corporate law, and at least once we discussed the challenges that corporate insolvency presented to international arbitrators. This discussion remains vivid in my mind and immediately provided the subject matter for this modest tribute to Guillermo.

International arbitration has undeniably become an increasingly popular means of resolving cross-border commercial disputes. In 1997, a total of 1,290 parties from 103 countries were involved in arbitration cases filed with the ICC.[1] More than two decades later, in 2020, the number of parties had almost doubled to 2,507 parties from 145 countries.[2] Parties choose international arbitration because of its efficiency, neutrality and adaptability to their needs, and because—as the statistics demonstrate—international arbitration is becoming the standard dispute resolution mechanism in global business.

* The author would like to thank the ICC for the opportunity to review unpublished awards for the purpose of drafting the present chapter. The author would also like to acknowledge the contribution of Kevin Cubeddu (associate at Latham & Watkins, Paris) and Aija Lejniece in the preparation of the present chapter.

1. ICC Statistical Report (1997), p. 4.
2. ICC Statistical Report (2020), pp. 9-10.

As globalization leads to more and more cross-border business relationships and their associated disputes, interactions between international arbitrations and insolvency proceedings affecting parties to an arbitration (or "parallel insolvency proceedings") are becoming increasingly common. However, while international arbitration is fundamentally a private dispute resolution mechanism—the cornerstones of which are party autonomy and detachment from national legal systems (or "delocalization") [3]—insolvency is a centralized and inherently public process governed by specific and often mandatory national rules.

As such, when one of the parties to an international arbitration is subject to parallel insolvency proceedings, the arbitral tribunal will necessarily face complex questions regarding the effects of such insolvency proceedings on the arbitration, which inevitably creates a strain between a very private procedure on the one hand and a very public procedure on the other. These questions concern, among other factors, the legal capacity of the insolvent party, the ongoing validity of the arbitration agreement, the obligation to stay the proceedings and the limits on the relief the tribunal is empowered to award.

The task of international arbitral tribunals is further complicated by the absence of global conflict of law rules or principles, both generally[4] and in relation to the effects of insolvency on arbitral proceedings.

Arbitrating disputes involving parallel insolvency proceedings is an intricate task that requires tribunals to be sensitive to both the conflicting interests that underpin arbitration as a private method of international dispute settlement and the public interests and priorities of state-centric insolvency proceedings.

This chapter first addresses the nature of international arbitral tribunals and the rules and principles they are bound to apply when faced with parallel insolvency proceedings—how an arbitral tribunal's "duty" to render an enforceable award may affect the legal principles it should take into account, and whether insolvency-specific conflict of law rules provide any guidance. The chapter then examines in more detail what principles tribunals and national courts have found to be relevant in the context of international arbitration and insolvency, and identifies several practical issues that an arbitral tribunal may face in a parallel insolvency context.

I LAW APPLICABLE TO THE EFFECTS OF PARALLEL INSOLVENCY PROCEEDINGS ON AN INTERNATIONAL ARBITRATION

Insolvency proceedings are almost entirely based on national laws, with each state taking different procedural and substantive approaches. No universal approach has ever been adopted despite regional attempts at harmonization and cooperation in

3. Gaillard, E. (2010) *Legal Theory of International Arbitration*. Leiden/Boston: Martinus Nijhoff Publishers.
4. Most arbitration rules and national laws simply defer to the parties' agreement when dealing with the law applicable to the merits of the dispute.

cross-border insolvency matters.[5] The 1997 UNCITRAL Model Law on Cross-Border Insolvency has been by far the most successful attempt but, even so, only fifty States have implemented (to varying degrees) the Model Law in their legislation.[6]

Further, there are no international instruments that directly guide international arbitral tribunals in the complex task of arbitrating a dispute involving parallel insolvency proceedings. Tribunals are nevertheless not left entirely to their own devices—as this chapter explores below, arbitrators are circumscribed by the parties' choice of law, international public policy, the tribunal's duty to ensure that the award it renders is enforceable and, in certain circumstances, mandatory rules of the seat of the arbitration and/or the place of insolvency proceedings.

A The Delocalized International Arbitral Tribunal

The first question that arises for an arbitral tribunal facing parallel insolvency proceedings is which law to apply when deciding on the recognition of such insolvency proceedings and their effect on the arbitration. An arbitral tribunal may be confronted with the possible application of at least five laws:

(1) the law applicable to the underlying contract;
(2) the law applicable to the merits of the dispute (either chosen by the parties or determined by the arbitral tribunal);
(3) the law of the seat of the arbitration;
(4) the law of the place where insolvency proceedings have been opened; and
(5) the law of the place of enforcement.

Strictly speaking, when recognizing an insolvency proceeding and assessing its effect on the arbitration, an arbitral tribunal is only bound to apply the law that the parties choose and to ensure that the application of that law is compatible with international public policy.

The fundamental difference between international arbitral tribunals and national courts is that the former are untethered to, and are not an institution of, the legal system of any state.[7] Unlike national court judges, international tribunals do not have a *lex fori*, and are detached from the substantive and procedural rules of any specific national law, including the seat of the arbitration. Awards rendered by such tribunals are therefore "delocalized" and "float" on the surface of national legal systems.[8]

5. *See, e.g.*, The Treaties of Montevideo of 1889 between Argentina, Bolivia, Paraguay, Peru and Uruguay, and the Nordic Bankruptcy Convention of November 7, 1933, between Denmark, Finland, Iceland, Norway and Sweden.
6. UNCITRAL Model Law on Cross-Border Insolvency (1997).
7. ICC Case No. 6379, Final Award of 1990 in van den Berg, A.J. (ed.) (1992) *Yearbook Commercial Arbitration* 17, pp. 212-220 ("ICC Case No. 6379"), at ¶ 21: "In international arbitration, an Arbitral Tribunal is not an institution under the legal system of a State."
8. *See* Gaillard, E. (2010) *Legal Theory of International Arbitration*. Leiden/Boston: Martinus Nijhoff Publishers, Chapter I(C); Fouchard, P. (1999). *Fouchard, Gaillard, Goldman on International Commercial Arbitration*. The Hague; Boston: Kluwer Law International ("Fouchard Gaillard

Nowhere is the delocalization of arbitration as strongly manifested as in France, where arbitral awards are considered to be so completely detached from the legal system of the seat of the arbitration that the French judicial system recognizes the existence of an *ordre juridique arbitral.*[9] French courts have expressly held that "[t]he place of the arbitral proceedings, chosen only in order to assure their neutrality, is not significant."[10] Most recently, the principle of delocalized arbitration was confirmed by the Paris Court of Appeal in *EGPC v. NATGAS*. In that case, the court found that the French legal system's approach to delocalization was applicable not just to foreign international arbitral awards that are recognized and enforced in France but also to foreign domestic arbitral awards (that is, awards that are considered domestic by the local jurisdiction in which the award was rendered).[11]

In *EGPC v. NATGAS*, an arbitration between two Egyptian parties, an award was rendered in Egypt in 2009 and granted recognition in France in 2010. The award was then annulled in Egypt later that year. Arguing before the Paris Court of Appeal, the parties disagreed as to whether or not the award was international. According to EGPC, the arbitration was a purely domestic Egyptian arbitration governed by Egyptian law. The annulment of the resulting award in Egypt was therefore justified, and the annulled award could not be enforced in France without violating international public policy. For NATGAS, the arbitration was international, and as a result, the annulment of the award in Egypt did not affect the validity of the award's recognition in France. The court ruled that regardless of whether Egyptian law considered the arbitration to be domestic or international, the rules of French law on the recognition of foreign arbitral awards applied uniformly.[12] The court thus confirmed that French courts will consider recognizing and enforcing foreign arbitral awards that have been annulled at the seat

Goldman"), 95-97; Lazić, V. (1998) *Insolvency Proceedings and Commercial Arbitration*. Kluwer Law International / T.M.C. Asser Instituut ("Lazić (1998)"), pp. 76, 80.

9. Gaillard, E. *Dialogue des ordres juridiques: ordre juridique arbitral et ordres juridiques étatiques* (2018) Revue de l'Arbitrage, p. 493. *See Société Ryanair et autre v. Syndicat mixte des aéroports de Charente (SMAC)*, July 8, 2015, Civ. 1, Cour de Cassation, Case No. 13-25.846 mentioning an "*ordre arbitral international.*" *See also Société PT Putrabali Adyamulia v. SA Rena Holding*, June 29, 2007, Case 1, Cour de Cassation, Case No. 05-18.053: "The international award, which is not attached to any state legal order, is a decision of international justice whose validity is only examined in light of the rules applicable in the country where its recognition and enforcement are requested" (translation) confirmed in *Société Ryanair et autre v. Syndicat mixte des aéroports de Charente (SMAC)*, July 8, 2015, Civ. 1, Cour de Cassation, Case No. 13-25.846. *See also Hilmarton v. OTV*, March 23, 1994, Civ. 1, Cour de Cassation, Case No. 92-15.137: "The award rendered in Switzerland was an international award that was not integrated into the legal order of this State, in the sense that it continued to exist even despite its annulment and its recognition in France was not contrary to international public policy [...]" (translation). *See also Norsolor v. Pabalk*, October 9, 1984, Civ. 1, Cour de Cassation, Case No. 83-11.355; *Polish Ocean Line v. Jolasry*, March 10, 1993, Cour de Cassation, Case No. 91-16.041.
10. *Société PT Putrabali Adyamulia v. SA Rena Holding*, June 29, 2007, Case 1, Cour de Cassation, Case No. 05-18.053.
11. *EGPC v. NATGAS*, May 21, 2019, Pôle 01 ch. 01, Cour d'Appel de Paris, Case No. 17/19850. *See also*, previously, *EGPC v. NATGAS*, November 24, 2011, Pôle 01 ch. 01, Cour d'Appel de Paris, Case No. 10/16525.
12. *EGPC v. NATGAS*, May 21, 2019, Pôle 01 ch. 01, Cour d'Appel de Paris, Case No. 17/19850: "[T]he provisions of Article 1498 and the following articles, which have now become Article 1514 and the following articles, on the recognition and enforcement of arbitral awards, are

of arbitration (whether domestic or international) and that, under French law, even foreign domestic arbitral awards are seen as unattached to the legal order from which they originated.

Canadian courts have also adopted a delocalized understanding of international arbitration. In *Dell Computer Corp*, the Supreme Court of Canada held that:

> Arbitration is an institution without a forum and without a geographic basis. Arbitration is part of no state's judicial system. The arbitrator has no allegiance or connection to any single country. In short, arbitration is a creature that owes its existence to the will of the parties alone.[13]

In contrast, courts in other jurisdictions still consider that a connection exists with the national jurisdiction in which the arbitration is seated and that the law of the seat plays a role in the proceedings. For example, English courts have found that:

> English law does not recognize the concept of a delocalized arbitration [...]. Accordingly, every arbitration process must have a seat or *locus arbitri* or forum which subjects its procedural rules to the municipal law which is there in force.[14]

And, even more stridently:

> Despite suggestions to the contrary by some learned writers under other systems, [English] jurisprudence does not recognize the concept of arbitral procedures floating in the transnational firmament, unconnected with any municipal system of law.[15]

The Singapore Court of Appeal has also rejected a delocalized view of international arbitration, holding that:

> The significance of the place of arbitration lies in the fact that for legal reasons the arbitration is to be regarded as situated in the state or territory. It identifies a state or territory whose laws will govern the arbitral process.[16]

In some instances, the U.S. courts' position has appeared receptive to a sort of "delocalized" view of international arbitration. Thus, in a 1996 decision, the U.S. District Court for the District of Columbia found that an award was valid as a matter of U.S. law, even though the award had been set aside at the seat.[17] While only a few years later, other U.S. courts had taken a different approach and refused to enforce arbitral

---

applicable to both international arbitral awards and foreign domestic arbitral awards, irrespective of whether the latter are considered as internal or international" (translation). *See also*, previously, *EGPC v. NATGAS*, November 24, 2011, Pôle 01 ch. 01, Cour d'Appel de Paris, Case No. 10/16525.

13. *Dell Computer Corp v. Union des consommateurs*, [2007] 2 SCR 801, at ¶ 51.
14. *Naviera Amazonica Peruano S.A. v. Compania Internacional de Seguros de Peru* [1988] 1 Lloyd's Rep 116.
15. *Bank Mellat v. HellinkiTechniki SA*, [1984] 1 QB 291, at p. 301. *See also SA Coppée-Lavalin NV v. Ken-Ren Chemicals and Fertilizers Ltd.*, [1995] 1 AC 38, at p. 52.
16. *PT Garuda Indonesia v. Birgen Air*, [2002] 1 SLR(R) 401 at ¶ 24.
17. *Matter of Chromalloy Aeroservices (Arab Republic)*, U.S. District Court for the District of Columbia, 939 F.Supp. 907 (1996).

awards set aside at the seat,[18] in 2016, in *COMMISA v. Pemex*, the U.S. Court of Appeals for the Second Circuit confirmed this position by recognizing an arbitral award that had been set aside by a court in Mexico, where the arbitration was seated.[19] This decision is the second in which a U.S. court recognized an arbitral award that had been annulled in the seat of arbitration.

The concept of delocalized arbitration is an ideal way to efficiently guarantee neutrality of forum, limit interference from national courts in the proceedings, eliminate national conflict of law problems and enable parties to create procedural rules that best fit their interests and the specific aspects of the dispute at hand. Indeed, it is difficult to see any reason why an international arbitral tribunal should be attached to the law of the seat, especially in light of the fact that "[p]arties frequently choose a seat of arbitration in a country where neither party's business interests are located" for convenience.[20]

Parties appear to have recognized the value of a delocalized approach to international arbitration. Notably, according to the 2020 ICC Dispute Resolution Statistics, France has remained one of the top four countries frequently selected for ICC arbitrations in the past several years.[21] Significantly, the ICC Rules, which do not contain a reference to the law of the seat as applicable to the arbitration,[22] are by far the most popular choice for arbitrating commercial disputes globally.[23] ICC tribunals have recognized the principle of delocalized arbitration,[24] including in an insolvency context. For example, an arbitral tribunal in a 2001 interim award rendered in ICC Case No. 10973 held that the ICC Rules "authorize[] [...] the parties and the arbitrators to conduct the arbitral proceedings outside any specific national procedural law."[25]

18. *Baker Marine (Nig.) Ltd. v. Chevron (Nig.) Ltd*, U.S. Court of Appeals for the Second Circuit, 191 F.3d 194 (2d Cir. 1999) and *Spier v. Calzaturificio Tecnica, S.p.A.*, U.S. District Court for the Southern District of New York, 71 F. Supp. 2d 279 (S.D.N.Y. 1999), *Termorío S.A. E.S.P. v. Electranta S.P.*, U.S. District Court for the District of Columbia, 487 F.3d 928 (D.C. Cir. 2007). *See also*: Mantilla-Serrano, F. *Case Note: Termorío S.A. E.S.P. et al. v. Electranta S.P.* (2008) 25 J. Int. Arb. 3, pp. 397-405.
19. *Corporación Mexicana de Mantenimiento Integral, S De RL De CV v. Pemex-Exploración y Producción*, U.S. Court of Appeals for the Second Circuit, 832 F.3d 92 (2d Cir. 2016).
20. Moses, M.L. (2008) *The Principles and Practice of International Commercial Arbitration*. Cambridge: Cambridge University Press, p. 56.
21. ICC Dispute Resolution Statistics (2020), p. 16.
22. Such a reference was contained in Article 16 of the 1955 ICC Rules, which provided: "The rules by which the arbitration proceedings shall be governed shall be these Rules and, in the event of no provision being made in these Rules, those of the law of procedure chosen by the parties or, failing such choice, those of the law of the country in which the arbitrator holds the proceedings."
23. *See* Queen Mary University of London, White & Case, 2021 International Arbitration Survey: Adapting arbitration to a changing world (2021), p. 9.
24. *See, e.g.*, ICC Case No. 6379, ¶ 21; ICC Case No. 11333, Interim Award of 2002, in van den Berg, A.J. (Ed.) (2006) *Yearbook Commercial Arbitration* 31, pp. 117-126 ("ICC Case No. 11333"), ¶ 6; ICC Case No. 13774, Partial Award of 2006, in van den Berg, A.J. (Ed.) (2014) *Yearbook Commercial Arbitration* 39, pp. 141-158, ¶ 29.
25. ICC Case No. 10973, Interim Award of 2001, in van den Berg, A.J. (Ed.) (2005) *Yearbook Commercial Arbitration* 30, pp. 77-84 ("ICC Case No. 10973"), ¶ 9. However, the tribunal also opined that "any mandatory provision" of the law of the seat still applies. *See also* ICC Case No. 5996, Final Award of 1991 in Jolivet. E. (2006) *Chronique de jurisprudence arbitrale de la Chambre de commerce international (CCI): Quelques exemples de traitement du droit des*

Indeed, because international arbitral tribunals are not attached to any specific local legal system, arbitrators must resolve disputes submitted to them in accordance with the terms of the arbitration agreement (which may include a choice of law by the parties) and the relevant contract. The only additional limit imposed on a tribunal is international public policy. However, while an international arbitral tribunal may only be bound to apply the law chosen by the parties and international public policy, it does have good reason to pay heed to the mandatory rules of the seat as well as the place of enforcement.

B Arbitral Tribunals' "Duty" to Render an Enforceable Award

An international arbitral tribunal's primary task is to resolve the dispute the parties have entrusted to it. Part of this task is to render an award that the parties may enforce—usually, this means rendering an award that will, ideally, not be set aside by the courts of the seat, and that will ultimately be enforceable in those courts and elsewhere. Considering that insolvency is one of the pillars of any national economic order, national insolvency laws are replete with mandatory rules and invoke national public policy principles.

Under Article 34(2)(b)(ii) of the 1985 UNCITRAL Model Law on International Commercial Arbitration, the violation of the public policy of the seat of the arbitration is a ground for setting aside an arbitral award.[26] Similarly, under Article V(2)(b) of the New York Convention, recognition and enforcement of an arbitral award may be refused if the competent authority in the country where recognition and enforcement are sought finds that recognition or enforcement of the award would be contrary to the public policy of that country.[27] However, not all national public policy principles form part of international public policy.[28] Nevertheless, an international arbitral tribunal (which, in principle, is only bound by international public policy) should consider national public policy, or at least try not to render awards that are incompatible with it.

While an international arbitral tribunal may not be tethered to a particular national jurisdiction, the courts of a national jurisdiction may ultimately have to recognize and enforce the arbitral award (and, potentially, set it aside). For example, the enforcement of an arbitral award in a jurisdiction where the debtor is insolvent may

procédures collectives dans l'arbitrage in Cahiers de l'arbitrage, Gazette du Palais No. 347-348 ("Jolivet"), p. 3762; ICC Case No. 5996, Final Award of 1997 in Jolivet, p. 3770.

26. 1985 UNCITRAL Model Law on Commercial Arbitration, Article 34(2)(b)(ii): "An arbitral award may be set aside by the court specified in Article 6 only if [...] the court finds that [...] the award is in conflict with the public policy of this State."

27. 1958 Convention on the Recognition and Enforcement of Foreign Arbitral Awards ("New York Convention"), Article V(2)(b): "Recognition and enforcement of an arbitral award may also be refused if the competent authority in the country where recognition and enforcement is sought finds that: [...] The recognition or enforcement of the award would be contrary to the public policy of that country."

28. *See* International Law Association, Committee on International Commercial Arbitration (2000) *Interim Report on Public Policy as a Bar to Enforcement of International Arbitral Awards*, p. 6; International Law Association, Committee on International Commercial Arbitration (2002) *Final Report on Public Policy as a Bar to Enforcement of International Arbitral Awards*, ¶ 11.

be subject to specific procedural rules for creditor claims based on an arbitral award.[29] Arguably, irrespective of which law the tribunal is bound to apply, the tribunal is, in any event, also bound to ensure that its award is compatible with the public policy of the seat and the likely place of enforcement, in order to guarantee the award's enforceability.[30]

An arbitral tribunal's "duty" to render an enforceable award is included in many arbitration rules. For example, the ICC Rules provide that an arbitral tribunal shall make "every effort to make sure that the award is enforceable at law";[31] the Stockholm Chamber of Commerce (SCC) Rules refer to a duty to make "every reasonable effort to ensure that any award is legally enforceable";[32] the London Court of International Arbitration (LCIA) Rules provide that a tribunal must make "every reasonable effort to ensure that any award is legally recognized and enforceable at the arbitral seat";[33] and the Singapore International Arbitration Centre (SIAC) Rules oblige a tribunal to make "every reasonable effort to ensure the fair, expeditious and economical conclusion of the arbitration and the enforceability of any Award."[34]

International arbitral tribunals have also recognized the duty to render an enforceable award when deciding disputes that involve parallel insolvency proceedings. The tribunal in ICC Case No. 6697 (in its award rendered in 1990) considered the eventual enforceability of the award in the country in which the award was likely to be enforced when assessing whether to recognize a foreign insolvency proceeding. The tribunal held:

> Arbitrators must not render an award that would violate the fundamental principles considered by the enforcement judge as international public policy, otherwise there is a risk that their award may be deprived of recognition or enforcement. The Arbitral Tribunal is therefore required under Article [42] of the ICC Rules to consider whether an award granting [the Claimant's] claim would be inconsistent with the 'stay of proceedings' rule which is one of the fundamental principles of insolvency law, widely recognized to be 'both national and international.[35]

While this award referred to international public policy (which an international arbitral tribunal is, in any event, bound to abide by), other tribunals have referred to national public policy and mandatory rules. For example, in an unpublished 2014 ICC award[36], the insolvent European Union (EU) respondent argued before a Swiss-seated tribunal that because the law of the state where the insolvency proceedings had been

29. For a comparative overview of such rules in major jurisdictions, *see* Vorburger, S. (2014). *International Arbitration and Cross-Border Insolvency: Comparative Perspectives*. Kluwer Law International ("Vorburger (2014)"), ¶¶ 689-720.
30. Fouchard, P. (1998) *Arbitrage et faillite*. Revue de l'Arbitrage, p. 471 ("Fouchard (1998)"), ¶¶ 20-22.
31. ICC Arbitration Rules, Article 42.
32. SCC Arbitration Rules, Article 2(2).
33. LCIA Arbitration Rules, Article 32(2).
34. SIAC Arbitration Rules, Rule 41(2).
35. ICC Case No. 6697, Award of December 26, 1990, in (1992) Revue de l'Arbitrage, p. 135 ("ICC Case No. 6697"), p. 142.
36. ICC Reference No. ICC-FA-2020-254.

commenced provided that the dispute was not arbitrable, the resulting award would breach that state's public policy, and would therefore be unenforceable in the EU. The respondent referred to Article V of the New York Convention and Article 42 of the 2012 ICC Rules.

In contrast, under Article 177 of the Swiss Private International Law Act (PILA), any dispute that relates to an "economic interest" may be the subject matter of an arbitration, including insolvency. The tribunal declined to apply the national law of the jurisdiction in which the insolvency proceedings had been brought, on the grounds that the dispute was arbitrable under the PILA. The tribunal nevertheless observed that "an international arbitral tribunal does not operate in a fictional world where national policies and public interest are neutralized and may be ignored." The tribunal referred to the practice of the Swiss Federal Supreme Court, which recognizes that public policy considerations may justify the application of the law of a different jurisdiction instead of the PILA. The tribunal noted that an arbitral tribunal's duty to render an enforceable award may also lead to a similar conclusion.

The sole arbitrator in an unpublished 2013 ICC case[37] involving parallel insolvency proceedings took a more drastic approach, holding that the arbitral proceedings should be terminated if the arbitration would result in an "inefficient award" in the country of the insolvency proceedings where enforcement was envisaged.

In practice, defining what constitutes an enforceable award is a daunting task. Demanding that arbitral tribunals render universally enforceable awards would be neither practicable nor possible because "a universally challenge-proof award is neither an absolute aim of arbitration, nor should it become the sole quest of the arbitrator to arrive to an award that may resist a challenge in almost every imaginable jurisdiction."[38] In fact, the language used in the various arbitration rules denotes, at most, a "best efforts" obligation or an obligation of conduct, not an obligation of result.[39] A tribunal cannot be expected to be aware of all potential places in which enforcement may occur, as now more than ever, parties may have a presence or relevant assets in a large number of jurisdictions and readily and easily move those assets. Tribunals are circumscribed by the arguments the parties present, and are required to decide the dispute based on the law and facts argued before them, not the law and public policy rules of all possible enforcement jurisdictions (which can be wide-ranging).

Tribunals should not be responsible for examining possible enforcement jurisdictions *sua sponte*, rather only if the parties have made arguments in this regard, thus fulfilling the tribunal's duty to allow both parties to express their views. The tribunal

37. ICC Reference No. ICC-FA-2020-256.
38. Mantilla-Serrano, F. (1995). *International Arbitration and Insolvency Proceedings*. Arbitration International 11(1) ("Mantilla-Serrano (1995)"), p. 74.
39. *See, e.g.*, Vorburger (2014), ¶¶ 176, 180; Derains, Y. & Schwartz, E. (2005). *A Guide to the ICC Rules of Arbitration* (2nd ed.). The Netherlands: Kluwer Law International ("Derains & Schwartz (2005)"), p. 385; Poudret, J.F. & Besson, S. (2007). *Comparative Law of International Arbitration* (2nd ed.). London, United Kingdom: Sweet & Maxwell, ¶ 147.

took this approach in ICC Case 10507,[40] in which a Dutch claimant commenced an arbitration against an Italian respondent who had been declared bankrupt in Italy. The respondent counterclaimed. The tribunal recalled its duty to "make every effort to make sure that the Award is enforceable at law" in accordance with the ICC Rules, and noted that both parties would only wish to seek enforcement of the award in the Netherlands. Accordingly, the tribunal did not have to ensure that the award would be enforceable in Italy.

Importantly, a party may not need to initiate enforcement proceedings to obtain the benefit of the award: rather, it may use the award as proof of debt as a creditor in insolvency proceedings, present it to its insurer in order to obtain compensation under a relevant policy or prove to its auditors that the arbitration has come to an end in order to write the claim off its balance sheet.[41]

C No Universal Conflict of Law Rules Applicable to Insolvency and Arbitration

If one is to assume that international arbitrators have no forum and are not bound to apply the national rules of the seat, "[i]t follows from this premise that arbitrators are not bound by the conflict of laws rules of a forum to choose the law applicable to the substance of the dispute."[42] Should the tribunal nevertheless consider any conflict of law rules?

At present, no universal international law rules or principles explicitly regulate which law an international arbitral tribunal should apply to the recognition of parallel insolvency proceedings or to the determination of the effect of such proceedings on the arbitration. The closest thing to an international—albeit regional—conflict of laws regime as regards insolvency may be found in the EU legal framework.

EC Regulation 1346/2000 ("Insolvency Regulation") was the first EU-wide instrument that established conflict of law rules for insolvency proceedings concerning EU debtors with operations in more than one EU Member State. The objective of the Insolvency Regulation was thus not to harmonize insolvency laws across different EU Member States, but rather to create a common framework for the commencement of insolvency proceedings and for the automatic recognition and cooperation between EU Member States in insolvency matters.

Article 4 provided that, in general, insolvency proceedings and their effects are governed by the law of the EU Member State where the insolvency proceedings are commenced.[43] Article 15 of the Insolvency Regulation contained an exception to this general rule, and provided that the effects of insolvency proceedings on a "lawsuit

40. ICC Case No. 10507, Interim Award in (2009) ICC Bulletin 20(1), p. 71 ("ICC Case No. 10507"), at ¶ 9.2.
41. Mantilla-Serrano (1995), footnote 12.
42. ICC Case No. 11333, ¶ 6.
43. EC Regulation 1346/2000, Article 4(1): "Save as otherwise provided in this Regulation, the law applicable to insolvency proceedings and their effects shall be that of the Member State within the territory of which such proceedings are opened, hereafter referred to as the 'State of the opening of proceedings.'"

pending" concerning an asset or a right that is the subject of insolvency "shall be governed solely by the law of the EU Member State in which that lawsuit is pending."[44] Given that the Insolvency Regulation did not explicitly refer to arbitration, its applicability was often debated by parties to international arbitrations and before national courts.[45] Several arbitral tribunals interpreted the term "lawsuit pending" in Article 15 of the Insolvency Regulation to include pending arbitral proceedings.[46] Other arbitral tribunals applied the Insolvency Regulation, but relied on Article 4, not Article 15, to determine the applicable law.[47] Interestingly, one tribunal seems to have preferred Article 4 because the law applicable on that basis was more favorable to the arbitral proceedings.[48]

44. EC Regulation 1346/2000, Article 15: "The effects of insolvency proceedings on a lawsuit pending concerning an asset or a right of which the debtor has been divested shall be governed solely by the law of the Member State in which that lawsuit is pending."
45. *See* Vorburger (2014), ¶ 396.
46. *See, e.g.*, ICC Case No. 12421, Final Award of 2005 in (2013) Arnaldez, J.J., Derains, Y. & Hascher, D. *Collection of ICC Arbitral Awards 2008-2011*. Wolters Kluwer Law & Business / International Chamber of Commerce, p. 79 (Barbadian and Italian parties, tribunal seated in the UK. The tribunal found that it was possible to regard the arbitration proceedings as a "lawsuit" within the meaning of the Regulation); VIAC Case No. SCH-5130, Final Award of 2011 in Vienna International Arbitral Centre of the Austrian Federal Economic Chamber (2015). *Selected Arbitral Awards* 1, pp. 207-210 (German and Ukrainian parties, insolvency initiated in Germany, tribunal seated in Austria. Tribunal found that the Regulation applied); ICC Case No. 10507 (Italian and Dutch Parties. Tribunal seated in Geneva, but referred to Regulation 1346 when concluding that Swiss law was applicable to the effects of a foreign insolvency on an arbitration seated in Geneva); two unpublished ICC awards from 2011, one by a tribunal seated in France (ICC Reference No. ICC-FA-2020-258), one by a tribunal seated in Austria (ICC Reference No. ICC-PA-2020-257).
47. *See, e.g.*, ICC Case No. 12553, Partial Award in (2013) Journal du droit international (Clunet) 1 Chron. 1; unpublished 2010 ICC award (ICC Reference No. ICC-FA-2020-260); unpublished 2011 ICC award (ICC Reference No. ICC-FA-2020-259).
48. In the unpublished 2010 ICC award mentioned in the preceding footnote, both parties were EU nationals and the tribunal was seated in France; French law applied to the contract. Insolvency proceedings had begun against the respondent in its country of origin. The tribunal found that the Insolvency Regulation applied by virtue of Article 4. By applying the law of the state where the insolvency proceedings took place, the tribunal noted that it would not be faced with the French law restriction on the scope of the arbitral award and would therefore be able to award payment. In another unpublished 2011 ICC case mentioned in the preceding footnote, both parties were EU nationals and the tribunal was seated in Poland where, at the time, any arbitration parallel to insolvency proceedings had to be terminated. Insolvency proceedings were commenced against the claimant in its state of origin (not Poland). The respondent argued that the arbitration should be terminated in line with the law of the seat in accordance with Article 15 of the Insolvency Regulation. While the tribunal did consider that Article 15 applied to international arbitrations, it also referred to Recital 24 of the Insolvency Regulation which referred to the protection of legitimate expectations and the certainty of transactions. The tribunal considered that this was the objective of Article 15, and that in the present case, applying the law of the seat of arbitration would run contrary to the protection of such legitimate expectations. The tribunal therefore held that the arbitration agreement was governed by Article 4 of the Insolvency Regulation, and the law of the state where insolvency proceedings had been opened should apply. The tribunal thus avoided the application of Polish law, which would have required termination of the proceedings (the tribunal nevertheless noted that this Polish law requirement was not a mandatory rule in relation to non-Polish insolvency proceedings).

The Insolvency Regulation provided for a review of its operation after 10 years, and in December 2012, the European Commission proposed updates to the Regulation.[49] On May 20, 2015, the European Parliament approved Regulation (EU) No. 2015/848 ("Recast Insolvency Regulation"), which entered into force on June 26, 2015, and applies to insolvency proceedings commenced on or after June 26, 2017.

The Recast Insolvency Regulation now explicitly refers to international arbitration, specifically instances in which an arbitral tribunal is seated within the EU, and parallel insolvency proceedings have been commenced in another EU Member State.[50] Article 18 provides that the effects of insolvency proceedings on pending arbitral proceedings concerning an asset or a right that forms part of a debtor's insolvency estate are governed by the law of the EU Member State where the arbitral tribunal is seated.[51]

One cannot conclude, however, that the Recast Insolvency Regulation is addressed to and binding on EU-seated arbitral tribunals.

Article 18 of the Recast Insolvency Regulation is essentially a conflict of laws rule that designates the seat of an arbitral tribunal as the connecting factor that leads to the application of the law of a specific EU Member State. As previously discussed, unlike national courts, international arbitral tribunals do not have a *lex fori* and are not attached to any national jurisdiction, be it in the EU or otherwise. International tribunals are bound only by the parties' agreement and international public policy. Accordingly, an international arbitral tribunal cannot be obliged to apply the Recast Insolvency Regulation merely on the grounds that the tribunal's seat is in an EU Member State.

Nor will an international arbitral tribunal be bound to apply the Recast Insolvency Regulation by virtue of the fact that the parties have chosen the law of an EU Member State as the law applicable to the contract and/or the merits of the dispute. A well-established principle of international arbitration law is that a reference to a law applicable to the merits of a dispute does not include the application of conflicts of law provisions in the applicable law.[52] This principle applies equally to EU regulations as it does to the national laws of a state. The conflict of laws provision enshrined in Article 18 therefore cannot bind an international arbitral tribunal. From the perspective of international arbitration, the Recast Insolvency Regulation is not addressed to international arbitral tribunals but rather to national EU Member State judges who may face an arbitral award that touches upon issues of an EU-based insolvency.

49. EC Regulation 1346/2000, Article 46.
50. Note that the United Kingdom is now considered a third state in newly initiated EU insolvency proceedings. *See* European Commission, *Notice to Stakeholders: Withdrawal of the United Kingdom and EU Rules in the Field of Civil Justice and Private International Law*, August 27, 2020, p. 11.
51. Regulation (EU) 2015/848, Article 18: "The effects of insolvency proceedings on a pending lawsuit or pending arbitral proceedings concerning an asset or a right which forms part of a debtor's insolvency estate shall be governed solely by the law of the Member State in which that lawsuit is pending or in which the arbitral tribunal has its seat."
52. *See* Mayer, P. (1998) *Droit international privé*. Paris: Montchrestien, ¶ 706; Fouchard Gaillard Goldman, ¶ 1429.

However, while arbitral tribunals are not bound by the conflict of laws rules in the Recast Insolvency Regulation, arbitrators would be ill-advised to dismiss them without careful analysis of the possible repercussions of its non-application. As discussed, arbitral tribunals should strive to ensure that their awards will be enforced and not be set aside (notably on the basis of public policy). An arbitral tribunal's approach to the Recast Insolvency Regulation may, in certain circumstances, either strengthen or weaken the position of its award vis-à-vis national EU judges in matters of enforcement and set-aside proceedings.

As a general matter, despite some harmonization of the approach to insolvency in EU Member States,[53] the insolvency legislation of each EU Member State remains different, with no guaranteed uniformity in the EU Member States' approach to arbitration and insolvency. Thus, the application of one EU Member State's law instead of another (whether on the basis of Article 18 of the Recast Insolvency Regulation or not) may lead to conflicting results. Such a situation may arise if the law of the seat and the law of the state of insolvency proceedings differ substantially (e.g., one deprives the debtor of legal capacity while the other does not; or one invalidates the arbitral agreement while the other does not).[54]

On the one hand, an arbitral tribunal's choice to follow the conflict of laws rule in Article 18 may be a safe option in terms of ensuring the enforceability of the award. The Recast Insolvency Regulation has been adopted under the umbrella of judicial cooperation in civil matters, which is enshrined in Article 81 of the Treaty on the Functioning of the European Union.[55] Accordingly, one may posit that even if the conflict of laws rule in Article 18 of the Recast Insolvency Regulation leads to the application of an EU Member State's law that is diametrically opposed to the law of the EU State where enforcement is being sought, the enforcement judge will nevertheless recognize and enforce the award; as indeed, the EU Member State judge is bound by the Recast Insolvency Regulation. However, the enforcement judge may refuse recognition and enforcement in order to protect the enforcing state's legal order if such recognition and enforcement would go against the international public policy of that state.

On the other hand, the mere fact that an arbitral tribunal has refused to follow the Recast Insolvency Regulation and not apply the law identified by Article 18 does not

53. *See, e.g.*, Directive (EU) 2019/1023 of the European Parliament and of the Council of June 20, 2019, on preventive restructuring frameworks, on discharge of debt and disqualifications, and on measures to increase the efficiency of procedures concerning restructuring, insolvency and discharge of debt, and amending Directive (EU) 2017/1132.
54. In principle, the primacy of EU law should guarantee that the Recast Insolvency Regulation would trump any conflicting national law. Nevertheless, the national judge enforcing such an award may consider that the application of the Recast Insolvency Regulation in the specific arbitral award conflicts with a national law or public policy to such an extent that it would warrant a refusal to apply EU law, or a referral of the issue for a preliminary ruling. Notably, while the Recast Insolvency Regulation points to the application of a certain national law in the context of insolvency and arbitration, it says nothing of the resulting award or its recognition and enforcement.
55. Recast Insolvency Regulation, Preamble and Recital 3.

automatically entail the set-aside and nonenforcement of the arbitral award.[56] While an EU Member State judge may be tempted to set aside or refuse the recognition and enforcement of an award that does not apply the law indicated by the conflict of laws rule in the Recast Insolvency Regulation, the judge will only do so if the law applied in contravention to Article 18 results in an award that conflicts with the public policy of the state of the seat or enforcement.

In terms of ensuring the enforceability of an award, the safer approach to the Recast Insolvency Regulation is difficult to predict. As yet, no decisions on the application of the Recast Insolvency Regulation have become publicly available, so there are no examples of how arbitral tribunals have ruled on its applicability.

Nevertheless, tribunals evidently must keep in mind that the EU Member State judge deciding on set-aside and enforcement will examine the award through the prism of the Recast Insolvency Regulation. For example, in a 2019 judgment, the Commercial Court of Santander (Spain) was seized pursuant to then Article 53(1) of the Spanish Insolvency Law with a request by an insolvent Spanish company to suspend the effects of a clause providing for international arbitration in London and had to determine whether Spanish law would apply[57]. The Commercial Court applied Article 18 of the Recast Insolvency Regulation, as well as its Article 7 (which succeeded to Article 4 of the Insolvency Regulation) and considered that, since no request for arbitration had been filed by either party, no arbitral proceeding was pending, and that Spanish law (*lex concursus*) thus applied to determine the effects of the insolvency on the arbitration agreement.[58] Tribunals must carefully analyze all facts and applicable laws in any given case as a thorough and detailed analysis of all eventualities will only strengthen the arbitral award in the eyes of the EU Member State judges who are ultimately tasked with enforcing it.

II PARALLEL INSOLVENCY PROCEEDINGS IN PRACTICE

As discussed above, parallel insolvency proceedings may substantially complicate the tribunal's task. While an arbitral tribunal is only obliged to apply the law that the parties choose and to abide by international public policy, some jurisdictions do not distinguish between national and international public policy. In these jurisdictions, violating mandatory local rules of the law of the seat may be grounds for setting aside the arbitral award[59] or refusing enforcement of the award.[60]

56. Note that Recital 73 of the Recast Insolvency Regulation provides that the rule contained in Article 18 "should not affect national rules on recognition and enforcement of arbitral awards." This presumably also includes the New York Convention, to which the EU Member States are party.
57. *Application of Delfuego Booking S.L.*, Judgment of September 30, 2019, Juzgado de lo Mercantil No. 1 de Santander, Case No, 427/2018, Judgment No. 266/2019.
58. *Ibid.*, ¶¶ 12-23.
59. *See* 1985 UNCITRAL Model Law on International Commercial Arbitration, Article 34(2)(b)(ii).
60. New York Convention, Article V(2)(b).

In many respects, arbitrating disputes that are affected by parallel insolvency proceedings is like arbitrating under the sword of Damocles—with many potentially dangerous pitfalls and almost no formal guidance for an arbitral tribunal to follow.

The following sections review which insolvency law principles have been found to constitute public policy (whether international or national), and the different types of situations in which the tribunal should take special care to consider the effects of a parallel insolvency proceeding on the arbitral proceedings.

A Public Policy and Mandatory Rules in the Context of Insolvency

International or transnational public policy can be described as a body of principles and rules recognized by the international community. A violation of international public policy on account of either the procedure pursuant to which the award was rendered or the award's contents may bar the recognition or enforcement of an arbitral award.[61] National public policy or mandatory norms will not always amount to international public policy.[62] International arbitral tribunals have the difficult task of identifying these principles. At the same time, they may also have to give due regard to national public policy and mandatory norms of the seat and other jurisdictions in order to ensure the enforceability of the award.

Insolvency proceedings are based on the protection of public interests and involve the intervention of the state in matters that, at their core, arise out of private law relationships. Inevitably, parallel insolvency proceedings may severely heighten the risk of set-aside or nonrecognition of an award since most insolvency laws are mandatory at the national level. There is no universally accepted list of which insolvency law principles have achieved the status of international public policy, and arbitral tribunals must thus make a case-by-case examination.

Although insolvency laws are by no means identical across all jurisdictions, certain principles are universal. Generally, insolvency entails the centralization of all claims under the supervision of a single bankruptcy court, and a limitation of the insolvent party's power to manage and dispose of its assets and assert its rights, which vest with a trustee appointed by the bankruptcy court to prevent further economic harm. The insolvency proceedings are designed to adjudicate in a collective and orderly manner the claims of competing categories of creditors against the insolvent debtor, and to distribute the proceeds of the insolvent estate in accordance with the principle of equality of creditors, or *pari passu*. This principle is one of the most

61. Mayer, P., Sheppard, A., *Final ILA Report on Public Policy as a Bar to Enforcement of International Arbitral Awards* (2003) Arbitration International 19(2), Recommendations 1(c) and 2(b).

62. *See, e.g.*, *Tampico Beverages Inc. v. Productos Naturales de la Sabans S.Z. Alqueria*, SC9909-2017, Case No. 11001-02-03-000-2014-01927-00. During the enforcement proceedings of an ICC award that had been challenged for violating public policy on the basis of an arbitrator's conflict of interest, the Supreme Court of Colombia acknowledged that this might violate Colombia's national, but not international public policy, and that the Supreme Court should turn to international authorities to make a determination. The Supreme Court referred to the 2014 IBA Guidelines on Conflicts of Interest to conclude that international public policy would be violated.

fundamental principles of insolvency laws around the world. An ICC arbitral tribunal went so far as calling it "a principle of equity which, for this reason, is universally known in insolvency law."[63] Under the principle of *pari passu*, creditors of the same category must be treated in the same manner with respect to their rights to the assets of the insolvent estate.

Certain insolvency law principles are so fundamental to insolvency proceedings that they may be considered to form part of international public policy. Such principles include:

- the validity, applicability and effectiveness of the arbitration agreement (notwithstanding the existence of insolvency proceedings);
- the need to bring under a single authority the control and preservation of the assets of the debtor in order to permit the insolvent party's rehabilitation or liquidation while respecting the rights of both unsecured and secured creditors;
- the principle of equal treatment of creditors belonging to the same class; and
- the need to properly notify the institution or individuals in charge of representing the insolvent party, and to grant sufficient opportunity to these individuals or institutions to appear and defend the interests of the insolvent party in the arbitration.[64]

As previously discussed, in addition to international public policy, arbitral tribunals should likewise be conscious of the pronouncements of national courts. From the perspective of national courts called upon to rule on set-aside or enforcement applications, no uniform approach has emerged as to which insolvency law principles form part of international public policy. For example, French courts have consistently held that insolvency law forms part of international public policy, in particular the principle of suspension of proceedings, the need to file a claim with the trustee and the principle of equality of creditors.[65] U.S. courts have also held that the "equitable and orderly distribution of local assets" that "requires assembling all claims against the limited assets in a single proceeding" is part of public policy in the U.S.[66] Conversely,

63. ICC Case No. 6697, p. 144: "Additionally, the arbitral tribunal considers that the principle of equality of non-privileged creditors is a principle of equity that [...] is universally known in insolvency law."
64. French courts have recognized many of these principles as part of international public policy. *See* Seraglini, C., Ortscheidt, J. (2019) *Droit de l'arbitrage interne et international* (2nd ed.). LGDJ: Issy-les-Moulineaux, ¶ 665. *See also* ICC Case No. 7289, Final Award of 1998 in Jolivet, p. 3767 where the tribunal considered that the equality of creditors and the need to preserve the assets of the debtor are fundamental principles that underpin insolvency proceedings.
65. *See Société Thinet v. Labrely ès-qualites*, March 8, 1988, Civ. 1, Cour de Cassation, Case No. 86-12015; *Société SARET v. SBBM*, February 4, 1992, Civ. 1, Cour de Cassation, Case No. 90-12569; *SAS IPSA Holding v. SCP Brouard Daude*, May 14, 2019, Cour d'Appel de Paris, Case No. 17/09133.
66. *Victrix S.S. Co., S.A. v. Salen Dry Cargo A.B.*, 825 F.2d 709 (2d Cir. 1987), p. 714.

in Germany, a breach of the principle that a claim must be filed with the trustee does not violate international public policy.[67]

B Navigating Treacherous Waters

A tribunal faced with an arbitration in which one or both of the parties have been declared insolvent needs to be especially vigilant in order to maximize the enforceability of the award. An arbitral tribunal may face a range of complex issues, some of which are explored below.

1 Legal Capacity and Representation of the Insolvent Party

The legal status and capacity of a company are determined by the law of the country of incorporation, which, in the vast majority of cases, is also the place of the insolvency proceedings.

The extent to which the commencement of insolvency proceedings against a party affects that party's capacity varies around the world, and according to each specific procedure under national laws. Most insolvency laws—such as Chapter 11 of the U.S. Bankruptcy Code relating to reorganization proceedings—uphold the debtor's capacity to a significant extent.

If the national law in question strips the insolvent party of legal capacity, that party may no longer be able to participate in the arbitral proceedings, and the tribunal may be compelled to dismiss the arbitration.[68]

In most cases, when an insolvent party loses the power to exercise its rights and obligations, and its capacity to participate as a party in arbitration proceedings, such power does not simply disappear—it vests *ex lege* with the trustee appointed to oversee the insolvency proceedings.[69] Accordingly, the arbitral tribunal should not discontinue the arbitration for want of a capable party, as the trustee can participate in the arbitration proceedings on behalf of the insolvent party and may intervene in the arbitral proceedings voluntarily. The participation of the trustee should cure any capacity/representation issues under most applicable laws.[70] If, after being duly called and served, the trustee does not participate, an award may still be rendered.

However, whichever principles the national jurisdiction has adopted in this regard, parties and arbitrators should always inform the trustee of the ongoing proceedings.[71]

67. Judgment of January 4, 2012, Higher Regional Court of Karlsruhe, Case No. 9 Sch 02/09. However, German courts consider that in a domestic arbitration, failing to file a claim with the trustee violates German national public policy. Judgment of January 29, 2009, Bundesgerichtshof, BGH III ZB 88/07.
68. Lazić (1998), pp. 36, 109-112; Vorburger (2014), ¶ 448.
69. Lazić (1998), pp. 109-112; Vorburger (2014), ¶ 488.
70. Vorburger (2014), ¶ 488.
71. *See* Mantilla-Serrano (1995), p. 62.

2 *Validity of the Arbitration Agreement*

The existence of parallel insolvency proceedings may affect the validity of the arbitration agreement from a domestic law perspective. The vast majority of laws, including French law, do not render an arbitration agreement void because of insolvency proceedings.[72] However, certain national insolvency laws do contain restrictive provisions.

For example, the former Polish Insolvency Law used to provide that "any arbitration clause concluded by the bankrupt party shall lose its legal effect as at the date bankruptcy is declared and any pending arbitration proceedings shall be discontinued."[73] This provision was widely considered to affect the validity of an arbitration agreement involving a Polish insolvent party[74] and led to contradictory parallel decisions by the English Court of Appeal and the Swiss Supreme Federal Court.[75] Poland amended its insolvency laws in 2016, and such provisions are becoming increasingly rare. Nevertheless, there are exceptions—for example, under Article 5(1)(8) of the Latvian Law on Arbitration, arbitral tribunals may not resolve disputes "relating to the rights and duties of persons with respect to whom insolvency or bankruptcy proceedings have been initiated."

The Spanish Recast Insolvency Law also deserves a mention. Although Spanish law does not automatically invalidate an arbitration agreement upon insolvency, pursuant to Article 140(3) of the Spanish Recast Insolvency Law the competent court may "grant a suspension of the effects of" arbitration agreements if it is satisfied that such agreements "would bring prejudice to the insolvency proceeding." This provision used to be Article 52(1) of the Insolvency Law that was applied in the most recent case law[76] in a very liberal manner in a judgment by the Commercial Court of Santander, cited above.[77] The Commercial Court determined that enforcing the arbitration agreement "would bring prejudice to the insolvency proceeding" and granted the suspension, thereby authorizing the insolvent party to pursue its claims before Spanish courts.[78] According to the Commercial Court, the vagueness of the arbitration clause, which provided for a seat in London but no institution or applicable rules, would have

72. This is also the case under German, English and U.S. laws. *See Société Soules v. Société Henry*, February 4, 1986, Com., Cour de Cassation, Case No. 84-16565; *T.A.G. v. B.M.P.C. et al.*, February 12, 1985, Com., Cour de Cassation, Case No. 83-14282; *Courrèges Homme v. Fleurot-Charvet et Fils*, October 19, 1982, Cour d'appel de Grenoble, Rev. Arb. 1983, pp. 321 et seq. *See* Fouchard (1998), ¶ 35; Lazić (1998), p. 231; Mourre, A. (2007) Arbitrage et droit de la faillite: Réflexions sur l'office du juge et de l'arbitre in Affaki, G. (Ed.) (2014) *Cross-Border Insolvency and Conflict of Jurisdictions: A US-EU Experience*. Bruylant, Brussels, ¶ 9; Vorburger ¶ 309.
73. Previous Polish Insolvency Law, Article 142 (translation).
74. Vorburger (2014), ¶ 306; Aslanowicz, M. & Jasiewicz, J. (2011). Report on Poland. In Thevenin, N. *Baker & McKenzie international arbitration yearbook: 2010-2011*, p. 333; minority in *Vivendi SA and others v. Deutsche Telekom AG and others*, Case No. 4A_428/2008, Swiss Supreme Court, March 31, 2009.
75. *Elektrim SA v. Vivendi Holdings* 1 Corp [2009] 2 All ER (Comm) 213; *Vivendi SA and others v Deutsche Telekom AG and others*, Case N° 4A_428/2008, Swiss Supreme Court.
76. *IBA Toolkit on Insolvency and Arbitration*, Questionnaire, National Report of Spain, p. 5.
77. *Application of Delfuego Booking S.L.*, Judgment of September 30, 2019, Juzgado de lo Mercantil No. 1 de Santander, Case No. 427/2018, Judgment No. 266/2019.
78. *Ibid.*, ¶¶ 35, 37.

entailed more delay in resolving the dispute, particularly in the initiation phase of the arbitration, than judicial proceedings in the Spanish courts.[79] The insolvent party would have likewise incurred substantial costs it would not have been able to assume, aggravating its insolvency and diminishing the value of its only asset, jeopardizing its creditors' ability to recover their claims.[80]

3 *Stay of Proceedings*

The vast majority of national insolvency laws provide for a stay of all pending proceedings upon the opening of insolvency proceedings.[81] Under French law, for example, pending proceedings are automatically suspended upon the insolvency of one of the parties, but can automatically resume when the creditor files its claim with, and duly summons, the trustee.[82]

In France, the principle is part of both domestic and international public policy, as has been settled in case law.[83] An arbitral tribunal that does not abide by such principles, when faced with a French insolvent party, would have its award set aside or denied recognition in France.[84] Nevertheless, in most circumstances, Article L. 622-22 allows arbitral proceedings to continue, as long as the claim is filed with the insolvent estate and the trustee is properly summoned—conditions that are not burdensome. Arbitral tribunals, particularly French-seated tribunals, have applied these principles when faced with the insolvency of a French party.[85] Nevertheless, not all tribunals with

79. *Ibid.*, ¶ 36.
80. *Ibid.*, ¶¶ 36-37.
81. *See, e.g.*, Swiss Federal Law on Bankruptcy, Article 207; U.S. Bankruptcy Code, § 362(a); German Code of Civil Procedure, § 240; U.K. Insolvency Act 1986, section 285.
82. Article L. 622-22 of the French Commercial Code: "Save for the provisions of Article L. 625-3, any pending proceedings shall be stayed until the creditor initiating the proceedings has filed its submission of claim. Such proceedings shall then be resumed *ipso jure* for the sole purpose of verifying the claims and determining their amount after having duly summoned the court-appointed receiver and, as the case may be, the administrator or the plan performance supervisor appointed in compliance with Article L. 626-25. [...]" (translation).
83. *See Société Thinet v. Labrely ès-qualites*, March 8, 1988, Civ. 1, Cour de Cassation, Case No. 86-12015; *Société SARET v. SBBM*, February 4, 1992, Civ. 1, Cour de Cassation, Case No. 90-12569; *SAS IPSA Holding v. SCP Brouard Daude*, May 14, 2019, Cour d'Appel de Paris, Case No. 17/09133.
84. IBA Toolkit on Insolvency and Arbitration (2021), National Report of France, pp. 7-8.
85. *See, e.g.*, ICC Case No. 10687, Final Award in (2010) ICC Bulletin 20(1) ("ICC Case No. 10687"), where the tribunal scrupulously applied Article 621-41 of the French Commercial Code (now Article L. 622-22) and the conditions set out therein: "It should first be determined whether the conditions for the resumption of the arbitration proceedings as set out above were fulfilled, namely the declaration by [the plaintiff] of his claim against [the defendant], and the joinder of the organs of the collective procedure to the proceedings" (translation). It found that such conditions were fulfilled since the claimant had effectively filed its claim with the French trustee who voluntarily intervened in the proceedings, although they were not summoned by the claimant. *See also* ICC Case No. 13845, Final Award in (2009) ICC Bulletin 20(1), where the appointed trustee decided to discontinue a contract with the claimant who filed its claim with the trustee and initiated arbitration. The tribunal applied French law, considering that for arbitration initiated after the commencement of insolvency proceedings, the arbitral tribunal's jurisdiction is dependent not only on the filing of the claim with the trustee but also on the end of the claim's admission procedure ("*procédure de vérification*").

seats outside France have applied these principles when invoked by an insolvent French respondent.[86]

The U.S. Bankruptcy Code provides for an automatic stay of proceedings when a debtor files for bankruptcy.[87] An automatic stay is meant to protect the debtor's estate by prohibiting new claims against it. This stay applies to arbitral tribunals seated in the U.S.,[88] but may also apply to arbitral tribunals seated outside the U.S. in proceedings involving U.S. parties (though the exact scope of this extraterritorial application is uncertain).[89]

Conversely, under Swiss law, most commentators consider the principle of suspension of proceedings as exclusive of arbitration, as the Swiss Supreme Federal Court decided in 2011 that the principle only binds national courts and authorities.[90]

Regardless of whether the law of the seat or the place of insolvency provides for a stay of pending arbitral proceedings, it may still be incumbent upon the arbitral tribunal to stay the proceedings at the tribunal's discretion to ensure procedural fairness, and in particular to ensure that the trustee be given sufficient time to prepare and to present its case.[91]

The arbitral tribunal must determine if and how long the arbitral proceedings should be suspended on a case-by-case basis, taking into consideration all relevant circumstances.

4 *Scope of Award*

The existence of parallel insolvency proceedings may limit the scope of the arbitral award or order that a tribunal may render. Accordingly, arbitral tribunals should consider carefully the parties' respective requests for relief.

Certain insolvency laws restrict the permissible scope of an arbitral award and the type of relief that an arbitral tribunal can grant against an insolvent party. French law in particular provides that an award against an insolvent party may only determine that a valid claim exists and quantify it, but may not order payment of the claim.[92] This

86. *See* Mantilla-Serrano (1995), p. 58, referring to ICC Cases No. 6057 and 5996.
87. U.S. Bankruptcy Code, § 362(a).
88. *In re U.S. Lines, Inc.*, 197 F.3d 631 (2d Cir. 1999); *In re Braniff Airways, Inc.*, 33 B.R. 33, Bankr. L. Rep. (CCH) P 69377 (Bankr. N.D. Tex. 1983).
89. *See In re Gucci*, 309 B.R. 679 (S.D.N.Y. 2004). *See also In re JSC BTA Bank*, 434 B.R. 334 (Bankr. S.D.N.Y. 2010); IBA Toolkit on Insolvency and Arbitration (2021), National Report of the United States, pp. 5-6.
90. Decision of the Swiss Federal Supreme Court of October 21, 2011, Case No. 2C_303/2010. *See*, Vorburger (2014), ¶¶ 568-569; Kaufmann-Kohler, G. & Lévy, L. (2006). Insolvency and International Arbitration, in: Peter, H., Jeandin, N. & Kilborn, J. (Eds.) *The Challenges of Insolvency Law Reform in the 21st Century*. Zurich, Switzerland: Schulthess, pp. 270-271; IBA Toolkit on Insolvency and Arbitration (2021), National Report of Switzerland, pp. 9-10.
91. *See* Nessi, S. (2018). Insolvency and Arbitration, in: Arroyo, M. (Ed.), *Arbitration in Switzerland: The Practitioner's Guide* (2nd ed.). The Netherlands: Kluwer Law International, ¶ 73; Vorburger (2014), ¶ 747; Lazić (1998), p. 317.
92. Article L. 622-22 of the French Commercial Code.

principle is considered part of French international public policy[93] and has been applied by arbitral tribunals.[94]

Generally, French courts will deny recognition of an award if the arbitral tribunal orders payment.[95] However, in 2019, the Paris Court of Appeal seems to have adopted a more nuanced approach. A Swiss arbitral tribunal had rendered an award ordering payment against a French respondent. Insolvency proceedings were initiated shortly thereafter in France. The claimant successfully obtained an exequatur from the *Tribunal de Grande Instance*. The insolvent respondent challenged the exequatur on the grounds that it contravened international public policy because the underlying award ordered payment. Instead of reversing the entirety of the lower court's decision, the Court of Appeal only reversed the part that ordered payment from the insolvent party, and upheld the tribunal's finding on the validity and quantum of the claim.[96] This decision may reflect a new approach in France to the permissible scope of an award, and arbitral tribunals faced with an insolvent French party may no longer need to limit their award to declaratory relief, as the national judge could impose such a limitation. In Germany, where insolvency law similarly limits the scope of an award when insolvency proceedings are involved, the German Federal Court of Justice has already adopted such a flexible approach by holding that an arbitral award ordering payment by the insolvent estate implicitly contains the declaration that the underlying claim is valid and existent and that declaration may be enforced—but that actual enforcement of the award can happen only in the insolvency proceedings.[97]

5 Setoff

Arbitral tribunals are normally entitled to set off successful claims brought by each party to a dispute if those claims fall within the tribunal's jurisdiction. However, the declaration of insolvency of one of the parties may limit this power. Under most insolvency laws, just as pending proceedings against the insolvent debtor are suspended, payment and performance of contracts entered into by the debtor are also

93. *See, e.g., SAS IPSA Holding v. SCP Brouard Daude*, May 14, 2019, Cour d'Appel de Paris, Case No. 17/09133.
94. In ICC Case No. 10687, the arbitral tribunal limited the scope of claimant's requests for relief in accordance with French law: "The above provision of the Commercial Code further specifies that the proceedings, once resumed, can only concern the recognition of the claims and the fixing of their amount, not the payment. The claims of [the plaintiff] are modified accordingly" (translation).
95. *Société SARET v. SBBM*, February 4, 1992, Civ. 1, Cour de Cassation, Case No. 90-12569 quashing *SARET v. SBBM*, February 5, 1991, Cour d'appel de Paris, Case No. 90-12569. *See also Société Thinet v. Labrely ès-qualites*, March 8, 1988, Civ. 1, Cour de Cassation, Case No. 86-12015; and most recently, *SAS IPSA Holding v. SCP Brouard Daude*, May 14, 2019, Cour d'Appel de Paris, Case No. 17/09133.
96. *SAS IPSA Holding v. SCP Brouard Daude*, May 14, 2019, Cour d'Appel de Paris, Case No. 17/09133.
97. Kroll, S.M. (2015). Part IV: Selected Areas and Issues of Arbitration in Germany, Insolvency and Arbitration—Effects of Party Insolvency on Arbitral Proceedings in Germany. In Nacimiento P., et al. (Eds.), *Arbitration in Germany: The Model Law in Practice* (2d ed.) Wolters Kluwer, ¶¶ 80-83.

suspended. For example, under Article L. 622-7 of the French *Code de Commerce*, the commencement of insolvency proceedings against the debtor prohibits the payment of all prior debts, unless authorized by the supervising judge on certain conditions.[98]

Setoff as a means of extinguishing a payment obligation (*compensation légale*) and as a means of avoiding cross-payments of the amounts awarded (*compensation judiciaire*) need to be distinguished in an insolvency context.[99] While tribunals have found that they can order setoff as a means of extinguishing a debt, several others have concluded that setoff to avoid cross-payments would contravene public policy. In ICC Case No. 6697, an arbitral tribunal considered that an order of setoff would violate French public policy as it would be tantamount to ordering payment, in violation of the principle that the arbitral award should only grant declaratory relief to validate and quantify the debt.[100] In an unpublished 2013 ICC case,[101] a solvent respondent raised a counterclaim against an insolvent claimant, to be set off against the claimant's claims. The tribunal held that while it had jurisdiction to decide on the claimant's claims, the respondent's counterclaim was subject to the relevant national insolvency law, which provided for a stay of all proceedings against the insolvent estate. The tribunal therefore decided that the setoff could not be pursued in arbitration.

6 Security for Costs

In most instances, the respondent will request security for costs orders against an insolvent claimant; more rarely, they will be requested by a claimant against an insolvent respondent who has raised a counterclaim. While the power of arbitral tribunals to order security for costs is now relatively undisputed, the criteria according to which security for costs should be granted still generate debate—in particular, to what extent the insolvency of the party against whom an order is sought should come into play. Is the mere fact that a party is insolvent sufficient to justify a security for costs order or, to the contrary, does it prohibit such an order?

In the case of an insolvent claimant, national courts have been cautious when ordering security for costs, for fear of stifling a genuine and serious claim by the claimant.[102] Likewise, arbitral tribunals have acknowledged the need to protect genuine claims by insolvent parties. As noted by the tribunal in ICC Case No. 15218:[103]

> [S]ecurity for costs in international arbitration is first and foremost an issue about the conflict between the (insolvent) plaintiff's right to have access to arbitral justice on the one hand and the defendant's interest to have a reasonable chance of being able to enforce a future cost award issued in its favour on the other. Deciding on an application for security for costs is therefore about the task of

98. French Commercial Code, Article L. 622-7.
99. Mantilla-Serrano (1995), p. 71.
100. ICC Case No. 6697, as described in Mantilla-Serrano (1995), pp. 70-71.
101. ICC Reference No. ICC-PA-2020-255.
102. *See, e.g.*, English High Court decision in *Absolute Living Developments Ltd v. DS7 Ltd and others* [2018] EWHC 1432 (Ch).
103. ICC Case No. 15218, Procedural Order of July 2008 in (2014) ICC Special Supplement 2014: Procedural Decisions in ICC Arbitration ("ICC Case No. 15218"), ¶ 17.

> arbitral tribunals to balance these two conflicting interests against each other and about determining, on the basis of all relevant circumstances of the case, which of them shall prevail over the other.

No uniform test exists for assessing security for costs applications, and arbitral tribunals "have to decide security for costs applications on the basis of the relevant standards under the applicable national law."[104] The Chartered Institute of Arbitrators' 2016 International Arbitration Practice Guidelines on Applications for Security for Costs that assess the "current best practice in international commercial arbitration in relation to applications for security for costs" recommends the following:[105]

> When deciding whether to make an order for security for costs, arbitrators should take into account the following matters: (i) the prospects of success of the claim(s) and defense(s) [...]; (ii) the claimant's ability to satisfy an adverse costs award and the availability of the claimant's assets for enforcement of an adverse costs award [...]; and (iii) whether it is fair in all of the circumstances to require one party to provide security for the other party's costs [...]. [A]rbitrators should also take into account any other additional considerations they may consider relevant to the particular situation of the parties and the circumstances of the arbitration.

The SCC Rules have adopted a similar position.[106]

When a tribunal faces an application for security for costs, the tribunal should first examine whether there is at least prima facie evidence that the claimant is unlikely to be able to pay an adverse costs award.[107] In principle, that initial step is satisfied in the case of an insolvent party. However, the insolvency of a party is a commercial risk inherent to business relationships and, on its own, will not be a sufficient basis for a security for costs order.[108]

Some authors have suggested that exceptional circumstances need to be established for a security for costs order to be made against an insolvent party,[109] for example, when "a party appears to have deliberately organized its insolvency while commencing what may prove to be lengthy and expensive arbitral proceedings."[110]

---

104. *Chapter 6: Costs and Security for Costs*, 2018 ICCA Reports No. 4: Report of the ICCA-Queen Mary Task Force on Third-Party Funding in International Arbitration 4, p. 145 ("ICCA Report") at p. 165.
105. Chartered Institute of Arbitrators (2016), *International Arbitration Practice Guideline: Applications for Security for Costs*, Introduction and Article 1. Retrieved from: https://www.ciarb.org/media/4196/guideline-5-security-for-costs-2015.pdf, last visited February 10, 2023.
106. SCC Arbitration Rules, Article 38(2).
107. ICCA Report, p. 168.
108. *See, e.g.*, ICC Case No. 15218, ¶ 17 ("The opening of bankruptcy would not be sufficient grounds as long as the estate of the bankrupt party has sufficient realizable assets in order to finance the arbitration and to honour a future cost award issued against it"); ICC Case No. 13359, Procedural Order of February 2006 in (2014) ICC Special Supplement 2014: Procedural Decisions in ICC Arbitration ("The Tribunal has concluded that financial weakness by itself is not a sufficient ground for granting security for costs[.]"); ICC Case No. 14355, Procedural Order of January 2007 in (2014) ICC Special Supplement 2014: Procedural Decisions in ICC Arbitration ("[T]here is no unanimous view as to whether financial difficulties of a claimant (with or without opening of insolvency proceedings) always justify the granting of security for costs").
109. Derains and Schwartz (2005), p. 297.
110. Fouchard Gaillard Goldman, ¶ 1256.

However, the tribunal in ICC Case No. 15218 held that while the behavior of the insolvent party "may well have an impact on whether security for costs should be granted or not [...], making an order for security for costs dependent on the condition that the insolvent party has deliberately and in view of the arbitration taken steps to deprive the other party from recovering its costs would be inappropriate."[111] According to the tribunal, such an approach would be "*one*-sided, putting all the weight of the decision on the (insolvent) plaintiff's interest to have access to arbitral justice (emphasis added)."[112] Consequently, the tribunal held that an objective analysis should prevail—if the respondent cannot reasonably enforce a future cost award in its favor, an order for security for costs should be granted, unless the insolvent claimant can prove that its financial troubles are directly connected to conduct by the defendant that is contrary to the principle of good faith.[113] According to the tribunal, this approach would not violate the claimant's right of access to arbitral justice.[114]

The tribunal likewise implied that a security for costs application against an insolvent party should be granted if there is a third-party funder—"the [claimant's] right to have access to arbitral justice can only be granted under the condition that [the third parties financing the claimant's arbitration costs] are also ready and willing to secure the other party's reasonable costs to be incurred."[115]

III CONCLUSION

International arbitral tribunals do not derive their powers and duties from any particular national legal order, and are bound only by the terms of the contract, the agreement of the parties and international public policy. Nevertheless, regardless of which rules an arbitral tribunal is *bound* to apply in the context of parallel insolvency proceedings, in order to fulfill its purpose and its best efforts obligation to resolve an arbitral dispute by rendering an enforceable award, the tribunal should carefully consider other factors, including the national public policy and mandatory rules of the seat and any other likely place of enforcement.

Nonuniform national insolvency laws and different approaches by national courts to public policy and mandatory rules in an insolvency context make the arbitrator's task particularly difficult. While most tribunals make an honest effort to preempt any possible set-aside or enforcement issues, without substantive insolvency principles in place, tribunals find it challenging to anticipate all of the possible standards against which an award will be tested when national courts are called upon to set it aside or enforce it.

While the globalization of business relationships in recent years has led to more and more interactions between international arbitration and insolvency proceedings, little has been done to help guide tribunals in arbitrating such cases, or to ensure a

111. ICC Case No. 15218, ¶ 18.
112. *Ibid.*
113. *Ibid.*
114. *Ibid.*, ¶ 20.
115. *Ibid.*, ¶ 21.

coherent and predictable approach is adopted universally. None of the major international instruments currently in place, such as the UNCITRAL Model Law on Cross-Border Insolvency, the UNCITRAL Model Law on International Commercial Arbitration or the New York Convention, provide substantive guidance to tribunals or contain uniform rules regarding the relationship between insolvency and arbitration proceedings. Although not applicable to international arbitral tribunals, the Recast Insolvency Regulation has been a valuable attempt to bring more clarity regarding applicable law on an EU level.

Arbitrating cases that are affected by insolvency would be easier if the parties to an arbitration agreement considered the possible ramifications of future insolvency proceedings when choosing the seat or the law applicable to the dispute. Nevertheless, such a gargantuan task should not be put on the shoulders of private parties that are often not in a position to take into account such considerations, at a time when they do not yet contemplate a dispute, let alone their own or their counterparty's potential insolvency.

The wider arbitration community has recognized the growing importance of the interplay between international arbitration and insolvency—UNCITRAL has a Working Group on Insolvency, and in September 2019, the Arbitration Committee of the International Bar Association established a new subcommittee on insolvency which, in 2021, published the IBA Toolkit on Insolvency and Arbitration with the goal of providing guidance to both counsel and arbitrators.[116]

Although Guillermo would admonish us against overregulation, no doubt he would be supportive of further research on the interaction of insolvency and international arbitration to foster arbitrators' awareness of crucial insolvency-related issues and help ensure consistent and predictable arbitral decisions in this regard.

116. IBA Toolkit on Insolvency and Arbitration (2021).

CHAPTER 9

The New NAFTA: Fulfilling Guillermo's Dream?

Brian Jacobi & Sara McBrearty

I INTRODUCTION

On January 1, 1994, the North American Free Trade Agreement (NAFTA) between the United States, Canada, and Mexico entered into force. Guillermo Aguilar Álvarez served as Mexico's "principal legal counsel to the [Mexican] government during the negotiation and implementation of NAFTA," and he "played a key role in shaping the chapters dealing with investor-state and state-to-state arbitration and countervailing duties disputes."[1] In the years after the enactment of NAFTA, Guillermo spent considerable time defending the investor-state dispute mechanism and the broad protection NAFTA granted to investors, protections which Guillermo adamantly insisted were vital to promote the economic enhancement of all three NAFTA members.

In recent years, public discourse has turned increasingly against investor-state dispute resolution. In August and September 2018, the three NAFTA members announced that they had reached a deal to replace NAFTA. The new United-States-Mexico-Canada Agreement (USMCA) significantly narrowed the protections afforded by NAFTA in a number of ways, including a significant limitation to the scope of international arbitration. Unfortunately, Guillermo passed away prior to the announcement of the USCMA. We therefore do not have any direct comment from Guillermo on the new treaty. Nonetheless, there is little doubt that Guillermo would be highly disappointed with, and critical of, this "new NAFTA."

1. B. Button-Stephens, *Guillermo Aguilar-Alvarez 1958-2017*, Global Arbitration Review (July 13, 2017).

II THE HULL AND CALVO DOCTRINES: THE HISTORICAL CONTEXT OF THE NAFTA NEGOTIATIONS

The legal precedent underlying NAFTA's dispute resolution provisions has its origins in two competing early twentieth-century foreign policy doctrines.

First, individuals and corporations historically could not bring direct claims against a foreign state.[2] Instead, a claimant would petition its own government to pursue the claim on its behalf.[3] A number of the capital-exporting states employed heavy-handed forms of this diplomatic protection on behalf of their subjects in the nineteenth and twentieth centuries—so much so that it became known as "gunboat diplomacy."[4] In response to what the capital-importing states viewed as an assault on state sovereignty, the Argentinian diplomat Carlos Calvo wrote an influential treatise on international law promoting the "Calvo Doctrine." He argued that "there is in international law no rule universally accepted in theory nor carried out in practice, which makes obligatory the payment of immediate compensation nor even of deferred compensation, for expropriations of a general and impersonal character."[5] Calvo further argued that "foreigners must bring property disputes to domestic courts without recourse to their home governments."[6]

In other words, "in investment and capital disputes with foreign nationals, the Calvo Doctrine emphasizes state sovereignty[,] ... rejects international law[,]"[7] and popularizes the view that "intervention by foreign governments on behalf of foreign investors violate[s] state sovereignty."[8]

Second, in the course of a debate with his Mexican counterpart, essentially in response to Mexico's assertion of the Calvo Doctrine after allegedly expropriating American investors' property, the United States' Secretary of State Cordell Hull argued that it was a "self-evident fact" that international law exists[9] and that under international law "no government is entitled to expropriate private property, for whatever purpose, without provision for prompt, adequate, and effective payment therefore."[10] This position became known as the Hull Doctrine.[11] While Hull did not explicitly demand that international expropriation disputes be settled outside the state parties' judicial systems, the doctrine would become closely associated with the United States'

2. N. Blackaby et al. (eds.), *Redfern & Hunter on International Arbitration* (Kluwer Int'l 6th ed. 2015) at 441.
3. *Ibid.*
4. *Ibid.*
5. H. Schrader, *Custom and General Principles as Sources of International Law in American Federal Courts*, 82 Colum. L. Rev. 751, 775 n. 170 (1982).
6. J. Liss, *The Origins, Purposes, and Negotiations of the NAFTA Investment Agreements: Implications for Renegotiations and Integration with China*, 46 Syracuse J. Int'l L. & Com. 261, 267 (2019).
7. *Ibid.*
8. *Ibid.*
9. *Ibid.* at 267-268.
10. J. Turk, *Compensation for 'Measures Tantamount to Expropriation' Under NAFTA: What It Means and Why It Matters*, 1 ILMR 41, 42 (2005).
11. J. Liss, *The Origins, Purposes, and Negotiations of the NAFTA Investment Agreements: Implications for Renegotiations and Integration with China*, 46 Syracuse J. Int'l L. & Com. 261, 267 (2019).

attempts to promote its investors' rights at the international level. This often involved a demand that such disputes be settled through international arbitration.

This international legal debate took on renewed importance in the wake of the dismantling of European colonies, as the newly independent states both sought to flex their independence within their territories and to gain control over the system of foreign direct investment. Most strikingly, a number of states expropriated foreign investments in the wake of the independence movement: "[f]rom 1960-1969 there were 136 expropriations in developing countries, but from 1970-1979 there were 423."[12]

The wave of expropriations in the late twentieth century presented a new test for American foreign policy. In response, the United States sought to promote both the principles of the Hull Doctrine and international arbitration. To that end, the United States created the Organisation for Economic Co-operation and Development (OECD) and adopted the binding Code of Liberalization of Capital Movements.[13] It also initiated a series of bilateral Friendship, Commerce and Navigation treaties containing investment protections.[14]

Meanwhile, Mexico began to retreat from its staunch defense of the Calvo Doctrine and, in the 1980s, began to liberalize its protectionist trade and investment policies in the face of a debt crisis.[15] "The trade liberalization measures that began in the mid-1980s shifted Mexico from one of the world's most protected economies into one of the most open."[16] Mexico viewed a free trade agreement with the United States as "a way to lock in the reforms of its market opening measures from the mid-1980s," and to "increase investment confidence in order to attract greater flows of foreign investment and spur economic growth."[17]

For the United States, NAFTA "represented an opportunity to expand the growing export market to the south, but it also represented a political opportunity for the United States and Mexico to work together in resolving some of the tensions in the bilateral relationships."[18] In addition to the trade and investment opportunities that NAFTA offered, an agreement with Mexico "would be a way to support the growth of political pluralism and a deepening of democratic processes in Mexico."[19]

With this shift in Mexican policy away from the Calvo Doctrine and greater openness to the United States' historical support of the Hull Doctrine, the ground was set for the negotiations that would eventually result in the NAFTA agreement.

12. *Ibid.* at 269.
13. *Ibid.* at 270-271.
14. *Ibid.* at 271.
15. M. Angeles Villarreal et al., *The North American Free Trade Agreement (NAFTA)*, Congressional Research Service (2017) at 3.
16. *Ibid.*
17. *Ibid.*
18. *Ibid.*
19. *Ibid.*

III THE NAFTA NEGOTIATIONS: GUILLERMO'S VISION

Though Guillermo does not appear to have ever publicly addressed the impact of the Calvo and Hull Doctrines on the NAFTA negotiations, there is no doubt that as Mexico's principal negotiator he was well aware of the historical context in which the NAFTA negotiations occurred. Indeed, Guillermo in many ways embodied the transitional period that Mexico itself was going through at the time, as he both appreciated the historical context underpinning the Calvo Doctrine and saw far more benefit in an international system based on Hull's ideas.

For instance, regarding the principles underlying the Calvo Doctrine, Guillermo has noted that "American multinationals imposed arbitration as the mechanism for settling investment disputes with foreign countries, particularly Latin America."[20] While those foreign investors viewed arbitration as a way to "level the playing field and to reduce the prospect of the host state 'hometown justice,' thereby safeguarding assets from exploitation without compensation,"[21] Guillermo was well aware that wealthy "nations were seen to control the arbitral process in a way that permitted it to be used simply as a tool for extracting concessions from the host country."[22]

Nonetheless, Guillermo acknowledged that international arbitration provides "a forum that is more neutral than host country courts, both politically and procedurally."[23] He noted that the "relative impartiality of international tribunals bolsters investor confidence and inspires greater certainty that the contract will be interpreted in line with the parties' shared ex ante expectations."[24] Investors and states knew that "[t]he greater the risk, the higher the cost of investment."[25] History taught that untrustworthy enforcement mechanisms "tend to chill cross-border economic cooperation to the detriment of those countries that depend most on foreign capital for development."[26] For the optimists, arbitration could promote "respect for implicit bargains between investor and host country, [and] it came to commend itself to developing countries as a matter of sound international economic policy."[27]

Guillermo had high hopes that including sound economic policy in NAFTA would benefit Mexico's economic development by "reduc[ing] poverty through international economic cooperation,"[28] and believed that robust investor protections, along with a neutral dispute resolution forum to enforce them, were key elements to doing so. Indeed, Guillermo believed that limiting dispute resolution to the domestic courts would "inevitably either thwart cross-border economic cooperation or add to its cost"

20. G. Aguilar-Alvarez & W. Park, *The New Face of Investment Arbitration: NAFTA Chapter 11*, 28 Yale J. Int'l L. 365, 369 (2003).
21. *Ibid.*
22. *Ibid.* at 367, 369.
23. *Ibid.* at 369.
24. *Ibid.*
25. *Ibid.* at 368.
26. *Ibid.*
27. *Ibid.*
28. *Ibid.* at 369.

because the "real or imagined bias of host country judges" would "inhibit[] wealth-creating transactions and discourage[] cross-border economic cooperation."[29]

IV ORIGINAL NAFTA: RISE OF THE HULL DOCTRINE

As noted above, the primary historical debate giving rise to the Hull and Calvo Doctrines centered on three questions: (1) whether disputes should be resolved in host state courts or an international forum; (2) whether investors had a right to a minimum standard of treatment; and (3) the extent to which host states should be liable for expropriation. There is little doubt that the Hull Doctrine, and the United States' preference for international arbitration, ultimately won out in the final text of the original NAFTA.

First, NAFTA provided that disputes between investors and the host state would be resolved through binding international arbitration, not through the host state's domestic courts. Specifically, NAFTA provides that "[a]n aggrieved investor may choose either (i) arbitration supervised by [the International Centre for Settlement of Investment Disputes (ICSID)] (part of the World Bank group) or (ii) a proceeding conducted under arbitration rules adopted by [the United Nations Commission on International Trade Law (UNCITRAL)]."[30] Like a bilateral investment treaty, NAFTA Chapter 11 gives investors from a member country the opportunity to arbitrate investment grievances with the government of another NAFTA country, regardless of whether an agreement to arbitrate actually exists between the investor and the state.

As Guillermo has noted, a preference for international arbitration ultimately prevailed for at least two reasons. For one, the business community's long-standing suspicion of litigation in a foreign forum made the negotiators eager to bolster confidence that investors would receive a "fair shake" in the event of a dispute with the host government.[31] Moreover, NAFTA stipulated "substantive standards of investment protection" that would require interpretation.[32] Reciprocal lack of trust among the three member countries "made it unlikely that host state courts would be acceptable to construe and apply these standards."[33]

Second, Hull's argument that foreign nationals are entitled to a "minimum standard of treatment" prevailed in the final text of NAFTA.[34] Specifically, Article 1105(1) of NAFTA requires each country to "accord to investments of investors of another Party treatment in accordance with international law, including fair and equitable treatment and full protection and security."[35] The article imposes the "substantive norms for cross-border investment, forbidding discrimination against

29. *Ibid.*
30. *Ibid.* at 373.
31. *Ibid.* at 371.
32. *Ibid.*
33. *Ibid.*
34. J. Liss, *The Origins, Purposes, and Negotiations of the NAFTA Investment Agreements: Implications for Renegotiations and Integration with China*, 46 Syracuse J. Int'l L. & Com. 261, 267 (2019).
35. NAFTA, Article 1105(1).

investors from another member country," "as well as compensation, for nationalized property."[36]

Third, NAFTA provided a fairly broad definition of expropriation, stipulating that a state may directly or indirectly expropriate private property provided that it does so for a public purpose and on a nondiscriminatory basis.[37] NAFTA's recognition of the possibility of an "indirect" expropriation was significant, as it "extend[ed] [the] protection against un-compensated expropriation to measures 'tantamount to nationalization or expropriation,' thus encompassing takings that have often been referred to as 'creeping' expropriation."[38]

Accordingly, under the original NAFTA, an indirect expropriation may occur if "the investor's expected entitlement to the benefits are impaired by host state interference, even if property is not legally taken by the State,"[39] or when the host state itself acquires nothing of value but "at least has been the instrument of its redistribution."[40] Moreover, as Guillermo has noted, "[w]hile 'tantamount to expropriation' is not defined in NAFTA, this well-established concept has been applied to cover not only openly avowed state takings of property, but also ... other actions that have the effect of 'taking' the property, in whole or in large part, outright or in stages [including] when [a state] subjects alien property to taxation, regulation, or other action that is confiscatory, or that prevents, unreasonably interferes with, or unduly delays, effective enjoyment of an alien's property."[41]

Notably, Mexico ceased to pursue its demand that the "time and manner of [compensation for expropriation] must be determined by [Mexico's] own laws."[42] Instead, NAFTA itself provides that such compensation "must be 'equivalent to the fair market value' of the investment at the date of the expropriation, must be 'paid without delay and be fully realizable,' and must bear interest at a commercially reasonable rate until the date of actual payment."[43] As Guillermo has stated, this compensation scheme was "intended to be compatible with standards traditionally advocated by the United States."[44]

The combined effect of these provisions meant that NAFTA was "the first multilateral treaty involving highly developed and lesser developed nations that

36. G. Aguilar-Alvarez & W. Park, *The New Face of Investment Arbitration: NAFTA Chapter 11*, 28 Yale J. Int'l L. 365, 373 (2003).
37. *Ibid.*
38. *Ibid.* at 378.
39. *Ibid.* at 379 (citing A. Mouri, *The International Law of Expropriation as Reflected in the Work of the Iran-U.S. Claims Tribunal* (1994)).
40. *Ibid.*
41. *Ibid.* at 378.
42. J. Liss, *The Origins, Purposes, and Negotiations of the NAFTA Investment Agreements: Implications for Renegotiations and Integration with China*, 46 Syracuse J. Int'l L. & Com. 261, 267 (2019).
43. G. Aguilar-Alvarez & W. Park, *The New Face of Investment Arbitration: NAFTA Chapter 11*, 28 Yale J. Int'l L. 365, 373 (2003).
44. *Ibid.*

incorporate[d] Hull Doctrine ideals and consensual international arbitration mechanisms as the standard means for determining compensation."[45]

V THE EFFECT OF NAFTA: MEXICAN JOY, U.S. AND CANADIAN DISTRESS

In the years after NAFTA was signed, a furious debate emerged over the benefits of the trade agreement. "On one side, critics of NAFTA argue[d] that the investment protections in Chapter 11 unduly interfered with legitimate government regulation and should be pared back."[46] On the other hand, NAFTA's defenders "assert[ed] that investment protections pose[d] no great threat to national sovereignty and [were] necessary to promote economic growth and development."[47]

There is no doubt that Guillermo was on the side of those who vigorously defended NAFTA and believed that it brought considerable benefits to Mexico. As Guillermo noted in 2000, "NAFTA has been the engine for growth in Mexico from the date of its implementation."[48] He also observed that Mexico "has experienced double digit growth since the NAFTA was implemented and in some of the years prior."[49] In Guillermo's view, "[p]eaks in trade in the case of Mexico and Canada as compared to the rest of the world can be explained primarily as a result of NAFTA."[50] He also believed that NAFTA created hundreds of thousands of new export jobs in Mexico in the early 1990s, and that these export jobs were higher-paying than the rest of the Mexican economy.[51]

Moreover, according to Guillermo, the enactment of NAFTA "[c]learly" had a "tremendous impact on Mexico's ability to capture foreign direct investment."[52] He noted that prior to NAFTA, the highest yearly foreign investment total was less than five billion dollars, while that number doubled to ten billion immediately after NAFTA went into effect.[53] Guillermo believed that NAFTA's investor-state dispute provisions were a significant part of the economic picture which allowed that general prosperity to manifest itself.[54]

More recent statistics confirm that Guillermo's view was correct: NAFTA did bring real economic benefits to Mexico. In dollar terms, "U.S. imports from Mexico

45. J. Daly, *Has Mexico Crossed the Border on State Responsibility for Economic Injury to Aliens? Foreign Investment and the Calvo Clause in Mexico After the NAFTA*, 25 St. Mary's L. J. 1147, 1174 (1994).
46. D. Price, *Some Observations on Chapter Eleven of NAFTA*, 23 Hastings Int'l & Comp. L. Rev. 421, 421 (2000).
47. *Ibid.*
48. G. Aguilar-Alvarez, *The Mexican View on the Operation of NAFTA for the Resolution of Canada-U.S.-Mexico Disputes*, 26 Can.-U.S. L.J. 219, 219 (2000).
49. *Ibid.*
50. *Ibid.*
51. *Ibid.* at 220.
52. *Ibid.*
53. *Ibid.*
54. G. Aguilar-Alvarez & W. Park, *The New Face of Investment Arbitration: NAFTA Chapter 11*, 28 Yale J. Int'l L. 365, 366 (2003).

increased from $39.9 billion in 1993 to $294.2 billion in 2016, an increase of 637%."[55] "U.S. private services imports from Mexico [also] increased from $7.4 billion in 1993 to $21.9 billion in 2015."[56] In fact, one study concludes that "[m]ost of the trade-related effects of NAFTA may be attributed to changes in trade and investment patterns with Mexico."[57]

NAFTA also brought enormous economic benefits to the United States and Canada. For instance, as of 2017, "U.S. trade with its NAFTA partners has more than tripled since [NAFTA] took effect."[58] Meanwhile, two-way investment between the United States and Canada has "increased markedly since NAFTA."[59] In fact, the flow of capital between all three members has grown over the course of NAFTA, and by 2011, trilateral trade among NAFTA partners reached USD 1 trillion.[60]

Unfortunately, despite these economic benefits, the United States and Canada were less sanguine about the effects of NAFTA's dispute resolution mechanism. As Guillermo stated, after January 1994, when NAFTA came into force, "the rifle sights" of investors' claims were turned toward the United States and Canada, who became respondents in cases brought by investors based in other NAFTA countries.[61] "After claims for unfair treatment were filed *against* the United States government, arbitration looked different than when Americans [sic] companies were the investors (emphasis in the original)."[62] As Americans and Canadians "began to understand the host state perspective, praise for arbitration's neutrality began to have competition in the form of complaints about infringement of national sovereignty and democracy."[63] The imagined "level playing field" no longer seemed like an "unconditional benefit."[64]

American officials, of course, framed their critiques in a different light, complaining that the investor-state dispute resolution process "sacrific[es] state and local laws at the altar of ill-defined international investor rights."[65] Indeed, according to Congressman Tierney during a debate in the United States Congress, a "good number" of U.S. Congressmen have "expressed [their] concerns about NAFTA because of provisions in that treaty that pose a threat to [the United States'] national interests in safeguarding [its] environment and upholding workers' rights."[66] It is clear from the transcript of the debate that the "provisions" referenced by the Congressman were NAFTA's dispute resolution mechanism, with Congressman Miller urging the U.S. Congress to take

55. M. Angeles Villarreal et al., *The North American Free Trade Agreement (NAFTA)*, Congressional Research Service (2017) at 15.
56. *Ibid.*
57. *Ibid.* at 11.
58. *Ibid.* at 11.
59. *Ibid.* at 24.
60. *Ibid.*
61. G. Aguilar-Alvarez & W. Park, *The New Face of Investment Arbitration: NAFTA Chapter 11*, 28 Yale J. Int'l L. 365, 370 (2003).
62. *Ibid.*
63. *Ibid.*
64. *Ibid.*
65. Debate on H.R. 2670, 145 Cong. Rec., HR, 106th Congress, 1st Session, August 5, 1999 at H-7368.
66. *Ibid.*

action so that "all levels of government are able to act in the public interest without the threat of trade lawsuits."[67]

That criticism has since become official White House policy, with the Trump administration's primary objection to NAFTA's dispute resolution mechanism being that it impinges on U.S. sovereignty. As the U.S. Trade Representative recently testified before the U.S. Senate, he is "always troubled by the fact that nonelected non-Americans can make the final decision that the United States law is invalid."[68]

Though Canadian officials had for years "repeatedly insisted that NAFTA's investor protections and investor-state dispute settlement do not interfere with the right to regulate," Canadian commentators have long complained that the Chapter 11 investor-state settlement process is one of "the most glaringly regressive parts" of NAFTA.[69] As one commentator has complained, "[t]he risk of investment treaty litigation and fines, even if uncertain, can deter governments from acting in the public interest or distort policy choices towards options that are more amenable to foreign commercial interests."[70] Much of that criticism has been aimed at tribunal decisions that have affected Canadian efforts to regulate in pro of the environment. In particular, the well-known *S.D. Myers* decision in which a corporate claimant successfully challenged a temporary Canadian ban on the export of toxic PCB wastes, ultimately receiving USD 6 million in damages.[71] More recently, Canadian officials have also begun to take exception to the effect of such decisions on their ability to enact public policy, stating that a revised NAFTA should "reinforce the right of governments to regulate in the public interest."[72]

The fact that awards such as *S.D. Myers* come from unelected international arbitral tribunals only adds fuel to this fire, with some NAFTA opponents complaining that their "worst fears about anonymous government have become reality."[73] As one New York Times editorial put it: "Their meetings are secret. Their members are generally unknown. The decisions they reach need not be fully disclosed. Yet the way a small group of international tribunals handles disputes between investors and foreign governments has led to national laws being revoked, justice systems questioned and environmental regulations challenged."[74]

These critiques from the Canadian perspective are somewhat unsurprising given Canada's track record in NAFTA arbitrations. As of January 1, 2018, "48% of the 85 known NAFTA claims were made by foreign investors against Canada."[75] This is

67. *Ibid.* at H-7369.
68. Public Citizen, *Selected Statements and Actions Against Investor-State Dispute Settlement (ISDS)* (2018) at 4.
69. S. Sinclair, *Canada's Track Record Under NAFTA Chapter 11*, Canadian Centre for Policy Alternatives (2018) at 1, 11.
70. *Ibid.* at 8.
71. *Ibid.* at 5.
72. Canadian House of Commons, 42nd Parliament, Standing Committee on International Trade (December 4, 2017) at 1534.
73. A. Depalma, *NAFTA's Powerful Little Secret; Obscure Tribunals Settle Disputes, but Go Too Far, Critics Say*, New York Times (March 11, 2001).
74. *Ibid.*
75. S. Sinclair, *Canada's Track Record Under NAFTA Chapter 11*, Canadian Centre for Policy Alternatives (2018) at 3.

"significantly more investor-state claims (41) then either Mexico (23) or the U.S. (21), even though the latter's economy is 10 times larger than Canada's."[76] In contrast, as of January 1, 2018, "[n]o Canadian investor ha[d] ever won a NAFTA case."[77]

The United States' aversion to NAFTA's dispute resolution provision is more perplexing. Of all the three NAFTA parties, "[o]nly the U.S. has an unbroken winning record, having won 11 concluded cases and lost none."[78]

VI GUILLERMO'S TAKE ON HOST STATE CONCERNS

Despite Guillermo playing a key role in shaping NAFTA's investor-state and state-to-state arbitration provisions, he recognized that "[m]any host state concerns about NAFTA arbitration are understandable."[79] Indeed, Guillermo conceded that "[a]s with any dispute resolution system, some elements of NAFTA investment arbitration may be open to improvement."[80] Nonetheless, Guillermo was of the view that "the nature of anti-NAFTA rhetoric often captures popular sentiment more easily th[a]n the sound arguments against distortion of cross-border capital flows."[81]

For instance, Guillermo did not fail to recognize the irony in the United States and Canada taking a distinctively Calvan stance toward investor-state dispute settlement. As Guillermo noted, "[m]ost of the current questions about investment arbitration did not originate with NAFTA."[82] Rather, "the perceived novelty of the issues derives from the new roles in which Canada and the United States find themselves."[83] These more-developed states suddenly found themselves "articula[ting] variations on themes long advanced by Latin American and African countries forced to arbitrate disputes over natural resources, the environment and other vital elements of national life."[84] Guillermo therefore saw no small irony in their sudden appreciation of the predicaments historically experienced by capital-importers.[85]

Moreover, Guillermo was not convinced that there was a risk that NAFTA dispute resolution would "sacrifice state and local laws at the altar of ill-defined international investor rights."[86] His lack of sympathy on this point was to some extent based on the fact that "the United States may have become a victim of its own success."[87] "In the past, Americans sometimes persuaded arbitrators to adopt broad standards providing

76. *Ibid.*
77. *Ibid.* at 11.
78. *Ibid.* at 4.
79. G. Aguilar-Alvarez & W. Park, *The New Face of Investment Arbitration: NAFTA Chapter 11*, 28 Yale J. Int'l L. 365, 387 (2003).
80. *Ibid.* at 398.
81. *Ibid.* at 396.
82. *Ibid.* at 393.
83. *Ibid.*
84. *Ibid.*
85. *Ibid.*
86. Debate on H.R. 2670, 145 Cong. Rec., HR, 106th Congress, 1st Session August 5, 1999 at H-7368.
87. G. Aguilar-Alvarez & W. Park, *The New Face of Investment Arbitration: NAFTA Chapter 11*, 28 Yale J. Int'l L. 365, 388 (2003).

'protection and security' that might override otherwise legitimate domestic laws."[88] Americans were, "in Shakespeare's words, 'hoist with their own petard,' having contributed to the creation of pro-investor substantive standards applied by international tribunals, and to a blurring of distinctions between state-private proceedings ... and commercial arbitration exclusively among private parties."[89]

That is not to say that Guillermo failed to recognize there are reasonable concerns with some international law standards. For instance, Guillermo mused that "[c]onsiderable ambiguity exists with respect to what constitutes 'fair and equitable' treatment."[90] Guillermo further believed that the law on expropriation is "relatively malleable, with little consensus on the standards that determine when administrative regulations rise to a governmental taking that requires compensation."[91] Ultimately, however, he believed that "an occasional 'wrong' decision is a small price for promoting aggregate gain to the public good through the type of broad cross-border investment fostered by arbitration."[92]

Guillermo was also unpersuaded by critiques that international arbitral tribunals were unelected officials silently eroding state sovereignty. Indeed, in his words, the United States' reaction to the dispute resolution mechanism is "pregnant with irony when one remembers how often the United States has imposed arbitration on other countries and how American negotiators advocated arbitration to promote the security of foreign investment over Mexico's longstanding opposition thereto."[93] Guillermo further opined that arbitrations imposed by multinational corporations on African and Latin American countries "often implicated natural resources and elements of industrial infrastructure no less critical to the economic sovereignty and well-being of those countries than the NAFTA cases that have caused controversy in the United States and Canada."[94] "A dispute resolution process that had been fair for the rest of the world came to be seen as a tool to put business before public interest."[95] In Guillermo's view, "[s]auce for the goose ought to be sauce for the gander."[96]

Accordingly, despite the rising cry against NAFTA arbitrations, Guillermo remained an ardent supporter of the international dispute settlement system and was not convinced that the criticisms lodged against it could outweigh its overall benefits. In his view, "[t]he lobby that invokes 'pure air and water' and 'sovereignty' has a message with a more urgent ring than the theme of international economic cooperation, notwithstanding the unfortunate aggregate consequences that flow from measures that discourage transnational wealth creation."[97]

As stated above, there is no doubt that Guillermo was correct that all three Member States have benefitted from increased foreign direct investment since the

88. *Ibid.*
89. *Ibid.*
90. *Ibid.* at 387.
91. *Ibid.*
92. *Ibid.* at 399.
93. *Ibid.* at 380.
94. *Ibid.* at 367.
95. *Ibid.* at 371.
96. *Ibid.* at 396.
97. *Ibid.*

implementation of NAFTA. He strongly believed that these economic benefits were "something that you have to bear in mind when we have these heated discussions about Chapter 11 of the NAFTA and how it protects investment."[98] Thus, while NAFTA opponents' complaints may make "great topic[s] for law review articles," Guillermo remained convinced throughout his life that "when you look at the impact of that protection on the investor's level of comfort, ... the cost benefit analysis is clearly favorable."[99]

VII NEW NAFTA: THE IRONIC RETURN OF THE CALVO DOCTRINE

Canadian concern that it was facing increasing claims under Chapter 11 of NAFTA led Canada's minister of international trade to write to his United States and Mexican counterparts in 2017 requesting "to begin a process of ... 'clarifying' the limits of [NAFTA's] investment protections and perhaps amending the agreement."[100] The Trump administration was happy to oblige, as President Trump had for months been complaining that "NAFTA is the worst trade deal maybe ever signed anywhere, but certainly ever signed in this country."[101] Accordingly, on May 18, 2017, Robert Lightizer, the U.S. Trade Representative, "sent a 90-day notification to the [U.S.] Congress of [the Administration's] intent to begin talks with Canada and Mexico to renegotiate [NAFTA]."[102] A review of the United States' and Mexico's negotiating goals highlights how far each had turned from its position in the 1938 disputes over Mexican oil nationalization.

For instance, Mexico, the formerly ardent supporter of Carlos Calvo's stance that "foreigners must bring property disputes to domestic courts without recourse to their home governments,"[103] now entered the second round of NAFTA negotiations with the aim of "bolster[ing]" NAFTA's dispute resolution mechanism.[104] In particular, Mexico's Congress backed a nonbinding motion urging the government to reject the Trump administration's proposal to scrap Chapter 19, a provision that grants binational panels the authority to hear complaints about illegal subsidies and dumping and to issue binding decisions.[105] According to the administration, the mechanism "has hindered

98. G. Aguilar-Alvarez, *The Mexican View on the Operation of NAFTA for the Resolution of Canada-U.S.-Mexico Disputes*, 26 Can.-U.S. L.J. 219, 220 (2000).
99. *Ibid.*
100. A. Depalma, *NAFTA's Powerful Little Secret; Obscure Tribunals Settle Disputes, but Go Too Far, Critics Say*, New York Times (March 11, 2001).
101. Patrick Gillespie, *Trump Hammers America's 'Worst Trade Deal'*, CNN Business (September 27, 2016).
102. M. Angeles Villarreal et al., *The North American Free Trade Agreement (NAFTA)*, Congressional Research Service (2017) at 24.
103. J. Liss, *The Origins, Purposes, and Negotiations of the NAFTA Investment Agreements: Implications for Renegotiations and Integration with China*, 46 Syracuse J. Int'l L. & Com. 261, 267 (2019).
104. G. Stargardter, *Mexico Sets Out NAFTA Goals Ahead of Re-negotiation Talks: Document*, Reuters (August 1, 2017).
105. *Ibid.*

the United States from pursuing anti-dumping and anti-subsidy cases against Mexican and Canadian firms."[106]

The United States, in contrast, entered the negotiations with the mindset that "NAFTA ha[d] fundamentally failed many, many Americans and need[ed] major improvement."[107] With regard to investment arbitration, the United States declared that it sought to establish a dispute settlement mechanism that would be "effective" and "timely,"[108] but notably took a page from the Calvo Doctrine in seeking to secure for U.S. investors "important rights consistent with *U.S. legal principles and practice* (emphasis in the original)," as opposed to international standards, "while ensuring that NAFTA country investors in the United States are not accorded greater substantive rights than domestic investors."[109]

On August 27, 2018, the United States and Mexico reached a bilateral agreement to replace NAFTA. Subsequently, on September 30, 2018, the United States and Canada reached a bilateral agreement to do the same. The resulting trilateral deal will be called the USMCA (it will not go into effect unless and until each member state domestically ratifies the agreement). The USMCA contains several changes with important consequences for investors.

First, the most significant change is that Canada has not signed on to the new investor-state arbitration provisions.[110] As a result, other than certain qualifying "legacy claims," U.S. and Mexican investors will not have the right to bring investment claims against Canada, and Canadian investors cannot bring claims against the United States or Mexico.[111]

Second, though the United States and Mexico have signed on to new investor-state provisions, the USMCA will significantly curtail the scope of investors' potential claims in a number of ways. For instance, the USMCA has greatly narrowed the definition of a potential "claimant" by excluding investors "owned or controlled by a person of a non-Annex Party that ... the other Annex Party has determined to be a non-market economy."[112] This is a broader exclusion of claimants than under NAFTA, which only denied benefits to claimants if they were *both* owned or controlled by investors of a non-Party *and* had "no substantial business activities in the territory of the Party under whose law it is constituted."[113] The USMCA therefore excludes claimants owned or controlled by a non-Party investor, even where the U.S. or Mexican company engages in substantial business activities in its state of incorporation. This

106. *Ibid.*
107. D. Gantz, *Addressing Dispute Resolution Institutions in a NAFTA Renegotiation* (México Center 2018) at 4 (quoting U.S. Trade Representative Robert Lightizer).
108. United States Trade Representative, *Summary Objectives for the NAFTA Renegotiation* (July 2017) at 17.
109. *Ibid.* at 9.
110. USMCA, Annex 14-D, Article 1.
111. Canadian investors in Mexico and Mexican investors in Canada will, however, have access to investment arbitration under the Comprehensive and Progressive Agreement for Trans-Pacific Partnership.
112. USMCA, Annex 14-D, Article 1 (defining "claimant").
113. NAFTA, Article 1113(2).

restriction appears to be directed at Chinese-owned or controlled investments in the United States and Mexico.

Furthermore, the USMCA has added a requirement that investors exhaust local remedies. While such provisions were once common in investment treaties, most modern treaties—including NAFTA—do not include them. USMCA bars investors from initiating an international arbitration claim unless the investor first challenges the measures alleged to breach the treaty in national courts, and the local proceeding is exhausted or has lasted thirty months.[114] This thirty-month time period is also unusually long, even for treaties with exhaustion requirements.

The exhaustion period, in combination with a new four-year statute of limitations for claims, effectively creates a 1.5-year statute of limitations. In other words, an investor must initiate a claim before local courts within eighteen months of when it knew or should have known about the claim. Otherwise, the four-year limitations period will expire before the claimant can exhaust the thirty-month local-remedy requirement.

Third, though the USMCA provides investors with a number of well-established treaty protections, including national treatment, most-favored-nation treatment, and protection against expropriation,[115] it limits those protections in three important and unusual ways.

For instance, the USMCA excludes national treatment and most-favored-nation claims concerning the "establishment or acquisition of an investment."[116] Claimants are therefore limited to discrimination claims relating to the "expansion, management, conduct, operation, and sale or other disposition of investments."[117] Furthermore, the most-favored-nation standard excludes "provisions in other international trade or investment agreements that establish international dispute resolution procedures or impose substantive obligations."[118] Rather, "treatment" only encompasses "measures adopted or maintained by the other Annex Party."[119] In other words, a claimant cannot import from another treaty a more favorable dispute resolution mechanism or more favorable protections. Additionally, the USMCA expressly excludes "indirect expropriation" claims.[120] This limitation, which runs counter to the development of international law on expropriation over the past half-century, means that short of an outright taking, a claimant cannot pursue a treaty claim for expropriation. Perhaps most notably, missing from the list of cognizable claims is a recognition that states must afford investments a minimum standard of treatment.[121]

These limitations on cognizable claims are important as they exclude or limit many of the most frequent claims brought under NAFTA—breaches of the minimum standard of treatment and indirect expropriation. As a result, Canada's withdrawal

114. USMCA, Annex 14-D, Articles 5(a), (b).
115. *Ibid.* Articles 14.4-14.8.
116. *Ibid.* Annex 14-D, Article 3(1)(a)(i)(A).
117. *Ibid.* Articles 14.4(1), 14.5(1).
118. *Ibid.* Annex 14-D, Article 3(1)(a)(i)(A) n. 22.
119. *Ibid.*
120. *Ibid.* Annex 14-D, Article 3(1)(a)(i)(B).
121. *Ibid.* Annex 14-D, Article 14.D.3.3(1)(a)(i)(B).

from the investor-state dispute resolution mechanism, combined with limitations on the cognizable claims, means that the USMCA provides significantly less substantive protection for investors than NAFTA.

In short, these reforms are profound and, if the treaty is ratified as it now stands, the number of investment disputes will likely be reduced significantly. That reduction in investment arbitrations will not be because such disputes will suddenly arise with less frequency; to the contrary, they are a normal part of international commerce and investment. Rather, investors will no longer have a forum—other than domestic courts—in which to resolve these disputes.

VIII DOES THE NEW NAFTA MEET GUILLERMO'S STANDARDS?

Guillermo would likely be disappointed by the "new NAFTA" in several respects.

First, he would likely be disappointed by a dispute resolution mechanism that did not include all three parties. In Guillermo's words, NAFTA's original dispute resolution mechanism was based on "equality of treatment among the three countries."[122] In his view, for Mexico "to accept arbitration of investment disputes within its borders, Canada and the United States had to respect a similar dispute resolution process."[123]

At first blush, Canada's absence from the USMCA dispute resolution mechanism may seem equitable: while Mexican investors cannot bring investment claims against Canada, Canadian investors also cannot bring claims against Mexico. However, in practice, the USMCA dispute resolution provision is likely to disadvantage Mexico to a disproportionate extent for one simple reason: no investor has ever won damages against the United States in a NAFTA case. Therefore, Mexico risks being the only state with significant legal exposure under the USMCA. Such a system hints at the problematic use of arbitration against capital-importing states that led to the rise of the Calvo Doctrine.

Second, Guillermo would be disappointed by the backlash against international arbitration that runs through the USMCA. He anticipated that some might criticize NAFTA arbitration tribunals "as courts of appeal on vital regulatory matters that discriminate against foreign investment or constitute illegal taking of an alien-owned property."[124] He emphasized, however, that such concerns were overblown because "Chapter 11 tribunals' power of review extends only to government measures that violate the NAFTA treaty obligations."[125]

Moreover, while Guillermo recognized that in certain circumstances "foreign claimants will receive better treatment than domestic courts give similarly situated local claimants," he cautioned that "[s]uch differences should not be surprising."[126] He also noted that investors have "traditionally favored arbitration" in cross-border

122. G. Aguilar-Alvarez & W. Park, *The New Face of Investment Arbitration: NAFTA Chapter 11*, 28 Yale J. Int'l L. 365, 371 (2003).
123. *Ibid.*
124. *Ibid.* at 393.
125. *Ibid.* at 394.
126. *Ibid.*

transactions for this very reason, and "investors from industrialized countries have long insisted on fair dealing for themselves, regardless of how poorly a host state might treat its own people."[127] In any event, as discussed above, Guillermo believed that the economic benefits of NAFTA, taken as a whole, outweighed the costs. The new NAFTA shows that the United States and Canada have come to the opposite conclusion, a development that would surely disappoint him.

Third, Guillermo would have disagreed with the new NAFTA's refusal to protect investors against indirect or creeping expropriations. Direct expropriations today are quite rare—and were already rare when the original NAFTA was enacted. Guillermo recognized that a prohibition on direct expropriation is of very limited utility because "not all discrimination is outright and abrupt."[128] When discussing Chapter 11 of NAFTA, Guillermo recognized that "[i]ndirect nationalization through improper administrative measures has long served as a back door to deprive the investor of its assets."[129] A state may arbitrarily take property in "a gradual fashion through abusive manipulation of the legal system," without committing a direct expropriation.[130] He recognized that such de facto nationalization is now known by many names under international law: "creeping expropriation," "indirect expropriation," and "constructive expropriation."[131] It is clear that Guillermo found such forms of expropriation troubling and would doubtless condemn the new NAFTA's failure to grant investors protection from such state action.

IX CONCLUSION

Guillermo candidly stated that it was "less than self-evident ... what exactly should be done to reduce the prospect of harsh legislative responses to NAFTA arbitration."[132] However, Guillermo believed that "[c]aution must remain a significant part of the process for bringing order to the resolution of investment disputes" as "overly general critiques of investment arbitration risk doing more harm than good, in the end backfiring to injure both the long- and short-term national interests."[133]

Unfortunately, the United States' and Canada's demands in the new NAFTA appear to embody Guillermo's fears and significantly erode the investment protections that Guillermo believed were essential to Mexico's (and the other NAFTA States') ability to reap the economic benefits of the treaty. There is little doubt that Guillermo would be disappointed that the dispute resolution process he worked so tirelessly to craft has "fall[en] prey to public pressure arising from a backlash against investor victories in some of the more visible NAFTA arbitration."[134]

127. *Ibid.*
128. *Ibid.* at 387.
129. *Ibid.*
130. *Ibid.*
131. *Ibid.*
132. *Ibid.* at 400.
133. *Ibid.* at 399-400.
134. *Ibid.* at 399.

CHAPTER 10

Internal and External Factors Fashioning Arbitral Authority

Horacio A. Grigera Naón

I INTRODUCTION

The authority of arbitrators has external and internal limitations, having as a common denominator the fact that the immediate source of arbitral authority is the will of the parties and not the constitutional organization of power.

Internal, because although party autonomy is the basis, *inter alia,* of arbitral authority, such authority is not unbound given the fact that arbitrators, unlike national courts, lack *imperium* to enforce their determinations. Within the four corners of the arbitral procedure, such authority is applied to the conduct of the arbitration, and because of the delicate factors that have to be weighed in fulfilling such mission, its scope and limitations (as will be shown in this chapter) depend on a balancing exercise that is more art than science: the art to persuade.

External, because unlike national courts, arbitrators are not a branch of government and therefore lack imperium to enforce their decisions as an external body situated above the parties. Unlike court decisions, arbitral determinations are effective to the extent that applicable national laws and courts lend their support to such determinations and awards. However, this chapter will explore situations in which arbitrators may be considered to have some degree of "external" authority to impose their determinations on the parties, which does not entirely depend on the ability of arbitrators to induce parties to spontaneously accept or abide by their directives.

There is an additional, at times preponderant, truly external and autonomous factor that has an impact on arbitral authority, which largely depends on ideological, political or pseudo-sociological considerations. This factor, by attempting to undermine the reliability and reputation of international arbitration as a dispute resolution mechanism, in practice, translates itself into an erosion of arbitral authority. This topic will be addressed in the last section of this chapter.

II INTERNAL FACTORS

Perhaps one of the most relevant internal factors conditioning arbitral authority is that arbitrators have to persuade (or induce) rather than impose.

Persuasion (or the ability to induce) is not a given and has to be built up step by step from the very inception of the procedure. It largely depends on: (i) the reasonableness of arbitral procedural determinations, (ii) the demeanor of the arbitral tribunal in its exchanges with the parties (courteous and firm at the same time, always ensuring that each party has been properly heard in connection with each procedural determination), and (iii) showing the parties they can trust that the arbitrators know and have studied the record, and that they will not take arbitral decisions carelessly or without reflection.

Another element contributing to the persuasiveness of arbitral procedural determinations—and thus reinforcing arbitral authority—is conveying to the parties the impression that the arbitral tribunal members, when addressing procedural matters, visibly operate as a united team. Showing internal dissensions to the parties and counsel (rather than addressing them within the four corners of the internal interactions among the members of the tribunal) undermines arbitral authority and alienates parties' and counsel's trust and respect.

The disconnect becomes more dramatic and harmful when one member of the arbitral tribunal openly takes positions (e.g., through questions during the hearing) only favoring the party that appointed him or her, but without reaching the level at which a party would feel comfortable challenging the arbitrator (after carefully balancing the possibility of success against the resulting disruption of the normal course of the arbitration and the risk of alienating the goodwill of that member of the arbitral tribunal if the challenge proves unsuccessful). That kind of attitude should prompt the president of the arbitral tribunal to have a private conversation with the relevant arbitrator (even if this requires pausing the hearing), in order to clearly impress upon the arbitrator that he or she must desist from such conduct which would otherwise taint the authority and integrity of the arbitral tribunal more broadly.

There is of course a psychological factor that positively contributes to the persuasiveness of arbitral determinations: the awareness of parties and counsel that the fate of their case is in the hands of the arbitral tribunal, and that it would be a mistake to alienate the arbitral tribunal's goodwill by conducting themselves improperly during the procedure with the potential effect of implicitly challenging arbitral authority and the arbitral tribunal's control over the procedure. For example, improper conduct may be evidenced by the use of guerrilla tactics, such as attempting to delay the procedure through baseless applications, unjustified requests to extend procedural deadlines, requests for the production of documents well after the deadline for doing so and, without showing due cause, multiplying procedural objections at the hearing, or trying to create procedural "booby traps" for possible future use in an application to set aside the award.

In this respect, external factors (particularly, the laws of the seat of the arbitration) converge with the internal factors already described to enhance arbitral authority and concomitantly deter parties from resorting to such tactics. Because of the limited means to attack or set aside arbitral determinations (at least in national jurisdictions interested in attracting arbitrations), parties and counsel know that arbitral decisions will finally dispose of their case both on procedural matters and on the merits, with very limited opportunities to attack such determinations before a court of law. For this reason, wise parties and their counsel will be inclined not to undermine arbitral authority during the arbitration by resorting to procedural tactics that may have an unintended adverse effect on the outcome of their case.

There is an additional factor that deserves separate treatment as it is, at the same time, both internal—since it is intimately associated with the internal interactions among the arbitrators—and external—because it is projected outside the four corners of the arbitral procedure with the negative effect (according to some opinions) of potentially weakening arbitral determinations or, in other words, eroding arbitral authority. I am referring to dissenting opinions.

III THE ARBITRAL TRIBUNAL'S INTERNAL CHEMISTRY: DISSENTING OPINIONS

In respect of dissenting opinions, there are different views.

The first advocates that dissenting opinions are impermissible since they tend to betray the secrecy of deliberations, undermine the persuasive value and the binding force of arbitral awards and do not contribute to the evolution of arbitral jurisprudence (if such a thing exists since international commercial arbitral awards are usually not published, and there is no arbitral *stare decisis*). Some statistics that show that in almost all cases dissenting opinions are made by the arbitrator chosen by the losing party are marshalled in support of this view. These statistics are also used in order to suggest that dissenting arbitrators are invariably partial to the case made by the party appointing them.

The second view (which I endorse) takes a more moderate approach.

As in many other areas of life, not all dissenting opinions belong in the same category: there are good ones, as well as the bad and ugly.

The latter include those dissenting opinions that are unprincipled in terms of their consideration of legal arguments put before the arbitrators and the record of the case, with the only purpose of weakening the award or perhaps of signaling to the party that appointed the dissenting arbitrator that he or she has sided with such party's position in the expectation of future appointments or as a *quid pro quo* within the context of some preexisting relationship with such party. Such dissents do not find support in sound legal reasoning based on the legal and factual questions raised by the dispute.

A good dissenting opinion arises when the basis for the dissent is an honest conviction that the majority are wrong, on either the law or the facts, or on both.

Professional integrity in fulfilling the arbitral function is part and parcel of the arbitral mission. An arbitrator's integrity (and also his or her reputation) suffers when endorsing awards that the arbitrator considers fundamentally wrong on the law or the facts. In such circumstances, particularly when the law is not applied or is misapplied by the majority, a dissent is justified.[1]

In any event, it is not appropriate to mechanically attribute to the dissenter a biased attitude in favor of the party who appointed him or her and who ultimately has not been favored by the majority decision. Particularly in connection with dissenting opinions, Mark Twain's skepticism regarding statistics seems justified.[2] In addition to cases in which the dissenting opinion may be explained in terms of the dissenter's sound legal reasoning supported by a correct evaluation of argument and evidence, there are many other instances where statistics fail to capture reality because the dissent is a direct consequence of inner situations or imbalances in the arbitral tribunal. For example, a weak or inexperienced president who is influenced by an astute and partial arbitrator to reach the wrong decision, thus prompting dissent by the other arbitrator; or an opinionated president who has a preconceived and ill-conceived vision of the case, which is promptly endorsed by one of the arbitrators who immediately sees that the party appointing him or her will have the upper hand, thus leaving the other arbitrator with no option but to dissent.

IV A PARTICULAR "EXTERNAL" FACTOR: ARBITRATORS' "COERCIVE POWERS"?

In theory, depending on the laws of the seat of the arbitration, the argument may be made that arbitrators may impose comminatory sanctions (*astreintes*) to induce a party to enforce arbitral procedural determinations. However, even if hypothetically the arbitral tribunal had the *authority* to do so under the applicable law, it would most likely lack the authority to *enforce* them, which would correspond to a national court of law. Be that as it may, in my experience I have never been confronted with a situation requiring *astreintes* or in which the arbitral tribunal was asked to impose *astreintes*, and I do not believe this to be a common occurrence.

Another facet of "external" arbitral authority is the right of arbitrators to police arbitral proceedings inherent to their mission that may go beyond their ability to persuade or induce referred to in section II above.

Because arbitrators are not judges, they lack certain powers for policing the arbitral procedure that judges have in connection with court proceedings. Perhaps the most evident power courts have and arbitrators lack is the authority to hold a party or

1. Recognizing that commercial arbitration awards that are not published are much less persuasive, the following words of Justice Ruth Bader Ginsburg also ring true in connection with international commercial arbitration: "To sum up, although I appreciate the value of unanimous opinions, I will continue to speak in dissent when important matters are at stake." R.B. Ginsburg, (2010). The Role of Dissenting Opinions. *Minnesota Law Review*, 428, p. 7.
2. Paraphrasing M. Twain: *There Are Three Types of Lies: Intentional, Unintentional and Statistics.*

counsel in contempt of court, as well as to impose fines on counsel, or even exclude counsel from the arbitration.

However, in extreme—perhaps exceptional—circumstances which arose in a bilateral investment treaty arbitration, the arbitral tribunal decided to exclude counsel from the case in a situation in which the presence of the excluded counsel was likely to undermine the fairness of the proceedings.[3]

Even if it were accepted that arbitrators enjoy such extended power under the applicable law (or eventually, arbitration rules[4]), such power should be exercised with the utmost care and caution, and only to safeguard the integrity and fairness of the arbitral procedure.[5] A party's freedom to have and maintain counsel of its own choice is closely associated with due process since it belongs to a party's fundamental right to advance and defend its case the way it sees fit. Such right cannot be denied except in the most extreme situations in which the very principle of due process would suffer because maintaining such counsel would contaminate the integrity of the proceedings and be a source of unfairness in the conduct of the arbitration, to the detriment of the opposing party's rights.

Another area in which the "external" authority of arbitrators may be tested is their powers to collect evidence. Arbitration rules' open-textured wording often suggests they do have such powers.[6] However, in practice they are seldom resorted to, and if they are, these powers should be exercised sparingly. For example, one thing is to require the incorporation of the full text of an incomplete document already in the record, or the incorporation of a document which has been cross-referred to in another document that is already in the record. It is a different matter if the arbitral tribunal *sua sponte* launches evidentiary measures aimed at establishing an arbitral record on the basis of its own investigative inclinations.

Arbitrators would be ill-advised to involve themselves in such conduct for at least two reasons: (1) by doing so, they are likely to advantage one party's case to the disadvantage of the opposing party's case, thus upsetting the apple cart contrary to due process and the duties of arbitrators to conduct themselves impartially and independently; and (2) evidentiary measures may be costly and time-consuming, and they are carried out at the expense of the parties—arbitrators must be very careful to not

3. *Hrvatska Elektroprivreda, d.d. v. The Republic of Slovenia* (ICSID Case No. ARB/05/24), Tribunal's Ruling regarding the participation of David Mildon QC in further stages of the proceedings, May 6, 2008.
4. International Bar Association (2013). *Guidelines on Party Representation in International Arbitration.* Guidelines 4-6 and their Comments, which in essence provide that once the arbitral tribunal has been constituted, a person should refuse to represent a party if a relationship exists with such party that would create a conflict of interest, unless no party objects after a proper disclosure of this fact. In case of breach, the arbitral tribunal is vested with the authority to take measures to safeguard the integrity of arbitral proceedings including the exclusion of the party's new representative in the arbitration.
5. ICC Arbitration Rules (2021) ("ICC Rules"), Article 22 (4): "In all cases, the arbitral tribunal shall act fairly and impartially and ensure that each party has a reasonable opportunity to present its case."
6. ICC Rules, Article 25(1): "The arbitral tribunal shall proceed within as short a time as possible to establish the facts of the case by all appropriate means"; *ibid.*, Article 25(4): "At any time during the proceedings the arbitral tribunal may summon any party to provide additional evidence."

unnecessarily increase arbitral procedure costs and duration by taking actions nobody has asked them to take.

V THE IMPACT OF POLITICAL AND IDEOLOGICAL FACTORS ON ARBITRAL AUTHORITY

It seems a truism to say that if the authority of international arbitration (i.e., its reputation and reliability as the most appropriate means for resolving international commercial and economic disputes) is undermined, the authority of arbitrators to adjudicate such disputes equally suffers. In that respect, the more international arbitration is exposed to pendulum-like ideological and political oscillations, the more this dispute resolution method is weakened and becomes mistrusted, in ways that are ultimately detrimental to arbitral authority.

Some of these problems originate in the area of investment arbitration, with their effects occasionally reaching international commercial arbitration more broadly.

On the one hand, developing States, in line with political decisions to open their economies to foreign capital, entered into a myriad of bilateral investment protection treaties (***BITs***), including international arbitration as the method to resolve investment disputes arising between foreign investors and the host State under such treaties. Because of a shift in their views as to the advantages provided by BITs, particularly as to the level of protection under international law afforded to the private investor and its investments thereunder, certain States have backtracked, or support backtracking, on some of the concessions made for the treatment of foreign investors and investments in BITs, including resorting to international arbitration for the resolution of investment disputes. This change of attitude has been accompanied by criticism of international arbitration and arbitral decisions, originating from different social and political sectors of opinion and academia.

On the other hand, developed States (so-called industrialized or first World States) have not been free from these pendular movements, responding to a change in their vision of the advantages offered by these treaties. In their origins, BITs were supposed to advance the economic interests of developed States since the flow of investments to the developing world would be substantially channeled under the protective umbrella of BITs, limiting the exercise of certain sovereign host State powers. Nevertheless, it did not take long for developed States to distance themselves from their original pro-BIT enthusiasm when the tables started to turn and they became exposed to international arbitration investment claims brought against them. This phenomenon was detected and for the first time highlighted in a seminal article coauthored by my dear and deeply missed friend Guillermo Aguilar Álvarez: when developed States are on the receiving end, they emulate developing States in resorting to Calvo-style arguments to, among other things, avoid international arbitration for the resolution of investment disputes and the application of international law by international arbitrators.[7]

The above circumstances give rise to the following reflections.

In the first place, international arbitration is a neutral method of dispute resolution requiring arbitrators to apply the rule of law as is (*de lege lata*), not as policy makers, political players or socioeconomic operators would like it to be (*de lege ferenda*). Arbitral determinations cannot be blamed if they reflect the law as is, not as it should be. It is for States, by using their treaty-making and other powers vested in them under international law, to fashion desirable rules that apply to international investment protection.

Second, it is a mistake to extend dissatisfaction with existing BIT standards for the substantive protection of foreign investors and investments to a criticism or outright rejection of international arbitration as a neutral or apt mechanism for the resolution of international commercial and investment disputes. As Aguilar Alvarez and Park incisively set forth in their paper on the matter of such standards: "Clarification and adjustment may be in order (....) it would be fundamentally unsound to call into question the use of neutral binding arbitration itself as the preferred means for resolving cross-border investment disputes."[8]

Third, the fundamental contributions of international commercial and investment arbitration to peace and the fostering of an appropriate environment governed by the rule of law for international trade and cross-border flows of economic resources are forgotten and blurred by ill-informed criticism or political shifts prompted more by shortsighted political objectives than long-term evaluations of the legal, social and economic benefits of international arbitration for the resolution of international investment disputes.

In this regard, it is useful to remember that international arbitration—particularly in the area of State disputes involving foreigners—was relied upon by developing States since the times of the *Alabama* decision[9] to secure the adjudication of such disputes under the aegis of the rule of international law rather than at the mercy of diplomatic protection (which was then often tantamount to gunboat diplomacy), or the decisions of the national courts of the strongest party.

---

7. Specifically referring to the USA (although this also applies to other traditionally capital-exporting countries): "To some observers a double standard seems to be creeping into American attitudes towards investment arbitration. Arbitration is good when it corrects misbehavior by foreign states, but not so desirable when claims are filed for alleged wrongdoing by the United States," in G. Aguilar Alvarez, W.W. Park (2003). The New Face of Investment Arbitration: NAFTA Chapter 11. *Yale Journal on International Law*, 28, pp. 368-369.
8. *Ibid.*, p. 398.
9. Claim by the USA against Great Britain for the latter's failure to honor its duties as a neutral in the Secession War by permitting the construction of ships in British yards used by the Southern states against the Northern states for bellicose purposes. It was settled through an arbitral award in favor of the USA dated September 14, 1872, reproduced in G. Wetter. *The International Arbitral Process: Public and Private*, Oceana Publications (1979), pp. 48-56. The USA, just emerging from a civil war and not yet a world power comparable to Great Britain, had a fair adjudication through arbitration of a case against the strongest land and maritime power at the time, which in principle was reluctant to go to arbitration, as recorded by the letter of September 25, 1869 from US Secretary of State Fish to US Minister Motley. *Ibid.*, pp. 28-35.

Indeed, Carlos Calvo has been misread and misquoted in connection with international arbitration involving State party disputes. Although he championed the principle that foreigners, like nationals, should be subject to the laws of the State in which they reside or conduct their activities,[10] his treatise only explicitly requires their submission to the exclusive jurisdiction of the national courts of such State regarding damages suffered as a result of civil wars or infighting within that very State; these scenarios therefore exclude or at least limit the possibility of diplomatic protection.[11] Outside that specific context, Carlos Calvo never denied the possibility of submitting disputes arising out of unequal treatment of foreigners to international arbitration.

On the contrary, already before the *Alabama* decision, certainly aware that the alternative to the peaceful resolution of disputes involving foreigners (e.g., through arbitration) was foreign military intervention, Carlos Calvo explicitly voiced his positive views regarding international arbitration in previous editions of his treatise:[12]

> Le jour où l'opinion par sa pression croissante sera parvenue à imposer aux nations le recours à l'arbitrage, ce jour-là l'opinion, par la même pression, sera en mesure d'imposer également aux parties contestantes le respect de décisions arbitrales, comme cela du reste a eu constamment lieu, car il n'est point de cas qu'on puisse citer où des Etats, ayant remis leur différend au jugement des arbitres, aient tenté même de se soustraire aux effets de la sentence prononcée contre eux.

Carlos Calvo's support for international arbitration is further illustrated by over 80 pages in his treatise which are dedicated to a favorable evaluation of decisions of international arbitral tribunals in a number of State party disputes, some of which originated (in one way or another) in the operations or conduct of private foreign

10. C. Calvo. III *Le Droit International Théorique et Pratique* (5th ed. Arthur Rousseau Ed. 1896), para. 1276, p. 138.
11. *Ibid.*, para. 1280, p. 142. This is confirmed, for example, by the intervention of Carlos Calvo appointed as Chargé d'affaires by the Paraguayan Government, before the British government in the Santiago Canstatt case. Mr. Canstatt took part in a conspiracy to kill the then Paraguayan president and was, with other accomplices, tried before a criminal court and sentenced to death (this was later commuted and he was freed in response to British intercession). Allegedly (although this is not free from doubt), the British government requested economic compensation for the deprivation of Mr. Canstatt's liberty due to his status as a British national. Through Calvo's intervention (he also secured three legal opinions from Robert Phillimore, Britain's then leading authority in international law, in support of the Paraguayan position), the Republic of Paraguay and Great Britain signed an agreement on October 14, 1862 putting an end to the dispute. Article 1 of this agreement recognized the jurisdiction of Paraguayan courts to apply its laws. However, this case, with direct intervention by Carlos Calvo, exclusively concerned the criminal jurisdiction of Paraguayan courts in a case involving a capital crime against the President of Paraguay. *Ibid.*, para. 1270, pp. 130-133. For a full file on the Canstatt case, including diplomatic correspondence and legal opinions, *see Cuestión Canstatt, Documentos Oficiales cambiados entre la Legación de la República del Paraguay y el Gobierno de su Majestad Británica con motivo de dicha cuestión, que terminó por la convención firmada en la Asunción el 14 de octubre de 1862* (1864). Besanzon [sic] José Jacquin printer.
12. Calvo, C. (1870-1872). *Le droit international théorique et pratique* III (4th ed. 1887). [Paris, G. Pedone Lauriel, Guillaumin et Cie, Arthur Rousseau, Marchal Billard Eds], para. 1806, pp. 514-515.

individuals.[13] The Calvo Doctrine should then be differentiated from the Calvo Clause (wrongly attributed to Carlos Calvo).

The importance of this evolution in the resolution of State party disputes found its way into world literature. See, for example, these lines from August Strindberg's *The German Lieutenant:*[14]

> "Ladies and gentlemen!" said the Englishman, raising his voice, while a waiter placed a tray with filled champagne glasses on the table. "Ladies and Gentlemen" he repeated, "this means, according to the telegram I have just received, that the first International Tribunal at Geneva has finished its work; this means that a war between two nations, *or what would have been worse—a war against the future,* has been prevented; that a hundred thousand Americans and as many Englishmen have to thank this day that they are alive. The Alabama Question has been settled not to the advantage of America, but of justice, not to the injury of England, but for the good of future generations" (emphasis added).

And most certainly bearing in mind the *Alabama* decision and Alexander II of Russia's award in the case of *Peruvian Barque María Luz,*[15] James Joyce wrote in *Ulysses* as follows:[16]

13. *Ibid.*, paras. 1706-1806, pp. 432-515.
14. A. Strindberg, *The German Lieutenant and Other Stories,* Echo Library (2014) at 30.
15. Award of Czar Alexander II in the Peruvian *Barque María Luz* case of 17 (29) May 1875 as cited in: J. Bassett Moore. V *History and Digest of the International Arbitrations to Which the United States Has Been a Party,* Washington Government Printing Office (1898), pp. 5035-5036. For antecedents of this case *see also* Authority of the Foreign Department of Japan. *Case of the Peruvian Barque Maria Luz.* Tokyo and Yokohama, Japan (1872). The dispute arose from actions taken by the Japanese authorities in connection with a Peruvian vessel, its crew and passengers. It was found that the vessel, which came to the Japanese coast in distress and was anchored in the port of Kanagawa for refitting, was transporting Chinese mostly illiterate *coolies*, who had been misled to believe that they had been legally hired to work in Peru when actually they were transported to that country as slave labor. By a decision of a Japanese court, which found that the *coolies* had been forcibly detained on board and cruelly treated by the captain and his crew, the Japanese authorities prevented the ship from leaving port, issued an order allowing all *coolies* to go ashore at Yokohama, refused to return those who had already fled to Japanese territory and found that the company owning the ship was guilty of wrongdoing. Notwithstanding the protestations of foreign consuls in Japan from practically all European powers, allegations that Japanese law was not up to the international law standards invoked by Japan (since it accepted certain forms of slave labor domestically), and accusations that Japanese courts lacked jurisdiction since the Chinese workers had been hired in Macao (then under Portuguese control which conditioned Japan's jurisdiction based on extraterritoriality agreements between Portugal and Japan), the arbitrator found that ".... the Japanese Government acted in good faith in virtue of its own laws and customs, without infringing the general prescriptions of the law of nations, or the stipulations of the particular treaties." It is worth mentioning that Czar Alexander II abolished serfdom in Russia (which may explain his abhorrence of slavery). However, despite some other progressive reforms, he did not abate police controls on dissenters who wanted to see more profound political changes (liberals, revolutionaries or anarchists), which led to the disenchantment of those who initially saw in him a democratizing force after the tyrannical rule of the previous Nicholas I. Czar, E.H. Carr. *The Romantic Exiles,* Serif London (1998), pp. 181-182, 191. Alexander II survived several attempts on his life until his final assassination in 1881.
16. J. Joyce. *Ulysses* (1946 ed.). Modern Library (1920), p. 574.

> Let us sit down somewhere and discuss, Struggle for life is the law of existence, but modern *philinerists*, notably the tsar and the king of England, have invented arbitration.[17]

Certainly, the historic background depicted above is not the same today. However, it serves as a useful reminder of the positive role played by international arbitration in contributing to the evolution of and respect for the rule of law in the international arena, including the area of investment disputes, and the importance of keeping that role alive and well.

Nevertheless, certain recent developments show an incipient different orientation, as illustrated, for example, by Article 8.27 of the Comprehensive Economic and Trade Agreement between Canada and the European Union (***CETA***), which entrusts decisions on investment disputes to a permanent tribunal (closer to an international court than to a real arbitral tribunal). This tribunal is composed of fifteen members (five Canadian, five EU nationals and five from third countries) elected for five-year terms that are renewable once; they are all appointed by the CETA Joint Committee, the members of which are appointed pursuant to CETA Article 26.1 by the CETA Member States. The members of the Appellate Tribunal are also appointed by the CETA Joint Committee, and pursuant to CETA Article 8.28.

Clearly, these provisions substantially depart from fundamental traits characterizing international arbitration, not only because the appointment of these tribunals' members is not made on a case-by-case basis but also because the private party involved has no say in the constitution of the tribunal that will hear the specific dispute at stake.

Only time will tell if developments like this will really be beneficial for the resolution of investment disputes—not only in terms of the substantive outcome of such disputes but also with regard to the neutrality and efficiency of the dispute resolution process and the fostering of the international circulation of capital and economic resources in accordance with standards of predictability and security. The replacement of a dispute resolution mechanism with a different one should be the result of a rational evaluation of what better serves the advancement of the rule of law against a background which elicits the trust of all those participating in the procedure rather than a response to political pressure or pseudoscientific or pseudo-sociological considerations.

In any case, this shift away from traditional investment arbitration does not seem to be substantiated by hard facts. If statistics are to be relied upon in this respect, out of 530 investor-State disputes concluded as of July 31, 2017, about one-third were decided in favor of the State, one quarter in favor of the investor, and the remaining cases were settled, discontinued or decided in favor of neither party.[18] Even in the cases decided in favor of investors, amounts awarded to them on average equaled 40% of the amounts claimed. From this data, it is not possible to conclude that arbitral decisions of investment disputes are arbitrary, biased or more favorable to a private party, or that

17. *Philinerists* (from the Greek) meaning "peace loving monarchs."
18. UNCTAD. *Issue 3: International Investment Agreements. Special Update on Investor-State Dispute Settlement: Facts and Figures* (2017), pp. 1, 3.

such party is unreasonably compensated when it succeeds in its claim. It would then seem that beyond political reasons leading to shifts in attitudes regarding international arbitration in investment disputes described above, there are no rational explanations for not resorting to traditional arbitration in this regard.

Consequently, it is submitted that the jury is still out on these matters. On the one hand, the apparent disrepute of traditional international arbitration and, as a result, the authority of international arbitrators to decide investment disputes is not proven and is unwarranted. On the other, it remains to be seen if the new tribunals set up in accordance with the recent developments described above will be free from the real or imaginary defects attributed to the existing system of international arbitration, or if they will contribute to the creation of an evenhanded, efficient and less costly dispute resolution mechanism for investment disputes. Another question is to what extent these tribunals will substantially depart in their decisions from the important contributions to the evolution of international law concerning foreign investments by awards made, and that continue to be made, within the traditional arbitration context. In this, like in so many other questions, the challenge is not only to prevent the unwise sacrifice of the past and present but first and foremost not (in Strindberg's words) to "war against the future."

CHAPTER 11

The Governance of Arbitral Institutions: How to Improve Standards Through Accreditation

Juan Fernández-Armesto[*]

Guillermo Aguilar Álvarez was my oldest friend in the world of arbitration. In the early 2000s, we discussed the possibility of jointly creating a boutique of arbitrators. Alas, it was not to be. He devoted a substantial part of his professional life to arbitral institutions: the International Chamber of Commerce (ICC) first and the Arbitration Center of Mexico (CAM) thereafter. We spoke many times about their governance. I am almost certain that, if he were still with us (as I fervently wish), he would have supported my proposal.

In June 2019, Alexis Mourre, the then President of the ICC Court, called for arbitral institutions to safeguard their legitimacy by agreeing internationally accepted standards of good governance. He admitted that there was a long way to go before the arbitral community reached a consensus on the scope of these standards, 'but the world is moving faster than we do, and such an effort would greatly contribute to establish the legitimacy of international arbitration as a global system of justice in the twenty years to come'.[1]

The world is indeed moving fast: since President Mourre spoke, the *Club Español del Arbitraje* has approved and published its 2019 'Code of Best Practices in Arbitration',[2] a compilation of soft law defining standards of conduct for arbitrators, lawyers

* I acknowledge the support of my colleague Melanie Riofrío in the preparation of this chapter.
1. Alexis Mourre, Keynote Address, GAR Live Istanbul, 20 June 2019, available for download at https://globalarbitrationreview.com/mourre-warns-against-nationalisation-of-arbitration (last accessed 12 December 2021).
2. Available in Spanish, English, and Portuguese at www.clubarbitraje.com.

and experts, and also for arbitral institutions. This is a world premiere: the first time that best practices for arbitral institutions have ever been compiled.[3]

It is indeed surprising that the governance and proper behaviour of arbitral institutions have received so little attention.[4] Historically, institutions arose as simple service providers: collecting fees from users and, in exchange, organizing the arbitration procedure. But nowadays, institutions have become much more than that. Arbitration has morphed into a transnational system of justice. And within this system, institutions perform a (growing) array of public functions, exercising both private and public regulatory powers. Institutions admit or reject claims, designate arbitrators, decide challenges, remove arbitrators, scrutinize awards and publish them. Warwas, who devoted her 2017 doctoral thesis to these issues, concludes that institutions, when exercising these public regulatory powers, suffer a 'democratic deficit', which 'call[s] for increasing public accountability'.[5]

There are two avenues which can be followed to fill this perceived gap in 'public accountability' of arbitral institutions. The first is enactment of legislation. The second is voluntary change through soft law:

(i) The UNCITRAL Model Law does not contain any provisions regulating the legal status of arbitration institutions. Neither does the New York Convention. The scarcity of rules is echoed at the domestic level: as a rule, municipal laws do not provide detailed requirements for the structure and operation of arbitration institutions; there are no mandatory characteristics or rules of governance. Most legal regimes also fail to impose a duty to obtain administrative authorization or registration. Finally, the inexistence of a government-controlled supervisory agency, with inspection and sanctioning powers, is also almost universal.

This *'laissez faire'* situation has been one of the factors which have permitted arbitration to grow into a truly transnational system of justice: international institutions regulated and supervised by the states of incorporation would have hamstrung the development of arbitration. In this largely unregulated area, arbitration consumers have been able to make informed decisions, choosing independent and impartial centres, and rejecting those of dubious reputation. That said, market forces have been unable to totally abolish disorganized and ill-equipped centres, which continue to operate, often at the expense of justice and to the prejudice of users. As Paulsson famously said:

3. The drafting committee included twenty-one experts, chaired by José Ricardo Feris, and advised by an expert committee with representatives of arbitration institutions.
4. An exception is Weber-Stecher's essay 'Principles of Good Governance and Organisation of Arbitral Institutions', in 'Arbitral Institutions under Scrutiny' (edited by Philipp Habegger, Daniel Hochstrasser, Gabrielle Nater-Bass and Urs Weber-Stecher), ASA Special Series No. 40, Juris, 2013.
5. Barbara Alicja Warwas: 'The Liability of Arbitral Institutions: Legitimacy Challenges and Functional Responses', T.M.C. Asser Press, 2017, p. 68.

> My observations of the world of arbitration lead me to believe that many if not most arbitral institutions are empty edifices waiting for someone to bother to dismantle them. Others cannot get away from features of cronyism, which were their *raison d'être* in the first place.[6]

But this situation of legislative '*laissez faire*' is changing.

As Galina Zukova has shown, a significant number of jurisdictions in Central and Eastern Europe, in Latin America as well as some countries in Africa and the Middle East, and finally China, are increasingly issuing detailed rules for the establishment, operation, and oversight of arbitral institutions.[7] The rationale for the detailed regulation and strong regulatory control is different across jurisdictions: for some countries, the main reason is to bring order into an otherwise wild market and to suppress abuse. For others, the rationale is diametrically opposite: to promote and encourage alternative dispute resolution services.[8]

(ii) The alternative to hard law is soft law: voluntary rules, codes of best practices not drafted by the legislator but rather by experts, at the instigation of trade associations, users, or supervisors. In the case of arbitral institutions, associations of arbitration users are probably best placed to prepare meaningful soft law because users have a heightened interest in improving and developing arbitration and are free of institutional conflicts of interest.

I THE CODE OF BEST PRACTICES OF THE SPANISH ARBITRATION CLUB

The background described above led the association of Spanish-speaking users of arbitration, the *Club Español del Arbitraje*, to take up in 2018 the challenge of preparing the first-ever code of best practices for arbitral institutions.

The Code is a lengthy instrument, with seven chapters divided into 156 Recommendations, which cover institutions, arbitrators, lawyers, experts, and financing. The first chapter, comprising Recommendations (Recitals) 1 through 64, is devoted to arbitral institutions. It is divided into five sections.

Section 1 defines the two overarching principles to which institutions are subject:

(1) institutions must be independent ('no third party shall participate in, or exercise any influence over, the taking of decisions', says Recitals 1); and

6. Jan Paulsson: 'Moral Hazard in International Dispute Resolution', ICSID Review - Foreign Investment Law Journal, Volume 25, Issue 2, Fall 2010, pp. 339-355 (Article based on the author's Inaugural Lecture as Holder of the Michael R. Klein Distinguished Scholar Chair, University of Miami School of Law, April 29, 2010).
7. Galina Zukova: 'Arbitration Institutions: Establishment, Attributes, Regulatory Supervision', IntALR, Volume 4, 2016, p. 102.
8. *Ibid.*, p. 111.

(2) institutions must be rule based, with bylaws governing their internal structure, and procedural rules for the arbitrations which they administer.

Nothing innovative so far. What is new is Recital 4, with an added requirement for 'integrated institutions', i.e., for those centres which lack legal personality and form part of larger organizations (normally Chambers of Commerce). These institutions must not only enjoy functional independence (they must have 'bodies that are independent of the parent organization' and the right to 'freely designate and remove' officers and employees) but also financial independence (they must have their own budget and annual accounts, 'to be approved by its bodies'). Money is king: without financial independence, functional independence is merely a façade.

Section 2 is much more prescriptive. It requires institutions to create four bodies and provides detailed regulation on how such bodies must operate. The four bodies are:

(1) the Board, responsible for overall governance and for all financial matters, to be chaired by its own President;
(2) the Court, which adopts all technical decisions regarding specific arbitration procedures, headed by a separate President;
(3) the Secretariat, entrusted with the day-to-day administration of procedures; and
(4) finally, the Appointments Committee, with the task of proposing candidates to fill vacancies in the other bodies.

The Code establishes a sophisticated system of checks and balances between these four bodies:

(1) vacancies can only be filled upon a proposal of the Appointments Committee, a small group of up to five independent outside experts, 'with a very lengthy career in arbitration', designated by the Board for a single term of six years, and which cannot be dismissed save in exceptional circumstances;
(2) the Board defines the overall policy of the Centre, approves the budget and designates the Secretary General and the members of the Court (always at the proposal of the Appointments Committee);
(3) the Court takes all relevant decisions regarding specific arbitrations procedures; its members cannot be dismissed save for good cause and (again) upon proposal of the Appointments Committee;
(4) the Secretary General heads the Secretariat, administers procedures under the supervision of the Court, and in administrative or financial matters reports to the Board.

Section 3 requires that each institution approve and publish a mandatory Code of Ethics to be applied to the members of its bodies and to all employees. The Code of Best Practices sets a minimum floor, with institutions being authorized to adopt stronger requirements:

- all members of bodies and all employees must disclose conflicts of interest regarding individual arbitration procedures, withdrawing from discussions and abstaining in decisions affected by such conflicts;
- there is a general prohibition of receiving gifts or any other form of compensations from parties, lawyers, experts, arbitrators;
- staff is prohibited from providing legal advice or from making recommendations;
- members and employees are not authorized to act as arbitrators (except if both parties agree once the dispute has arisen);
- various 'Chinese walls' must be created to thwart improper access to confidential information.

The next section is devoted to the administration of arbitration procedures.

The designation of arbitrators is one of the key functions of any arbitral institution.

As a general rule, the Code discourages the use of a list of arbitrators – but if the institution opts for a list, the Code provides detailed criteria (Recitals 54 and 55).

Instead, the Code opts for a dual approach:

- designations of candidates made by the parties will be respected (subject to the candidates meeting the tests of availability, independence, and impartiality);
- subsidiarily, the designation will be made by the Court, using an enhanced list procedure: candidates will be proposed by both parties, the list will be topped up by the institution, parties are then entitled to veto one-third of the proposed names, and to rank the rest in order of preference; the preferred candidate will be chosen.

The aim of this (complex) list procedure is to create a system of checks and balances: the power to propose candidates is shared between the parties and the institution; parties additionally enjoy the right to veto certain names proposed by others; and the ranking creates an objective system for selecting the most acceptable candidate.

As an exception, in expedited and small amount disputes, the Code permits that arbitrators be directly appointed by the Board of the institutions – without resorting to the list procedure. The underlying reason is to streamline the process, and to permit the incorporation into the system of younger, less well-known arbitrators: the enhanced list procedure tends to favour designations from a small pool of arbitrators with a long track record.

The Code also devotes a subsection (Recitals 56 through 59) to the financial management of the proceedings, providing that fee schedules must be public, that institutions are prohibited from charging fees to arbitrators (a commonplace malpractice in certain jurisdictions), and that advances of funds made by parties must be held in separate bank accounts (to minimize insolvency risk).

The last section is devoted to transparency.

Here the Code breaks with one of the most negative, but at the same time most resilient, traditions of arbitration: secrecy. The insistence on secrecy in arbitration was instilled into the system by the founding fathers. In 2009 Serge Lazareff still said: 'If, as Ihering wrote, form is the twin sister of freedom, then confidentiality is the twin sister of arbitration.'[9]

In the present times, this position is untenable: we – thankfully – live in a world where citizens are not cowed by authority, but demand knowledge, as an instrument for increased assertiveness. The quest extends to all walks of life and all areas of society: patients require to be fairly informed about their illness and their chance of recovery; investors demand to be provided with all relevant information affecting listed companies; 'Freedom of Information' Acts grant citizens the right to inspect government records. In all jurisdictions, judgments are public – there is no rule of law if justice is not publicly administered, and in the most progressive countries, the entire judicial records are open to inspection by citizens.[10]

The Code, aware of these changes in perception, requires institutions to adopt a policy of full transparency (set forth in Recitals 60 through 64):

> *First*, institutions must operate a corporate webpage, providing full information regarding their governance system; indicating the names and curriculum vitae of the members of the various corporate bodies; identifying sponsors, and the amounts received. The page must also include a calculator of fees and costs. Additionally, institutions are required to publish their annual accounts, as well as detailed statistics on arbitrator appointments, broken down by age, gender, and geographic origin.
> *Second*, institutions must publish on their webpage a list of all cases administered; the names of the parties can be anonymized, but those of arbitrators and counsel must be identified; the webpage must also identify the dates when the arbitration was commenced and when the award was rendered – permitting parties to judge the relationships between parties and arbitrators and the efficiency of the procedure.
> *Third*, the Code establishes, as a general rule, that institutions must publish awards within a brief period following their approval, anonymizing the names of the parties but keeping the names of the arbitrators and counsel.[11] The Code only permits an exception if a party expressly objects (or the institution considers that there are relevant grounds justifying confidentiality). But even in those cases, a summary or redacted extract, with the names of arbitrators and lawyers, may (and should) be published.

The general rule of publicity also applies to the Court's decisions on arbitrator challenges and replacements.

9. Serge Lazareff, 'Confidentiality and Arbitration' in 'Confidentiality in Arbitration 2009 Special Supplement ICC Bulletin', p. 81.
10. For a full discussion of secrecy and transparency in arbitration, *see* Juan Fernández-Armesto: 'The Time Has Come: A Plea for Abandoning Secrecy in Arbitration', in CAPJA2012-3-002 Cahiers de l'Arbitrage, July 1, 2012 No. 3, p. 583.
11. The advantages of publishing awards are set forth in Juan Fernández-Armesto, *supra* n. 10, pp. 585-587.

II ENFORCEMENT OF THE CODE

The great advantage, and at the same time, the greatest weakness of soft law is its voluntary character. The Code is not legislation; it simply reflects the opinion of the *Club Español del Arbitraje*. The Club's opinions may carry certain weight because the Club is the main association of Spanish-speaking arbitration users, and the rules were developed through a careful process of research and consultation, weighing various alternatives and selecting the best for fostering the use of arbitration. But institutions are, of course, free to comply with the Code in part or in full, or even to totally disregard it (hopefully not!).

Does this mean that the Code is useless? That it will never achieve its aim of improving the governance of arbitral institutions?

An answer to this question may be found in a parallel area, the reform of governance in listed companies. The movement to improve corporate governance started in the last decades of the 20th century, and soft law proved a valuable tool in fostering improvement in an area traditionally reluctant to change. The United Kingdom was the first jurisdiction to advocate the use of a voluntary corporate governance code (the so-called *Cadbury Code*), and the idea then spread to many other jurisdictions, including Spain (where the *Código Olivencia* was the first step in a succession of soft-law regulations).[12] These codes were voluntary, and listed companies were free to comply or not with their recommendations. But securities regulators developed the 'comply or explain' principle: listed companies were obliged to publicly explain the reasons justifying non-compliance. The expectation was that markets would punish those companies which failed to adapt their governance structure to the recommended best practices, and that eventually, compliance would become universal – as in fact it did.

In his recent keynote address, Alexis Mourre proposed a similar approach for international arbitration: he advocates an accreditation procedure for institutions, 'based on internationally accepted standards of independence, good governance and transparency'.[13] He further proposes that the International Council for Commercial Arbitration (ICCA) and the International Federation of Commercial Arbitration Institutions (IFCAI) join forces to perform this task.

I wholeheartedly support his approach. Arbitral institutions require reform. Their governance structure must be updated. Users demand additional information. Transparency must become the norm. The Code of the *Club Español del Arbitraje* is a bold step in the right direction. It will not be the last: it is likely that other players within the arbitration community will embark on similar projects. I would hope that these new codes, if and when they arrive, result in standards being watered-up, not watered-down.

12. For an analysis of the early developments in Spain, *see* Fernández-Armesto/Hernández: 'El gobierno de las sociedades cotizadas: situación actual y reformas pendientes', Papeles de la Fundación FAES núm 56, 2000.
13. Alexis Mourre, *supra* n. 1, p. 18.

In any case, the enforcement impasse will remain. The way forward is the principle 'comply or explain', borrowed from the area of corporate governance of listed companies. An independent third party - be it the *Club Español del Arbitraje* or ICCA - should assume the task of assessing whether individual arbitral institutions are or not applying best practices in their internal governance - as reflected in the Club's Code or a future alternative regulation. Non-compliant institutions must be given the opportunity to explain their choice. Users will have full information. And in the end, they will dictate judgment by taking their cases to those institutions which offer the best mix of efficiency and legitimacy.

Periculum est in mora. Up to now, arbitral institutions have been - to a very large extent - outside the scope of domestic legislation. This has proved a bonus: under this '*laissez faire*' approach, institutions have thrived, and arbitration has developed into a global system of justice. A reform of the institutions' governance has now become urgent. Soft law and the principle of 'comply or explain' offer a way ahead. The arbitration community should follow it. If not, domestic legislators will fill the vacuum.

CHAPTER 12

Proving Corruption in International Arbitration: The Utility of "Red Flags"

Edward G. Kehoe & Aloysius Llamzon[*]

Corruption has been a ubiquitous and mendacious reality in international commerce for hundreds of years,[1] but its centrality as a legal issue whose consequences can affect the entire outcome of a case is only now emerging as the international community, particularly the influential financial centers such as the U.S., U.K, and Switzerland, take more seriously the thorny issue of combatting corruption. The emergence of international arbitration as one of the few areas in the international legal order that can effectively punish corruption[2] is to be celebrated, but presents complications of its own. Among these is a basic issue: *how does one prove corruption?*

---

* We dedicate this chapter to the memory of our friend, colleague, and teacher Guillermo Aguilar Álvarez. He was, simply, a gentleman and a scholar, who practiced with passion and integrity, and was devoted to family. His absence continues to be felt deeply. The area of transnational anti-corruption was one of the final acts of service Guillermo pursued outside the daily practice of law—we knew of his dedicated work toward creating an anti-corruption framework under North American Free Trade Agreement (NAFTA), a fitting extension to his many years of dedication to that treaty and to international law and public order.

For their influence on the authors' thinking on red flags, they thank Lucinda Low, James Castello, Doak Bishop, and Rami Chahine. Our gratitude also to the editors, Michael Reisman and Nigel Blackaby. All errors are our own, of course.

1. For multinational enterprise, that history goes back to the East India companies and the corruption it engendered in South and Southeast Asia, as well as in European capitals. *See* ALOYSIUS LLAMZON, CORRUPTION IN INTERNATIONAL INVESTMENT ARBITRATION 6-7 (2014); Padideh Ala'i, *The Legacy of Geographical Morality and Colonialism: A Historical Assessment of the Current Crusade Against Corruption*, 33 VAND. J. TRANSN'L. L. 877 (2000).
2. *See* ALOYSIUS LLAMZON, CORRUPTION IN INTERNATIONAL INVESTMENT ARBITRATION 81-82 (2014) ("Having examined the international legal framework currently governing transnational corruption, one realizes that there are few provisions with real teeth from which a truly effective *international* system of control can be built. [...] Because the political will to bring these programmes into reality does not exist (and may well never do so), a more effective and realistic proposition may be to utilize the existing mechanisms already established in international law. Perhaps the area with the most potential among these is international arbitration, particularly arbitration under

Because bribery is bilateral in nature,[3] requiring cooperation between the supplier of the bribe and its recipient (often a public official), *both* sides of the corrupt transaction have an incentive to hide the evidence, which they often do under the veneer of legal transactions designed to withstand initial scrutiny. As arbitral tribunals decide issues of bribery and influence peddling through reasoned written awards, the case law shows that corruption generally is difficult to prove. While there have been a few important instances where the key elements of bribery were openly admitted during the proceedings,[4] corruption issues are more often made on the basis of probabilities arising from circumstantial evidence. The "smoking gun" evidence of the quid pro quo that characterizes bribery[5] rarely comes to light, befitting its clandestine nature. Recognizing this reality, the UN Convention Against Corruption does not require direct evidence of bribery, trading in influence, and other offenses—inferences built on objective facts are permitted.[6] As Article 28 of the Convention states: "[k]nowledge, intent or purpose required as an element of an offense established in accordance with this Convention *may be inferred from objective factual circumstances*."[7]

Compounding the difficulty of proving corruption is another reality embedded in the nature of transnational commerce and investment: that doing business in unfamiliar jurisdictions is difficult, and often requires transactional relationships with prominent local businesses and individuals that, at least in part, have the objective of reducing friction in government interactions. Sometimes these relationships take the form of consultancy and agency relationships, but they also oftentimes are more involved, with joint venture or partnership relationships that would give the local

bilateral and multilateral investment treaties that by definition involve the primary actors in transnational corruption—foreign investors and host States").

3. *See* Aloysius Llamzon & Anthony Sinclair, *Investor Wrongdoing in Investment Arbitration: Standards Governing Issues of Corruption, Fraud, Misrepresentation and Other Investor Misconduct, in* LEGITIMACY: MYTHS, REALITIES, CHALLENGES, ICCA INTERNATIONAL ARBITRATION CONGRESS SERIES NO. 18 460-61 (A.J. van den Berg ed., 2015) ("The inherently bilateral nature of corruption is unique among the species of investor wrongdoing, unlike fraud, misrepresentation or other forms of wrongdoing that are essentially unilateral acts perpetrated by an investor against the host State. Often but not always in violation of the host State's national legislation, corruption is only consummated when there is a meeting of offer and acceptance between the investor and public officials of the host State (often via intermediaries)").
4. *See* World Duty Free Company Limited v. The Republic of Kenya (ICSID Case No. ARB/00/7), Award, October 4, 2006; Metal-Tech Ltd. v. Republic of Uzbekistan (ICSID Case No. ARB/10/3), Award, October 4, 2013.
5. Under the UN Convention Against Corruption, Article 16(1) defines bribery: "*Any promise, offering, or giving* to a (foreign) public official, directly or indirectly, of an undue financial or other advantage *in order that* the official act or refrain from acting in the exercise of his or her official duties, *for the purpose of* obtaining business advantages" [emphasis supplied]. Quid pro quo is one of the key differentiators of bribery from trading in influence (or influence peddling, in more common parlance), the other key form of corruption that is relevant to transnational commerce and investment. *See* Aloysius Llamzon, *Trading in Influence, in* UNITED NATIONS CONVENTION AGAINST CORRUPTION: A COMMENTARY (C. Rose et al. eds., 2019).
6. Michael Kubiciel and Cornelia Spörl, *Article 28, in* UNITED NATIONS CONVENTION AGAINST CORRUPTION: A COMMENTARY 292 (C. Rose et al. eds., 2019).
7. UN Convention Against Corruption, Article 28 ("Knowledge, Intent, and Purpose as Elements of an Offense").

partners a stake in the business.[8] These relationships are not particularly problematic in and of themselves—it has long been recognized by arbitrators that such relationships are necessary if transnational investment is to be made at scale.[9]

But anyone who has engaged with these phenomena in practice understands that these relationships can take on forms that are similar to those used by corrupt parties disguising corruption: local parties are promised or paid sizeable sums of money in order to help ensure the success of the business and the relevant agreements that document this intention often can invite puzzlement over what might appear to be a lack of overt, hard "value" brought into the new enterprise. Not surprisingly, such relationships have, in fact, been the subject of intense scrutiny in a number of recent corruption-related decisions in international arbitration.[10]

Arbitrators are thus under considerable pressure to ascertain the truth from circumstantial evidence, an undeniably subjective enterprise whether one uses an ordinary or heightened standard of proof.[11] It is out of the desire to introduce a greater sense of objectivity into the decision-making process that the concept of "red flags" of corruption was embraced and used in arbitral decision-making. But the "red flags" concept is one imported from the world of regulatory compliance, a tool developed to warn private businesses (and the private and public institutions that fund them) about certain practices that need to be taken into account as exposing that enterprise to a heightened risk of corruption. Can those "red flags" effectively be employed in a manner that is consistent with established rules for proving whether an offense has or has not been committed, i.e., proving the legal elements of bribery or influence peddling? And if so, how?

---

8. *Compare, e.g.*, Metal-Tech v. Uzbekistan (consultancy agreement alleged to be evidence of bribery) *with* Unión Fenosa Gas S.A. v. Arab Republic of Egypt, ICSID Case No. ARB/14/4, Award, August 31, 2018 (joint venture agreement with local shareholder and joint venture partner alleged to be evidence of bribery).
9. *See* International Thunderbird Gaming Corporation v. The United Mexican States, NAFTA/UNCITRAL, Award, January 26, 2006, Separate Opinion of Professor Thomas Wälde, para. 147 ("[t]here is no foreign investment where a close interaction, mostly with use of local consultants, with the government can be avoided. The whiff of corruption can therefore be made to appear in virtually any foreign investment project").
10. *See* Metal-Tech Ltd. v. Republic of Uzbekistan (ICSID Case No. ARB/10/3), Award, October 4, 2013; Spentex Netherlands BV v. Republic of Uzbekistan, ICSID Case No. ARB/13/26, Award, December 27, 2016; Vladislav Kim v. Republic of Uzbekistan, ICSID Case No. ARB/10/3, Decision on Jurisdiction, March 8, 2017; Unión Fenosa Gas S.A. v. Arab Republic of Egypt, ICSID Case No. ARB/14/4, Award, August 31, 2018.
11. Both the heightened, "clear and convincing" standard as well as the ordinary "preponderance of evidence" standard have existed side by side in the case law for some time. Some arbitral tribunals have chosen one or the other; others seem unwilling to commit to a particular standard. A recent award that attempts to bridge this divide is found in *Niko v. Bangladesh*, where the Tribunal stated: "... the less formalistic sensibility of Rompetrol and Metal-Tech towards the evidentiary rules to be applied to corruption issues is helpful. Because corruption is a serious charge with serious consequences attached, the degree of confidence a tribunal should have in the evidence of that corruption must be high. However, this does not mean that the standard of proof itself should necessarily be higher, or that circumstantial evidence, inferences, or presumptions and indicators of possible corruption (such as 'red flags') cannot come to the aid of the fact-finder. Tribunals are given the freedom and burden of choice, which they should not abdicate by rote reference to an abstract 'heightened' standard of proof" (*quoting* LLAMZON, CORRUPTION IN INTERNATIONAL INVESTMENT ARBITRATION para. 9.26 (2014)).

These are particularly important questions in light of the very serious consequences attendant on a finding of corruption, particularly in investment treaty arbitration. Although there are indications that the ground is shifting toward a more proportional and merits-based treatment of corruption's consequences,[12] the case law, for the most part, continues to treat corruption as potentially fatal to a claimant's ability to obtain any redress at all in international arbitration: a finding that bribery was committed would result in a denial of jurisdiction, no matter what harm might have been caused by the State to the investor.

The remainder of this brief chapter will look into both the theory and recent case law concerning the use of red flags, before offering a few observations in conclusion. In so doing, we honor the memory of Guillermo Aguilar Álvarez, who always insisted on considering the underlying reasons behind doctrine, probing whether particular principles effectively perpetuated public order and combining theory and practice in a way that is particularly needed when considering the use and potential misuse of "red flags" in international arbitration.

I WHAT KIND OF "CORRUPTION" ARE RED FLAGS UTILIZED FOR?

Before discussing the origins and applications of "red flags" analysis, it is important to first define the specific forms of corruption to which that analysis should be employed. Corruption is a polyvalent word that serves as a catchall for a variety of distinct offenses—from trading in influence, to money laundering, to bribery, among others.[13] There is no offense of "corruption" as such.

12. Examples of this can be found in both contract-based and treaty-based arbitration. In contract-based arbitration, the English law precedents that supported *World Duty Free v. Kenya*'s finding that a concession contract tainted by corruption must require dismissal of those claims outright (arguably an inadmissibility finding on grounds of unclean hands) has been overturned expressly by the U.K. Supreme Court in Patel v. Mirza, 2016 UKSC 42. In the realm of treaty arbitration, *see* Vladislav Kim and others v. Republic of Uzbekistan, ICSID Case No. ARB/13/6, Decision on Jurisdiction, March 8, 2017, para. 20 ("Tribunal must balance the object[ive] of promoting economic relations by providing a stable investment framework with the harsh consequence of denying the application of the BIT in total when the investment is not made in compliance with legislation. The denial of the protections of the BIT is a harsh consequence that is a proportional response only when its application is triggered by noncompliance with a law that results in a compromise of a correspondingly significant interest of the Host State"); In the words of Professor Cremades in Fraport I, "[i]f the legality of the Claimant's conduct is a jurisdictional issue, and the legality of the Respondent's conduct is a merits issue, then the Respondent Host State is placed in a powerful position. In the Biblical phrase, the Tribunal must first examine the speck in the eye of the investor and defer, and maybe never address, a beam in the eye of the Host State." Bernardo Cremades, Dissenting Opinion, Fraport v. Philippines (ICSID Case No. ARB/03/25, July 19, 2007, para. 37). *See also* Zachary Douglas, *The Plea of Illegality in Investment Treaty Arbitration,* 29 ICSID Review—Foreign Investment L.J., 176 *(2014)*.
13. The UN Convention Against Corruption has no distinct offense of "corruption"; instead, it identifies a number of offenses that call within the ambit of the term, including Bribery of Domestic Officials (Article 15); Bribery of Foreign Public Officials and Officials of Public International Organizations (Article 16); Embezzlement, Misappropriation or Other Diversion of Property by a Public Official (Article 17); Trading in Influence (Article 18), etc. United Nations Convention Against Corruption, Adopted: October 31, 2003; Entry into force: December 14, 2005.

Although international commercial and investment arbitrators increasingly have been dealing with issues of money laundering and trading in influence, bribery is the most common form of corruption found in the arbitral case law. To be even more precise, the bribery typically involved is "transnational bribery," the most widely accepted definition of which is found in Article 16 of the UN Convention Against Corruption, which in turn was inspired by the OECD Anti-Bribery Convention.[14] The elements of transnational bribery are found in Article 16(1) of United Nations Convention Against Corruption. The article states:

> *Article 16. Bribery of foreign public officials and officials of public international organizations*
>
> 1. Each State Party shall adopt such legislative and other measures as may be necessary to establish as a criminal offence, when committed intentionally, the promise, offering or giving to a foreign public official or an official of a public international organization, directly or indirectly, of an undue advantage, for the official himself or herself or another person or entity, in order that the official act or refrain from acting in the exercise of his or her official duties, in order to obtain or retain business or other undue advantage in relation to the conduct of international business.[15]

The offense of bribery under Article 16(1) thus contains the following elements:

(1) the person committing the offense
(2) "intentionally" (*mens rea)*
(3) "the promise, offering, or giving" (*actus reus)*
(4) "of an undue advantage"
(5) the recipient, who is either "the official himself or herself or another person or entity"
(6) "in order that the official act or refrain from acting in the exercise of his or her official duties" (quid pro quo)
(7) so that the person committing the offense can "obtain or retain business or other undue advantage in relation to the conduct of international business."

All of these elements must be met for bribery to be found—this is true whether one seeks to prove bribery in a criminal court, in a civil court, or before an arbitral tribunal. There is no such thing as a stand-alone offense of "corruption" that arbitrators can identify and punish in civil cases. Some forms of corruption (such as bribery) are universally considered to be serious violations of national and transnational public

14. OECD Convention on Bribery of Foreign Public Officials in International Business Transactions (Adopted: November 21, 1997; Entry into force: February 15, 1999).
15. Notably, UNCAC Article 16(2) contains a nonmandatory provision that states as follows:

> 2. Each State Party shall consider adopting such legislative and other measures as may be necessary to establish as a criminal offence, when committed intentionally, the solicitation or acceptance by a foreign public official or an official of a public international organization, directly or indirectly, of an undue advantage, for the official himself or herself or another person or entity, in order that the official act or refrain from acting in the exercise of his or her official duties.

policy, but others are not so universally proscribed, such as trading in influence, in which it may be difficult to distinguish between legal lobbying and the illegal peddling of influence.[16] The point of emphasis is that the elements necessary to prove bribery do not change in scope whether decided upon in criminal or civil (or even administrative) fora.

What does change, of course, is the standard of proof: the graver consequences of a criminal finding of corruption requires a much higher standard—beyond reasonable doubt—vis-à-vis the primarily economic consequences arising from corruption findings in civil cases. But whatever standard of proof is employed, or under what circumstances the burden of proof (or persuasion) shifts, the first question asked is: what must be proven? Must the elements of a specific form of corruption—bribery, trading in influence, or other offenses—be shown? Or is it sufficient to point to red flags under the idea that once a number of those exist, "corruption" is proven or at least leads to a shifting of the burden of proof (or persuasion) from the party alleging corruption to the party defending against it?

For criminal proceedings, of course, proof beyond reasonable doubt is necessary, given the penalties involved, which often can involve imprisonment for many years, in addition to fines for companies and individuals that can reach hundreds of millions of US dollars. By contrast, in most civil courts—as well as in international arbitration—bribery can be shown by a standard of proof that requires less moral certainty. The exact standard—whether it is a "preponderance of evidence" (roughly, a 51 % likelihood that the evidence weighs in favor of bribery) *or* a heightened standard that is often called "clear and convincing evidence" (something significantly more than a 51 % likelihood, if one is even capable of weighing evidence in this manner)—is one that is debated ceaselessly in the case law and in scholarship.[17] There are good arguments for both sides. The impetus for a heightened standard makes sense when the consequences are high, as they tend to be particularly in investment treaty arbitration, where corruption often is treated as a jurisdiction or admissibility issue, the

16. *See* Kim v. Uzbekistan, ICSID Case No. ARB/13/6, Decision on Jurisdiction, March 8, 2017 ("… the OECD Convention, which Respondent cites as indicative of international public policy, takes as its focus the bribery of government officials. Thus, the titular concern of the OECD Convention is 'Combating Bribery of Foreign Public Officials in International Business Transactions' and the substantive provisions of the Convention bear out this conclusion. The UN Convention, which Respondent also cites, also has this focus. Simultaneously, the Tribunal acknowledges that the effort to combat corruption is an evolving area. Insofar as the UN Convention makes broader reference to '*Trading in Influence,*' or 'Bribery in the Private Sector,' the relevant articles of the Convention use the language *'consider making.'* This language matches the evolving and serious effort to combat corruption. It also suggests a *lower level of consensus* amongst the parties to the Convention as to corruption within the private sector, a sector governed by a broad range of criminal statutes").

    See further Aloysius Llamzon, *Article 18: Trading in Influence, in* The United Nations Convention Against Corruption: A Commentary 192, 193-194 (C. Rose et al. eds., 2019) ("Thus influence peddling—unlike bribery—is not automatically prohibited as a matter of international law and transnational public policy").

17. For a helpful summary, *see* David Weiss, *Distorted Mirrors: Perceived Disagreements Obfuscate the General Principle of law that a Heightened Standard of Proof Applies to Corruption Allegations in Investment Arbitration, in* Investment Treaty Arbitration and International Law 291 (Ian Laird, et al., eds., 2016).

practical effect of which would be a denial of any remedy, no matter how serious a violation of investment protections under the treaty might have occurred. That said, the most recent expressions of the case law seem to indicate that an ordinary standard is applied, albeit with greater care that the quality of the evidence is strong.[18]

Ascertaining the standard of proof is only one part of the decision-making exercise, however. Indeed, it may not even be the starting point of the inquiry. In international *commercial* arbitration, most corruption-related cases involve simulated intermediary agreements—typically agency or consultancy agreements.[19] These contracts are entered into in relation to a larger commercial relationship, usually an investment or sales transaction with a government entity enabled by bribes paid to public officials. An intermediary—sometimes a family member or close associate—facilitates those bribes, with the bribe payment transmitted through the agency or consultancy fee. The agreement that documents the fee would have an arbitration clause; arbitration often is (though not always) part of the scheme. To further mask the illicit nature of the agreement, arbitration is initiated in order to secure a binding award requiring payment. In this way, many corruption issues in commercial arbitration actually involve contracts *for* corruption, that is, simulated agency or consultancy agreements that in reality are created to mask bribes under the guise of legitimate fees. Benefitting the serious rupture in public policy that such contracts cause, the Civil Law Convention on Corruption treats such contracts providing for corruption as void *ab initio*.[20] Usually, none of the parties to the contract of corruption will raise the issue of bribery even when there are disputes about other aspects of the relationship, leaving arbitral tribunals with real challenges, not least to determine the degree to which they must be proactive in ascertaining whether the agency or consultancy agreement is legitimate or simulated. In such situations, having a laundry list of "typical" indicators of corruption—red flags—may be very useful.

By contrast, corruption in *investment* arbitration (as well as in a minority of commercial arbitration cases) involves an assessment of rights and obligations arising from the main investment agreement itself, not any other ancillary agreement. Bribery allegations in these cases typically are focused on whether the principal investment—often a concession or other long-term or high-value contract with the government—was entered into by the State because bribes were paid by the foreign investor to the State's public officials, whether directly or through intermediaries. And unlike arbitrations involving simulated contracts for corruption, in these cases one party—most often the respondent State—accuses the other side of having paid bribes

18. *See* David Weiss, *Distorted Mirrors: Perceived Disagreements Obfuscate the General Principle of law that a Heightened Standard of Proof Applies to Corruption Allegations in Investment Arbitration*, in Ian Laird, *et al.*, eds., INVESTMENT TREATY ARBITRATION AND INTERNATIONAL LAW 291 (2016).
    See discussion in Niko v. Bangladesh, *supra* n. 11 and accompanying text.
19. For a comprehensive survey of corruption cases in international commercial arbitration, *see* ABDULHAY SAYED, CORRUPTION IN INTERNATIONAL TRADE AND COMMERCIAL ARBITRATION (2004).
20. Council of Europe Civil Law Convention on Corruption (Adopted: November 4, 1999; Entry into force: November 1, 2003).

to secure the investment contract.[21] There is, therefore, no need at the outset for arbitrators to look *propio motu* to red flag indicia of corruption because it is the accusing party that brings its evidence of corruption to the proceedings in order to meet its burden of proving that bribery did in fact take place. Curiously, however, it also is within this context—where red flags would seemingly be unnecessary given direct allegations of corruption that can be examined using ordinary rules of evidence—that the idea of employing red flags to facilitate proving corruption has taken the greatest hold. There seems to be no cogent reason for assigning an outsized role to red flags, and yet, as Section III demonstrates, their use persists. To understand why requires a deeper understanding of the original intent behind red flags in the 1970s.

II THE ORIGINAL INTENT OF "RED FLAGS" AND ITS CURRENT USAGE

The concept of "red flags" of corruption originates from efforts spanning several decades to foster greater compliance with national and international anti-corruption norms. The U.S. Foreign Corrupt Practices Act in the 1970s was the first national legislation of wide effect that prohibited and penalized bribery done outside the country's territorial jurisdiction.[22] "Red flags" in corruption analysis originated with the Foreign Corrupt Practices Act (FCPA) as warning signs of possible illicit activity and are focused on the activities of intermediaries in foreign jurisdictions.[23] In the decades that followed, in an increasingly competitive and globalized economy, international anti-corruption efforts gained further momentum, most notably with the 1997 OECD Anti-Bribery Convention, which attempted for the first time to put nationals of the major capital-exporting countries under the same set of rules prohibiting bribery in foreign jurisdictions. With these new treaties and statutes in place, intergovernmental organizations and nongovernmental organizations committed to anti-corruption began to issue guidelines designed to alert companies to factors that may lead to greater risks of corrupt practices.[24] These numerous soft law instruments are preventive tools used to warn a company of potential risks that, if ignored, may result in liability under

21. There is also a subset of corruption-related treaty arbitrations (about 1/3 of all) where it is the investor who claims corruption, usually because of some form of extortion or solicitation of corruption perpetrated by one against the other. *See* ALOYSIUS LLAMZON, CORRUPTION IN INTERNATIONAL INVESTMENT ARBITRATION 199-200 (2014). *That* form of corruption—which some might consider a form of corrupt solicitation (only by the person with influence instead of by the foreign investor)—is not typically the concern of red flags analysis.
22. For a contemporaneous analysis of the FCPA, *see* W Michael Reisman, Folded Lies: Bribery, Crusades, and Reforms (1979).
23. Lucinda Low, *Dealing with Allegations of Corruption in International Arbitration*, 113 AJIL UNBOUND 341, 343 (2019).
24. *See, e.g.*, U.S. Department of Justice and U.S. Securities and Exchange Commission, A Resource Guide to the Foreign Corrupt Practices Act (2012); International Chamber of Commerce, Guidelines on Agents, Intermediaries, and Third Parties (2010).

national anti-corruption statutes, whether due to knowledge or willful ignorance (the oft-used "head in sand" metaphor).[25]

Thus, red flags of corruption originate from the world of compliance. Their form is that of a list of factors—some very broad (such as the general reputation of a country) and others more specific (such as the close family relationship existing between an intermediary hired as agent or consultant and a public official). This wide range of factors sometimes can be useful in an arbitral setting. In fact, they often are not. As Lucinda Low has noted, "[p]arties alleging corruption have seized upon red flags, sometimes arguing that the mere presence of numerous red flags establishes corruption. But red flags are only indicators that must be pursued to determine what evidence they yield. General red flags—relating to the country or sector—have little probative value, and prove nothing in an individual case, while those that are more specific to a counterparty or transaction—for example, a lack of services provided by a third party in return for significant compensation—have more probative value."[26]

Thus, rather than corral varying red flags lists together, it is more useful to look at red flag lists that arbitral tribunals have actually found to have probative value. In *Metal-Tech v. Uzbekistan,* the tribunal elaborated on one such list—that drafted by Lord Woolf, the former Chief Justice of England and Wales. Selecting a number of relevant risk factors, "among other things," the Tribunal identified the following red flags:

(1) "an Adviser has a lack of experience in the sector";
(2) "non-residence of an Adviser in the country where the customer or the project is located";
(3) "no significant business presence of the Adviser within the country";
(4) "an Adviser requests 'urgent' payments or unusually high commissions";
(5) "an Adviser requests payments be paid in cash, use of a corporate vehicle such as equity, or be paid in a third country, to a numbered bank account, or to some other person or entity";
(6) "an Adviser has a close personal/professional relationship to the government or customers that could improperly influence the customer's decision."[27]

These factors are practical in nature and proactive in stance: although they may not in themselves mean that corruption exists, they are cause for greater precaution on the part of employees of companies that do business in unfamiliar countries. An in-house counsel or compliance officer who attempts to safeguard a company about to do business abroad is engaged in an act of prediction: the factors set guidelines in order to spot potential issues that may occur in the company's business relationship. The

25. Lucinda Low, *Dealing with Allegations of Corruption in International Arbitration,* 113 AJIL Unbound 341, 343 (2019).
26. Lucinda Low, *Dealing with Allegations of Corruption in International Arbitration,* 113 AJIL Unbound 341, 343 (2019).
27. Metal-Tech v. Uzbekistan, para. 293, *citing* Woolf Committee Report on Business Ethics, Global Companies and the Defence Industry: Ethical Business Conduct in BAE Systems Plc 25-26 (2008).

motivation is to minimize risk that the company will be entering into relationships that may expose it to corruption. This is an *ex ante*, preventive approach to corruption which may lead to the conclusion: do not engage in this activity or proceed with the transaction, as there are too many red flags.

Thus, unlike transnational bribery, which is defined by its legal elements, "red flags" of corruption identify a broad range of factors that *may* be present in commercial arrangements that suffer from corruption. Red flags were not designed by legislative minds intent on identifying and proscribing specific human activities under pain of incarceration. And "red flags" never were contemplated for use in the manner for which they predominantly are used now in international arbitration—as potentially decisive indicators of corruption whose presence amounts to circumstantial evidence that bribery tainted the investment or transaction. Notably, no international anti-corruption treaty references "red flags."

Of course, the arbitral tribunal is engaged in an adjudicative function, not compliance. It is seeking to understand, *ex post*, whether under the specific circumstances of the case before it, bribery occurred. The question the arbitrator must answer is whether there is sufficient probative evidence of bribery. The only proper way to answer that is not by reference to red flags designed to warn about potential "corruption" in the general and generic sense. Proving particular forms of corruption requires methodical reference to the elements of the offense, to determine through direct or circumstantial evidence whether those elements are present to the standard of proof required under the particular national law (or determined by the tribunal applying international legal principles). Red flags—no matter how many—do not constitute an element of the offense.

What *is* an element of bribery—perhaps the key and often the most hotly contested element—is the quid pro quo—giving something to a public official—whether directly or indirectly (through an intermediary) —in exchange for an undue advantage. There needs to be knowledge (or willful, "head in sand" ignorance) that the briber knew that the intermediary was going to exchange the "quid" for an official act or omission.

This is not to say that red flags have no use. They fall under the category of potential circumstantial evidence, and as with all indirect forms of evidence, the probity of the red flag circumstance, once found to exist as a fact, lies in how that fact ties together with other pieces of circumstantial evidence in order to advance an overall conviction that bribery was or was not committed. In our experience, arbitration practitioners and decision-makers understand and sympathize with the difficulties in proving the quid pro quo of bribery. Few awards have insisted, before finding bribery, on the actual smoking gun of an exchange of money, caught on tape, or some version of the words "if you do this, I will pay you," was uttered.

That said, open admissions of corruption can and in fact do occur in a surprising number of cases. Most notably in *World Duty Free,* no need for weighing of evidence was necessary in light of the free admission by the Claimant's controlling shareholder that he paid a USD 4 million bribe.[28] The case between Chevron and Ecuador[29] is another obvious exception to this because the fraudsters recorded their corrupt behavior in high-definition, movie quality tape. In most other cases, however, findings on bribery will be built on circumstantial evidence. If certain red flags that have probative value are found to exist, tribunals are well within their power to ask further questions to ferret out whether bribery occurred. To use the red flags cited by Lord Woolf above, evidence pointing to funds paid to the bank account of an intermediary abroad (a numbered account), and especially if that intermediary is a family member of a public official, forms a series of circumstantial evidence that, together with further evidence that points to governmental action done in a manner favorable to the principal, amounts to significant, even compelling evidence of a quid pro quo, and thus strong evidence of bribery based on its elements.

Overall, red flags can be indicators that bribery may have occurred, but those flags alone are insufficient proof. They are circumstantial evidence that must be considered against the definition of transnational bribery, including the elements of intent (not necessarily *mens rea* within the meaning of criminal law) and quid pro quo. In other words, the elements of the offense must be the ultimate guidepost with respect to which circumstantial evidence is weighed against: "red flags", no matter how many, in and of themselves, are not proof of corruption without their reference back to the elements of the offense.

In this regard, some French courts recently have taken an increasingly permissive turn toward the use of "red flags" to prove corruption (specifically money laundering), considering them to be squarely within the concept of "*faisceau d'indices*" or "evidence based on inference and not on personal knowledge or observation."[30] This jurisprudence has been built upon the review of corruption issues in relation to the set-aside cases of Paris-seated arbitral awards, over which the Paris Court of Appeal exercises jurisdiction. The seeming willingness of the Court of Appeal to annul awards with findings on corruption that they disagree with upon a *de novo* appreciation of the facts under a French international public policy analysis is perhaps unusual, but falls within the parameters of acceptable public policy review under the New York Convention and Model Law. A significant divergence of this strand of case law from the view the authors have espoused above lies in the way corrupt conduct is found to exist. Crucially, the Court of Appeal does not refer to the definition of corruption or related offenses under French criminal law, referring instead to international anti-corruption conventions, particularly the 1997 OECD Convention on Combating Bribery of Foreign Public Officials in International Business Transactions and the UN Convention Against

---

28. World Duty Free v. Kenya, Award, ICSID Case No. ARB/00/7, Award, October 4, 2006. Indeed, apart from *World Duty Free,* the other leading case in the modern era of anti-corruption case law, *Metal-Tech v Uzbekistan,* is also arguably an instance where free admissions made led to the finding of bribery. *See* LLAMZON, CORRUPTION IN INTERNATIONAL INVESTMENT ARBITRATION 117-122 (2014).
29. Chevron Corporation (USA) and Texaco Petroleum Company (USA) v the Republic of Ecuador, UNCITRAL.
30. Domitile Baizeau & Tessa Hayes, *The Arbitral Tribunal's Duty and Power to Address Corruption Sua Sponte, in* INTERNATIONAL ARBITRATION AND THE RULE OF LAW: CONTRIBUTION AND CONFORMITY: 19 ICCA CONGRESS SERIES 225, 258 (A. Menaker ed., 2017).

Corruption. In one case, the Paris Court of Appeal stated that "it is not this Court's role [...] to determine whether a party to the arbitration is guilty of a corruption offense pursuant to the laws of a domestic legal system, but only to determine whether the enforcement of the award contravenes the objective of combatting corruption in the sense that the compensation ordered by the award would have the effect of financing an activity corruption or influence peddling."[31]

That passage might be read as a sanction for parsing the facts within the framework of the elements of the offense of transnational bribery as it is defined under the OECD and UN Conventions. Indeed, the Court stated in that same case that "combatting corruption is an objective of the [OECD Convention] and the [UN Convention Against Corruption]" and provided a definition of bribery that is consistent with "the international consensus expressed by those instruments."[32] The Paris Court of Appeal took this approach in the *Alstom* case: in its decision to reopen the proceedings and to seek additional evidence, the Court provided a list of typical "red flags" that may lead to a finding of corruption. These were identified as: (i) the lack of elements showing that the intermediary performed actual work; (ii) his lack of resources; (iii) the disproportion between the intermediary's remuneration and his services; (iv) the fact that the intermediary is paid on a percentage basis; (v) the fact that the intermediary's accounting is incomplete or insincere; (vi) the unlikeliness that the underlying contract would be awarded to the suspected bribe-giver; and (vii) the fact that the relevant country or sector is notoriously corrupt.[33] Crucially, in its subsequent 2019 decision on the merits, the Court of Appeal held in *Alstom* that "the examination by the enforcement judge of an allegation that an arbitral award has granted sums destined to finance a corrupt activity can only entail, in light of the hidden nature of corruption facts, the gathering of a range of indicia [*faisceau d'indice*]. It is on the admissibility [...] of the evidence submitted by the appellant, the reality of the indicia, and on their sufficiently serious, precise and convergent character, and not on precisely identified corruption facts, that the defense rights are exercised in this case."[34]

The Court then relied on several of the red flag indicators to find that corruption was proved, namely: (i) that the fact that the intermediary's company had no prior existence and was only a shell company; (ii) that the remuneration of many of the services to be rendered by the intermediary was disproportionate; (iii) that the only services actually rendered (and for which remuneration was not disproportionate) consisted in the communication of confidential documents; (iv) that the remuneration received by the intermediary company was its unique source of revenue and was almost entirely distributed to its shareholders, who were all members of the same family, and through opaque channels; (v) that the accounting of the intermediary

31. French Supreme Court, Case n° 16-25.657, SA Ancienne Maison Marcel Bauche v. Indagro, September 13, 2017.
32. *Ibid.*
33. Paris Court of Appeal, Case no° 16/11182, Sté Alstom Transport SA et al. v. Sté Alexander Brothers Ltd., April 10, 2018.
34. Paris Court of Appeal, Case no° 16/11182, Sté Alstom Transport SA et al. v. Sté Alexander Brothers Ltd., May 28, 2019.

company revealed suspicious expenses such as pieces of art or furniture which were not properly registered as company assets; and (vi) that Alstom had been awarded one of the contracts despite being less highly ranked than its competitors.[35]

Another pivotal step toward the French court system's reliance on "red flags" without any explicit reference to the criminal offenses most closely associated with corruption, including bribery, trading in influence, and money laundering, occurred a little earlier with the Paris Court of Appeal's February 2017 decision in *Kyrgystan v Belokon*.[36] Unlike *Alstom*, where corruption did not figure prominently in the original arbitral award (and involved an intermediary contract, and thus a contract *for* corruption), *Belokon* was a UNCITRAL investment treaty arbitration under the Kyrgyztan-Latvia investment treaty where issues of corruption figured prominently. The Latvian investor had acquired a bank in the Kyrgyz Republic following a public tender organized by the Kyrgyz National Bank. After the government changed, Kyrgyzstan placed the investor's bank and four other banks under temporary administration to stabilize the banking sector. But the following year, Kyrgyzstan imposed a sequestration regime on the investor's bank because criminal proceedings related to suspicious transactions had been instituted. The investor commenced treaty arbitration, but as the investment treaty did not identify a seat of arbitration, the tribunal selected Paris as the seat. The treaty tribunal ultimately awarded over USD 15 million in damages to the investor, finding that Kyrgyzstan had violated the treaty by expropriating the investor's investment. As to the issue relating to corruption, the Tribunal acknowledged Kyrgyzstan's criminal investigation into the investor's bank's suspicious transactions. However, it also noted that after investigating the investor for four years, without evidentiary support or cogent explanations, insufficient evidence of money laundering or other wrongdoing had been presented to justify the investor's treatment.

The State sought to set aside the award before the Paris Court of Appeal, arguing that the award breached the French concept of international public policy because the tribunal had awarded damages based on the value of a money-laundering enterprise and the enforcement of an award would negate efforts to fight money laundering. The Court of Appeal reviewed the factual record *de novo* and ultimately disagreed with the tribunal's findings. After conducting an in-depth analysis of the underlying facts, which importantly involved new evidence (the Latvian authorities having imposed a EUR 1.1 million fine against a bank affiliated with Mr. Belokon for breaching Latvian anti-money laundering rules), the court concluded that the award allowed Mr. Belokon to benefit from the product of money laundering, which contravened French international public policy. In this respect, the court confirmed that its "investigation [of the money laundering allegation], carried out in defense of international public policy, is not limited to the evidence submitted to the arbitrators or bound by the findings, assessments and qualifications made by them."[37]

35. *Ibid.*
36. République du Kirghizistan v. M. Valeriy Belokon, Paris Court of Appeal, Case n° 15-01650, February 21, 2017.
37. *Ibid.*

Reviewing the facts first decided by the arbitral tribunal in greater depth, the tribunal's conclusion that the State had not shown that the investor's business relationship with the Kyrgyz' President's son was inappropriate was set aside. The Court considered the relationship to be inappropriate.[38]

Going even further into detail, the Court ruled that the tribunal overlooked evidence that the auditor of the investor's bank had rented seven safe deposit boxes in the same bank, containing a significant amount of cash and stamps for companies in the British Virgin Islands and various Kyrgyz tax authorities; these were considered confirmation of the State's arguments, undermining the credibility of the auditors' reports. The Court also considered the investor's ownership of another bank that Latvian authorities had fined for breach of anti-money laundering rules (even though the fine postdated the arbitral award by over a year). Finally, the Court found inexplicable from the viewpoint of orthodox banking practices the fact that a bank that had been insolvent upon acquisition was then able to realize USD 5.2 billion in transactions in a short two years and eight months' period, equivalent to 80% of the Kyrgyz Republic's gross domestic product.

The cumulation of these red flags led the Paris Court of Appeal to conclude that "there are serious, precise and convergent indicia that [the bank] was purchased by the buyer to develop, in a State where its privileged relationship with the holder of the economic power guaranteed him no real control over its activities, money-laundering practices."[39]

Thus (and unless overturned by the French Supreme Court), it seems that the contemporaneous view prevalent in French courts is that in demonstrating the existence of corruption, courts primarily will resort to circumstantial, "red flags" evidence., i.e., "annulment would be justified only if it was demonstrated by serious, precise and convergent indicia that the award has the effect of enforcing a contract obtained by corruption."[40] Critically, that convergent evidence of corruption need not—at least for French courts acting in review of arbitral awards—precisely identify and fill out the elements of a particular criminal offense. Is this manner of proving particular modalities of corruption found in recent arbitral awards as well?

III RED FLAGS IN PRACTICE: SOME RECENT CASES

Recent case law suggests that a considerable lack of uniformity remains as to how red flags are utilized. One way to depict their utilization in the case law is to set two poles. First, arbitrators can use red flags merely as indicators, a starting point for analysis that proceeds into a more detailed examination of whether the facts support a finding of

38. And while the tribunal concluded that Kyrgyzstan failed to establish that the tender process that led to the awarding of the underlying contract was fraudulent, the Court reversed that finding as well, concluding that the tender process occurred in irregular circumstances.
39. République Démocratique du Congo v. Sté Customs and Tax Consultancy LLC, Paris Court of Appeal, Case n° 15/17442, May 16, 2017.
40. *Ibid.*

transnational bribery or other specific corruption-related offenses. The "connect-the-dots" approach, a methodology discussed and adopted in the *Methanex* and *UFG* cases,[41] is one articulation of this approach. "Connecting dots" is a metaphor that helps to visualize how circumstantial evidence is used to arrive at a full factual picture, taking proper account of each relevant fact. But the ultimate derived "picture" arrived at is one that is grounded on meeting the elements of the offense alleged, such as transnational bribery. In *Methanex,* the tribunal held that the connect-the-dots approach must consider other plausible explanations based on the facts established, and if the dots can form alternate lines, the exploration of those alternative explanations is important.[42] A donation to a candidate's reelection campaign can demonstrate the quid pro quo that exchanges the donation for governmental action. Or it can be the simple desire to curry favor without any specific commitment or promise of future benefit. Those two alternative explanations are both plausible, and it is only with the addition of further dots and the examination of those dots against the elements of the offense of transnational bribery that a conclusion is rendered legally *and* factually sound.

Second, and alternatively, case law such as that emerging from the Paris Court of Appeal discussed above suggests an alternative and opposing pole in the use of red flags. An arbitral tribunal's written analysis can be so focused on the red flags themselves that insufficient treatment of those points of circumstantial evidence against the constitutive elements of the offense occurs, leaving most readers with the impression that red flags analysis alone is sufficient to lead to a finding of "corruption" —in its generic sense. This also may have occurred in the *Spentex v. Uzbekistan* case, where the (still confidential) award seems to have reached the conclusion that the investment was obtained through corruption based on the presence of a number of red flags.[43]

---

41. Methanex Corp. v. United States of America, UNCITRAL (NAFTA), Final Award on Jurisdiction and Merits (August 3, 2005); Unión Fenosa Gas S.A. v. Arab Republic of Egypt, ICSID Case No. ARB/14/4, Award, August 31, 2018.
42. Methanex Corporation v. United States of America, NAFTA/UNCITRAL, Final Award on Jurisdiction and Merits, August 3, 2005, Part III, Ch. B. In that case, the tribunal adopted a "connect the dots" methodology (Methanex, Part III, Ch. B, para. 2 ("while individual pieces of evidence when viewed in isolation may appear to have no significance, when seen together, they provide the most compelling of possible explanations of events...")), with the caveat that each "dot" (i.e., key event) be examined in its own context as well as within the overall pattern, and that the tribunal must ultimately determine what the "dots" are from the evidence presented by both parties:

> Connecting the dots is hardly a unique methodology; but when it is applied, it is critical, first, that all the relevant dots be assembled; and, second, that each be examined, in its own context, for its own significance, before a possible pattern is essayed. Plainly, a self-serving selection of events and a self-serving interpretation of each of those selected, may produce an account approximating verisimilitude, but it will not reflect what actually happened. Accordingly, the Tribunal will consider the various 'dots' which Methanex has adduced—one-by-one and then together with certain key events (essentially additional, noteworthy dots) which Methanex does not adduce—in order to reach a conclusion about the factual assertions which Methanex has made.

43. *See* Vladislav Djanic, *In Newly Unearthed Uzbekistan Ruling, Exorbitant Fees Promised to Consultants on Eve of Tender Process Are Viewed by Tribunal As Evidence of Corruption, Leading*

The reality emerging from a brief review of five recent, publicly available international arbitral awards involving corruption issues[44] is that while tribunals employ a red flags analysis that do not perfectly fall in one of these two opposed polarities, red flags have been put in proper context. By and large, red flags have not been allowed to operate as a form of or substitute for proving the elements of bribery, influence peddling, or money laundering.

A *Metal-Tech v. Uzbekistan*[45]

Metal-Tech v. Uzbekistan was the first known investment treaty arbitration where a finding of corruption (specifically bribery) resulted in the case being dismissed for lack of jurisdiction due to an absence of consent to arbitrate on the State's part based on a "legality clause" in the Israel-Uzbekistan bilateral investment treaty. The specific corruption-related allegation concerned the investor's hiring of a consultant, Mr. Sultanov, who was the brother of the then-Prime Minister of Uzbekistan. That brother was found to have no experience in the field, and his actual services provided were undocumented; in the eyes of the tribunal, these facts "impose the conclusion that Mr. Sultanov was paid to use his family relationship to facilitate the establishment of Metal-Tech's investment in Uzbekistan."[46] Another person, Mr. Chijenok, who was a public official, also was engaged as consultant—this also was found to be a clear violation of Uzbek law.[47] Mr. Chijenok had worked in the office of the President at the time the claimant began vying to have its investment approved, and the claimant failed

---

to Dismissal of All Claims under Dutch BIT, IA Reporter, June 22, 2017. From this article, it appears that the *Spentex* tribunal was able to return a finding of "corruption" on the basis of a number of red flags that arose in relation to the investment's acquisition, particularly payments made to the two consulting firms in relation to the tender process. These red flags included: (1) the suspiciously high amounts paid to the two consultancy firms, i.e., 2% and 9% of the purchase price (amounting to USD 1.62 million and USD 7.29 million, although the latter was actually paid USD 6 million), relative to the services provided, particularly for the second consultant; (2) the claimant failed to disclose the consulting contracts to the tribunal, despite being requested to do so; (3) the consultants lacked qualifications in the industry involved (one company was headed by the 22-year-old brother of the Kazakh-British Chamber of Commerce, without any other obvious qualifications); (4) the lack of evidence that specific services were provided, especially by the higher-paid consultant; (5) The fact that payment was made to offshore accounts in Luxembourg and the British Virgin Islands, and without any invoices.

44. Other cases that employ red flags analysis but are not fully discussed in this brief survey include: (i) *Karkey Karadeniz v. Pakistan*: In that case, the arbitral tribunal indicated in its award that was not satisfied that red flags consisting solely of questions are of sufficient weight and credibility to shift the State's burden of proving its allegations of corruption to the claimant so as to require the claimant to exonerate itself; (ii) *Churchill and Planet v. Indonesia*. *Churchill* was primarily a case where the investor's claims were considered inadmissible by reason of forgery. As to corruption, the tribunal found that the evidence on record was insufficient to establish that the disputed documents were issued as a result of corrupt practices. And while the *Churchill* tribunal readily acknowledged that corruption is inherently difficult to prove, sufficient facts on the record, at least in the form of circumstantial evidence or red flags signaling corruption, must exist before those allegations can be given serious consideration.
45. Metal-Tech v. Uzbekistan, Award, ICSID Case No. ARB/10/3.
46. *Ibid.*, para. 351.
47. *See ibid.*, paras. 325-327.

to offer a persuasive explanation as to what actual services were rendered by this individual.

The tribunal noted that "corruption is by essence difficult to establish and [...] it is thus generally admitted that it can be shown through circumstantial evidence."[48] The tribunal found corruption to have been established "with reasonable certainty"[49] on the basis of a number of red flags that helped supplement the black letter of Uzbek anti-bribery statutes. These circumstantial factors included: (1) very large payments to consultants (the aggregate consultancy fees paid amounted to USD 4 million); (2) no proof of services rendered by those consultants;[50] (3) the consultants' lack of qualifications; (4) the fact that the consulting contracts were a "sham"; (5) lack of transparency of payments to the consultants; and (6) the fact that the consultants had close connections with public officials in charge of claimant's investment. The case suggests that the evidentiary standard of "reasonable certainty" can be met through a cumulation of these red flag indicators. However, the tribunal explicitly considered Articles 210-12 of the Uzbek Criminal Code on bribery, summarizing the content of Uzbek law on the payment of a relative of an official as being the equivalent of payment to the official himself,[51] and found that the investor had violated Uzbek law against bribery.

B *Niko Resources v. Bapex and Petrobangla*[52]

With its depth of reasoning concerning various issues relating to corruption, including attribution, clean hands, and causation, the *Niko v. BAPEX and Petrobangla* tribunal had, in its 2013 decision on jurisdiction, already generated some of the most detailed analyses on corruption-related issues found in the existing case law. The tribunal ultimately rejected the respondents' corruption allegations as a jurisdictional issue.[53] At the time, the claimant Niko Resources had pleaded guilty before Canadian authorities (for which it paid a USD 9.5 million fine in 2011) to bribing Bangladesh's energy minister in relation to the Chattak gas field in northern Bangladesh, which Niko operated under a joint venture agreement it signed with Bapex.

The bribes admitted to came in the form of a Toyota Land Cruiser as well as foreign trips, both of which went to the direct benefit of the Energy Minister. Those bribes were made for purposes of obtaining the underlying joint venture and gas sale agreements. The tribunal found, however, that the bribes paid did not affect the State's consent to the agreement itself, and thus the contract remained valid. Equally important, the tribunal ruled that Niko's plea before the Canadian authorities did not bar it from bringing claims in the arbitration—and in doing so, the tribunal rejected the

48. *Ibid.*, para. 243.
49. *Ibid.*
50. *Ibid.*, para. 206.
51. *Ibid.*, paras. 288-290.
52. Niko Resources (Bangladesh) Ltd. v. Bangladesh Petroleum Exploration & Production Company Limited ("Bapex") and Bangladesh Oil Gas and Mineral Corporation ("Petrobangla"), Decision on the Corruption Claim, ICSID Case No. ARB/10/11 and No. ARB/10/18.
53. For an extended discussion of this case's Decision on Jurisdiction, *see* Llamzon, Corruption in International Investment Arbitration 188-192 (2014).

applicability of the clean hands doctrine.[54] The tribunal found nothing illegal and then stated that the consequences of the bribes were a matter for the merits phase.

Six years later, and after further corruption allegations were made, the tribunal rendered its *Decision on the Corruption Claim* in 2019. The *Niko* tribunal continued to analyze corruption issues deeply, this time considering new allegations of corruption within an almost-600 page decision devoted to corruption issues in a dedicated phase that lasted some three years, including a weeklong hearing dedicated to the corruption allegations in April 2017.[55]

Focusing on the red-flags-related issues, the *Niko* tribunal went into considerable detail in outlining the parties' respective positions on how red flags, when present, might affect the shifting of the burden of proof. The claimant's position was that the mere presence of red flags was insufficient to shift the burden of proof; red flags may indicate that a transaction merits particular scrutiny, but are not, in themselves, evidence of corruption. The claimant cited *Kim v. Uzbekistan's* holding that red flags of themselves cannot "substantiate the most basic requirements of the crime of bribe giving [to government officials] as set forth in Article 211 [of the Uzbek Criminal Code]."[56] The respondents' position was the opposite: in their view, the case law showed that red flags "are not to be taken lightly and tribunals frequently have ruled against claimants after they failed to produce evidence sufficient to rebut a presumption of illegality that arises from them."[57] The respondents then focused on one particular red flag—the supposed disproportion between the commission or fee paid to the consultant in relation to services rendered, *citing* the Metal-Tech award *supra.*[58] The respondents then cited the December 2016 *Spentex v. Uzbekistan* Award (which, at the time of this chapter's submission, remains outside the public domain) as supposedly "the most recent award addressing the issue of red flags [in which] an ICSID tribunal found that the red flag of large payments to consultants was alone sufficient proof of corruption."[59]

The *Niko* tribunal refused to be drawn into deciding this issue of burden-shifting as a purely doctrinal matter: "the difference between the Parties concerning the burden of proof and the question whether it has been shifted in the present case is not an issue of principle which can be decided in the abstract."[60] The tribunal concluded that its duty was to "examine whether (i) the circumstances on which the Respondents rely as red flags are established and, if so, (ii) what evidentiary conclusions should be drawn from them, taken individually and collectively. In this process, the Tribunals will also have to consider circumstances which point in the opposite direction."[61]

54. *See discussion in* Llamzon, Corruption in International Investment Arbitration 191 (2014).
55. *See* Damien Charlotin, *Schneider, Paulsson and McLachlan in Newly-Surfaced 600 Page ICSID Decision, See No Proof of Corruption by Canadian Investor, Niko—Merely Engagement of Local "Lobbyists" in Bangladesh,* IA Reporter, Aug. 1, 2019.
56. Niko, Decision on the Corruption Claim, para. 787, *citing Vladislav Kim v. Republic of Uzbekistan,* para. 589.
57. Niko, Decision on Corruption Claim, para. 791, citing Respondent's submission R-RC, para. 94.
58. *Ibid.*, para. 793.
59. *Ibid.*, para. 794.
60. *Ibid.*, para. 796.
61. *Ibid.*, para. 797.

Delving into the "red flags" themselves, the respondents argued that the reputation of Bangladesh at that time (a previous regime), including the country's energy ministry specifically, was a legitimate "red flag" that needed to be taken into account. The tribunal was not willing to extend this kind of generalized "red flag" as probative: "[i]t is not the role of these Tribunals to pass judgment on the Government of Bangladesh during a certain period and the general corruption allegations made by the Respondents and their experts."[62]

The main red flag at play was Niko's use of consultants and intermediaries at the time the contracts were entered into. The respondents alleged that Niko used local consultants to execute its corrupt scheme, with payments to officials allegedly channeled through these consultants. The *Niko* tribunal examined the consultancy agreements in great detail, and in that sense, it can be said that the red flags analysis served its purpose of focusing the tribunal's attention. The tribunal noted that the Respondents themselves assumed red flags to be "warning signals and possible clues but not evidence."[63]

As a threshold matter, the tribunal found that the engagement of consultants is not alone evidence that bribery was afoot. Indeed, the tribunal approached the question from the outset with a sense of realism, acknowledging that in the oil and gas industry, and particularly when first investing in a country that the investor was new to, employing in-country consultants is "sensible," stating: "[i]n these circumstances the Tribunals conclude that, especially in the initial phase of the project development and the negotiations, the engagement of consultants by Niko was not unusual in the oil and gas industry."[64]

The tribunal then concluded that "it was reasonable for Niko to engage one, or possibly several, consultants" in pursuit of the business venture, as the "engagement of consultants in itself is no evidence that bribery was intended or committed."[65] But in so concluding, the tribunal was also willing to see the opposite perspective: while Niko's "recourse to consultants was justified," that "does not exclude that through these consultants acts of bribery were committed. The Tribunals therefore must examine, one by one, the consultancy agreements concluded by Niko in order to determine whether their engagement aimed at the performance of corruption or, when procuring the JVA and the GPSA, the consultants committed acts of corruption."[66]

The tribunal then proceeded to analyze the three sets of consultants Niko employed:

(i) Niko first employed Five Feathers, a local consultant, which it hired in 1997 to obtain a contract from the Bangladeshi government without going through the competitive bidding process. Five Feathers was paid USD 1 million plus a running commission to do so;

62. *Ibid.*, para. 1455.
63. *Ibid.*, para. 1477.
64. *Ibid.*, paras. 1487-1488.
65. *Ibid.*, para. 1494.
66. *Ibid.*

(ii) Niko also employed Stratum, a consultancy it hired in 1998. Stratum was paid USD 4 million in success fees plus an interest in the project's profits (Stratum's running costs were subtracted from the success fee, and its principal, Mr. Sharif, eventually became president of one of Niko's Bangladeshi subsidiaries); and

(iii) finally, Niko hired Nationwide, which they contracted for "marketing and logistical support to Niko in securing the JVA and Gas Purchase and Sale Agreement (GPSA)," including explicit obligations to liaise with Bapex, Petrobangla, and the Ministry of Energy & Mineral Resources.[67] While some of the details were redacted in the public version of the Award, Nationwide stood to make USD 500,000 coming from Stratum's success fee upon conclusion of the Joint Venture Agreement (JVA).

The last consultancy arrangement, in particular, was said to be a front to bribe a known personal friend of the Prime Minister's son.

Ultimately, the tribunal unanimously found that Niko's use of consultants had been for the legitimate purpose of overcoming bureaucratic obstacles, and not as a conduit for bribe payments. A number of factors led to that conclusion. On the question of whether compensation for the consultants was disproportionate—the red flag that was pushed most strongly—the tribunal concluded that none of the amounts involved in each of the three consultancies was disproportionate to the size of the project. The first consultancy with Five Feathers, for example, required convincing the government to enter into an entirely new venture, and no compensation was payable should the consultants have failed. Neither was there significant evidence that the consultant bribed any government official. And as to Stratum and Mr. Sharif, the tribunal took into consideration their first mover status—it was Mr. Sharif who had brought up the idea of developing Bangladesh's marginal fields, which was a crucial component of the project. Nor were Mr. Sharif's qualifications to assist Niko with respect to the project seriously challenged—and here, evidence of Mr. Sharif's actual work done on the ground was persuasive. And the USD 4 million compensation was not disproportionate considering the expected revenue. *A fortiori*, the USD 500,000 compensation promised to Nationwide out of Stratum's USD 4 million was not considered excessive either. The tribunal was "not impressed" by the Nationwide contract's enumeration of services, but it did not conclude that nationwide's principals—Messrs. Mamoon and Bhuyian—were used to "layer" the transaction or to funnel bribes. Although both individuals had influence, and may even be considered lobbyists, the offense found in Section 163 of the Bangladeshi Penal Code required the use of "personal influence," which was unclear, and indeed, there was no evidence that such influence led to the JVA being signed.

Other allegations, including that a series of bribe payments were made to government officials to obtain the joint venture, were rejected as unfounded. For example, right before the Joint Venture Agreement was to be signed, Niko was asked

67. *Ibid.*, para. 1758.

to perform a feasibility study at its own cost, which would not have occurred had bribes been paid.

C *Kim v. Uzbekistan*[68]

The claimants in *Kim v. Uzbekistan*, Mr. Kim and eleven other individuals had made significant investments in two cement plants in Uzbekistan, acquiring majority stakes in each. According to these investors, starting in 2010, they were subjected to a campaign of harassment by the Uzbek government in the form of criminal and regulatory investigations, resulting in criminal convictions and a transfer of ownership in one of the cement plants back to the Uzbek State. For Uzbekistan, however, the claimants were embroiled in serious criminal activity, including coercion, tax evasion, and corruption.

As seen from the *Niko* decision above, *Kim v. Uzbekistan's* March 2017 Decision on Jurisdiction contained significant illegality and corruption-related findings. Citing Article 211 of Uzbekistan's Criminal Code, which punishes bribery, the tribunal began by noting that the proper standard of proof for bribery would be under the host State's law, but that neither party argued what the applicable standard of proof for bribery would be under Article 211. The tribunal did not consider this problematic, however, as whatever standard of proof between "reasonable certainty" (*a la Metal-Tech)* or "clear and convincing evidence" (the traditional standard of proof for fraud-related allegations utilized in, e.g., *Siag v. Egypt)*, the allegations were not proven.[69]

The tribunal then went into an extended discussion of red flags, noting at the outset that a "central part of the evidence" put forward by Uzbekistan was certain identified red flags "in relation to Claimants' alleged dealings with Ms. Karimova and Mr Bizakov,"[70] the former being the daughter of then-President Islam Karimov, and the latter a prominent Kazakh businessman. The State identified the following red flags: (i) the urgency of the payments made; (ii) the lack of formal due diligence or site visits; (iii) payments were made through a third-party intermediary; (iv) those payments were sent to bank accounts in a third country; (v) multilayered corporate structures were involved; (vi) different prices were set out in the various contracts; and (vii) some of those hired were subsequently involved in other illegal acts.[71] Uzbekistan then cited several International Chamber of Commerce (ICC) awards that relied on red flags in concluding that "corrupt practices were involved."[72] These red flags also were coupled

68. Vladislav Kim et al. v. Republic of Uzbekistan, ICSID Case No. ARB/13/6, Decision on Jurisdiction, March 8, 2017, paras. 595-596.
69. *Ibid.*, para. 545.
70. *Ibid.*, para. 546.
71. *Ibid.*
72. *Ibid., citing* ICC Case No. 13914 dated March 2008, ICC Bulletin Vol. 24, Special Supplement 2013, pp. 77-79; ICC Case No. 8891, Final Award of 1998, *reprinted in* 4 Journal du Droit International 1076 (2000), pp. 1080-1082; Principality of Lichtenstein v. Federal Republic of Germany, ICC Case No. 6497, Final Award of 1994, *reprinted in* 24a Y.B. Comm. Arb. (1999) 71, 75, paras. 17-29.

with a request for adverse inferences on corruption grounded on the failure to provide requested documents during the document production phase.

For their part, the claimants sought to counter each of the red flags identified above. They argued that complicated acquisition structures as well as the layering of companies are common in transactions involving the Commonwealth of Independent States (CIS) region and do not violate any laws. They also pointed out that some of the facts identified as red flags actually were required by the counterparty. As to the evidentiary value of red flags themselves, claimants argued that "a mere existence of red flags may assist a fraud examiner in formulating a hypothesis and focus its investigation. However, [...] the red flags, of themselves, do not constitute actual evidence of fraud or corruption. Claimants further contend that many of the above listed flags are in fact normal features of transactions in the business environment in the CIS region."[73]

Having considered these arguments, the *Kim* tribunal viewed red flags as potentially helpful, but they cannot result in corruption findings in and of themselves, even when the red flags are proven to exist. The tribunal's nuanced reasoning merits direct quotation:

> 549. The Tribunal first finds that red flags most often provide only circumstantial, as opposed to direct, evidence. *As circumstantial evidence, red flags can play an important supporting role in the assessment of guilt. Whether red flags can directly establish, for example, an element of a crime depends on the legal system applicable. There is not a universal answer.*
>
> 550. The Tribunal second finds *red flags useful in triggering an awareness that a transaction does not conform with the characteristics usually found in comparable transactions. Simultaneously, an examination of circumstances that give rise to red flags must take the surrounding context into consideration.* In this sense, the Tribunal finds persuasive Claimants assertion that the business and personal safety considerations in the CIS countries at the time in question in this dispute justified the taking of extra measures so as not to call attention to any individual's wealth or business dealings. This explanatory *surrounding context does not negate the red flags in their entirety, but rather may lessen the strength of the red flags identified.*
>
> 551. The Tribunal has concerns about several aspects of the transactions that led to Claimants' investment. These concerns relate to some—albeit as set out below not all—of the red flags that Respondent contends are present in this dispute. As a result of its concerns, the Tribunal has taken particular steps throughout its consideration of this objection to subject those transactions to heightened scrutiny.
>
> 551. First, the Tribunal acceded to an expansive additional document request by Respondent as regards financial aspects of the purchase of the shares, and undertook itself to examine for relevancy the documents requested by Respondent (despite a lack of apparent relevancy or materiality).
>
> 552. Second, the Tribunal has conducted a rigorous examination of Respondent's allegations as regards Claimants' alleged interactions with both Ms. Karimova and Mr. Bizakov. In doing so the Tribunal has examined the allegations in relation to both national law and international public policy.

73. Kim, para. 547.

> 553. As a final point, the Tribunal notes that its focus, at this stage of these proceedings, is on jurisdictional matters and therefore on bribery or corruption only that pertains to Claimants' initial investment. Any matters as regards bribery or corruption that arose later are more appropriately addressed at the merits stage.[74]

In essence, the *Kim* tribunal correctly considered red flags as circumstantial (not direct) evidence, and as such, red flags can have explanatory power, providing "an important supporting role in the assessment of guilt." They can also be good indicators of a need to expose parties and their transactions to further scrutiny in the arbitral process. Even if not entirely novel, this is a lucid articulation of the value of red flags.

Where *Kim* gives further insight, however, is in its linkage of red flags to *what a party needs to prove*. For the tribunal, red flags, as circumstantial evidence, have value insofar as they are traced to the "elements of a crime," which in turn depend "on the legal system applicable." In this case, the respondent State alleging bribery must prove the elements of bribery by reference to the law applicable in that State, as well as to "international public policy" articulating bribery—most notably in the UN Convention Against Corruption.

In keeping with the serious red flags raised, the *Kim* tribunal performed a detailed analysis of the evidence adduced. Ms. Karimova was both an intermediary and an owner of the cement assets being sold. Expounding on the nature of bribery under Article 211 of the Uzbek Criminal Code (prohibiting the transfer of "tangible valuables to an official, [...] for performance or nonperformance of certain action, which the official must or could have officially performed, in the interests of the person giving a bribe."),[75] the tribunal identified four questions that needed to be answered, dividing them into objective elements and mixed questions of fact and law: "[t]he first two elements are objective: (a) did Claimants make an overpayment as a part of the purchase price; and (b) was that overpayment made to Ms Karimova? The second two elements are mixed questions of fact and law: (c) was Ms Karimova an 'official' of the Government and (d) was the overpayment intended 'for performance or nonperformance of certain action, which the official must or could have officially performed, in the interests of the person giving a bribe'?"

As to the first element, the respondent State had alleged that there was an alleged overpayment for shares to Ms. Karimova of USD 8.2 million (the actual value of the shares being USD 25.8 million vis-à-vis payment of USD 33.98 million), from which disguised bribery could be inferred. The tribunal was not willing, however, to second-guess the value of the shares, pointing out that those shares were difficult to value and that overpayment due to bribery could also be explained by their own valuation of their shares (or even pure lapse of judgment). The second element was easier—the tribunal concurred with the respondent State that Ms. Karimova was the recipient of the "overpayment," notwithstanding her not being named in the documentation. In part, this finding was animated by the claimants' own statements that they sought a relationship of trust with Ms. Karimova because she was considered a

74. *Ibid.*, paras. 549-53.
75. Kim, para. 556.

powerful player in Uzbekistan who could either protect or jeopardize their investment. As to the third element, however, the tribunal decided that Ms. Karimova had no official role in the Uzbek government and thus bribery could not have occurred as defined under Uzbek law if those payments were meant for her (and crucially, the tribunal found that while it is possible for bribery to occur had Ms. Karimova only been a conduit for bribes to public officials, Uzbekistan did not make that argument, maintaining that she was the ultimate beneficiary).

Uzbekistan raised additional corruption allegations against Mr. Bizakov; specifically that a USD 3 million payment to him for consultancy services was proof of corruption—his service had been to introduce the claimants to the investments in the concerned companies. The tribunal, however, was not persuaded that Mr. Bizakov could not perform those services, as it had been shown that he previously helped the claimants with the acquisition of other cement industry investments (albeit outside Uzbekistan). The amount itself (USD 3 million) appeared to the tribunal to be justifiable—it seemed to agree with the investors' explanation that Uzbekistan's conditions at the time made it critical that intermediaries be involved, without whom such transactions might not take place—and with that necessity came large fees.

In this finding, the *Kim* tribunal seemed to diverge from *Metal-Tech's* findings, which also involved intermediaries acting within the Uzbek economic and political environment. Uzbekistan argued these parallels strongly, and the tribunal acknowledged the similarities while also pointing to distinguishing factors, most notably that Mr. Bizakov did not appear to have any specific relationship with the Uzbek government.

D *Unión Fenosa Gas v. Egypt*

Finally, the *Unión Fenosa Gas v. Arab Republic of Egypt* Award merits careful study for its significant *dicta* on the utility of red flags. Because of the authors' direct involvement in *UFG v. Egypt*, of which publication remains pending (Egypt having filed for annulment before an *ad hoc* Committee), no further commentary will be made beyond a synopsis and mention of the relevant passages that illustrate the divergent views of the majority (Messrs. Veeder and Rowley) who found for the claimant, and the minority (Mr. Clodfelter).

The dispute's corruption-related issues centered on the claimant's predecessor having entered into a long-term natural gas purchase agreement, which was part of a larger project involving a gas liquefaction plant built to convert that gas into liquefied natural gas (LNG), which would then be sold to foreign markets (particularly in Spain, as claimant was part of the third-largest electricity producer in that country and the LNG would serve as power plant fuel). Egypt alleged that the gas purchase agreement was obtained by the claimant through corruption via the intermediation of a local company, Egyptian Arab Trading Company (EATCO), headed by local businessman Yehia El Komy. Mr. El Komy was alleged to have been close to the then-Minister of

Petroleum (Mr. Fahmy) and to have facilitated the Ministry's approval of the agreement in exchange for bribe payments, funneled through many millions of dollars in fees and equity paid (or potentially to be paid) to EATCO.

Setting aside two other allegations for which Egypt had no evidence (and which, in the tribunal's eyes, supported the conclusion that Egypt's corruption allegations were meant to serve a "tactical purpose"),[76] the *UFG* tribunal focused on the red flag allegations Egypt made in relation to the claimant's relationship with Mr. El Komy, particularly a "joint venture agreement" that Egypt had obtained from the claimant via document production. And as with the *Kim* tribunal, the *UFG* tribunal took significant additional steps upon being confronted with red flags of corruption, including the reopening of the evidentiary record after the hearing and while the tribunal was deliberating in order to analyze, in great detail, documents that explained the relationship between the claimant and Mr. El Komy, which had been revealed in a related commercial arbitration proceeding (called the "six documents" in the arbitral award).[77]

The redactions to the public version of the UFG award make a comprehensive discussion of the corruption-related issues challenging. On red flags, in particular, of the eight identified, only three were entirely unredacted: (i) the "Project [had taken] place in a country known for corrupt payments, namely Egypt at the time of the events in question"; (ii) "the agent has a close personal or family relationship, or business relationship, with a public official or relative of such official (such as that between Mr. El Komy and the Respondent's Minister Mr Fahmy), which is the only qualification the agent brings to the venture"; and (iii) "[t]he agent is a shell company or has some other non-transparent corporate structure (EATCO is a shell entity owned by members of Mr El Komy's family)." Partially unredacted is a fourth red flag, (iv) "[t]here is no substantial time lag between [redacted] and the date when the main contract is awarded to the principal."[78]

As to the first red flag, from the visible text of the award the tribunal does not seem to have given any weight to the argument that generalized corruption in Egypt at the time is cogent evidence that the relationship between Mr. El Komy and the claimant was corrupt at the time.[79] Similarly, the third and fourth red flags above were not the topic of extended analysis.

The second red flag—the existence or nonexistence of a personal relationship with the public official (Minister Fahmy), and the absence of any other skill or qualification as consultant or agent—was considered carefully. As to the supposed

76. UFG v. Egypt, Award, para. 7.112 ("Third, the belated plea of corruption, raised by the Respondent as a jurisdictional objection after the commencement of this arbitration, raises a suspicion that the plea serves a convenient tactical purpose. This suggestion is strengthened by the weakness of the Respondent's two other pleas relating to Halliburton and Mr Hussein Salem, both of which seemed only to serve a tactical purpose in seeking to defeat or delay the Claimant's claims against the Respondent. These two pleas should not have been made by the Respondent based on the materials presented by it to the Tribunal").

77. UFG, Award, Part I, paras. 1.74-1.78; Part II, para. 2.5.

78. UFG, Award, Part II, para. 2.5.

79. This is in keeping with the case law. *See, e.g.*, Rumeli Telekom AS and Telsim Mobil Telekomunikasyon Hizmetleri AS v. Republic of Kazakhstan (ICSID Case No. ARB/05/16), Award, July 29, 2008, paras. 446, 715.

relationship between the supposed intermediary—Mr. El Komy—and Minister of Petroleum Fahmy, the tribunal decided that while he had a prior relationship with the Minister's *father* a few years before the contract was negotiated and entered into, he had no relationship with the Minister personally at the relevant time (1999 onward). And as to Mr. El Komy's supposed lack of relevant qualifications, "[a]lthough Mr El Komy's experience did not include natural gas projects before the SPA, the Tribunal accepts that both he and EATCO had some professional and business experience with oil and petrochemical projects."[80]

Importantly for this chapter, the *UFG* tribunal's majority discussed the relationship between red flags, circumstantial evidence, the connect-the-dots approach, and "black flags." The majority ruled:

> the Respondent and its legal representatives should not be criticised for raising its allegations of corruption in this arbitration in regard to Mr El Komy. These allegations were not frivolous. Several were *classic "red flags"; but even the reddest of red flags does not suffice without proof of corruption before the tribunal.* Whilst it can be relatively easy to allege corruption, it is less easy to prove it, as observed in the *Metal-Tech* award (2013). Suspicion is not equivalent to proof. Unanswered queries may have innocent explanations, not amounting (in the absence of explanations) to proof of corruption. With hindsight, what business people agree not infrequently defies logic or commonsense to non-business people, again without amounting to proof of corruption. The legal burden of proving corruption rests upon the party alleging corruption; and it is not discharged by placing the burden on the adverse party to prove the absence of corruption.
>
> Moreover, with a case dependent upon circumstantial evidence (as in the present case), it is often a question of joining up the dots; but there have first to be dots in the evidence adduced before the tribunal. In this case, so the Tribunal decides, there are insufficient dots; and the red flags are outnumbered by *neutral black flags*.[81]

By contrast, the Dissenting Opinion of Mark Clodfelter found the red flag (the amount of compensation of the local partner) to be sufficient to require a plausible and credible explanation from the claimant. And since the claimant's explanations were neither plausible nor credible in his view, the only inference that could be drawn is that the high compensation was for the purpose of exerting improper influence upon government officials in allowing the project.

IV CONCLUSION

When faced with allegations of corruption, tribunals and counsel alike often confront a messy set of facts capable of multiple competing explanations, all of which are plausible to some degree. In such situations, legal minds often revert to abstractions that would impose order and move decision-making forward. That impetus may partly be behind the increasing use of red flags of corruption in international arbitration. From the reputation of a country or a particular industry for endemic corruption; to the use

80. UFG, Award, Part VII, para. 7.71.
81. *Ibid.*, paras. 7.113-7.114.

of agents, consultants, and other intermediaries with personal relationships with government officials; to the amounts paid to those consultants and where they are paid, arbitral case law has allowed red flags to play a role in identifying and punishing corruption.

Agency and consultancy relationships, in particular, have taken on an outsized role in red flags analysis. As seen from the cases discussed in section III above, the presence of such agents quickly leads to more red flag questions. But the answers often can be only partially satisfying, and doubts can remain as to whether (for example) a large success fee for helping secure a concession contract is justifiable. The conclusions made depend a lot on the perspective of the viewer: decision-makers squinting at the evidence many years after the fact can in good faith come to very different legal conclusions. The problem might well be reduced to this truism: *while proving corruption is difficult, it is also difficult to disprove.* Foreign corporations that move into new and unfamiliar markets need to deal with regulatory, political, and commercial realities that they are often unfamiliar with, and the tendency to deal with the problem through the mediation of prominent local persons is real. The line between having a well-connected local consultant or partner who can help smooth over the issues legally and one who is an influence peddler is often very difficult to draw. Similarly, the line between a businessman making campaign contributions in order to indirectly benefit from favorable policy predispositions of the supported politician, and an outright quid pro quo, is difficult to locate.

Kim v. Uzbekistan is particularly insightful as to what the next step must be following the presence of certain red flags. There, the tribunal acknowledged that red flags, as circumstantial evidence, have value only insofar as they are traced to the "elements of a crime," which in turn, depends "on the legal system applicable." In investment treaty cases, therefore, the party alleging bribery cannot rely on red flags alone, and must prove the elements of bribery by reference to the national law where the act was committed, as well as international anti-corruption legal principles such as those found in the UN Convention Against Corruption (given the direct applicability of international law and transnational public policy in investment treaty cases).

The reality, therefore, is that while red flags can often be a useful first step, they often relate to the easiest part of the analysis: they confirm the need to ask more questions, but provide no further answers.

CHAPTER 13

Consent to Arbitration Given Through Investment Treaties

María Inés Corrá[*]

Consent is the cornerstone of arbitration.[1] It is the pillar and main feature of this mechanism of dispute resolution, which is itself based on unanimous consensus.[2]

There are three main ways to give consent to arbitration for the settlement of investment disputes: (i) consent by direct agreement, (ii) consent through host State legislation and (iii) consent through bilateral investment treaties (BITs) or multilateral investment treaties (MITs).[3]

This contribution will focus on the nature and effects of consent given through bilateral or MITs, going through some of the old and new issues arising from that consent. Several reasons justify the selection of this topic. First, this technique has been the main tool used by States in the last three decades to provide neutral forums to

* The author would like to thank to Santiago Peña, senior associate at Bomchil, for his appreciated collaboration in the elaboration of this contribution and to Celina Urabayen for her valuable assistance. The author would also like to thank to Prof. G.S. Tawil for leading her in the vast and challenging field of investment arbitration.

1. *See* Report of the Executive Directors of the World Bank on the ICSID Convention, § 23: "Consent of the parties is the cornerstone of the jurisdiction of the Centre." (available at: https://icsid-archive.worldbank.org/en/Documents/resources/2006%20CRR_English-final.pdf).
2. G. Aguilar Álvarez, "Article II(2) of the New York Convention and the Courts," in A. J. Van den Berg (ed.), *Improving the Efficiency of Arbitration Agreements and Awards: 40 Years of Application of the New York Convention* (ICCA Congress Series, vol. 9, Kluwer Law International, 1999), 68; Ch. F. Amerasinghe, *Jurisdiction of specific international tribunals* (Martinus Nijhoff Publishers, 2009), 437; Ch. Schreuer, "Consent to Arbitration," in P. Muchlinski, F. Ortino & Ch. Schreuer, *The Oxford Handbook of International Investment Law* (Oxford University Press, 2008), 831; Z. Douglas, *The International Law of Investment Claims* (Cambridge University Press, 2009), 151.
3. Ch. Schreuer, "Consent to Arbitration," in P. Muchlinski, F. Ortino & Ch. Schreuer, *The Oxford Handbook of International Investment Law* (Oxford University Press, 2008), 831.

resolve investment disputes in the context of an increasing globalization process.[4] Second, tribunal practice has shown the existence of different views and positions on the scope, limits and temporal validity of consent to arbitration granted by States through the BITs, evidencing the need to make more efforts to harmonize that practice.[5] Third, the topic was addressed with authority in the widely known *Lanco* precedent, one of the decisions which confirms the legacy of Professor G. Aguilar Álvarez, to whom this chapter intends to pay a humble tribute, as adjudicator.[6]

This chapter will address (I) the main features of consent to arbitration given through investment treaties and the influence of the *Lanco* decision on the appropriate understanding of that consent; (II) the procedural requirements and limits to consent to arbitration given in investment treaties and their impact; (III) the interaction between dispute resolution provisions in investment treaties and dispute forum clauses in investment-related agreements; (IV) new discussions arising from States' denunciation of investment treaties or the ICSID Convention; and (V) our concluding remarks.

I CONSENT TO ARBITRATION GIVEN THROUGH INVESTMENT TREATIES

Consent of the parties is a fundamental prerequisite for the existence of arbitration jurisdiction. This applies equally to commercial and investor-State arbitration.[7]

Consent must be obtained from all parties, in writing, although it is not necessary for the consent to be included in a single document signed by all of them.[8]

As regards States, in the last decades, the most common way to give consent to arbitration has been through either BITs between the host State and the investor's home State (BITs) or MITs.[9]

4. G. S. Tawil, "Los Conflictos en Materia de Inversión, la Jurisdicción del CIADI y el Derecho Aplicable: a Propósito de las Recientes Decisiones en los Casos 'Vivendi', 'Wena' y 'Maffezini'," *Revista Brasileira de Arbitragem* (Kluwer Law International, 2003), 125.
5. Ch. Schreuer, "Consent to Arbitration," in P. Muchlinski, F. Ortino & Ch. Schreuer, *The Oxford Handbook of International Investment Law* (Oxford University Press, 2008), 835/849 and 867.
6. *See Lanco International Inc. v. The Argentine Republic*, ICSID Case No. ARB/97/6 (Preliminary Decision on Jurisdiction, December 8, 1998) (hereinafter "*Lanco v. Argentine Republic*"). Awards and decisions quoted in this chapter are available at https://icsid.worldbank.org/cases/concluded and https://www.italaw.com/
7. Ch. Schreuer, "Consent to Investment Arbitration" (Transnational Dispute Management vol. 2, issue 05, 2007), 3; Z. Douglas, *The International Law of Investment Claims* (Cambridge University Press, 2009), 151; A. M. Steingruber, *Consent in International Arbitration* (Oxford University Press, 2012), 189/190.
8. L. Reed et al., *Guide to ICSID Arbitration* (Kluwer Law International, 2010), 36.
9. Several MITs have clauses expressing consent to arbitrate investor-State disputes, such as: North American Free Trade Agreement (NAFTA) (Article 1122), the current United States-Mexico-Canada Agreement (USMCA) (Chapters 14.C, 14.D and 14.E), and the Energy Charter Treaty (ECT) (Article 26.3), among others. Consent of the host State may also be expressed in investment promotion law or in investment agreements between States and foreign investors. *See* for all: Ch. Schreuer, "Consent to Arbitration" in Muchlinski, F. Ortino & Ch. Schreuer, *The Oxford Handbook of International Investment Law* (Oxford University Press, 2008), 831, 835/836 and 851.

Consent to a neutral and efficient arbitration forum offered by the contracting States to investment treaties is an important part of the protection pursued by foreign investors through them.[10]

The mechanism is similar in the majority of the BITs. The contracting parties offer their consent to arbitration to investors that are nationals of the other contracting State. As in any arbitration, an agreement between the parties is needed. Thus, the State's offer of consent has to be accepted by a qualifying investor in order to perfect the consent to arbitration.[11]

A Nature and Effects of the State's Consent to Arbitration Given in Investment Treaties

1 The Lanco *Decision*

The nature of a State's consent to arbitration expressed through a BIT was conclusively addressed in the Preliminary Decision on Jurisdiction in *Lanco* v. *Argentine Republic.*[12]

The case involved a dispute between a US investor, Lanco International Inc., and the Republic of Argentina in connection with a claim for damages arising out of the alleged violation of the US-Argentina BIT on several grounds.[13]

Lanco (as awardee and guarantor of the grantee's obligations) and Argentina had entered into a concession agreement for the development and operation of Terminal No. 3 of the New Port of Buenos Aires.[14]

The investor relied on the consent to arbitrate offered by Argentina in Article VII (4) of the US-Argentina BIT, which reads as follows:

> Each Party hereby consents to the submission of any investment dispute for settlement by binding arbitration in accordance with the choice specified in the written consent of the national or company under paragraph 3. Such consent, together with the written consent of the national or company when given under paragraph 3 shall satisfy the requirement for:

10. G. S. Tawil, "Los Conflictos en Materia de Inversión, la Jurisdicción del CIADI y el Derecho Aplicable: a Propósito de las Recientes Decisiones en los Casos 'Vivendi', 'Wena' y 'Maffezini'," *Revista Brasileira de Arbitragem* (Kluwer Law International, 2003), 127/128; Ch. Schreuer, "Consent to Investment Arbitration" (Transnational Dispute Management vol. 2, issue 05, 2007), 6. *See also Siemens A.G. v. The Argentine Republic*, ICSID Case No. ARB/02/8 (Decision on jurisdiction) August 3, 2004 (hereinafter "*Siemens v. Argentine Republic*"). §§ 181/182; *Gas Natural SDG, S.A. v. The Argentine Republic*, ICSID Case No. ARB/03/10 (Decision of the Tribunal on Preliminary Questions on Jurisdiction), June 17, 2005 (hereinafter "*Gas Natural v. Argentine Republic*"), § 49.
11. *See*, among others, Ch. Schreuer, "Consent to Arbitration," in P. Muchlinski, F. Ortino & Ch. Schreuer, *The Oxford Handbook of International Investment Law* (Oxford University Press, 2008), 836; C. F. Dugan, D. Wallace Jr., N.D. Rubins & B. Sabahi, *Consent to Arbitral Jurisdiction* (Oxford University Press, 2008), 219.
12. *See Lanco v. Argentine Republic*, *supra* n. 6.
13. *See Lanco v. Argentine Republic*, § 1.
14. The concession agreement for Port Terminal No. 3 was signed on June 6, 1996 and was awarded to Terminal Portuarias Argentinas S.A., which Lanco was owner of 17,4% of the capital stock (*see Lanco v. Argentine Republic*, § 5). The co-bidders and awardees formed part of the grantee company and signed the concession agreement as awardees and guarantors (*ibid.*, §§ 15/16).

(a) written consent of the parties to the dispute for purposes of Chapter II of the ICSID Convention (Jurisdiction of the Centre) and for purposes of the Additional Facility Rules; and
(b) an 'agreement in writing' for purposes of Article II of the United Nations Convention on the Recognition and Enforcement of Foreign Arbitral Awards, done at New York, June 10, 1958 ("New York Convention").

Argentina claimed that there was an absence of consent to arbitrate for the purposes of Article 25(1) of the ICSID Convention,[15] based on the fact that the parties had agreed to resolve their disputes before the Federal Contentious-Administrative Courts of Buenos Aires, pursuant to the concession agreement dispute resolution clause.[16]

Argentina argued that "the generic offer that the States Parties formulate in Article VII(2) for accepting arbitral jurisdiction is residual or has effect where there is no stipulation by the parties to the contrary, pursuant to Article 26 of the ICSID Convention. While according to the BIT that choice is to be made by the investor once the dispute arises, it is unquestionable that the investor may only exercise that right to choose 'unless otherwise stated', in the terms of Article 26 of the ICSID Convention."[17]

The arbitral tribunal rejected the objections to jurisdiction put forward by Argentina, based on several findings of particular interest for investment arbitration.

The tribunal addressed the nature of the consent given by the State in a BIT and stated that *such consent was an invitation or a "generic" offer to arbitrate directed to the investors.*[18]

That offer was not binding for covered investors, who had to accept it by giving their consent in writing.[19]

The Tribunal further stated that *the consent of the investor, along with that of the Argentine Republic*, expressed in Article VII(4), *created the consent needed to provide ICSID with jurisdiction* over the dispute, pursuant to Article 25(1) of the ICSID Convention.[20]

15. Argentina alleged that: "The general offer or open invitation of Argentina and of the United States of America to U.S. and Argentine investors, respectively, or the fact of considering that the investor expresses its consent in writing upon submitting a dispute to ICSID, does not constitute the written consent required by Article 25(1) of ICSID, when subsequent to that generic offer there is an agreement between parties by which they freely consent to select a forum to settle any dispute related to the Concession Agreement" (*Lanco v. Argentine Republic*, § 34).
16. The concession agreement dispute resolution clause stated: "For all purposes derived from the agreement and the BID CONDITIONS, the parties agree to the jurisdiction of the Federal Contentious-Administrative Tribunals of the Federal Capital of the ARGENTINE REPUBLIC" (*Lanco v. Argentine Republic*, § 6).
17. *See Lanco v. Argentine Republic*, § 34.
18. *See ibid.*, § 32: "The States that are signatories to the ARGENTINA-U.S. Treaty make a generic offer in Article VII(4) to submit to international arbitration as selected by the investor pursuant to Article VII(3)."
19. *See Lanco v. Argentine Republic*, § 43.
20. *See ibid.*, § 33. Relying on the *American Manufacturing & Trading, Inc. v. Republic of Zaire*, ICSID Case No. ARB/93/1 (Award), February 21, 1997, the *Lanco* tribunal remarked that: [The consent for the purpose of Article 25 (1)] "is understood to be given by the State party to the dispute in the bilateral investment treaty from the moment the State extends a generic invitation to all the investors who are nationals of the other Contracting State to submit the settlement of

Once this was decided, the *Lanco* tribunal then referred to the exclusive remedy presumption set out in Article 26 of the ICSID Convention[21] and found that "when the parties give their consent to ICSID arbitration, they lose their right to seek to settle the dispute in any other forum, domestic or international, and it therefore presupposes the non-interference of any other forum with the ICSID arbitration proceedings once such proceeding has been instituted."[22]

The tribunal also examined the second sentence of Article 26 of the ICSID Convention. In the tribunal's view, the exclusivity rule established in the first sentence means that there is no need to exhaust domestic procedures before initiating ICSID arbitration, unless otherwise stipulated. To this end, the second sentence of Article 26 allows the State to require prior exhaustion of its administrative or judicial remedies as a condition for its consent to arbitration under the ICSID Convention.[23]

The tribunal found that stipulation to the contrary, if it exists (which was not found in the case), *does not replace consent* but instead dilutes the presumption of exclusivity of ICSID arbitration set forth in Article 26 of the ICSID Convention.[24]

Having concluded that no such stipulation to the contrary existed in the case, the tribunal recalled the irrevocability of consent once the arbitration was accepted by the investor,[25] and remarked that *the offer of consent expressed by the State under the Argentina-US BIT could not be diminished by the submission to Argentina's domestic courts to which the concession agreement remitted.*[26]

their possible disputes to ICSID jurisdiction. In contrast, the consent of the investor who is a national of the other Contracting State must be given by the investor in writing, since the consent of the State is not binding on the investor." *See Lanco v. Argentine Republic,* § 43.

21. *See* ICSID Convention, Article 26: "Consent of the parties to arbitration under this Convention shall, unless otherwise stated, be deemed consent to such arbitration to the exclusion of any other remedy. A Contracting State may require the exhaustion of local administrative or judicial remedies as a condition of its consent to arbitration under this Convention."
22. *See Lanco v. Argentine Republic,* § 36.
23. The Tribunal disregarded the existence of such condition in the case since the applicable BIT did not require the prior exhaustion of local remedies and the concession agreement invoked by Argentina merely set forth a jurisdiction which would be available for the investor in any case (*ibid.*, §§ 37/40).
24. *See Lanco v. Argentine Republic,* §§ 38/40. According to the tribunal, the stipulation to the contrary, if any, would result in a concurrence of jurisdiction, which would have to be resolved in the light of the provision of the second sentence of Article 26 of the ICSID Convention. Having found that such stipulation to the contrary did not exist in the case, the tribunal concluded that "In our case, the Parties have given their consent to ICSID arbitration, consent that is valid, there thus being a presumption in favor of ICSID arbitration, without having first to exhaust domestic remedies. In effect, once valid consent to ICSID arbitration is established, any other forum called on to decide the issue should decline jurisdiction. The investor's consent, which comes from its written consent by letter of September 17, 1997, and its request for arbitration of OCTOBER 1, 1997, and the consent of the State which comes directly form the ARGENTINA-U.S. Treaty, which gives the investor the choice of forum for settling its disputes, indicate that there is no stipulation contrary to the consent of the parties." *See Lanco v. Argentine Republic,* § 40.
25. *See Lanco v. Argentine Republic,* §§ 40/41. Article 25(1) *in fine* of the ICSID Convention states: "When the parties have given their consent, no party may withdraw its consent unilaterally." Based on this finding, the tribunal asserted that Argentina could not withdraw the consent given through the BIT after the investor had accepted ICSID jurisdiction (*ibid.*, § 40).
26. *See Lanco v. Argentine Republic,* § 40. Although the *Lanco* tribunal did not develop the distinction between contractual-based claims and treaty-based claims in order to support this finding—as done by several tribunals afterward—the examination carried out by the tribunal

Therefore, the *Lanco* decision not only shed light on the nature and effects of the State's consent given through BITs but also asserted the prevalence of the BIT dispute settlement provision over the contractual forum selection clauses, as far as BIT claims concern.[27]

Further, the *Lanco* tribunal highlighted the *rule of judicial abstention of local courts* (that is, the duty of non-interference) resulting from Article 26 of the ICSID Convention once the consent to ICSID arbitration is perfected. It also recalled the State's exposure to international liability that may result from courts' failure to comply with that duty.[28]

2 *The Offer of Consent Given in Investment Treaties*

The wording of investor-State dispute resolution provisions contained in investment treaties may vary significantly.[29] For that reason, the analysis must pay careful attention to the text of the specific treaty under examination.

Investment treaties frequently use unequivocal terms, stating that each contracting party "hereby consents,"[30] or that "the dispute shall be submitted to arbitration"[31]

was at the outset based on the finding that the Argentina-US applied to the case "given the existence of an investment dispute." That was the reason that led the Tribunal to examine whether the requirements for an investor to be able to recourse to the ICSID arbitration under Article VII of that treaty had been met (*ibid.*, § 20). Therefore, *Lanco* finding applies to treaty-based disputes.

27. *See* S. Alexandrov, "Introductory Note to ICSID: Lanco International Inc. v. Argentine Republic (Preliminary Decision on Jurisdiction of the Arbitral Tribunal)," 40ILM. 454 (2001), 454. The *Lanco* doctrine has been followed by several tribunals and commented by scholars. *See*, among others, *CMS Gas Transmission Company v. The Argentine Republic*, ICSID Case No. ARB/01/8 (Decision of the Tribunal on Objections to Jurisdiction), July 17, 2003 (hereinafter "*CMS v. Argentine Republic*"); *Azurix Corp. v. The Argentine Republic,* ICSID Case No. ARB/01/12 (Decision on Jurisdiction), December 8, 2003 (hereinafter "*Azurix v. Argentine Republic*"); *LG&E Energy Corp., LG&E Capital Corp., and LG&E International, Inc. v. Argentine Republic,* ICSID Case No. ARB/02/1 (Decision of the Arbitral Tribunal on Objections to Jurisdiction), April 30, 2004 (hereinafter "*LG&E v. Argentine Republic*"). *See also* B. M. Cremades & D. J. A. Cairns, "Contract and Treaty Claims and Choice of Forum in Foreign Investment Disputes," in B. M. Cremades & J. D. M. Lew (eds.), *Parallel State and Arbitral Procedures in International Arbitration* (Dossiers of the ICC Institute of World Business Law, vol. 3, Kluwer Law International, 2005), 3; Ch. Schreuer, "Consent to Investment Arbitration" (Transnational Dispute Management vol. 2, issue 05, 2007), 2; E. Gaillard, "The Denunciation of the ICSID Convention" (New York Law Journal vol. 237 n° 122, 2007), 2/3, among others.
28. *See Lanco v. Argentine Republic,* § 40.
29. B. M. Cremades & D. J. A. Cairns, "Contract and Treaty Claims and Choice of Forum in Foreign Investment Disputes," in B. M. Cremades & J. D. M. Lew (eds.), *Parallel State and Arbitral Procedures in International Arbitration* (Dossiers of the ICC Institute of World Business Law, vol. 3, Kluwer Law International, 2005), 14; Ch. Schreuer, "Consent to Investment Arbitration" (Transnational Dispute Management vol. 2, issue 05, 2007), 2; E. Gaillard, "The Denunciation of the ICSID Convention" (New York Law Journal vol. 237 n° 122, 2007), 3.
30. That is the case, inter alia, of the United Kingdom-United Republic of Tanzania BIT (1994), Article 8(1); and the Argentine Republic-Kingdom of the Netherlands BIT (1992), Article 10(3).
31. Ch. Schreuer, "Consent to Investment Arbitration" (Transnational Dispute Management vol. 2, issue 05, 2007), 4. That is the case, *inter alia*, of The Republic of Lebanon and The Republic of Chile BIT (1999), Article IX.2.2; and the Argentine Republic-Costa Rica BIT (1997), Article 5(b).

or alike. Such provisions constitute binding offers of consent made in writing by the host State.[32]

However, some treaties use other expressions, such as the host State "shall consent"[33] to arbitration in case of a future dispute. Such wording does not signify binding consent to arbitration. The parties (investor and State) need to enter into a separate agreement to arbitrate.[34] In those cases, the State does not express consent to arbitration but undertakes the commitment to give consent to arbitration in a future time.[35] The term "shall" means that the contracting State has a legal obligation under the relevant treaty to proceed as determined in those provisions.

As explained by Schreuer, in the above cases, if the host State refuses to give its consent, it would be in breach of its obligations under the BIT, and, thus, any remedy would lie with the other contracting party to the treaty.[36]

A weaker formulation may be found in the so-called "agreements to agree" clauses (like "disputes shall, upon the agreement by both parties, be submitted to arbitration to [ICSID]").[37] It has been confirmed that the intention of those clauses is to express a preference for arbitration of investment disputes while preserving a sovereign independence in the State parties to deal with investment disputes on a case-by-case basis as they arise.[38] A similar conclusion extends to clauses which state that the State "may consent" instead of "shall consent." These clauses would not be enforceable, even by the treaty partner of the BIT.

32. Ch. Schreuer, "Consent to Arbitration," in *Dispute Settlement. International Center for Settlement of Investment Dispute* (UNCTAD, 2003), 6.
33. That is the case, *inter alia*, of the Japan-Pakistan BIT (1998), Article 10(2); the Australia-Indonesia BIT (1992), Article 4(2); and the Australia-Lituania BIT (1998), Article 13.3.(a).
34. B. M. Cremades & D. J. A. Cairns, "Contract and Treaty Claims and Choice of Forum in Foreign Investment Disputes," in B. M. Cremades & J. D. M. Lew (eds.), *Parallel State and Arbitral Procedures in International Arbitration* (Dossiers of the ICC Institute of World Business Law, vol. 3, Kluwer Law International, 2005), 33.
35. Ch. Schreuer, "Consent to Arbitration," in P. Muchlinski, F. Ortino & Ch. Schreuer, *The Oxford Handbook of International Investment Law* (Oxford University Press, 2008), 836. Though the investor may be unable to claim directly against the host State, it may have access to diplomatic espousal by its home State or a claim under the State-State arbitration provision of the relevant treaty triggered by the latter (*see* C. F. Dugan, D. Wallace Jr., N. D. Rubins & B. Sabahi, *Consent to Arbitral Jurisdiction* (Oxford University Press, 2008), 238).
36. Ch. Schreuer, "Consent to Arbitration," in P. Muchlinski, F. Ortino & Ch. Schreuer, *The Oxford Handbook of International Investment Law* (Oxford University Press, 2008), 836.
37. *See* Serbia-Sweden BIT (1978), Article 6; and Sri Lanka-Switzerland BIT (1981), Article 9(1).
38. B. M. Cremades & D. J. A. Cairns, "Contract and Treaty Claims and Choice of Forum in Foreign Investment Disputes," in B. M. Cremades & J. D. M. Lew (eds.), *Parallel State and Arbitral Procedures in International Arbitration* (Dossiers of the ICC Institute of World Business Law, vol. 3, Kluwer Law International, 2005), 34; C. F. Dugan, D. Wallace Jr., N. D. Rubins & B. Sabahi, *Consent to Arbitral Jurisdiction* (Oxford University Press, 2008), 237. As regards the so-called agreement to agree clause, the former ICSID Secretary-General, Aron Broches, explained "[s]uch a provision does not, of course, constitute consent to arbitration by the States concerned ... Nor does it impose a legal obligation on these States to give such consent" (A. Broches, "Bilateral Investment Protection Treaties and Arbitration of Investment Disputes," in J. C. Schultsz & A. J. Van der Berg (eds.), *The Art of Arbitration* (Kluwer Law and Taxation, 1982), 63 and 65).

3 *Perfection of Consent*

Consent to arbitration must be mutual and reciprocal and must be obtained from both or all parties.[39]

The acceptance of the State's offer by a covered investor, also given in writing, perfects the consent, thus creating the agreement needed to submit the dispute to arbitration.[40] As stated in *Lanco*, once perfected, consent to arbitration becomes irrevocable unilaterally. This is not only an explicit rule under Article 25(1) of the ICSID Convention, but a consequence of the *pacta sunt servanda* principle, which applies equally whether an offer of consent is contained in national legislation or in a treaty[41] and whether it refers to ICSID jurisdiction or other international arbitration forums.[42]

a *Investor's Acceptance*

The investor's acceptance of consent can be given only within the limits of the offer (though it would be possible for the investor to narrow the scope of the offer and limit its acceptance only to certain matters or to a specific investment transaction).[43]

The investor may take up the State's offer of consent to arbitrate by filing the request for arbitration and, thus, instituting the arbitral proceeding. However, the acceptance may take place at an earlier, and perhaps more convenient, time.

Unless otherwise provided in the applicable treaty, nothing prevents covered investors expressing their acceptance to the arbitral forum offered in the investment treaty in an earlier stage and before the dispute arises or becomes mature enough to trigger the arbitration proceedings.[44] This could be done even at the time the investment is established, acquired, or during its development.[45]

39. Ch. Schreuer, "Denunciation of the ICSID Convention and Consent to Arbitration," in M. Waibel, A. Kaushal, K. L. Chung & C. Balchin (eds.), *The Backlash against Investment Arbitration: Perceptions and Reality* (Kluwer International, 2010), 357.
40. Ch. Schreuer, "Consent to Investment Arbitration" (Transnational Dispute Management vol. 2, issue 05, 2007) 5; A. M. Steingruber, *Consent in International Arbitration* (Oxford University Press), 190; B. M. Cremades & D. J. A. Cairns, "Contract and Treaty Claims and Choice of Forum in Foreign Investment Disputes," in B. M. Cremades & J. D. M. Lew (eds.), *Parallel State and Arbitral Procedures in International Arbitration* (Dossiers of the ICC Institute of World Business Law, vol. 3, Kluwer Law International, 2005), 33. *See also Tenaris S.A. and Talta: Trading e Marketing Sociedade Unipessoal Lda. v. Bolivarian Republic of Venezuela*, ICSID Case No. ARB/12/23 (Award), December 12, 2016 (hereinafter "*Tenaris v. Venezuela*"), § 59.
41. J. Sicard-Mirabal & Y. Derains, *Introduction to Investor-State Arbitration* (Kluwer Law International, 2018), 51/52; L. Reed et al., *Guide to ICSID Arbitration* (Kluwer Law International, 2010), 38.
42. Other institutions used for investment arbitration are: the ICC Court, the LCIA (London Court of International Arbitration), and for noninstitutional arbitration, the most common rules are those of the UNCITRAL.
43. Ch. Schreuer, "Denunciation of the ICSID Convention and Consent to Arbitration," in M. Waibel, A. Kaushal, K. L. Chung & C. Balchin (eds.), *The Backlash against Investment Arbitration: Perceptions and Reality* (Kluwer International, 2010), 358.
44. *See* in this sense, L. Reed et al., *Guide to ICSID Arbitration* (Kluwer Law International, 2010), 36 ("Consent may be given in advance with respect to a defined class of future disputes or with respect to an existing dispute"). Likewise, when consent is given in investment treaties, its perfection may take place, by a notice of acceptance given by the protected investor to the host

Investors may decide to accept the State's offer of consent before initiating arbitration proceedings and have the consent perfected at an earlier stage in order to prevent risks in case the States party to the BIT decide to amend or terminate the treaty in the future.[46] Although this is not the most usual way to proceed, depending on the circumstances (and, particularly, the likelihood of a future modification or unilateral termination of the relevant treaty or the ICSID Convention), an earlier acceptance could become an appropriate measure in order to preserve the covered investor's right to access the neutral arbitral forum offered in the applicable BIT. Once perfected, consent will remain in force even if the contracting parties decide to modify or terminate the treaty in the future.[47]

b *Date of Consent*

The date of consent is determined by the date on which the parties have agreed to arbitration.[48] In case the State's consent is anticipated in a BIT or an MIT, the investor's acceptance to the State's offer of consent will determine the date of the consent perfection.[49] In principle, there are no time constraints to accept the offer unless the offer expressly provides for acceptance within a certain period of time.[50]

State before the dispute arises. However, any provision to the contrary established in the applicable treaty will of course prevail. *See*, for instance, Article 1121(3) of the NAFTA and Articles 14.D.3(b)(2) and 14.D.5.1(d) of the USMCA for Mexico-United States disputes.

45. *See* Ch. Schreuer, "Consent to Arbitration," in P. Muchlinski, F. Ortino & Ch. Schreuer, *The Oxford Handbook of International Investment Law* (Oxford University Press, 2008), 837.
46. Ch. Schreuer, "Consent to Arbitration," in P. Muchlinski, F. Ortino & Ch. Schreuer, *The Oxford Handbook of International Investment Law* (Oxford University Press, 2008), 837. *See also* section [E.1] related to the State's denunciation of the applicable investment treaty or the ICSID convention.
47. *See* E. Gaillard, "The Denunciation of the ICSID Convention" (New York Law Journal vol. 237 n° 122, 2007), 2.; and Ch. Schreuer, "Consent to Arbitration," in P. Muchlinski, F. Ortino & Ch. Schreuer, *The Oxford Handbook of International Investment Law* (Oxford University Press, 2008), 837.
48. Ch. Schreuer, "Consent to Investment Arbitration," in P. Muchlinski, F. Ortino & Ch. Schreuer, *The Oxford Handbook of International Investment Law* (Oxford University Press, 2008), 832. In addition, this criterion was enshrined under the ICSID Institution Rules, Rule 2 which provides: "(3) "Date of consent' means the date on which the parties to the dispute consented in writing to submit it to the Center; if both parties did not act on the same day, it means the date on which the second party acted."
49. M. D. Nolan & F. G. Sourgens, "Limits of Consent—Arbitration without Privity and Beyond," in M. A. Fernández-Ballester & D. Arias Lozano (eds.), *Liber Amicorum Bernardo Cremades* (Wolters Kluwer España, 2010), 874.
50. A recent example of a time constraint can be found in the new USMCA (2020), Article 14.D.5.1 (c) setting out a four-year term, running as from the date on which the claimant first acquired, or should have first acquired, knowledge of the breach alleged, for a claim to be submitted to arbitration. *See also* Ch. Schreuer, "Consent to Arbitration," in P. Muchlinski, F. Ortino & Ch. Schreuer, *The Oxford Handbook of International Investment Law* (Oxford University Press, 2008), 855.

The determination of the time of consent is of particular importance since it is accepted that a mere offer of consent to arbitration may be withdrawn before its acceptance, unless it is irrevocable by its own terms.[51]

However, States are not allowed to withdraw the binding offer of consent unilaterally and on a case-by-case basis. A mutual amendment of the treaty by the contracting States or a valid cause for termination under the law of the treaties is required.[52]

For this reason, the State cannot indirectly modify the treaty offer by substituting it for a domestic forum clause in an agreement entered into with the investor (or an investment vehicle).[53] The offer given through the investment treaty will prevail for purposes of settling treaty-based claims.[54]

Consent must exist at the date of the institution of the arbitral proceedings. Consent to arbitration that is subsequent to the date of institution of the arbitral proceedings may not be enough, and the claim could be rejected for that reason.[55]

c *Legal Effects: Transfer of Investment Issues*

The moment in which the consent of the parties is satisfied becomes critical for several reasons.[56]

---

51. Ch. Schreuer, "Denunciation of the ICSID Convention and Consent to Arbitration," in M. Waibel, A. Kaushal, K.L. Chung & C. Balchin (eds.), *The Backlash against Investment Arbitration: Perceptions and Reality* (Kluwer International, 2010), 362. The withdrawal of an offer of consent given in a treaty may only take place before the perfection of consent and through a valid termination of the relevant treaties. Therefore, the general principle applicable to the matter may be found in Article 70 of the VCLT (relating to the consequences of the termination treaty).
52. Ch. Schreuer, "Consent to Arbitration," in P. Muchlinski, F. Ortino & Ch. Schreuer, *The Oxford Handbook of International Investment Law* (Oxford University Press, 2008), 837.
53. *See* B. M. Cremades & J. D. M. Lew (eds.), *Parallel State and Arbitral Procedures in International Arbitration* (Dossiers of the ICC Institute of World Business Law, vol. 3, Kluwer Law International, 2005), footnote 51 (stating that "The point is that a State party cannot withdraw its open offer or general consent to arbitrate by agreement with a particular investor (...) The right of forum selection arguably continues until an investment dispute arises, at which time any election of forum is irrevocable"). *See also* Ch. Schreuer, "Consent to Arbitration," in P. Muchlinski, F. Ortino & Ch. Schreuer, *The Oxford Handbook of International Investment Law* (Oxford University Press, 2008), 837.
54. *See Lanco v. Argentine Republic*, §§ 38/40, and the comment in section [I.A.1] above. *See also* S. Alexandrov, "Introductory Note to ICSID: Lanco International Inc. v. Argentine Republic (Preliminary Decision on Jurisdiction of the Arbitral Tribunal)," 40 ILM 454 (2001), 454.
55. In *Tradex v. Albania*, the ICSID tribunal rejected the BIT as a basis for its jurisdiction because it had come into force after the request for arbitration had been filed. According to the arbitral tribunal, it was clear that at the time of submitting the request for arbitration, Tradex could not rely on the tribunal jurisdiction only by the provisions of the BIT, since it entered into force several months after the request for arbitration was filed. Nevertheless, the tribunal also analyzed whether the later entry into force of the BIT could, with delay, be a basis in order to justify its jurisdiction. With respect to this issue, the tribunal noted that it could be arguably that Article 8 of the BIT (according to which the treaty also applied to investments made prior to its entry into force) provided a sufficient ground for the arbitral tribunal's jurisdiction and, therefore, based on the wording of the applicable BIT, also dismissed jurisdiction on that ground (*see Tradex Hellas S.A. v. Republic of Albania*, ICSID Case No. ARB/94/2 (Decision on Jurisdiction), December 24, 1996, § D.1).
56. Ch. Schreuer, "Consent to Arbitration," in P. Muchlinski, F. Ortino & Ch. Schreuer, *The Oxford Handbook of International Investment Law* (Oxford University Press, 2008), 856.

Consent to arbitration creates an exclusive forum that excludes all other remedies, unless express reservation is made.[57] This consequence is expressly set out in Article 26 of the ICSID Convention, although it is also generally applicable to non-ICSID disputes as well, to the extent that no explicit reservation to the contrary has been made.[58]

Similarly, diplomatic protection by the State of the investor nationality is no longer permitted once the parties have consented to the ICSID jurisdiction (Article 27(1) of ICSID Convention).[59]

The date of consent also fixes the parties' mutual rights and obligations with respect to proceedings under the ICSID Convention and other rules. Thus, no subsequent change in the arbitration rules can be applied to a proceeding initiated pursuant to an earlier consent, unless both parties agree otherwise.[60]

Further, under the ICSID Convention, the nationality of the foreign investor is generally determined by reference to the date of consent. Thus, national or legal persons must be nationals of another contracting State on the date of consent. If consent is based on a general offer in a treaty, the relevant date for the determination of the nationality is the date of the investor's acceptance.[61]

The nationality of the investor has led to new debates and issues, particularly in cases where investments have been transferred. During the last decades, several decisions have addressed controversial topics related to the validity of the assignment of treaty claims and the creation of new juridical entities in third States by the initial investor, in order to be able to invoke and take advantage of a BIT executed by third States with the host State of the investment.[62] Those tribunals reached different conclusions regarding the "treaty shopping" objection.[63]

---

57. Ch. F. Amerasinghe, *Jurisdiction of specific international tribunals* (Martinus Nijhoff Publishers, 2009), 446.
58. *See CME Czech Republic B.V. (The Netherlands) v. The Czech Republic*, UNCITRAL (1976) (Partial Award), September 31, 2001 and (Final Award), March 14, 2003, §§ 306/308; *Yaung Chi OO Trading PTE LTD. v. Government of the Union of Myanmar*, ASEAN I.D. Case No. ARB/01/1 (Award), March 31, 2003, § 41; *Nykomb Synergetics Technology Holding AB v. The Republic of Latvia*, SCC (Award), December 16, 2003 and *Mytilineos Holdings SA v. 1. The State Union of Serbia & Montenegro 2. Republic of Serbia*, UNCITRAL (Partial Award on Jurisdiction), September 8, 2006, §§ 221/225.
59. As the *Lanco* tribunal stated: "when the parties give their consent to ICSID arbitration, they lose their right to seek to settle the dispute in any other forum. In other words, once the investor accepted the state's offer to bring the matter to ICSID tribunal, this deprives any other tribunal or court of its jurisdiction" (*Lanco v. Argentine Republic*, § 36).
60. Ch. Schreuer, "Consent to Investment Arbitration" (Transnational Dispute Management vol. 2, issue 05, 2007), 29 and Ch. Schreuer, "Denunciation of the ICSID Convention and Consent to Arbitration," in M. Waibel, A. Kaushal, K. L. Chung & C. Balchin (eds.), *The Backlash against Investment Arbitration: Perceptions and Reality* (Kluwer International, 2010), 364.
61. Ch. Schreuer, "Denunciation of the ICSID Convention and Consent to Arbitration," in M. Waibel, A. Kaushal, K. L. Chung & C. Balchin (eds.), *The Backlash against Investment Arbitration: Perceptions and Reality* (Kluwer International, 2010), 361.
62. W. L. Lawton, "The transfer of Treaty Claims and Treaty-Shopping in Investor-State Disputes" (The Journal of World Investment & Trade, vol. 10, issue 03, 2009), 429.
63. Notwithstanding the absence of a unique definition, treaty shopping is usually seen as a legal operation aimed at making certain (more beneficial) investment treaty provisions accessible to the investor, including all legal operations aimed at invoking or creating a qualifying nationality and / or a qualifying investment (e.g., by structuring or restructuring an investment or by

Treaty or nationality planning cannot be deemed illegal as such,[64] and when it takes place before the investment is made or the alleged treaty breach occurs, it is usually accepted unless the applicable treaty states otherwise and the host State laws and BIT provisions for nationality are complied with.[65]

However, the practice shows several cases in which nationality planning has led to denial of jurisdiction. The *Banro v. Congo* case constitutes a clear example of this. In that case, the transfer of ownership of an investment was carried out from a company registered in a non-ICSID party (Canada) to an affiliate company in the United States (a party to the ICSID Convention). The transfer was made after the dispute had arisen and only days before instituting arbitration proceedings. Assuming that this served the purpose of obtaining access to ICSID and that the contracting investor could not transfer a better right than what he had, the tribunal refused to accept jurisdiction.[66]

Likewise, in *Société Générale v. Dominican Republic*, the tribunal stated that any transfer of rights should be a *bona fide* transaction and not be devised "to allow a national of a State not qualifying for protection under a treaty to obtain an inappropriate jurisdictional advantage otherwise unavailable by transferring its rights after-the-fact to a qualifying national." The tribunal found in that case that nothing suggested that the transaction had been designed in order to obtain inappropriate jurisdictional advantages. However, it also stated that Claimant became a beneficiary of the relevant treaty as of the time it acquired the investment.[67]

In *Autopista v. Venezuela*, the tribunal accepted its jurisdiction despite the fact that the original investors were from Mexico (a State that did not have a BIT with Venezuela) and had transferred their shares to a company in the United States (a State that did have a BIT with Venezuela), insofar as such transfer was accepted by Venezuela and the country expressed its consent to such operation.[68]

---

transferring claims) with a view to benefitting from a particular international investment agreement, granting an investor *ius standi* (J. Baumgartner, *Treaty Shopping in International Investment Law* (Oxford University Press, 2016), 10/12).

64. R. Dolzer & Ch. Schreuer, *Principles of International Investment Law* (Oxford University Press, 2012), 52.
65. E. Zuleta Jaramillo et al., "Treaty Planning: Current Trends in international Investment Disputes that Impact Foreign Investment Decisions and Treaty Drafting," in M. A. Fernández-Ballester & D. Arias Lozano (eds.), *Liber Amicorum Bernardo Cremades* (Wolters Kluwer España, 2010), 1250.
66. *See Banro American Resources, Inc. and Société Aurifère du Kivu et du Maniema S.A.R.L. v. Democratic Republic of the Congo*, ICSID Case No. ARB/98/7 (Award), September 1, 2000, § 5. In the same sense, *see Mihaly International Corporation v. Democratic Socialist Republic of Sri Lanka*, ICSID Case No. ARB/00/2 (Award), March 15, 2002, § 24; *Phoenix Action, Ltd. v. The Czech Republic*, ICSID Case No. ARB/06/5 (Award), April 15, 2009, § 93; and *Cementownia 'Nowa Huta' S.A. v. Republic of Turkey*, ICSID Case No. ARB(AF)/06/2 (Award), September 17, 2009, § 154.
67. *See Société Générale in respect of DR Energy Holdings Limited and Empresa Distribuidora de Electricidad del Este, S.A. v. The Dominican Republic*, LCIA Case No. UN 7927 (Award on Preliminary Objections to Jurisdiction) September 19, 2008, §110 (hereinafter "*Société Générale v. Dominican Republic*"). The tribunal further found that it had jurisdiction over acts and omissions that took place after the time the investor became beneficiary of the treaty (§ 107/111).
68. *See Autopista Concesionada de Venezuela, C.A. v. Bolivarian Republic of Venezuela*, ICSID Case No. ARB/00/5 (Decision on Jurisdiction), September 27, 2001, § 129.

In light of the existing case law, in order to avoid the appearance of treaty shopping, it is advisable for any change of nationality of an investor whose State does not have a BIT with the host State of the investment—either by way of the transfer of shares or assignment of claims or otherwise—to take place as early as possible and be grounded on good reasons.[69] Otherwise, if that transfer is made after the alleged BIT's breach occurs, it may be viewed with skepticism and find the jurisdiction denied,[70] even if the transfer takes place before the date of consent.

B Scope of Consent to Arbitration. Impact of the Umbrella Clause

Consent to arbitration offered in investment treaties may vary in scope. The dispute resolution provision may encompass "all disputes arising from an investment,"[71] or limit the scope to claims for violations of certain clauses of the treaty[72] or to certain disputes, excluding others.[73]

Broad formulations like "all disputes related to an investment" or "related to investment made under the treaty" have not been interpreted uniformly. While some tribunals have adopted an objective interpretation, others have interpreted them restrictively.[74]

---

69. W. L. Lawton, "The transfer of Treaty Claims and Treaty-Shopping in Investor-State Disputes" (The Journal of World Investment & Trade vol. 10, issue 03, 2009), 446.
70. E. Zuleta Jaramillo et al., "Treaty Planning: Current Trends in international Investment Disputes that Impact Foreign Investment Decisions and Treaty Drafting," in M. A. Fernández-Ballester & D. Arias Lozano (eds.), *Liber Amicorum Bernardo Cremades* (Wolters Kluwer España, 2010) 1252 ("...once the breach occurs, a transfer to a party with jurisdiction will be viewed with skepticism and almost certainly denied jurisdiction").
71. *See* the Pakistan-Switzerland BIT (1996), Article 9(1); the Argentine-France BIT (1993), Article 8(1); the China-Benin BIT (2004), Article 8(1); the Egypt-Tanzania BIT (1997), Article 10(1).
72. *See* Annex 14.C, Article 1 and Article 14.D.3.1 of the USMCA. *See also* Ch. Schreuer, "Consent to Investment Arbitration" (Transnational Dispute Management vol. 2, issue 05, 2007), 23/24 and 40.
73. *See* Article VII of the Argentine Republic-United States treaty where the consent is offered for investment disputes which are defined as follows: "a dispute between a Party and a national or company of the other Party arising out of or relating to (a) an investment agreement between that Party and such national or company; (b) an investment authorization granted by that Party's foreign investment authority (if any such authorization exists) to such national or company; or (c) an alleged breach of any right conferred or created by this Treaty with respect to an investment."
74. In *SGS v. Pakistan* the tribunal was required to decide in the light of Article 9 of the Switzerland-Pakistan BIT, which refers to "dispute with respect to investments." The *SGS v. Pakistan* tribunal stated that the phrase did not relate to the legal basis of the claims or cause of action asserted in the claims and no implication necessarily arises that both BIT and purely contractual claims are intended to be covered in the dispute settlement clause. *See SGS Societé Générale de Surveillance S.A. v. Islamic Republic of Pakistan*, ICSID Case No. ARB/01/13 (Decision on Objection to Jurisdiction), August 6, 2003 (hereinafter "*SGS v. Pakistan*") § 171. On the opposite way, in *SGS Société Générale de Surveillance SA v. the Republic of the Philippines*, ICSID Case No. ARB/02/6 (Decision on Jurisdiction), January 29, 2004 (hereinafter "*SGS v. Philippines*"), the tribunal concluded that the terms "dispute with respect to investments" included disputes arising from an investment contract, thus departing from the *SGS v. Pakistan* restrictive construction. *See SGS v. Philippines*, § 116. *See also Salini Costruttori S.p.A. and Italstrade S.p.A. v. The Hashemite Kingdom of Jordan*, ICSID Case No. ARB/02/13 (Decision on Jurisdiction), November 9, 2004 (hereinafter "*Salini v. Jordan*"), § 154; and *Compañia de Aguas*

In some investment treaties, the offer of consent to arbitration explicitly limits the scope to investments that have complied with certain requirements.[75] In some cases, the scope of consent is limited only to the amount of compensation for expropriation.[76] This kind of limit leads to the need for the arbitral tribunals to do substantial findings on facts and rights in order to determine their jurisdiction.

Further, consent to arbitration in investment treaties may be impacted by the umbrella clause contained in those treaties. Under the umbrella clause, the State parties undertake to observe any obligations they might have entered into with respect to investments.[77] As explained by Schreuer, through the umbrella clause, contractual obligations are put under the umbrella of the treaty protection. Therefore, violations of the contract related to the investment become treaty violations.[78]

However, arbitral tribunals have not come to a uniform position in respect of umbrella clauses. For instance, in *SGS v. Pakistan*, the tribunal found that the umbrella clause in the Pakistan-Switzerland BIT[79] did not purport to state that breaches of contracts alleged by an investor in relation to a contract had to be automatically "elevated" to the level of breaches of the international treaty law.[80] In *SGS v. Philippines*, the tribunal came to the opposite conclusion and affirmed that the umbrella clause in the Philippines-Switzerland BIT[81] made the host State's failure to observe binding commitments, including contractual commitments which it had assumed with regard to specific investments, a breach of the BIT.[82]

---

del Aconquija S.A. and Vivendi Universal S.A. v. The Argentine Republic, ICSID Case No. ARB/97/3 (Decision on Annulment), July 3, 2002, § 95. *Mobil Exploration and Development Inc. v. The Argentine Republic*, ICSID Case No. ARB/04/16 (Award), February 25, 2016, § 102.

75. The Belgium-Luxembourg-Malaysia BIT requires that the investment to which the dispute relates must have been specifically approved in writing as a condition for consent (*see* Belgium-Luxembourg-Malaysia BIT (1982), Article 10(2)). *See Philippe Gruslin v. Malaysia*, ICSID Case No. ARB/99/3 (Award), November 27, 2000, § 5.
76. *Telenor Mobile Communications A.S. v. The Republic of Hungary* ICSID Case No. ARB/04/15 (Award), September 13, 2006 (hereinafter "*Telenor v. Hungary*"), § 102. *See also*, the China-Hungary BIT (1993).
77. The most usual wording of umbrella clauses provides that each contracting party "shall observe any obligation it may have entered into with regard to investments." *See*, among others, the Argentine Republic-United States BIT (1994), Article 2(2)(c); the Argentine Republic-United Kingdom (1993), Article 2(2); the Kingdom of Netherlands-Republic of Paraguay BIT (1994), Article 3(4); the Kingdom of Netherlands-Republic of Peru BIT (1996), Article 3(4); the Germany-Pakistan BIT (1962), Article 7; the Denmark-Korea BIT (1988), Article 3; the Japan-Hong Kong BIT (1997), Article 2(3); the Ecuador Republic-United States BIT (1997), Article II.3.(c); and the Finland-Estonia BIT (1992), Article 4.
78. Ch. Schreuer, Consent to Arbitration, in P. Muchlinski, F. Ortino & Ch. Schreuer, *The Oxford Handbook of International Investment Law* (Oxford University Press, 2008), 839.
79. Pakistan-Switzerland BIT, Article 11.
80. *See SGS v. Pakistan*, §§ 166/167. The tribunal in *Joy Mining v. Egypt* also held a narrow view, stating that the umbrella clause in the Egypt-United Kingdom BIT could not have the effect of transforming all contract disputes into investment disputes under the Treaty, "unless of course there could be a clear violation of the Treaty rights and obligations or a violation of contract rights of such a magnitude as to trigger the Treaty protections, which is not the case." *See Joy Mining Machinery Limited v. The Arab Republic of Egypt*, ICSID Case No. ARB/03/11 (Award on Jurisdiction), August 6, 2004, § 81.
81. Philippines-Switzerland BIT, Article X(2).
82. *See SGS v. Philippines*, §§ 127/128. The tribunal made a distinction between the observance and performance of State obligations, such as a contract concluded with the investors, and the

Other tribunals, based on an effective interpretation of umbrella clauses, have recognized additional obligations arising therefrom, the breach of which has been considered a violation of the BIT, irrespective of whether it could also be framed as a breach of the BIT's other standards.[83]

Divergences have also appeared in several cases involving Argentina. In *El Paso v. Argentina*, the tribunal held a narrow interpretation and, drawing the distinction between commercial contracts and investment agreements, found that the umbrella clause did not extend the treaty protection to breaches of ordinary commercial contracts entered into by the State or a State-owned entity, but covered additional investment protections contractually agreed by the State as a sovereign (such as a stabilization clause) inserted in an investment agreement.[84] On the opposite direction, in *Siemens v. Argentina*, the tribunal dismissed the alleged distinction between different types of agreements (in that case, between investment agreements and contracts of administrative nature). The tribunal stated that "[a]ny agreement related to an investment that qualifies as such under the Treaty would be part of the obligations covered under the umbrella clause."[85]

Finally, in *LG&E v. Argentina*, the tribunal found that the umbrella clause covered not only obligations toward investments assumed in contracts but also specific undertakings assumed in domestic legislation.[86]

C Consent under an MFN Clause

Most investment treaties contain Most-Favored-Nation (MFN) clauses through which the beneficiaries of the treaty are entitled to claim the better treatment granted to a third State or its nationals.[87] One of the main questions regarding the application of the MFN

"extent or content" of these obligations, which remained contractual in nature, and thus, should be governed by the applicable national law.

83. *CMS Gas Transmission Company v. The Argentine Republic*, ICSID Case No. ARB/01/8 (Award), May 12, 2005, § 303; *Eureko B.V. v. Republic of Poland* (Partial Award), August 19, 2005 (hereinafter "*Eureko v. Poland*"), §§ 244/260; *Noble Ventures, Inc. v. Romania*, ICSID Case No. ARB/01/11 (Award), October 12, 2005, §§ 61/62.
84. *El Paso Energy International Company v. The Argentine Republic*, ICSID Case No. ARB/03/15 (Decision on Jurisdiction), April 27, 2006, §§ 66/86. In the same line, *see Pan American Energy LLC and BP Argentina Exploration Company v. The Argentine Republic*, ICSID Case No. ARB/03/13 (Decision on preliminary objections), July 27, 2006, §§ 92/115; *Joseph C. Lemire v. Ukraine* II, ICSID Case No. ARB/06/18 (Decision on Jurisdiction and Liability), January 14, 2010, § 498; *Ioan Micula and others v. Romania I*, ICSID Case No. ARB/05/20 (Award), December 11, 2013, §§ 417/418; *Oxus Gold plc v. Republic of Uzbekistan*, UNCITRAL (Final Award), December 17, 2015, § 365; and *Garanti Koza LLP v. Turkmenistan*, ICSID Case No. ARB/11/20 (Award), December 19, 2016, § 244.
85. *Siemens A.G. v. The Argentine Republic*, ICSID Case No. ARB/02/8 (Award), January, 17, 2007, § 206.
86. *LG&E v. Argentine Republic*, § 175.
87. Ch. Schreuer, Consent to Arbitration, in P. Muchlinski, F. Ortino & Ch. Schreuer, *The Oxford Handbook of International Investment Law* (Oxford University Press, 2008), 851. G. S. Tawil, *Los Conflictos en Materia de Inversión, la Jurisdicción del CIADI y el Derecho Aplicable: a Propósito de las Recientes Decisiones en los Casos 'Vivendi", 'Wena" y 'Maffezini"* (Kluwer International Law, 2003), 154/155.

clause has been whether its effects extend only to more favorable substantive protections granted in third treaties or also to most favorable dispute settlement provisions set forth therein.[88] More precisely, the debate has dealt with two main issues: whether it is possible to avoid the limitations attached to consent to arbitration in a treaty by relying on the MFN clause to apply another treaty that does not have those limitations or, going even further, whether it is admissible to take advantage of the MFN clause to create the consent to arbitration that is absent in the basic treaty.[89]

It is possible to find two clear different views on the matter. One view that understands that the MFN clause applies to dispute settlement provisions because that provision is a key element of the investment protection framework set forth in those treaties. And the opposite one, according to which the application of the MFN clause extends only to substantive protections, unless otherwise stated in a clear and unambiguous way in the basic treaty.

The decision adopted by the ICSID tribunal in *Maffezini v. Spain* constituted the starting point for this debate. The tribunal in that case ruled in favor of the claimant, allowing him to avoid the eighteen-month period of domestic courts litigation set out in the Argentine-Spain BIT by relying on the dispute resolution clause of the Chile-Spain BIT.[90]

The tribunal found that dispute settlement arrangements were part of the protection of foreign investors.[91] Therefore, the tribunal was satisfied that the MFN clause included in the Argentine-Spain BIT embraced the dispute settlement provision of the treaty, and thus the claimant had the right to submit the dispute to arbitration without passing through the Spanish courts first.[92]

After *Maffezini*, case law evidences that, while a number of decisions have followed the *Maffezini* reasoning,[93] other arbitral tribunals have departed from it and

88. Ch. F. Dugan, D. Wallace Jr., N. D. Rubins & B. Sabahi, *Investor-State Arbitration* (Oxford University Press, 2008), 217; A. Reinisch, "How Narrow are Narrow Dispute Settlement Clauses in Investment Treaties?" (Journal of International Dispute Settlement, Vol. 2, No. 1, 2011), 115/174.
89. Ch. Schreuer, Consent to Arbitration, in P. Muchlinski, F. Ortino & Ch. Schreuer, *The Oxford Handbook of International Investment Law* (Oxford University Press, 2008), 852/854.
90. *See Emilio Agustín Maffezini v. The Kingdom of Spain*, ICSID Case No. ARB/97/7 (Decision on Objections to Jurisdiction), January 25, 2000 (hereinafter "*Maffezini v. Spain*"), § 64.
91. *See Maffezini v. Spain*, § 50/54.
92. *See ibid.*, § 61/64. The tribunal made a distinction between the legitimate extension of rights and benefits and disruptive treaty-shopping and remarked that the MFN clause should not override public policy considerations that the contracting parties had in mind as fundamental conditions for their acceptance of the agreement (which were not present in the case). *See Maffezini v. Spain*, § 61/64.
93. *See Siemens v. Argentine Republic*, § 120; *Gas Natural v. Argentine Republic*, § 49; *Hochtief AG v. The Argentine Republic*, ICSID Case No. ARB/07/31 (Decision on Jurisdiction), October 24, 2011, § 73; *Suez, Sociedad General de Aguas de Barcelona, S.A. and Vivendi Universal, S.A. v. The Argentine Republic*, ICSID Case No. ARB/03/19 (Decision on Jurisdiction), August 3, 2006 (hereinafter "*Suez v. Argentine Republic*"), § 57; *National Grid plc v. The Argentine Republic*, UNCITRAL (Decision on Jurisdiction), June 20, 2006 (hereinafter "*National Grid v. Argentine Republic*"), § 93; *RosInvestCo v. Russian Federation*, §§ 155/156.

narrowed the scope of the MFN clauses, extending them only to substantive protections.[94]

For instance, the tribunal in *Wintershall v. Argentina* rejected the extension of the MFN clause to the dispute settlement clause and considered that the eighteen-month domestic litigation requirement was an essential preliminary step to the institution of ICSID arbitration, and constituted an integral part of the standing offer of the host State, which had to be accepted on the same terms.[95]

Another set of decisions also rejected the application of the MFN to dispute settlement displaying a restrictive view. However, differently from the abovementioned decisions, these cases dealt with treaties where the matter at issue was not the possibility to override procedural obstacles to the institution of arbitration proceedings but the absence of arbitration jurisdiction offered in the basic treaty. In *Plama v. Bulgaria*, the tribunal rejected the use of the MFN clause of the Bulgaria-Finland BIT to establish ICSID's jurisdiction. The tribunal held that the MFN provision did not incorporate by reference dispute settlement provisions, in whole or in part, set forth in another treaty, "unless the MFN provision in the basic treaty leaves no doubt that the Contracting Parties intended to incorporate them."[96]

D Interpretation of Consent to Arbitration

Expressions of consent to arbitration contained in investment treaties (or domestic legislation) have been interpreted through different approaches.[97] Although arbitral

94. *See Salini v. Jordan*, §§ 112/119; *Plama Consortium Limited v. Republic of Bulgaria*, ICSID Case No. ARB/03/24 (Decision on Jurisdiction), February 8, 2005 (hereinafter "*Plama v. Bulgaria*"), § 215; *Telenor v. Hungary*, §§ 83/101; *Vladimir Berschader and Moïse Berschader v. The Russian Federation*, SCC Case No. 080/2004 (Award), April 21, 2006 (hereinafter "*Berschader v. Russian Federation*"), § 181; *Wintershall Aktiengesellschaft v. Argentine Republic*, ICSID Case No. ARB/04/14 (Award), December 8, 2008 (hereinafter "*Wintershall v. Argentine Republic*"), §§ 160/167; *ICS Inspection and Control Services Limited (United Kingdom) v. The Republic of Argentina*, UNCITRAL, PCA Case No. 2010-9 (Award on Jurisdiction), February 10, 2012 (hereinafter "*ICS v. Argentina*"), §§ 274/318.
95. *Wintershall v. Argentine Republic*, §§ 160/167. Likewise, the tribunal in *ICS v. Argentina* rejected the invocation of the MFN clause based on the specific terms of the MFN clause of the Argentine Republic-United Kingdom BIT. The tribunal understood that the applicable MFN clause was not applicable to international arbitration since the MFN clause was only applicable to treatment "in the territory of the host State." Therefore, that treatment outside the territory of the host state did not fall within the scope of the clause (*ICS v. Argentina*, §§ 308/309). The argument based on the "place" of the treatment seems implausible. The place refers to the place of the investment, which is by definition made in the territory of the host State.
96. *Plama v. Bulgaria*, § 204 and § 223. Likewise, in *Telenor v. Hungary*, the offer of consent to arbitration was limited to the compensation or other consequences of the expropriation. The tribunal rejected the use of the MFN clause to benefit from wider dispute resolution provisions between the respondent State and third countries, by sustaining that the MFN clause referred to substantive but not to procedural rights (*see Telenor v. Hungary*, §§ 90/100). Further, in *Salini v. Jordan*, the tribunal also rejected to apply the MFN clause to extend jurisdiction over contract claims (*see Salini v. Jordan*, §§ 115/119).
97. *See Southern Pacific Properties (Middle East) Limited v. Arab Republic of Egypt*, ICSID Case No. ARB/84/3 (Decision on jurisdiction), April 14, 1988, § 143 (hereinafter "*SPP v. Egypt*"); *OPIC Karimum Corporation v. The Bolivarian Republic of Venezuela*, ICSID Case No. ARB/10/14 (Award), May 28, 2013 (hereinafter "*OPIC v. Venezuela*"), among others.

tribunals have not followed a uniform criterion, the balanced approach, according to which the interpretation shall be neither broad nor restrictive, but rather objective and consistent with the principle of good faith, has generally prevailed.

In *Amco v. Indonesia*, the tribunal rejected the respondent's argument that there was a presumption against the conferment of jurisdiction with respect to a sovereign State and stated that "...a convention to arbitrate is not to be construed restrictively, nor, as a matter of fact, broadly or liberally. It is to be construed in a way which leads to find out and to respect the common will of the parties... Moreover—and this is again a general principle of law—any convention, including conventions to arbitrate, should be construed in good faith, that is to say by taking into account the consequences of their commitment the parties may be considered as having reasonably and legitimately envisaged."[98]

A similar approach was applied by the tribunal in *Mondev v. United States*, where the tribunal supported the interpretation in accordance with the applicable rules of interpretation of treaties set out in Articles 31-33 of the Vienna Convention on the Law of Treaties (VCLT).[99]

In *SOABI v. Senegal*, the tribunal stated that consent to arbitral proceedings constituted a derogation of the right to have recourse to national courts, and thus such consent should not be presumed. However, the tribunal also noted that the correct view was an interpretation consistent with the principle of good faith: "interpretation must take into account the consequences which the parties must reasonably and legitimately be considered to have envisaged as flowing from their undertakings...."[100]

In *SPP v. Egypt*, the restrictive interpretation was invoked in connection with an arbitration clause contained in national legislation. The tribunal found that there was not a presumption in favor of or against the conferment of jurisdiction. Arbitral jurisdiction only exists insofar as consent has been given by the parties.[101]

Some tribunals have gone even further and sustained an extensive interpretation of the consent clause.[102]

98. *See Amco Asia Corporation and others v. Republic of Indonesia*, ICSID Case No. ARB/81/1 (Decision on jurisdiction), September 25, 1983 (hereinafter "*Amco v. Indonesia*"), § 24.
99. *See Mondev International LTD. v. United States of America* ICSID Case No. ARB(AF)/99/2 (Award), October 11, 2002 (hereinafter "*Mondev v. United States*"), §§ 42/43.
100. *Société Ouest Africaine des Bétons Industriels v. Senegal*, ICSID Case No. ARB/82/1 (Award), February, 25, 1988, § 4.08/4.10. Endorsing a balanced approach of interpretation, *see also Duke Energy International Peru Investments No. 1 Ltd. v. Republic of Peru*, ICSID Case No. ARB/03/28 (Decision on Jurisdiction), February 1, 2006, § 76/78; *El Paso Energy International Company v. The Argentine Republic*, ICSID Case No. ARB/03/15 (Award), October 31, 2011, § 68/70.
101. *SPP v. Egypt*, § 63; *Inceysa Vallisoletana S.L. v. Republic of El Salvador*, ICSID Case No. ARB/03/26 (Award), August, 2, 2006, § 176.
102. Ch. Schreuer, "Consent to Investment Arbitration" (Transnational Dispute Management vol. 2, issue 05, 2007), 37. *See also*: *Methanex Corporation v. United States of America*, UNCITRAL (Preliminary Award on Jurisdiction), August 7, 2002, § 7; *Aguas del Tunari, S.A. v. Republic of Bolivia*, ICSID Case No. ARB/02/3 (Decision on Jurisdiction), October 21, 2005, § 91; *SGS v. Philippines*, § 8 and 116; *Eureko v. Poland*, § 248; and *Suez v. Argentine Republic*, § 59 and § 64; *Tradex v. Albania*, § D.6.

More recently, this discussion arose in the *OPIC Karimun v. Venezuela* case, in connection with the interpretation of Article 22 of Venezuela's Investment Law.[103] The cornerstone of the debate was whether the Respondent had provided consent to ICSID jurisdiction through that provision.[104]

As a starting point, the tribunal supported a balanced view, stating that "the correct approach to interpretation of Article 22 of the Investment Law is to apply the rules of international law governing the interpretation of treaties and of unilateral acts formulated within the framework and on the basis of a treaty, namely the ICSID Convention, having regard to the ICSID jurisprudence where relevant."[105]

However, since the wording of Article 22 of the Investment Law was ambiguous, the tribunal looked for the evidence submitted by the Parties in order to determine whether the evidence established with "sufficient clarity" that Venezuela intended to consent to ICSID arbitration when it passed Article 22 of the Investment Law.[106] The majority of the tribunal concluded that, although some inferences of consent could exist, *there was no direct evidence* before it to establish the intention of the Venezuelan legislator to grant consent to ICSID jurisdiction through Article 22 of the Investment Law, *as required* by Article 25 of the ICSID Convention.[107]

The dissenting opinion reached a different conclusion.[108] It agreed on the applicable standard for the interpretation of consent and the need to look beyond the wording of Article 22 of Venezuela Investment Law in order to determine Venezuela's intention when enacting the Law. However, it rejected the assertion of the majority of the tribunal that "consent should be expressed in a manner that leaves no doubt" (since that standard of proof limited evidence of consent exclusively to the wording of the text), as well as the denial of jurisdiction based on the absence of 'direct evidence' of consent that could only take the form of documents in possession, custody or control of the Respondent, duly requested and not produced by the latter. That threshold of proof imposed by the majority of the tribunal was deemed too high.[109] The dissenting opinion further recalled that an offer of consent to arbitrate had to be interpreted neither restrictively nor expansively, but rather objectively and in good faith,[110] as stated by the tribunal in the *SPP v. Egypt* case and others.[111]

103. Article 22 of the Venezuela's Investment Law states: "Disputes arising between an international investor whose country of origin has in effect with Venezuela a treaty or agreement on the promotion and protection of investments, or disputes to which are applicable the provisions of the Convention Establishing the Multilateral Investment Guarantee Agency (OMIGI-MIGA) or the Convention on the Settlement of Investment Disputes between States and Nationals of Other States (ICSID), shall be submitted to international arbitration according to the terms of the respective treaty or agreement, if it so provides, without prejudice to the possibility of making use, when appropriate, of the dispute resolution means provided for under the Venezuelan legislation in effect" (*see OPIC v. Venezuela*, §§ 66/67).
104. *See OPIC v. Venezuela*, § 68.
105. *See ibid.*, § 76.
106. *See ibid.*, § 165.
107. *See ibid.*, § 178.
108. *See OPIC v. Venezuela*, Dissenting Opinion of Prof. Dr. Guido S. Tawil, May 16, 2013 (hereinafter "*OPIC v. Venezuela—Dissenting Opinion*").
109. *See ibid.*, §§ 4/6 and § 13.
110. *See ibid.*, §§ 3/4.
111. *See ibid.*, §§ 11/13.

Finally, arbitral tribunals have consistently found that interpretation of consent to arbitration contained in investment treaties shall be governed by the rules of treaty interpretation and international law. Likewise, questions about whether the parties have consented to ICSID jurisdiction (even when the clause is included in legislation or agreements) are not to be answered by reference to national law but rather to international law, as set out in Article 25(1) of the ICSID Convention.[112] Tribunals have also held that the law applicable to the merit of the case does not apply to this matter.[113]

E Consent in Multiparty Arbitration

As explained above [I], consent must be obtained from all parties, in writing.

Multiparty investment arbitrations need to find consent in some of the instruments which are appropriate for that purpose (i.e., treaty, legislation or contracts). In treaty-based disputes, consent is more likely to be found in the applicable investment treaty (BIT or MIT) or the rules of arbitration that they incorporate by reference.[114]

Arbitral tribunals have not required additional consent from States for multiparty proceedings when the applicable BIT contains a clause related to consent to multiparty arbitration[115] or consent to have the pending disputes arising from the same overall economic transaction resolved in one and the same arbitration could be implied.[116] In *Abaclat v. Argentina*, *Ambiente Ufficio v. Argentina*, and *Alemanni v. Argentina*, additional consent was not required since the Argentina-Italy BIT granted the arbitral jurisdiction over disputes "between the Contracting Party and the *investors*" (emphasis added). In those cases, the arbitral tribunals considered that the use of the word

112. *See SPP v. Egypt*, § 61.
113. *See CMS v. Argentine Republic*, § 88.
114. C. Lamm, P. Hansel & A. Bay. "Consent and Due Process in Multiparty Investor-State Arbitrations," in C. Binder, U. Kriebaum, A. Reinisch & S. Wittich (eds.), *International Investment Law for the 21st Century: Essays in Honour of Christoph Schreuer* (Oxford University Press, 2009), 55/56. Examples of investment treaties containing specific provisions on the matter are the 2004 US Model BIT, Article 33, NAFTA, Article 1126(2) and (3) and more recently, USMCA, Article 14.D.12, which reads as follows: "If two or more claims have been submitted separately to arbitration under Article 14.D.3.1 (Submission of a Claim to Arbitration) and the claims have a question of law or fact in common and arise out of the same events or circumstances, any disputing party may seek a consolidation order in accordance with the agreement of all the disputing parties sought to be covered by the order or the terms of paragraphs 2 through 10." Further, the most modern arbitration rules frequently referred to in investment treaties contain explicit provisions on multiparty arbitrations and consolidation (*see* UNCITRAL Arbitration Rules (2013), Article 17.5 and ICC Arbitration Rules (2021), Articles 7 to 10).
115. *Canfor Corporation and others v. United States*, UNCITRAL (Order of the Consolidation Tribunal), September 7, 2005, § 79.
116. *Noble Energy and Machala Power v. Ecuador and Conelec*, ICSID Case ARB/05/12 (Decision on Jurisdiction), March 5, 2008, § 194. Other precedents admitting the consolidation are: *Ambiente Ufficio S.p.A. and others v. Argentine Republic*, ICSID Case No. ARB/08/9 (Decision on Jurisdiction and Admissibility), February 8, 2013 (hereinafter "*Ambiente Ufficio v. Argentine Republic*"), § 133; *Guaracachi America, Inc. and Rurelec PLC v. Bolivia*, PCA Case No. 2011-17 (Award), January 31, 2014, § 343.

investor in plural was sufficient to prove the implied consent to multiparty arbitration.[117]

Under the new United States-Mexico-Canada Agreement (USMCA), consolidation of multiparty arbitrations can be requested by any disputing party when the claims both have a question of law or fact in common *and* arise out of the same events or circumstances.[118]

When considering whether multiparty arbitrations can be consolidated, arbitral tribunals have considered several factors, including whether: (i) there are common legal or factual grounds; (ii) the investment is the same or was made jointly by the claimants; (iii) the underlying facts or the overall economic transaction was the same; (iv) the investors or the claims were affiliated; (v) the alleged harm was caused by similar measures of the same State; (vi) the same respondents were named; and (vii) the remedies sought were aligned. In general terms, it could be said that the more related the cases are, the more likely a Tribunal is to treat them together—even over a party's objection.[119]

With the purpose of providing a more modern solution to this issue, the Proposals for Amendment of the ICSID Rules admit the possibility of multiple claims by establishing that the expression "party" may include all parties acting as claimants or respondents. Pursuant to the proposed amended rules, consolidation will require the agreement of the parties of two or more pending arbitrations.[120]

Investment treaties do not generally provide for joinder of third parties. Requests for joinder have been made on the basis of the applicable arbitration rules. The criterion for admitting the third-party joinder has been restrictive in investment

117. *See* Italy-Argentina BIT Article 8(3). *See also, Ambiente Ufficio v. Argentine Republic*, § 133; *Abaclat and Others (Case formerly known as Giovanna a Beccara and Others) v. Argentine Republic*, ICSID Case No. ARB/07/5 (Decision on Jurisdiction and Admissibility), August 4, 2011 (hereinafter "*Abaclat v. Argentine Republic*"), § 541; and *Giovanni Alemanni and others v. Argentine Republic*, ICSID Case No. ARB/07/8 (Decision on Jurisdiction and Admissibility), November 17, 2014, § 186.

118. *See* Article 14.D.12 of USMCA. If proceedings are consolidated the arbitration will be conducted under the UNCITRAL Rules (Article 14.D.12.8).

119. *See* the Proposals for Amendment of the ICSID Rules, Working Paper #4, vol. 3, Schedule 7, 834/ 840. *See also Noble Energy and Machala Power v. Ecuador and Conelec*, ICSID Case No. ARB/05/12 (Decision on Jurisdiction), March 5, 2008, § 186/207 (which also stated that " resolving different disputes in a single proceeding does not mean merging disputes, or applicable laws, or remedies"; *ibid.*, §206).

120. *See* Proposals for Amendment of the ICSID Rules, Working Paper#4, vol. 3, 87/88 (https://icsid.worldbank.org/sites/default/files/amendments/WP_4_Vol_1_En.pdf). The amended Rule 2 (Chapter II) reads as follows: "Meaning of Party and Party Representation (1) For the purposes of these Rules, "party" may include, where the context so admits: (a) all parties acting as claimants or as respondents; and (b) an authorized representative of a party (...)." Amended Article 87 also states the following: "Rule 38 Consolidation or Coordination on Consent of Parties (1) Parties to two or more pending arbitrations administered by the Centre may agree to consolidate or coordinate these arbitrations. (2) The parties referred to in paragraph (1) shall provide the Secretary-General with written terms of reference, specifying the terms of consolidation or coordination to which they would consent. (3) The Secretary-General shall take all necessary administrative steps to implement the agreement of the parties if the consolidation or coordination requested would promote a fair and efficient resolution of all or any claims asserted in the arbitrations."

arbitration. Instead, submissions of non-disputing parties or *amicus curiae* have been admitted under certain conditions and limits.[121]

F Applicability of Consent in Investment Treaties *Ratione Temporis*

Investment treaties may provide that they shall apply to investments made before their entry into force. Some of them also set forth that they shall not apply to disputes arising before their entry into force.[122] In those cases, the time at which the dispute has arisen becomes decisive for the applicability of the consent to arbitration. Several tribunals have dealt with this matter. In order to decide, tribunals have distinguished the existence of a dispute from the chain of events that may lead to it or the damage that may result therefrom.

In *Maffezini v. Spain*, the tribunal distinguished between the facts and events that might have led to the dispute and taken place before the BIT's entry into force and the existence of the dispute. The tribunal found that "the conflict of legal views and interests will only be present in the latter stage, even though the underlying facts predate them."[123]

In *Helnan v. Egypt*, the tribunal differentiated between the terms "divergence" and "dispute" and stated that, although both required the existence of a disagreement between the parties on specific points, they did not imply the same degree of animosity: "[I]n case of a dispute, the difference of views forms the subject of an active exchange

121. *See* ICSID Arbitration Rule 37(2). *See also* the recent USMCA, Article 14.D.7.3 (which provides for the *amicus curiae* participation as follows: "After consultation with the disputing parties, the tribunal may accept and consider written *amicus curiae* submissions regarding a matter of fact or law within the scope of the dispute… ." *See also* UNCITRAL Rules on Transparency in Treaty-based Investor-State Arbitration (2013), Articles 4 and 5. *See also Suez, Sociedad General de Aguas de Barcelona, S.A., and Vivendi Universal S.A. v. The Argentine Republic,* ICSID Case No. ARB/03/19 (Order in Response to a Petition by Five Non-governmental Organisations for Permission to Make an Amicus Curiae) Submission), February 12, 2007, § 24 ("As a general proposition, an amicus curiae must have sufficient information on the subject matter of the dispute to provide perspectives, expertise and arguments which are pertinent and thus likely to be of assistance to the tribunal"). The readiness revealed by the tribunal in *Suez* shows that the arbitrators felt competent to decide on the question of access by non-disputing parties to the case file, without the need to obtain the consent of the parties to the dispute. The tribunal in *Biwater v. Tanzania* expressed their decision on this issue in similar terms (*see Biwater Gauff (Tanzania) v. United Republic of Tanzania,* ICSID Case No. ARB/05/22 (Procedural Order No. 5), February 2, 2007, § 62. However, in absence of a rule stating otherwise (ICSID Arbitration Rules as amended in 2006 were not yet in force), the ICSID arbitral tribunal in *Aguas del Tunari v. Bolivia* informed the amicus petitioners that their request was "beyond the power or the authority of the Tribunal to grant. The interplay of the two treaties involved . . . and the consensual nature of arbitration places the control of the issues you raise with the parties, not the Tribunal. In particular, it is manifestly clear to the Tribunal that it does not, absent the agreement of the Parties, have the power to join a non-party to the proceedings" (*see Aguas del Tunari, S.A. v. Republic of Bolivia,* ICSID Case No. ARB/02/3 (Decision on Jurisdiction), October 21, 2005) § 17).
122. *See,* for instance, the Argentine Republic-Kingdom of Spain BIT (1992), Article II.2; the Australia-Oriental Republic of Uruguay BIT (2019), Article 2.(1); the Republic of Peru-Republic of Chile BIT (2001), Article 2.
123. *See Maffezini v. Spain,* § 96.

between the parties under circumstances which indicate that the parties wish to solve the difference, be it before a third party or otherwise."[124]

Where the consent to arbitration is limited to claims based on the violation of the treaty that contains the consent, the date of the treaty's entry into force is also the date from which acts and events are covered by the consent.[125] In those cases, some tribunals have endorsed the concept of "continuing breach"—that is, an act that commenced before the treaty's entry into force and persisted thereafter,[126] and have distinguished between an act of a continuing character and an act already completed which continues to cause loss or damage.[127] Likewise, tribunals have also pointed out that prior acts or conduct may play a role since they may be considered a constituting part, concurrent factor or aggravating or mitigating element of conduct, acts or omissions of the respondent State that took place after the date the treaty entered into force. This is so provided that such subsequent conduct constitutes a breach of the treaty.[128]

II PROCEDURAL REQUIREMENTS AND LIMITS TO CONSENT TO ARBITRATION GIVEN IN INVESTMENT TREATIES

Most investment treaties set out certain procedural requirements which must be met by investors to submit a claim to arbitration. Such requirements usually refer to waiting periods for amicable settlement[129] and, sometimes, mandatory resort to domestic courts in order to attempt to settle the dispute within a certain period of time.[130]

As for the waiting periods for amicable settlement, arbitral tribunals have most frequently found that the requirement had been fulfilled by the claimant. In some cases, tribunals found that noncompliance with waiting periods did not affect their jurisdiction, and allowed the claimant to avoid them if the insistence would have been an excessive formalism or would be futile.[131] However, in other cases, tribunals

124. *Helnan International Hotels A/S v. Arab Republic of Egypt*, ICSID Case No. ARB/05/19 (Decision of the Tribunal on Objection to Jurisdiction), October 17, 2006, § 52.
125. *Société Générale v. Dominican Republic*, § 90/94 and §111 (pointing out the rule of nonretroactivity of the treaty rights to acts and omissions occurred before the treaty entry into force and the claimant became an investor under the treaty).
126. Ch. Schreuer, "Consent to Arbitration," in P. Muchlinski, F. Ortino & Ch. Schreuer, *The Oxford Handbook of International Investment Law* (Oxford University Press, 2008), 860.
127. *See Mondev v. United States*, §§ 57/58. *See also Société Générale v. Dominican Republic*, § 94.
128. *Técnicas Medioambientales Tecmed, S.A. v. The United Mexican States*, ICSID Case No. ARB/00/2 (Award), May 29, 2003, §§ 64/65. *See also*, *Mondev v. United States*, § 70.
129. This requirement is subject to certain time limits ranging from three to twelve months and, if no settlement is reached within that period, the claimant may proceed to arbitration (Ch. Schreuer, "Consent to Arbitration," in P. Muchlinski, F. Ortino & Ch. Schreuer, *The Oxford Handbook of International Investment Law* (Oxford University Press, 2008), 844).
130. Ch. Schreuer, "Consent to Arbitration," in P. Muchlinski, F. Ortino & Ch. Schreuer, *The Oxford Handbook of International Investment Law* (Oxford University Press, 2008), 847.
131. *See Ronald S. Lauder v. The Czech Republic*, UNCITRAL (Final Award), September 3, 2001 (hereinafter "*Lauder v. Czech Republic*"), §§ 188/191; *SGS v. Pakistan*, § 184.

expressed a contrary view and pointed out that the waiting period was a jurisdictional requirement.[132]

Nevertheless, the most common understanding is that, unless an amicable agreement has been frustrated by the submission of the request for arbitration ahead of time, fulfillment of the waiting period requirement is not required, and has not generally been considered an essential prerequisite in order to define the tribunal's jurisdiction.[133]

States may also require the exhaustion of local remedies as a condition of consent to arbitration.[134] However, the exhaustion of local remedies has lost popularity in modern investment treaties, and Article 26 of the ICSID Convention explicitly excludes it "unless otherwise stated."[135] As pointed out in *Lanco*, the first sentence of Article 26 means that there is no need to exhaust domestic procedures before initiating ICSID arbitration, unless otherwise stipulated.[136]

The exhaustion of local remedies was replaced by a requirement to attempt to settle the dispute in domestic courts for a certain period of time (not necessarily to exhaust recourses available in domestic courts).[137]

---

132. *Enron Corporation and Ponderosa Assets, L.P. v. Argentine Republic*, ICSID Case No. ARB/01/3 (Decision on jurisdiction), January 14, 2004 (hereinafter "*Enron v. Argentine Republic*"), § 88. *See also Antoine Goetz et consorts v. République du Burundi*, ICSID Case No. ARB/95/3 (Award), February 10, 1999, §§ 90/93.
133. *See Ethyl Corp v. The Government of Canada*, UNCITRAL (Award on Jurisdiction), June 24, 1998, § 76/88; *Wena Hotels Ltd. v. Arab Republic of Egypt*, ICSID Case No. ARB/98/4 (Decision on jurisdiction), June, 29, 1999, § 74/87; *Bayindir Insaat Turizm Ticaret Ve Sanayi A.S. v. Islamic Republic of Pakistan*, ICSID Case No. ARB/03/29 (Decision on jurisdiction), November 14, 2005, §§ 99/102; *Lauder v. Czech Republic*, §§ 171/175; *SGS v. Pakistan*, §§ 185/189.
134. Ch. Schreuer, "Consent to Arbitration," in P. Muchlinski, F. Ortino & Ch. Schreuer, *The Oxford Handbook of International Investment Law* (Oxford University Press, 2008), 847. The exhaustion of local remedies requirement prevents the investor from filing its claim before an arbitral tribunal until remedies have been exhausted before domestic courts (*see* E. Sipiorski, *Good Faith in International Investment Arbitration* (Oxford International Arbitration Series, 2019), 118). It constitutes an indirect restrain of the *Calvo* doctrine, according to which "foreigners could seek redress from grievances only before local courts." The doctrine gave rise to the *Calvo Clause*, which precluded arbitration and instead required disputes to be resolved in national courts, *see* G. Biggs, "Bernardo Cremade's Contribution to the Development of Arbitration Law in Latin America," in M. A. Fernández-Ballester & D. Arias Lozano, *Liber Amicorum Bernardo Cremades* (Wolters Kluwer España; 2010), 216; and G. S. Tawil *On the Internationalization of Administrative Contracts, Arbitration and the Calvo Doctrine*, in Albert Jan Van den Berg (ed.), Arbitration Advocacy in Changing Times, ICCA Congress Series, Volume 15 (Kluwer Law International 2011) 328/334).
135. *See* Ch. Schreuer, "Consent to Arbitration," in P. Muchlinski, F. Ortino & Ch. Schreuer The Oxford Handbook of International Investment Law (Oxford University Press, 2008), 847/848; Ch. Schreuer, "Calvo's Grandchildren: The Return of Local Remedies in Investment Arbitration" (The Law and Practice of International Courts and Tribunals 1, 2005), 1; and J. Sicard-Mirabal & Y. Derains, *Introduction to Investor-State Arbitration* (Kluwer Law International, 2018), 53.
136. *See Lanco v. Argentine Republic*, § 38. The tribunal in *Generation Ukraine v. Ukraine* followed the same reasoning, adding that a State requirement to exhaust local remedies as a condition of consent to ICSID arbitration "*must be contained in the instrument in which such consent is expressed, i.e., the BIT itself*" (*Generation Ukraine, Inc. v. Ukraine*, ICSID Case No. ARB/00/9 (Award), September 16, 2003, § 13.5).
137. *See* among others, E. Sipiorski, *Good Faith in International Investment Arbitration* (Oxford International Arbitration Series, 2019) 118. A similar requirement has been introduced in the USMCA (2020), Article 14-D.5.1.(a) and (b) for a period of thirty months.

Claimants have consistently relied on the MFN clause in order to avoid such requirement of resorting to domestic courts for a period of time (usually eighteen months) by importing more favorable dispute settlement provisions from third-party BITs. They have also invoked the futility exception to override the requirement.[138] Tribunal decisions have been neither uniform nor consistent regarding this issue, as explained in [I.C] above.

While some tribunals have waived the requirement through the application of the futility exception, emphasizing that the relief sought in local courts was patently unavailable,[139] others have rejected the exception based on the fact that futility was not patent enough.[140] Notably, the futility exception has been explicitly recognized in the recent USMCA,[141] stating that the requirement to obtain a final decision from a court of last resort by the respondent or that a thirty-month term has elapsed from the date the proceeding[142] does not apply when the recourse to domestic remedies is obviously futile.[143]

A large number of modern BITs exclude the exhaustion of local remedies requirement or the limited recourse to local courts for a certain period of time and, instead, include clauses that allow an investor to choose between the local courts of the host State and international arbitration. The so-called *fork-in-the-road* provision.[144] Under that provision, the investor is offered a choice between the host State's domestic courts and international arbitration,[145] but once the claimant chooses one forum, it automatically excludes the other one.[146]

138. A related argument is that the eighteen-month recourse to local courts is not a jurisdictional requirement but a procedural rule directed at facilitating the dispute settlement within a limited timeframe. Therefore, it should not be deemed binding should it become futile. *See* G. S. Tawil, "Los Conflictos en Materia de Inversión, la Jurisdicción del CIADI y el Derecho Aplicable: a Propósito de las Recientes Decisiones en los Casos 'Vivendi', 'Wena' y 'Maffezini'," Revista Brasileira de Arbitragem (Kluwer Law International, 2003), 159. *See also* Ch. F. Amerasinghe, *Jurisdiction of specific international tribunals* (Martinus Nijhoff Publishers, 2009), who explains, with regard to the exhaustion of internal remedies, that it is a condition of admissibility ("properly interpreted and applied, the nature of the rule [exhaustion of local remedies] is entirely procedural and in no circumstances substantive") (*ibid.* 119/120).
139. *Abaclat v. Argentine Republic*, § 582. *See also Ambiente Ufficio v. Argentine Republic*, § 607.
140. *See ICS v. Argentina*, § 269. *See also Wintershall v. Argentine Republic*, § 128.
141. *See* USMCA (2020), Article 14.D.5.1 (b).
142. *See ibid.*, Article 14.D.5.1 (a) ("the claimant (for claims brought under Article 14.D.3.1(a) (Submission of a Claim to Arbitration)) and the claimant or the enterprise (for claims brought under Article 14.D.3.1(b)) first initiated a proceeding before a competent court or administrative tribunal of the respondent with respect to the measures alleged to constitute a breach referred to in Article 14.D.3").
143. *See* USMCA (2020), Annex 14.D, footnote 25 ("The provisions in subparagraphs (a) and (b) do not apply to the extent recourse to domestic remedies was obviously futile").
144. E. Sipiorski, *Good Faith in International Investment Arbitration* (Oxford International Arbitration Series, 2019), 119/120. Ch. Schreuer, "Calvo's Grandchildren: The Return of Local Remedies in Investment Arbitration" (The Law and Practice of International Courts and Tribunals 1, 2005), 4.
145. Ch. Schreuer, "Consent to Arbitration," in P. Muchlinski, F. Ortino & Ch. Schreuer, *The Oxford Handbook of International Investment Law* (Oxford University Press, 2008), 848.
146. Z. Douglas, *The International Law of Investment Claims* (Cambridge University Press, 2009), 152.

The purpose of the fork-in-the-road provision in international investment arbitration is to avoid situations of uncertainty and unpredictability that dispute resolution at multiple fora may bring. In addition to a possible violation of the principle of *ne bis in idem* (not twice the same thing) it may give rise to contradictory decisions on the same matter and between the same parties, and double enforcement and execution proceedings.[147]

As regards the applicable test in order to identify whether the investment dispute is the same, some tribunals have relied on the triple identity test (examining whether the domestic proceedings concern the same cause of action and object, and are brought among the same parties as those involved in the international arbitration forum).[148] Other tribunals have relied instead on whether or not the "fundamental basis of a claim" or the "cause of action" are identical in the two lawsuits or are autonomous one from the other. The latter standard has been confirmed by recurring case law.[149]

The most critical issue arising from these requirements is whether they should be considered precedent conditions to consent that impede the tribunal's power to adjudicate (that is, for being of jurisdictional natural) or whether they pertain to the admissibility of the claim.[150] Doctrine and case law are not uniform on the matter (mainly in respect of the resort to domestic courts for a limited period of time).[151] However, the futility exception has been admitted in both cases, and has even been explicitly recognized in recent investment treaties (i.e., the USMCA). This may lead to a more stable and accepted practice in favor of extending the applicability of the futility

147. J. Sicard-Mirabal & Y. Derains, *Introduction to Investor-State Arbitration* (Kluwer Law International, 2018), 71.
148. *See Occidental Exploration and Production Company v. The Republic of Ecuador*, LCIA Case No. UN3467 (Final Award), July 1, 2004, § 52; *Alex Genin, Eastern Credit Limited, Inc. and A.S. Baltoil v. The Republic of Estonia*, ICSID Case No. ARB/99/2 (Award), June 25, 2001, §§ 330/331; *CMS v. Argentine Republic*, § 80; *Azurix v. Argentine Republic*, § 88; *Víctor Pey Casado and President Allende Foundation v. Republic of Chile*, ICSID Case No. ARB/98/2 (Award I), May 8, 2008, §§ 483/486, *Enron v. Argentine Republic*, §§ 97/98; *AES Corporation v. Argentine Republic*, ICSID Case No. ARB/02/17 (Decision on Jurisdiction), April 26, 2005, §§ 95/97, among others.
149. This test was first set out by the *Woodruff Case, United States v. Venezuela*, American Venezuelan Mixed Commission (IX RIAA 213, 1903), and adopted by the arbitrator Jan Paulsson in the case *Pantechniki S.A. Contractors & Engineers (Greece) v. The Republic of Albania*, ICSID Case No. ARB/07/21 (Award), July 30, 2009, § 61. The fundamental basis test was further applied in recurring case law, such as, *H&H Enterprises Investments, Inc. v. Arab Republic of Egypt*, ICSID Case No. ARB 09/15 (Award), May 6, 2014, § 368; *AES Corporation and Tau Power B.V. v. Republic of Kazakhstan*, ICSID Case No. ARB/10/16 (Award), November 1, 2013, §§ 226/230; and *Yuri Bogdanov and Yulia Bogdanov v. Republic of Moldova*, SCC Case No. V091/2012 (Final Award), April 16, 2013, §§ 171/174. Ch. Schreuer, "Consent to Arbitration," in P. Muchlinski, F. Ortino & Ch. Schreuer, *The Oxford Handbook of International Investment Law* (Oxford University Press, 2008), 849.
150. Z. Douglas, *The International Law of Investment Claims* (Cambridge University Press, 2009), 152.
151. *See Maffezini v. Spain*, §§ 61/64; *Siemens v. Argentine Republic*, § 120; *Gas Natural v. Argentine Republic*, § 49; *Suez v. Argentine Republic*, § 57; *National Grid v. Argentine Republic*, § 93; *RosInvestCo UK Ltd. v. The Russian Federation*, SCC Case No. V079/2005 (Award on Jurisdiction), October 1, 2007 (hereinafter "*RosInvestCo v. Russian Federation*"), §§ 155/156. And on the other hand: *See Salini v. Jordan*, §§ 112/119; *Wintershall v. Argentine Republic*, §§ 160/167; *ICS v. Argentina*, §§ 274/318.

exception to all prior requirements established for the submission of the dispute to arbitration.

III INTERACTION BETWEEN CONSENT IN INVESTMENT TREATIES AND INVESTMENT AGREEMENTS

As anticipated in section [I.A.1] *supra*, in *Lanco* the tribunal concluded that the stipulation to the contrary foreseen in Article 26 of the ICSID Convention only eliminates the presumption as to the exclusivity of ICSID arbitration and does not replace the consent to arbitration—which, once it has been given by the parties, prevails over any other forum called on to decide the dispute.[152] Thus, since the parties had validly given their consent to ICSID arbitration and the investor had not agreed to submit the investment dispute to any other forum, the arbitral tribunal concluded that it had jurisdiction to hear and decide on the case.[153]

Several ICSID tribunals have followed the *Lanco* doctrine, affirming that, although contractual disputes may belong to the exclusive jurisdiction of local courts, that does not prevent the investor party to a contract from initiating arbitration proceedings to enforce its rights under a BIT.[154] The breach of a contract is not enough to transform the dispute into a non-international contractual claim,[155] and if the fundamental basis of a claim is a treaty, a forum selection clause inserted in a contract does not prevent the application of a conventional rule.[156]

In addition, a different view could lead to situations of abuse by States.[157] This is more evident where (as frequently happens) the terms and conditions of licenses, concession agreements and governmental authorizations are unilaterally imposed by the State party, the contractors not being enabled to depart from or modify them at their own will and in their own benefit.[158] Therefore, States would have the chance to easily bypass their treaty obligations and duties—including the duty to arbitrate in a neutral forum selected by the investor—if they were allowed to disregard the consent offered

152. *See Lanco v. Argentine Republic*, §§ 38/40.
153. *See ibid.*, § 28 and §§ 38/40.
154. *See Suez v. Argentine Republic*, § 44.
155. *See TSA Spectrum Argentina S.A. Claimant v. The Argentine Republic* ICSID Case No. ARB/05/5 (Award), December 19, 2019, § 51.
156. *See Enron Creditors Recovery Corp. Ponderosa Assets, L.P. v. The Argentine Republic*, ICSID Case No. ARB/01/3 (Decision on the Application for Annulment of the Argentine Republic), July 30, 2010, § 132.
157. Ch. Schreuer, "Calvo's Grandchildren: The Return of Local Remedies in Investment Arbitration" (The Law and Practice of International Courts and Tribunals 1, 2005), 1; J. Sicard-Mirabal & Y. Derains, *Introduction to Investor-State Arbitration* (Kluwer Law International, 2018), 49/63.
158. The award of concession agreements and licenses through international public tender is the rule and the most frequent mechanism to grant governmental contracts in energy, public infrastructure, public services, airport, among others sectors of public interest. Under the public law regime governing State's activity, governmental contracts are generally awarded in accordance with the terms and conditions designed by the State, without allowing the private parties to change them in order to preserve the principles of legality and equal treatment (with regard to the public law general principles governing the State's activity, *see* G.S. Tawil, *Administración y Justicia* (Depalma, 1993), 43/44).

in a BIT by simply establishing a domestic dispute forum (or any other limitation or conditions absent in the treaty) in contracts, licenses or authorizations related to the investment.

IV NEW ISSUES ARISING FROM DENUNCIATION OF TREATIES AND THE ICSID CONVENTION

During the last decade, the denunciation of investment treaties has given rise to several issues regarding the impact of that decision on the State's offer of consent to arbitration contained in the relevant treaty and the rights of foreign investors protected by such international instrument.

Pursuant to Article 42 (2) of the VCLT, "the termination of a treaty, its denunciation or the withdrawal of a party, may take place only as a result of the application of the provisions of the treaty or of the present Convention." Article 54(a) adds that termination of a treaty or the withdrawal of a party may take place in conformity with the provisions of the treaty. These rules reflect customary international law.[159]

Thus, in dealing with this issue, the denunciation provisions of the relevant treaty prevail as *lex specialis*.[160]

As an example, the US Model BIT (2012) prescribes: "A Party may terminate this Treaty at the end of the initial ten-year period or at any time thereafter by giving one year's written notice to the other Party."[161]

Where the BIT does not contain a provision as to the manner in which it may be terminated or withdrawn from, Article 56 of the VCLT allows States to withdraw from international treaties unilaterally as long as there was an express or implied intention to permit such withdrawal and the withdrawing party provides a no less than twelve-month notice to the other contracting parties.[162]

The notice period has a direct impact on the denunciation's effectiveness. During the notice period, the parties remain bound by the provisions of the treaty and the investors remain the beneficiaries of the treaty's protections. Upon the conclusion of that notice period, contracting States are released from any obligations under the treaty but remain actively involved in any pending arbitration proceedings to which they are a party.[163]

159. Ch. Schreuer, "Denunciation of the ICSID Convention and Consent to Arbitration," in M. Waibel, A. Kaushal, K. L. Chung & C. Balchin (eds.), *The Backlash against Investment Arbitration: Perceptions and Reality* (Kluwer International, 2010), 353.
160. That is confirmed by Article 44 of the VCLT which provides "A right of a party, provided for in a treaty or arising under article 56, to denounce, withdraw from or suspend the operation of the treaty may be exercised only with respect to the whole treaty unless the treaty otherwise provides or the parties otherwise agree."
161. *See* United States Model BIT (2012), Article 22.2.
162. Article 56(2) of the VCLT states: "A party shall give not less than twelve months' notice of its intention to denounce or withdraw from a treaty under paragraph 1."
163. Ch. B. Wychera & W. Mimnagh, "Investment Arbitration. The Nature of State Consent Expressed in BITs," in Ch. Klausegger & P. Klein, et al. (eds.), *Austrian Yearbook on International Arbitration 2019* (Manz'sche Verlags- und Universitätsbuchhandlung, 2019) 409.

a Sunset clauses

Many investment treaties include the so-called sunset or survival clause, which are designed to prolong the benefits and protections afforded under such treaty to investors who invested before the termination date.[164]

The purpose of sunset clauses is to protect an investor's legitimate expectations and therefore to prevent host States from abruptly changing the entire investment regime upon which the investors relied.[165] A sunset clause protects investors that have already made an investment in the territory of the host State before the expiry date of the treaty. Those clauses typically prolong investment protections for a period between five and twenty years.[166]

Some States, with the purpose of terminating their BITs, may first amend their BIT in order to remove its sunset clause and only subsequently terminate the BIT in its entirety. An amendment of this kind is directed at allowing the contracting parties to avoid the activation of the sunset clause and immediate termination of the BIT.[167]

As long as the BIT remains in force, the State's offer of consent is, in principle, maintained and binding.[168] That offer is extended to the sunset clause period in respect of investments made prior to the treaty's expiry date. In other words, in principle, the treaty protections and rights remain with regard to investments already made, including the investor's right to accept the offer of consent to arbitration contained in the investor-State dispute resolution clause.[169]

---

164. A recent example of this is Article 26(3) of the draft Dutch Model BIT (2018), which contemplates the following sunset clause: "In respect of investments made before the date of the termination of the present Agreement, this Agreement shall continue to be in effect for a further period of fifteen years from that date."
165. Ch. B. Wychera & W. Mimnagh, "Investment Arbitration. The Nature of State Consent Expressed in BITs," in Ch. Klausegger et al. (eds.), *Austrian Yearbook on International Arbitration 2019* (Manz'sche Verlags- und Universitätsbuchhandlung, 2019) 408/410.
166. For instance, the Italy-Romania BIT (1995) in its Article 11.3 provides that "In the case of investments made before the expiry date of this Agreement, such as provided for in this Article 11, the provisions of articles 1 to 1) will remain in force for others *five years* after the aforementioned dates" (emphasis added). Further, pursuant Article 13.3 of the Netherlands-Poland BIT (1994): "In respect of investments made before the date of the termination of this Agreement the foregoing Articles thereof shall continue to be effective for a further period of *15 years* from that date" (emphasis added). Also, Article 12.3 of the Czech Republic-Malta BIT (2003) provides that "In respect of investments made prior to the termination of this Agreement, the provisions of this Agreement shall continue to be effective for a period of *ten years* from the date of termination" (emphasis added) and the Japan-Ukraine BIT (2015) in its Article 28.4 states "Notwithstanding paragraph 2, in respect of investments acquired prior to the date of termination of this Agreement, the provisions of this Agreement shall continue to be effective for a period of *ten (10) years* from the date of termination of this Agreement" (emphasis added).
167. Such was the case of the amendment made by Denmark and the Czech Republic in 2011 to its 1991 BIT. Through the amendment, the parties removed Article 16(2) of the Czech Republic-Denmark BIT which kept the effect of the substantive provisions of that BIT for ten years.
168. Ch. Schreuer, "Consent to Arbitration," in P. Muchlinski, F. Ortino & Ch. Schreuer, *The Oxford Handbook of International Investment Law* (Oxford University Press, 2008), 836.
169. It has been argued that sunset clauses create an independent treaty right that once accepted by an investor, cannot be revoked by the State as part of a separate agreement with its BIT counterparty (*see* M. Paparinskis, "*Analogies and Other Regimes of International Law*," in Z. Douglas, J. Pauwelyn & J. E. Vinuales (eds.), *The Foundations of International Investment Law*

b Denunciation of ICSID Convention

The denunciation of the ICSID Convention by Ecuador, Bolivia and Venezuela has triggered a further deep debate in this field.[170] Doubts arose primarily about the effects that such denunciation causes on the offer to ICSID arbitration contained in BITs and investment laws enacted by the denouncing State.[171]

Articles 71 and 72 of the ICSID Convention deal with the denunciation of that treaty in the following terms:

> "Article 71: Any Contracting State may denounce this Convention by written notice to the depositary of this Convention. The denunciation shall take effect six months after receipt of such notice.
>
> Article 72: Notice by a Contracting State pursuant to Articles 70 or 71 shall not affect the rights or obligations under this Convention of that State or of any of its constituent subdivisions or agencies or of any national of that State arising out of consent to the jurisdiction of the Centre given by one of them before such notice was received by the depositary."

Pursuant to Article 71, the denunciation has effect after a six-month period as of its notice. On the other hand, according to Article 72 of the ICSID Convention, rights and obligations arising out of "consent to the jurisdiction of the Centre" given by that contracting State, its constituent subdivisions or agencies, or any national of that State, before the notice of denunciation, shall remain unaffected.

The interpretation of Articles 71 and 72 and their impact on binding BITs have led to different views by scholars and case law. Discussions deal first with the question of whether the consent mentioned in Article 72 refers to consent perfected by the acceptance of the investor, which is therefore irrevocable, or if it refers to the general consent given by an ICSID contracting party in an investment treaty. The other question deals with the interaction between Articles 71 and 72, to the extent that the former prolongs the effectiveness of the ICSID Convention for a six-month period after the denunciation date. The third question relates to the impact of the denunciation of the ICSID Convention on the dispute resolution provisions referring to ICSID jurisdiction contained in BITs or investment treaties that are still in force.

According to some scholars and case law, the acceptance of the offer of the State to consent ICSID arbitration should be done before the denunciation date to trigger the

(Oxford University Press, 2014), 81/82). The discussion deals with the general rule set forth in Article 70(1)(b) of the VCLT, pursuant to which, unless otherwise provides in the (original) treaty, the termination or withdrawal of a treaty does not affect any right, obligation or legal situation of the parties created through the execution of the treaty prior to its termination.

170. On May 2, 2007, the World Bank received a notice of denunciation of the ICSID Convention from the Republic of Bolivia (https://icsid.worldbank.org/en/Pages/News.aspx?CID=103); on July 2, 2009, Ecuador denounced the ICSID Convention (https://icsid.worldbank.org/en/Pages/News.aspx?CID=87), although it subsequently rejoined on August 4, 2021 (https://icsid.worldbank.org/news-and-events/news-releases/ecuador-ratifies-icsid-convention) and; on January 24, 2012, Venezuela's Ministry of Foreign Affairs submitted a written notice of denunciation of the ICSID Convention before the World Bank (https://icsid.worldbank.org/en/Pages/News.aspx?CID=47).
171. A. Mezgravis, "El estándar de interpretación aplicable al consentimiento y a su revocatoria en el arbitraje de inversión" (Revista Internacional de Arbitraje, Bogotá, Colombia, 2010), 151.

protection under Article 72. On the other hand, it has been sustained that the acceptance of the offer of consent by an investor after the notice of denunciation but before the six-month expiration of Article 71 should also be unaffected since, during that additional term, the ICSID Convention continues in force and the denouncing State remains party to the ICSID Convention.[172]

The divergence has been reflected in recent cases involving Venezuela. In *Blue Bank v. Venezuela*,[173] *Venoklim v. Venezuela*[174] and *Fábrica de Vidrios and Owens Illinois v. Venezuela*,[175] the claimants filed their request for arbitration during the six-month period of Article 71 and, therefore, their consent had not yet perfected before the notice of Venezuela's denunciation of the ICSID Convention.

Applying the rules of treaty interpretation as set out in the VCLT, the majority of the tribunal in *Blue Bank*[176] understood that the plain reading of Article 71 of the ICSID Convention required that denunciation become effective as of the expiry of the six-month notification period.[177] Thus, the majority concluded that the agreement to arbitrate was validly perfected before the expiry of the six-month period during which Venezuela, despite its denunciation, was still a party to the ICSID Convention.[178] Hence, the State's offer of consent was still in force and binding and could therefore be accepted by the investor.[179] For that reason the majority of the tribunal did not need to address the interpretation of the expression "consent to the jurisdiction of the Centre" included in Article 72 of the ICSID Convention.[180]

Further, in *Venoklim v. Venezuela* the tribunal concluded that Article 72 of the ICSID Convention could not be interpreted to give immediate effects to Venezuela's

172. For an overview of the discussion *see* Ch. Schreuer, "Denunciation of the ICSID Convention and Consent to Arbitration," in M. Waibel, A. Kaushal, K. L. Chung & C. Balchin (eds.), *The Backlash against Investment Arbitration: Perceptions and Reality* (Kluwer International, 2010), 353 et seq.; and E. Gaillard, in The Denunciation of the ICSID Convention (New York Law Journal vol. 237 n° 122, 2007), 2.
173. *See Blue Bank International & Trust (Barbados) Ltd. v. Bolivarian Republic of Venezuela*, ICSID Case No. ARB 12/20 (Award), April 26, 2017 (hereinafter "*Blue Bank v. Venezuela*").
174. *See Venoklim Holding B.V. v. Bolivarian Republic of Venezuela*, ICSID Case No. ARB/12/22 (Award), April 3, 2015 (hereinafter "*Venoklim v. Venezuela*").
175. *See Fábrica de Vidrios Los Andes, C.A. and Owens-Illinois de Venezuela, S.A. v. Venezuela*, ICSID Case No. ARB/12/21 (Award), November 13, 2017 (hereinafter "*Fábrica de Vidrios and Owens Illinois v. Venezuela*").
176. As stated in the award, the three members of the Tribunal reached the same result regarding the Tribunal's jurisdiction *ratione voluntatis*, and agreed on this conclusion unanimously, but the President of the Tribunal adopted a different approach to this issue and appended a separate opinion to the Award in this regard (*Blue Bank v. Venezuela*, §101).
177. The majority of the tribunal highlighted that the term "shall" of Article 71 of the ICSID Convention is mandatory and, stated that: "Any other interpretation of this provision would render the reference to a six-month time period devoid of any meaning, and would run directly contrary to the principle of *effet utile* (*ut res magis valeat quam pereat*), which is one of the fundamental tenets of treaty interpretation. If the intention was for the denunciation to take immediate effect, it would have made no sense to specify, in the second sentence of Article 71, that there should be a further waiting period of six months after receipt of the notice before the denunciation becomes effective" (*see Blue Bank v. Venezuela*, § 119).
178. *See Blue Bank v. Venezuela*, § 120.
179. See *ibid.*, § 110.
180. See *ibid.*, § 119.

denunciation of the ICSID Convention, noting that an interpretation as such would be in direct contradiction of Article 71 of the ICSID Convention.[181]

The tribunal further distinguished the scope and meaning of Articles 71 and 72, stating that while Article 71 brings solutions for problems that may arise after the denunciation, Article 72 sets out the preservation of acquired rights and duties arising before the denunciation, confirming the nonretroactivity rule.[182]

In *Fábrica de Vidrios and Owens Illinois v. Venezuela*, the tribunal departed from the *Venoklim* and *Blue Bank* precedents and made a distinction between Article 71 and Article 72 of the ICSID Convention, pointing out that Article 71 is addressed to Venezuela as a contracting State to the ICSID Convention, while Article 72 is addressed to the State as a party (or potential party) in ICSID arbitration proceedings.[183] Weighing the nature of a State's consent expressed in a BIT, the tribunal concluded that the mere inclusion of an expression of consent in a BIT does not generate any rights under the ICSID Convention. Rights under the ICSID Convention only exist when the offer of consent is perfected.[184] According to the tribunal, "it is only where consent to arbitration to the jurisdiction of the Centre is perfected, such that it generates rights and obligations under the ICSID Convention that those rights and obligations persist following the receipt of a notice of denunciation by a Contracting State pursuant to Article 71."[185] Thus, the tribunal interpretation of Article 72 of the ICSID Convention was that "consent to the jurisdiction of the Centre" is only preserved if it was given and perfected prior to the notice of denunciation being received by the depository pursuant to Article 71 of the ICSID Convention.[186]

The analysis of the tribunal in this case follows, in general terms, Prof. Schreuer's position on the matter. Schreuer also relies on the discussion of the *travaux préparatoires* to Article 72 of the ICSID Convention where it was stated that a unilateral statement of consent by a State that had not been accepted by the investor was not binding and that it would be made ineffective by a denunciation.[187]

181. See *ibid.*, § 62.
182. See *ibid.*, § 64. The *Blue Bank v. Venezuela* tribunal followed a similar approach, adding: "If, as the majority finds, an agreement to arbitrate was formed between the Claimant and the Respondent before denunciation under Article 71 took effect, there is no reason to inquire further into Article 72, inasmuch as Article 72 deals only with the post-termination survival of certain of a State's rights or obligations" (*Blue Bank v. Venezuela*, §108).
183. *See Fábrica de Vidrios and Owens Illinois v. Venezuela*, § 269.
184. *See ibid.*, § 275. *See also* Ch. B. Wychera & W. Mimnagh, "Investment Arbitration. The Nature of State Consent Expressed in BITs," in Ch. Klausegger et al. (eds.), *Austrian Yearbook on International Arbitration 2019* (Manz'sche Verlags- und Universitätsbuchhandlung, 2019), 413.
185. *Fábrica de Vidrios and Owens Illinois v. Venezuela*, § 282.
186. *Ibid.*, §§ 271/282.
187. Ch. Schreuer, "Denunciation of the ICSID Convention and Consent to Arbitration," in M. Waibel, A. Kaushal, K.L. Chung & C. Balchin (eds), *The Backlash against Investment Arbitration: Perceptions and Reality* (Kluwer International, 2010), 365. *See also Fábrica de Vidrios and Owens Illinois v. Venezuela*, § 292. In truth, Prof. Schreuer pointed out that at the time of the ICSID Convention's drafting, treaties, such as BITs containing offers of consent to arbitration were still unknown (*ibid.*, 357). Prof. Schreuer's main reasoning is based on the interpretation of Article 72 of the ICSID Convention as a special intertemporal rule that preserves the rights and obligations arising out from the consent from the consequences of the denunciation (*ibid.*, 364).

However, the assertion does not deny the binding effect of commitments and undertakings arising from BITs and investment treaties—including the unequivocal offer of consent to arbitration—until the denunciation or valid termination of the relevant treaty takes effect. This leads the discussion back to the starting point, that is, the determination of the date the denunciation becomes effective.[188]

The wording of Article 71 of the ICSID Convention does not give rise to controversy. Indeed, the discussion arises from the more complex wording of Article 72. Article 71 does not contain any expression subjecting or conditioning that provision to any other rule. It does not make any distinction as regards the Convention's effectiveness until the six-month period elapses and the denunciation takes effect. Instead, Article 72 explicitly relies on the former by providing: "Notice by a Contracting State *pursuant to* Article ...71 shall not affect the rights or obligations under this Convention ... ."

In this context, the interpretation sustained in *Blue Bank v. Venezuela* and *Venoklim v. Venezuela*—according to which the consent perfected before the denunciation takes effect shall be deemed valid and effective—seems to better conciliate both provisions without depriving any of them of their scope and meaning.[189]

Another discussion relates to whether the consent shall be deemed perfected when the applicable treaty sets out prior steps to submit a dispute to arbitration and they have not been fulfilled at the time of the denunciation of a State party.

This matter arose in the *Tenaris and Talta v. Venezuela* case[190] where the claimants—part of the Techint Group—initiated an arbitration proceeding against Venezuela for the alleged violation of the BITs signed by Venezuela with Luxemburg and Portugal in relation to two of their companies: "*Tavsa*" (Luxembourgish) and

188. Additional views have been brought to the table. For instance, M. Potestá has stated that "[t]he principle that a written or oral declaration made by a state official, without any reciprocal commitment or response and outside the context of formal negotiations, may give rise to binding obligations is well established under international law and was affirmed by the International Court of Justice (ICJ) in the Nuclear Tests cases (...)" and that "[t]here is no reason why the same legal principles could not be applied to unilateral declarations made by states to private entities" (*see* M. Potestá, The Interpretation of Consent to ICSID Arbitration Contained in Domestic Investment Laws, *Arbitration International* (LCIA Volume 27, Issue 2, June 1, 2011), 162).

189. The consent perfected during the six-month period set out in Article 71 will be covered anyway by the principle of irrevocability established in Article 25(1) of the ICSID Convention and also by the general rule set forth in Articles 44 and 70(1)(b) and (2) of the VCLT, which explicitly preserve any right, obligation or legal situation of the parties created through the execution of the treaty prior to its termination, stating that, in MITs, the termination applies to the relations between that State and each of the other parties to the treaty *from the date* when such denunciation or withdrawal *takes effect*. *See also* E. Gaillard, "The Denunciation of the ICSID Convention" (New York Law Journal vol. 237 n° 122, 2007), 2 ("When the investor has accepted the state's general consent prior to the receipt of the notice of denunciation by the centre or within the six-month period set forth in Article 72, the effectiveness of the existing rights and obligations should raise little difficulty as the host state is still a contracting party at those times").

190. *See Tenaris v. Venezuela*, §§ 52/57. The key question was to determine whether the Claimants had accepted the offer of consent prior to the denunciation date (*ibid*, §65).

"*Comsigua*" (Portuguese). The consent perfection date was the cornerstone of the discussion.[191]

The debate dealt with the consent given by Tenaris to arbitrate in respect of "*Comsigua*" under the Luxemburg-Venezuela BIT. The issue arose in view of the particular wording of Article 9.2 of the Venezuela-Luxemburg BIT, which set out that the six-month negotiation period started running *from the date of notification* (unlike the Portugal-Venezuela BIT, which provided that the six-month negotiation period commenced as from the start of the negotiation). While claimants filed their notification under Article 9 of the Venezuela-Luxemburg BIT on December 2, 2011; Venezuela denounced the ICSID Convention on January 24, 2012. Therefore, the six-month negotiation period elapsed on June 2, 2012, and thus, after the denunciation notice.[192]

Venezuela alleged that the consent to arbitrate could not be perfected until the mandatory period of six months of negotiations had elapsed and, therefore, Tenaris had not perfected the consent with respect to its investment in Comsigua.[193] On the other hand, Tenaris sustained that consent had been perfected as regards Comsigua through the notice of dispute and consent to arbitration, and that the negotiation period constituted a simple procedural requirement that only affected the admissibility of the claim; therefore, until it expired, the investor was forbidden to file a claim, but that waiting period did not affect the perfection of the consent previously given.[194]

The arbitral tribunal found that in Article 9 of the Venezuela-Luxembourg BIT, each contracting party explicitly provided it "irrevocable" consent to arbitrate in advance, without preventing the investor from notifying the dispute, expressing its consent beforehand and simultaneously declaring its option to ICSID arbitration.[195] Therefore, the investor's notice perfected the parties' consent to arbitrate through an ICSID tribunal; therefore, the consent was validly locked before Venezuela decided to withdraw from the ICSID Convention.[196]

The matter has led to further views in doctrine as well. Prof. Schreuer, from a purely contractual perspective—offer and acceptance—indicates that, as with the formation of contracts, the irrevocability of the arbitration agreement only occurs once the offer has been accepted and the consent has been "perfected."[197] Without objecting to the contractual nature of consent given by Schreuer, Gaillard warns of the particular

191. Through the notification dated December 2, 2011, Tenaris and Talta informed Venezuela on the existence of a dispute in the terms of Article 9 of the Venezuela-Luxemburg BIT and Article VIII.2 of the Portugal-Venezuela BIT with respect to their investments "*Comsigua*" and "*Tavsa*," respectively. In the case of Tenaris-Tavsa and Talta-Consigua, the tribunal found that in both cases the notification of the dispute and the termination of the negotiation period had taken place before the denunciation notice (*see Tenaris v. Venezuela*, §§ 91 and 97).

192. *See Tenaris v. Venezuela*, § 95, §101/102. The *Tenaris v. Venezuela* tribunal seemed to adhere to the position that required the consent to be perfected before the denunciation notice to remain unaffected under Article 72 of the ICSID Convention.

193. *See Tenaris v. Venezuela*, §§ 104/106.

194. *See ibid.*, §§ 115/121.

195. *See ibid.*, §§ 123/124 and 136/137. The tribunal added that that interpretation was the most consistent with the context, the objective and purpose of the States in the Treaty, and the good faith principle (*ibid.*, §§138/142).

196. *See Tenaris v. Venezuela*, §§ 143/144.

197. Ch. Schreuer, *The ICSID Convention: A Commentary* (Cambridge University Press, 2001), 219.

meaning that should be given to the word "consent" contained in Article 72 of the ICSID Convention, and states that the possibility of resorting to the jurisdiction of the ICSID will depend on the terminology used in the arbitration clause contained in the respective BIT.[198]

As explained in this chapter, the State's consent to arbitration given in investment treaties is perfected once it is taken up by the investor. The arbitral agreement validly exists upon acceptance. In the absence of wording in the treaty that implies those requirements are suspensive conditions of the consent's effectiveness, their fulfillment does not affect the consent's perfection.[199]

V CONCLUDING REMARKS

This chapter examines some of the old and new questions relating to States' consent to arbitration given in investment treaties. While the old questions have not yet come to be totally settled, new questions have arisen in the last decade giving rise to new debates. A clear example of this are the recent developments and issues concerning, *inter alia*, multiparty arbitration or the effects of denunciation of BITs or the ICSID Convention on the consent already provided and/or offered under those treaties.

In times that may be considered a pivotal moment for investor-State arbitration, special efforts have to be made in order to definitely settle old debates and find appropriate answers to novel issues. This could contribute to the improvement and harmonization of the investor-State arbitration practice and preserve it as the most neutral and balanced way to settle foreign investment disputes.

198. Prof. Gaillard sustains that, for the purposes of Article 72, it is important to ensure that the wording of the arbitration clause in each investment protection treaty in effect constitutes a State's prior consent to the jurisdiction of the ICSID. Where an unqualified consent exists, as opposed to an agreement to consent, the rights and obligations attached to this consent should not be affected by the denunciation of the ICSID Convention (E. Gaillard, *The Denunciation of the ICSID* Convention (New York Law Journal vol. 237 n° 122, 2007), 3).

199. *See Tenaris v. Venezuela*, §§122, 126 and §136. As explained in section [I.A.3.a] above, except otherwise stipulated in the relevant treaty, the investor's acceptance may be given before the institution of the arbitral proceedings. As regards the rights and duties arising out of consent, *see* Ch. Schreuer, "Denunciation of the ICSID Convention and Consent to Arbitration," in M. Waibel, A. Kaushal, K. L. Chung & C. Balchin (eds.), *The Backlash against Investment Arbitration: Perceptions and Reality* (Kluwer International, 2010), 364. The conclusion is not irrelevant, to the extent that, in case the mutual consent exists before the timeframe set out in Articles 71 and 72 of the ICSID Convention, rights and obligations under the ICSID Convention would not be affected, irrespective of when the arbitral proceedings are commenced.

CHAPTER 14

Legal Fictions in the Language of International Arbitration

Eduardo Silva Romero

I INTRODUCTION

Memo, philosopher of law. Guillermo ('**Memo**') Aguilar Alvarez once discussed with me the deep roots of what I then called the 'international arbitration system'. Memo, I recall, started contesting politely the characterization of 'system' that I, without giving it too much thought, had proposed for the legal rules and practices which form the framework of what, to put it in colloquial terms, 'we do'. He then added that many such legal rules and practices were illogical and, as such, could not really be said to form a 'logical system'. He, in short, suggested that the appellation of 'system' was abusive in the circumstances. He was right.

The fragility of arbitration and its legal fictions. My (rather indirect—not to say off point) response to Memo's argument was at the time two-fold: (i) arbitration has always been and still is a fragile legal institution and, as a consequence, (ii) the (so to speak) 'theory', not to say 'system', of arbitration is made up of several propositions which do not seem to be logical at first sight because they are in fact 'legal fictions'. The 'international arbitration system', I said, rests on myriad 'legal fictions'. The legal language has the incredible power of often times derogating from the logic of ordinary language. Be that as it may, I now gather what I suggested at the time was the somewhat extraordinary proposition that the international arbitration theory is—on purpose—not logical. This proposition, however, is true as a matter of fact:

Arbitration has always been under attack. (i) On the one hand, the history of arbitration shows that arbitration has always been and still is under attack. Arbitration has always struggled and is still struggling for life. The vanishing of arbitration in France for more than eighty years after the issuance of the 1843 *Prunier* judgment by the French *Cour de cassation*[1] is a telling illustration of that constant, aggressive attack. It took the entry into force of the Geneva Protocol of 1923 and the enactment of new legislation in France recognizing the validity of arbitration clauses in 1925 for arbitration to reappear in the landscape of French dispute resolution. To properly understand its context, it is worth recalling what one of the judges of the French *Cour de cassation* wrote at the time of the rendering of the *Prunier* decision. Judge Troplong wrote that:

> *l'arbitrage est une manière de juger si défectueuse, si dépourvue de garanties, qu'on aurait dû laisser les parties maîtresses d'y recourir ou de le répudier, suivant les occasions. Quant à moi qui a été arbitre quelque fois, je déclare, par expérience, que, dans un procès de quelque gravité, je ne conseillerais à personne de se faire juger par des arbitres ; un tribunal, qui se croit le droit d'être plus équitable que les lois les plus équitables du monde, me paraît ne pouvoir s'adapter qu'à un petit nombre de questions de fait et à des intérêts médiocres.*[2]

Achmea. More recently, the stance adopted by the European Union (EU) toward investment arbitration provides us with yet another example of the fragility of arbitration. In that case, the European Court of Justice, in sum, decided to vanish intra-EU investment arbitration.[3] More generally, it is a historical premise of arbitration that its very existence depends entirely on its acceptance by the relevant public authorities, that is, the legislator, the executive branch (the government), and the judiciary; in short, arbitration cannot exist without the State's recognition and support. After all, we must recognize, despite all universalist and internationalist doctrines, that the more intense legal power (the so-called sovereignty) on earth still belongs, for better or worse, to the States.

'Legal fictions'. (ii) On the other hand, there are many definitions in the legal literature of 'legal fiction'.[4] For the purposes of the present chapter, we will understand that a 'legal fiction' is "[...] an assumption that something is true even if it may be untrue, made especially in judicial reasoning to alter how a legal rule operates [...]."[5] In our field, a 'legal fiction' is a means for international arbitration to struggle for life. More specifically, a 'legal fiction' has traditionally been a tool by which the architects of the international arbitration theory have overcome obstacles to the existence of or the access to international arbitral justice. The image that could come to mind when thinking of a 'legal fiction' is that of a military bridge ingeniously built when the road reaches an abyss.

'As if'. To return to my conversation with Memo, a 'legal fiction' is not a logical proposition but may 'pretend' to be one. The expression '*as if*' evokes well the sense of

1. Civ. July 10, 1843, *Compagnie l'Alliance c/ Prunier*, in: I. Fadlallah and D. Hascher, *Les grandes décisions du droit de l'arbitrage commercial*, Paris: Dalloz (Coll. Objectif Avocat !), 2019, pp. 3 et seq.
2. R.-T. Troplong, "*Du contrat de société civile et commerciales*," Paris, 1843, t. 2, n° 520, cited by I. Fadlallah and D. Hascher, *supra*, p. 6.
3. European Court of Justice, *Slovak Republic v. Achmea BV*, Case C-284/16, Judgment, March 6, 2018.
4. On 'legal fictions', *cf.*, for instance, M. Del Mar and W. Twining (eds.), *Legal Fictions in Theory and Practice*, New York: Springer, 2015.
5. B. A. Garner, ed., *Black's Law Dictionary*, St. Paul: West Group, 1999, Seventh Edition, p. 904.

the notion of 'legal fiction'. In definitive, any fiction,[6] including legal fictions, plays out '*as if*' it were true, or real, or logical, even if it ultimately is not. 'Pretending' belongs to the essence of the notion of 'fiction'. A 'legal fiction' is always a good actor. A 'legal myth' is, among all 'legal fictions', a wonderful comedian.

The job of legal fictions. The presence of a legal fiction in the legal language is never capricious. Any legal fiction has a purpose or does a job within that language. Every military bridge aims at filling in a gap. A vivid anecdotal example of legal fiction is the *Mostyn v. Fabrigas* case:

> [...] Fabrigas, a resident of the Mediterranean island of Minorca then occupied and controlled by England, was imprisoned by Mostyn, at the time the governor of the island. Because no suit could be brought against Mostyn in Minorca without the approval of the governor, and because the governor was the defendant in the very lawsuit Fabrigas wished to pursue, Fabrigas sued instead in the Court of Common Pleas in London for trespass and false imprisonment, and proceeded to win a jury verdict of 3 000 £. On appeal, Mostyn claimed, correctly, that the trial court had been granted jurisdiction only in cases brought by residents of London, but Lord Mansfield, recognizing that denying jurisdiction here would leave someone who was plainly wronged without a legal remedy, concluded that Minorca was part of London for purposes of this action. That conclusion was plainly false and equally plainly produced a just result, and thus Mostyn v. Fabrigas represents the paradigmatic example of using a fiction to achieve what might in earlier days have been done through the vehicle of equity.[7]

This case shows us that, at least to some extent, a legal fiction in the legal language is the equivalent to axioms in geometry; its job is to appear when legal reasoning comes to a dead end; a manifestly unfair result is a dead end (a 'legal fiction' may also be represented as a handy ladder).

Abuse of legal fictions. Sometimes, however, legal fictions are taken as if they were logical propositions. As a result, some legal fictions are forced to accomplish from time to time a purpose or to do a job for which they were not created in the first place. This is a mistake. One good example of this kind of error is found in the field of international arbitration when one relies on the autonomy or separability of the arbitration clause to argue that the arbitration clause must be separately (in respect of the main contract) assigned.[8] The purpose of the autonomy or separability of the arbitration agreement, however, is to ensure its existence or validity despite the potential inexistence or invalidity of the main contract; in other words, the job that the autonomy or separability of the arbitration agreement accomplishes in the language of international arbitration is granting the arbitrators jurisdiction to adjudicate any dispute relating to the existence or validity of the main contract; as a consequence, the job of that rule is not to render the arbitration agreement autonomous or separable for all purposes or in all circumstances, including in connection with the assignment of the main contract. Interestingly, however, in the context of the assignment of a contract,

6. *Cf.*, for instance, L. Menoud, *Que'est-ce que la fiction ?*, Paris: Vrin, 2005.
7. F. Schauer, "Legal Fictions Revisited," in: M. Del Mar and W. Twining (eds.), *Legal Fictions in Theory and Practice*, *supra*, p. 122.
8. For further reference to the separability "fiction" *see* section II.C *infra*.

the legal language counters the potential abuses of the autonomy or separability of the arbitration clause rule by adopting another legal fiction, which is that 'the accessory follows the fate of the principal'. In this sense, the arbitration clause does not need to be assigned separately from the main contract because the former would be characterized as an 'accessory' of the latter. There are in this sense counter-legal fictions.

Typologies of legal fictions. The legal literature also contains several typologies of legal fictions. French doctrine, for instance, classifies them into legal fictions aimed at creating new legal rules and legal fictions aimed at interpreting existing legal rules.[9] The legal fictions in the language of international arbitration may also be classified in several ways. We, however, have come to the conclusion that the most illustrative typology of legal fictions in the language of international arbitration is that between legal fictions aimed at ensuring the existence of international arbitration (section II), and those aimed at ensuring access to international arbitration (section III) (both types of legal fictions serving international arbitration's struggle for life).

II LEGAL FICTIONS AIMED AT ENSURING THE EXISTENCE OF INTERNATIONAL ARBITRATION

The paradigm of the judicial process. We have all been educated to perceive the State's judiciary system as the paradigm of the administration of justice.[10] This is the reason why, in its struggle for life, international arbitration has always tried to resemble the paradigm of the judicial process. Sentences such as 'an arbitrator is like a judge', 'the arbitral proceedings are like a judicial process', and 'the arbitral award is like a judgment' are very common in the language of international arbitration. All these expressions point to the contra-*Prunier* idea (Troplong was wrong) that 'arbitration cannot be 'that bad' if it resembles so much the judicial process that we all cherish'.

Arbitration is like the judicial process. It is in our view through this attempt to resemble the paradigm of the judicial process that international arbitration has, at least to some extent, ensured its efficiency and autonomy, that is, the two required qualities without which international arbitration could simply not exist as an effective means for resolving disputes. The phrases quoted in the preceding paragraph reveal the five elements of the judicial process that international arbitration has always tried—as a means for survival—to resemble: a foundational theory (section II.A); the assimilation of international arbitrators to State judges (section II.B); the assimilation of the arbitral proceedings to the judicial process; the assimilation of the arbitral award to the State judge's judgment; and the autonomy of international arbitral justice (section II.C).

Proceedings and decisions. Only two words are needed on the assimilation of proceedings and decisions referred to in the preceding paragraph. The arbitral proceedings need to be assimilated to the judicial proceedings for the former to be perceived as a proceeding which, at the very least, does not contravene the principle of due process of law. The arbitral award, in turn, needs to be assimilated to the judgment rendered by

9. A.-J. Arnaud (ed.), *Dictionnaire encyclopédique de théorie et de sociologie du droit*, Paris: LGDJ, 1993, Second Edition, pp. 259-261.
10. *Cf*, for instance, M. Weber, *Sociologie du droit*, Paris: PUF, 1986, esp. pp. 207 et seq.

State judges for the former to produce the legal effects of res judicata and enforceability. Without these two fictional assimilations, international arbitration could not be an effective means of dispute resolution and, hence, would not exist.

A Some Fictional Foundational Theories of International Arbitration

The need for a foundational theory. *First*, there is a need for a foundational theory responding to the following question: where does the legitimacy of international arbitration come from? By essence, that theory will be a 'legal fiction' and, even, a 'legal myth'. From a French perspective, for instance, the deep roots of the State and its judicial process are to be found in the fictional notion of 'social contract' (*contrat social*).[11] The idea of a 'social contract' is a 'fiction' because the members of a society never met around a table or otherwise to negotiate and execute such a contract. By the same token, there are several foundational theories of international arbitration. Two of them are, from our perspective, particularly interesting:

The foundational theory of the advantages of international arbitration. (i) The first legal fiction / foundational theory very often used in arbitration's struggle for life is the affirmation that international arbitration has many advantages in comparison with other dispute resolution methods, which justify users' recourse to it. The affirmation, in general terms, is that 'international arbitration is better than other methods for dispute resolution, including, in particular, the judicial process before State courts'. This general affirmation comes with a paradox: arbitration is sold to be better than the judicial process which it needs to resemble to survive. This contradiction is, in our view, not perceived very often because of the different levels—not to say the fragmentation—of the human mind. The human mind fails too often to see the big picture.

A marketing strategy? In many books devoted to international arbitration,[12] one of the first chapters—normally before or after the definition of 'arbitration'—is devoted to a relatively long list of the so-called advantages of arbitration. Among these advantages, one may often find neutrality, the expertise / specialization of arbitrators, efficiency (time and cost) and confidentiality. We know how much these 'advantages' and many others have been attacked and criticized in recent years. What interests us for the purpose of this chapter is that those lists contain affirmations with no demonstration of their truthfulness. In fact, the 'advantages of international arbitration' are not supported by empirical evidence; conversely, they are rather blunt statements in which arbitration practitioners have traditionally believed. Believing in the 'advantages of international arbitration' is *in fine* equivalent to an '*acte de foi*'.

The advantages of international arbitration as legal fictions. Why is the affirmation of the advantages of international arbitration a legal fiction? Three reasons may respond to this question: (a) such affirmation arises out of the fictional premise that international arbitration is, *in abstracto*, better than other mechanisms of dispute

11. *Cf.*, for instance, L. Althuser, *Sur le contrat social*, Paris: Manucius, 2009.
12. *Cf.*, for instance, G. Born, *International Commercial Arbitration*, Volume I, Alphen aan den Rijn: Kluwer, 2009, esp. pp. 71 et seq.

resolution (in particular, the foundational theory of the 'advantages of international arbitration' is arbitrarily developed '*as if*' arbitration were better than the judicial process; any comparison, however, can only operate on a case-by-case basis, that is, *in concreto*); (b) the so-called arbitration community has commonly taken those advantages for granted, that is, '*as if*' they were axioms of the 'arbitration geometry' (in fact, those advantages are legal fictions given that they assume as true or real what has not been demonstrated with empirical evidence to be true or real); and (c) there is no doubt that the job of the 'advantages of international arbitration' as legal fictions is to preserve arbitration's life within arbitration's struggle for life. The expression 'we have to believe in the advantages of arbitration' conveys well its true nature.

The example of confidentiality. One of the 'advantages of international arbitration' most broadly promoted in the language of international commercial arbitration was its purported confidentiality. How many times did arbitration practitioners indeed affirm (without providing any evidence of that proposition) that international arbitration was confidential? We now know that such affirmation did not have any legal basis in many jurisdictions. There is, in fact, no universal, inherent principle of confidentiality in international arbitration, commercial or otherwise. Conversely, we increasingly live in a 'transparency society'[13].

The evolution of the advantages of international arbitration. The foundational theory of the 'advantages of international arbitration' has evolved over time. In short, international arbitration was presented under a much better light twenty years ago. It perhaps had to be. The incessant, aggressive attacks against the institution of arbitration, however, have left many wounds. The number of advantages of arbitration has decreased in these last two decades. Neutrality, expertise / specialization, and some efficiency seem to be the surviving qualities of the institution.[14]

The downsides of international arbitration. Interestingly, recent textbooks have introduced a chapter on the 'problems or downsides of arbitration.'[15] This is, in our view, unprecedented. Are we, as a result, experiencing the end of the legal fictions which are the 'advantages of international arbitration'? The answer should be in the negative. It rather seems that the 'arbitration community' is cleverly attempting to convey the impression that the remaining (those which have not been destroyed yet) advantages of the institution are true and real by criticizing only some of the other advantages 'to some extent'. In short, international arbitration practitioners may no longer give users of the system the impression that they believe irrationally in its goodness; some moderate '*esprit critique*' is always a good marketing tool.

The foundational theory of the 'arbitral legal order'. (ii) The second legal fiction / foundational theory of international arbitration which deserves some comment is the one pertaining to the existence of an autonomous 'arbitral legal order'. This foundational theory is complex in the sense that it is based on many premises and may have several corollaries.

---

13. *Cf.*, for instance, B.-Ch. Han, *The Transparency Society*, Stanford: Stanford University Press, 2015.
14. *Cf.*, for instance, G. Born, *International Commercial Arbitration*, *supra*.
15. *Cf.*, for instance, J.-B. Racine, *Droit de l'arbitrage*, Paris: PUF, pp. 85 et seq.

The implicit premises of the 'arbitral legal order'. The three premises of this second foundational theory of international arbitration are these:

- there would exist a society of international merchants that, to lend credence to its existence, some authors call the '*societas mercatorum*', where its members trade and conduct business; it is interesting to note that some investment arbitral decisions and awards refer to the existence of a 'community of investors and States hosting investments',[16] which is not without resemblance to the idea of the '*societas mercatorum*';
- it is then added that '*ubi societas, ibi ius*' (any society must have its law) and that the law applicable in the '*societas mercatorum*' is the '*lex mercatoria*'; and
- all societies must have a 'natural judge'; the 'natural judges' of the '*societas mercatorum*' are international arbitrators.

The premises of the 'arbitral legal order' are legal fictions. These very attractive premises (especially those formulated in Latin) are legal fictions (if not 'legal myths'):

- international merchants are not organized in a society (neither are host States and investors for that matter); in other words, this second foundational theory of international arbitration operates '*as if*' international merchants interacted in a society—the '*societas mercatorum*' is a legal fiction;
- the '*lex mercatoria*' is, in turn, an invention of some clever professors that has not been universally recognized as a legal order; as a consequence, this premise operates '*as if*': (a) there were a '*societas mercatorum*', and (b) such a society had a legal order, that is, the '*lex mercatoria*'[17]—the '*lex mercatoria*' is yet another legal fiction; and
- it is also fictional to hold that international arbitrators are the 'natural judges' of the '*societas mercatorum*'. In fact, international arbitration does not apply automatically to disputes arising out of international commerce and investment; rather, the participants in international commerce and investment have by law or treaty a choice—when drafting the dispute resolution clause of an international contract or choosing to rely on a bilateral investment treaty—of the dispute resolution forum before which they want to submit potential

16. *Cf.*, for instance, *Burlington Resources Inc. c/ Republic of* Ecuador, ICSID Case No. ARB/08/5, Decision on Liability, December 14, 2012, para. 187 ("As stated in the Decision on Jurisdiction, the Tribunal considers that it is not bound by previous decisions. Nevertheless, the majority considers that it must pay due regard to earlier decisions of international courts and tribunals. It believes that, subject to compelling contrary grounds, it has a duty to adopt solutions established in a series of consistent cases. It further believes that, subject to the specifics of a given treaty and of the circumstances of the actual case, it has a duty to seek to contribute to the harmonious development of investment law, and thereby to meet the legitimate expectations of the community of States and investors towards the certainty of the rule of law. Arbitrator Stern does not analyze the arbitrator's role in the same manner, as she considers it her duty to decide each case on its own merits, independently of any apparent jurisprudential trend").
17. *Cf.*, for instance, B. Goldman, "Frontières du droit et 'lex mercatoria'," in: *Archives de Philosophie du Droit, Le droit subjectif en question*, Paris: Sirey, 1964, pp. 177 et seq.

disputes. Conversely, State judges are 'natural judges' because their jurisdiction applies automatically to disputes arising within the territory of their State. As a result, the idea that international arbitrators are somewhere (*societas mercatorum*) 'natural judges' is at best used as a 'metaphor' in the circumstances ('*as if*').

The 'arbitral legal order'. These three legal fictions form in any event the basis for the existence of an 'arbitral legal order'. To summarize this idea, one can argue that not only would the *societas mercatorum* have its own material or substantive law, the *lex mercatoria*, but it would also have its natural judges, the international arbitrators, who in turn would be supported by their own legal order, independent from any national legal order, which would be the so-called 'arbitral legal order'. In this sense, the validity (legal force) of international arbitration would come from the 'arbitral legal order'. This theory has been developed, in particular, by French case-law and doctrine.

The 'arbitral legal order' in French case law. (a) The most famous French decision on the notion of 'arbitral legal order' is perhaps the *Putrabali* Decision. In that Decision, the French *Cour de Cassation* held that: "[...] *la sentence internationale, qui n'est rattachée à aucun ordre juridique étatique, est une décision de justice internationale* [...]."[18] Even if this holding does not refer explicitly to the 'arbitral legal order', its characterization of an international award as a 'decision of international justice' unequivocally implies it.

French doctrine on the 'arbitral legal order'. (b) As to French doctrine, The Hague Academy course delivered by Professor Emmanuel Gaillard deserves a special mention. This is how Professor Gaillard describes the 'arbitral legal order':

> *La troisième représentation de l'arbitrage est celle qui accepte de considérer que la juridicité de l'arbitrage puisse être puisée non dans un ordre juridique étatique, qu'il s'agisse de celui du siège ou de celui du ou des lieux d'exécution, mais dans un ordre juridique tiers, susceptible d'être qualifié d'ordre juridique arbitral. Elle correspond à la perception forte chez les arbitres du commerce international qu'ils ne rendent pas la justice au nom d'un Etat quelconque, mais qu'ils n'en exercent pas moins une fonction juridictionnelle au service de la communauté internationale. Compte tenu du vaste mouvement de reconnaissance du bien-fondé du recours à l'arbitrage international comme mode de règlement des différends du commerce international, la légitimité de l'exercice de cette fonction n'est pas douteuse [...].*[19]

'International community' and '*lex mercatoria*' are synonymous.

The 'arbitral legal order' is a legal fiction. In definitive, the 'arbitral legal order' is yet another legal fiction for, at least, three main reasons:

18. Civ. 1ere, June 29, 2007, *Sté PT Putrabali Adyamula c/ Sté Rena Holding*. In: I. Fadlallah and D. Hascher, *supra*, p. 325.
19. E. Gaillard, *Aspects philosophiques du droit de l'arbitrage international*, Maubeuge: Martinus Nijhoff Publishers (Coll. Les livres de poche de l'Académie de droit international de La Haye), 2008, p. 60.

(1) all the premises (*'societas mercatorum'*; *'lex mercatoria'*; and international arbitrators as 'natural judges' of the international commercial society) leading to its affirmation are legal fictions themselves;
(2) the theory of the 'arbitral legal order' has some corollaries that are, in turn, legal fictions as well; these corollaries are the 'principle of validity of the international arbitration agreement' (*cf.*, for instance, the *Dalico* and *Zanzi* decisions of the French *Cour de Cassation*) and the possibility of enforcing arbitral awards annulled at their country of origin (*cf.*, for instance, the *Putrabali* Decision of the French *Cour de Cassation*);[20] and
(3) the foundational theory of the 'arbitral legal order' is not universally recognized.

The 'arbitral legal order' of the ICSID Convention. There is, however, an arbitration system in which the theory of the 'arbitral legal order' fits very well: the ICSID Convention arbitration system. As a matter of positive law, the ICSID Convention encompasses an autonomous arbitration system (including an annulment proceeding) whose legal force arises out of an international treaty. Comparing the International Centre for Settlement of Investment Disputes (ICSID) 'legal order' with the French 'arbitral legal order', one can conclude that the problem of the foundational theory of the 'arbitral legal order' as developed by French case law and doctrine is that the source of that 'order' remains, from a positive law perspective, unclear; is, in sum, the French *Cour de cassation* legally entitled to create an autonomous 'arbitral legal order' for international arbitrations?

Another *acte de foi*. Professor Gaillard appears to be well aware of that lack of clarity. In his book following his course delivered at The Hague Academy of International Law, he somehow recognized that the 'arbitral legal order' is a 'legal fiction' / 'legal myth'. At the very end of his book, Professor Gaillard writes that:

> *[...] qu'en présence de trois conceptions de l'arbitrage international qui, toutes, ont vocation à expliquer l'entier phénomène, on pourrait être tenté de se demander suivant quels critères il y aurait lieu de les départager. Une telle question n'aurait en réalité aucun sens s'agissant de représentations, de visions de l'institution qui, en tant que telles, relèvent du domaine de la croyance, sinon de la foi, et non de celui de la vérité scientifique. On n'insistera jamais assez sur le fait que, dans ce registre, il ne saurait être question de vrai ou de faux mais seulement de cohérent ou d'incohérent, d'efficace ou d'inefficace [...].*[21]

One may link this statement with the introductory idea that arbitration has always struggled and is still struggling for life. There can be no doubt that the best way to fend off the many attacks against international arbitration is for it to be based on an international, autonomous 'arbitral legal order', which would prevail over national

20. Civ. 1ere, December 20, 1993, *Comité populaire de la municipalité de Khoms El Mergeb c/ Dalico Contractors*, in: I. Fadlallah and D. Hascher, *supra*, p. 22; Civ. 1ere, January 5, 1999, *M. Zanzi ès qualités c/ M. de Coninck et autres*, in: I. Fadlallah and D. Hascher, *supra*, p. 23; Civ. 1ere, June 29, 2007, *Sté PT Putrabali Adyamula c/ Sté Rena Holding*, in: I. Fadlallah and D. Hascher, *supra*, p. 325.
21. E. Gaillard, *supra*, p. 209.

legal orders. Thus, for instance, the existence of an 'arbitral legal order' would entail that, independently from what the public powers of the States might decide against the legal institution of international arbitration (for instance, national judges annulling arbitral awards for 'exotic' reasons), international arbitration and the resulting award would be valid in accordance with the 'arbitral legal order'. Nothing is more powerful than a good theory.

B The Fictional Assimilation of International Arbitrators to State Judges

The international arbitrator must be assimilated to the State judge. *Second*, the arbitrator needs to be—at the very least—assimilated to the judge; in other words, arbitrators need to be perceived to be as respectable as judges would be. Troplong's preconceptions need to be effectively countered. The rationale for the need of that assimilation is that the judicial process is still in our minds the paradigm of the administration of justice.

Abundance of fictions. One may preliminarily wonder what the legal foundation is of the main proposition arising out of that paradigm, that is, the idea that the State must have the monopoly of the administration of justice. Is it the legal fiction of Rousseau's 'social contract'? It is worth noting at this point that many of the institutions that form the modern society and its Rule of Law rest on fictions, 'legal' or otherwise. This truth shows us the power of the human mind and its language.

Corollaries of the assimilation of international arbitrators to State judges. Be that as it may, the expression 'assimilation of international arbitrators to State judges' has two main meanings and, hence, legal consequences which, among other things, explain why it is a 'legal fiction'.

International arbitrators must be '*as good*' as State judges. (i) The assimilation of international arbitrators to State judges first entails that international arbitrators must meet the same requirements that must be met by a State judge. In particular, international arbitrators, '*as if*' they were State judges, shall be independent and impartial.

'Independence' and 'impartiality'. The term 'independence', as applied in the international arbitration language, is yet another legal fiction. 'Independence' is indeed said to be an 'objective notion', setting forth an 'objective test', which, if met by the international arbitrator, entails that he or she may be deemed to be 'impartial'. 'Impartiality', in turn, is meant to be a 'subjective notion' or a 'state of mind' that only the international arbitrator can have knowledge of.[22]

The legal fiction of 'independence'. The objective legal test arising from the notion of 'independence' may be characterized as a legal fiction. Some, however, would prefer to characterize it as a 'presumption' or, simply, as a 'legal test'. Be that as it may, that test would be a legal fiction because, if met, it produces the legal effect of deeming that the international arbitrator is impartial; one, however, cannot know in

22. *Cf.*, for instance, G. Born, *International Commercial Arbitration*, *supra*, pp. 1474 and 1475.

reality whether he or she is impartial; an independent international arbitrator would be taken '*as if*' he or she were impartial.

The powers of international arbitrators. (ii) The second corollary of the assimilation of international arbitrators to State judges is that international arbitrators have some of the powers that State judges have to fulfill their jurisdictional mission. What are those powers?

- First, international arbitrators, like State judges, have the *jurisdictio*, that is, the power of administering justice (adjudicating a dispute). From this perspective, there can be no doubt that international arbitrators must be and are 'like State judges'; if they were not, international arbitration would not be an efficient means for resolving disputes but, at most, an alternative dispute resolution method such as mediation.
- International arbitrators, also like State judges, have the power of adopting interim measures of protection upon request of one of the parties. This international arbitrators' power, however, is limited in comparison to the State judges' power to adopt such measures. In sum, international arbitrators are not entitled in most jurisdictions to adopt interim measures which could affect the parties' rights of property. More specifically, international arbitrators are in principle not entitled to seize assets of the parties in dispute. Conversely, State judges are entitled to do so. In legal, sophisticated terms, this difference between international arbitrators and State judges is often formulated in the following manner: international arbitrators do not have *imperium*, whereas State judges do.

The dangers of the total assimilation of arbitrators to State judges. The international arbitrators' powers described above make clear that international arbitrators (and, in many jurisdictions, even domestic arbitrators) 'are like' State judges but are not equal to them. It results from this proposition that fictional assimilation of international arbitrators to State judges is needed for international arbitration to survive but not 'total' assimilation. 'Total assimilation', in our view, would make international arbitration less attractive as a means for resolving disputes because it would lose its flexibility and, as a result, any appealing difference with the judicial process. 'Total' assimilation may destroy international arbitration.

Some domestic arbitrators are State judges. It is, however, interesting to mention that, in some Latin American jurisdictions, domestic (not international) arbitrators are almost totally assimilated to State judges to the point that domestic arbitrators there are entitled to: (a) seize assets of the parties with a view of guaranteeing compliance with the arbitral award; (b) ask directly for assistance from the police to bring reluctant witnesses to testify at the hearing; and (c) even enforce their own decisions. The Colombian Arbitration Statute, in its domestic arbitration section, provides, for instance, the following:[23]

23. Colombian Arbitration Statute, Law 1563 of 2012.

> *Artículo 32. Medidas cautelares. A petición de cualquiera de las partes, el tribunal podrá ordenar las medidas cautelares que serían procedentes de tramitarse el proceso ante la justicia ordinaria o la contencioso administrativa, cuyos decreto, práctica y levantamiento se someterán a las normas del Código de Procedimiento Civil, el Código de Procedimiento Administrativo y de lo Contencioso Administrativo y a las disposiciones especiales pertinentes [...].*

The philosophy underlying the 'total assimilation' of domestic arbitrators to State judges. This extraordinary empowerment of domestic arbitrators in some jurisdictions responds in our view to a philosophy which is different from the one underlying international arbitration. Under that philosophy, domestic arbitration is a judicial process, and domestic arbitrators are inserted into the State's judiciary for the time of their mission. In definitive, domestic arbitrators, from such standpoint, are no longer 'like State judges' but in fact 'are State judges on a temporary basis'. Experience shows that this representation of arbitration may entail some (perhaps) negative consequences:

- Those domestic arbitrators are considered State judges for all criminal law purposes ('*delito de prevaricato*',[24] for instance), which, in comparison with international arbitrators, means that domestic arbitrators in some jurisdictions are not protected by arbitrator immunities that are recognized in most of the modern arbitration jurisdictions (England, France, Switzerland, U.S., etc.).
  The domestic arbitral procedure in those jurisdictions are as formalistic as proceedings before State judges. Flexibility is not a feature of that kind of domestic arbitration. The notion of due process in those domestic proceedings is far more demanding than the one most commonly applied in international arbitration.
- Those domestic arbitrators render their decisions, as any State judge does, 'in the name of the State'.

Domestic arbitration as an improved judicial process. In conclusion, domestic arbitration in those jurisdictions is not really meant to be an '*alternative*' to the judicial process, as international arbitration is always presented to be, but, rather, an '*improved judicial process*', where judges called 'private arbitrators' may devote more time than a State judge to resolving the dispute that they have been entrusted with. All in all, this domestic arbitration system arises from the fact that the judiciary in those jurisdictions may not be adequate to handle some complex matters or is simply too busy to administer justice in some sensitive cases with the necessary speed and, perhaps, experience; sadly, that domestic arbitration system is sometimes also the only solution to avoid corrupted judges.

---

24. *Cf.*, for instance, Article 413 of Colombian Penal Code. "*Prevaricato por acción. El servidor público que profiera resolución, dictamen o concepto manifiestamente contrario a la ley, incurrirá en prisión de cuarenta y ocho (48) a ciento cuarenta y cuatro (144) meses, multa de sesenta y seis punto sesenta y seis (66.66) a trescientos (300) salarios mínimos legales mensuales vigentes, e inhabilitación para el ejercicio de derechos y funciones públicas de ochenta (80) a ciento cuarenta y cuatro (144) meses.*"

The impact of the 'total assimilation' of international arbitrators to State judges on international arbitration. What is the relevance of the analysis of the domestic arbitration system described above? From an international arbitration perspective, the problem is that the underlying philosophy of that domestic arbitration system still has a very important influence on how many arbitration practitioners and judges in those jurisdictions perceive and approach international arbitration. A very illustrative example of such an impact is the publication of the 'Prague Rules' on the Effective Conduct of Arbitration. Despite some descriptions of this set of rules, they do not pertain to the taking of evidence. In summary, the Prague Rules contain a proposal to transform the international arbitration procedure into a civil law process, in which the arbitrator, like a civil law judge, would have inquisitorial powers. In this sense, the Prague Rules do not correspond to the philosophy underlying international arbitration. Conversely, the International Bar Association (IBA) Rules on the Taking of Evidence do. The rationale behind the IBA Rules is the creation of procedural rules for international arbitration which are not civil law or common law rules but, to the extent possible, a combination of both systems.

C Legal Fictions Aimed at Ensuring the Autonomy of International Arbitration

The autonomy of arbitral justice. The basic proposition for this third category of legal fictions aimed at ensuring the existence of international arbitration is this: international arbitration as an efficient means for dispute resolution cannot exist if the international arbitration system is not autonomous to the greatest extent possible. This, in particular, means that international arbitration must not suffer from constant and unwarranted interventions from, in particular, the judiciary of the State where the seat of the arbitration is located. In sum, the autonomy of arbitral justice is an essential feature of its existence.

The two most popular legal fictions in the language of international arbitration. Perhaps, the most important and, in any event, the most popular legal fictions in the language of international arbitration are those aimed at ensuring its autonomy (especially from the State judiciary). These legal fictions are nowadays recognized by most arbitration legislations and relevant case law worldwide. These two legal fictions are: (i) the autonomy or separability of the arbitration agreement (we will henceforth refer to the autonomy of the arbitration agreement) and (ii) the Kompetenz-Kompetenz rule.

The autonomy of the arbitration agreement. *First*, the autonomy of the arbitration agreement has been formulated, for instance, under French law as follows:

> *La convention d'arbitrage est indépendante du contrat auquel elle se rapporte. Elle n'est pas affectée par l'inefficacité de celui-ci.[...].*[25]

25. French Code of Civil Procedure, Article 1447.

This famous legal fiction calls for four observations:

The job of the autonomy of the arbitration agreement. (i) The immediate job that this legal fiction accomplishes is granting the arbitrators jurisdiction to adjudicate disputes relating to the existence or validity of the main contract. As already noted, its job is not to render the arbitration agreement autonomous or separable for all purposes, including the assignment of the main contract.

The purpose of the autonomy of the arbitration agreement. (ii) The mediate job of the autonomy of the arbitration agreement is to prevent the State justice to interfere in an international arbitration when one of the parties to the arbitral proceedings alleges that the main contract does not exist or is invalid. International arbitration would simply not be an efficient method for resolving disputes if it had to be suspended while a State court decides whether the main contract exists or is valid.

The autonomy of the arbitration agreement in the typology of legal fictions. (iii) The autonomy of the arbitration agreement is, pursuant to one of the French typologies of legal fictions, a legal fiction aimed at creating a rule.[26] Legislators and courts have decided to support arbitration by granting, through the autonomy of the arbitration agreement rule, jurisdiction to arbitrators for them to adjudicate all disputes relating to the existence or validity of the main contract. Any legal system recognizing the legal fiction of the autonomy of the arbitration agreement has explicitly or implicitly adopted a policy to promote the resolution of disputes through arbitration.

The autonomy of the arbitration agreement is a legal fiction. (iv) As we already mentioned, it is a mistake to assume that the autonomy of the arbitration agreement is a logical proposition. It is not. This point has been made not only by, for instance, the French courts but also by French doctrine. Professor Pierre Mayer, in his seminal article on the limits to the separability of the arbitration clause, pointed to the boundaries of that legal fiction.[27] These limits underscore the fictional nature of the autonomy of the arbitration agreement. Professor Mayer's conclusion, however, is incorrect. The conclusion should not be that legal systems should recognize limits to the rule for it to be a logical proposition. The conclusion, in our view, should rather be that the rule of the autonomy of the arbitration agreement is not a logical proposition and that, as a consequence, legislators and State courts can arbitrarily frame the scope of the rule as they deem fit. Legal language has the incredible power of derogating from ordinary language. There can in any event be no doubt that the rule of the autonomy of the arbitration agreement is a legal fiction, that is, a tool created by the human mind in order for arbitration to prevail in its struggle for life.

---

26. *Cf.* for instance, A.-J. Arnaud (ed.), *Dictionnaire encyclopédique de théorie et de sociologie du droit*, Paris: LGDJ, 1993, Second Edition, pp. 259-261.
27. *Cf.* P. Mayer, "Les limites de la séparabilité de la clause compromissoire," in: *Revue de l'arbitrage*, 1998, p. 359.

A misleading labeling. A natural conclusion from the developments above should be that the appellation of the rule may be misleading. Words are never innocent. The word 'autonomy' means that an entity issues its own rules. The word 'separability', in turn, conveys the meaning that the arbitration clause is independent from the main contract. We, however, know that the only job of the autonomy of the arbitration agreement rule is to grant arbitrators jurisdiction to adjudicate disputes relating to the existence or validity of the main contract. It was not and is not in our view necessary to resort to the shortcuts of 'autonomy' or 'separability' to enunciate the rule.

The Kompetenz-Kompetenz principle. *Second*, the so-called (not to say wrongly called) 'principle' of Kompetenz-Kompetenz completes the rule of the autonomy of the arbitration agreement in order to ensure the overall autonomy of arbitral justice. The rule of the autonomy of the arbitration agreement is not sufficient to ensure that autonomy. In particular, the rule of the autonomy of the arbitration agreement does not grant arbitrators jurisdiction to resolve disputes concerning the existence or validity of the arbitration agreement itself. While the rule of the autonomy of the arbitration agreement prevents the intervention of State courts in an arbitration when one of the parties alleges the inexistence or invalidity of the main contract, the Kompetenz-Kompetenz principle prevents the same intervention when one of the parties argues that the arbitration agreement itself is inexistent or invalid. In other words, the rule of the autonomy of the arbitration agreement grants arbitrators jurisdiction to adjudicate disputes as to the existence or validity of the main contract, whereas the Kompetenz-Kompetenz principle, in turn, grants jurisdiction to the arbitrators to adjudicate disputes relating to the existence or validity of the arbitration agreement itself.

Description of the principle. French law, for instance, describes this 'principle' as follows:

> *Le tribunal arbitral est seul compétent pour statuer sur les conditions relatives à son pouvoir juridictionnel.*[28]

The Kompetenz-Kompetenz principle is a legal fiction. Why is the principle of Kompetenz-Kompetenz is a legal fiction? A demonstration in four stages may support this characterization:

(1) The Kompetenz-Kompetenz principle consists in empowering arbitrators to make any decision upon their own jurisdiction, which is equivalent to saying that arbitrators are entitled to make any decision upon the existence or validity of the arbitration agreement.

(2) One knows, however, that the very source of arbitrators' jurisdiction arises out of such arbitration agreement. The question at this point of the demonstration should therefore be this: how could arbitrators decide upon the existence or validity of the arbitration agreement from which their jurisdiction arises?.

28. French Code of Civil Procedure, Article 1465.

(3) The answer to this question is that arbitrators are entitled to decide upon the existence or validity of the arbitration agreement because the State, through its legislative or judicial organ, has so decided by adopting the Kompetenz-Kompetenz principle in its arbitration legislation or case law. Kompetenz-Kompetenz is, in sum, a legal fiction because, from its perspective, arbitral jurisdiction would be established 'as if' it arose from beyond the arbitration agreement.

(4) It is thus undeniable that international arbitration cannot exist (that is, cannot prevail in its struggle for life) without the support of the State.

Another misleading labeling. It is lastly interesting to note that the sophisticated way in which this arbitral power is presented, that is: (i) as a 'principle' and (ii) through its formulation in German, projects the wrong impression that Kompetenz-Kompetenz is a 'logical principle' or, at the very least, that it comes from a relevant historical background. This is misleading. On the one hand, Kompetenz-Kompetenz, as suggested above, is not a 'principle'. To put it in geometrical terms, Kompetenz-Kompetenz is not an axiom or theorem from which a logical systemic edifice has been erected. On the other hand, it is our view that, instead of resorting to a German expression, it would have been much simpler to: (i) assert that arbitral jurisdiction results from the arbitration agreement and (ii) add that, however, should disputes regarding the existence or validity of the arbitration agreement be brought before arbitrators, they have jurisdiction by law to adjudicate them with a view of ensuring the autonomy of arbitration as a means of resolving controversies, its efficiency and, ultimately, its very existence. Linguistic shortcuts often create confusion.

The expansion of the scope of international arbitration. Once one can establish that the latest battle in the struggle for life has been won by international arbitration (the war is never won; arbitration's struggle for life is as long as human history), one may then focus on how legal fictions have also been used to ensure access to international arbitration.

III LEGAL FICTIONS AIMED AT ENSURING ACCESS TO INTERNATIONAL ARBITRATION

Expansion as a means for survival. Granting increasing access to international arbitration is yet another means for fighting for its survival. It is a matter of common-sense that international arbitration can be better defended should it be increasingly employed by more and more users in more and more sectors. International arbitration has always attempted to become an indispensable method for dispute resolution in order to survive.

Legal fictions aimed at expanding the scope of international arbitration. Expansion of the scope of international arbitration has given rise, according to the job that they may do, to two categories of legal fictions in the language of international arbitration: legal fictions aimed at creating legal rules so as to ensure access to international arbitration (section III.A), and legal fictions aimed at interpreting legal rules so as to ensure access to international arbitration (section III.B).

A Legal Fictions Aimed at Creating Legal Rules So as to Ensure Access to International Arbitration

Several examples of legal fictions granting access to arbitral justice. One may find in the language of international arbitration several examples of legal fictions aimed at creating legal rules so as to ensure access to international arbitration. These examples can be found both in international commercial arbitration and in international investment arbitration.

The 'fundamental right to arbitrate'. There is, however, one legal fiction which seems to apply to all types of international arbitration. It is what has been called, especially under some Constitutional laws, the 'fundamental right to arbitrate'. This fundamental right may be found in some laws as well as in some judicial decisions in several jurisdictions. In Germany, for instance, the Supreme Court held that "Article 2(1) of the Basic Law guarantees personal freedom and private autonomy. This fundamental right requires that the arbitrability of the matter and the resulting waiver of the right of access to national courts must be based on the parties' voluntary agreement."[29] Article 86 of the 1793 French Constitution, in turn, provided that "no encroachment can be made upon the right of citizens to have their matters in dispute decided by an arbitrator of their own choice."

It is worth noting here that the main defender today of the existence of a 'fundamental right to arbitrate' is Professor Gary Born. In a paper written in 2015, Professor Born concludes that:

> In summary, courts and tribunals from around the globe have repeatedly recognized the central importance of the right to arbitrate to the rule of law. That right has properly been founded on constitutionally-protected liberties—freedom of contract, freedom of association and other individual rights. Denials of the right of citizens to arbitrate their disputes is no less a threat to the rule of law and individual liberties than denials of the freedom to contract or associate.[30]

Some observations regarding the fictional nature of the 'fundamental right to arbitrate' and its job within the language of international arbitration are needed at this point:

The 'fundamental right to arbitrate' is a legal fiction. That the 'fundamental right to arbitrate' is a legal fiction may be demonstrated through two series of propositions:

- First, the fictional nature of this right arises out of the adjective 'fundamental' in its formulation. This word qualifies rights which are conquests of humanity

29. Judgment of April 3, 2000, II ZR 373 / 98, cited by G. Born, "The Right to Arbitrate: Historical and Contemporary Perspectives," in: *Asian Disputes Review*, Hong Kong: HKIAC, 2015, Volume 17, Issue 2, p. 58.
30. G. Born, "The Right to Arbitrate: Historical and Contemporary Perspectives," *supra*, p. 60.

and, as such, are essential to any human being and can be characterized as 'human rights'. The question, therefore, is this: is the right to arbitrate (which arises out of an arbitration agreement) a 'fundamental' right? The answer seems to be in the negative; the right to arbitrate simply does not seem to be essential for any human being and, hence, cannot be characterized as a 'human right'. As a consequence, the 'fundamental' nature of the right to arbitrate is a legal fiction because such right would be taken '*as if*' it were a 'fundamental' right.

- Second, one of the arguments which is provided to support the 'fundamental' qualifier is that the 'right to arbitrate' is somewhat subsumed into the 'fundamental right to access the administration of justice'. This argument, however, is incorrect. In our view, the 'fundamental right to access the administration of justice' only refers to the State's judicial organ and not to the exceptional arbitral justice. In fact, in some instances in which an arbitration agreement was executed through economic duress, such arbitration agreement has been invalidated by State courts because it prevented one of the parties (for instance, an employee on whom the employer imposed an arbitration clause in its labor contract) from accessing the justice administered by the State's judicial organ.

The job of the 'fundamental right to arbitrate'. What is in the end the job accomplished by the legal fiction of the 'fundamental right to arbitrate'? Its main role seems to be, at least in those jurisdictions where some constitutional remedies may, rightly or wrongly, be used to attack arbitral awards, to provide the State's judicial organ with an argument according to which those recourses could be rejected. In short, placing the right to arbitrate at the same constitutional, fundamental level as the right to access the administration of justice and, more generally, due process rights allows the State court seized with a constitutional recourse against an arbitral award to reject it more easily by referring to the constitutional, fundamental right to arbitrate.

Another '*acte de foi*'. There are, in the end: (i) legal fictions which have been universally adopted such as the autonomy of the arbitration agreement rule or the principle of Kompetenz-Kompetenz and (ii) legal fictions which have been adopted by one or, at best, by a few legal orders and that, as a result, can at most become '*actes de foi*' on the international plane. In this sense, the legal fiction of the 'fundamental right to arbitrate' is of the same nature as the legal fiction of the 'arbitral legal order'. We may, in other words, want to believe in the 'fundamental' importance of the right to arbitrate.

International commercial and investment arbitration. One can better explain other legal fictions aimed at granting access to international arbitration by analyzing them within the context of the type of international arbitration in which they appear, that is, international commercial arbitration (section III.A.1) or international investment arbitration (section III.A.B).

1 *Legal Fictions Aimed at Creating Rules So as to Ensure Access to International Commercial Arbitration*

A myriad of legal fictions aimed at granting access to international commercial arbitration. There are many legal fictions of the kind referred to in the title above. There are, however, two of them which, given their relevance in the language of international arbitration, deserve special comment, that is: (i) the 'extension of the arbitration agreement to non-signatories' and (ii) the notion of 'subjective arbitrability'.

Natural selection. As a consequence, we will not discuss *in extenso* in these pages less relevant legal fictions such as: (i) the '*mandat apparent*' theory regarding representation of legal entities in the execution of arbitration agreements; (ii) the arbitration agreement 'by reference'; and (iii) the 'circulation' (more technically, the 'assignment') of the arbitration agreement.

Confirmation of the nature of legal fictions. In brief fashion, however, it is worth addressing why the notions referred to in the preceding paragraph are legal fictions:

- The theory of 'apparent mandate' provides access to international commercial arbitration in the following factual situation: the representative of a company or of a State or a State entity who executes the contract containing the relevant arbitration agreement did not have the legal authority or the legal power to bind the supposedly represented company, State or State entity. If, however, the purported representative who executed the contract has within the company, State or State entity sufficient status to project the 'appearance' that he or she may represent the company, State or State entity, one may conclude, on the basis of the 'apparent mandate' legal fiction, that the represented company, State or State entity should be bound by the contract containing the arbitration agreement '*as if*' the purported representative was 'really' entitled to execute it on its behalf. The theory of the apparent mandate assumes as true and real a situation which is neither true nor real.
- The legal fiction of the 'arbitration agreement by reference' is interesting in two ways: it is first worth noting that this notion assumes that a general reference to general conditions for contracting, which, in turn, contain an arbitration agreement, is a reference to that arbitration agreement; in other words, the reference to the general conditions for contracting is taken '*as if*' it were a specific reference to the arbitration agreement contained therein. This legal fiction is also interesting because, as is the case with respect to the circulation or assignment of the arbitration agreement, it demonstrates that the legal fiction of the autonomy of the arbitration agreement cannot be taken as a logical proposition. Should it be a logical proposition, a general reference to the general conditions for contracting containing an arbitration clause would not be sufficient for this autonomous or separate clause to be binding upon the parties.

- Lastly, the legal fiction of the circulation or assignment of the arbitration agreement assumes, in turn, that the arbitration agreement is an accessory to the main contract. This means that there is no need for a specific agreement to assign the arbitration clause in that main contract; that is, the arbitration clause is assigned together with the main contract which contains it. This assumption also makes clear that the autonomy of the arbitration agreement rule cannot be taken as a logical proposition.

The legal fiction of the 'extension of the arbitration agreement to non-signatories'. *First,* the legal fiction of the so-called extension of the arbitration agreement to non-signatories deserves special attention within the language of international commercial arbitration. This legal fiction is perhaps as famous as the autonomy of the arbitration agreement rule and the Kompetenz-Kompetenz principle.

The factual scenario of the 'extension of the arbitration agreement'. The factual scenario in which this legal fiction is relied upon is this: the contract containing the arbitration agreement is signed by parties A and B. B may be a special corporate vehicle or an empty shell created, with a rather insignificant capital, by its parent company B-1. B-1 has somehow participated in the negotiation, execution or performance of the contract containing the relevant arbitration agreement. B breaches the contract. A, given that B does not have the funds to respond for the breach, commences arbitration against B and B-1. The question arising out of this factual scenario is this: given that B-1 did not sign the contract containing the relevant arbitration agreement, can that arbitration agreement be legally 'extended' to B-1?

The fictional nature of the 'extension of the arbitration agreement'. Essentially, the legal fiction of the 'extension of the arbitration agreement' consists in assuming that, because of its behavior during the negotiation, execution and, in particular, the performance of the contract containing the relevant arbitration agreement, the non-signatory (B-1) implicitly gave its consent to that arbitration agreement and, as a result, to participating in any international arbitration arising therefrom. In other words, the legal fiction of the 'extension of the arbitration agreement' operates '*as if*' the non-signatory had signed the contract containing the relevant arbitration agreement, and, hence, had consented to being a party to the ensuing arbitration.

The evolution of the 'extension of the arbitration agreement'. The legal fiction described above has observed an interesting evolution under French law. One may indeed identify three different moments of such evolution:

(1) The first stage of this evolution coincides with the Paris Court of Appeals decision in the *Dow Chemical* case.[31] According to this judgment, the participation in the negotiation, execution or performance of a contract by a non-signatory belonging to the group of companies of one of the signatory parties to that contract was taken '*as if*' the non-signatory had signed that contract. Under this first test of French case law, the 'extension of the

31. Paris, October 21, 1983, *Sté Isover St-Gobain c/ Stés Dow Chemical France et autres,* in: I. Fadlallah and D. Hascher, *supra*, pp. 15 et seq.

arbitration agreement' could only occur if: (i) the non-signatory belonged to the group of companies of one of the signatory parties and (ii) the non-signatory had participated in the negotiation, execution or performance of the contract containing the relevant arbitration agreement. This first theory, called the 'group of companies theory', was based on the idea (perhaps another legal fiction) that the companies belonging to the same group formed the 'same economic reality'.

(2) The second stage of the evolution of this legal fiction corresponds to the rendering of the *Jaguar* Decision of the Paris Court of Appeals.[32] The test changed in its second iteration. Pursuant to the *Jaguar* case, there is no longer a need for the non-signatory to belong to the group of companies of one of the signatories of the contract containing the relevant arbitration agreement; the non-signatory party should only have participated in, in particular, the performance of the contract containing the relevant arbitration agreement for it to be 'extended' to it. Under this modified test, the participation of the non-signatory party in the performance of the contract containing the relevant arbitration agreement is taken '*as if*' that party had signed such contract. This second theory has been called the 'implicit consent' theory.

(3) The third and latest test of the 'extension of the arbitration agreement' legal fiction results from the *Dallah* Decision of the Paris Court of Appeals.[33] In this case, the theory of 'implicit consent' seems to have been abandoned. Under this third iteration of the test, the 'extension of the arbitration agreement' to a non-signatory party depends on the purpose of avoiding a denial of justice situation.[34] It is in my view important to summarize the facts of the *Dallah* case to understand the current state of the French theory of the 'extension of the arbitration agreement' to nonsignatories:
   - the contract containing the relevant International Chamber of Commerce (ICC) arbitration agreement had been signed by Dallah and a Trust, whose beneficiary was the State of Pakistan;
   - the fact that such contract was to be signed by the Trust and not by the State was known by Dallah since the very beginning of the relevant negotiations, including that the Trust expired at some point in time;
   - the Trust did not fulfill its contractual obligations and expired; as a consequence, Dallah commenced ICC arbitration against the State of Pakistan;
   - the State of Pakistan objected to the jurisdiction of the ICC tribunal on the basis that it did not consent to any ICC arbitration anywhere; Dallah, in turn, invoked the theory of 'implicit consent' and, hence, Pakistan's

32. Paris, December 7, 1994, *Jaguar*, R.T.D. Com., 1995, p. 401.
33. Paris, February 17, 2011, *Gouvernement de Pakistan, ministère des affaires religieuses c/ Sté Dallah Real Estate and Tourism Holding Company*, in: *Revue de l'arbitrage*, Paris : Litec, 2012, pp. 369 et seq.
34. *Cf.*, for instance, P. Mayer, *The Extension of the Arbitration Clause to Non-Signatories—The Irreconcilable Positions of French and English Courts*, in: *American University International Law Review*, 2012, Volume 27, Issue 4, pp. 831 et seq.

participation in the dealings relating to the Trust in order to seek the extension of the arbitration agreement to the State;

- the Arbitral Tribunal—with great hesitation made explicit in a Partial Award—rejected the jurisdictional objection raised by Pakistan, and proceeded to the examination of the merits of the case; then, in the Final Award, the Arbitral Tribunal found in favor of Dallah;
- Pakistan did not comply spontaneously with the Final Award; as a result, Dallah commenced enforcement proceedings against Pakistan in England; in their three instances, the English courts rejected the enforcement requested on the ground that the arbitration agreement had been wrongly extended to Pakistan and, as a consequence, the Arbitral Tribunal did not have jurisdiction over the State; and
- Pakistan also filed a set-aside action against the Final Award in Paris, the seat of the arbitration, on the same ground of lack of jurisdiction; the Paris Court of Appeals rejected that action adopting the 'denial of justice' test.

In this third and last iteration of the legal fiction of the 'extension of the arbitration agreement to non-signatories', the Paris Court of Appeals treats Pakistan *as if* it had signed the contract containing the arbitration agreement in order to avoid a denial of justice.

The hidden fiction behind the word 'extension'. The word 'extension' deserves special comment. The use of that word shows the fictional nature of the theory of the 'extension of the arbitration agreement'. A contract cannot in reality be 'extended' to a party. Either that party: (i) consented to the contract and, hence, is a party to it, and it makes no sense 'to extend' it to it or (ii) did not consent to that contract and, as a result, it is not a party to it, and it cannot be extended to it either. 'Extension' is in this sense synonymous to '*as if*'.

The legal fiction of 'subjective arbitrability'. *Second*, another remarkable legal fiction created to ensure access to international commercial arbitration is that of 'subjective arbitrability'. This concept, also created in France,[35] refers to international commercial arbitration involving States or State entities, that is, to the aptitude of States or State entities to enter into an international arbitration agreement.

The factual matrix in which 'subjective arbitrability' plays out. The factual situation in which this legal fiction plays a role is this: a private entity and a State or a State entity entered into a contract containing an international arbitration agreement; when a dispute arises out of that contract, the State or the State entity objects to the jurisdiction of the arbitral tribunal on the ground that it did not have the 'capacity' under the law of the State to enter into international arbitration agreements; the law of the State may, for instance, encompass a provision stating that the State or any State entity cannot submit to arbitration disputes arising out of administrative contracts or administrative acts. The private entity, for its part, has no choice but to argue that a law

35. *Cf.*, for instance, Ch. Séraglini and J. Ortscheidt, *Droit de l'arbitrage interne et international*, Paris: Montchrestien, 2013, pp. 530 et seq.

other than the law of the State applies to the jurisdictional objection raised by the State or the State entity.

The job accomplished by the 'subjective arbitrability' legal fiction. The premise of this legal fiction is that the aptitude of a State or a State entity does not raise an issue of 'capacity' of entering into an international arbitration agreement. Rather, it raises an issue of 'subjective arbitrability'. The rationale behind the change of characterization has traditionally been that 'capacity' regimes are aimed at protecting physical persons who, for reasons of age or disability, do not have the free and informed will to enter into contracts; conversely, States and State entities are not physical persons and, as a consequence, there is no point in assessing whether their discernment was free and informed when entering into a contract. This change of legal characterization operates a change in the applicable law to resolve the issue. The applicable law to issues of capacity is the law of the person alleging that it did not have the capacity of entering into a contract; under this scenario, the arbitral tribunal would have no choice but to declare that it does not have jurisdiction over the State or the State entity. The applicable law to issues of arbitrability is, in turn, the applicable law to the arbitration agreement; given that the applicable law to the arbitration agreement may be different from the law of the State or the State entity (the applicable law to the arbitration agreement is often—under comparative law—the law of the seat of the arbitration), the arbitral tribunal may, under this second scenario, reject the jurisdictional objection raised by the State or the State entity.

The fictional nature of 'subjective arbitrability'. 'Subjective arbitrability' is a legal fiction because it assumes that a clear capacity issue is an arbitrability issue; in other words, 'subjective arbitrability' is fictional because it operates '*as if*' the aptitude of States and State entities to submit disputes to international arbitration was an arbitrability issue. Interestingly, the legal fiction operates in this case through an arbitrary change of the legal characterization of the issue. One can at this point conclude that one of the methods by which legal fictions are created is the arbitrary change of the legal characterization of issues.

The rule pursuant to which a State or a State entity cannot rely on its own, internal law to escape the legal effects of an international arbitration agreement. An interesting rule—which may also be considered to be a legal fiction—completes the legal fiction of 'subjective arbitrability'. This is the rule according to which a State or a State entity cannot rely on its own internal law to escape the legal effects of an international arbitration agreement. It is worth recounting the history of this rule:

- It seems that the first time this rule was somewhat adopted in a legal text was in 1961, when the Geneva Convention on International Commercial Arbitration was adopted; its Article II.1 indeed provided that, "[i]n cases referred to in Article I, paragraph 1, of this Convention, legal persons considered by the law which is applicable to them as 'legal persons of public law' have the right to conclude valid arbitration agreements."
- A second period of the application of this rule occurred in ICC arbitrations where the arbitrators inferred it from either 'international public policy' or the

'principle of good faith.'[36] This application especially arose out of cases in which National Iranian Oil Company (NIOC), the Iranian State-owned oil company, entered into an international arbitration agreement and, then, when a dispute arose, raised a jurisdictional objection on the ground that it was not permitted to execute that international arbitration agreement because the Iranian Constitution required prior parliamentary approval which had not occurred in the circumstances. It seems indeed against our intuition of what good faith is for a State or a State entity to sign a contract including an international arbitration agreement to then attempt to escape its legal effects. A question which, to our knowledge, remains unsolved is, however, what should be the legal consequence in cases where the private entity is aware of the fact that the State or the State entity is entering into an international arbitration agreement in contravention of that State's own, internal law.
- The rule has been adopted by States' case law (the *Gatoil* case of the French *Cour de cassation* is a good example[37]) and legislation (Switzerland in 1987, Spain in 2003, Colombia in 2013[38]).

The legal fictions aimed at ensuring access to international commercial arbitration against States and State entities. The rule described above completes the legal fiction of 'subjective arbitrability' in two different ways. On the one hand, it ensures that the dispute be arbitrated when: (i) the seat of the arbitration is located in the State raising a 'lack of capacity' jurisdictional objection and (ii) as a result, the law applicable to 'subjective arbitrability' is the one of that State. On the other hand, the rule is also useful in those jurisdictions where the notion of 'subjective arbitrability' is not recognized. In sum, the conjunction formed by 'subjective arbitrability' and the rule pursuant to which a State or a State entity cannot rely on its own internal law to escape the legal effects of an international arbitration agreement should ensure the access of private entities to international commercial arbitration against States or State entities. The legal fictions aimed at granting access to investment arbitration are also of interest.

2 Legal Fictions Aimed at Creating Rules So as to Ensure Access to Investment Arbitration

A myriad of legal fictions in bilateral investment treaties. The relatively recent field of investment law is full of legal fictions. Given that it is a field created to favor foreign

36. *Cf.*, for instance, E. Silva Romero, "Some Remarks on the Contribution of ICC Arbitrators to the Development of International Commercial Arbitration Involving States and State Entities," in: *International Arbitration Under Review, Essays in honor of John Beechey*, Paris: ICC Publication, 2015, pp. 401 et seq.
37. Paris, December 17, 1991, *Gatoil*, in: *Revue de l'arbitrage*, 1993, pp. 281 et seq.
38. Article 177(2) of the Swiss Private International Law Act provides that, "*si une partie à la convention d'arbitrage est un Etat, une entreprise dominée ou une organisation contrôlée par lui, cette partie ne peut pas invoquer son propre droit pour contester l'arbitrabilité du litige ou sa capacité d'être partie à l'arbitrage.*" This text was copied by the Spanish and Colombian legislators.

investment, its policies often clash with logic or, even, with orthodox legal reasoning. These clashes are normally solved by the creation of a legal fiction. Three examples may help illustrate this proposition:

The legal fictions in the notion of 'investment'. *First*, most bilateral investment treaties attempt to derogate from ordinary language by including within the notion of 'investment' what it is not. These treaties, for instance, provide that:

> 'investment' means every kind of asset and in particular, though not exclusively, includes: (i) movable or immovable property and any other property rights [...] (ii) shares in and stock and debentures of a company [...] (iii) claims to money [...] (iv) industrial and intellectual property rights, technical processes, knowhow and goodwill; (v) business concessions [...].[39]

This definition of 'investment' contradicts with what 'investment' means in ordinary language. As put by the tribunal in the *Saba Fakes* case:

> the criteria of (i) a contribution, (ii) a certain duration, and (iii) an element of risk, are both necessary and sufficient to define an investment [...] These three criteria derive from the ordinary meaning of the word 'investment,' be it in the context of a complex international transaction or that of the education of one's child: in both instances, one is required to contribute a certain amount of funds or know-how, one cannot harvest the benefits of such contribution instantaneously, and one runs the risk that no benefits would be reaped at all, as a project might never be completed or a child might not be up to his parents' hopes or expectations.[40]

In short, 'investment' means for most people the 'activity of investing' in the expectation of obtaining—in a 'period of time', which implies a 'risk'—a 'return'. The lists of 'investments' in bilateral investment treaties treat 'invested objects' such as property rights, shares and claims to money *'as if'* they were 'investments'; taking 'invested objects' as 'investments' is a legal fiction.

The return of the real notion of investment. The legal fictions in these lists of investments in bilateral investment treaties have encountered some resistance by States and arbitral tribunals. There seems to be a current trend toward recognizing the existence of an objective notion of investment beyond the 'objects invested' as listed in bilateral investment treaties. As put by some tribunals,[41] 'investment' is not only the

39. Agreement between the United Kingdom and the Republic of Turkey for the Promotion and Protection of Investments, March 15, 1991, Article 1(a).
40. *Saba Fakes v. Republic of Turkey*, ICSID Case No. ARB/07/20, Award, July 14, 2010, para. 110.
41. *Quiborax S.A., Non Metallic Minerals S.A. and Allan Fosk Kaplún v. Plurinational State of Bolivia*, ICSID Case No. ARB/06/2, Decision on Jurisdiction, September 27, 2012, para. 233 ("According to Bolivia, a distinction should be made between the objects of an investment, 'such as shares or concessions [...] and the action of investing'. The Tribunal agrees"); *Clorox Spain S.L. v. Bolivarian Republic of Venezuela*, PCA Case No. 2015-30, Award, May 20, 2019, para. 815 ("*el Tratado requiere que para constituir una inversión protegida, la tenencia de acciones resulte de un acto de invertir por un inversor de una Parte Contratante*"); *Malicorp Limited v. Arab Republic of Egypt*, ICSID Case No. ARB/08/18, Award, February 7, 2011, para. 110 ("There must be 'active' economic contributions, as is confirmed by the etymology of the word 'invest'").

'object invested' but also the 'action of investing'. 'Investing', in turn, supposes a 'contribution', a 'duration' and a 'risk.'[42]

Local may be deemed to be foreign. *Second,* bilateral investment treaties often encompass the legal fiction, based on the notion of 'control', that a company of the nationality of the State hosting the investment shall be treated as a national of the other, foreign State party to the treaty for the purpose of benefiting from its protections. This is, for instance, the case of the 2008 Model Bilateral Investment Treaty of the United Kingdom:

> A company which is incorporated or constituted under the law in force in the territory of one Contracting Party and in which before such a dispute arises the majority of shares are owned by nationals or companies of the other Contracting Party shall in accordance with Article 25 (2) (b) of the Convention be treated for the purposes of the Convention as a company of the other Contracting Party.[43]

The existence of 'control' entails, in accordance with those treaties, that a company of one nationality is taken '*as if*' it had a different nationality. This legal fiction is equivalent to the one establishing, for the purpose of avoiding a denial of justice, that Minorca is part of London.

Treaty claims and contract claims. *Third,* perhaps the most relevant legal fiction in investment law is the distinction between treaty claims and contract claims. In the landmark case, *Vivendi,* in which this rule was first formulated, the ICSID ad hoc annulment committee stated the following:

> A treaty cause of action is not the same as a contractual cause of action; it requires a clear showing of conduct which is in the circumstances contrary to the relevant treaty standard. The availability of local courts ready and able to resolve specific issues independently may be a relevant circumstance in determining whether there has been a breach of international law (especially in relation to a standard such as that contained in Article 3). But it is not dispositive, and it does not preclude an international tribunal from considering the merits of the dispute.[44]

The job of the treaty claims / contract claims legal fiction. Much has been written about the distinction between treaty claims and contract claims.[45] For the purposes of this chapter, suffice it to say that the job of the distinction is to provide investors with access to investment arbitration. This legal fiction, however, has been mistakenly considered to be a logical proposition. As a consequence, there are far too many cases in which the investor and the host State have debated whether the dispute is merely 'contractual' or whether the 'dispute is serious enough to breach the treaty'.

42. *LESI, S.p.A. and Astaldi, S.p.A. v. People's Democratic Republic of Algeria,* ICSID Case No. ARB/05/3, Decision, July 12, 2006, para. 72; *Víctor Pey Casado and President Allende Foundation v. Republic of Chile,* ICSID Case No. ARB/98/2, Award, May 8, 2008, para. 233; *Quiborax S.A., Non Metallic Minerals S.A. and Allan Fosk Kaplún v. Plurinational State of Bolivia,* ICSID Case No. ARB/06/2, Decision on Jurisdiction, September 27, 2012, para. 227.
43. United Kingdom Model Bilateral Investment Treaty, 2008, Article 8(2).
44. *Compañiá de Aguas del Aconquija S.A. and Vivendi Universal S.A. v. Argentine Republic,* ICSID Case No. ARB/97/3, Decision on Annulment, July 3, 2002, para. 113.
45. J. Crawford, "Treaty and Contract in Investment Arbitration," *Arbitration International,* 2008, Volume 24, Issue 3, pp. 351 et seq. (delivered as the 22nd annual Freshfields Lecture).

These debates are particularly complex when the relevant contract contains a dispute resolution clause in favor of a mechanism of dispute resolution different from investment arbitration. Was it not easier and simpler to clearly establish either: (i) that investors may choose between the contractual dispute resolution mechanism in the contract or investment arbitration or (ii) that the dispute resolution clause in the contract prevents the investor from resorting to investment arbitration? Once more, one may observe that treating legal fictions as logical propositions, labeling with shortcuts, may be a source of confusion.

B Legal Fictions Aimed at Interpreting Legal Rules So as to Ensure Access to International Arbitration

Many examples in investment arbitration. In a purer sense, legal fictions are tools created to adapt existing rules to an unforeseen reality in which a strict application of the law may lead to injustice. From this standpoint, legal fictions are close to the notion of 'equity'. It is in our view the investment arbitration field which provides the two best examples of this category of legal fictions.

The 'triple identity test' in the construction of 'fork-in-the-road' provisions. *First*, investment case law has created a legal test[46] to interpret and apply fork-in-the-road provisions in bilateral investment treaties. As an example, these provisions commonly read as follows:

> Once an investor has submitted the dispute either to the jurisdiction of the Contracting Party involved or to international arbitration, the choice of one or the other of these procedures shall be final.[47]

Importing from another legal language. Imported from the language of civil procedure, the so-called triple identity test (for the rule to apply, there should be identity of parties, subject matter, and cause of action) takes the fork-in-the-road rule '*as if*' it belonged to the family of legal institutions such as '*res judicata*' and '*lis pendens*'. That assumption, however, would make it almost impossible for the fork-in-the-road rule to apply.

The fork-in-the-road facts. The factual matrix to which such rule applies is this: the group of the investor commences at least two different proceedings against the host State or its relevant agency. Only very rarely those proceedings are between the same parties and result from the same cause of action. Commonly, one case is a lawsuit commenced before the courts of the host State, whereas the second one is the investment arbitration in which the fork-in-the-road objection is raised by the host State. The *effet utile* principle on the interpretation of treaties has produced new case

---

46. *Víctor Pey Casado and President Allende Foundation v. Republic of Chile*, ICSID Case No. ARB/98/2, Award, May 8, 2008, para. 482 et seq. ("*[...] les demandes portées respectivement devant les juridictions nationales et devant le Tribunal arbitral doivent avoir à la fois le même objet et le même fondement et être présentées par les mêmes parties*").
47. Agreement between the French Republic and the Argentine Republic for the Reciprocal Encouragement and Promotion of Investments, July 3, 1991, Article 8(2).

law in which the triple identity test is either replaced or, at the very least, moderated. In, for instance, the *Pantechniki* case, the Sole Arbitrator adopted the following test:

> [it must be determined] whether or not 'the fundamental basis of a claim' sought to be brought before the international forum is autonomous of claims to be heard elsewhere.[48]

The legal fiction of the 'umbrella clause'. *Second*, another interesting legal fiction has been used to interpret what has been called in investment arbitration an 'umbrella clause'. Umbrella clauses commonly read as follows:

> Each Contracting Party shall observe any obligation it may have entered into with regard to investments of nationals or companies of the other Contracting Party.[49]

A fictional 'elevation'. In their interpretation of these provisions, arbitral tribunals and scholars[50] have stated that the umbrella clause 'elevates' the municipal or contractual dispute to the treaty level. The legal fiction lies in the use of the verb 'to elevate'. As a matter of fact and law, the relevant bilateral investment treaty does not 'elevate' anything. The word 'elevation' projects in our view the wrong impression that the municipal or contractual dispute changes in nature by operation of the umbrella clause. It should not. The main effect of the umbrella clause is to provide the investor with the avenue of investment arbitration to solve its municipal or contractual dispute with the host State. In short, 'elevation' in the construction of umbrella clauses reminds us of 'autonomy' in the expression 'autonomy of the arbitration agreement'. Shortcut labels should be avoided.

IV CONCLUSIONS

Another typology of legal fictions. In conclusion, a new typology of legal fictions in the language of international arbitration may be inferred from the analyses above. I would submit that those legal fictions can in the end be classified into two main categories.

Legal fictions aimed at ensuring the survival of international arbitration. *First*, there are legal fictions in the language of international arbitration aimed at ensuring the survival of international arbitration. These legal fictions are, for instance, the 'arbitral legal order'; the assimilation of arbitrators to judges; the autonomy of the arbitration agreement; the Kompetenz-Kompetenz principle; the fundamental right to arbitrate; the extension of the arbitration agreement to nonsignatories; and 'subjective

48. *Pantechniki S.A. Contractors & Engineers (Greece) v. The Republic of Albania*, ICSID Case No. ARB/07/21, Award, July 30, 2009, para. 61.
49. United Kingdom Model Bilateral Investment Treaty, 2008, Article 2(2).
50. *Ioan Micula and others v. Romania*, ICSID Case No. ARB/05/20, Award, December 11, 2013, para. 417 ("The purpose of the umbrella clause is to cover or 'elevate' to the protection of the BIT an obligation of the state that is separate from, and additional to, the treaty obligations that it has assumed under the BIT"); R. Dolzer and C. Schreuer, *Principles of Investment Law*, Oxford: Oxford University Press, 2008, p. 155 ("[...] the purpose of the clause as a means to elevate violations of investment contracts to the level of international law").

arbitrability'. All these notions seek to make the international arbitration system more robust.

Effective legal fictions are based on belief. We may, in particular, believe or not (we should refer again to the '*acte de foi*' mentioned by Emmanuel Gaillard) in the theories of the arbitral legal order and the fundamental right to arbitrate. The fact of the matter, however, is that these two theories clearly seek to reinforce the international arbitration system and, as a result, ensure its survival.

Effective legal fictions become legal rules. It is worth noting that all the legal fictions aimed at ensuring the survival of international arbitration have with time become legal rules.

Legal fictions are not logical propositions. There is a danger in those legal fictions, however. They can produce undesirable legal effects if they are taken as if they were logical propositions. Despite their misleading labeling (remember, for instance, the word 'autonomy' in the 'autonomy of the arbitration agreement', and the characterization of Kompetenz-Kompetenz as a 'legal principle'), they are not. Well understood as legal fictions, there should not be any need for relying on counter-legal fictions such as the 'accessory follows the fate of the principal'.

Legal fictions which endanger the survival of international arbitration. *Second*, there are legal fictions in the language of international arbitration which endanger the survival of the international arbitration system. These are, for instance, the affirmation without demonstration of the advantages of international arbitration; the total, unwarranted assimilation of arbitrators to State judges; the rationales proposed by ICC arbitrators of the rule pursuant to which a State or a State entity cannot rely on its own, internal law to escape the legal effects of an international arbitration agreement; the list of 'investments' (invested objects) in bilateral investment treaties; the distinction between treaty claims and contract claims; the 'triple identity test' imported to construe fork-in-the-road provisions; and the use of the verb 'to elevate' when interpreting umbrella clauses.

The crisis of investment arbitration. Interestingly, many of these legal fictions are aimed at constructing legal rules. In fact, these legal fictions in the end actually distort those rules. Most of these legal fictions are to be found in the language of investment arbitration. The crisis of investment arbitration may as a consequence also be explained by the fact that most of those legal fictions are used to distort, that is, to modify the text of the relevant treaties.

Throwing the ladder away. To close, one should, after the analyses above, paraphrase Ludwig Wittgenstein,[51] and submit that the propositions of this chapter could only be useful in the following manner: they should form a ladder (Memo

51. *Cf.* L. Wittgenstein, *Tractatus Logico-Philosophicus*, Translated by D. F. Pears and F. McGuiness, London: Routledge, 2000, proposition 6.54, p. 74: "My propositions serve as elucidations in the following way: anyone who understands me eventually recognizes them as nonsensical, when he has used them—as steps—to climb up beyond them. (He must, so to speak, throw away the ladder after he has climbed up it.) He must transcend these propositions, and then he will see the world alright."

provided me with a ladder during our discussion referred to above) from which the reader should be able to look at the world of international arbitration under a clearer light; then, the reader should throw that ladder away.

CHAPTER 15

Law and Simplicity: The Art of the Samurai

Santiago Montt

Simplicity is about subtracting the obvious, and adding the meaningful.

John Maeda, *The Laws of Simplicity* (MIT Press, 2006, p. 1).

I INTRODUCTION

The remarkable character you see above is Guillermo Aguilar Álvarez's signature, evidence of the extraordinary person Guillermo was. This short chapter is a eulogy for Guillermo. It reflects on one of Guillermo's outstanding characteristics as a legal writer: his commitment to simplicity in his argumentation style.

I nicknamed Guillermo "the Samurai." His implacable and impeccable minimalism, coupled with that beautifully reduced signature, led me to this name. This nickname was also in reaction to the thousands of hours of discussions and debate we had on the right length and complexity of argumentation in legal practice.

I worked alongside Guillermo for three years. We jointly prepared a number of briefs and academic articles. Many times he would read my drafts and ask, somewhat disapprovingly, "what did you *really* try to say here?" After listening to my attempts to explain, he would materially reduce my paragraphs, dropping all but one or two lucky arguments. The resulting text would be materially shorter, far more succinct, and contain only the strongest arguments, as not many survived his demanding and honest scrutiny.

Even now, when I write legal opinions or business memos, in my mind I talk endlessly with Guillermo. He always challenges me to commit to the Samurai's law: *to say the minimum number of things, each of them in the most simple and shortest possible way*.

In this short note, I will discuss simplicity and its role in legal argumentation. I will argue that the arbitrator has more room for parsimony than the judge—at least, the high court judge—and within arbitration, a commercial arbitrator more than an investment arbitrator. Guillermo, my admired Samurai mentor, was one of the best arbitrators of his generation, and his commitment to parsimony reflects his deep vocation as an arbitrator.

II ON SIMPLICITY

As Kant explains, there are two competing principles at stake, simplicity and explanatory sufficiency. "Principles must not be unnecessarily multiplied" and "the variety of entities should not be rashly diminished." A similar tension appears in empirical sciences and considerations of "how exactly simplicity ought to be balanced against empirical adequacy. Simple but wildly inaccurate theories are not hard to come up with. Nor are accurate theories which are highly complex."[1]

Finding the right balance between simplicity and explanatory sufficiency is a challenging art in both science and the humanities, including the law. Simplicity comes at a cost. Guillermo, in one of the finest expressions of our profession, adopted and promoted a strong position in favor of simplicity in legal argumentation. I cannot but continue to admire its elegance, a true mark of his genius.

Paradoxically the concept of simplicity is not simple. After working for three years with Guillermo, I keep wondering why is it the case that simple theories are *better*? Why should we prefer them? The virtue of simplicity may seem, in principle, self-evident: if the outcome is not affected, we should prefer simpler theories or simpler justifications. This principle is usually identified with Occam's Razor, but it has been codified since by more recent philosophers and scientists:

> Aristotle: We may assume the superiority ceteris paribus of the demonstration which derives from fewer postulates or hypotheses.
>
> Aquinas: If a thing can be done adequately by means of one, it is superfluous to do it by means of several; for we observe that nature does not employ two instruments where one suffices.
>
> Newton: We are to admit no more causes of natural things than such as are both true and sufficient to explain their appearances.
>
> Einstein: The grand aim of all science ... is to cover the greatest possible number of empirical facts by logical deductions from the smallest possible number of hypotheses or axioms.[2]

Simplicity encompasses two different concepts: elegance—syntactic simplicity or theory simplicity, which refers to the number and complexity of hypotheses—and parsimony—ontological simplicity or simplicity of the world, which refers to the number and complexity of things being postulated. Unfortunately, elegance and

1. Alan Baker, "Simplicity," in *Stanford Encyclopedia of Philosophy* (October 2004, substantively reviewed on December 2016), available at https://plato.stanford.edu/entries/simplicity/ (last visited November 2, 2019).
2. All quoted in Baker, "Simplicity."

parsimony do not always pull in the same direction. The following explanation of this tension helps to explain these two concepts:

> Postulating extra entities may allow a theory to be formulated more simply, while reducing the ontology of a theory may only be possible at the price of making it syntactically more complex. For example, the postulation of Neptune, at the time not directly observable, allowed the perturbations in the orbits of other observed planets to be explained without complicating the laws of celestial mechanics. There is typically a trade-off between ontology and ideology—to use the terminology favored by Quine—in which contraction in one domain requires expansion in the other. This points to another way of characterizing the elegance/parsimony distinction, in terms of simplicity of theory versus simplicity of world respectively.[3]

The postulation of Neptune made the theory ontologically more complex, as a new entity was introduced into the system. Not postulating, Neptune would have required a much more complex set of laws of mechanics.

There are three general approaches to look for simplicity justifications: a priori justifications, naturalistic or empirical justifications, and probabilistic justifications.[4]

As Baker explains, a priori justifications—that is, deriving from reason alone, independent of experience—are theological (based on views of God), metaphysical (that is, belonging to a more general metaphysical frame), intrinsic-value (circular in nature) or based on the principle of rationality (that is, characteristic of rational inquiry). One line of argument among the latter, worth considering here as we will come back to it, is "epistemic conservatism": "Parsimony in a theory can be viewed as minimizing the number of 'new' entities and mechanisms which are postulated. This preference for old mechanisms may in turn be justified by a more general epistemological caution, or conservatism, which is characteristic of rational inquiry."[5]

Naturalistic justifications look, from an empirical perspective, at scientific practices. According to Baker, during the twentieth century, philosophy had been understood by some, in comparison with science, as encompassing concerns that are not fundamentally different from scientists'. For this school of thought, philosophy should look into patterns of acceptance and rejections of competing theories in science and discover the place of simplicity in those existing practices.

Even more interesting for the purpose of this note are probabilistic justifications. These statistical approaches provide an interesting perspective in understanding the trade-offs between simplicity and empirical adequacy (goodness of fit, an empirical version of explanatory sufficiency). As already noted, both excessively simple theories that are highly inaccurate and highly complex theories that are accurate are equally dissatisfactory. Finding the right middle point is not a trivial or simple exercise, and statistics shed light on this fundamental problem:

> The standard case in the statistical literature on parsimony concerns *curve-fitting*. We imagine a situation in which we have a set of discrete data points and are

3. Baker, "Simplicity."
4. *Ibid.*
5. *Ibid.*

> looking for the curve (i.e. function) which has generated them. The issue of what family of curves the answer belongs in (e.g. in LIN [linear function] or in PAR [parabolic function]) is often referred to as *model-selection*. The basic idea is that there are two competing criteria for model selection—parsimony and goodness of fit. The possibility of measurement error and "noise" in the data means that the correct curve may not go through every data point. Indeed, if goodness of fit were the only criterion then there would be a danger of "overfitting" the model to accidental discrepancies unrepresentative of the broader regularity. Parsimony acts as a counterbalance to such overfitting, since a curve passing through every data point is likely to be very convoluted and hence have many adjusted parameters.[6]

What is the application of these concepts in the law? Personally, I found a priori and naturalistic justifications difficult to accept, and will therefore focus here on the probabilistic approach. Simplicity in legal argumentation postulates in favor of less arguments, and within each, the most succinct possible form. I identify the first part of that statement with parsimony, and the second with elegance. For those who espouse simplicity, simple arguments are *better*. A better argument can be defined as one that is more persuasive.

Put in concrete terms, how should lawyers—including judges and arbitrators—confront the preparation and argumentation of their legal cases, given all the potential facts and legal theories applicable to those cases? Should the balance be in favor of parsimony or goodness of fit? In the first case, a lawyer would choose a few strong legal theories or arguments, and a limited number of key facts to structure his or her case. The price is "noise": there will be several arguments and facts that, given the distance to the selected theories and arguments, weaken the position adopted.

The reverse is also true. An approach excessively focused on goodness of fit will risk overfitting. If all the facts and theories are postulated in an equally relevant way, or even if all of them get space in a brief or legal piece, the excessive amount will end up eroding simplicity, and unquestionably impacting the position's persuasiveness.

In the end, the fundamental question of simplicity, in science and in the law is, in Baker's words, "how much accuracy should be sacrificed for [the benefit of] simplicity?"[7] I think this question is equally valid in descriptive or normative spaces: as there are trade-offs between descriptive accuracy and simplicity, there are comparable trade-offs between normative accuracy and simplicity. As the next section explains, answering this question, in the law, requires paying attention to context.

III SIMPLICITY IN ARBITRATION AND JUDICIAL ADJUDICATION

For many, parsimony is not an absolute value. A priori black or white attempts of justification are not acceptable. Parsimony seems to depend on context and operates a posteriori: "The legitimacy of parsimony stands or falls, in a particular research context, on subject matter specific (and *a posteriori*) considerations… What makes

6. *Ibid.*
7. *Ibid.*

parsimony reasonable in one context may have nothing in common with why it matters in another."[8]

Persuasiveness in legal argumentation is also certainly context dependent. Different contexts, roles and positions, as well as differing audiences, will require different forms of argumentation, with diverging levels of simplicity. Still, there is always a maximum level of simplicity that can be achieved as permitted per each specific context. Simplicity continues to hold as a value but operates on a relative scale.

My thesis in this note is that there are differences between the levels of simplicity that an arbitrator and a judge—at least a high court judge—can aim for and achieve. To prove this point, it is useful to bring Ronald Dworkin to the fore. In his famous 1982 article, *Law as Interpretation*, Dworkin explain judges' role in reference to the metaphor of a "chain novel":[9]

> [In hard cases] [e]ach judge is then like a novelist in the chain. He or she must read through what other judges in the past have written not simply to discover what these judges have said, or their state of mind when they said it, but to reach an opinion about what these judges have collectively done, in the way that each of our novelists formed an opinion about the collective novel so far written... Each judge must regard himself, in deciding the new case before him, as a partner in a complex chain enterprise of which these innumerable decisions, structures, conventions, and practices are the history; it is his job to continue that history into the future through what he does on the day... He *must* interpret what has gone before because he has a responsibility to advance the enterprise in hand rather than strike out in some new direction of his own.[10]

There are two steps in this "chain novel" interpretative process: fit and integrity. Notwithstanding the critiques that have been formulated against Dworkin for this division, I continue to believe in its usefulness. First, the step of *fit* determines whether there are clear and straightforward legal rules and principles that provide the outer limits to the decision of the case: "A judge's duty is to interpret the legal history he finds, not to invent a better history. The dimension of fit will provide some boundaries. There is, of course, no algorithm for deciding whether a particular interpretation sufficiently fits that history not to be ruled out."[11]

The second and more difficult step is the step of *integrity*. We are now working within the boundaries provided by the test of fit, where there are no clear and straightforward rules of principle that allow us to prefer one response to another:

> It should be apparent, however, that any particular judge's theory of fit will often fail to produce a unique interpretation ... Just as two readings of a poem may each find sufficient support in the text to show its unity and coherence, so two principles may each find enough support in the various decisions of the past to

8. E. Sober, "Let's Razor Ockham's Razor," in *From a Biological Point of View*, Cambridge University Press, pp. 136-157, cited in Alan Baker.
9. Ronald Dworkin, "Law as Interpretation," 60 *Texas Law Review* 527 (1982).
10. *Ibid.*, pp. 542-543.
11. *Ibid.*, p. 544.

> satisfy any plausible theory of fit. In that case substantive political theory (like substantive consideration of artistic merit) will play a decisive role.[12]

In the first step of *fit*, the roles of the arbitrator and judge do not substantially differ. Both are equally bound. If the outer boundaries of legal interpretation are crossed, then the decision will be *contra legem* and will fail to meet any reasonable and rational standard. Yet, things are different at the second step of *integrity*. Here, the metaphor of the chain novel is relevant, and at this point the judge innovates—within the boundaries of fit—and provides new answers.

The judge belongs to a jurisdiction where his or her decisions are public and therefore open to the scrutiny of the public of that jurisdiction. The judge speaks not only to the parties but also to the community, legal and beyond. The judge is, using Dworkin's language, a "partner" in the chain enterprise. Backward looking, his or her job is to engage in the understanding of the applicable legal materials and precedents; forward looking, his or her decisions will become, once published, new links of the chain novel.

More importantly, the judge is a state officer, and has the formal authority, and in several cases, substantive legitimacy, to provide the political and policy analysis demanded in the *integrity* step. I believe this is valid even in civil law countries, where cases are not binding precedents, but carry weight for future decisions. The decision-making power in adjudication may seem small and incremental, as compared with legislation and administrative rulemaking—which can more radically alter the status quo—but it is nevertheless a material form of state power.

By contrast, the arbitrator has only one duty: to solve the dispute between the parties that lies before him or her. Arbitration is rooted in commercial practices and is therefore, in most instances, private and confidential. The arbitrator is not an officer of any state and does not engage with the public at large. At least in commercial arbitration, there are no "chain novel" duties, or no material ones, and maybe to a lesser extent only some duties concerning procedural matters.

The authority and legitimacy to provide an integrity account of his or her decisions is thin for the arbitrator, as their duty to provide reasons beyond the boundaries of the fit test is minimal. There is certainly no need to do so, as scrutiny from courts of the site will rarely result in an annulled decision for not having strong integrity argumentation.

In commercial arbitration, the parsimony principle speaks against multiplying the arguments beyond the minimum required to achieve the fundamental purpose of validly resolving the dispute among the parties. Following the principle of rationality justification of parsimony—"epistemic conservatism"—the arbitrator should minimize new "entities and mechanisms," and prefer existing ones. Avoid innovation and stick to the accepted. Stay in the first step of fit and minimize exercises in the second step of integrity.

12. *Ibid.*, p. 545.

IV THE CASE OF INTERNATIONAL INVESTMENT LAW

Investment arbitration practices derive from the thousands of bilateral investment treaties (BITs) that exist today, all of which are worded in similar terms. There is a common professional practice surrounding international investment treaties. "This system of treaties has given way to a common vocabulary, framework of argumentation, and epistemic community."[13] This is due to the close proximity of treaties, which allows decisions rendered under one particular BIT to influence arbitration decisions under other BITs. This was a key point in my *descriptive* theory of the BIT Generation as a virtual network:[14]

> BIT interpretation has given rise to a genuine constitutional jurisprudence, by which I mean a process of judicial norm-creation that gives actual specific content to the overly general provisions of the treaties. Indeed, we can see today how, since the first arbitral award was rendered in 1990, international investment law has gradually become its own distinct field of international law. There is, beyond doubt, "a genuine arbitration case law specific to the field of investment."[15]

If this network theory is descriptively right, it follows that, as a matter of fact (e.g., descriptively speaking), there is indeed a chain novel. Reading investment treaty awards demonstrates the point that it can be empirically proven that there is constant reference to previous decisions.

At this point, it is relevant to discuss a series of normative question: what are the duties of arbitrators toward this chain enterprise? Does investment treaty law change the nature of arbitral decision-making, as postulated above, moving arbitrators further into the realm of the second step of integrity? If yes, to the same extent as judges, or to a lesser degree? All are difficult questions, as investment treaty law is a platypus:[16] part commercial arbitration, part international law, part public law.

Interestingly, Guillermo Aguilar Álvarez and Michael Reisman did confront some of these questions in an academic piece, and defended that investment arbitrators do have a duty to go beyond commercial arbitration:

> Unlike international commercial arbitration, which is conducted entirely by and for professionals and whose awards are only rarely published, international investment awards may have a major political impact on an entire country. In some cases, the economic consequences of investment awards may have long-term implications for the economic vitality of the state concerned. Citizens, as "stakeholders" who may have to bear the consequences of an award, are entitled to know why a decision was made. Similarly, the political opposition in democratic states will wish to understand why a decision was made. The quality of internal political debate about investment policy, which is surely one of the most vital

13. Santiago Montt, *State Liability in Investment Treaty Arbitration* (Hart Publishing, Oxford, 2009), p. 19.
14. Santiago Montt, "Chapter 2. The BIT Generation's Emergence as a Collective Action Problem: Prisoner's Dilemma or Network Effects?," in Santiago Montt (ed.), *State Liability in Investment Treaty Arbitration* (Hart Publishing, Oxford, 2009), pp. 83 ff.
15. *Ibid.*, pp. 84-85.
16. Anthea Roberts, "Clash of Paradigms: Actors and Analogies Shaping the Investment Treaty System," 107 *American Journal of International Law* 45 (2013).

> issues for developing countries, can hardly proceed if the reasons for decisions that are being taken are not clear. Thus, the reasons requirement, as a control mechanism in other sectors of arbitration, acquires a greater importance in international investment arbitration. Indeed, these considerations should lead to the drafting of awards that are accessible to reasonably intelligent people and are not so recondite that none but a small group of specialists can comprehend them.[17]

I want to reconnect with a personal anecdote. When I worked with Guillermo between 2005 and 2008, I was a young scholar in the field of international investment law. I spent a significant amount of time on the topic of "fair and equitable treatment." I witnessed how it became the dominant standard in international investment law, and I dedicated a full chapter of my book *State Liability in Investment Treaty Arbitration* (2009) to it ("Chapter 6. Controlling Arbitrariness Through the Fair and Equitable Treatment Standard").

Several pages of that Chapter were focused on the question of whether the fair and equitable treatment standard is an autonomous standard, or if it is constrained by the so-called international minimum standards. I strongly advocated for the latter and considered the "autonomous standard" theory completely unacceptable. Guillermo and I debated this academic abstract point under all possible angles, testing all possible answers.

Guillermo, as the presiding member of the BG Tribunal,[18] had a leading role in a decision that found Argentina in breach of the fair and equitable standard. Yet, there was no decision on the autonomy dilemma. In a great example of parsimony, that Tribunal held that "[T]he measures adopted by Argentina fall below the international minimum standards and it is consequently not necessary for this award to examine whether the Argentina-U.K. BIT provides a more generous independent standard of protection."[19]

17. Guillermo Aguilar Álvarez and W. Michael Reisman, "How Well Are Investment Awards Reasoned?" in Guillermo Aguilar Álvarez and W. Michael Reisman (eds.), *The Reasons Requirement in International Investment Arbitration. Critical Case Studies* (Martinus Nijhoff Publishers, Leiden 2008) p. 1, 2. *See also* p. 29 ("International investment arbitration, as we said, may present special circumstances with respect a reasons requirement. Unlike international commercial arbitrations, which occur between two private parties both of whom have elected arbitration because they wish confidentiality and for both of whom the issue is essentially commercial, international investment arbitration involves a much wider cast of players. In addition to the government of the host state, which is the invariable respondent, and its loyal opposition, international investment arbitrations involve local industries, non-governmental groups, which may be quite active within the state, and, in a significant number of cases, broad strata of the population, which may be profoundly affected by the outcome of the award. Precisely because awards in international investment law cut so deeply into the national political economy and have such profound and potentially continuing effects on national political processes, their acceptability depends on their persuasiveness, that is, the extent to which they manifest a good faith application of the law. In this respect, a higher threshold for the reasons requirement than might obtain for international commercial arbitration, rather than a lower or more modest one, would seem to commend itself").
18. *BG Group Plc. v. Argentina*, UNCITRAL Ad Hoc Arbitration (arbitration materials available at https://www.italaw.com/cases/143, last visited June 7, 2020).
19. *BG Group Plc. v. Argentina*, UNCITRAL Ad Hoc Arbitration, Award (December 24, 2007), para. 291.

In contrast with other expansive tribunals that enjoyed getting into lengthy doctrinal discourses, the BG Tribunal held a minimal position. There was no attempt to go into the integrity step and defend one of the two theories in this field. If the lowest common denominator-threshold of the two competing theories was met, parsimony demanded that there was no need to examine whether the autonomous theory—that is, the more generous—applied.

I am of the view that the BG Tribunal established the right approach in investment treaty arbitration. This is because, beyond our own personal doctrinal preferences, arbitrators only have light duties toward the chain novel in international investment law. On the one hand, as Guillermo and Michael rightly explain, they have heightened duties toward providing reasons,[20] but on the other hand, they must minimize innovation at the political level of the integrity step.

Several arguments support this conservative approach. First, investment treaty arbitration panels have the delicate duty to apply a new form of global constitutional and administrative law. This is the thesis I strongly defended in my book. The development of this new area of the law, as is the case more generally in constitutional and administrative law, is full of political and policy challenges. This demands that arbitrators be guided by a principle of "judicial restraint": paraphrasing Justice Breyer, an investment arbitrator "when interpreting such open-ended provisions, must avoid being 'willful, in the sense of enforcing individual views'."[21] If Breyer recommends that principle for US Supreme Court Justices, then we should conclude that it is a far stronger imperative at the international investment law level.

Second, the decisions of investment arbitration panels—as those of commercial arbitration—are subject to challenge before either state courts or other annulment committees, depending on the regime they are subject to. The proper application of the parsimony principle minimizes the chances that the award is later annulled. Excessive rhetoric or argumentative innovation is usually the source of trouble for arbitral awards. Argumentative caution, a form of conservatism—as previously explained—works in favor of the stability of the award, especially considering that the integrity step includes a significant amount of political and policy analysis (always a subjective matter of taste and disagreement).

Third, there are aesthetic reasons. Baker cites the philosopher W.V.O. Quine's note on his "taste for 'clear skies' and 'desert landscapes'."[22] In this sense, the genius of adjudication comes from its incremental nature, as important innovation stems from the particular way a set of disputed facts are resolved, irrespective of the reasoning (assuming the fit test is complied with). Particularly in a new field of the law, like investment treaty arbitration, arbitrators should be timid in venturing into risky and potentially unsound argumentations.

20. Aguilar Alvarez and Reisman, *supra* n. 17, pp. 1, 2, and 29.
21. Stephen Breyer, *Active Liberty. Interpreting Our Democratic Constitution* (New York, Knopf, 2005) p. 17.
22. Baker, "Simplicity."

I am not arguing for arbitrary decisions that are devoid of content. Arbitrators are not global supreme justices freely defining a new body of substantive global constitutional and administrative law. The authority and legitimacy of the arbitrator is small compared with that of the member of a high national court.

Following the example of the BG Tribunal decision, I advocate in favor of parsimony in investment arbitration decision-making. Put in another way, I argue for the right balance between parsimony and explanatory sufficiency. Panels must be mindful of the minimum duties toward the parties and of passing post-decision judicial scrutiny, both pillars of the explanatory sufficiency principle in the arbitration space. Panels must also provide proper and solid explanations at the *fit* step, but minimize arguments that enter into the dangerous and innovative territory of the *integrity* step.

V CONCLUSIONS

I have no doubt that I continue to fail to meet Guillermo's expectations of simplicity. As I write and continue to talk to Guillermo in my mind, I will try my best to question myself as Guillermo would have. In my defense, simplicity is not a simple proposition.[23] Philosophers and scientists continue to struggle to comprehend its foundations and limits, and to determine the right balance against the competing principle of explanatory sufficiency.

Guillermo left us the Samurai law: to say the minimum number of things, each of them in the most simple and shortest possible way. Simplicity in legal argumentation requires taking parsimony seriously, without crossing the limits demanded by explanatory sufficiency. The most remarkable part of all was that he achieved this Samurai status of analytical rigor with a deep Mexican soul, full of the most colorful and fascinating baroque tradition.

You are deeply missed, dear Professor.

23. As Maeda notes in his "Law 9. Failure," "Some things can never be made simple."

CHAPTER 16

Les contre-procès internationaux dans l'histoire judiciaire contemporaine

Alexis Mourre

I INTRODUCTION

L'histoire des grands contre-procès internationaux paraîtra sans doute être un sujet surprenant dans un ouvrage consacré à la mémoire d'un grand praticien de l'arbitrage international. Mais l'arbitrage est une justice, qui saurait d'autant moins se désintéresser de la société qui l'entoure que celle-ci paraît porter sur lui un regard de plus en plus critique. Guillermo Aguilar Álvarez était de plus une personnalité profondément éprise de justice, à la vaste culture historique et politique, qui n'aurait peut-être pas trouvé les quelques réflexions qui vont suivre totalement étrangères à ses préoccupations de juriste international.

Les grands procès judiciaires ont souvent contribué à modeler la psychologie collective, à forger l'identité nationale, voire à l'écriture ou à la réécriture de l'histoire. Le procès de Galilée aura ainsi beaucoup fait pour noircir la relation complexe et souvent féconde que nourrissait alors l'Eglise avec la science, et pour alimenter l'imputation, à bien des égards excessive, d'obscurantisme qui lui a ensuite été faite. Celui de Louis XVI aura pour longtemps associé monarchie et tyrannie, et discrédité en France les élites, posant ainsi les bases d'un populisme justicialiste dont les effets perdurent encore aujourd'hui. Les procès de Moscou, dont il sera question ici, ont pour longtemps instillé dans la société soviétique une culture de la peur, de la servilité et de la délation.[1] Plus positivement, le procès de Nuremberg a fait entrer dans notre droit la notion de crime contre l'humanité et fondé l'idée d'une justice naturelle reposant sur

1. André Gide écrira en octobre 1936, dans *Retour de l'U.R.S.S.* « *Je doute qu'en aucun autre pays aujourd'hui, fût-ce dans l'Allemagne de Hitler, l'esprit soit moins libre, plus craintif, plus vassalisé* », Gallimard, 1978, p. 55.

des droits universels et imprescriptibles. D'innombrables autres exemples pourraient ici être cités pour illustrer l'empreinte profonde laissée dans la culture politique et dans l'imaginaire collectif par de grandes décisions de justice. La solennité du procès, l'éminence des juges et la légitimité politique ou historique revendiquée par eux à l'appui de leurs décisions ont sans aucun doute contribué à l'impact profond de ces décisions dans la mémoire collective des peuples. Mais le dialogue entre justice et société est entré à l'époque moderne dans une dimension nouvelle, avec l'avènement de la presse et la montée en puissance de l'opinion publique. Le procès va alors être soumis, de façon toujours plus intense, au jugement des intellectuels, des médias et plus largement de la société civile. La magistrature morale de Voltaire et des philosophes avait certes à elle seule permis d'obtenir la révision du procès injuste de Jean Calas ; mais lorsque la voix de Zola s'est élevée dans les colonnes d'un grand organe de la presse quotidienne pour innocenter Dreyfus, l'Affaire a pris les dimensions d'un drame national. A bien des égards Zola a mené ce qui s'apparente à un contre-procès, réunissant des témoignages, mobilisant l'opinion, s'appuyant sur la presse et en appelant, face à l'injustice de l'Etat, au droit naturel, à la raison et aux valeurs du procès équitable. Depuis, les prétentions exercées par la justice sur la vérité auront souvent à se confronter à un débat public, non plus seulement judiciaire, mais aussi politique et moral.

Cette critique s'est souvent exercée en dehors du procès, et à bien des égards contre lui. Elle procédait alors d'une démarche qui ne doit pas être confondue avec la défense de rupture, telle que les avocats des militants algériens du FLN la pratiquèrent plus tard, de l'intérieur du prétoire, en récusant la défense de connivence que leur imposait la juridiction militaire d'exception, et qui donna lieu au pamphlet resté fameux de Jacques Vergès.[2] La défense de rupture, on le sait, fut pour la première fois mise en œuvre par Dimitrov lors du procès de l'incendie du Reichstag, puis théorisée par son avocat Marcel Willard dans un ouvrage paru en 1938 sous le titre *La défense accuse*.[3] Le même avocat, stalinien convaincu, fera aussi plus tard l'apologie des procès de Moscou, mais la thèse qu'il développe alors devant le tribunal nazi est que face à un tribunal de classe, instrument d'oppression d'un régime de dictature, le militant accusé doit se transformer en accusateur et faire du prétoire une tribune politique. On voit ainsi ce qui sépare cette idée de défense tribunicienne de celle de contre-procès dont nous parlerons ici : il s'agit d'un côté de renverser le procès de l'intérieur, et de l'autre de le refaire.

L'idée d'un contrepoint au procès injuste débouche sur la création d'instances totalement informelles, mais revendiquant pour les besoins de leur cause certains des attributs d'une juridiction : indépendance et impartialité de ses membres, procès contradictoire, droits de la défense, auditions de témoins et application de la règle de droit.[4] Ces instances n'ont aucune *jurisdictio*, et bien entendu aucun pouvoir

2. Jacques Vergès, *De la stratégie judiciaire*, Editions de Minuit, Paris, 1968.
3. Marcel Willard, *La défense accuse, de Babeuf à Dimitrov*, Editions Sociales Internationales, Janvier 1938.
4. Le sujet a fait l'objet d'une étude par Arthur et Judith Klinghoffer : *International Citizen's Tribunals : Mobilizing Public Opinion to Advance Human Rights*, Palgrave, 2002.

contraignant. Elles se reconnaissent pourtant le droit d'acquitter l'accusé injustement condamné. Cette prétention n'est fondée sur aucune autorité, pas plus qu'elle devrait se fonder sur une posture idéologique ; elle puise sa légitimité dans la seule existence d'une injustice et la nécessité d'y remédier. Cela a été parfaitement expliqué par John Dewey dans la déclaration introductive de la Commission d'enquête sur le procès de Léon Trotsky : « *In this case there exists no legally constituted court before which the accused may plead his case* [...] *Therefore, it became part of the function of this defense committee to initiate the formation of an impartial body before which his side of the case could be heard* ».[5] Trotsky, alors exilé au Mexique, ne pouvait se défendre à Moscou ; privé du droit d'être entendu, et n'ayant accès à aucune juridiction qui puisse lui rendre justice, il fallait lui offrir un for devant lequel plaider sa défense. Cet état de nécessité légitimait donc la constitution d'une commission d'enquête internationale investie de fonctions proches de celles d'un tribunal, en dehors de tout rattachement à un ordre juridictionnel.

La création de telles commissions doit encore être distinguée d'une autre notion, bien connue des praticiens du droit international, qui est celle des commissions d'enquête pour l'établissement de faits litigieux fondées sur un accord entre Etats. Ces commissions, dont le principe fut établi lors des deux Conférences de La Haye de 1899 et 1907, ont d'abord conduit à l'établissement dans un grand nombre de traités,[6] de commissions d'enquête permanentes composées de membres indépendants, ainsi qu'à un certain nombre de commissions spéciales ayant enquêté sur des affaires diverses, puis à l'inclusion de pouvoirs d'enquête dans le Pacte de la Société des Nations,[7] la Charte des Nations Unies,[8] et le Statut de la Cour Internationale de Justice.[9] L'histoire de ces commissions d'enquête a fait l'objet de plusieurs études, désormais anciennes.[10] Celles-ci, qui ont été parfois rapprochées de l'arbitrage,[11] se distinguent du sujet qui nous occupe par plusieurs traits fondamentaux : au premier chef, le consentement qui y est donné par les Etats parties, mais aussi leur fonction, qui est de préparer le procès et non d'en renverser le résultat.

Une des manifestations de l'essor, après la seconde guerre mondiale, du droit international des droits de l'Homme, a été la multiplication d'enquêtes visant à établir l'existence de faits de génocide, de discrimination, ou d'autres violations des droits humains. Nombre de ces enquêtes ont été menées par des commissions créées sous

5. Introductory Statement of the Commission of Inquiry, in J. Dewey, *Works*, Vol. 11 (1935-1937), p. 307.
6. Dont le premier fut celui signé entre les Etats-Unis et le Royaume Uni le 11 janvier 1909 relatif aux frontières dans les eaux limitrophes des Etats-Unis et du Canada ; suivi par une trentaine de traités signés par les Etats-Unis en 1913 et 1914 sous l'impulsion du Secrétaire d'Etat William J. Bryan.
7. Articles 12, 15 et 17 du Pacte de la Société des Nations.
8. Article 34 de la Charte des Nations Unies.
9. Article 50 du Statut de la Cour Internationale de Justice.
10. Tabrizi Bensalah, *L'enquête internationale dans le règlement des conflits* ; Thèse, Paris, LGDJ, 1976, qui cite plusieurs études datant du début du siècle dernier ; M. Bokanowski, *Les Commissions internationales d'enquête*, Paris, 1908 ; A. Beaucourt, *Les Commissions Internationales d'enquête*, Thèse, Paris 1909 ; A. Le Ray, *Les Commissions internationales d'enquête au XXème siècle*, Thèse, Paris, 1910, signe de l'intérêt que la question a suscité avant la première guerre mondiale.
11. Bensalah, *op. cit.* p. 115.

l'égide des Nations Unies, comme en 1992 sur les crimes commis en ex-Yougoslavie, en 1994 pour le Rwanda, en 2004 pour le Darfour, sur le Burundi en 2016 ou sur le Mali en 2018. De nombreuses enquêtes ont aussi été menées à l'initiative d'ONG ; le Comité International de la Croix-Rouge a ainsi déployé une activité importante pour alerter l'opinion sur l'existence de violations des Conventions de Genève de 1949, et on mentionnera parmi de nombreux autres exemples l'action de la Commission Internationale des Juristes sur des questions telles que l'occupation du Tibet,[12] les massacres de Bizerte[13] ou l'apartheid en Afrique du Sud.[14] La nature privée de ces dernières initiatives, et l'ambition qu'elles se donnaient d'alerter l'opinion publique, les rapprochent dans une certaine mesure de celles que nous nous proposons d'étudier ici, mais elles restaient néanmoins cantonnées dans un rôle d'enquête sans prétendre se constituer en tribunaux d'opinion, ni invalider le jugement rendu par un tribunal compétent.

II GENÈSE DES CONTRE-PROCÈS D'OPINION

Les contre-procès d'opinion ont leurs racines historiques aux Etats-Unis. Le procès et la condamnation des militants socialistes Warren Billings et Thomas Mooney pour un attentat qu'ils n'avaient pas commis, survenu à San Francisco en juillet 1916, provoqua un mouvement de protestation et de solidarité au sein du mouvement syndical californien.[15] Un comité de défense fut créé, à l'initiative de militants anarchistes[16], dans les mois suivant l'arrestation des deux militants. La solidarité ouvrière permit d'engager William B. Cockran, grand avocat d'origine irlandaise et membre de la Chambre des représentants pour l'Etat de New-York, qui examina le dossier et conclut que les témoignages retenus contre les deux militants étaient faux. Un mouvement national de protestation se développa alors ; la date de l'exécution de Mooney approchant, un « Mooney day » fut organisé en juin 1918, avec des centaines de manifestations dans toutes les villes des Etats-Unis,[17] conduisant le président Woodrow Wilson à commuer en 1918, la veille de l'exécution, la peine de mort en détention à perpétuité. Le mouvement avait également pris une dimension internationale, avec en particulier des manifestations organisées en avril 1917 à Petrograd. Aux Etats-Unis, le Comité de défense, qui était resté largement inactif depuis la décision du président Wilson de commuer la peine, fut reconstitué à la fin des années vingt, très largement

12. Commission Internationale des Juristes, *La question du Tibet et la primauté du droit*, Genève, 1959.
13. Rapport de la Commission Internationale des Juristes sur les massacres de Bizerte, Genève, 1961.
14. Commission Internationale des Juristes, *L'Afrique du Sud et la primauté du droit*, Genève, 1961.
15. Warren Billings fut condamné en septembre 1916 à la prison à perpétuité. Tom Mooney fut condamné à mort en Janvier 1917. Tous deux seront grâciés en 1939 et réhabilités en 1961. Sur l'ensemble de l'affaire, on lira le livre passionnant de Richard H. Frost, *The Mooney case*, Stanford University Press, Stanford, 1968.
16. Notamment Alexander Berkman et Emma Goldman, deux anarchistes russes émigrés aux Etat Unis.
17. L'affaire Mooney inspira le roman d'Upton Sinclair, paru en 1920, *100%, the story of a patriot*, mais elle ne mobilisa pas autrement les milieux intellectuels.

sous l'impulsion du parti communiste et de l'*International Labor Defense*, émanation du Secours Rouge International, et se réunit en congrès à Chicago en mai 1932. John F. Finerty, avocat réputé à Washington,[18] prit alors en charge la défense et organisa, avec le Comité de défense et le soutien financier de *l'American Civil Liberties Union*, une contre-enquête réunissant preuves et témoignages, qui permit d'établir le caractère frauduleux du jugement - et notamment la fausseté des témoignages retenus par le tribunal de San Francisco -, ouvrant ainsi la voie à une demande d'*habeas corpus* ; cette dernière fut cependant rejetée par la Cour suprême de Californie en octobre 1937, puis par la Cour suprême des Etats-Unis en décembre 1938. Le Comité n'entreprit jamais de prononcer lui-même l'innocence de Mooney et Billings, mais ses activités contribuèrent à alerter l'opinion sur le déni de justice dont avaient été victimes les deux accusés, ouvrant la voie à leur libération, puis à leur réhabilitation.

La campagne pour innocenter Mooney préfigure et poursuit à certains égards celle à laquelle donna lieu le procès de Sacco et Vanzetti. Les deux militants anarchistes italiens, accusés à tort d'un vol à main armée et de meurtres commis dans le Massachussetts en 1919 et 1920, furent arrêtés en mai 1920. Immédiatement après leur arrestation fut créé le premier Comité de défense des deux accusés, composé d'anarchistes italiens mobilisés par Carlo Tresca, et qui sera dirigé par un journaliste nommé Aldino Feliciani.[19] Le journal italien de Boston *La Notizia* deviendra ensuite la plate-forme de la campagne pour établir l'innocence des deux accusés. Le Comité organisa une grande campagne de presse, financée par les associations de défense des ouvriers et les syndicats, au premier rang desquels ceux de l'hôtellerie, de la boucherie et de la couture, au sein desquels les anarchistes exerçaient une influence importante. Les milieux libéraux ne tardèrent cependant pas à rejoindre la campagne, notamment avec le Comité de la Nouvelle-Angleterre pour les libertés civiles et la Ligue bostonienne pour le contrôle démocratique d'Elizabeth Evans. En juillet 1921, les deux accusés furent condamnés à mort. La campagne prit alors une dimension internationale. Anatole France, en octobre 1921, adressa un appel au peuple américain dénonçant la nature politique du procès.[20] Les meetings et manifestations de soutien aux accusés se multiplièrent, comme à Paris où la gauche et les syndicats rassemblèrent le 21 octobre 8.000 personnes à la salle Wagram, au point que le gouvernement fit protéger l'ambassade américaine par 10.000 policiers et 18.000 soldats.

La mobilisation marca ensuite le pas, jusqu'à la création en 1926, autour de la Ligue des Droits de l'Homme, d'un second comité de défense. Le 11 octobre 1926, la fédération syndicale américaine *American Federation of Labor* adopta une résolution demandant la révision du procès. John Dos Passos s'engagea, menant une véritable contre-instruction, analysant les 3.900 pages des procès-verbaux du procès de 1921, pointant les contradictions dans les témoignages retenus par l'accusation, les erreurs des expertises, les vices de procédure et la partialité du jury. Son enquête sera publiée en 1927 par le Comité de défense sous le titre *Facing the Chair : Story of the*

18. Finerty avait participé à la défense de Sacco et Vanzetti et sera plus tard conseil de la Commission Dewey.
19. Ronald Creagh, *Sacco et Vanzetti*, Ed. La Découverte, 1984, p. 145.
20. Anatole France to the People of America, *The Nation*, 23 Nov. 1921.

Americanization of Two Foreign Born Workmen. Elle intervient immédiatement après le rejet par la Cour Suprême du Massachussetts, en avril 1927, de la demande de révision du procès qui était pourtant fondée sur les confessions d'un gangster – Celestino Madeiros – qui disculpaient totalement Sacco et Vanzetti. Le mois précédent, une figure importante de l'élite conservatrice bostonienne, Felix Frankturter, professeur à Harvard et futur juge à la Cour Suprême des Etats-Unis, publia dans l'*Atlantic Monthly* un article dénonçant le caractère biaisé et injuste du procès. Son intervention donna lieu à la création d'un comité consultatif chargé de donner un avis au Gouverneur, présidé par Abbott Lawrence Lowell, président de l'Université d'Harvard. Le comité consultatif, dans le doute, refusa pourtant de recommander la clémence, et les deux accusés furent électrocutés le 23 août 1927, malgré la multiplication aux Etats-Unis, en Europe, mais aussi en Amérique Latine et en Australie, d'un mouvement sans précédent de grèves de solidarité, de pétitions, de meetings et de manifestations. Michael Dukakis, alors Gouverneur du Massachussetts et futur candidat à la présidence des Etats-Unis, réhabilitera les deux italiens en 1977.

L'affaire Sacco et Vanzetti ne donna pas véritablement lieu à un contre-procès. Comme cela avait le cas dans la campagne pour Mooney, les divers comités de défense qui s'étaient constitués aux Etats-Unis et en Europe s'étaient plus donné pour objectif de mobiliser l'opinion que d'instruire les faits reprochés aux accusés. Mais le travail minutieux accompli par Dos Passos était bien une tentative de réfuter, sur le plan technique et juridique et non pas seulement politique, l'instruction à charge menée par les tribunaux du Massachussetts. Le procès de Sacco et Vanzetti est aussi le premier qui ait suscité une campagne de protestation véritablement internationale et une réaction massive de l'opinion publique mondiale. Les comités de défense de Mooney et Billings, puis de Sacco et Vanzetti, ouvrirent la voie à l'idée de véritables contre-procès. Il est à cet égard intéressant de constater que de nombreuses personnalités qui participèrent aux campagnes pour Mooney et Sacco et Vanzetti se retrouveraient ensuite dans l'organisation des contre-tribunaux dont il sera maintenant question.

III LE CONTRE-PROCÈS DE L'INCENDIE DU REICHSTAG

L'incendie du Reichstag, survenu le 27 février 1933, moins d'un mois après l'accession d'Hitler au pouvoir, donna lieu à une féroce répression, qui visa particulièrement l'opposition communiste et sociale-démocrate. Dans les jours qui suivirent l'incendie, attribué à un complot communiste, des milliers d'opposants furent arrêtés, et des milliers d'autres prirent le chemin de l'émigration tandis qu'Hindenburg signait, le 28 février, des ordonnances suspendant les droits garantis par la Constitution de Weimar. Le 3 mars fut arrêté Ernst Thälmann, secrétaire général du Parti communiste allemand, et le 9 mars furent arrêtés trois dirigeants communistes bulgares qui se trouvaient alors en exil à Berlin, dont Georges Dimitrov, alors membre suppléant du Comité exécutif de l'Internationale communiste et du Bureau Ouest-européen du Komintern. Les deux autres bulgares arrêtés étaient Blagoï Popov et Vassili Tanev, tous deux membres du Comité central du Parti communiste bulgare. Tous trois avaient été condamnés à mort en Bulgarie pour avoir organisé une tentative de coup d'Etat en 1923. Un quatrième dirigeant communiste, l'allemand Ernst Torgler – lequel deviendra plus tard un agent de la Gestapo –, s'était livré volontairement le lendemain de l'incendie. Tous furent accusés d'être les organisateurs de l'acte criminel, imputé à un maçon hollandais nommé Marinus van der Lubbe, déséquilibré au passé d'agitateur d'extrême-gauche qui fut arrêté sur les lieux du sinistre et avoua peu après avoir provoqué l'incendie.

L'instruction du procès débuta à Leipzig le 31 mars 1933.[21] A la mi-mars, le parti communiste s'employa à organiser la riposte, dont le maître d'œuvre fut Willi Münzenberg ; celui-ci, ex-député au Reichstag et responsable au sein de l'Internationale Communiste du travail envers les intellectuels et les artistes, avait déjà été chargé de superviser l'activité communiste dans la campagne en défense de Sacco et Vanzetti. Il avait aussi fondé un groupe de presse populaire important, acquis la maison d'édition du Carrefour, et disposait du soutien financier du Secours Ouvrier International. Münzenberg s'attela tout d'abord à la publication d'un livre anti-nazi, qui sera publié en août 1933 sous le titre *The Brown Book of the Hitler Terror and the Burning of the Reichstag.* Ce livre, rédigé par un groupe de journalistes dont faisait partie Arthur Koestler,[22] s'efforçait de montrer, au prix d'ailleurs de multiples approximations et d'informations non vérifiées, que l'incendie avait été provoqué par des nazis ayant utilisé un souterrain reliant le Reichstag au palais de la présidence, alors occupé par Göring.[23] Le livre, qui était accompagné d'une préface de Lord Marley, membre de la Chambre des Lords, ainsi que de contributions de Sherwood Anderson, André Gide, Henri Barbusse, Romain Rolland, Ernst Toller et Ellen Wilkinson, eut un retentissement immédiat et important.

Münzenberg prit aussi une autre initiative, qui nous intéresse ici plus directement : il s'agit de la création, en mars 1933, du Comité international d'aide aux victimes du fascisme. Albert Einstein avait accepté d'en être le président d'honneur, tandis que Lord Marley en était le président. Le Comité, qui comptait parmi ses membres André Gide, André Malraux, Romain Rolland et Paul Langevin, constitua le mois suivant une Commission d'enquête internationale sur l'incendie du Reichstag. La Commission, installée à Londres sous la présidence de l'avocat anglais Dennis N. Pritt, comptait parmi ses membres les français de Moro-Giafferi et Gaston Bergery, le belge Piet Vermeylen, la hollandaise Betsy Bakker-Nort, le suédois Georges Branting, l'américain Arthur Garfield Hays et le danois Vald Hvidt. Dennis N. Pritt était un brillant avocat d'affaires qui devint plus tard député du *Labour* et fut approché pour représenter le point de vue soviétique devant la Commission Dewey sur le procès de Moscou de 1936, auquel il avait assisté et qu'il avait publiquement soutenu. De Moro Giafferi, ténor du barreau et député, avait été signataire d'appels en faveur de Sacco et Vanzetti en 1927,

21. Sur le procès de Leipzig et le contre-procès de Londres, on lira Gilbert Badia, *Feu au Reichstag, L'acte de naissance du régime nazi*, Editions Sociales, 1983 ; ainsi que Ch. Roulette et A. Langevin, *Le procès Dimitrov, l'incendie du Reichstag dans la presse et l'histoire*, Ed. Croix de Chavaux, 1983.
22. Ainsi qu'Alexander Abusch, Albert Norden, Rudolf Fürth, Wilhelm Koenen, Max Schröder, Alfred Kantorowicz et le dirigeant communiste Otto Katz.
23. Information fondée sur une note, connue comme le *Mémorandum Oberfohren*, rédigée par un député conservateur et dont de larges extraits furent publiés par le *Manchester Guardian* en avril. Oberforhen fut assassiné le mois suivant, très probablement par les nazis qui cherchèrent à maquiller le meurtre en suicide.

fondé l'Association juridique internationale, et avait contribué au *Brown book* ; il quittera cependant la Commission à l'issue de sa première journée d'audience. Bergery, ancien directeur de cabinet d'Edouard Herriot au Ministère des affaires étrangères, et qui deviendra plus tard vichyste, était alors un militant antifasciste engagé. L'avocat belge Vermeylen, qui détiendra après la guerre les portefeuilles de l'intérieur et de la justice, avait été dirigeant des jeunesses communistes dans les années vingt, avant de quitter le parti communiste belge en 1930 tout en restant actif au sein du Secours Rouge International. La militante féministe hollandaise Bakker-Nort était parlementaire du parti libéral progressiste et n'avait pas de liens particuliers avec le mouvement communiste. L'avocat suédois Branting était un parlementaire social-démocrate, fondateur de la banque russo-suédoise, qui était intervenu en faveur de Sacco et Vanzetti et fut plus tard suspecté d'être un agent soviétique. Arthur Garfield Hays, également avocat, était un des fondateurs en 1920 de l'*American Civil Liberties Union* et avait, tout comme Branting, participé à la défense de Sacco et Vanzetti.[24] Quant à l'avocat d'affaires danois Vald Hvidt, il ne parait avoir laissé trace d'aucune activité politique significative.

Le contre-tribunal installé à Londres était ainsi composé, pour l'essentiel, de personnalités indépendantes du mouvement communiste. Deux d'entre elles étaient des sympathisants communistes déclarés, et les autres des personnalités libérales ou sociales-démocrates, ou encore des juristes de renom sans attaches politiques comme l'était Vald Hvidt. Tous étaient des juristes qualifiés. La Commission d'enquête comprenait aussi, dans sa composition initiale, deux membres qui durent par la suite renoncer à la suite de pressions exercées par leurs gouvernements respectifs : l'ancien président du conseil italien, le radical Francesco Nitti, et le social-démocrate suisse Johannes Huber.[25] La défense des accusés était assurée devant la Commission par l'avocat communiste allemand et ancien député au Reichstag Kurt Rosenfeld.

La Commission se livra, en mai et juin 1933, à sa propre instruction de l'affaire, rassemblant des preuves et entendant plus de cent témoins. Elle annonça début juillet la tenue d'une audience à La Haye. Elle ne put cependant jamais avoir accès à l'acte d'accusation du tribunal de Leipzig. A la suite de pressions exercées par les nazis sur le gouvernement hollandais, celui-ci refusa les visas nécessaires et l'audience se tint en définitive à Londres, malgré de vigoureuses protestations du gouvernement allemand

24. Hays agit comme intermédiaire dans les échanges qui eurent lieu entre la Commission d'enquête et le tribunal de Leipzig, dont il sera question ci-après. Il participa aussi, après le verdict, à diverses campagnes antinazies, en particulier un *mock trial* de Hitler organisé en mars 1934 par l'*American Federation of Labor* et l'*American Jewish Congress*, « procès » au cours duquel furent entendus divers témoins et à l'issue duquel une assemblée de vingt-mille personnes constituée en « jury » condamna Hitler du chef de crimes contre la civilisation. Hays invita l'ambassadeur allemand aux Etats-Unis, Hans Luther, à participer à ces « audiences » comme observateur ou comme avocat d'Hitler, ce que ce dernier refusa. Hays joua ensuite un rôle, sur lequel nous reviendrons, dans la Commission d'enquête sur les procès de Moscou, en sorte qu'il s'était engagé tant dans l'enquête concernant Sacco et Vanzetti que dans celles concernant l'incendie du Reichstag et les procès de Moscou. Hays, qui n'était pas marxiste, était en revanche convaincu de la légitimité de tribunaux citoyens constitués par des intellectuels ou des représentants de la société civile. A ce sujet, cf. Klinghoffer, *op. cit.*, p. 49 et 74-75.

25. La Neue Züricher Zeitung écrira que « *le procés du Reichstag est une affaire intérieure allemande et personne n'a confié à Mr J. Huber le soin d'être juge dans ce procès* », Badia, *op. cit.* p. 102.

auprès du gouvernement britannique. Signe de l'inquiétude suscitée par le contre-procès, le Secrétaire d'Etat auprès du Ministre des affaires étrangères du Reich adressera le 18 août 1933 une circulaire à toutes les représentations diplomatiques allemandes à l'étranger, indiquant que la Commission d'enquête de Londres n'avait « *aucun caractère officiel* » et que les conclusions auxquelles elle pourrait parvenir ne sauraient « *tenir lieu de preuve* » ; dans le même temps, curieusement, le gouvernement du Reich indiquait avoir pris contact avec Georg Branting et Romain Rolland « *en les invitant à communiquer* [au procureur général de Leipzig] *les documents dont ils disposaient et à lui désigner des témoins éventuels pour qu'ils puissent être cités à comparaître* ».[26] Branting répondit immédiatement que les preuves en possession de la Commission pourraient être remises non pas au procureur mais à la défense des accusés de Leipzig pour être soumises au tribunal, à la condition toutefois que les accusés puissent choisir librement leur défenseur, y compris parmi des avocats étrangers, que ces derniers puissent librement accéder au dossier, que l'immunité des témoins soit garantie et que le procès soit public. Le procureur répondit en renvoyant Branting aux dispositions du code de procédure allemand, qui garantissait formellement la sécurité des défenseurs et des témoins. Mais la Commission avait de solides raisons de douter de ces garanties : nombre d'avocats défenseurs d'opposants au régime avaient déjà été torturés ou emprisonnés, et le procureur lui-même s'était livré, à propos du procès du Reichstag, à des déclarations publiques sur la nécessité d'extirper la peste rouge. Branding annonça donc que la Commission communiquerait publiquement ses conclusions, et que le tribunal de Leipzig en serait informé à l'avance. Cet échange entre le tribunal et le Commission, le premier de cette nature dans l'histoire de la justice moderne, reçut une large couverture dans la presse internationale.

La Commission tint audience publique à Londres, du 14 au 18 septembre 1933, sous la présidence de Pritt. Deux cents personnes, observateurs, journalistes et membres du public, y assistaient. Sir Stafford Cripps, qui sera ambassadeur britannique en Union soviétique pendant la guerre et plus tard Chancelier de l'Echiquier, présenta le point de vue de l'accusation. Gilbert Badia décrit ainsi le déroulement des travaux : « *Le tribunal entendit les rapports des sous-commissions préalablement désignées – par exemple le rapport de l'enquête menée en Hollande du 5 au 7 septembre* [...] *examina les notes établies par divers experts (en pyrotechnie notamment), vérifia la validité et le contenu des déclarations faites devant des hommes de loi... Mais surtout, la Commission entendit un grand nombre de témoins... Des Hollandais qui fournirent des renseignements précis sur l'appartenance et les activités politiques de van der Lubbe, sur son emploi du temps aussi, pendant les mois de janvier-février 1933. Un Yougoslave apporta la preuve que Dimitrov était à Munich le soir de l'incendie.* [...] *Le tribunal de Londres entendit l'ancien rédacteur en chef de la Vossische Zeitung, Georg Bernhard, ex-député au Reichstag, de tendance libérale et fort connu à l'étranger. Il entendit trois dirigeants sociaux-démocrates : Hertz, membre de la direction social-démocrate en exil à Prague, Rudolf Breitscheid, ancien ministre et Albert Grzesinski, ancien préfet de*

26. Badia, *op. cit.* p. 105.

police de Berlin et ancien ministre de l'Intérieur de Prusse [...]. *Du côté communiste, le tribunal entendit deux députés, Otto Kühne et Wilhem Koenen* [qui] *avait passé plusieurs heures dans l'après-midi du 27 février au Reichstag en compagnie de Torgler... Vinrent témoigner enfin outre l'écrivain Ernst Toller, le jeune fils de Torgler, Kurt, et surtout la sœur de Dimitrov, Elena Dimitrova* [...]. *Les commissaires leur posaient des questions, contestant tel point, obligeant le témoin à préciser une affirmation. Certains furent récusés...* ».[27] Le rapport final de la Commission notera « [qu']*il existe certainement un grand nombre de témoignages qui n'ont pu être recueillis... ou qui se sont offerts trop tard pour être reçus et pris en considération... La Commission, d'autre part, n'a pas eu la possibilité de lire l'acte d'accusation présenté à la Cour du Reich. Enfin, il n'a naturellement pas été possible de soumettre les témoignages à un 'contre-interrogatoire' par des avocats s'attachant à établir une thèse opposée à celle des témoins ; la Commission a eu à juger de la crédibilité des témoins, surtout en considérant le contenu de leurs témoignages, les faits par lesquels ils sont corroborés, l'attitude des témoins eux-mêmes et leurs réponses aux questions posées par les membres de la Commission* ». La Commission prenait ainsi soin de souligner le caractère incomplet de l'instruction à laquelle elle s'était livrée. Elle avait aussi dû prendre garde aux provocations destinées à la décrédibiliser, notamment par l'utilisation de faux témoins, et prendre soin d'éviter, en veillant à ce qu'elles restent autant que possible confinées au terrain juridique et factuel, que ses audiences se transformassent en tribune politique. L'écrivain H.G Wells, qui assista à la première journée d'audience, déclara n'avoir jamais assisté à un spectacle aussi ennuyeux, ce qui fut légitimement pris par le président de la Commission comme une marque de sérieux. Fait remarquable, la Commission invita le tribunal de Leipzig à envoyer un observateur à participer à ses sessions, ce que dernier – fait plus remarquable encore – accepta en déléguant un de ses employés.

Les audiences publiques furent closes le 18 septembre. Le 20 septembre, soit la veille de l'ouverture du procès de Leipzig, la Commission conclut publiquement à l'innocence de Dimitrov, Popov et Tanev, et à l'existence d'indices de suspicion graves à l'encontre de personnalités dirigeantes du parti nazi. Ces conclusions furent immédiatement envoyées au tribunal de Leipzig. Le jugement du tribunal de Londres eut un grand retentissement international, au point qu'une partie de la presse et de l'opinion estimèrent que l'affaire était d'ores et déjà jugée. L'édition du 23 septembre du *Wiener Allgemeine Zeitung* notait par exemple que « *le jugement de Londres a purement et simplement annulé par avance le prochain jugement de Leipzig* ». Dans le même temps, une campagne d'opinion internationale se développa. Le 11 septembre, un grand meeting eut lieu à la salle Wagram, à Paris, avec une intervention de de Moro-Giafferi accusant Göring ; des manifestations, rassemblant des dizaines de milliers de participants, eurent lieu partout en Europe et aux Etats-Unis, et jusqu'à Tunis ou Calcutta. La presse mondiale – à l'exception de la presse allemande - se faisait le relais des conclusions du *Brown book* et de la Commission d'enquête. Cette dernière, qui s'était réservée le droit de continuer à siéger, se réunit à nouveau le 4 octobre sous la

27. *Op. cit.* pp. 111-115.

présidence de de Moro-Giafferi pour entendre certains témoins qui n'avaient pu déposer en septembre, faute de visas. La Commission, à ce moment, avait eu accès à l'acte d'accusation de Leipzig, qu'elle étudia minutieusement, ce qui donna lieu à des conclusions additionnelles selon lesquelles Van der Lubbe n'avait pu agir seul – conclusion au demeurant partagée par les juges de Leipzig. La Commission se réunit encore le 18 décembre, soit l'avant-veille du verdict de Leipzig, pour annoncer ses conclusions définitives, qui seraient publiées sous la forme d'une petite brochure intitulée *Le Verdict*. Trente mille personnes participèrent à Paris, le 19, à un grand meeting organisé par la Ligue de Droits de l'Homme et par tous les partis de gauche. Le procès de Leipzig s'était quant à lui, par le talent, le courage et l'opiniâtreté de Dimitrov, transformé en tribune antinazie, faisant clairement apparaître l'inconsistance de l'accusation. Avec les conclusions du tribunal de Londres, la tentative nazie de donner un semblant de légitimité judiciaire à sa politique de répression et de censure avait irrémédiablement échoué : le 23 décembre, Dimitrov, Popov, Tanev et Torgler furent acquittés à Leipzig. Van der Lubbe, dont le rôle exact ne fut jamais éclairci, fut quant à lui condamné et exécuté.

Le tribunal de Londres, malgré les imperfections de l'instruction qu'il mena – et qu'il reconnut lui-même – est le premier exemple dans l'histoire d'un contre-tribunal dont la légitimité, incontestable aux yeux de l'opinion publique mondiale, ne reposait que sur l'autorité morale de ses membres et sur le caractère manifeste de l'injustice que les juges allemands s'apprêtaient à commettre. Son verdict n'avait techniquement aucune autorité de chose jugée, mais il a fini par s'imposer aux yeux de l'opinion publique et de l'histoire, et peut-être du tribunal compétent lui-même, qui n'eut d'autre choix que d'acquitter les prévenus.

IV LA COMMISSION DEWEY

Le 19 août 1936 s'ouvrit le premier des trois grands procès de Moscou, dit du « centre terroriste trotskyste-zinovieviste », ou « procès des seize ». Les principaux accusés étaient deux des dirigeants historiques du parti bolchévique et de la révolution russe, Grigori Zinoviev et Léon Kamenev. Un deuxième procès, dit du « centre antisoviétique trotskyste de réserve », s'ouvrit le 23 janvier 1937, dont les principaux accusés furent Georges Piatakov, Karl Radek et Grigori Sokolnikov. Un troisième procès se déroula en mai et juin 1937, visant des généraux de l'armée rouge, dont Mikhaïl Toukhatchevski. Enfin, le procès dit du « bloc des droitiers et des trotskystes antisoviétiques » se tint du 2 au 13 mars 1938, avec comme principaux accusés Nicolas Boukharine, Alexeï Rykov et Christian Rakovsky. Toute l'accusation de ces quatre procès tournait autour de la thèse – entièrement fabriquée – d'un complot organisé par Trotsky en coopération avec la Gestapo pour abattre le régime soviétique. Leon Trotsky – qui avait quitté la Norvège en décembre 1936 pour s'installer au Mexique – et son fils Leon Sedov – réfugié en France – étaient explicitement visés par l'acte d'accusation.[28]

28. Acte d'accusation du premier procès: "*L. Trotsky and his son L.L. Sedov, both of whom are abroad, having been exposed by the materials in the present case as having directly prepared and*

Ces quatre procès étaient extraordinaires à de multiples égards. La liste des accusés comprenait pratiquement tous les dirigeants communistes historiques de la révolution russe, en sorte que les procès visaient à effacer la mémoire et l'histoire vivante du parti bolchévique. La plupart des accusés, soumis à des mois de torture physique et psychologique, avouèrent des crimes inconcevables, au-delà de toute crédibilité, devançant même parfois les incroyables accusations fabriquées de toutes pièces par l'accusation, ainsi que l'a montré Arthur Koestler à travers le personnage de Roubatchef dans son magnifique roman *Le zéro et l'infini*.[29] Enfin, les procès – qui avaient pris pour prétexte l'assassinat de Serge Kirov en 1934[30] – dont les responsabilités n'ont jamais été élucidées et qui fut immédiatement instrumentalisé par Staline pour lancer l'offensive contre l'opposition – visaient autant à décapiter l'élite historique du parti bolchévique qu'à légitimer l'instauration d'un régime de terreur, avec des millions d'arrestations arbitraires, de déportations et d'exécutions sommaires. Le contexte international dans lequel ils intervenaient était aussi très différent de celui du procès du Reichstag. Les procès de Moscou n'étaient à l'évidence qu'une épouvantable machination, mais à la différence du gouvernement allemand de 1933, le régime soviétique, en raison de son soutien aux fronts populaires, de la crainte suscitée par la montée du nazisme et de la guerre en Espagne, suscitait une relative sympathie dans les milieux de gauche et parmi les intellectuels,[31] en sorte que la mobilisation contre la machination organisée par Vychinsky et Iejov[32] se heurta à une résistance très forte, à laquelle les organisateurs du contre-procès de Londres n'avaient pas eu à faire face.[33]

Trotsky, qui se trouvait interné en Norvège, s'employa dès août 1936 à encourager dans la mesure de ses moyens la création d'une commission d'enquête internationale qui pût montrer la fausseté des accusations contre les accusés du premier

personally guided the work of organizing in the U.S.S.R. terroristic acts against the leaders of the C.P.S.U. and of the Soviet State, in the event of being discovered on the territory of the U.S.S.R., are subject to immediate arrest and trial by the Military Collegium of the Supreme Court of the U.S.S.R."; une formulation identique se trouve dans l'acte d'accusation du procès de 1937.

29. Le personnage de Roubatchef était inspiré de Boukharine.
30. Dont Victor Serge s'inspirera dans son roman *L'Affaire Toulaev*, publié en 1939.
31. Jean Gehenno écrivit : « *Nous n'avons pas quant à nous à être staliniens ni trotskytes : ce sont là des affaires spécifiquement russes* » ; Romain Rolland : « *Je n'ai aucune raison de douter des condamnations qui frappent en Zinoviev et Kamenev des personnages depuis longtemps méprisés... Je ne vois pas comment on peut rejeter comme inventées ou arrachées des déclarations faites publiquement par les accusés* » ; André Malraux : « *Pas plus que l'Inquisition n'a diminué la dignité fondamentale du christianisme, les procès de Moscou n'ont diminué la dignité fondamentale du communisme* » ; George Bernard Shaw : « *Il me paraît tout aussi impossible de considérer Staline comme un vulgaire gangster que de voir en Trostsky un vulgaire assassin* » ; cf. Nicolas Werth, *Les procès de Moscou*, Ed. Complexe, 2006, pp. 57-60. Albert Einstein dira quant lui, lorsqu'il fut approché pour devenir membre de la Commission Dewey : « *From my point of view both Stalin and Trotsky are political gangsters* ».
32. Iejov avait remplacé Iagoda en Septembre 1936 au poste de Commissaire du peuple à l'intérieur ; l'architecte des procès de Moscou et l'organisateur des grandes purges sera fusillé en février 1940.
33. Pritt, qui avait présidé le contre-procès de l'incendie du Reichstag, participa comme observateur au premier procès de Moscou et déclara que le procès avait été équitable et que les accusés étaient coupables.

procès de Moscou.[34] Des personnalités socialistes - comme l'américain Norman Thomas, qui fut candidat à six reprises aux élections présidentielles, et qui se prononça en faveur du droit de Trotsky « *de se faire entendre devant une commission spéciale pour donner son propre témoignage* », s'élevèrent contre la persécution dont faisaient l'objet les trotskystes. En octobre 1936, un « Comité provisoire pour la défense de Leon Trotsky » fut formé aux Etats-Unis. Le nom du Comité de défense était une claire référence aux comités de défense de Tom Mooney, puis de Sacco et Vanzetti, héritage auquel John Dewey lui-même en appela dans la déclaration introductive de la Commission d'enquête qui sera constituée en mars de l'année suivante : « *In the United States, it has long been customary for public spirited citizens to organize committees for the purpose of securing fair trials in cases where there was a suspicion concerning the impartiality of the courts. Such committees are traditionally known as « Defense Committees » and include in their title the name of the defendant. I just cite two instances in this connection; the Tom Mooney Defense Committee and the Sacco-Vanzetti Defense Committee, with which many members of the American Committee for the Defense of Leon Trotsky cooperated. Membership on such committees does not, of course, imply anything more than the belief that the accused is entitled to a fair trial*".[35]

Le Comité provisoire comprenait, outre le philosophe John Dewey et Norman Thomas, les journalistes socialistes Devere Allen et Freda Kirchwey, le philosophe Horace Kallen, l'anthropologue Franz Boas, le critique littéraire Edmund Wilson, les journalistes Dwight MacDonald et Felix Morrow, l'écrivain Louis Adamic, Herb Solow et le critique d'art dramatique Joseph W. Krutch. L'écrivain et journaliste Mauritz Hallgren, après avoir adhéré au Comité, en démissionna publiquement en janvier 1937, le dénonçant comme instrument d'une offensive antisoviétique et se déclarant convaincu de la culpabilité de Zinoviev, Kamenev et des autres accusés du procès des seize.

Le Comité se mit immédiatement au travail. Des dizaines d'intellectuels libéraux ou antistaliniens y adhérèrent. Un bureau exécutif fut constitué avec Sidney Hook, l'écrivain et poète James Rorty – qui avait été arrêté lors des manifestations en faveur de Sacco et Vanzetti –, le romancier James T. Farrell, le journaliste Benjamin Stolberg, la journaliste féministe Suzanne La Follette, qui deviendra secrétaire de la Commission d'enquête, et le trotskyste James Burnham. Le 18 décembre 1936, un meeting public fut organisé à l'hôtel Center de New York, avec plus de trois mille participants. Un autre se tiendra le 9 février 1937 au vieil hippodrome de New York, avec six mille personnes, au cours duquel un discours de Trotsky sera lu, dans lequel il appela une nouvelle fois de ses vœux la constitution d'une commission d'enquête et déclara que si une telle commission devait le reconnaître coupable d'une partie seulement des faits qui lui étaient imputés par Moscou « *I pledge in advance to place myself voluntarily in the hands of the executioners of the G.P.U.* ». Les communistes réagirent par une violente campagne de presse dénonçant Dewey et ses collègues du Comité comme fascistes,

34. Sur l'histoire de la naissance de la Commission Dewey, cf. la thèse de Thomas Ray Poole, *Counter-Trial, Leon Trotsky on the Soviet Purge Trials*, University of Massachussetts, 1974 ; *Les procès de Moscou dans le Monde*, Cahiers Leon Trotsky, Institut Leon Trotsky, n°3, Paris, 1979.
35. Introductory Statement of the Commission of Inquiry, in J. Dewey, Works, Vol. 11 (1935-1937), p. 306.

accompagnée d'appels et de pétitions en faveur des procès de Moscou qui furent signés par un nombre important de socialistes et de radicaux favorables à l'Union soviétique. Les membres du Comité furent aussi victimes de multiples tentatives d'intimidation et de menaces individuelles. L'écrivain Louis Adamic se vit ainsi menacer d'interdiction de publication en Union Soviétique,[36] tandis que Dewey se vit plus tard offrir un voyage officiel en Union Soviétique à l'occasion du vingtième anniversaire de la révolution d'octobre, qu'il refusa bien entendu.[37]

Un Comité de même nature fut créé en Angleterre - auquel Bertrand Russell adhéra mais ne participa pas activement, et auquel George Bernard Shaw, qui condamnait pourtant les procès de Moscou, n'accepta quant à lui pas de participer - ainsi qu'en Tchécoslovaquie. En France, un « Comité pour l'enquête sur les procès de Moscou et pour la défense de la liberté d'opinion dans la révolution » fut créé avec le soutien de nombreux intellectuels, parmi lesquels André Breton, Jean Giono, Daniel Guérin et Victor Serge.[38]

Le parti pro-soviétique réagit en préemptant la commission d'enquête internationale dont Trotsky réclamait avec force la constitution par la création d'un organe qui pût contrebalancer la campagne contre les procès de Moscou. Le 18 octobre 1936, au moment même où était créé le Comité provisoire américain, était constituée à Paris, sur proposition du Comité central de la Ligue des Droits de l'Homme, une Commission d'enquête sur le procès des seize. Cette Commission, placée sous la direction de l'avocat Raymond Rosenmark, ancien conseiller juridique de l'ambassade d'U.R.S.S. à Paris, était composée de Victor Basch, cofondateur et alors président de la Ligue des Droits de l'Homme, qui sera assassiné en 1944 par la Milice, de Boris Mirkine-Guetzévitch, exilé russe et secrétaire général de l'Institut de droit comparé, de l'historien Albert Bayet et de l'avocat et Maurice Paz, ancien trotskyste, ami de Léon Blum et membre de la Commission administrative permanente de la Section française de l'Internationale ouvrière, lequel démissionnera cependant pour ne pas être associé à ce qu'il qualifia de « simulacre d'enquête ». En réalité, la Commission de la LDH ne mena aucune enquête, ce qui n'empêcha pas Rosenmark de conclure, dans son rapport du 15 novembre 1936,[39] que les débats devant le Collège militaire de la Cour Suprême de l'Union Soviétique avaient été réguliers ; le rapport notait que les accusés avaient tous avoué et qu'il serait « *contraire à toutes les données de l'histoire de la justice criminelle de supposer que par des tortures ou des menaces de torture on fasse avouer des innocents dans la proportion de seize sur seize* ». Le rapport Rosenmark notait aussi que le « *salut d'une révolution est parfois justifié par des mesures exceptionnelles* », et qu'il serait contraire à « *l'expérience historique de la révolution française* » de dénier à une

36. Klinghoffer, *op. cit.* p. 68.
37. George Dykhuizen, *The Life and Mind of John Dewey*, Southern Illinois University Press, 1973, p. 281.
38. Auquel Romain Rolland refusa de participer ; cf. Romain Pudal, *Pour une analyse comparée de l'engagement politique des intellectuels en France et aux Etats-Unis lors des procès de Moscou de 1936-1938*, Sociétés Contemporaines, 2006/4 pp. 95-113 ; Ch. Jacquier, *La gauche française, Boris Souvarine et les procès de Moscou*, Revue d'histoire moderne et contemporaine, 1998, pp. 451-465.
39. Cahiers des droits de l'homme, 15 novembre 1936.

nation le droit de « *réprimer ceux qui conspirent contre elle en intelligence avec des puissances ennemies* ». Ce rapport, qui avait été rédigé par Rosenmark seul, fut désapprouvé par plusieurs des membres de la Commission, comme Basch et Mirkine-Guetzevitch.[40] Il fut néanmoins entériné par le Bureau de la LDH, ce que Trotsky qualifiera de « tache indélébile » sur l'histoire de la Ligue. Aux Etats-Unis, le philosophe Corliss Lamont se déshonora en acceptant d'orchestrer, avec l'appui du journal libéral *The New Republic* de Malcolm Cowley, une campagne en faveur des procès de Moscou.[41]

Trotsky, face à cette offensive et au retard que prenait la constitution d'une commission internationale capable de mener une véritable contre-enquête, s'orienta alors un instant vers d'autres stratégies. Il envisagea un moment de porter son cas devant La Commission de la Ligue des Nations sur le terrorisme politique, qui avait été créée à l'initiative de Staline lors de l'adhésion de l'U.R.S.S. à la Ligue.[42] Il décida ensuite de saisir un tribunal étatique d'une plainte en diffamation contre les organes de presse qui véhiculaient les fausses accusations dont lui-même et les accusés du procès de seize étaient l'objet. Son choix se porta sur les tribunaux suisses, qu'il jugeait indépendants, et il fut décidé de saisir le tribunal correctionnel de Bâle, lieu de parution du journal du parti communiste suisse. Me Erwin Strobel fut chargé de préparer une plainte dirigée contre Georges Dimitrov et les rédacteurs en chef des principaux journaux communistes suisses. La plainte aurait dû être déposée en février 1937, mais l'avocat, sans doute soumis à des pressions politiques, décida de démissionner. Entretemps, la perspective de constitution d'une commission d'enquête internationale présidée par John Dewey était devenue plus concrète, et Trotsky renonça à l'action judiciaire peu après que la plainte ait été déposée.[43]

La Commission d'enquête fut officiellement constituée en mars 1937, à la suite d'une réunion préparatoire de coordination tenue le mois précédent par les comités de défense de Grande-Bretagne, de France et de Tchécoslovaquie. Le deuxième procès de Moscou venait à peine de s'ouvrir. Les fonds nécessaires à son fonctionnement avaient été réunis grâce à des dons de sympathisants, en particulier Margaret Burnham De Silver – compagne de Carlo Tresca, un des membres de la Commission – et Suzanne La Follette, qui en sera la secrétaire. Ses membres étaient, outre John Dewey, le journaliste libéral John P. Chamberlain ; Alfred Rosmer, qui avait été dans les années vingt membre du Comité exécutif de l'Internationale Communiste et rédacteur en chef de l'Humanité ; le sociologue Edward Alsworth Ross ; l'écrivain communiste Otto Ruehle ; le journaliste et syndicaliste Benjamin Stolberg ; l'éditeur et ancien député communiste Wendelin Thomas ; l'anarcho-syndicaliste italien Carlo Tresca, qui avait activement participé à la défense de Sacco et Vanzetti ; le journaliste et syndicaliste mexicain

40. Maurice Paz en avait démissionné le 27 juin 1937.
41. Frank Warren, *Liberals and communism: the red decade revisited*, Columbia University Press, 1993, p. 167.
42. Klinghoffer, *op. cit.* p. 57.
43. Le président du tribunal de Bâle suspendit la procédure immédiatement après le dépôt de la plainte, pour une question de validité de la procuration donnée par le plaignant à ses représentants : Daniel Vogelsanger, Tentative de contre-procès à Bâle, Cahiers Léon Trotsky, *op. cit.* p. 109.

Francisco Zamora Padilla, Herb Solow et Suzanne La Follette, dont il a déjà été question.[44] Un des membres de la Commission, le journaliste et spécialiste de l'Amérique latine Carleton Beals, démissionna en avril à la suite d'un incident avec Trotsky.[45] Il fut convenu que les comités européens tiendraient des audiences sur le continent, tandis que le comité américain se chargerait d'entendre Trotsky au Mexique.

La Commission était présidée par John Dewey. Dewey, qui avait alors 76 ans, était une personnalité libérale majeure aux Etats-Unis et un intellectuel de dimension internationale. Il avait été approché par son collègue et ancien élève Sidney Hook, professeur de philosophie à Columbia et militant marxiste, qui le convainquit, avec l'aide des militants trotskystes James Cannon et George Novack – qui deviendrait le secrétaire du Comité –, d'accepter la présidence du Comité. L'engagement de Dewey est d'autant plus remarquable qu'en libéral convaincu, il ne voyait pas de différence de nature entre communisme et fascisme, les deux régimes étant pour lui caractérisés par une absence de liberté, et qu'il considérait qu'au pouvoir, Trotsky n'aurait sans doute pas agi de façon très différente de Staline. Mais ce qui comptait à ses yeux était la vérité et l'exigence de justice, non le combat politique entre trotskystes et staliniens.[46]

Il est frappant de constater que la Commission ne comprenait, à l'exception de Dewey, pas d'intellectuels d'envergure internationale, et qu'à la différence de la commission d'enquête sur l'incendie du Reichstag, qui était intégralement composée de juristes qualifiés, elle n'en comprenait aucun.[47] Il s'agissait d'un groupe éminemment politique, sur la composition duquel Trotsky avait certainement exercé une vigilance étroite, qui devait se montrer capable de résister aux pressions politiques considérables qui ne manqueraient pas de s'exercer sur lui.

Le 2 avril, Dewey et les membres de la Commission d'enquête[48] quittèrent New York par le train pour le Mexique. Dewey mit à profit le voyage pour étudier les

---

44. Norman Thomas refusa de faire partie de la Commission, considérant que sa participation au Comité de défense américain affectait son impartialité. Les historiens Charles Beard et Carl Becker refusèrent également, l'un en raison de doutes sur la procédure envisagée, et l'autre pour des raisons personnelles. La Commission envisagea aussi d'inclure parmi ses membres Arthur Garfield Hays, lequel offrit plutôt d'intervenir comme conseil de la Commission. André Gide et Albert Einstein furent également approchés, sans succès (Klinghoffer, *op. cit.* pp. 74-76).
45. Cf. ci-après.
46. Les équilibres politiques au sein de la Commission ne manquèrent d'ailleurs pas d'inquiéter Trotsky, qui s'en ouvrit en mars 1937 auprès de George Novack et de plusieurs de ses camarades; Trotsky, *Œuvres*, Vol. 13, Institut Leon Trotsky, Paris, 1982, not. pp. 56 ss ; pp. 135 ss.
47. George Novack, qui avait été secrétaire du Comité provisoire pour la défense de Leon Trotsky créé en octobre de l'année précédente, et qui avait contribué à convaincre Dewey de prendre la présidence de la Commission d'enquête, avait également approché l'avocat américain Alfred Garfield Hays, dont il a été question plus avant, pour en devenir membre. Hays cependant estima que la Commission ne devait pas se fixer pour objectif de statuer sur la culpabilité ou l'innocence de Trotsky, mais d'évaluer les procès de Moscou dans leur ensemble, ce sur quoi Dewey était en désaccord. Hays demanda alors à intervenir comme conseil de la Commission, ce que Dewey accepta, mais il ne put en définitive participer à ses travaux en raison d'autres engagements professionnels.
48. Tous ne purent faire le voyage. Se déplacèrent au Mexique La Follette, Stolberg et Novack, ainsi que le romancier James Farrell. Beals voyagea séparément. Otto Ruehle se trouvait déjà sur place. John F. Finerty, qui avait été avocat de Tom Mooney et de Sacco et Vanzetti, et agissait comme conseil de la Commission, était également du voyage.

transcrits des audiences tenues à Moscou. Ils arrivèrent le 6 et tinrent le 10 avril leur première séance dans la Maison bleue de Diego Rivera à Coyoacan, où vivait Trotsky, laquelle était entourée pour l'occasion d'un impressionnant dispositif de sécurité.[49] La famille de Dewey avait émis de sérieuses réserves sur ce voyage, en raison de l'âge du philosophe et des craintes d'attentats de la part d'agents soviétiques. Mais Dewey, qui croyait en l'importance historique d'établir la vérité sur les procès de Moscou, ne se laissa pas dissuader.

La Commission tint à la Maison bleue, entre le 10 et le 17 avril, treize sessions d'une durée de trois à cinq heures, dont chacune fut présidée par Dewey.[50] Ces audiences furent entièrement consacrées à l'interrogatoire de Trotsky et dans une moindre mesure de son secrétaire Jan Frankel. Trotsky fut interrogé par son conseil Albert Goldman, un avocat trotskyste spécialiste de droit du travail et de questions syndicales,[51] et ensuite contre-interrogé par le conseil de la Commission John F. Finerty. La Commission invita sans succès le gouvernement de l'Union soviétique, à travers son ambassade à Washington, à participer aux débats et à lui communiquer les procès-verbaux des audiences tenues à Moscou.[52] Le Parti communiste américain, le Parti communiste mexicain, le Parti communiste français et le Ligue de Droits de l'Homme déclinèrent également une invitation à participer aux débats de la Commission. Enfin, les principales organisations syndicales mexicaines - dont certaines acceptèrent -, furent également invitées à dépêcher des observateurs. Un correspondant du Secrétariat de la Société des Nations, Mr Louis Sanchez Ponton, ainsi qu'un représentant de la Ligue culturelle Israélite, acceptèrent également de participer aux travaux comme observateurs.

La Commission créa une sous-commission parisienne, composée de l'avocat italien Giuseppe Modigliani, qui avait défendu la veuve de Matteotti, de l'avocat socialiste Maurice Delépine, et à laquelle participèrent Alfred Rosmer, André Breton et le syndicaliste Fernand Charbit. Cette sous-commission se réunit en France à onze

49. Les fenêtres de la salle d'audience, pouvant accueillir cinquante personnes, avaient été murées de crainte d'un attentat.
50. Les audiences se déroulèrent en anglais, sans interprétation, et firent l'objet d'une transcription intégrale qui fut publiée dans un livre de 837 pages : *The Case of Leon Trotsky*, Pathfinder Press, New York, 1938, réédité en 2006. La Commission avait aussi un chargé de relations presse en la personne de Charlie Walker.
51. Goldman, ancien communiste, avait rompu avec le parti communiste après un voyage en U.R.S.S. en 1931. Il fut condamné et emprisonné en 1941 pour ses activités pacifistes et radié du barreau en 1943, où il ne sera réintégré qu'en 1956, quelques années avant sa mort.
52. La question de la défense de l'Union Soviétique devant la Commission se posa avec acuité. Hays avait recommandé à Dewey, ce que ce dernier accepta, d'inviter l'avocat Joseph Brodsky à représenter l'accusation. Brodsky était un avocat communiste, conseil de l'*International Labor Defense* (organisation liée au Secours Rouge International qui avait été active dans la défense de Mooney et de Sacco et Vanzetti) et co-fondateur de l'*International Juridical Association*. Il avait assuré la défense des noirs américains, notamment lors de l'affaire des *Scottsboro boys*. Brodsky ayant refusé, Pritt fut invité à son tour, mais refusa également de se rendre au Mexique. On demanda alors à l'ambassadeur russe Troyanovsky de désigner un conseil, qui répondit qu'il ne transmettrait pas même la demande à son gouvernement, considérant que la Commission était manipulée par Trotsky (« *it means that Trotsky will lead the inquiry about himself and afterward will probably be his own judge with the assistance of his advocates* » - *The case of Leon Trotsky*, *op. cit.* p. 594).

reprises du 12 mai au 22 juin 1937, entendant cinq témoins, dont le fils de Trotsky, Léon Sedov, et recueillant des preuves écrites. Une autre sous-commission se réunit à New York les 26 et 27 juillet 1937, recevant – à plusieurs reprises à huis clos – onze témoignages, parmi lesquels celui d'Arben Davitian (dit Tarov), qui fut l'un des premiers à alerter sur la répression politique en U.R.S.S., et qui sera plus tard un des dirigeants du groupe Manouchian, et celui d'Ante Ciliga, qui décrira son expérience dans les camps soviétiques dans un livre resté célèbre : *Au pays du grand mensonge*, paru en 1938.[53]

Un observateur décrivit ainsi la conduite des audiences par John Dewey : « *Dewey's attention was unflagging. In a most unobtrusive way, he guided the proceedings when guidance was necessary. He was alert to see to it that all that was needed was put into the record. He would intervene when any points required clarification. When he cross-questioned Trotsky, his questions were apt, and they were part of a logical structure of questions which led to some clear and significant point or idea. He addressed Mr Trotsky politely, and usually in the casual tone which marks so much of his conversation. Once or twice, in instances where Trotsky's own statements ran clearly counter to Dewey's own democratic ideas, there was a scarcely noticeable change of tone. In these rare instances, Dewey's own independence of mind, in the face of Trotsky's brilliance, was apparent. At the same time, there was here no violation of his role, no tactlessness* ».[54]

Les procès-verbaux d'audition témoignent du souci qu'avait la Commission de reproduire aussi fidèlement que possible la procédure qui aurait été suivie devant un véritable tribunal. Chaque session était ainsi ouverte par un « interrogatoire direct » conduit par Albert Goldman, suivi d'un « contre-interrogatoire » mené par les membres de la Commission sous le contrôle de John Dewey. Le fait que l'accusation moscovite ne soit pas représentée, ainsi que la façon dont la Commission avait été constituée, ne permettent bien entendu pas de rapprocher cette procédure d'une véritable procédure judiciaire.[55] La Commission elle-même en était consciente. Dans le rapport qu'elle établira à la suite de ses auditions d'avril, elle dira – façon d'ailleurs contradictoire avec ses propres conclusions finales sur l'innocence de Trotsky –, que : « *your subcommission was in Mexico neither as prosecutor or as judge. We did not regard Mr*

53. Le livre fut augmenté par la suite à plusieurs reprises, sa version définitive portant le titre *Dix ans au pays du mensonge déconcertant*, Ed. Champ Libre, 1977.
54. James T. Farrell, *Dewey in Mexico*, in *John Dewey, Philosopher of Science and Freedom*, ed. Sidney Hook, Dial Press, New York, 1950, p. 364.
55. Arthur et Judith Klinghoffer écrivent à ce propos, à juste titre : « *Finerty* [qui était chargé de contre-interroger Trotsky] *was acting more like an independent magistrate than a prosecutor. When questioning Trotsky, he referred to 'alleged acts' – usage generally associated with the legal defense. When Finerty had agreed to serve as counsel, he had been assured that he could treat Trotsky as a hostile witness. Trotsky concurred. Finerty was so impressed with Trotsky during the hearings, however, that he came to treat him rather gently... The Manchester Guardian Weekly reported: 'if in the Moscow trials there was, for Trotsky, no means of defense, in Mexico there was, on the other hand, no prosecutor'. This was to a considerable extent true, but was surely not part of the tribunal's design. It had clearly recognized the need for pro-Stalinist participation, but entreaties had been rejected by both Brodsky and Troyanovsky. This was similar to the Reichstag countertrial's failure to attract German government participation"; International citizen's tribunals, op.cit.*, pp. 82-83.

Trotsky as defendant or accused [...]. *Therefore, we were in Mexico solely as an investigative body, to take Mr Trotsky's testimony on the accusations made against him in the confessions of the Moscow defendants; to accept such documents as he had to submit in his own defense; and to report to the full Commission on the basis of this evidence our decision whether or not Mr Trotsky has a case warranting further investigation* ».[56] Le rapport final précisera aussi: "*The procedure of this Commission has been similar to that of such bodies as Senate investigating committees, the National Labor Relations Board, and the unofficial international commission which investigated the Reichstag Fire case*".[57] La Commission était ainsi consciente que son rôle ne pouvait être assimilé à celui d'un Tribunal ; dans le même temps, elle s'inscrivait pleinement dans la continuité de l'action du contre-tribunal de Londres sur l'incendie du Reichstag.

La Commission chercha d'ailleurs à adopter des procédures et des règles de preuve semblables à celles admises devant les tribunaux. Le rapport de la sous-commission chargée d'interroger Trotsky dira ainsi « *It is an established rule even in legally constituted courts that the bearing of the witness may be taken into account in weighing the value of his testimony. We are guided by the same principle* ».[58] Dans son rapport final de décembre 1937, la Commission ira même jusqu'à définir le standard de preuve appliqué par elle : « [The Commission] *has been concerned with bringing to light all available facts in the case, whether favorable or unfavorable to Trotsky and Sedov. In accepting evidence it has been guided by the so-called 'best evidence rule', under which it has received the best evidence which the circumstances made available*".[59]

La Commission devança aussi l'argument avancé par ceux qui soutenaient que, dès lors que les procès de Moscou avaient été réguliers au regard de la loi procédurale en vigueur en Union Soviétique, leur résultat devait nécessairement être accepté : « *The argument most generally advanced in defense of the conduct of the Moscow trial is that they conformed to Soviet legal procedure ; and that any impression of unfairness that they may have created abroad is due to differences between Soviet procedure and that of other countries. In the opinion of the Commission, adherence to a given legal procedure is not the basic criterion in judging any trial. The basic criterion is fairness and honesty in the attempt to ascertain the truth. It is quite possible, as history has proved, for accused persons to be falsely convicted without departure from the letter of the law governing criminal trials. This question can be approached only in the light of what must be the theory of criminal procedure in any system of jurisprudence, namely: that its purpose is to enable the establishment of an ascertainable truth in any given case. Only in so far as prosecutor and court conform to the spirit as well as the letter of a justifiable procedure can they be held to safeguard the right of accused persons to be convicted or acquitted on the basis of the truth concerning the charges against them. If the procedure in the Moscow trials had in fact conformed to Soviet law, the conclusion would in our opinion be inescapable that Soviet procedure is not designed to develop the ascertainable*

56. *The case of Leon Trotsky*, *op. cit.* p. 25.
57. *Not Guilty, Findings of the 1937 Commission chaired by John Dewey investigating the charges against Leon Trotsky in the Moscow Trials*, Pathfinder Press, New York, 1938, p. 30.
58. *Op. cit.* p. 28.
59. *Not Guilty, Findings of the 1937 Commission chaired by John Dewey investigating the charges against Leon Trotsky in the Moscow Trials*, *op. cit.* p. 30.

truth. In fact, however, the conduct of the trials violated Soviet law in every important point ».[60] La Commission, sous la plume de Dewey, exprimait ainsi une conception beaucoup plus substantielle que formelle du déni de justice.

Il reste cependant que la procédure était profondément tronquée par l'absence à l'audience de représentants de l'accusation, et par le fait que pour cette même raison, la totalité des preuves sur lesquelles la Commission pouvait s'appuyer étaient fournies par le camp trotskyste. Ces défauts furent augmentés par le manque de communication entre la sous-commission siégeant au Mexique et la sous-commission française, et par le fait que le secrétariat de Trotsky, plutôt qu'une équipe indépendante, fut chargée de traduire les preuves rédigées en langue originale russe. Les représentants de la presse qui avaient assisté aux audiences se montrèrent soit sceptiques sur le caractère équitable de la procédure – ce fut le cas du *New York Times* –, soit franchement hostiles pour la presse influencée par les communistes, au premier chef le *New Republic*.

Les faiblesses de la Commission furent illustrées par l'épisode qui conduisit à la démission de Carleton Beals en Avril 1937. Beals estimait nécessaire de se livrer à un contre-interrogatoire agressif de Trotsky, portant sur l'ensemble de sa vie, et c'est bien ce qui se serait produit devant un tribunal ordinaire. Lors d'une séance de la Commission, il lui posa la question de savoir s'il avait participé aux efforts de l'Internationale Communiste, en 1919, pour fomenter un mouvement révolutionnaire au Mexique, question clairement destinée à l'embarrasser dès lors que Trotsky s'était engagé, pour obtenir l'asile au Mexique, à se tenir à l'écart de la politique mexicaine. La Follette et Finerty objectèrent alors à ces questions. Dewey autorisa Beals à poursuivre, mais celui-ci annonça son retrait, malgré l'offre de Dewey de soumettre une opinion dissidente aux conclusions de la Commission. Beals rendit alors publique une lettre qualifiant les travaux de la Commission de « *pink tea party with anyone but me ushering sweet platitudes* ». Quoiqu'il n'existe aucune preuve en ce sens, Trotsky et Diego Rivera l'accuseront plus tard d'avoir travaillé au compte du Gosudarstvennoe Politicheskoe Upravlenie (G.P.U.).

Les preuves reçues par la Commission étaient par la force des choses partielles, la Commission n'ayant aucun pouvoir contraignant et ne pouvant ni convoquer des témoins à comparaître contre leur volonté, ni contraindre le gouvernement soviétique à lui remettre les preuves produites à Moscou. Le travail de la Commission permit cependant d'infirmer un certain nombre de faits tenus pour établis par le Collège militaire de la Cour Suprême de l'Union Soviétique sur la base des faux aveux extorqués aux accusés. Par exemple, Edouard Holtzman, l'un des accusés du procès de seize, avait affirmé avoir rencontré le fils de Trotsky, Leon Sedov, à l'hôtel Bristol de Copenhague en 1932, alors que l'hôtel avait été détruit des années avant cette rencontre supposée.[61] Autre exemple : Piatakov avait déclaré s'être rendu par avion spécial de Berlin à Oslo dans la première moitié de décembre 1935, où Trotsky lui aurait

60. *Op. cit.* pp. 46-47.

61. L'accusation tenta de rectifier ce témoignage en affirmant que la rencontre avait eu lieu à la pâtisserie Bristol de Copenhague, affirmation impossible à vérifier dès lors que Holtzman avant entretemps été fusillé, et infirmée par le fait que Sedov prouvera devant la Commission ne pas s'être rendu au Danemark, faute de visa; *The Case of Leon Trotsky, op. cit.* pp. 250 ss.

fait part d'instructions que Rudolf Hess lui aurait données. La Commission obtint cependant la preuve par l'aérodrome de Kjeller, où Piatakov avait déclaré être arrivé, qu'aucun avion étranger n'y avait atterri en décembre 1935 ; la Commission obtint également la déclaration du député socialiste Knudsen, chez qui Trotsky était hébergé, démentant l'existence de tels entretiens.[62] Autre exemple encore : un certain Vladimir Romm, ancien correspondant des *Izvestia* à Paris, avait témoigné à Moscou avoir rencontré Trotsky au bois de Boulogne à Paris en juillet 1933. Or, Trotsky apporta devant la Commission la preuve qu'il se trouvait alors à Saint-Palais, près de Royan, localité qu'il n'avait quitté qu'en octobre pour se rendre à Barbizon.[63]

La suite des travaux de la Commission fut rendue très difficile par l'absence de moyens et de structure administrative. Un nouveau membre, en la personne d'Angelica Balabanova, qui avait été secrétaire de l'Internationale communiste en 1919 et avait ensuite rompu avec le stalinisme, fut nommée pour remplacer Carleton Beals, ce qui n'était pas un choix de nature à rassurer sur l'impartialité de la Commission. La sous-commission française parvint néanmoins à se réunir du 12 mai au 22 juin 1937, et interrogea cinq témoins, parmi lesquels le fils de Trotsky, Leon Sedov – qui sera assassiné l'année suivante par le G.P.U. –, dont les déclarations écrites avaient été produites au Mexique. Des audiences se tinrent ensuite à New York les 26 et 27 juillet, en présence de La Follette, Rosmer, Tresca et Wendelin Thomas, au cours desquelles furent entendus onze témoins, parmi lesquels Herb Solow et Max Shachtman. La Commission se réunit ensuite en septembre, pour adopter le procès-verbal des audiences du Mexique. Les transcriptions furent rendues publiques le 21 septembre, et ensuite publiées sous le titre *The case of Leon Trotsky : Trotsky's testimony before the 1937 Dewey Commission investigating charges made against him in the Moscow trials.*

Le verdict final fut lu par John Dewey, le 12 décembre 1937, dans un meeting à New York en présence des membres de la Commission, déclarant Trotsky et Sedov non coupables des crimes qui leur étaient imputés à Moscou. Malgré les faiblesses et les défauts inhérents de la procédure suivie, les cinq-cents pages du rapport final de la Commission[64] témoignent du sérieux avec lequel l'enquête fut conduite. Devant l'histoire, le rapport Dewey apporta un démenti formel aux accusations délirantes portées à Moscou contre Trotsky et les autres accusés, dans des conditions où – à la différence de ce qui s'était produit à l'égard du gouvernement allemand lors du procès du Reichstag – la vaste majorité des milieux intellectuels et de l'opinion publique internationale avait une attitude plutôt bienveillante envers l'Union Soviétique.

V LE TRIBUNAL RUSSELL

L'histoire des contre procès-internationaux pourrait s'arrêter là, mais cet article ne serait pas complet sans mentionner le « tribunal » constitué à l'initiative du philosophe

62. *The Case of Leon Troksky, op. cit.* pp. 765 ss.
63. *Op. cit.* pp. 725 ss.
64. Le rapport fut publié en 1938 sous le titre *Not Guilty, Findings of the 1937 commission chaired by John Dewey investigating the charges against Leon Trotsky in the Moscow trials* et réédité en 2006 par Pathfinder Press, New York.

Bertrand Russell pour juger les actes commis par l'armée américaine au Viêt Nam. Cette instance, qui prit le nom de « tribunal Russell », se distinguait du tribunal de Londres sur l'incendie du Reichstag et de la Commission Dewey par plusieurs traits fondamentaux. En premier lieu, son but n'était pas d'enquêter sur la culpabilité ou l'innocence d'individus victimes d'un déni de justice, mais d'établir la responsabilité d'un Etat - les Etats-Unis - pour ses actes commis au cours d'un conflit armé. Il ne s'agissait donc pas d'un contre-procès destiné à rétablir un déni de justice. En second lieu, le « tribunal Russell » n'eut jamais, à la différence du tribunal de Londres et de la Commission Dewey, le souci d'affirmer son impartialité ; il s'agissait au contraire d'une instance ouvertement politique au service de la lutte du Front national de libération du Sud Viêt Nam. Mais Russell s'était dans une certaine mesure inspiré des travaux de la Commission Dewey, qu'il connaissait bien pour avoir été membre du comité anglais de défense de Trotsky. De plus, il entendait s'inspirer du modèle de Nuremberg, ce qui le conduisait à vouloir adopter les formes et le fonctionnement d'un organe juridictionnel.

L'idée de juger les actes commis par les Etats-Unis au Viêt Nam avait déjà été avancée par des activistes radicaux comme Ralph Miliband - père de David et Ed Miliband - et M.S. Arnoni.[65] En 1966, Russell, qui avait évolué vers des positions pacifistes et anti-américaines et qui avait créé en 1963 la Fondation Bertrand Russell pour la paix, se lança avec fougue dans ce combat. Il avait alors quatre-vingt-treize ans. En février, Russell dépêcha son secrétaire Ralph Schoenman à Hanoï pour recueillir le soutien d'Ho Chi Minh à l'initiative, lequel offrit de collaborer à l'enquête et de fournir des témoins. Le 16 juin, le vieux philosophe adressa à un certain nombre de personnalités de gauche une invitation à participer à un « tribunal des crimes de guerre » devant enquêter sur le Viêt Nam.

Répondirent favorablement l'historien et biographe de Trotsky, Isaac Deutscher, le dissident Yougoslave Vladimir Dedijer, Jean-Paul Sartre[66] et Simone de Beauvoir, le philosophe Gunther Anders, l'écrivain américain David Dellinger, le mathématicien français Laurent Schwartz, l'avocat pakistanais Mahmood Ali Kasuri, le président de l'Union des travailleurs turcs Mehmet Ali Aybar, le syndicaliste et poète philippin Amado Hernandez, l'avocat et vice-président du *Japan Civil Liberties Union* Kinju Morikawa, le physicien japonais Shoichi Sakata, l'ancien président du Mexique Lazaro Cardenas, Stokely Carmichael, président de l'association étudiante américaine SNCC (*Student Non-violent Co-ordinating Committee*), et le parlementaire socialiste italien Lelio Basso. Le tribunal Russell tint une première réunion du 13 au 15 novembre 1966 à Londres, au cours de laquelle Russell fut élu président d'honneur, Sartre président exécutif, tandis que Vladimir Dedijer présiderait les sessions et que Laurent Schwartz en assurerait la coprésidence. Un certain nombre d'autres membres seraient cooptés par la suite : l'écrivain James Baldwyn, le syndicaliste anglais Lawrence Daly, le président de l'organisation étudiante américaine *Students for a Democratic Society* Karl Oglesby, le politologue allemand Wolfgang Abendroth, le dramaturge allemand Peter

65. Klinghoffer, op.cit. p. 106.
66. Qui se fit parfois représenter aux audiences par Claude Lanzmann.

Weiss[67] et la présidente du Comité cubain de solidarité avec le Viêt Nam, Melba Hernandez.

Le tribunal était ainsi largement dominé, à l'exception des avocats Ali Kasuri et Kinju Morikawa, par des intellectuels, des artistes et des personnalités politiques engagés dans la campagne contre la guerre au Viêt Nam, et se caractérisait par une totale absence en son sein de spécialistes du droit international, qu'il avait pourtant l'ambition d'appliquer. Le tribunal créerait ensuite une « commission juridique » - fait en soi curieux pour un tribunal - constituée des avocats Leo Matarasso et Gisèle Halimi.

La liste des personnalités qui refusèrent l'invitation de Russell est tout aussi intéressante. On y trouve Arthur Miller, qui trouva le groupe trop partisan, l'historien Lewis Mumford et le critique théâtral Kenneth Tynan, qui estimèrent qu'un tribunal ne pouvait opérer en l'absence des accusés, Herbert Marcuse, qui craignait de perdre sa chaire à l'université de San Diego, les journalistes Tom Wicker, Raymond Walter Apple et Harrisson Salisbury, ainsi que Che Guevara et Vyacheslav Molotov.[68]

Le 13 novembre 1966, Russell s'adressa aux membres du tribunal en des termes qui ne laissaient guère augurer favorablement de l'impartialité des débats : « *Nous entamons notre enquête avec un dossier considérable de preuves* prima facie, *dont les éléments n'ont pas été fournis par les victimes, mais recueillis dans les publications favorables à la politique qui a conduit à ces crimes. Je crois que nous sommes en droit de conclure à la nécessité de réunir un tribunal solennel, composé d'hommes éminents non par la puissance mais en vertu de leur contribution intellectuelle et morale à ce qu'il est convenu, sur le mode optimiste, d'appeler la 'civilisation humaine'.* [...] *Puisse ce Tribunal empêcher le crime du silence de s'accomplir* ».[69]

Le groupe envisagea d'abord de tenir ses audiences à Paris, et Sartre intervint en ce sens auprès de De Gaulle, lequel refusa en considérant que le prétendu tribunal était privé de toute légitimité.[70] La Grande Bretagne et la Suisse refusèrent à leur tour d'accueillir le tribunal, lequel obtint enfin l'accord du gouvernement suédois. Les audiences se tinrent donc à Stockholm, dans les locaux du parti social-démocrate, du 2 au 10 mai 1967. Les dates d'audiences ayant été modifiées à la dernière minute, de nombreux membres du tribunal, parmi lesquels James Baldwyn et Lazaro Cardenas, ne purent y participer. Russell lui-même n'était pas présent à Stockholm. Le président Lyndon Johnson et le Secrétaire d'Etat Dean Rusk furent invités à venir présenter leur défense, lesquels refusèrent évidemment.

Dans son discours inaugural, Sartre se plaça d'emblée dans la continuité du tribunal de Nuremberg pour établir la légitimité du tribunal : « *Le Tribunal Russell est né de cette double constatation contradictoire : la sentence de Nuremberg a rendu nécessaire l'existence d'une institution destinée à enquêter sur les crimes de guerre et,*

67. Sur la constitution du tribunal, cf. *Tribunal Russell, Le jugement de Stockholm*, Gallimard, Paris, 1967, p. 19 ; Weiss et Carmichael avaient dans un premier temps refusé de participer à la réunion de novembre 1966, le premier faisant valoir qu'il était à ses yeux préférable que le groupe fut composé de juristes, et le second par manque de temps ; Klinghoffer, *op. cit.* p. 112.
68. Klinghoffer, pp. 112-113.
69. *Tribunal Russell, Le jugement de Stockholm, op. cit.* pp. 10-11.
70. Annie Cohen-Solal, *Sartre*, Gallimard, 1985, p. 583.

s'il y a lieu, à en juger ; ni les gouvernements ni les peuples ne sont aujourd'hui en mesure de la créer. Nous sommes parfaitement conscients de n'avoir été mandatés par personne, mais si nous avons pris l'initiative de nous réunir, c'est que nous savions aussi que personne ne pouvait *nous mandater. Certes notre Tribunal n'est pas une institution. Mais, il ne se substitue à aucun pouvoir institué : il est issu, au contraire, d'un vide et d'un appel. Nous n'avons pas été recrutés et investis de pouvoirs réels par des gouvernements : mais, nous avons vu, tout à l'heure, que cette investiture à Nuremberg n'a pas sufi à donner aux magistrats une légitimité incontestable... Le Tribunal Russell estime au contraire que sa légitimité vient à la fois de sa parfaite impuissance et de son universalité.* [...] *Ces dernières remarques permettent de répondre à une critique que nous faisait, sans malveillance d'ailleurs, un journal parisien : 'quel étrange tribunal : des jurés et pas de juge !'. C'est vrai : nous ne sommes que des jurés, nous n'avons le pouvoir ni de condamner, ni d'acquitter personne. Donc, pas de ministère public. Il n'y aura pas même d'acte d'accusation à proprement parler. Me Matarasso, président de la commission juridique, va vous lire un exposé des griefs qui en tient lieu : les jurés en fin de session, auront à se prononcer sur ces griefs : sont-ils fondés ou non ? Pourtant, les juges existent partout : ce sont les peuples, en particulier le peuple américain. Et c'est pour eux que nous travaillons ».*[71] Le rapport de Matarasso était quant à lui beaucoup plus juridique, appliquant aux faits l'article 6 du statut de Nuremberg, les articles 2, 3 et 4 de la Charte des Nations Unies, les résolutions de l'Assemblée Générale et le droit pénal international, pour conclure que « *la guerre menée par les Etats-Unis au Vietnam est criminelle, au sens du droit international positif, tant dans son principe que dans sa conduite* ».[72]

Le tribunal statua sur la base de rapports d'expertise de nature juridique, politique, historique, mais aussi scientifique et médicale, parfois suivis de contre-interrogatoires menés par les membres du tribunal. Des témoins nord-vietnamiens, incluant des enfants, furent également entendus, notamment sur les ravages causés par les bombardements aériens, les mines antipersonnel, les bombes à fragmentation et la destruction de digues, ainsi que des représentants du Front National de Libération du Sud Viêt Nam et personnalités y ayant séjourné, comme l'écrivain Alejo Carpentier.[73] Norodom Sihanouk, chef de l'Etat du Cambodge, adressa un message de soutien au tribunal.

Le tribunal délibéra dans la nuit du 9 au 10 mai 1967, et rendit un premier jugement déclarant les Etats-Unis coupables de génocide envers le peuple vietnamien, d'emploi de traitements inhumains et interdits par les lois de la guerre, et de violation du droit international dans le traitement des prisonniers de guerre. Les Etats-Unis étaient également reconnus coupables d'agression envers le Laos, et les gouvernements de Thaïlande, des Philippines et du Japon (pour ce dernier à une majorité de 11 contre 3) de complicité.

---

71. *Tribunal Russell, Le jugement de Stockholm, op. cit.* pp. 28-31.
72. *Ib.* p. 41.
73. L'intégralité de ces rapports et témoignages est reproduite dans *Tribunal Russell, Le jugement de Stockholm, op. cit.*

La section japonaise de la Fondation Russell pour la Paix organisa ensuite des audiences à Tokyo, du 28 au 30 août 1967, qui se focalisèrent sur des accusations de complicité du gouvernement japonais avec les Etats-Unis. Le tribunal Russell se réunit ensuite à nouveau à Roskilde, au Danemark, du 20 novembre au 1er décembre 1967,[74] pour connaître de l'usage au Viêt Nam de napalm, de défoliants et d'armes au phosphore. Encore une fois, le tribunal entendit le témoignage d'experts, de victimes vietnamiennes, de soldats américains et de journalistes,[75] et émit à l'issue de ses travaux un rapport établissant « *que des méthodes inhumaines et illégales sont quotidiennement utilisées par les forces armées américaines et leurs satellites contre les populations civiles ainsi menacées d'extermination* ».[76]

Bertrand Russell décéda en 1970, à l'âge de quatre-vingt-dix-sept ans. Lelio Basso et Vladimir Dedijer, avec l'appui de la veuve du philosophe, Edith, et du socialiste anglais Ken Coates, décidèrent alors de reconstituer le tribunal, qui se réunira à trois reprises entre 1973 et 1976, d'abord pour connaître de la répression d'extrême-droite en Amérique latine, puis des entraves à la liberté d'opinion en République Fédérale Allemande et enfin de la condition des indiens d'Amérique. Lelio Basso, qui avait présidé ces séances du tribunal, lança alors l'idée de créer une instance permanente. Basso décéda en 1978, mais son initiative déboucha le 24 juin 1979 sur la création du « Tribunal Permanent des Peuples » (TPP). Le TPP se dota d'une liste permanente de « juges », et d'un règlement prévoyant les modalités de traitement de plaintes pouvant être déposées par des ONG ou des victimes de faits contraires au droit international, lesquelles sont alors entendues et jugées par des panels de sept membres. Le TPP s'est ainsi, depuis 1979, intéressé à des sujets aussi divers que les droits des femmes, le droit d'asile, le traitement des maladies mentales, les droits des peuples indigènes, la tragédie de Bhopal, ou encore les effets des plans de restructuration financière du FMI et de la Banque Mondiale. En dernier lieu, le TPP se réunit à Paris en 2018 pour « juger » de la politique migratoire européenne, « condamnant » la France et l'Union européenne du chef de complicité de crime contre l'humanité pour le traitement réservé aux migrants.[77]

L'idée du tribunal d'opinion, qui avait été portée par les animateurs du tribunal de Londres sur l'incendie du Reichstag ou les membres de la Commission Dewey sur les procès de Moscou, était ainsi – de façon parfois grotesque – dévoyée à des fins propagandistes qui n'avaient plus rien à voir avec l'administration de la justice. Cette dérive ne datait d'ailleurs pas de la création du TPP ; elle se trouvait clairement en germe dans le tribunal Russell lui-même qui, dès son origine en 1966, avait nettement affirmé son parti-pris et sa volonté de contribuer au combat politique contre la guerre du Viêt Nam plutôt que d'agir avec impartialité.

74. Dans la même composition que lors des audiences de Stockholm, à l'exception de Deutscher, qui était décédé en août.
75. L'intégralité des transcriptions de ces audiences a été publié dans *Tribunal Russell, le jugement final*, Gallimard, Paris, 1968.
76. *Ib.* p. 348.
77. « Migrants : au "Tribunal permanent des peuples", l'Etat prend cher » Journal *Libération*, 7 janvier 2018.

VI CONCLUSION

La tension entre l'absence de pouvoir juridictionnel de ces « tribunaux » et leur ambition d'émettre un jugement sur les faits qui leurs étaient soumis s'est manifestée dès l'enquête sur l'incendie du Reichstag, et tout au long des activités de la Commission Dewey, ainsi qu'en témoignent les débats qui agitèrent cette dernière sur l'emploi des termes « commission d'enquête » et la contradiction entre les déclarations initiales de Dewey, selon lesquelles la Commission n'agirait pas comme tribunal, et les conclusions finales de la Commission déclarant Trotsky et Sedov « non coupables ». Le tribunal de Londres sur l'incendie du Reichstag et la Commission Dewey ne disposaient d'aucune investiture. Pour autant, ces instances ont dans une large mesure cherchées à fonctionner comme des tribunaux, manifestant le souci de leur impartialité, établissant des procédures se voulant contradictoires – même si elles ne pouvaient techniquement l'être –, et prononçant des jugements formulés en termes de culpabilité ou d'innocence. Leur volonté était de rendre justice devant l'histoire et devant la communauté internationale. La mesure dans laquelle ils y sont parvenus doit être appréciée à l'aune de leur légitimité morale, de la nature de leurs objectifs, et des conditions historiques particulières dans lesquelles ils ont été amenés à agir. La totale objectivité et l'intégrité morale d'un intellectuel de dimension internationale comme John Dewey ont beaucoup fait pour établir la légitimité des conclusions de la Commission sur le procès de seize. La même observation vaut pour le Dos Passos du procès de Sacco et Vanzetti. Par contraste, le parti-pris et l'activisme politique souvent extrême des membres du tribunal Russell ont largement contribué à affaiblir l'impact international de ses conclusions, pour ne pas dire à le discréditer, même si les transcrits des audiences de Stockholm et de Roskilde restent un des témoignages les plus frappants des horreurs commises par l'armée américaine au Viêt Nam.

Il est permis de dire que le tribunal de Londres de 1933 comme la Commission Dewey auront atteint leur objectif : celui d'établir l'innocence d'individus injustement accusés et victimes de dénis de justice. La légitimité morale qu'ils ont opposée à la légitimité politique et institutionnelle des accusateurs était entière. Ces expériences sont sans doute, en raison du caractère unique des conditions historiques dans lesquelles elles s'inscrivaient, irrépétibles ; elles posent néanmoins des questions de portée générale auxquelles quiconque s'intéresse à la justice ne peut rester insensible, au premier chef celle de savoir s'il est concevable qu'un groupe de personnes privées dépourvu de toute investiture puisse se constituer en tribunal, c'est-à-dire en organe juridictionnel. La réponse est évidemment négative, dès lors que le pouvoir de juger de façon contraignante ne saurait dériver que d'un Etat, d'un traité, de la volonté des parties en matière contractuelle, ou dans certains cas de la coutume. Lelio Basso, en proposant la création d'un tribunal permanent s'inscrivant dans la continuité de Nuremberg, eut certainement une intuition féconde ; mais c'est la création en 1998 de la Cour Pénale Internationale, plutôt que le « tribunal des peuples », qui y a vraiment répondu, quoique de façon imparfaite.

Pour autant, la légitimité morale et historique de commissions d'enquête internationales ou de jurys d'honneur peut être supérieure à celle d'un tribunal étatique agissant de façon partiale, voire servile : on a vu comment le « jugement » du « tribunal de Londres » a contraint celui de Leipzig à acquitter Dimitrov et ses co-accusés bulgares, qu'il aurait certainement autrement condamnés. Et il est parfaitement concevable de voir de telles commissions adopter les formes et les procédures en vigueur devant les juridictions internationales pour prévenir un déni de justice manifeste ou y remédier. L'impartialité de telles commissions, la participation de juristes qualifiés, et un respect aussi scrupuleux que possible des principes d'égalité des parties et du contradictoire, sont alors indispensables pour atteindre le but désiré ; le tribunal de Londres et la Commission Dewey, pour des raisons qui ne leur étaient qu'en partie imputables, ont dans une large mesure échoué à respecter ces principes, tandis que le Tribunal Russell les a complètement ignorés. L'expérience de ces contre-tribunaux montre que la justice et la politique ne font jamais bon ménage. Plus positivement, ces initiatives nous enseignent que la justice n'est pas qu'une affaire de juristes, et que l'engagement d'intellectuels, d'artistes, et plus généralement de la société civile, est indispensable à la protection des principes fondamentaux du procès équitable.

CHAPTER 17

Abuse of Rights in Corporate Restructuring: An Unruly Horse in Investment Treaty Arbitration?*

Nartnirun Junngam & Amnart Tangkiriphimarn

> It is not every injury that the law prohibits. A person or a State may, when exercising a legal right, legitimately and justifiably injure another person or State. Law is not an ethical code of mutual sacrifice and forbearance. But it must step in when the injury arising from the exercise of a right is disproportionately grave, and especially when it is obvious that the particular right is used for a purpose different from or opposed to that for which it has been granted.
>
> —Hersch Lauterpacht[1]

I INTRODUCTION

The principle of good faith (bona fide) is not an anomaly in international investment law. Numerous investor-state tribunals have applied this principle, generally treating it as a general principle of law. In a large number of cases, good faith is mentioned as a

* This chapter is part of our research entitled "The Doctrine of Abuse of Rights and Corporate Restructuring: Drawing the Line between Legitimate and Abusive Exercises of Rights to Access International Investment Arbitration." It is current as of September 2019. We wish to acknowledge with gratitude the support and care provided by the late Guillermo Aguilar Álvarez, who jointly taught us with Professor W. Michael Reisman at Yale Law School. His support and care are an essential part that has made us who we are today. It is with sadness that we untimely contribute to this memorial project rather than show him our gratitude by other means. We thank Professor Reisman for kindly guiding us since our very first step in the field of international investment law and arbitration.

1. Hersch Lauterpacht, *International Law: General Works* 385 (Cambridge: E. Lauterpacht ed., 1970).

fundamental guiding principle of how international investment agreements (IIAs) must be interpreted in light of Article 31 of the Vienna Convention on the Law of Treaties (VCLT).[2] In particular, tribunals have observed that an obligation to act in good faith is part of a state's substantive obligation concerning its treatment of investment in accordance with, for example, the fair and equitable treatment (FET)[3] and expropriation clauses.[4] Concomitantly, good faith also governs how the arbitration proceedings should be conducted[5] and how the costs should be allocated.[6]

To comply with the principle of good faith, every right is to be exercised honestly and loyally; a failure to do so may constitute an abuse of right (*abus de droit*).[7] This applies to every relevant party. Accordingly, it can be either respondent states or claimant investors who degenerate their exercising of rights into an abuse. Thus, tribunals have occasionally tackled this matter from different aspects. For instance, in their assessment of states' behavior, some tribunals consider whether states have abused their sovereign or regulatory authority.[8] Sometimes, tribunals have to address whether claimants' claim should or must be dismissed given respondents' allegation

2. Metalclad Corporation v. The United Mexican States, ICSID Case No. ARB(AF)/97/1, Award, para. 70 (August 30, 2000); Methanex Corporation v. United States of America, UNCITRAL, Partial Award on Jurisdiction and Admissibility, paras. 97-98 (August 7, 2002); Patrick H. Mitchell v. Democratic Republic of the Congo, ICSID Case No. ARB/99/7, Award, para. 50 (January 26, 2004).
3. S.D. Myers, Inc. v. Government of Canada, UNCITRAL, Partial Award, para. 134 (November 13, 2000); CME Czech Republic B.V. v. The Czech Republic, UNCITRAL, Partial Award, para. 156 (September 13, 2001); United Parcel Service of America Inc. v. Government of Canada, ICSID Case No. UNCT/02/1, Award on Jurisdiction, para. 46 (November 22, 2002); Técnicas Medioambientales Tecmed, S.A. v. The United Mexican States, ICSID Case No. ARB (AF)/00/2, Award, paras. 153-154 (May 29, 2003); Ceskoslovenska Obchodni Banka, A.S. v. The Slovak Republic, ICSID Case No. ARB/97/4, Award, para. 153 (December 29, 2004); MTD Equity Sdn. Bhd. and MTD Chile S.A. v. Republic of Chile, ICSID Case No. ARB/01/7, Award, para. 109 (May 25, 2004) (*citing* the Opinion (Witness Statement) of Judge Stephen Schwebel, para. 23); Waste Management, Inc. v. United Mexican State, ICSID Case No. ARB(AF)/00/3, Award, para. 138 (April 30, 2004).
4. Azurix Corp. v. The Argentine Republic, ICSID Case No. ARB/01/12, Award, para. 310 (July 14, 2006); The Third Restatement of the Foreign Relations Law of the United States of 1987, § 712, Comment g.
5. Marvin Roy Feldman Karpa v. United Mexican States, ICSID Case No. ARB(AF)/99/1, Award, para. 33 (December 16, 2002); Methanex Corporation v. United States of America, UNCITRAL, Final Award of the Tribunal on Jurisdiction and Merits, Part II Chapter I para. 54 (August 3, 2005) ("*Methanex*").
6. Waste Management, Inc. v. United Mexican States, ICSID Case No. ARB(AF)/98/2, Award, para. 31 (May 26, 2000); Bayview Irrigation District et al. v. United Mexican States, ICSID Case No. ARB(AF)/05/1, Award, para. 125 (June 19, 2007); Jan de Nul N.V. and Dredging International N.V. v. Arab Republic of Egypt, ICSID Case No. ARB/04/13, Award, para. 281 (November 6, 2008); Sistem Mühendislik In aat Sanayi ve Ticaret A. v. Kyrgyz Republic, ICSID Case No. ARB(AF)/06/1, Award, para. 203 (September 9, 2009).
7. Bin Cheng, *General Principles of Law as Applied by International Courts and Tribunals* 123, 136 (Cambridge: Cambridge University Press, 1953).
8. Compañiá de Aguas del Aconquija S.A. and Vivendi Universal S.A. v. Argentine Republic, ICSID Case No. ARB/97/3, Award, para. 58 (November 21, 2000); Link-Trading Joint Stock Company v. Department for Customs Control of the Republic of Moldova, UNCITRAL, Final Award, para. 64 (April 18, 2002); Middle East Cement Shipping and Handling Co. S.A. v. Arab Republic of Egypt, ICSID Case No. ARB/99/6, Award, paras. 155, 161 (April 12, 2002); CMS Gas Transmission Company v. The Republic of Argentina, ICSID Case No. ARB/01/8, Award, para. 321 (April 20, 2005); PSEG Global, Inc., The North American Coal Corporation, and Konya Ingin Electrik Üretim

that their action constitutes an "abuse of process."[9] Increasingly, tribunals' jurisdiction has been challenged on the ground that investors' acquisition of relevant nationality constitutes an abuse.[10]

It is in the last-mentioned context of a nationality requirement that one tribunal expressed its concern about treaty shopping,[11] which later served as a platform for an ongoing discussion on an abusive exercise of rights in relation to corporate restructuring. Thus, this chapter regards as its premise the concept of treaty shopping and proceeds to demonstrate how the doctrine of abuse of rights has been brought into play. It then examines a theoretical foundation of the doctrine and its expansive application. Last, the chapter presents an appraisal and proposed alternatives for decision-makers.

II TREATY SHOPPING

Treaty shopping has long been a subject of much controversy. It denotes a situation whereby, in order to obtain more favorable rights or protections under a particular investment treaty, an investor, usually a juristic entity, deliberately devises its corporate structure so as to acquire the nationality of a "home country of convenience,"[12] which is not closely connected with it.[13] This "shopping" activity is highly contentious. On the one hand, it is asserted that there is nothing wrong with treaty shopping per se.[14] "[A] prudent investor," Professors Dolzer and Schreuer note, "may organize its investment in a way that affords maximum protection under existing treaties."[15] According to Professor Schill, treaty shopping is in line with the objective of the

---

ve Ticaret Limited Sirketi v. Republic of Turkey, ICSID Case No. ARB/02/5, Award, paras. 227-228, 247, 252 (January 19, 2007).

9. Ronald S. Lauder v. The Czech Republic, UNCITRAL, Final Award, paras. 169-179 (September 3, 2001); CME Czech Republic B.V. v. The Czech Republic, UNCITRAL, Partial Award, paras. 172-177, 302-310, 396-400, 412 (September 13, 2001); Waste Management, Inc. v. United Mexican State, ICSID Case No. ARB(AF)/00/3, Decision of the Tribunal on Preliminary Objection Concerning the Previous Proceedings, paras. 48-49 (April 30, 2004).
10. Saluka Investments B.V. v. The Czech Republic, UNCITRAL, Partial Award, paras. 231-241 (March 17, 2006) ("*Saluka*"); Compañiá de Aguas del Aconquija S.A. and Vivendi Universal S.A. v. Argentine Republic, ICSID Case No. ARB/97/3, Award, para. 7.2.2 (August 20, 2007).
11. *Saluka*, *supra* n. 10, para. 240 ("[A] possibility lends itself to abuses of the arbitral procedure, and to practices of 'treaty shopping' which can share many of the disadvantages of the widely criticized practice of 'forum shopping'").
12. Martin J. Valasek & Patrick Dumberry, *Developments in the Legal Standing of Shareholders and Holding Corporations in Investor-State Disputes*, 26 ICSID Rev. 34, 59 (2011).
13. Matthew Skinner, Cameron A. Miles & Sam Luttrell, *Access and Advantage in Investor-State Arbitration: The Law and Practice of Treaty Shopping*, 3 J. World Energy L. & Bus. 260, 260 (2010); Eunjung Lee, *Treaty Shopping in International Investment Arbitration: How Often Has It Occurred and How Has It Been Perceived by Tribunals?*, 1 (2015), http://www.lse.ac.uk/internationalDevelopment/pdf/Dissertations/WP167.pdf (accessed January 28, 2019).
14. In this regard, the term "nationality planning" is sometimes used to avoid any bad impression associated with "treaty shopping." *See, e.g.*, Christoph Schreuer, *Nationality Planning*, in Arthur W. Lovine (ed.) *Contemporary Issues in International Arbitration and Mediation: The Fordham Papers 2012* (Leiden: Martinus Nijhoff, 2013), 17.
15. Rudolf Dolzer & Christoph Schreuer, *Principles of International Investment Law*, 2nd edition (Oxford: Oxford University Press, 2012), 52.

international investment law regime, which is to promote the flow of capital, regardless of where the capital originates.[16] Similarly, Professor Vandevelde, a once prominent negotiator of international investment treaties for the USA, observes that to allow treaty shopping is consistent with the goal of bilateral investment treaties (BITs) to "create a liberal international investment regime."[17] On the other hand, it is maintained that treaty shopping is an unfavorable phenomenon. Namely, it undermines the principle of reciprocity, as host states would have to give benefits to investors whose original home states do not provide the same benefits to the host states' nationals in return.[18] For Professor Sornarajah, this jurisdiction shopping is contrary to, and is an abuse of, the objectives of the ICSID Convention and the network of IIAs.[19] Also, the practice may forestall states' attempts to reform investor-state dispute settlement (ISDS), given that investors remain capable of incorporating a corporate entity in a state with old-style investment treaties to bypass this effort.[20]

To date, the practice of treaty shopping is generally acknowledged and endorsed by investment arbitral tribunals. Particularly, most tribunals have exclusively focused on their textual and consensual basis of jurisdiction. By so doing, they typically conclude that, given the liberal approach adopted in the relevant legal instruments (i.e., IIAs, investment contracts, and domestic laws), the jurisdictional requirement *ratione personae* is satisfied. Two leading cases illustrating such acknowledgment and endorsement are *Aucoven v. Venezuela*[21] and *Tokios Tokelès v. Ukraine.*[22]

Focusing on the text of clause 64 in the concession agreement between Autopista Concesionada de Venezuela, C.A. (Aucoven) and Venezuela, the *Aucoven* tribunal dismissed Venezuela's contention that the ICSID Convention's purposes had been abused. Having found that clause 64 constituted a valid agreement to commence ICSID arbitration, the tribunal then considered whether the ICSID Convention imposes any additional objective jurisdictional requirements.[23] As the Convention does not define the terms "nationality" and "foreign control," the tribunal held that it would focus on

16. Stephan W. Schill, *The Multilateralization of International Investment Law* (Cambridge: Cambridge University Press, 2009), 234-235; *see also* Zeynep Tekin, *International Investment Law and Treaty Shopping Through Corporate Nationality Structuring* (2017), http://pennjil.com/international-investment-law-and-treaty-shopping-through-corporate-nationality-structuring/ (accessed January 28, 2019).
17. Kenneth J. Vandevelde, *Case Comments: Aguas del Tunari, S.A. v. Republic of Bolivia*, 101 Am. J. Int'l L. 179, 183-184 (2007).
18. Roos van Os & Roeline Knottnerus, *Dutch Bilateral Investment Treaties: A Gateway to "Treaty Shopping" for Investment Protection by Multinational Companies* 11 (2011), https://www.somo.nl/wp-content/uploads/2011/10/Dutch-Bilateral-Investment-Treaties.pdf (accessed February 16, 2019); Jan Primec, *Enemy of the State: Is Treaty Shopping in Contradiction with the Rationale of Investment Law?* 3 (2015), http://scriptiesonline.uba.uva.nl/document/621905 (accessed February 17, 2019).
19. M. Sornarajah, *The International Law on Foreign Investment*, 4th edition (Cambridge: Cambridge University Press, 2017), 385-386.
20. John Lee, *Resolving Concerns of Treaty Shopping in International Investment Arbitration*, 6 J. Int'l Disp. Set. 355, 361 (2015).
21. Autopista Concesionada de Venezuela, C.A. v. Bolivarian Republic of Venezuela, ICSID Case No. ARB/00/5, Decision on Jurisdiction (September 27, 2001) ("*Aucoven*").
22. Tokios Tokelès v. Ukraine, ICSID Case No. ARB/02/18, Decision on Jurisdiction (April 29, 2004) ("*Tokios Tokelès*").
23. *Aucoven*, *supra* n. 21, para. 96.

the disputing parties' own definitions of the terms, as long as they were "reasonable and not totally inconsistent with the purpose of the Convention."[24] In this case, Aucoven and Venezuela agreed to define "foreign control" only by reference to the nationality of the majority shareholder of Aucoven and not to the effective or ultimate control test as argued by Venezuela.[25] As this majority shareholding test is one of the reasonable criteria commonly used to determine who controls a corporation, the tribunal ruled that it must respect the parties' choice on this matter.[26] The tribunal also found that the transfer of shares here could be justified by economic reasons as it was driven by the investor's attempt to alleviate the difficulties caused by the peso crisis.[27]

A central subject of controversy in *Tokios Tokelès* is concerned with a "round-tripping" situation—"an investor transferring funds to another state and then redirecting the funds into his own home state" to gain international protection from the investor's own home state.[28] As the respondent argued, Tokios Tokelès was not "a 'genuine entity' of Lithuania first because it is owned and controlled predominantly by Ukrainian nationals, [...] has no substantial business activities in Lithuania and maintains its *siège social*, or administrative headquarters, in Ukraine."[29] The tribunal held that, given the ICSID Convention's silence on the definition of "investor," it would defer to the BIT parties' intention.[30] Regarding the fact, the parties did not dispute that the claimant was founded in the Lithuanian territory and legally registered under Lithuanian law. Thus, considering the ordinary meaning of Article 1(2) of the BIT, the claimant was a Lithuanian investor.[31] As for the respondent's argument that the tribunal should also take into account the control test and the substantial business criterion in determining the claimant's nationality, the tribunal ruled that "it is not for tribunals to impose limits on the scope of BITs not found in the text, much less limits nowhere evident from the negotiating history."[32] Therefore, the tribunal concluded that, pursuant to the BIT, the *ratione personae* jurisdictional requirement was satisfied.[33]

This award was accompanied by a strong dissenting opinion of the presiding arbitrator, who later announced his withdrawal from the case. In his dissent, the late Professor Weil noted that the tribunal's decision was incompatible with the primary object and purpose of the ICSID Convention, i.e., to "stimulate a larger flow of private international investment into territories."[34] In other words, for him, the ICSID dispute settlement mechanism was meant to apply to resolve *international* "disputes between

24. *Ibid.*, paras. 97, 99.
25. *Ibid.*, para. 117.
26. *Ibid.*, paras. 119-120.
27. *Ibid.*, paras. 122-224.
28. Sornarajah, *supra* n. 19, at 328.
29. *Tokios Tokelès*, *supra* n. 22, para. 21.
30. *Ibid.*, paras. 24-25.
31. *Ibid.*, para. 29.
32. *Ibid.*, paras. 30-36, 52.
33. *Ibid.*, para. 38.
34. Tokios Tokelès v. Ukraine, ICSID Case No. ARB/02/18, Prosper Weil's Dissenting Opinion, paras. 1-3 (April 29, 2004) ("*Tokios Tokelès* Dissent"), *referring to* Report of the Executive Directors, paras. 10-13.

States and *foreign* investors (emphasis added)."[35] Accordingly, the origin of the capital of the relevant investment must be taken into consideration.[36]

One observation that should not be neglected is that *Aucoven* is one of the very first cases, if not the first, in the series where the argument of "abuse of the ICSID Convention purposes" was raised by the respondent state in relation to the investor's restructuring of its corporate structure. Nevertheless, the tribunal did not particularly discuss the concept of abuse. Rather, it merely viewed the text of the concession agreement as an expression of the parties' intention and essentially held that the ICSID Convention gave the parties substantial autonomy to deal with *ratione personae* matters. As for *Tokios Tokèles*, whereby the tribunal's conclusion is similar to that of *Aucoven*, it nonetheless showed some reluctance to fully endorse its liberal textualist approach. Namely, to support its conclusion, the tribunal noted that:

> none of the Claimant's conduct with respect to its status as an entity of Lithuania constitutes an abuse of legal personality. The Claimant made no attempt whatever to conceal its national identity from the Respondent. [...] The Claimant manifestly did not create Tokios Tokelès for the purpose of gaining access to ICSID arbitration under the BIT against Ukraine, as the enterprise was founded six years before the BIT between Ukraine and Lithuania entered into force. Indeed, there is no evidence in the record that the Claimant used its formal legal nationality for any improper purpose.[37]

By stating this, it remains unclear whether the tribunal implied that if Tokios Tokelés had been established after the BIT became effective for the purpose of gaining access to ICSID arbitration, it would have ignored the company's state of incorporation and instead pierced the corporate veil by looking at the company's ultimate shareholders as argued by the respondent to determine the nationality.[38]

That said, despite the reservation made in *Tokios Tokèles*, it is safe to say that an investor is entitled to form its corporate structure as it deems appropriate. As has been endorsed by numerous tribunals, there is nothing inherently wrong with the investor's attempt to attain treaty rights, including access to ISDS, by acquiring a certain nationality, provided that it meets the textual requirements stipulated in the treaty.[39]

35. *Ibid.*, para. 5.
36. *Ibid.*, para. 20.
37. *Tokios Tokelès, supra* n. 22, para. 56.
38. Nartnirun Junngam, *The Decision on Jurisdiction in Tokios Tokeles v. Ukraine*, in Guillermo Aguilar Álvarez & W. Michael Reisman (eds), The Reasons Requirement in International Investment Arbitration: Critical Case Studies (The Hague: Martinus Nijhoff, 2008), 206-208.
39. *See, e.g.*, CME Czech Republic B.V. v. The Czech Republic, UNCITRAL, Partial Award, para. 419 (September 13, 2001); Aguas del Tunari, S.A. v. Republic of Bolivia, ICSID Case No. ARB/02/3, Decision on Respondent's Objections to Jurisdiction, para. 330(d) (October 21, 2005) ("*AdT*"); Saluka Investments B.V. v. The Czech Republic, UNCITRAL, Partial Award, paras. 241-242 (March 17, 2006); ADC Affiliate Limited and ADC & ADMC Management Limited v. The Republic of Hungary, ICSID Case No. ARB/03/16, Award, paras. 356-362 (October 2, 2006) ("*ADC*"); Mobil Corporation, Venezuela Holdings, B.V., et al. v. Bolivarian Republic of Venezuela, ICSID Case No. ARB/07/27, Decision on Jurisdiction, para. 204 (June 10, 2010) ("*Venezuela Holdings*"); Tidewater Inc., Tidewater Investment SRL, Tidewater Caribe, C.A., et al. v. The Bolivarian Republic of Venezuela, ICSID Case No. ARB/10/5, Decision on Jurisdiction, para. 184 (February 8, 2013) ("*Tidewater*").

Yet, likely due to a backlash movement against ISDS in general, in a recent trend, investment arbitral tribunals have introduced new nonwritten constraints into their scrutiny as to whether the gates to investment treaty should be further restricted.[40] One of these added jurisdictional requirements is the examination as to whether the investor has abused its rights by restructuring its investment to gain access to investment treaty arbitration. The first case bringing this possibility to light is *Phoenix v. Czech Republic*,[41] the case to which we now turn.

III ABUSE OF RIGHTS AWAKENED

Metaphorically, as a sleeping giant, the doctrine of abuse of rights was awakened by the tribunal in *Phoenix v. Czech Republic*. Then, other tribunals have kept it awake and made it even more aggressive. Let us first consider the awakening case. Phoenix, an Israeli company, invested in two Czech companies—Benet Praha (BP) and Benet Group (BG)—on December 26, 2002. At the time of the investment, BP and BG had already been involved in a number of disputes with some authorities of the Czech Republic. BP's dispute concerned the state's freezing of its funds and the seizure of accounting and business documents in connection with the police and the prosecutorial authorities' investigation of its former executive's misconduct. As for BG, it was involved in a dispute with a Czech national with regard to ownership in two Czech companies; the dispute, argued the claimant, led to the bankruptcy of BG's properties resulting from Czech courts' failure to resolve it promptly. Given the continuing post-acquisition damage to BP and BG, the claimant delivered a notice of dispute to the respondent on March 2, 2003, and subsequently submitted a request for arbitration dated February 15, 2004, to ICSID pursuant to the Israel-Czech BIT.

The tribunal had no difficulty finding that it did not have jurisdiction *ratione temporis* to consider claims arising before the date of investment, i.e., December 26, 2002.[42] The main question thus concerned whether it had jurisdiction *ratione materiae* (as framed by the tribunal)—"whether there is a legal dispute arising directly out of an investment"—to consider claims arising thereafter.[43] Applying the "double-barreled test" endorsed by some previous tribunals,[44] the tribunal focused on whether there was

40. Diane A. Desierto, *Arbitral Controls and Policing the Gates to Investment Treaty Claims against States in Transglobal Green Energy v. Panama and Philip Morris v. Australia*, EJIL Talk (June 22, 2016), https://www.ejiltalk.org/arbitral-controls-and-policing-the-gates-to-investment-treaty-claims-against-states-in-transglobal-green-energy-v-panama-and-philip-morris-v-australia/ (accessed January 28, 2019).
41. *Phoenix Action, LTD v. The Czech Republic*, ICSID Case No. ARB/06/5, Award, paras. 67-71 (April 15, 2009) ("*Phoenix*"); Tania Voon, Andrew Mitchell & James Munro, *Legal Responses to Corporate Manoeuvring in International Investment Arbitration*, 5 J. Int'l Disp. Set. 41, 64 (2014); Xiao-Jing Zhang, *Proper Interpretation of Corporate Nationality under International Investment Law to Prevent Treaty Shopping*, 6 Contemp. Asia Arb. J. 49, 63 (2013).
42. *Phoenix*, *supra* n. 41, paras. 67-71.
43. *Ibid.*, para. 73.
44. *See* Salini Costruttori S.p.A. and Italstrade S.p.A. v. Kingdom of Morocco, ICSID Case No. ARB/00/4, Decision on Jurisdiction (July 31, 2001) ("*Salini*"); Malaysian Historical Salvors, SDN, BHD v. The Government of Malaysia, ICSID Case No. ARB/05/10, Award on Jurisdiction (May 17, 2007).

an investment as required by the ICSID Convention and the Israel-Czech BIT in light of relevant public international law and its general principles.[45] Against this backdrop, the tribunal concluded that, for an investment to be entitled to treaty protection, there must be:

(1) a contribution in money or other assets;
(2) a certain duration;
(3) an element of risk;
(4) an operation made in order to develop an economic activity in the host State;
(5) assets invested in accordance with the laws of the host State;
(6) assets invested bona fide.[46]

Our focus here will be on the tribunal's discussion of the sixth element. The timing of the investment, the timing of the claim, the substance of the investment transaction, and the nature of the business operation were factors that the tribunal took into consideration as to whether the investment was made in good faith.[47] Having found that: (1) the damage to the claimant had already occurred when the investment was made;[48] (2) the claim was brought only two months after the date of investment;[49] (3) the share transfers were made internally within a family;[50] and (4) the investments had no economic performance,[51] the tribunal concluded that "the whole 'investment' was an artificial transaction to gain access to ICSID"[52] and that the claimant's pursuit of this arbitration was "an abuse of the system of international ICSID investment arbitration."[53]

Notwithstanding a myriad of reasons cited by the tribunal, should one read the award carefully, it was rather obvious that the principal reason behind this conclusion was the timing of the investment—that the investment was made after the damage had occurred. This point was emphasized frequently in the award. For example, in paragraph 92, having discussed the ICSID awards in *Banro v. Congo*[54] and *Mihaly v. Sri Lanka*,[55] the tribunal stated that "a corporation cannot modify the structure of its investment for the sole purpose of gaining access to ICSID jurisdiction, *after damages*

45. *Phoenix*, *supra* n. 41, para. 78.
46. *Ibid.*, para. 114. The first four elements were pronounced by the tribunal in *Salini v. Morocco*. *See Salini*, *supra* n. 44, para. 52. On this matter, the *Salini* tribunal relied heavily on Schreuer's commentary in Christoph Schreuer et al., *The ICSID Convention: A Commentary*, 2nd edition (Cambridge: Cambridge University Press, 2009), para. 153. The last two elements derive from the Tribunal's interpretation of "the international principle of good faith as applied to the international arbitration mechanism of ICSID."
47. *Ibid.*, paras. 136-140.
48. *Ibid.*, para. 136.
49. *Ibid.*, para. 138.
50. *Ibid.*, para. 139.
51. *Ibid.*, para. 140.
52. *Ibid.*, para. 143.
53. *Ibid.*, para. 144.
54. Banro American Resources, Inc. and Société Aurifère du Kivu et du Maniema S.A.R.L. v. Democratic Republic of the Congo, ICSID Case No. ARB/98/7, Award (September 1, 2000).
55. Mihaly International Corporation v. Democratic Socialist Republic of Sri Lanka, ICSID Case No. ARB/00/2, Award (March 15, 2002).

[sic] *have occurred.*"[56] Again, in paragraph 95, the tribunal stated that "an international investor cannot modify downstream the protection granted to its investment by the host State, *once the acts which the investor considers are causing damages* [sic] *to its investment have already been committed.*"[57] Subsequently, the tribunal expressed its agreement with one of the respondent's comments that "the manifest purpose behind [the claimant's] purchase of the Benet Companies was an attempt to render their purely domestic disputes subject to the protections of the BIT rather than to conduct business."[58] Lastly, it noted that "[i]f it were accepted that the tribunal has jurisdiction to decide Phoenix's claim, then *any pre-existing national dispute* could be brought to an ICSID tribunal by a transfer of the national economic interests to a foreign company in an attempt to seek protections under a BIT."[59]

Whereas *Phoenix* might not be the first case in which the concept of abuse is discussed by a tribunal in determining its jurisdiction, it has become a seminal case where the respondent's objection to this point was upheld for the first time. In so doing, the tribunal elaborated the notion of abuse in detail. In particular, having cited the principle of good faith as part of the general principles of international law, the tribunal expounded that an investment not made in good faith could not be protected.[60] According to the tribunal, this principle could be inferred from both the national legal order[61] and the international legal order.[62] Nonetheless, it should be noted that, in spite of applying the principle of good faith as an autonomous legal principle,[63] the tribunal merely applied it in connection with the type of investment that could satisfy the tribunal's jurisdictional requirement—*ratione materiae*.[64] Ultimately, the tribunal concluded that, as the putative investment was made only to seek protections under the Israel-Czech BIT vis-à-vis preexisting national disputes, this is an "abusive manipulation of the system of international investment protection under the ICSID Convention and the BITs," and, as a result, the tribunal lacked jurisdiction.[65]

That the tribunal lacked jurisdiction over the dispute was undoubtedly a proper verdict. No investor should be able to transform what was hitherto a purely national dispute into an international dispute by way of acquiring a new nationality after the

56. *Phoenix*, *supra* n. 41, para. 92 (emphasis added).
57. *Ibid.*, para. 95 (emphasis added).
58. *Ibid.*, para. 141.
59. *Ibid.*, para. 144 (emphasis added).
60. *Ibid.*, paras. 100, 106-107.
61. *Ibid.*, para. 109, noting that "[t]he principle of good faith is also recognized in most, if not all, domestic legal systems."
62. *Ibid.*, paras. 107-113, *citing* A. D'Amato, *Good Faith*, in Encyclopedia of Public International Law (Vol. 7) 107 (R. Bernhardt ed. 1984); Hersch Lauterpacht, *The Development of International Law by the International Court* 164 (Cambridge 1958); Amco Asia Corporation et al v. Indonesia, ICSID Case No. ARB/81/1, Decision on Jurisdiction, para. 14 (September 25, 1983); Inceysa Vallisoletana, S.L. v. Republic of El Salvador, ICSID Case No. ARB/03/26, Award, paras. 230, 243, 249 (August 2, 2006); Plama Consortium Limited v. Bulgaria, ICSID Case No. ARB/03/24, Award, paras. 143-144 (August 27, 2008); World Duty Free Company Limited v. The Republic of Kenya, ICSID Case No. ARB/00/7, Award, paras. 148, 157 (October 4, 2006).
63. Duncan Watson & Tom Brebner, *Nationality Planning and Abuse of Process: A Coherent Framework*, 33 ICSID Rev. 302, 307 (2018).
64. *Phoenix*, *supra* n. 41, para. 114.
65. *Ibid.*, paras. 144-145.

dispute had occurred. That being said, it is doubtful if the tribunal needed to apply this imprecise principle of good faith or the doctrine of abuse of rights to reach such a conclusion.[66] An investor's attempt to transform an existing dispute not originally governed by the relevant IIA and investor-state arbitration provision therein was not novel when the *Phoenix* award was rendered.[67] For instance, in *Société Générale v. Dominican Republic*,[68] the tribunal had to consider whether it had jurisdiction *ratione temporis*, as the respondent argued that the complained acts occurred before the relevant BIT became effective and before the claimant as a French corporation made its investment.[69]

The *Société Générale* tribunal examined two issues in its *ratione temporis* analysis: the retroactive application of the France-Dominican Republic BIT and the time that the investor acquired its investment. As for the retroactive application of the treaty, the tribunal referred to Article 28 of the VCLT, which expressly states that unless the contracting states agree otherwise, the treaty would be applicable only to events taking place after its entry into force.[70] Also, this nonretroactivity principle is supported by the principle of intertemporal law reflected in the *Island of Palmas* award:[71] "A juridical fact must be appreciated in the light of the law contemporary with it, and not of the law in force at the time when a dispute in regard to it arises or falls to be settled."[72] Thus, the tribunal concluded that it did not have jurisdiction for any complained acts happening prior to the entry into force of the treaty.[73] As for the respondent's argument in relation to the investor's nationality, the tribunal held that only the nationals and companies of the contracting states were a designated beneficiary of the treaty:[74]

66. Sanja Dajic, *Mapping the Good Faith Principle in International Investment Arbitration: Assessment of Its Substantive and Procedural Value*, 46 Zbornik Radova 207, 209 (2012).
67. As for a study on treaty shopping in the context of assignment of claims, *see* William Lawton Kirtley, *The Transfer of Treaty Claims and Treaty-Shopping in Investor-State Disputes*, 10 J. World Inv. & Trade 427 (2009). In this article, Kirtley examines the following awards in detail: Banro American Resources, Inc. and Société Aurifère du Kivu et du Maniema S.A.R.L. v. Democratic Republic of the Congo, ICSID Case No. ARB/98/7, Award (September 1, 2000); Mihaly International Corporation v. Democratic Socialist Republic of Sri Lanka, ICSID Case No. ARB/00/2, Award (March 15, 2002).
68. Société Générale In respect of DR Energy Holdings Limited and Empresa Distribuidora de Electricidad del Este, S.A. v. The Dominican Republic, LCIA Case No. UN 7927, Award on Preliminary Objections to Jurisdiction (September 19, 2008) ("*Société Générale*").
69. *Ibid.*, para. 13.
70. *Ibid.*, para. 79.
71. *Ibid.*, paras. 85-86, *referring to* Island of Palmas (U.S./Neth.), Award (April 4, 1928), reprinted in 2 Rep. Int'l Arb. Award 829 (1928); Max Sorensen, *The Intertemporal Problem in Public International Law* (1975), http://www.idi-iil.org/app/uploads/2017/06/1975_wies_01_en.pdf (accessed February 18, 2019); Impregilo S.p.A. v. Islamic Republic of Pakistan, ICSID Case No. ARB/03/3, Decision on Jurisdiction, para. 311 (April 22, 2005). *See also*, Zachary Douglas, *The International Law of Investment Claims* (Cambridge: Cambridge University Press, 2009), 329-330.
72. Island of Palmas (U.S./Neth.), Award (April 4, 1928), reprinted in 2 Rep. Int'l Arb. Award 829, 845 (1928).
73. *Société Générale, supra* n. 68, para. 84.
74. *Ibid.*, para. 106.

> As with most investment treaties, the meaning of this provision is that the investment might have been made before or after the date of the Treaty, but that the treaty violation falling under the Tribunal's jurisdiction must have occurred after the entry into force of the Treaty and the investor became its beneficiary as an eligible national of the relevant Contracting Party. One would expect any derogation of this principle to be express and not implied. The Treaty could thus not apply to any acts or omissions that occurred before that date because the investor's nationality was different from that required by the treaty and did not permit it to qualify as a protected investor under the Treaty.[75]

For this reason, the tribunal concluded that it did not have jurisdiction over events taking place before the claimant as a French national made its investment.[76]

A comparison between *Phoenix* and *Société Générale* shows that while both tribunals reached the same conclusion that they lacked jurisdiction over disputes arising before the change of nationality, their pathways are totally different. Whereas the *Société Générale* tribunal applied the relatively precise concept of *ratione temporis*, the *Phoenix* tribunal instead applied the ambiguous doctrine of abuse of rights derived from the general principle of good faith. One could further question if it was necessary for the *Phoenix* tribunal to take this winding path in the first place. Indeed, scholars have convincingly argued that this approach is flawed, as, in order to find an abuse of rights, one would have to establish first that the right exists; should the claimant investor fail to assert that the tribunal has jurisdiction, what rights could it possess or exercise, let alone abuse?[77]

Notwithstanding its problematic methodology, the *Phoenix* approach has been followed by other tribunals. In *Mobil Corporation, Venezuela Holdings, B.V. et al. v. Venezuela*,[78] among its various jurisdictional objections to the tribunal's jurisdiction under the Netherlands-Venezuela BIT, Venezuela contended that "Venezuela Holdings is a 'corporation of convenience' created [...] for the sole purpose of gaining access to ICSID jurisdiction [and] 'this abuse of the corporate form and blatant treaty-shopping should not be condoned.'"[79] This assertion was based on the fact that the claimants decided in early 2005 to restructure their investments (by inserting Venezuela Holdings, a Dutch entity, into their corporate chain) in response to Venezuela's first hostile fiscal measure adopted in late 2004.[80] Thus, it was clear, stated the tribunal, that "the main, if not the sole purpose of the restructuring was to protect Mobil investments from

75. *Ibid.*, para. 105.
76. *Ibid.*, para. 107.
77. Eric De Brabandere, *"Good Faith", "Abuse of Process" and the Initiation of Investment Treaty Claims*, 3 J. Int'l Disp. Set. 609, 620, 628-629 (2012); Yuka Fukunaga, *Abuse of Process under International Law and Investment Arbitration*, 33 ICSID Rev. 181, 183 (2018); Emmanuel Gaillard, *Abuse of Process in International Arbitration*, ICSID Rev. 17, 21-22 (2017); Stephen Jagusch, Anthony C. Sinclair & Manthi Wickramasooriya, *Restructuring Investments to Achieve Investment Treaty Protection*, in Meg Kinnear et al (eds.), Building International Investment Law: The First 50 Years of ICSID (Maryland: Aspen Publishers, 2015), 179; Stephan W. Schill & Heather L. Bray, *Good Faith Limitations on Protected Investments and Corporate Structuring*, in Andrew D. Mitchell, M. Sornarajah & Tania Voon (eds.), Good Faith and International Economic Law (Oxford: Oxford University Press, 2015), 112.
78. *Venezuela Holdings*, *supra* n. 39.
79. *Ibid.*, para. 27.
80. *Ibid.*, para. 189.

adverse measures in getting access to ICSID arbitration through the Dutch-Venezuela BIT."[81]

According to the tribunal, whether this restructuring was "legitimate corporate planning" or an "abuse of right" depended on the circumstances.[82] It then considered Venezuela's reaction to the restructuring and the timings of the restructuring and the dispute. The tribunal found that several disputes concerning Venezuela's fiscal measures had already arisen in mid-2005 before the restructuring took place, unlike the Nationalization Decree, which was implemented in early 2007 after the restructuring. Therefore, the tribunal concluded that it had jurisdiction only over disputes occurring after the date of the restructuring:[83]

> [T]he aim of the restructuring of their investments in Venezuela through a Dutch holding was to protect those investments against breaches of their rights by the Venezuelan authorities by gaining access to ICSID arbitration through the BIT. The tribunal considers that *this was a perfectly legitimate goal as far as it concerned future disputes*.
>
> *With respect to pre-existing disputes, the situation is different* and the tribunal considers that to restructure investments only in order to gain jurisdiction under a BIT for such disputes would constitute, to take the words of the Phoenix tribunal, "an abusive manipulation of the system" of international investment protection under the ICSID Convention and the BITs.[84]

Subsequently, the tribunals in *ST-AD v. Bulgaria*[85] and *Transglobal v. Panama*[86] reached a similar conclusion. That is, in *ST-AD*, the tribunal correctly concluded that it did not have jurisdiction *ratione temporis* over the dispute as there was not any alleged treaty violation arising after the claimant had become a qualified investor.[87] Whereas this could have been the end of its analysis, the tribunal further addressed the respondent's claim of abuse of process and observed that there were "the major or substantial issue of systemic abuse and the more minor one of procedural abuse."[88] As for the issue of systemic abuse ("a claim of bad faith in the initiation of the arbitration"),[89] the tribunal noted that the possibility to initiate this investment arbitration was the main reason why the claimant acquired shares in a domestic company[90] and emphasized that the damage to the investment had already occurred prior to such share acquisition.[91] Based on these findings and the *Phoenix* and

81. *Ibid.*, para. 190.
82. *Ibid.*, para. 191.
83. *Ibid.*, para. 206.
84. *Ibid.*, paras. 204-205 (emphasis added in *italic*).
85. ST-AD GmbH v. The Republic of Bulgaria, PCA Case No. 2011-06, Award on Jurisdiction (July 18, 2013) ("*ST-AD*").
86. Transglobal Green Energy, LLC and Transglobal Green Energy de Panama, S.A. v. The Republic of Panama, ICSID Case No. ARB/13/28, Award (June 2, 2016) ("*Transglobal*").
87. *ST-AD, supra* n. 85, para. 333.
88. *Ibid.*, para. 404.
89. *Ibid.*, para. 405.
90. *Ibid.*, para. 415.
91. *Ibid.*, para. 419.

Venezuela Holdings awards, the tribunal concluded that the claimant's action constituted an abuse of process, as the transfer of shares took place in the aftermath of the preexisting national dispute.[92]

For *Transglobal*, its underlying dispute concerned the claimants' (Transglobal (U.S.) and Transglobal Panama) concessionary rights, which were originally held by La Mina, a Panamanian company owned by Mr. Lisac, a Panamanian national, to design, build, and operate a hydroelectric power plant. The relevant Panamanian authority, the so-called Ente Regulador de los Servicios Públicos (ASEP), terminated the concession on December 20, 2006, and later conferred the rights to another company, Ideal. Mr. Lisac brought the dispute before Panama's court on March 16, 2007, which subsequently ruled in his favor and ordered the restitution of the concession to La Mina on November 11, 2010. After the judgment, on September 30, 2011, Mr. Lisac entered into the Partnership and Transfer Agreement (PTA) with Transglobal (U.S.) and assigned the concessionary rights to Transglobal Panama, which was incorporated on October 6, 2011. This PTA was a final product of an MOU signed by the parties on December 17, 2010, roughly one month after the date of the judgment. On May 1, 2012, ASEP, with the Panamanian cabinet's approval, declared the *rescate administrativo* of the concession.

The respondent argued that the claimants abused the process as Transglobal Panama was put into the picture "at a time when the project was already embroiled in a domestic dispute" and thus requested that the tribunal decline jurisdiction.[93] Having reviewed, *inter alia*, the terms of the PTA[94] and the claimants' conduct in the arbitration proceedings,[95] the tribunal held that the PTA was signed when there was obviously a problem with the execution of the court's judgment.[96] Therefore, it concluded that the claimants abused the investment treaty arbitration system "by attempting to create artificial international jurisdiction over a pre-existing domestic dispute."[97]

Like *Phoenix*, the tribunals in *Venezuela Holdings*, *ST-AD*, and *Transglobal* focused on the issue of timing—whether the restructuring occurred before or after the adoption of each disputed sovereign measure—in its determination of whether the claimants' conduct constituted an "abuse of right." Therefore, the abovementioned

92. *Ibid.*, para. 423.
93. *Transglobal*, *supra* n. 86, para. 85.
94. *Ibid.*, paras. 110-112 ("ASEP had failed to comply with the Third Chamber Judgment and its enforcement takes a prominent place in the object of the PTA and the obligations of the Parties. [...] The PTA provisions on the distribution of the proceeds of an eventual sale of the power plant or of receipt of compensation reflects the predominant role of Mr. Lisac disproportionate to his shareholding in [Transglobal] Panama. [...] [T]here is no record of [Transglobal] ever making any contribution other than the US$50,000 paid to Mr. Lisac at the time of the signing of the PTA").
95. *Ibid.*, para. 113 ("The procedural developments related to the pursuit by Mr. Lisac of the execution of the Third Chamber Judgment in Panama prompted Claimants twice to request the suspension of this arbitration. Both suspension requests reveal the intimate relationship of the ongoing court proceedings in Panama and this proceeding, and confirm the intent of Mr. Lisac to internationalize his domestic dispute with Panama").
96. *Ibid.*, para. 116.
97. *Ibid.*, para. 118.

observation in *Phoenix* also applies to these tribunals' analysis as to the need to rely upon the broad doctrine of abuse of rights instead of the established legal rule of *ratione temporis*;[98] the latter clearly requires that, for a tribunal to have jurisdiction over a dispute, the investor's acquisition of nationality or its making of investment must take place before the dispute arises.[99]

Leaving aside the suitability or validity of its application to particular events for a moment, let us now turn to where this doctrine of abuse of rights derives from in the context of international investment law.

IV THEORETICAL FOUNDATION OF ABUSE OF RIGHTS

To begin with, our focus is on the *Phoenix* award in which the genesis of the doctrine of abuse of rights was fairly elaborated. Therein, the tribunal noted that international treaties must "be analyzed with due regard to the requirements of the general principles of law."[100] Hence, any investment made inconsistently with general principles of international law should not be protected under the IIAs regime. As the principle of good faith forms part of these general principles of international law, it accordingly means that, to be eligible for the protection, the investment must be bona fide.[101] The tribunal's survey of preceding cases and domestic legal systems (according to the approach called the "Janus Concept"—"one face looking at the national legal order and one at the international legal order") also supports this explanation.[102] The tribunal then referred to the works of D'Amato and Lauterpacht to conclude that the good faith principle requires that no investor abuse the rights conferred upon it by the relevant investment treaty.[103] Many commentators seem to agree with the "Janus Concept" proposed by the *Phoenix* tribunal.[104]

98. *See* n. 77.
99. *See Société Générale*, *supra* n. 68; Banro American Resources, Inc. and Société Aurifère du Kivu et du Maniema S.A.R.L. v. Democratic Republic of the Congo, ICSID Case No. ARB/98/7, Award (September 1, 2000); Mihaly International Corporation v. Democratic Socialist Republic of Sri Lanka, ICSID Case No. ARB/00/2, Award (March 15, 2002).
100. *Phoenix*, *supra* n. 41, paras. 77-80, *citing* Joost Pauwelyn, *Role of Public International Law in the WTO Law*, 95 Am. J. Int'l L. 535, 539 (2001); United States - Standards for Reformulated and Conventional Gasoline, WT/DS2/AB/R (April 29, 1996), 18.
101. *Ibid.*, para. 106.
102. *Ibid.*, paras. 108-113, *referring to* Amco Asia Corporation and others v. Republic of Indonesia, ICSID Case No. ARB/81/1, Decision on Jurisdiction, para. 14 (September 25, 1983); Inceysa Vallisoletana S.L. v. Republic of El Salvador, ICSID Case No. ARB/03/26, Award, paras. 230, 243, 249 (August 2, 2006); Plama Consortium Limited v. Bulgaria, ICSID Case No. ARB/03/24, Award, paras. 143-144 (August 27, 2008).
103. *Ibid.*, para. 107, *referring to* Lauterpacht, *supra* n. 62; D'Amato, *supra* n. 62.
104. *See, e.g.*, Brabandere, *supra* n. 77, at 612; Fukunaga, *supra* n. 77, at 183; Gaillard, *supra* n. 77, at 34; Voon, Mitchell & Munro, *supra* n. 41, at 60; Hervé Ascensio, *Abuse of Process in International Investment Arbitration*, 13 Chi. J. Int'l L. 763, 777 (2014); Yael Ribco Borman, *Treaty Shopping through Corporate Restructuring of Investments: Legitimate Corporate Planning or Abuse of Rights*, 24 Hague Y.B. Int'l L. 359, 368 (2011); John P. Gaffney, *Abuse of Process in Investment Treaty*, 11 J. World Inv. & Trade 515, 523 (2010); Juan Garay, *Abuse of Process Through Corporate Restructuring of Assets: The Legal Standard for the Multinational Investor*, 35 B.U. Int'l L.J. 397, 410-411 (2017); Brigitte Stern, *Are There New Limits on Access to International Arbitration?*, 25 ICSID Rev. 26, 29 (2010).

Interestingly, a good number of those commentators cite Professor Cheng's classic manuscript in their works.[105] Having examined an abuse of rights in relations between states, Cheng defined it as "an exercise of the right contrary to the principle of good faith."[106] Simply put, it is a corollary of good faith,[107] and its key aspect is to prohibit malicious injury.[108] This prohibition extends to the exercise of a right or a supposed right that ceases to exist, the sole purpose of which is to cause injury to others.[109] Put in Cheng's words, "[e]very right is the legal protection of a legitimate interest. An alleged exercise of a right not in furtherance of such interest, but with the malicious purpose of injuring others can no longer claim the protection of the law."[110]

In addition, to comply with the principle of good faith, every right is to be exercised honestly and loyally. An abuse of rights occurs if the rights are exercised *fictitiously* to evade laws or contracts.[111] To determine the existence of an abuse of rights, international courts and tribunals must consider the purpose of the exercise of rights. If such an exercise is to pursue the legitimate interest destined to be protected by that right and not aimed at unfairly prejudicing the right and legitimate interests of the other party, it is consistent with the principle of good faith and does not constitute an abuse.[112] This is to keep a fair and reasonable balance between the conflicting rights and interests of the parties, protecting the legitimate interests of the holder of the rights while imposing some limitations on it for the sake of the legitimate interest of the other party, whether the interest is secured by treaties or general international law. In other words, states must exercise their rights consistently with their obligations under treaties or general international law. As their rights and obligations are interdependent and correlative, one must exercise their rights reasonably, giving due regard to those of others. Therefore, a line is drawn to delimit one's rights and obligations. Any exercise of rights that crosses the line or exceeds its limits is likely to cause an abuse of rights.[113] However, due to the general presumption of good faith, an abuse of rights cannot be presumed.[114]

Apart from the preceding explanation, some commentators argue that the doctrine of abuse of rights can also be derived from tribunals' inherent power.[115] For example, having examined some important studies on the inherent power of judicial

105. *See, e.g.*, Fukunaga, *supra* n. 77, at 183; Gaillard, *supra* n. 77, at 17.
106. Cheng, *supra* n. 7, at 127.
107. Mark Villiger, The 1969 Vienna Convention on the Law of Treaties-40 Years after (Volume 344) in Collected Courses of the Hague Academy of International Law 117, 152 (2009).
108. Cheng, *supra* n. 7, at 121.
109. *Ibid.*, at 122, 136.
110. *Ibid.*, at 122 (footnote omitted).
111. *Ibid.*, at 123, 136.
112. *Ibid.*, at 128-129.
113. *Ibid.*, at 129, 131-132 (1953); V. S. Mani, Humanitarian Intervention Today (Volume 313), in Collected Courses of the Hague Academy of International Law 178 (2005).
114. *Ibid.*, at 136.
115. Fukunaga, *supra* n. 77, at 185-192; Gaffney, *supra* n. 104, at 521-523; Utku Topcan, *Abuse of the Right to Access ICSID Arbitration*, 29 ICSID Rev. 627 (2014); John P. Gaffney, *Is an Investment Treaty Tribunal Entitled to Dismiss a Claim Where It Amounts to an "Abuse of Process"?* Kluwer Arbitration Blog (August 4, 2009), http://arbitrationblog.kluwerarbitration.com/2009/08/04/is-an-investment-treaty-tribunal-entitled-to-dismiss-a-claim-where-it-amounts-to-an-abuse-of-process/ (accessed May 3, 2019); *see also* Pac Rim Cayman LLC v. The

institutions and past practice of investment tribunals, Professor Brabandere observes that "declaring a claim inadmissible because it constitutes an 'abuse of process' lies within the power of an arbitral tribunal, even without an express power to do so."[116] That a judicial tribunal has this inherent competence to decline to exercise jurisdiction, according to Professor Lowe, is common and necessary for the effectiveness of its adjudicative function.[117]

Moreover, as several scholars argue, the prohibition of abuse of rights in investment treaty arbitration is also warranted from a policy perspective. That is, the goal of preventing investors from bringing "egregious," "malicious," or "abusive" claims (i.e., situations whereby the rights granted are exercised to achieve results contrary to their intended purposes) against states justifies the application of the doctrine to corporate maneuvering adopted to gain access to investment treaty arbitration.[118] Particularly, Professor Sornarajah submits that it is in the international community's interest to apply the good faith principle to prevent an abuse instead of strictly adhering to the written black letter law:

> Good faith is an amorphous concept without specific content. Its application can be scoffed at for its uncertainty, lack of definite content, use as a vehicle for subjective preferences, and as a last ditch attempt at substantiating a difficult argument. But its inner core as a doctrine that deters obvious fraud and ensures that only those with clean hands are afforded a remedy can hardly be contested. In this core sense, it has an overarching presence that deters decisions in disputes that feature even a hint of fraud or malevolence on the part of the claimant. It is in that narrow and well-accepted sense that it needs to be used in considering the issue of corporate nationality in investment arbitration.[119]

Similarly, Professor Gaillard notes that "it is perfectly suited to tackle circumstances in which parties to international arbitrations engage in tactics that do not violate any hard and fast rules, but which are nevertheless objectionable in the

Republic of El Salvador, ICSID Case No. ARB/09/12, The Republic of El Salvador's Memorial Objections to Jurisdiction, para. 89 (October 15, 2010) ("*El Salvador's Memorial*").

116. Brabandere, *supra* n. 77, at 621, *referring to* Chester Brown, *A Common Law of International Adjudication* (Oxford: Oxford University Press, 2007), 245; Chester Brown, *The Inherent Powers of International Courts and Tribunals*, 76 Brit. Y.B. Int'l L. 195 (2005); Martins Paparinski, *Inherent Powers of ICSID Tribunals: Broad and Rightly So*, in Todd J. Weiler & Ian A. Laird (eds.), 5 Investment Treaty Arbitration and International Law (New York: JurisNet, 2012), 11; Yuval Shany, *The Competing Jurisdictions of International Courts and Tribunals* (Oxford: Oxford University Press, 2003), 255.
117. Vaughan Lowe, *Overlapping Jurisdiction in International Tribunals*, 20 Aust. Y.B. Int'l L. 191, 202-203 (1999).
118. Ascensio, *supra* n. 104, at 764-765; Gaillard, *supra* n. 77, at 32; Jean-François Hébert, *Issues of Corporate Nationality in Investment Arbitration*, in Armand de Mestral & Céline Lévesque (eds.), Improving International Agreements (New York: Routledge, 2013), 235-236; M. Sornarajah, *Good Faith, Corporate Nationality, and Denial of Benefits*, in Andrew D. Mitchell, M. Sornarajah & Tania Voon (eds.), Good Faith and International Economic Law (Oxford: Oxford University Press, 2015), 126; Tania Voon, Andrew D. Mitchell & James Munro, *Good Faith in Parallel Trade and Investment Disputes*, in Andrew D. Mitchell, M. Sornarajah & Tania Voon (eds.), Good Faith and International Economic Law (Oxford: Oxford University Press, 2015), 75; Tekin, *supra* n. 16; *Venezuela Holdings*, *supra* n. 39, para. 169.
119. Sornarajah, *supra* n. 118, at 117.

particular circumstances of the case."[120] In addition, the tribunal in *ConocoPhillips v. Venezuela* pointed out that the element of "equality of position" between the respondent state and the claimant corporation also justifies its examination as to whether an abuse occurs.[121]

Regardless of these justifications, some advocates of the abuse of rights doctrine acknowledge several drawbacks of its application in the context of corporate restructuring. They criticize the doctrine for its broad and ambiguous scope of application.[122] More importantly, the number of prominent scholars who are skeptical about the doctrine, or even deny its existence, should not be overlooked.[123] For instance, Scerni stated that the only theoretical foundation of the doctrine of abuse of rights would be "the social and solidaristic conception of the subjective rights, a conception which is out of the question on account of the highly individualistic character of international law."[124] In Fitzmaurice's view, the doctrine "is still in a rudimentary condition in international law, both as to its content and the method of its application—so much so as to have led to the question whether there is any real room for it."[125] In other words, the doctrine is not "definitely established." Nor is it regarded by many as a principle of international law.[126] Another distinguished authority, Schwarzenberger, held that "outside the field of treaty relations, the place of the prohibition of abuse of rights is, as yet, highly precarious."[127] Brownlie pointed out in the last self-edited edition of his treatise that there is no such thing as the principle of abuse of rights:

> It may be said that the doctrine is a useful agent in the progressive development of the law, but that, as a general principle, it does not exist in positive law. Indeed it is doubtful if it could be safely recognized as an ambulatory doctrine, since it

120. Gaillard, *supra* n. 77, at 34.
121. ConocoPhillips Petrozuata B.V. et al. v. Bolivarian Republic of Venezuela, ICSID Case No. ARB/07/30, Decision on Jurisdiction and the Merits (September 3, 2013) ("*ConocoPhillips*").
122. Dajic, *supra* n. 66, at 209 ("[T]he [good faith] principle itself is an empty shell and far from the legal certainty and predictability which should be inherent to the very same principle"); Primec, *supra* n. 18, at 41 ("It is arguable whether a notion so abstract and devoid of graspable meaning can have a place in the investment protection legal order"); Sornarajah, *supra* n. 118, at 117 ("Good faith is an amorphous concept without specific content. Its application can be scoffed at for its uncertainty, lack of definite content, use as a vehicle for subjective preferences, and as a last ditch attempt at substantiating a difficult argument").
123. *See, e.g.*, Gerald Fitzmaurice, *The Law and Procedure of the International Court of Justice* (Volume One) 12, 183-184 (1986); Georg Schwarzenberger, *International Law as Applied by International Courts and Tribunals* (Volume II): *The Law of Armed Conflict* 79 (1968); Georg Schwarzenberger, *The Fundamental Principles of International Law* (Volume 87), in Collected Courses of the Hague Academy of International Law 304-306 (1955); Ian Brownlie, *Principles of Public International Law* 445, 7th edition (Oxford University Press 2008).
124. F.V. Garcia Amador, State Responsibility: Some New Problems (Volume 94) in Collected Courses of the Hague Academy of International Law 379 (1958) (citing Scerni, *L'Abuso di Diritto nei Rapporti Internazionali* (1930), Cavaglieri, *Corso di Diritto Internazionale*, 3rd edition (1934), p. 508.)
125. Gerald Fitzmaurice, The General Principles of International Law Considered from the Standpoint of the Rule of Law (Volume 92) in Collected Courses of the Hague Academy of International Law 54 (1957).
126. Fitzmaurice, *supra* n. 123, at 12.
127. Schwarzenberger, *supra* n. 123, at 79.

> would encourage doctrines as to the relativity of rights and result, outside the judicial forum, in instability.[128]

Thus, there is also a strong policy argument that an investment treaty tribunal should avoid applying this broad principle of good faith or the doctrine of abuse of rights to deny treaty protection to an investment or investor that indisputably satisfies the jurisdictional requirements expressly prescribed in the relevant IIAs.[129] This is especially the case should one accept that the investor's right to bring a claim to the tribunal is a fundamental right of access to justice (a fair and neutral tribunal).[130] However, if one views this entitlement not as a right but as a special privilege conferred upon the foreign investor (in relation to the right ordinarily held by the host state's national), this argument may not hold. Therefore, how one perceives this matter may ultimately rest on his or her opinion concerning the use of investment treaty arbitration, rather than domestic legal proceedings, to resolve international investor-state disputes in general.[131]

Probably because the International Court of Justice (ICJ) views the right to bring a dispute to a judicial entity as a fundamental right of access to justice, it has treated this matter with care and reserve. Although the Court has not rejected the existence of the abuse of rights concept, it has never upheld the respondent state's argument in this regard.[132] Perhaps the case most relevant to our discussion here is the *Right of Passage* case,[133] whereby the Court allowed Portugal to initiate proceedings against India just three days after its deposit of its optional-clause declaration accepting the compulsory jurisdiction of the Court:

128. Brownlie, *supra* n. 123, at 445.
129. Schill & Bray, *supra* n. 77, at 98.
130. Ascensio, *supra* n. 104, at 765, 782; Richard Kreindler, *Are Tribunals Setting New Limits on Access to International Jurisdiction?*, 25 ICSID Rev. 37, 42-43 (2010).
131. For a similar argument in the field of international arbitration in general, *see* Emmanuel Gaillard, *Legal Theory of International Arbitration* (Leiden: Martinus Nijhoff, 2010), 11; Emmanuel Gaillard, *The Representations of International Arbitration*, 1 J. Int'l Disp. Set. 271, 272 (2010). In these works, Professor Gaillard argues that:

    > There is not a single representation, a single vision, of international arbitration. It is precisely because there are several visions, several competing representations of international arbitration, that the controversies on a number of apparently purely technical topics remain so vivid. Not surprisingly, certain authors always agree with one another no matter how different the issues at hand, while others will always disagree with the former on the same issues. This is because they belong to different schools of thought, because they embrace different visions of arbitration. The controversies are all the more intense that, in reality, what is at stake are not matters that may be disposed of by scientific demonstration, but rather matters that belong to the realm of belief, of faith.

132. Fukunaga, *supra* n. 77, at 186; Gaffney, *supra* n. 104, at 520-521; Robert Kolb, *General Principles of Procedural Law*, in Andreas Zimmerman et al. (eds), The Statute of the International Court of Justice: A Commentary, 2nd edition (Oxford: Oxford University Press, 2012), 904.
133. Right of Passage over Indian Territory (Portugal/India), ICJ Reports (1957) ("*Right of Passage*") *see* also, Certain German Interests in Polish Upper Silesia (Ger. v. Pol.), 1925 P.C.I.J. (ser. A) No. 7, 30, at 37-38 (August 25).

> A State accepting the jurisdiction of the Court must expect that an Application may be filed against it before the Court by a new declarant State on the same day on which that State deposits with the Secretary-General its Declaration of Acceptance. For it is on that very day that the consensual bond, which is the basis of the Optional Clause, comes into being between the States concerned.
>
> [...]
>
> Moreover, unlike some other instruments, Article 36 provides for no additional requirement, for instance, that the information transmitted by the Secretary-General must reach the Parties to the Statute, or that some period must elapse subsequent to the deposit of the Declaration before it can become effective. Any such requirement would introduce an element of uncertainty into the operation of the Optional Clause system. The Court cannot read into the Optional Clause any requirement of that nature.[134]

Thus, the Court did not view this "surprise attack" as an abuse of rights.[135] Had this same rationale (i.e., that an international tribunal cannot read into an international instrument upon which its jurisdiction is based, a concept serving to avoid bringing in "an element of uncertainty" into the system) been followed in investment treaty arbitration, one could argue that an investment arbitral tribunal should not refuse to exercise its jurisdiction due to the mere fact that a putative investor modifies its corporate structure to acquire a certain nationality prior to a dispute arises.

Moreover, there is another argument that the tribunal's application of the doctrine of abuse of rights in this circumstance is unjustified. Casas makes a detailed analysis on this point.[136] He focuses on an element of abuse that has been missing in contemporary scholarly discussions and arbitral awards, i.e., *harm*. Having researched extensively on this issue, reviewing both domestic and international materials,[137] Casas maintains that "[a]n abuse of rights does not necessarily occur simply because a right is used in a way different from its original purpose."[138] Rather, it requires harm, which must be concrete: there must exist: (1) subjective intent (of the person exercising the right to cause harm) and (2) objective consequence that such an exercise of right causes unnecessary or excessive harm.[139]

Hence, a question arises as to whether, by bringing a claim to an international arbitral tribunal against a state, an investor causes any unreasonable harm to that state. Again, the answer to this question may depend on how one perceives the ISDS system.

134. *Right of Passage*, *supra* n. 133, at 125, 146-147.
135. Kolb, *supra* n. 132, at 905.
136. Manuel Casas, *Nationalities of Convenience, Personal Jurisdiction, and Access to Investor-State Dispute Settlement*, 49 N.Y.U. J. Int'l L. & Pol. 63, 114-125 (2016).
137. *Ibid.*, at 117-124, *referring to*, for example, Cheng, *supra* n. 7, at 122; M. Byers, *Abuse of Rights: An Old Principle, A New Age*, 47 McGill L. J. 389 (2002); H. C. Gutteridge, *Abuse of Rights*, 5 Cambridge L. J. 22 (1933); Preservation of Fur Seals (U.K. v. U.S.), 27 R.I.A.A. 263, 266 (1893); Certain German Interests in Polish Upper Silesia (Ger. v. Pol.), 1925 P.C.I.J. (ser. A) No. 7, 30, at 37-38 (August 25); Free Zone of Upper Savoy and the District of Gex (Fr. v. Switz.), 1932 P.C.I.J. (ser. A/B) No. 46, at 167 (June 7); *cf.* Lauterpacht, *supra* n. 62, at 298-300; Louis Josserand, De L'esprit des Lois et de leur Relativité: Theorie dite de l'abus des Droits (2 ed. 1939); Nicolas Politis, *Les Probléme des Limitations de la Souveraineté et la Théorie de l'abus des Droits dans les Rapports Internationaux*, 6 *in* Collected Courses of the Hague Academy of International Law 1 (1925).
138. *Ibid.*, at 117.
139. *Ibid.*

For some, the fact that, in investor-state arbitration, a state is responsible for legal fees and costs in defending a treaty claim and subject to the risk of being ordered to remedy the investor alone would suffice to conclude that harm occurs. Yet, are these conceivable impairments the type of harm sufficient to establish an abuse? On this point, Casas convincingly argues, and we concur, that by bringing a dispute to an arbitration tribunal, the investor exercising the right does not deliberately harm the state.[140] Rather, the investor's fundamental objective is to gain access to a neutral judicial forum, and this goal arguably outweighs the overall costs borne by the disputing parties,[141] especially when there are other alternatives available to address this concern, e.g., the tribunal's power to order security for costs and allocate costs at the end of the proceedings.[142] However, while Casas disagrees with the investment treaty tribunals' approach to the problem, he tends to agree with the final outcome, considering their refusal to exercise jurisdiction "reasonable" and their determination of the timing of the corporate restructuring "nuanced."[143] For him, these tribunals should have applied the principle of continuous nationality found in the law of diplomatic protection instead.[144]

Notwithstanding such arguably theoretical flaw(s), the doctrine of abuse of rights seems to have been firmly entrenched in the present investment treaty arbitration jurisprudence with respect to investors' corporate restructuring for the purpose of securing jurisdiction. Most scholars writing on this topic have merely examined how tribunals apply the concept and discussed factors each tribunal took account of when considering whether an abuse exists. It is only rarely that these commentators disagree with the current trend.[145] Indeed, after *Phoenix* and *Venezuela Holdings*, the threshold of abuse of rights has been lowered in certain subsequent cases. While the *Phoenix* and *Venezuela Holdings* tribunals rendered the doctrine applicable to a situation where a restructuring takes place *after* a dispute arises, some later tribunals applied it to a situation where a restructuring takes place *before* a dispute occurs provided that the

140. *Ibid.*, at 119, 124.
141. *See* W. Michael Reisman, *The Past and Future of the Great Compact*, 33 ICSID Rev. 56, 58, 64-65 (2018) (Professor Reisman argues that the requirement that an investor-state dispute be submitted to international arbitration is a fundamental component of the Great Compact whereby "investors' States waiving the deployment of their superior power to protect their investors in return for host States' agreeing to submit the disputes with those investors to international arbitration by independent third party determination." This Great Company, he continues, "has proven itself an efficient and fair program of dispute resolution supporting transnational productive economic activity").
142. For a further discussion on this point, *see* section VI, *infra*.
143. Casas, *supra* n. 136, at 116.
144. *Ibid.*, at 124-125, *referring to* arts. 4 and 5 of Draft Articles on Diplomatic Protection with Commentaries, Int'l Law Comm'n, U.N. Doc. A/61/10 (2006).
145. *See, e.g.*, Casas, *supra* n. 136; Schill & Bray, *supra* n. 77; International Chamber of Commerce, *Symposium on Abuse of Process in International Arbitration*, ICC Digital Library (2017), https://library.iccwbo.org/dr-noaccount.htm?reqhref=/content/dr/ICCActivities/IA_0007.htm?l1=ICCActivities%252612=Symposium+on+Abuse+of+Process+in+International+Arbitration (accessed May 14, 2019) (Noah Rubins disagreed with Emmanuel Gaillard's comment that an acquisition of "a particular nationality or engaging in corporate restructuring for the sole purpose of securing jurisdiction under a particular bilateral investment treaty" constitutes abuse).

investor could *foresee* the possibility of the dispute at the time of restructuring ("foreseeability test"). This development was introduced in *Pac Rim v. El Salvador*[146] and subsequently followed by *Tidewater v. Venezuela*, *ConocoPhillips v. Venezuela*, *Lao Holdings v. Lao*, *Gremcitel v. Peru*, and *Philipp Morris v. Australia*.

V ABUSE OF RIGHTS UNCHAINED

In *Pac Rim*, Pac Rim Cayman LLC (PRC) was a U.S. subsidiary of Pacific Rim Mining Corporation (Pacific Rim), a Canadian mining company. On April 30, 2009, it brought an ICSID claim against El Salvador under the Dominican Republic-Central America-United States Free Trade Agreement (CAFTA), which became effective on March 1, 2006. El Salvador challenged the tribunal's jurisdiction on the ground that the claimant had "abused the provisions of CAFTA and the international arbitration process by changing Pac Rim Cayman's nationality to a CAFTA Party to bring a pre-existing dispute before this tribunal under CAFTA"[147] by changing its nationality from Caymanian to American on December 13, 2007. Apart from the claimant's alleged goal of cost saving, the tribunal found that the principal purpose of the restructuring was to gain access to CAFTA protection.[148]

Against this backdrop, the tribunal then determined whether the disputed measure occurred before or after December 13, 2007.[149] Such determination was somehow complicated given that the respondent's "practice [...] comprise[s] a multiplicity of pre- or co-existing acts or omissions."[150] The temporal point of departure here was then President Saca's speech on March 11, 2008, expressing his intention not to grant any new mining permits, which the claimant described as the respondent's *de*

146. Pac Rim Cayman LLC v. The Republic of El Salvador, ICSID Case NO. ARB/09/12, Decision on the Respondent's Jurisdictional Objections (June 1, 2012) ("*Pac Rim*"). While some observers may argue that the foreseeability test did not really appear for the first time in *Pac Rim* but had actually been floating around since the *Aguas del Tunari v. Bolivia* ("AdT") award was rendered in 2005, the authors opine that the AdT tribunal's discussion on this point was only in passing, as the matter did not seem to be seriously challenged by Bolivia (paras. 206-213) The tribunal succinctly summarizes the parties' arguments on this point in one paragraph (para. 212), stating that the claimant objected "Respondent's suggestions that [the relevant entities] are mere 'shell' created solely for the purpose of gaining ICSID jurisdiction" and argued that the "change in structure occurred before the events that would so severely affect the Concession were foreseeable." Moreover, the tribunal did not examine this issue until the very last paragraphs located in the Concluding Observation section of its jurisdictional decision (paras. 328-333). In so doing, it swiftly rejected Bolivia's suggestion that an abuse of corporate form took place as a result of the claimant's corporate restructuring in November to December 1999, which might be done in anticipation of the injurious events occurring in the Spring of 2000, and no attempt was made to explain what the abuse means. It then succinctly concluded that there was not enough evidence to support such an allegation for the following reasons: (1) the planning likely predated the restructuring for a long time; (2) it was unlikely that the dispute was foreseeable in late 1999; (3) the restructuring could be done for other purposes, such as taxation, apart from gaining access to treaty arbitration (para. 330) *AdT*, *supra* n. 39.
147. *Pac Rim*, *supra* n. 146, para. 2.17.
148. *Ibid.*, para. 2.41.
149. *Ibid.*, paras. 2.45, 2.52.
150. *Ibid.*, para. 2.58.

facto ban on the claimant's mining operations[151] and was thus allegedly the moment when the dispute crystallized.[152] The tribunal noted nonetheless that it had to focus on the "effective beginning of a practice causing injury to the claimant" and not on the speech itself.[153] It then categorized government measures in general into three types: "one time act," "continuous act," and "composite act."[154] The question here was whether the disputed act was a continuous one (i.e., "the same act extending throughout a period of time") or a composite one (i.e., "a series of different acts that extend over that period").[155] In this regard, the tribunal found that El Salvador's alleged failure to grant permits was not conclusive before December 13, 2007, because there remained the possibility that they might be granted later.[156] In other words, for the tribunal, "an omission to act does not necessarily affect the parties as long as it is not definitive; and an omission could remain non-definitive throughout a period during which it could be cured by a positive act."[157] The tribunal did not view this omission as a composite act since it was not "a different legal animal from the several acts that comprise it."[158] Rather, it was a continuous act that commenced after the claimant filed the request for a permit and continued after the change of nationality[159] as "the controversy began with a problem over the non-granting of the permits and concession; and it remained a controversy over a practice of not granting the mining permits and concession."[160]

Based on the parties' submissions, the claimant's corporate restructuring could be considered an abuse of process, had it been done after one of these three suggested critical moments or dividing lines: (1) when the dispute was foreseeable; (2) when the dispute occurred; and (3) when the dispute was submitted to a tribunal.[161] The tribunal swiftly dismissed the third option as it agreed with the respondent's contention that this moment "would always be after the change of nationality and the change could thus never be abusive."[162] Then, it differentiated between "abuse of process" and jurisdiction *ratione temporis*.[163] Jurisdiction *ratione temporis* concerns the principle of nonretroactivity application of treaties. That is, the relevant BIT is applicable only when the dispute occurs after a claimant becomes a national of one of the contracting parties of the BIT.[164] Hence, the critical moment is when the dispute occurs. As for

151. *Ibid.*, para. 2.55.
152. *Ibid.*, paras. 2.58, 2.60.
153. *Ibid.*, para. 2.61.
154. *Ibid.*, para. 2.67, *referring to* Draft Articles on Responsibility of States for Internationally Wrongful Acts, with commentaries, 2001, Yearbook of the International Law Commission, 2001, vol. II, Part Two, pp. 59-64 ("ILC Commentaries").
155. *Ibid.*, paras. 2.69-2.70, 2.72.
156. *Ibid.*, para. 2.84.
157. *Ibid.*, para. 2.91.
158. *Ibid.*, para. 2.88.
159. *Ibid.*, para. 2.94.
160. *Ibid.*, para. 2.92.
161. *Ibid.*, para. 2.96.
162. *Ibid.*, paras. 2.98-2.99.
163. *Ibid.*, para. 2.101.
164. *Ibid.*, para. 2.103.

abuse of process, the relevant date "must necessarily be earlier in time" than that.[165] Accordingly, the tribunal concluded that had the claimant "changed its nationality during that continuous practice knowing of an actual or specific future dispute, thus manipulating the process under CAFTA and the ICSID Convention in bad faith to gain unwarranted access to international arbitration," it would be precluded from exercising jurisdiction.[166] Concerning this condition of the claimant's awareness of the dispute, the tribunal explained in an oft-cited paragraph:

> [T]he dividing-line occurs when the relevant party can see an actual dispute or can foresee a specific future dispute as a very high probability and not merely as a possible controversy. In the Tribunal's view, before that dividing-line is reached, there will be ordinarily no abuse of process; but after that dividing-line is passed, there ordinarily will be. The answer in each case will, however, depend upon its particular facts and circumstances, as in this case. As already indicated above, the Tribunal is here more concerned with substance than semantics; and it recognises that, as a matter of practical reality, this dividing-line will rarely be a thin red line, but will include a significant grey area.[167]

As the relevant continuous act (the disputed measure) took place from March 2008 onward and became known to the claimant only after the delivery of President Saca's speech on March 11, 2008, the tribunal held that the claimant could not foresee such an act before its corporate restructuring on December 13, 2007. Therefore, the tribunal concluded that the restructuring was not an abuse of process.[168]

The *Pac Rim* tribunal, so it seems, has notably lowered the temporal threshold of what constitutes an abuse as compared with that of the *Phoenix* tribunal. It found that an abuse could happen earlier in time—before a dispute occurred. An abusive corporate restructuring can be found even if there is no preexisting dispute, provided that the investor foresees the potential dispute at the time of restructuring. This is different from *Phoenix*, where an abuse was found to happen later in time—after a dispute occurred. Hence, applying the *Pac Rim* standard, in order to gain access to investment treaty arbitration, a potential claimant must prepare itself much in advance before its relationship with the state turns sour. A careful reading as to how the respondent framed its argument on this point may shed some light on the tribunal's findings.

At first glance, one may find the respondent's arguments in line with the decisions in *Phoenix* and its progeny. Namely, in part of its memorial, which was reproduced in the award in verbatim,[169] the respondent argued that the claimant abused the arbitration system by engaging in "a *retrospective* gaming of the system to gain jurisdiction for an *existing* dispute based on *existing* facts (emphasis in the original)."[170] Likewise, in its reply, the respondent contended that "by initiating CAFTA arbitration for a dispute that had already begun before Pac Rim Cayman's

165. *Ibid.*, para. 2.107.
166. *Ibid.*
167. *Ibid.*, para. 2.99.
168. *Ibid.*, paras. 2.109-2.110.
169. *Ibid.*, para. 2.19.
170. *El Salvador's Memorial, supra* n. 115, para. 18.

change of nationality,"[171] the claimant had committed an abuse. Lastly, in part of its post-hearing brief reproduced in the award,[172] the respondent wrote that the abuse resulted from the claimant's change of nationality "to initiate ICSID arbitration proceedings for a pre-existing dispute."[173] However, a close reading of these pleadings reveals that the respondent's understanding of the terms "existing dispute" or "pre-existing dispute" extended to cover the dispute that is foreseeable.[174] In so doing, the respondent relied heavily on the *AdT* award.

How the respondent shaped its argument significantly affected the tribunal's analysis, which noted that an abuse of process would be found when the disputed measure was completed before the restructuring:

> The Tribunal considers first whether the relevant measure or measures constitute one-time acts that were completed before the Claimant's change of nationality in December 2007. If this were the case, in the Tribunal's view, it would follow on the particular facts of this case, that the Claimant's change of nationality would be an abuse of process by the Claimant. However, if the relevant one-time acts all took place after such change of nationality in or after March 2008, in the Tribunal's view, it would follow on the particular facts of this case, that such change would not be an abuse of process.[175]

Nonetheless, later in the award, the tribunal added that an abuse might also occur when the restructuring was made by a claimant being "fully aware of [a] future dispute."[176] Having explained the doctrine of abuse of rights, the tribunal then applied it to the facts of the case. As the disputed measure concerned the respondent's omission to issue permits, which was a negative measure, it was difficult to pinpoint the exact moment when the omission was definitive as it might always be possible that the permits would be granted.[177] Finally, the tribunal treated President Saca's speech on March 11, 2008, as the critical date on which the claimant could be aware of "an actual or specific future dispute with the Respondent" and thus concluded that there was no abuse.[178] Given the tribunal's lack of explanation regarding the application of the abuse of process doctrine, it was unclear whether (and to what extent) the fact that the claimant's request for permits had never been granted affected the final outcome.[179]

That a change of nationality prior to a dispute could constitute an abuse was followed in subsequent cases. Roughly eight months after the *Pac Rim* award was

---

171. Pac Rim Cayman LLC v. The Republic of El Salvador, ICSID Case NO. ARB/09/12, The Republic of El Salvador's Reply Objections to Jurisdiction, para. 9 (January 31, 2011) ("*El Salvador's Reply*").
172. *Pac Rim, supra* n. 146, para. 2.20.
173. Pac Rim Cayman LLC v. The Republic of El Salvador, ICSID Case NO. ARB/09/12, The Republic of El Salvador's Post-Hearing Brief Objections to Jurisdiction, para. 2 (June 10, 2011) ("*El Salvador's PHB*").
174. *El Salvador's Memorial, supra* n. 170, paras. 85-87; *El Salvador's Reply, supra* n. 171, paras. 39-40; *El Salvador's PHB, supra* n. 173, paras. 3, 44.
175. *Pac Rim, supra* n. 146, para. 2.79.
176. *Ibid.*, para. 2.100.
177. *Ibid.*, para. 2.84.
178. *Ibid.*, para. 2.109.
179. The tribunal's explanation on this point was remarkably short (paras. 2.107-2.109), considering the length of the whole "Abuse of Process" part (paras. 2.1-2.111).

rendered, the *Tidewater v. Venezuela* tribunal, a member of which was Professor Stern, approved this approach.[180] This case concerned Venezuela's alleged maltreatments and eventually, in early May 2009, expropriation of the claimants' investment in marine support services to the oil industry.[181] Venezuela argued that the claimants committed an abuse as, in anticipation of the dispute, they incorporated Tidewater Barbados to own and control their business in Venezuela on March 9, 2009, so that they could arbitrate under the Barbados-Venezuela BIT.[182] Citing Professor Douglas' work as its authority, the tribunal said it would determine whether "the objective purpose of the restructuring was to facilitate access to an investment treaty tribunal with respect to a claim that was within the reasonable contemplation of the investor."[183]

Subsequently, the tribunal held that it could not find any evidence showing that there was a reasonable prospect of expropriation in December 2008 (when the restructuring process commenced) and March 2009 (when the restructuring was completed). In so doing, it discussed both parties' behaviors during the period. It noted that the claimants continued to make additional investment in their business,[184] and there was no sign that the business would have been expropriated, notwithstanding the fact that the respondent seized an unrelated company's oil rig in January 2009.[185] In particular, in the tribunal's opinion, the expropriation "was introduced without warning and passed into law over just three days from 4 to 7 May 2009."[186] Therefore, the tribunal had jurisdiction and the case was admissible.[187]

It should be noted that, despite the timing of the award, the *Tidewater* tribunal surprisingly did not refer to the *Pac Rim* award to support its legal analysis. Rather, it merely cited the *Venezuela Holdings* tribunal's observation that a corporate restructuring made to obtain BIT protections with respect to a preexisting dispute would be considered, as the *Phoenix* tribunal wrote, "an abusive manipulation of the system" of investment treaty arbitration.[188] Yet, as discussed earlier, the *Phoenix* and *Venezuela Holdings* awards did not mention the foreseeable dispute or the dispute that was reasonably in contemplation. As such, the tribunal seemed to have created new jurisprudence based largely on Professor Douglas' observation.

Pac Rim's distinction between the lack of jurisdiction *ratione temporis* and the abuse of rights was later endorsed and elaborated in *ConocoPhillips v. Venezuela*[189] and *Lao Holdings v. Lao*.[190] In the former award, the tribunal opined that it was justified to add extra limits to textual jurisdictional requirements to prevent any treaty abuse.[191]

180. *Tidewater, supra* n. 39. Yet, the *Tidewater* tribunal did not cite the *Pac Rim* award.
181. *Ibid.*, paras. 6, 171-173.
182. *Ibid.*, para. 144.
183. *Ibid.*, para. 150, *citing* Douglas, *supra* n. 71, at 465.
184. *Ibid.*, para. 194.
185. *Ibid.*, para. 195.
186. *Ibid.*, para. 196.
187. *Ibid.*, para. 198.
188. *Ibid.*, para. 146, *citing Venezuela Holdings, supra* n. 39, paras. 204-205; *Phoenix, supra* n. 41, para. 144.
189. *ConocoPhillips, supra* n. 121.
190. Lao Holdings N.V. v. The Lao People's Democratic Republic, ICSID Case No. ARB(AF)/12/6, Decision on Jurisdiction (February 21, 2014) ("*Lao Holdings*").
191. *ConocoPhillips, supra* n. 121, para. 274.

However, it held that the disputed measures were not "in prospect at the times of the restructurings."[192] Moreover, it noted that the claimants' intention to continue operating and investing in the businesses was another essential factor showing that there was no abuse.[193] Therefore, the tribunal dismissed the respondent's jurisdictional challenge[194] despite its finding that the sole purpose of the corporate restructuring was to secure access to ICSID arbitration.[195] In *Lao Holdings*, the tribunal, referring to the *Pac Rim* award, eloquently differentiated abuse of rights and jurisdiction *ratione temporis* objections as follows:

> [I]f a company changes its nationality in order to gain ICSID jurisdiction at a moment when things have started to deteriorate so that a dispute is highly probable, it can be considered an abuse of process, but for an objection based on *ratione temporis* to be upheld, the dispute has to have actually arisen before the critical date to conform to the general principle of non-retroactivity in the interpretation and application of international treaties.[196]

Nonetheless, as the respondent did not raise an objection on the ground of abuse of rights, it was not necessary for the tribunal to consider the matter.[197]

Although the legal possibility that a tribunal may not exercise jurisdiction due to its finding of abuse of rights had seemingly been firmly established in the awards previously discussed, it should be noted that no corporate restructuring done *before* a dispute arose had been found to constitute an abuse of rights therein. Namely, in *Phoenix*, *ST-AD*, and *Transglobal*, the tribunals treated the investors' changes of nationality as abuses because the modifications were made to transform *preexisting* domestic disputes into international ones. On the other hand, while the *Pac Rim*, *Tidewater*, and *ConocoPhillips* tribunals expressly stated that a restructuring completed before a dispute occurs could also constitute an abuse, no such abuse was identified. It was not until the tribunal in *Gremcitel v. Peru*[198] rendered its award that a genuine abuse of rights objection was for the first time upheld.

The dispute in *Gremcitel* concerned the government's treatment of land owned by Gremcitel, a Peruvian subsidiary, which was ultimately controlled by Ms. Renée Rose Levy, a French national. The respondent alleged that the claimants were not investors under the France-Peru BIT as Ms. Levy's shareholding in Gremcitel was fabricated, and thus the tribunal lacked jurisdiction *ratione temporis*. Also, it contended that the claimants' transfer of shares was made in a hurry with "the sole purpose of attracting the France-Peru BIT protection at a time the dispute had either already arisen or was at least entirely foreseeable" and accordingly constituted an abuse of right.[199] On the relationship between these two objections, the tribunal stated that "[i]f a claimant

192. *Ibid.*, para. 279.
193. *Ibid.*, para. 280.
194. *Ibid.*, para. 281.
195. *Ibid.*, para. 279.
196. *Lao Holdings*, *supra* n. 190, para. 76.
197. *Ibid.*, para. 83.
198. Renée Rose Levy and Gremcitel S.A. v. Republic of Peru, ICSID Case No. ARB/11/17, Award (July 9, 2015) ("*Gremcitel*").
199. *Ibid.*, para. 69.

acquires an investment after the date on which the challenged act occurred, the tribunal will normally lack jurisdiction *ratione temporis* and there will be no room for an abuse of process."[200]

The tribunal acknowledged that the BIT did not specify at what time a claimant must have acquired an investment for it to be protected under the treaty.[201] Nonetheless, it asserted that the nonretroactivity of treaties principle applied[202] and that an investment must be acquired before an alleged breach occurred for the tribunal to have jurisdiction over the dispute.[203] According to the tribunal, the critical date—the date that the alleged treaty breach occurred—would be the date "on which the State adopts the disputed measure, even when the measure represents the culmination of a process or sequence of events which may have started years earlier."[204] It found that the critical date here was October 18, 2007, which was the date on which a Peruvian authority enacted a resolution allegedly affecting the claimants' rights.[205] The tribunal observed that "the moment when the challenged acts occurred is not necessarily the same as the one when the dispute arose," given that "a breach or violation does not become a 'dispute' until the injured party identifies the breach or violation and objects to it." In any case, it found that these two moments were identical in this case as it accepted the claimants' understanding that October 18, 2007, was the date on which the dispute arose.[206]

Having considered whether Ms. Levy was either a direct or indirect interest (or share) holder of Gremcitel before the critical date, the tribunal held that the claimants failed to prove that Ms. Levy acquired any indirect control over Gremcitel in 2005.[207] But it accepted the claimants' evidence that Ms. Levy became a majority shareholder of Gremcitel on October 9, 2007.[208] As a consequence, the tribunal concluded that it had jurisdiction *ratione personae* and *ratione temporis*.[209] Notwithstanding this finding, it proceeded to consider whether an "abuse of process" had occurred.

Having observed that the parties had not discussed whether an abuse of process objection is a matter of jurisdiction or admissibility, the tribunal decided not to touch upon the issue. It concurred with the *Pac Rim* tribunal that this differentiation was "a distinction without a difference" since it would have had no impact on the case outcome.[210] While the tribunal acknowledged that some corporate restructurings could be tantamount to abuses,[211] it confirmed the general understanding that a restructuring with an aim to acquire treaty benefits is not an illegitimate activity per se.[212] To be

200. *Ibid.*, para. 182.
201. *Ibid.*, para. 143.
202. *Ibid.*, para. 147.
203. *Ibid.*, para. 146.
204. *Ibid.*, para. 149.
205. *Ibid.*, para. 150.
206. *Ibid.*, paras. 166-167.
207. *Ibid.*, paras. 152-155.
208. *Ibid.*, paras. 156-160.
209. *Ibid.*, paras. 169-173.
210. *Ibid.*, paras. 180-181, *citing Pac Rim*, *supra* n. 146, para. 2.10.
211. *Ibid.*, para. 183, *citing Phoenix*, *supra* n. 41, para. 144.
212. *Ibid.*, para. 184, *citing Tidewater*, *supra* n. 39, para. 184.

considered an abuse, a restructuring must be made when a specific future dispute is foreseeable "as a very high probability and not merely as a possible controversy,"[213] and the tribunal must take into account "all the circumstances of the case."[214]

The timing of the restructuring was of particular importance in this case because the date of the restructuring (October 9, 2007) was very close to the date of the dispute (October 18, 2007). For the tribunal, this proximity was not a coincidence[215] as the conflict had been looming since 2005 when a number of claimants' acquaintances became aware of a report issued in 2005 on which the disputed 2007 resolution was based.[216] The tribunal also thoroughly scrutinized the hastiness of the share transfer in 2007. As one of the claimants' consultants had learned about the formalization of the measure and must have had informed the claimants of this fact, the tribunal found that the only reason for the transfer of shares was Ms. Levy's French nationality.[217] Having disapproved of this action in 2007 and the claimants' attempt to prove the alleged transfer of shares in 2005, which turned out to be untrustworthy (or even deceitful), the tribunal held that the claimants' behavior showed "a pattern of manipulative conduct that casts a bad light on their actions."[218] It therefore concluded that the 2007 restructuring constituted an abuse of process[219] and ordered that the claimants be responsible for the costs of proceedings and pay the respondent a reasonable amount of money as a contribution to its fees and expenditures.[220]

The next award holding that the claimant's corporate restructuring is an abuse is that of *Philip Morris v. Australia*.[221] Yet, unlike the situation in *Gremcitel*, where the interval between the restructuring and the disputed measure was very brief (less than ten days), the interval in this case was approximately one year. Due to the importance of the substantive legal controversy at stake (whether Australia's adoption of tobacco plain packaging measures violated its investment treaty obligation), the incident has been a subject of much discussion both before and after the award was rendered.[222]

213. *Ibid.*, para. 185.
214. *Ibid.*, para. 186.
215. *Ibid.*, para. 188.
216. *Ibid.*, para. 189.
217. *Ibid.*, paras. 190-191.
218. *Ibid.*, para. 194.
219. *Ibid.*, para. 195.
220. *Ibid.*, paras. 201-202.
221. Philip Morris Asia Limited v. The Common Wealth of Australia, PCA Case No. 2012-12, Award on Jurisdiction and Admissibility (December 17, 2015) ("*Philip Morris*").
222. *See, e.g.*, Voon, Mitchell & Munro, *supra* n. 41; Jarrod Hepbern & Luke Nottage, *Case Comments: A Procedural Win for Public Health Measures*, 18 J. World Inv. & Trade 307 (2017); Deborah Gleeson & Sharon Friel, *Emerging Threats to Public Health from Regional Trade Agreements*, 381 Viewpoint 1507 (2013); Ankita Ritwik, *Tobacco Packaging Arbitration and the State's Ability to Legislate*, 54 Harv. Int'l L.J. 523 (2013); Tania Voon & Andrew D. Mitchell, *Implications of International Investment Law for Plain Tobacco Packaging: Lessons from the Hong Kong-Australia BIT*, in Tania Voon et al. (eds.), Public Health and Plain Packaging of Cigarettes (Cheltenham: Edward Elgar, 2012), 137; Tania Voon & Andrew Mitchell, *Time to Quit? Assessing International Investment Claims Against Plain Tobacco Packaging in Australia*, 14 J. Int'l Econ. L. 515 (2011); Tania Voon & Andrew D. Mitchell, *Philip Morris vs. Tobacco Control: Two Wins for Public Health but Uncertainty Remains* (September 12, 2016), http://ccsi.columbia.edu/files/2013/10/No-182-Voon-and-Mitchell-FINAL.pdf (accessed May 17, 20 19); Luke Nottage, *Consumer Product Safety Regulation and Investor-State Arbitration Policy*

The dispute revolved around the Australian Parliament's enactment of the Tobacco Plain Packaging Act (TPPA) on November 21, 2011. Australia challenged the tribunal's competence to hear this case on the ground that Philip Morris Asia, a Hong Kong company, acquired its interest in Philip Morris' business in Australia only after the government had announced its plan to reform the laws concerning tobacco control. It argued, *inter alia*, that this practice constituted an abuse of right and as such Philip Morris Asia was barred from exercising its right to bring the dispute to arbitration.[223] It explained that "the exercise of the right in such a manner as to prejudice the interests of the other contracting party arising out of the treaty is unreasonable and is considered as inconsistent with the *bona fide* execution of the treaty obligation, and a breach of the treaty."[224] According to the tribunal, the concept of foreseeability applied.[225] Thus, the tribunal's factual findings, especially those concerning temporal elements (i.e., When did the "specific dispute" arise? When could the investor foresee the dispute? When did the restructuring take place?) were crucial to its final decision.

Referring to the *Gremcitel* award, the tribunal confirmed the difference between *ratione temporis* jurisdiction and abuse of rights objections.[226] Whereas the former concerned whether the investment was made before the alleged treaty violation,[227] the latter concerned whether the investment was made before the dispute became foreseeable. Hence, regarding the *ratione temporis* objection, the critical date was relatively obvious. It was when Australia adopted the disputed measure or when the claimant's rights were affected.[228] As it was clear in this case that the investment was made before the adoption of the TPPA, the tribunal concluded that it had jurisdiction *ratione temporis*.[229]

On the abuse of rights matter, the tribunal first surveyed pertinent cases. To begin with, it indicated that the threshold of this test, which was of an objective character, was high,[230] and the mere fact of corporate restructuring to gain access to investment arbitration did not automatically constitute an abuse of rights.[231] Yet, while "it is legitimate for an investor to seek to protect itself from the *general risk of future disputes*,"[232] "a restructuring undertaken to gain treaty protection in light of a *specific dispute* can constitute an abuse."[233] For this reason, the time of restructuring (in relation to the time of dispute) was of critical importance. A number of incidents could be significant to the tribunal's analysis: (1) the date when the restructuring plan was introduced; (2) the date when the restructuring was decided; (3) the date when the

and Practice after Philip Morris Asia v Australia (2012), https://papers.ssrn.com/sol3/papers.cfm?abstract_id=2041680 (accessed May 17, 2019).

223. *Philip Morris*, *supra* n. 221, para. 400.
224. Philip Morris Asia Limited v. The Common Wealth of Australia, PCA Case No. 2012-12, Statement of Defence, Vol. A, para. 138, reproduced in *Philip Morris*, *supra* n. 221, para. 400.
225. *Philip Morris*, *supra* n. 221, para. 554.
226. *Ibid.*, para. 527.
227. *Ibid.*, para. 529.
228. *Ibid.*, paras. 530-533, referring to *Gremcitel*, *supra* n. 198, para. 149.
229. *Ibid.*, paras. 533-534.
230. *Ibid.*, paras. 539, 550.
231. *Ibid.*, paras. 540-544.
232. *Ibid.*, para. 545 (emphasis added).
233. *Ibid.*, para. 549 (emphasis added).

restructuring was successfully implemented; (4) the date when the specific dispute became foreseeable; and (5) the date when the specific dispute materialized. In this regard, the tribunal usefully "juxtaposed" relevant incidents within Philip Morris group of companies and political developments in Australia. Specifically, the tribunal noted that Australia began considering to adopt tobacco control measures in 2008;[234] Philip Morris group discussed legal advice as to possible corporate restructuring and investment treaty protection in mid-2010;[235] the Rudd government announced its intention to introduce plain packaging legislation on April 29, 2010;[236] Philip Morris group internally approved the plan to transfer Australian subsidiaries to Philip Morris Asia on September 3, 2010;[237] the restructuring was formally completed on February 23, 2011;[238] the tobacco plain packaging bill was introduced into the parliament on April 6, 2011;[239] and the TPPA was finally enacted on November 21, 2011.[240]

Notwithstanding the factual complexity, the tribunal's analysis is somewhat cursory. The tribunal swiftly held that the time when the dispute was foreseeable was on April 29, 2010, when "Prime Minister Rudd and Health Minister Roxon unequivocally announced the Government's intention to introduce Plain Packaging Measures," as "there was no uncertainty about the Government's intention to introduce plain packaging [...] and there was a reasonable prospect that legislation equivalent to the Plain Packaging Measures would eventually be enacted."[241] The tribunal arrived at this conclusion although it was considerably uncertain as to whether the government would have had enough votes in the parliament to pass the bill. As the tribunal itself acknowledged, there was a huge gap of nineteen months between such an announcement and the passing of the legislation.[242] Many crucial events happened during that period: Prime Minister Rudd was replaced by Deputy Prime Minister Julia Gillard (June 24, 2010);[243] the House of Representatives was dissolved (July 19, 2010);[244] following the federal election, the proponent party (the Labor Party) and the opposition coalition of the plain packaging measures had an equal number of members in the House (August 21, 2010);[245] the Parliament dropped the Fielding Bill, which was TPP's predecessor (August 26, 2010);[246] the new Labor Party-led minority government was formed with insufficient votes to pass the TPP (September 14, 2010);[247] and Health Minister Roxon admitted that the government confronted a "very big fight on [its] hands" to pass the law (May 22, 2011).[248] It was not until May 26, 2011, that a press

234. *Ibid.*, para. 556.
235. *Ibid.*, para. 557.
236. *Ibid.*
237. *Ibid.*, para. 560.
238. *Ibid.*, para. 563.
239. *Ibid.*, para. 564.
240. *Ibid.*, para. 565.
241. *Ibid.*, para. 566.
242. *Ibid.*, para. 567.
243. *Ibid.*, para. 557.
244. *Ibid.*
245. *Ibid.*, para. 560.
246. *Ibid.*
247. *Ibid.*, para. 561.
248. *Ibid.*, para. 564.

report surfaced that the Labor Party had secured enough votes to pass the legislation.[249] Yet, the tribunal trivialized this uncertainty of the outcome and instead focused on the certainty of the government's intention to push forward the tobacco control measures.[250] It thus concluded:

> [A]t the time of the restructuring, the dispute that materialised subsequently was foreseeable to the Claimant. Indeed, at least after the 29 April 2010 announcement, it was reasonably foreseeable that legislation equivalent to the Plain Packaging Measures would eventually be enacted and, consequently, a dispute would arise.[251]

In addition to these temporal elements, the tribunal also discussed the claimant's motivation to modify its corporate structure. It expounded that no abuse of rights would have been found had it been that, regardless of the timing, "the restructuring was justified independently of the possibility of bringing such a claim."[252] It then considered the claimant's arguments that the restructuring was put in place to: (1) complete Philip Morris' group-wide process of restructuring; (2) improve the group's management structure; (3) minimize its tax liabilities; (4) optimize its cash flow; and (5) gain access to the BIT protection.[253] Having considered the parties' arguments on these contentions, the tribunal held that factors (1) to (4) were not "determinative" factors, as the claimant's submitted evidence was unconvincing.[254] It thus concluded that obtaining the BIT protection was the main and probably the sole reason for the restructuring.[255] The tribunal relied on this finding as a supplementary reason[256] for its final conclusion that the claimant's commencement of this arbitration proceedings was an abuse of rights as the restructuring occurred when the dispute had already been foreseeable.[257] Therefore, the case was inadmissible.[258]

VI APPRAISAL AND PROPOSED ALTERNATIVES

It seems that the doctrine of abuse of rights vis-à-vis corporate restructuring to gain access to ISDS has been firmly established in investment arbitration jurisprudence. It would not be an overstatement to assert that this development has been fostered by two leading figures in the field, Professors Brigitte Stern and Gabriel Kaufmann-Kohler, who served as arbitrators in almost every case discussed in this chapter. The former was the presiding arbitrator in *Phoenix* and *ST-Ad* and the respondent-appointed arbitrator in *Pac Rim*, *Tidewater*, and *Lao Holdings*. The latter was the presiding

249. *Ibid.*
250. *Ibid.*, paras. 567-568.
251. *Ibid.*, para. 569.
252. *Ibid.*, para. 570.
253. *Ibid.*, paras. 571-581.
254. *Ibid.*, paras. 582-583.
255. *Ibid.*, para. 584.
256. *Ibid.*, para. 587 ("The Tribunal's conclusion is reinforced by a review of the evidence regarding the Claimant's professed alternative reasons for the restructuring").
257. *Ibid.*, para. 585.
258. *Ibid.*, para. 588.

arbitrator in *Gremcitel* and the claimant-appointed arbitrator in *Venezuela Holdings* and *Philip Morris*.[259]

Even though only two jurists were the principal architects of this doctrine of abuse of rights, its future application is unpredictable due to inconsistencies in terminology and in the specific factors which indicate abuse. First, the legal terminologies adopted by tribunals to denote this particular situation have been inconsistent. Two phrases are of particular importance and sometimes used interchangeably:[260] "abuse of rights" and "abuse of process."[261] While it may be obvious that the "right" allegedly abused here is the investor's treaty right to submit its claim to arbitration, it is quite unclear as to what "process" is being abused here, as the term "process" can mean different things, including the arbitration process (or procedure) in a particular arbitration case and the arbitration process (or system) in general. When using the phrase "abuse of process," many tribunals, in fact, exclusively refer to the latter situation—"abuse of the system of international investment arbitration."[262]

In addition, the concept of abuse of process (or system) is vague as it could cover both the lack of jurisdiction *ratione temporis* and the abuse of rights in the context of corporate restructuring. This conflation can clearly be seen in *Phoenix* where the tribunal ruled that a supposedly simple case of lack of jurisdiction *ratione temporis* was also tantamount to an abuse. It was not until the *Pac Rim* award was rendered that these two scenarios were explicitly delineated.

Given the confusion caused by this reality, we suggest that tribunals adopt the phrase "abuse of rights" when they discuss the investor's attempt to gain access to international investment arbitration by way of corporate restructuring. The phrase "abuse of process" should be reserved for a situation where the disputing parties abuse their procedural rights before an arbitral tribunal, e.g., frivolous challenges and delay tactics.[263] This categorization would conform to the recent ICJ judgment in *Immunities and Criminal Proceedings*, in which the Court noted that there is a distinction between an abuse of rights and an abuse of process; although their underlying justifications are the same, their consequences may be different.[264] All abuses of process seem to be abuses of rights, but not all abuses of rights are necessarily abuses of process. Particularly, an abuse of process, according to the Court, "goes to the procedure before a court or tribunal,"[265] whereas an abuse of rights can involve both substance and

259. One may also add Dr. Andrés Rigo Sureda to this group, as he sat as the presiding arbitrator in *Transglobal* and the claimant-appointed arbitrator in *Tidewater*. However, in the authors' opinion, the precedential effect of these two cases are much less compared to cases like *Phoenix*, *Gremcitel*, and *Philip Morris*.

260. *See, e.g.*, *Phoenix*, *supra* n. 41, paras. 93, 100, 107, 143; *Gremcitel*, *supra* n. 198, para. 183.

261. For example, whereas the *Pac Rim* and *ST-AD* tribunals used the phrase "abuse of process," the *Tidewater* and *Philip Morris* tribunals adopted the phrase "abuse of rights." Notwithstanding these different nomenclatures, these tribunals were talking about the same scenarios.

262. *Phoenix*, *supra* n. 41, para. 144; *Pac Rim*, *supra* n. 146, para. 2.107.

263. Robert Pfeiffer & Stephan Wilske, *Introduction to Guerrilla Tactics in International Arbitration*, in Günther J. Horvath & Stephan Wilske (eds), Guerilla Tactics in International Arbitration (Alphen aan de Rijn: Kluwer Law International, 2013), 9-11.

264. Immunities and Criminal Proceedings (Equatorial Guinea v. France), Preliminary Objections, Judgment, I.C.J. Reports 2018, p. 335.

265. *Ibid.*, at 336.

procedure.[266] In this sense, an abuse of process is just a special application of the prohibition of abuse of rights.[267] This distinction would also alleviate the risk of conflating the issues of jurisdiction *ratione temporis* and abuse, originally found in *Phoenix* and, most recently, in *Transglobal*.

Next, ambiguity persists as to the factors that tribunals should take into consideration when addressing a claimant's alleged abuse. According to the current jurisprudence, it is indisputable that timing is the most crucial factor in determining whether an abuse occurs. To be considered a bona fide exercise of right, the investor's corporate restructuring must be made prior to the moment the dispute is foreseeable. Thus, the proximity of the time of restructuring and the time of dispute is a critical indicator as to whether the investor could have expected the dispute at the time of restructuring. On this point, the *Gremcitel* award may represent the most suitable situation in which the abuse of rights objection could succeed, given that the date of the corporate restructuring (had it actually happened as the claimants' alleged manipulation of evidence suggested) and the date on which the disputed sovereign measure became public were only nine days apart.[268] The situation was utterly different in *Philip Morris* as the period in question, according to the tribunal's evaluation, lasted roughly for nine months.[269]

Accordingly, how a tribunal selects the point at which a dispute becomes foreseeable will materially affect its verdict. A comparison between the tribunals' findings on this point in *Pac Rim* and *Philip Morris* is illustrative. In the *Pac Rim* dispute, which concerned the state's omission to issue permits, the tribunal chose the time when the head of the government declared its categorical intention not to grant any new mining permits (March 11, 2008) as the critical moment at which the claimant became aware of the dispute. In so doing, it ignored the respondent's previous refusals of the claimant's requests for relevant permits, a significant part of which had occurred before the date of the claimant's corporate restructuring (December 13, 2007). By contrast, the *Philip Morris* tribunal treated the date on which two prominent cabinet members announced their intention to adopt plain packaging measures (April 29, 2010) as the critical moment, elaborating that it was the point in time when there was a reasonable prospect that the contentious measures would be eventually adopted. Hence, the tribunal ignored subsequent events demonstrating the uncertainty that the parliament might not have passed the bill at issue. The finding led to its conclusion that the restructuring within the Philip Morris group (completed on February 23, 2011) took place roughly ten months after the dispute became foreseeable.

There are a number of relevant temporal points in this analysis: (1) the moment when the restructuring plan is initially considered; (2) the moment when the plan is approved internally by the investor; (3) the moment when the restructuring is formally completed; (4) the moment when the disputed measure is first discussed by the relevant government authority; (5) the moment when the relevant authority announces its intention to impose the measure; (6) the moment when it is certain that the

266. Kolb, *supra* n. 135, at 904.
267. *Ibid.*
268. *Gremcitel, supra* n. 198, para. 188.
269. *Philip Morris, supra* n. 221, paras. 563, 565.

measure will be adopted; (7) the moment when the measure is completely adopted; and (8) the moment when the dispute between the investor and the state arises. Whereas points (1), (2), and (3) concern the timing of corporate restructuring, points (4), (5), (6), (7), and (8) are related to the timing of dispute. Which two alternatives, then, should the tribunal treat as the time of restructuring and the time when the dispute is foreseeable? The current trend seems to be that tribunals usually treat point (3) as the time of restructuring and either point (5) or point (6) as the time when the dispute is foreseeable. Thus, the time gap between these two moments is getting shorter. Consequently, it is more likely that a tribunal finds an abuse as exemplified in *Philip Morris*.

A number of questions persist. First, having studied these relevant awards, we observe that the element of the claimant's *animus nocendi* is a vital factor in the tribunal's analysis. That is, in every case where the tribunal finds an abuse, the claimant's intention to transform a preexisting or foreseeable dispute that could not be brought before ISDS to a qualified one can be perceived. In other words, the claimant's awareness of the possible dispute at the time of restructuring must necessarily be proven to be its principal or sole motivation to change its corporate structure. Accordingly, if a focus here is on the motivation behind the restructuring, it should not be point (3) but either point (1) or point (2) (the claimant's internal proposal to restructure or its subsequent internal approval of the operation), which is considered a decisive restructuring moment.

Second, as for the element of dispute foreseeability, the possible findings are even more uncertain. In *Pac Rim*, the tribunal treated the date on which the head of state's unequivocal statement that no permits shall be granted was made as the date when the dispute became known or foreseeable.[270] In *Tidewater*, the tribunal did not consider the state's expropriation of other similar investments as a sign indicating the foreseeability of the expropriation of the claimant's investment.[271] Lastly, in *Philip Morris*, the tribunal treated the timing of the Prime Minister's and Minister of Health's announcement of their policy decision, despite its uncertain support, as the moment at which the dispute became fairly certain.[272] Apparently, the tribunals in *Pac Rim* and *Tidewater* disregarded certain circumstantial evidence showing the respondent states' conceivable animus toward the investors—El Salvador's prior constant refusals to grant mining permits and Venezuela's expropriation of other comparable investments—and ruled in favor of the investors. By contrast, the *Philip Morris* tribunal highlighted the importance of the executive declaration to introduce the allegedly unlawful measure despite the uncertainty as to whether the effort would eventually materialize.

The problem can be more complicated, given the difficulty of determining what constitutes a dispute and when it erupts. On this matter, the Permanent Court of International Justice's (PCIJ) judgment in *Mavrommatis* has often been cited as a point of departure. According to the Court, a dispute "is a disagreement on a point of law or

270. *Pac Rim*, *supra* n. 146, paras. 2.109-2.110.
271. *Tidewater*, *supra* n. 39, paras. 196-198.
272. *Philip Morris*, *supra* n. 221, para. 566.

fact, a conflict of legal views or of interests between two persons."[273] The Court in *Peace Treaties* adopted a similar view, noting that a dispute involves "a situation in which the two sides hold clearly opposite views concerning the question of the performance or non-performance of certain treaty obligations."[274] Subsequently, in *South West Africa*, the ICJ wrote that a dispute occurs when "the claim of one party is positively opposed by the other."[275] Against this backdrop, there must be disagreements between the parties for a dispute to exist. Hence, in investment treaty arbitration, a dispute could arise either at the time the state's allegedly unlawful action occurs or thereafter.[276] Yet, the reality may not be straightforward. As the award in *Pac Rim* shows, in the case of a state's omission, it may not be simple to pinpoint an exact moment at which a dispute erupts. It goes without saying that, in this kind of case, to prove whether a dispute is foreseeable at a certain point could be particularly onerous and lead to ambiguities. A similar observation applies where the investor's injury results from a series of measures covering an extended period, i.e., creeping expropriation.[277]

Apart from the temporal factor, the question remains if other factors should play any role in the tribunal's deliberation. Notably, the fact as to whether the investor continues investing has frequently been mentioned. For instance, having found that the claimant had not been involved in any economic activity following the restructuring, the *Phoenix* tribunal affirmed that the claimant simply rearranged its business operation to gain access to ICSID arbitration, and therefore the investment was not made in good faith.[278] In *ConocoPhillips*, after its detailed discussion on the timeline of relevant events,[279] the tribunal succinctly stated in one paragraph that the claimant's record of continuing expenditure "is evidence telling strongly against any finding of treaty abuse."[280] The *Tidewater* tribunal considered the claimant's unceasing investment and submission of bids for new concessions to be an indication that the claimant could not foresee the dispute at the time of restructuring, which commenced approximately five months before the expropriation.[281] This observation shows that tribunals usually take into account the presence of the investor's financial contribution following the restructuring as indicative of whether the investor could foresee the dispute. Their

273. Mavrommatis Palestine Concessions (Greece v. U.K.), Judgment, 1924 P.C.I.J. (ser. B) No. 3 at 11 (August 30).
274. Interpretation of Peace Treaties with Bulgaria, Hungary and Romania, Advisory Opinion, March 30, 1950, p. 74.
275. South West Africa (Ethiopia v. South Africa; Liberia v. South Africa), Preliminary Objections, Judgment, I.C.J. Reports 1962, p. 328; *see* also Armed Activities on the Territory of the Congo (New Application : 2002) (Democratic Republic of the Congo v. Rwanda), Jurisdiction and Admissibility, Judgment, I.C.J. Reports 2006, p. 40, para. 90; Application of the International Convention on the Elimination of All Forms of Racial Discrimination (Georgia v. Russia) Preliminary Objection, Judgment of April 1, 2011, p. 84, para. 30.
276. Garay, *supra* n. 104, at 408.
277. W. Michael Reisman & Robert D. Sloane, *Indirect Expropriation and Its Valuation in the BIT Generation*, 75 Brit. Y.B. Int'l L. 115, 122-123 (2004).
278. *Phoenix*, *supra* n. 41, paras. 140-142.
279. *ConocoPhillips*, *supra* n. 121, paras. 276-279.
280. *Ibid.*, para. 280.
281. *Tidewater*, *supra* n. 39, paras. 193-194.

preliminary assumption is that a rational investor discerning any potential harm would not make additional investment given the looming business and political exposures. Nonetheless, this assumption might not always be correct, given the investor's opportunity to obtain returns in the form of compensation awarded by an investment treaty tribunal.

Another possible factor that could have played a vital role in the tribunal's deliberation process is the nature of dispute. As aforementioned, the *Philip Morris* case is probably the most obvious case whereby the abuse of rights doctrine has been loosely applied. The outcome has not prompted much criticism, however, particularly because of the substance of the claim, which concerned the government's police power to protect public health. Indeed, Australia's plain packaging effort falls in line with the international community's normative expectation of the need to regulate how tobacco products should be marketed to curb its consumption. The measure had been endorsed by the Framework Convention on Tobacco Control (FCTC), to which 181 states are contracting parties,[282] a number of whom have taken meaningful steps to implement it.[283] Thus, naturally, there had been much pressure on the tribunal that it reach the "right" verdict. Moreover, this case reinforced the contemporaneous growing antagonism against ISDS in general, as in April 2011 (two months before the filing of the notice of claim), the Gillard Government issued its trade policy statement declaring that ISDS clauses would no longer be included in any future trade and investment agreements.[284] Since then, Australia's policy toward ISDS has shifted to a moderate one, however.[285] The country had entered into a number of international agreements that contain ISDS provisions, including the Comprehensive and Progressive Agreement for Trans-Pacific Partnership (CPTPP) and the bilateral investment agreement with Uruguay. Currently, the Department of Foreign Affairs and Trade explains on its website that ISDS is not a threat to Australia's sovereignty.[286] Yet, regarding the CPTPP, the contracting parties have notably agreed to exclude claims concerning tobacco control measures from ISDS. Indisputably, the *Philip Morris* case has meritoriously raised public awareness that foreign investors could challenge Australia's and other

282. Article 11 of the FCTC (https://treaties.un.org/doc/Treaties/2003/05/20030506%2002-12%20PM/Ch_IX_04p.pdf); Guidelines for implementation of Article 11: Packaging and Labelling of Tobacco Products (https://www.who.int/fctc/treaty_instruments/adopted/Guidelines_Article_11_English.pdf?ua=1) https://treaties.un.org/pages/ViewDetails.aspx?src=TREATY&mtdsg_no=IX-4&chapter=9&clang=_en.
283. World Health Organization, Tobacco Plain Packaging: Global Status Update, v (2018) https://apps.who.int/iris/bitstream/handle/10665/275277/WHO-NMH-PND-NAC-18.9-eng.pdf?ua=1.
284. Jurgen Kurtz & Luke Nottage, *Investment Treaty Arbitration 'Down Under': Policy and Politics in Australia*, 30 ICSID Rev. 465, 469 (2015), *citing* Australian Government, Department of Foreign Affairs and Trade, Gillard Government Trade Policy Statement: Trading Our Way to More Jobs and Prosperity 14 (2011).
285. *Ibid.*, at 468.
286. About foreign investment, https://dfat.gov.au/trade/investment/Pages/investor-state-dispute-settlement.aspx (last visited September 22, 2020).

states' public policy laws and regulations before international tribunals[287] and thus has had a significant impact on their endorsement of ISDS.

By contrast, other tribunals seemed to be more lenient when sitting on disputes relating to clearly unlawful sovereign measures. For instance, in direct expropriation cases, where states expressly seize targeted investments without compensation, a number of tribunals tend to ignore relevant circumstantial evidence of deteriorated relationships between states and investors and choose critical dates that are more favorable to the investors. To illustrate, in *Venezuela Holdings*, in which Venezuela issued a nationalization decree to take the claimants' investment, the tribunal restrictively applied the doctrine of abuse of rights and merely declined to exercise its jurisdiction with respect to disputes arising prior to the restructuring, calling it "an abusive manipulation of the [ISDS] system."[288] As for the post-restructuring disputes, which include the dispute in relation to the nationalization decree, the tribunal did not consider whether the claimants could have foreseen them at the time of restructuring. A similar approach was adopted by the tribunal in *Tidewater*, in which Venezuela passed a statute to expropriate the claimants' operations and assets.[289]

Indeed, one may reasonably question, had the controversy in *Philip Morris* not concerned such a crucial public policy measure as the tobacco plain packaging arrangement, whether the tribunal's verdict would have been different. One may also ask if the doctrine of abuse of right, as it stands today, should be applied in a situation where a dispute concerns an obviously egregious state measure. For instance, suppose that a government has considered expropriating an investment, probably without paying full or even partial compensation, and announces today that it intends to do so at the earliest moment. A week later, the investor comes up with a resolution that restructuring must be done to ensure access to investment treaty arbitration. The restructuring is completed a month later, just before the government passes an expropriation decree. The application of the doctrine of abuse of rights in this situation could hinder the investor from attaining the only available remedy. Would not the investor in this situation deserve protection under international law? What harm against the state does its restructuring action cause? Simply put, is there a meaningful abuse here?

All in all, tribunals' deliberations on this abuse of right vis-à-vis corporate restructuring issue in investment treaty disputes involve a myriad of legal and policy considerations and require fact-intensive examination. As a result, each tribunal assigned with the task is expected to exercise considerable discretion, and rightly so, given the nature of the doctrine of abuse of rights. In the current jurisprudence, tribunals axiomatically treat investors' abuse as an admissibility issue. Hence, the tribunals' finding of an abuse generally leads to their refusal to hear the case, despite the fact that they have jurisdiction. We agree with this result, as the investor in this situation usually satisfies the jurisdictional requirements stipulated in the underlying

287. Leon E. Trakman, *Investor-State Arbitration: Evaluating Australia's Evolving Position*, 15 J. World Inv. & Trade 152, 162-163 (2014).
288. *Venezuela Holdings*, *supra* n. 39, para. 205.
289. *See supra* nn. 180-187.

treaties (i.e., *ratione voluntatis*, *ratione materiae*, *ratione personae*, and *ratione temporis*). In any case, as the ultimate outcome here is case dismissal, the *Pac Rim* tribunal rightly pointed out that the tribunal's decision as to whether an abuse concerns "the existence of jurisdiction" or "the exercise of jurisdiction" does not lead to different implications; it is "a distinction without a difference."[290]

Some controversies remain, however. First, is there an abuse at all in this scenario of corporate restructuring? Second, if one perceives the investor's action as an abuse, should relevant participants solve the uncertainty resulting from the application of such a far-reaching doctrine, and if so, how? Last, should one consider the investor's conduct inappropriate, are there any better alternatives than the tribunal's order that the case be dismissed, as the jurisprudence currently stands? These points shall be examined in turn.

First, as briefly discussed earlier, whether the tribunal's application of the doctrine of abuse of rights here is legally justified remains questionable.[291] For many commentators, an abuse of rights occurs when the right is abnormally exercised in contradiction with its goal or intended purpose.[292] In this regard, the investor's subjective intention (i.e., bad faith) is crucial to the tribunal's finding of an abuse, and as such many factors (e.g., timing and the investor's economic contribution to the restructured investment) are taken account of to establish such a malign intent. Yet, these factors only concern the subjective maliciousness of the investor but ignore the objective maliciousness or concrete unfavorable impact upon the state against which the right is exercised. In other words, should the element of harm be considered in establishing an abuse of rights? At this point, it is worth recalling Judge Read's dissenting opinion in *Nottebohm*.

In *Nottebohm*, Judge Read assumed that the existence of a right was the basis for abuse of rights. It was assumed that Liechtenstein had the right under international law to naturalize Mr. Nottebohm. However, given the special circumstances and the manner in which Liechtenstein exercised its right, such exercise was improper, "outrageous and unconscionable."[293] Thus, Liechtenstein could not invoke its result, i.e., the conferment of the national status on Mr. Nottebohm, against Guatemala.[294] The preceding assumption was not an end in itself. As Judge Read continued, in order

290. *Pac Rim*, *supra* n. 146, para. 2.10. The differentiation of jurisdiction and admissibility can be important in other contexts, however. For instance, some BITs require that the investor follow certain pre-arbitration procedures, including negotiation and resolving disputes domestically for a certain period of time, before it could submit its case to arbitration. If the investor fails to comply with this prerequisite, notwithstanding that the tribunal has jurisdiction over the dispute, it may not admit the case, i.e., the case is inadmissible. Nevertheless, this shortcoming leading to the case inadmissibility can be *cured*. Namely, once the first tribunal dismisses the case based on the said admissibility ground, should the investor go back and subsequently follow the procedure stipulated, a new case concerning the same matter can be brought to a new tribunal.

291. *See supra* nn. 136-144.

292. Ascensio, *supra* n. 104, at 764-765; Gaillard, *supra* n. 77, at 32; Sornarajah, *supra* n. 118, at 126; Voon, Mitchell & Munro, *supra* n. 118, at 75.

293. Nottebohm Case (second phase), Judgment of April 6th, 1955, I.C. J. Reports 1955, Dissenting Opinion of Judge Read, Nottebohm Case (Second Phase), p 37.

294. *Ibid.*, para. 37.

to invoke the doctrine of abuse of rights, proof of damage caused was required. In his own words, "[t]he doctrine of abuse of right cannot be invoked by one State against another unless the State which is admittedly exercising its rights under international law causes damage to the State invoking the doctrine."[295] As Liechtenstein did not exercise its right to naturalize Mr. Nottebohm in a way that caused damage to Guatemala, the latter could not invoke the doctrine.[296] Judge Read did not think that "international law, apart from abuse of right and fraud, permits the consideration of the motives which led to naturalization as determining its effects."[297] Judge Read's view on the qualified applicability of the notion of abuse of rights was supported by Judge Klaestad, who stated that the notion, if applicable in international law, would "presuppose the infliction of some kind of injury upon the legitimate interests of Guatemala by the naturalization of Mr. Nottebohm."[298]

Adopting and applying the Judges' view here, we propose that the element of harm should be proven before any abuse of rights is confirmed. And we have difficulty accepting that the mere fact that a host state has to appear before international arbitration is indicative of harm. Particularly, in order to establish harm, the respondent state would have to prove that the claimant investor, by exercising its right to submit disputes to arbitration, which has been recognized by most participants as a neutral option for settlement of international dispute, causes harm. For the host state, to defend its case before the arbitral tribunal and to bear certain burdens (i.e., financial costs, time, and human resources) is not necessarily harm. Rather, they are merely a corollary of any investor's regular exercise of right to bring investment dispute to arbitration or any other adjudicating body. And this investor's right should not be easily outweighed by the state's burdens.

Moreover, should the main concern here be about the state's responsibility in relation to the costs of the proceedings, other alternatives might be used to address it. Specifically, arbitral tribunals generally have considerable discretion in allocating the costs. For instance, Article 61 of the ICSID Convention provides that the tribunal is entitled to decide how the incurred expenses and fees shall be allocated. Similarly, this approach can be found in most leading arbitration rules. Article 42 of the UNCITRAL Arbitration Rules (as revised in 2010), despite its default premise that the costs should follow the event, and Article 38 of the International Chamber of Commerce (ICC) Arbitration Rules (2017) allow the tribunal to apportion the costs as it deems appropriate, taking into account the circumstances of the case, such as the parties' conduct and the case outcome. In practice, several tribunals have not hesitated to wield this authority.[299] Therefore, even if the aggregate costs suffered may not be wholly compensable in every case, the problem could be much alleviated.

295. *Ibid.*
296. *Ibid.*, at 38.
297. *Ibid.*, at 42.
298. Nottebohm Case (second phase), Judgment of April 6th, 1955, I.C. J. Reports 1955, Dissenting Opinion of Judge Klaestad p. 31.
299. Susan D. Franck, *Arbitration Costs: Myths and Realities in Investment Treaty Arbitration* (Oxford: Oxford University Press, 2019), 215-217.

Assuming that the doctrine of abuse of rights is necessary or desirable in this context, how should we deal with the uncertainty resulting from its application? One possible solution is to stipulate in the relevant treaties the circumstances in which an abuse would occur. Investment treaties do not normally include provisions on this issue. Nonetheless, a noteworthy development in this respect can be found in the recently published final version of the Netherlands model BIT (2019). Article 16(2) thereof provides that "[t]he Tribunal shall decline jurisdiction if the investment has been made through fraudulent misrepresentation, concealment, corruption, or similar bad faith conduct amounting to an abuse of process."[300] No elaboration of the term "abuse of process" is offered. Hence, what the Dutch government does here is endorsing the current investment treaty arbitration jurisprudence on "abuse of process" while leaving the issue to be solved on a case-by-case basis by investment treaty tribunals. Uncertainty therefore persists.

All in all, on the one hand, the current jurisprudence may prove effective in signaling that such behavior is not acceptable and thus deterring the investor from engaging in jurisdictional maneuvering. On the other hand, the doctrine's unsettled application could leave both states and investors in a murky situation, which could increase the quantity of disputes on this particular matter. As the Award on Costs in *Philip Morris* shows, the expenses associated with this controversy can be high.[301] For this reason, states negotiating a treaty should consider this issue. One possibility would be to stipulate clearly in the relevant ISDS provision that the tribunal *shall* decline jurisdiction if the investor obtains the requisite nationality within a certain period of time (e.g., three or six months). Another would be to secure the host state's approval for restructuring as in *Aucoven*[302] prior to the date of dispute, which should normally be the date when the challenged sovereign measure takes place. Agreeing will not be easy. Additionally, the agreed period may not necessarily be suitable in every case. For example, had the six-month condition been implemented in *Tidewater*, the tribunal would have had to decline jurisdiction.[303] As such, the parties might prefer to give the tribunals some flexibility by replacing the term "*shall*" with "*should*."[304]

300. https://www.rijksoverheid.nl/binaries/rijksoverheid/documenten/publicaties/2019/03/22/nieuwe-modeltekst-investeringsakkoorden/nieuwe+modeltekst+investeringsakkoorden.pdf (accessed August 15, 2019).
301. Philip Morris Asia Limited v. The Common Wealth of Australia, PCA Case No. 2012-12, Final Award Regarding Costs, July 8, 2017. The award's unredacted version can be found at https://www.iareporter.com/wp-content/themes/iareporter/download.php?post_id=33052 (accessed August 15, 2019).
302. *Aucoven, supra* n. 21, paras. 127-132, 143.
303. *See supra* nn. 184-187.
304. It should be noted that the Netherlands has incorporated a provision address this point in its recently published draft investment agreement. However, the provision (Article 16(2)) is drafted in a so broad manner that in essence it merely endorses the tribunal's power to dismiss cases provided it finds "bad faith conduct amounting to an abuse of process." Article 16(2) reads: "The Tribunal shall decline jurisdiction if the investment has been made through fraudulent misrepresentation, concealment, corruption, or similar bad faith conduct amounting to an abuse of process." https://globalarbitrationreview.com/digital_assets/820bcdd9-08b5-4bb5-a81e-d69e6c6735ce/Draft-Model-BIT-NL-2018.pdf (accessed August 15, 2019).

Last but not least, whereas we acknowledge and sympathize with a barrage of criticisms for an investor's corporate maneuvering, a tribunal's dismissal of a dispute at the preliminary objection stage may not be the best alternative given its draconian effect. As a result, we suggest that tribunals rather consider tackling this matter either at the merits or quantum stage.

As for the merits, the timing of investment could be crucial in the tribunal's finding as to the detrimental effect of the disputed measure(s) on the investment. That is, the investment climate or the legal framework in which an investment is made is a critical factor in assessing whether the state has breached treaty obligations. Particularly, the investor's "legitimate expectation" (especially at the time of investment) is generally considered a vital factor in the tribunal's determination of whether there is a breach of the FET provision.[305] Similarly, a number of IIAs have clarified that, in determining whether indirect expropriation occurs, the tribunal must take into account "the extent to which the measure or series of measures interferes with distinct, reasonable investment-backed expectations."[306] In this case, the legitimate expectation in question is that of the new investor inserted into the corporate chain (rather than that of the original investor), as the relevant treaty only applies after "the investor became its beneficiary as an eligible national of the relevant Contracting Party."[307] As such, if the state could exhibit that the investor restructures its investment in anticipation of the dispute, the investor's claim that its investment had been unlawfully undermined would fundamentally be weakened.

Next, despite the investor's weakened legitimate expectation, in case the government measure is so egregious that the tribunal still finds the investor's claim meritorious, it could address the timing of restructuring at the quantum phase. The deteriorating relationship between the state and the investor at that time, which naturally reduces the market value of the investment, would affect the tribunal's valuation. Under IIAs, the prescription on how to calculate compensation can be found in the expropriation clause. One representative clause is Article 4(2) of the Cyprus-Hungary BIT—the applicable treaty in the well-known *ADC v. Hungary* case[308]—which stipulates that "[t]he amount of compensation must correspond to the market value of the expropriated investments at the moment of expropriation." In general, this market value should be based on the discount cash flow (DCF) valuation method as it is in alignment with the empirical reality that "[v]alue is the present worth of future

305. Todd J. Grierson-Weiler & Ian A. Laird, *Standards of Treatment*, in Peter Muchlinski, Federico Ortino & Christoph Schreuer (eds.), The Oxford Handbook of International Investment Law (Oxford: Oxford University Press, 2008), 275-277; Campbell McLachlan, Laurence Shore & Matthew Weiniger, *International Investment Arbitration: Substantive Principles*, 2nd edition (Oxford: Oxford University Press, 2017), 279-280; Rudolf Dolzer & Christoph Schreuer, *Principles of International Investment Law*, 2nd edition (Oxford: Oxford University Press, 2012), 145-149.
306. *See, e.g.*, Annex 8-A of the Comprehensive Economic and Trade Agreement; Annex 9-B of the CPTPP.
307. *Société Générale, supra* n. 68, para. 105.
308. *ADC, supra* n. 39.

benefits."[309] Two important steps are thus necessary. The first is to project the amount of future net cash flow. The second is to bring the future net cash flow back to the present value by applying the appropriate discount rate.

The fact that the restructuring has taken place shortly before the dispute arises could significantly impact the projected net cash flow. Indeed, this repercussion—that the disputed measure has substantially deprived the expected financial gain of the investment—is a reason why the investor submits its claim in the first place. Moreover, the existence of anticipated dispute also means the investment is encountering a higher risk, which consequently results in a higher applicable discount rate. As a result, because of the reduction of projected net cash flow and the increase in discount rate, the market value will inevitably lessen. It thus follows that the state will have to pay less compensation to the investor in this circumstance. Whereas this explanation focuses on compensation for expropriation, the same logic *mutatis mutandis* applies to the calculation of damages for other forms of treaty violation whereby several tribunals have found that the full reparation standard pronounced in *Chorzów*[310] applies.[311]

Applying this proposed alternative to *Philip Morris* will change the outcome of the case. Philip Morris Asia, which was inserted into the corporate chain, entered the Australian political economy, being aware of the government's inclination to adopt a new tobacco control regulatory framework.[312] Later, it participated in the regulatory process and ultimately failed to prevent the legislative change from happening. This situation could affect the tribunal's consideration of Philip Morris Asia's legitimate expectation at the time of investment (restructuring), and Philip Morris Asia would face an uphill task of proving that the plain packaging measure came as a surprise and caused unreasonable damage to its investment. Thus, there is a high probability that the state would not be found in breach of the treaty's substantive obligations. In the state's worst-case scenario, should the tribunal uphold the claimant's allegation, it would order the state to pay less compensation given the diminished market value of the investment caused by the public anticipation, at the time of restructuring, of potential adverse measures.

VII CONCLUSION

A close reading of the decisions finding an abuse of rights in relation to corporate restructuring reveals that their health is frail. First, in the case of disputes that had arisen before treaty protection was available, there is no need to invoke the doctrine of abuse of rights. In this regard, jurisdiction *ratione temporis* serves its purpose well. Second, in the case of disputes that arose after treaty protection had been available, the

309. Shannon Pratt & Alina V. Niculita, *The Lawyer's Business Valuation Handbook*, 2nd edition (Chicago: American Bar Association, 2013), 45.
310. Factory at Chorzów (Ger. v. Pol.), 1928 P.C.I.J. (ser. A) No. 17, Judgment No. 13 (September 28) (page 47). This principle is incorporated into Article 36 of the International Law Commissions' Articles on State Responsibility for Internationally Wrongful Acts.
311. Sergey Ripinsky & Kevin Williams, *Damages in International Investment Law* (London: British Institute of International and Comparative Law, 2008), 89-90.
312. *See Methanex*, *supra* n. 5, Part IV Chapter D paras. 9-10.

application of the doctrine is questionable. In dismissing a claim at an early stage for abuse of rights, the tribunals were not justified in randomly selecting the elements that they thought relevant for establishing an abuse.

If our suspicion is correct that the *Philip Morris v. Australia* tribunal was swayed by public opinion opposing its review of Australia's plain packaging measure, one might also frame this incident as the tribunal's missed opportunity to affirm the legitimacy of the measure. To illustrate, if the final award in *Philip Morris v. Uruguay*[313] had not been rendered a year later, the question as to whether the plain packaging imposition complies with treaty obligations would have remained unsettled. By unanimously deciding that Uruguay's plain packaging measure was not in violation of the FET provision[314] and was a legitimate exercise of the state's *police power*,[315] the tribunal has put the matter to rest and reinforced the global consensus on the need to control how tobacco companies market their products.

In our opinion, corporate restructuring in response to foreseeable disputes per se is not objectionable. As a policy matter, we are inclined to support the lesser of two evils. We favor allowing the investor to avail itself of investment treaty arbitration (notwithstanding the foreseeability of dispute at the time of restructuring) instead of depriving it of the said forum and forcing it through a relatively partial domestic counterpart. Corporate restructuring in this circumstance should not be viewed as an abusive exercise of rights but a legitimate one. If the host state deems it undesirable, it should deal with this matter by way of treatification. Leaving the issue with arbitral tribunals is not a preferred alternative. Metaphorically said, the abuse of rights doctrine is an unruly horse by its nature, and arbitral tribunals are its jockeys. We never know where they will carry us.

313. Phillip Morris Brand Sárl, Phillip Morris Products S.A., and Abal Hermanos S.A. v. Oriental Republic of Uruguay, ICSID Case No. ARB/10/7, Award (July 8, 2016).
314. *Ibid.*, at para. 420.
315. *Ibid.*, at para. 307.

CHAPTER 18

Policy-Oriented Analysis on Foreign Investment Disputes Within the USMCA Chapter 14: A Backlash on the Great Compact

Jaime Olaiz-González

A quarter-century ago, Mexico looked very promising thanks to a series of radical transformations: they were ushered in by a new generation of policy-makers that decided to undertake momentous structural legal reforms. They may represent, in time, Mexico's admission to the global economy, the door being the North American Free Trade Agreement (NAFTA).[1] Nowadays, it accounts for nearly USD 1.2 trillion in annual trade of goods and services. Guillermo Aguilar Álvarez was part of that generation, and he played a fundamental role as one of Mexico's principal NAFTA negotiators. Once the Agreement entered into force, Guillermo became a prominent arbitrator and an authority on international investment law.

This chapter is about one of Guillermo's main interests: the future of investment protection globally and the future prospects of the Agreement that he contributed to.

The context could hardly be more auspicious: the outcome of the renegotiation of NAFTA that has resulted in a modernized 2.0 version of the original agreement has changed fundamentally the arrangements that Guillermo's generation helped to install. The growing disidentifications among the partnering countries of NAFTA undermined their original consensus, and the erosion of their trading and investing practices has created a radically new setting that significantly contrasts with that of twenty-five years ago.

1. NORTH AMERICAN FREE TRADE AGREEMENT (NAFTA), U.S.-CAN.-MEX., December 15, 1992, https://www.nafta-sec-alena.org/Home/Texts-of-the-Agreement/North-American-Free-Trade-Agreement, accessed November 8, 2019.

However, if we embrace the notion of law as a continuous process of controlling and authoritative decision,[2] fundamentally influenced by the perspectives of the relevant participants, as well as by the situations, bases of power, strategies and outcomes that are inherent to any decision-making process, the present United States-Mexico-Canada Agreement (USMCA) and its Chapter 14,[3] represent an evolution in the dialectic process of legal construction of the North American countries' arrangements in promoting and protecting their respective direct investments in one another.

To identify the distinctive dynamics that this dialectic process brought about, we will employ the intellectual tools provided by the policy-oriented jurisprudence, also known as *The New Haven School,*[4] and which was very close to Guillermo over much of his academic and professional trajectory.

I PRINCIPLES OF CONTENT

In order to frame the context in which decision-making and constitutive processes[5] take place more comprehensively, the policy-oriented jurisprudence has articulated a systematic methodology to identify critical elements and functions of a given situation to enable decision-makers to enlarge their scope of inquiry to gain a greater insight of the problem at hand.

Policy-oriented jurisprudence helps to map the constitutive process pertaining to the transition of the former NAFTA Chapter 11 to the new USMCA Chapter 14. Assuming as an observational standpoint that of a scholar and adviser of the relevant actors in this matter, we can identify as *participants* those that are, in varying degrees, critical to the process of promoting investment between NAFTA/USMCA countries and resolving investment disputes that may arise between investors and States.

---

2. W. Michael Reisman, Siegfried Wiessner & Andrew R. Willard, *The New Haven School: A Brief Introduction,* 32 Yale J. Int'l L. 576 (2007).
3. Agreement between the United States of America, the Mexican United States, and Canada Text (USMCA), November 30, 2018, https://ustr.gov/trade-agreements/free-trade-agreements/united-states-mexico-canada-agreement, accessed November 8, 2019.
4. W. Michael Reisman, Siegfried Wiessner & Andrew R. Willard, *supra* note 2, at 575.
5. W. Michael Reisman, *A Jurisprudence from the Perspective of the "Political Superior,"* 23 N. Ky. L. Rev. 605 (1996). According to Reisman, the term *constitutive process* refers "to that portion of a group's activity concerned with establishing, maintaining, or changing the fundamental institutions and procedures of decision-making. From the perspective of a jurisprudence for those making choices, a focal lens which clearly identifies when constitutive decisions are being taken and how they are likely to impact on and shape the constitutive process in the future is important." The constitutive process is also defined as "authoritative power exercised to provide an institutional framework for decision and for allocating indispensable functions; the particular decisions emerging from this process, which we call 'public order' decisions, may be specialized to the shaping and sharing of wealth, enlightenment, respect, and all other values." *Authoritative decision* refers to "a process of decision characterized both by expectations of authority and by effective control." *See* Myres McDougal, Harold D. Lasswell & W. Michael Reisman, *The World Constitutive Process of Authoritative Decision,* in Myres S. McDougal & W. Michael Reisman, International Law Essays: A Supplement to International Law in Contemporary Perspective (1981). The original version of this article was published in 19 J. Legal Ed. 253, 403 (1967).

This description may comprise, on the one hand, investors in the form of multinational corporations, venture capitalists, conglomerates, systemic banks and financial institutions, individual or multiple independent capitalists, associations of traders and producers, among others. On the other hand, there are the States that are parties of the Agreement, embodied in their respective governments at the central, state and local levels. A central participant in this process is the arbitrators who conduct and resolve the investment disputes. Additionally, there are also businesses, unions, nongovernmental organizations and other members of the public that, in different forms, may be peripheral participants in the process of investment.

These participants have distinctive *perspectives,* which include "specific patterns of identification and disidentification, their matter-of-fact expectations of past and future, and the value demands they project."[6] With respect to promoting investment and enhancing the mechanisms for resolving investment disputes, the perspectives are especially influenced by the goals and strategies implemented by the respective governments. All parties coincide in creating a favorable environment toward investment, by establishing rules that reduce and eliminate reciprocal barriers that may impede investment in fair, equitable and nondiscriminatory terms; and in providing meaningful procedures for resolving investment disputes. However, their expectations and demands tend to differ: The United States is mainly concerned with assuring conditions that will protect its investors in accordance with U.S. legal principles and practices consistent with minimum standards of treatment under customary international law, ensuring protection of U.S. sovereignty and enhancing U.S. domestic industries. Mexico is mainly focused on improving and enhancing the mechanism for investment disputes to provide legal certainty and predictability to investors. Bradly J. Condon describes these varying expectations:

> NAFTA Chapter 11 dispute settlement for foreign investors was always more important for Mexico than for Canada. For Mexico, NAFTA's primary importance was not in providing market access to the United States, which already applied low tariff rates under GATT. NAFTA's primary importance was in providing investor protections to foreign direct investment, with the possibility of using NAFTA Chapter 20 to enforce arbitral awards against governments under Chapter 11 of NAFTA. In this regard, NAFTA was instrumental in increasing foreign direct investment in Mexican manufacturing, by lowering political risk. [In] Canada, which has relatively low political risk, eliminating NAFTA Chapter 11 should not make much difference in its attractiveness to foreign investment. However, it will allow Canadian governments to regulate in the public interest without running the risk that the messiness of modern democratic politics might lead to compensation for foreign investors.[7]

Canada and Mexico are frequently at odds in terms of their expectations and demands in the region. As Condon puts it:

6. W. Michael Reisman, Siegfried Wiessner & Andrew R. Willard, *supra* note 2, at 578.
7. Bradly J. Condon, *From NAFTA to USMCA: Two's Company, Three's a Crowd,* 2 LATIN AM. J. TRADE POL'Y 45 (2018).

> [Canadian] and Mexican interests do not always coincide. The reality is that they are competitors in the trilateral arena, both economically and politically. Economically, they compete for foreign investment and trade. Each country sells itself to multinational firms as the best base from which to serve the North American market. Politically, they compete for the attention of the U.S. government on bilateral issues when their interests differ. For example, the issue of cross-border labor movement is a problem for Mexico, not Canada.[8]

Arbitrators, for their part, expect to operate with a mechanism that maximizes their liberty to decide solely on legal grounds,[9] free of political pressure and interference.

Situations are the spaces, areas or arenas where the investment process takes place. They include government agencies, such as the U.S. Trade Representative, the Foreign, Finance and Trade Ministries of the three USMCA state parties, to the international organizations, such as the World Bank's International Centre for the Settlement of Investment Disputes (ICSID) and ad hoc international arbitral tribunals. As explained below, a fundamental feature of the new mechanism prescribes full transparency of the arbitration as well as public hearings and the possibility of filing amicus curiae briefs from other relevant participants equally concerned in the investment dispute.

According to Wiessner and Willard, "the assets or *base values* that participants draw on in their efforts to achieve their demanded values are inventoried in terms of authority to perform certain functions and control over access to and use of values."[10] Most compliance with the mechanism is based upon reciprocal expectations shared by the foreign investor and its home state, on the one hand, and the importing state and its central, state and local governments, on the other. The expectations chiefly rely on power and rectitude as values, and a sense of mutual convenience in preserving a cross-border environment favorable to foreign investment and its protection. As we will explore, the new mechanism is designed to narrow the spectrum for interpretation in resolving investment disputes.

The *strategies* at the participants' disposal "are considered in terms of a persuasive-coercive continuum and their reliance on [diplomatic and economic instruments]."[11] The prospect for a capital-importing state to have to pay monetary damages and compensate a claimant for breaching the agreement has proved to be a restraint on national abuses on foreign investment.

Finally, with respect to the *outcomes* of this constitutive process, there is overall optimism in Mexico and the United States over the new regulation of investment and investment disputes. As long as Mexico continues receiving the same rate of U.S. investment in critical and strategic areas of its economy and U.S. investors feel

8. *Ibid.*, at 36.
9. W. Michael Reisman, *The Past and Future of the Great Compact: White & Case International Arbitration Lecture (Lamm Lecture, University of Miami School of Law, 9 February 2017)*, in 33(1) ICSID REV. 56-66 (2018).
10. Siegfried Wiessner & Andrew R. Willard, *Policy-Oriented Jurisprudence and Human Rights Abuses in Internal Conflict: Toward a World Public Order of Human Dignity*, 93 AM. J. INT'L L. 324 (1999).
11. *Ibid.*

protected by an efficient and predictable mechanism, the prospects are auspicious. But, if political alienation continues to grow on both sides of the border, investments will be at risk and the mechanisms will prove futile.

II PRINCIPLES OF PROCEDURE: RECALIBRATING THE MECHANISM

Once we have framed the content of the constitutive process under scrutiny, policy-oriented jurisprudence requires setting forth modalities of implementation. Five intellectual tasks are recommended for this endeavor: goal clarification, trend description, factor analysis, projection of future decisions and the invention of alternatives.[12] We will proceed then to apply them to the terms of the new USMCA Chapter 14.

A Clarification of Goals

After almost a quarter of century without revision, NAFTA Chapter 11 required a considerable overhaul. Based on the experience accumulated within that period and aiming to bring the mechanism up to date, the U.S. Trade Representative was the leading force in promoting the modernization of the agreement. In November 2017, it issued a Summary of Objectives for the NAFTA Renegotiation. It specified the objectives which the U.S. administration had set to review and renegotiate the terms of the free trade mechanism in the region. For the chapter on foreign investment, the Office of the U.S. Trade Representative set as goals:

- Secure for U.S. investors in the NAFTA countries important rights consistent with U.S. legal principles and practice, while ensuring that NAFTA country investors in the United States are not accorded greater substantive rights than domestic investors.
- Establish rules that reduce or eliminate barriers to U.S. investment in all sectors in the NAFTA countries, including the following rules:
  - National treatment and most-favored-nation treatment;
  - Prohibitions on restrictions on transfers of investment-related capital;
  - Prohibition on performance requirements, including forced technology transfer and technology localization;
  - Prohibition on expropriation without prompt, adequate and effective compensation, consistent with U.S. legal principles and practice; and
  - A minimum standard of treatment under customary international law, consistent with U.S. legal principles and practice.
- Provide meaningful procedures for resolving investment disputes, while ensuring the protection of U.S. sovereignty and the maintenance of strong U.S. domestic industries.
- Improve procedures for resolving investment disputes, including ensuring that arbitrators act impartially and independently, allowing arbitrators expeditiously to review and dismiss frivolous claims, and providing the NAFTA countries with tools to ensure the coherence and correctness of the interpretation of investment rules.

12. W. Michael Reisman, Siegfried Wiessner & Andrew R. Willard, *supra* note 2, at 576.

- Ensure that dispute settlement hearings are open to the public and that all key documents related to the proceedings are promptly made public.
- Establish a mechanism to allow amicus curiae submissions in dispute settlement proceedings from businesses, unions, nongovernmental organizations, and other members of the public.[13]

These goals reflected the distinctive attitudes of the Trump administration toward free trade, in general, and the promotion and protection of U.S. investments abroad, in particular. In contrast to its predecessors, the Administration focused on protecting domestic investors as opposed to the treatment that NAFTA country investors were receiving in the United States. This renegotiation sought to redress the balance between the growing interest in enhancing the protection of its investors in the region with the interest in ensuring a preferential treatment to its domestic constituents by promoting policies and tax incentives to keep its larger corporations investing in the United States, instead of south of the border.

In this respect, it is important to note that the renegotiation of NAFTA Chapter 11 evinced from the beginning a bilateral—rather than a trilateral—interplay: the United States and Mexico produced a de facto BIT between both countries due to Canada's opt-out from the new USMCA Chapter 14. As Bradly Condon explains:

> [For] the most part, economic, political and cultural relations in the NAFTA countries are bilateral in nature. [Twenty-five] years after the North American Free Trade Agreement (NAFTA) was signed, the regional relationship consists of two bilateral interactions on two very different borders, with the exception of those sectors in which supply chains have become integrated on a trilateral basis and beyond. [Beyond] these trilateral sectors, the relationship between Canada and Mexico plays a relatively minor role. However, replacing NAFTA with bilateral agreements would have placed Canada and Mexico at a disadvantage, relative to the United States, in terms of attracting foreign direct investment. Nevertheless, Canadian and Mexican interests do not always coincide, nor do their negotiating positions. [Canada] was willing to give up NAFTA Chapter 11 on foreign investment disputes, whereas Mexico accepted a modified version. The result is a trilateral agreement with significant bilateral elements.[14]

On the Mexican side, goals were similar. In a *communiqué* issued by the Trade Ministry on July 2017, the Mexican stance for the negotiations was as follows:

> [NAFTA] is a factor or certainty in the integration of North-America. That is why it is essential to keep and maintain regulations contributing to make foreign trade and investments more predictable. Here, controversial solution mechanisms play a crucial role, which throughout more than two decades have tried its effectiveness as an instrument that allows making regional trade more predictable, in addition to incorporating the most recent elements on transparency and participation of other relevant actors.

13. Office of the United States Trade Representative. Executive Office of the President, *Summary of Objectives for the NAFTA Renegotiation*, pp. 8-9, November 2017. *See* https://ustr.gov/sites/default/files/files/Press/Releases/Nov%20Objectives%20Update.pdf, accessed November 8, 2019.
14. Bradly J. Condon, *supra* note 7, at 30-31.

For all that, it is necessary to:

- Consolidate the legal framework regulation State productive enterprises, which allow them to achieve effective trade procedures.
- Modernize all the controversy-solution mechanisms provided in the NAFTA (investor-State, State-State, as well as antidumping and countervailing duties, and financial services) to make them more agile, transparent, and effective.
- Promote free competition through the improvement of cooperation and exchange of information among authorities of the NAFTA countries, in order to keep the efficiency of the markets and to protect consumers' rights.
- Provide legal certainty to Mexican providers in the (public) procurement procedures in North America.[15]

When the Mexican government issued these priorities for the renegotiation, the Peña administration was entering its final year as presidential elections were scheduled for July 2018. The outcome of that election was the landslide victory of the leftist candidate Andrés Manuel López Obrador. In the beginning, AMLO had maintained an elusive attitude toward the renegotiation of NAFTA, but as his inauguration approached, members of his team on trade joined the Mexican delegation to assure a continuity of the terms and policies that had been on the table. To the surprise of many, López Obrador concluded by fully embracing the new USMCA. The Mexican Congress was the first legislative body of the three partnering countries to approve the agreement.

In sum, the common goals were set to promote a minimum public order in the region that promotes foreign direct investment (FDI) in accordance with customary international law.

B Trend Description

FDI has played a critical role in North American economic dynamics over the last quarter of century. This is totally due to NAFTA. In many ways, NAFTA triggered not only radical economic and political transformations in the region, but also deep cultural and societal changes that have redefined the social process.

FDI in Mexico is only second to Brazil as the top destination in Latin America. Nearly half of Mexico's total FDI in 2018 (USD 31.6 billion) came from its North American trade partners. More than half of this investment went to the manufacturing sector, followed by the finance and insurance industries, and the energy sector.[16]

The United States is the largest source of FDI in Mexico. According to data from the Bureau of Economic Analysis of the U.S. Department of Commerce, United States' direct investment in Mexico increased almost 6.5 times, from USD 17.0 billion in 1994 to a historical peak of USD 109.7 billion in 2017. Mexico's FDI in the U.S. has also

15. Secretaría de Economía, *Prioridades de México en las negociaciones para la modernización del Tratado de Libre Comercio de América del Norte,* 2 de agosto de 2017. *See* https://www.gob.mx/se/articulos/prioridades-de-mexico-en-las-negociaciones-para-la-modernizacion-del-tratado-de-libre-comercio-de-america-del-norte?idiom=es, accessed November 8, 2019.
16. *See* https://www.as-coa.org/articles/chart-breakdown-foreign-direct-investment-mexico, accessed November 8, 2019.

increased around nine times over this period, going from USD 2.1 billion in 1994 to USD 18 billion in 2017.[17]

This steady increment of FDI is thanks to NAFTA's provisions on investment. It gradually boosted the confidence of U.S. investors. It also strengthened Mexico's attitude toward global FDI, transforming its former protective policies in the 1970s and 1980s to a complete liberalization of most sectors of its economy.[18] From the Mexican vantage point, the key trend over these years has been to afford investors nondiscriminatory treatment by means of NAFTA's Most-Favored-Nation (MFN) and Minimum Standard of Treatment (MST) clauses and its protections against uncompensated expropriation. The main disputes occurred when these protections collided with Government regulation on environment, health and safety.[19]

Under the protection of NAFTA Chapter 11, any investor of the Parties who alleged having been impaired in her investment rights due to a breach of the chapter's protections has been able to submit a claim for arbitration to a neutral decision-maker in the form of a three-member arbitration tribunal, one appointed by each of the conflicting parties and a third appointed by the agreement of both, or ultimately, by ICSID's Secretary-General.

Over these 25 years, 61 cases were initiated under NAFTA Chapter 11: 16 have been against the United States; 26 against Canada; and 19 against Mexico. Of those, the United States has won all its cases (mostly against Canada, with 15 cases), while Mexico and Canada have secured eight favorable decisions respectively.[20] As of January 2018, ten cases have been decided against the State, 5 against Canada and 5 against Mexico. Six cases have been settled; Canada settled 3 cases with damages and 2 without. The United States has settled one without damages. Twenty-five cases were dismissed and nine withdrawn by the claimant. The remaining eleven cases are ongoing as of this date. Canada has paid a total compensation of USD 181 million, while Mexico has paid nearly USD 205 million.[21] Notwithstanding the fact that Mexico is the State that has paid the highest share of awarded compensations, in the NAFTA renegotiation it was Canada that has the party most interested in eliminating Chapter 11.

The major claim against the substance and operation of Chapter 11 focused on the award of damages against states without going through the domestic courts of the capital-importing State. As portrayed by Scott Sinclair:

> NAFTA's controversial ISDS mechanism allows foreign investors to bypass the domestic courts and sue governments directly before private international arbitration tribunals. Historically, ISDS had been a feature of bilateral investment treaties

17. M. Angeles Villareal, *U.S.-Mexico Economic Relations: Trends, Issues, and Implications*, Congressional Research Service, March 26, 2019, p. 5.
18. *Ibid.*
19. M. Angeles Villareal & Ian F. Fergusson, *NAFTA Renegotiation and the Proposed United States-Mexico-Canada Agreement (USMCA)*, Congressional Research Service, February 26, 2019, p. 22.
20. *Ibid.*, at 25.
21. Scott Sinclair, *Canada's Track Record Under NAFTA Chapter 11: North American Investor-State Disputes to January 2018*, Canadian Centre for Policy Alternatives, January 2018, at 46.

> between developed and developing countries, but the signing of NAFTA marked the first time investment arbitration was integrated into a comprehensive regional trade agreement. While national governments alone are responsible for defending ISDS cases, government measures at the federal, provincial, state and local levels can and frequently *have been targeted by investors.* [Arbitration] can be invoked unilaterally by foreign investors from the three NAFTA countries. Investors do not need to seek consent from their home governments and are not obliged to try to resolve a complaint through the domestic court system before launching a NAFTA claim. Under Chapter 11, all three parties have given their "unconditional, prior consent" to submit investor claims to binding arbitration, allowing investors to simply bypass the domestic courts. [Tribunal] decisions are final and not appealable through any court.[22]

This is not entirely accurate inasmuch as the exhaustion of domestic remedies was not required in NAFTA Chapter 11.

There were additional problematic issues, such as:

- NAFTA's Chapter 11 broad definition of key concepts such as investment, national treatment, MFN treatment, MST and expropriation, has produced an equally broad interpretation from arbitrators that has frequently been criticized;[23]
- lack of regulation in cases of armed conflict and civil strife;
- potential conflicts of interest of some arbitrators in the absence of stricter rules for eligibility;[24]
- predominance of national criteria in cases of expropriation for regulatory purposes.[25] This view is very much influenced by the decisions in the cases of *Philip Morris v. Uruguay*[26] and *Eli Lily v. Canada*;[27]
- lack of publicity and transparency in some cases which have undermined the integrity of the mechanism;
- problematic execution of the awards when they are reviewed by the domestic courts of the place of arbitration since most domestic judges are specialized neither in the subject matter of the arbitration nor in international investment law and customary international law.

As explained below, each of these issues was addressed in the formulation of new prescriptions for USMCA Chapter 14.

---

22. *Ibid.*, at 2-3. Emphasis added by the author.
23. Oscar Cruz Barney & Carlos H. Reyes Díaz, *El T-MEC/USMCA: solución de controversias, remedios comerciales e inversiones*, Instituto de Investigaciones Jurídicas de la UNAM, Serie Opiniones Técnicas sobre Temas de Relevancia Nacional, núm. 1, 2018. *See* https://archivos.juridicas.unam.mx/www/bjv/libros/11/5499/8.pdf, accessed November 8, 2019.
24. *Ibid.*, at 50.
25. *Ibid.*, at 44, 55-56.
26. *See* https://icsid.worldbank.org/en/Pages/cases/casedetail.aspx?CaseNo=ARB/10/7, accessed November 8, 2019.
27. *See* https://icsid.worldbank.org/en/Pages/cases/casedetail.aspx?CaseNo=UNCT/14/2, accessed November 8, 2019.

C Analysis of Conditioning Factors

Regional economic growth and development flourished over the last two decades, in good part thanks to NAFTA. This became more evident in the case of Mexico as growing FDI there helped to reduce historical migration flows of Mexican workers to the United States. As Condon explains pertaining to NAFTA effects on Mexico's FDI:

> Capital flows in the form of foreign direct investment have had a major impact on merchandise trade by stimulating intra-firm trade. In the NAFTA region, foreign direct investment in the maquiladoras has stimulated considerable growth in cross-border flows of goods across the Mexico-U.S. border. Similarly, the regional integration of the automotive sector has sparked considerable foreign direct investment and merchandise trade between the NAFTA countries. With greater foreign direct investment in Mexico's manufacturing sector, there are more jobs to keep Mexican workers at home. Export-led growth has the potential to reduce the wage gap between Mexico and the United States, reducing incentives for Mexicans to seek work in the northern neighbor.[28]

These investment-trade-migration dynamics coincided with the emergence of an elite deeply believing in free trade and foreign investment protection as necessary for further economic integration and development, and trusting in international institutions' economic, political and legal processes. In NAFTA's renegotiation two decades later, perspectives based upon nationalist, protectionist and in some cases, isolationist views are rejecting the very foundations of what Michael Reisman refers to as the *Great Compact*:

> Now, one of the girders of the economic system that has allowed for the unprecedented production and wider distribution of wealth—the international trade and investment system—seems to be wobbling. Whether it is actually buckling or is only adjusting, as part of the ongoing dialectic of all law, requires us to identify and trace the origins of what I will call "the Great Compact", the foundational normative arrangement that undergirds the contemporary international investment system.[29]

The *Great Compact* then tracks back to the Porter Convention of 1907, by which "investors' States waived the deployment of their superior power to protect their investors in return for host States' agreeing to submit the disputes with those investors to international arbitration by independent third-party determination."[30] This arrangement was later refined by the creation of the World Bank's International Centre for Settlement of Investment Disputes (ICSID) in the 1965 Washington Convention, which signaled a consensus decision between developing and developed States that upgraded the Porter Convention. As Reisman explains:

> [A] critical addition (to the original version of the Great Compact) was that the initiative to establish a tribunal, theretofore through the agreement of both State parties, was henceforth to be at the instance of the foreign investors themselves.

28. Bradly Condon, *supra* note 7, at 38.
29. W. Michael Reisman, *supra* note 9, at 1.
30. *Ibid.*, at 3.

> Powerful governments of capital-exporting States, which were already removed from the process of forcefully implementing customary international law's standards of protection of aliens, were also excluded from any role in establishing and managing the arbitral process. Now the responsibility for their application was assigned to international tribunals, constituted on the initiative of the private foreign investor. [The] package that comprised the Great Compact, in its 2.0 version, had something for everyone. From the perspective of the capital-importing State, the Compact exorcised the specter of coercive collection. From the perspective of the Foreign Office of the capital-exporting State, the Compact depoliticized investment disputes by transferring the politically expensive burden of espousing national claims to a reliable external applier. From the perspective of the foreign investor, it dispelled uncertainty about whether its own government would be willing, when needed, to bear the political cost of bringing a claim against another State. And from the perspective of the arbitrators to whom the exclusive responsibility for resolving the dispute was being assigned, it cleared the way for deciding solely on legal grounds. This was, in sum, the Great Compact on which the modern system of international investment law was built. And I might say that all States—developed, developing, liberal, socialist and communist —participated on an equal footing in fashioning it.[31]

The instrument per excellence to make the modern version of the Great Compact operative was the Investor-State Dispute Settlement (ISDS) mechanism, which represented the core protective component of Bilateral Investment Treaties (BITs). BITs represented an efficient means for promoting "stable, favorable and transparent conditions for investment [in] the territory of the other contracting Party."[32]

The renegotiation of NAFTA and the expected approval of the new USMCA actualizes both the perspectives of the U.S. and Mexico administrations transpire. In the case of Mexico, a social welfare agenda is based on the strategic relevance of promoting and protecting FDI. Despite the López Obrador administration signaling in favor of the renegotiated NAFTA, the cancelation of the major infrastructure project and its related contracts which had been initiated by its predecessor raised serious concerns among foreign investors about the true colors of the new Mexican government. This is currently reflected in the 0.1 % projection of economic growth for 2019 in Mexico. With respect to the United States, besides its present political turmoil due to the impeachment procedures against President Trump and the ever-present instability in a presidential election year, the prospects are equally concerning. As Condon puts it in reference to an opinion of Petros Mavroidis:

> President Trump's trade policy is a decisive turn towards unilateralism followed by bilateral deals. This combination is a blow to the multilateral edifice the US has helped establish. Only time will tell how serious this turn to unilateralism is. This Administration has accustomed the world to an erratic behavior, so a turn in the opposite direction—a lifting of tariffs and respect for multilateral treaties—cannot be excluded out of hand.[33]

31. *Ibid.*, at 4-5.
32. *Ibid.*, at 5. Professor Reisman takes this language from the trilateral investment treaty between South Korea, China and Japan, underscoring their deep differences in political economy, but nonetheless coincident in their approach toward international investment.
33. Bradly Condon, *supra* note 7, at 38-39.

Notwithstanding these conditioning factors, public support of NAFTA and its new version remains solid in the region. According to a survey conducted by the Chicago Council of Global Affairs and the Mexican pollster Buendía & Laredo, 80% of Mexicans and 70% of Americans thought that the new agreement would be beneficial to their respective countries.[34] Condon offers slightly different figures favoring NAFTA: 74% in Canada, 60% in Mexico and 51% in the United States.[35] Nonetheless, it remains clear that in general, public opinion in the region favors the free trade mechanism started in 1994.

D Strategies for Recalibration

As a result of careful observation and thoughtful analysis of the trends that have shaped and the factors that have conditioned NAFTA Chapter 11, the process of renegotiating and predicating a modern regulation of investment in the region succeeded in crafting an updated mechanism for investment and investment disputes that reflects and accommodates the distinctive views and perspectives of the participants involved.

As explained above, the new mechanism, which only applies to Mexico and the United States, preserves critical parts of the foundational arrangement in NAFTA, in particular the linkage with the ICSID and UNCITRAL systems. The novelties in the new mechanism are mainly focused on narrowing the interpretative scope of arbitrators by introducing more specific (and functional) definitions of investment,[36] covered investment,[37] national treatment,[38] MFN treatment,[39] MST[40] and expropriation.[41] It has also introduced rules related to treatment in case of armed conflict and civil strife.[42] Chapter 14 also prescribes an obligation for transparency and publicity of the arbitral proceedings by ensuring that dispute settlement hearings and all key documents are open to the public.[43]

Another distinctive addition is the amicus curiae submission as an integral part of the arbitration.[44] This measure enhances an inclusive perspective as it enables interested third parties to have a say in the arbitral proceedings. By enabling all relevant actors to provide their insight in the matter, this maximizes the ultimate correctness and fairness of the award.

In connection with the eligibility of arbitrators, Chapter 14 prescribes that they have to comply with the International Bar Association Guidelines on Conflicts of

34. *See* https://www.thechicagocouncil.org/sites/default/files/report_mexicans-americans-share-positive-views-usmca-trade-agreement_20190506.pdf, accessed November 8, 2019.
35. Bradly Condon, *supra* note 7, at 37.
36. Article 14.1.
37. *Ibid.*
38. Article 14.4.
39. Article 14.5.
40. Article 14.6.
41. Article 14.8 and Annex 14-B.
42. Article 14.7.
43. Annex 14-D, Article 8.
44. Annex 14-D, Article 7.3.

Interest in International Arbitration.[45] It also provides as general rule, and unlike NAFTA, that nondiscriminatory regulatory action to protect legitimate public welfare objectives will not constitute indirect expropriation.[46]

The downside of the renegotiation and its implication for the ISDS mechanism is the USMCA Chapter 14's precondition of exhaustion of domestic remedies before a claim for arbitration may be pursued.[47] Even though this measure is consistent with customary international law and U.S. legal principles and practice,[48] it represents a setback to the Great Compact, inasmuch as the competence and independence of national courts are not the same among the three USMCA countries. The ISDS mechanism was an efficient tool to compensate for the lack of confidence of American and Canadian investors in Mexican courts. Nonetheless, in Annexes 14-C and 14-E, the United States and Mexico agreed on a series of matters in which the ISDS under NAFTA Chapter 11 will remain operational: (1) *legacy claims by investors* still pending decision under NAFTA Chapter 11. This will survive for a period of three years;[49] and (2) cases related to government contracts on covered investments with respect to oil and natural gas, power generation, telecommunications, transportation services, and infrastructure (roads, railways, bridges or canals).[50] According to David Gantz, the preservation of ISDS for these areas is critical:

> The full ISDS protections, including the frequently cited denial of fair and equitable treatment and indirect expropriation, remain only for investors in Mexico that have concluded contracts with the government or government entities in oil and gas, infrastructure projects, power generation, transportation, and telecommunications. Given the importance for Mexico in attracting foreign investment to the hydrocarbons sector, the preservation of ISDS for that sector will probably afford potential investors a greater level of confidence when they invest in long-term projects. For investors in the relatively unprotected sectors, questions arise as to whether there will be a substantial impact on investment levels, given the relatively few ISDS actions (less than 20 in 25 years) against Mexico.[51]

E Projection of Future Trends

In light of this factor analysis, the prospects of a successful implementation of the USMCA Chapter 14 are elusive. The developmental constructs that we foresee are the following.

45. Annex 14-D, Article 5 (a), (b).
46. Annex 14-B, Article 3 (b).
47. Annex 14-D, Article 5.1 (a), (b).
48. The *Interhandel* (Switzerland v. United States of America) and *Elettronica Sicula* (United States of America v. Italy) cases are illustrative in this respect. *See* https://www.icj-cij.org/en/case/34 and https://www.icj-cij.org/en/case/76, respectively, accessed November 8, 2019.
49. Annex 14-C, Article 3.
50. Annex 14-E, Article 2, 6 (a), (b).
51. David A. Gantz, *The United States-Mexico-Canada Agreement: Overview and Analysis*, Baker Institute Report no. 12.11.18, Rice University's Baker Institute for Public Policy, Houston, Texas. *See* https://www.wita.org/wp-content/uploads/2018/12/bi-report-121118-mex-gantz.pdf, accessed November 8, 2019.

In the case of Mexico and its present administration, the historical concerns of foreign investors about political risk acquire a renewed significance. In the United States, the supportive attitude toward free trade mechanisms is declining and in an electoral year will not be reversed. Canada's rejection of Chapter 14 has also undermined the trilateral consensus around the ISDS system.[52] It will be up to dialogue between the relevant actors and State authorities to promote its refinement and recalibration. As Cruz Barney argues, a permanent arbitral court on investor-State disputes as the one that is being explored in the renegotiation of the Free Trade Agreement between Mexico and the European Union[53] may be worth considering for improving the resulting mechanism prescribed in USMCA Chapter 14.

F A Closing Caveat

Guillermo's generation's legacy is at risk. As his dear friend and colleague, Michael Reisman indicates:

> A coalition of States, which I have referred to figuratively as "The Empire", is striking back at some current trends and tendencies. Until now and for the most part, the agitation for adjustments has taken place within the Great Compact and has not shaken its foundational arrangements, but every moment of a constantly eroding present contains a wide range of embryonic futures. We cannot assume a straight-line projection from the past or an organic extension of the current situation into the future. Especially in view of the political and economic vicissitudes that the world is now experiencing, there is no assurance that the Great Compact will survive intact. If it does not, the Empire will have struck back at its own interests. [Most] proponents of international investment law, no matter where they stand on particular issues, seek a future that promises enhanced production and the efficient use of the resources of our planet in ways that sustain the environment, a future in which everyone is net better off and in which there are efficient and timely procedures for the adjustment of arrangements that benefit all yet have downsides for some and in which there are internationally supervised modes of dispute resolution. The resulting interdependence, one hopes, will also act as a restraint on the unilateral use of violence, one of the objectives of the Great Compact and, in my view, an ancillary objective of all economic integration. [At] the moment, however, it seems to have become fashionable in some quarters to see everything in zero-sum terms.[54]

There is always a need to hope. Part of a better future in the region relies upon the maximization of our identifications and common interests. Such undertaking should start by having a clearer understanding of the historical differences in legal traditions and practices between Canada, Mexico and the United States. Perhaps a major mistake in trying to integrate these three countries over the last quarter of century was to overlook the relevance of clarifying their respective approaches toward the law and its implications in a given polity. I owe such clarification to Guillermo, who enlightened me while I was doing doctoral studies at Yale Law School. In framing the continuous

52. *Ibid.*, at 5.
53. Oscar Cruz Barney & Carlos H. Reyes Díaz, *supra* note 24, at 50-51.
54. W. Michael Reisman, *supra* note 9, at 10.

deficit of the rule of law in Mexico, Guillermo explained that the huge gap between Mexican legal culture and those of developed countries is that Mexico has historically undertaken the lengthy and strict formulation of all kinds of laws, but when it comes time to applying them, it has opted for a lax and selective approach. In more developed countries, the situation is very much the reverse: the rule of law is characterized by a minimalist and flexible legislation, with ample room for interpretation, and a strict, nonselective and egalitarian application of the law where all citizens are treated in the same way regardless of their position in the political, social or economic structures.[55]

With this clarity, Guillermo revealed the unceasing conundrum of Mexico in relating itself with countries with a customary legal tradition such as that of the United States and Canada. His legacy in creating NAFTA as an instrument for common understanding in the region must be preserved by new generations as an inspiration for a brighter common future.

55. Jaime Olaiz-González, *At the Turn of the Tide: A Framework for a Policy-Oriented Inquiry into Strategies for the Transformation of the Constitutive Process of Authoritative Decision in Mexico*, Yale Law School Dissertations, 6, at 259 (2015). *See* http://digitalcommons.law.yale.edu/ylsd/6, accessed November 8, 2019.

CHAPTER 19

The Building of Space Environment: Note on Customary International Law in the Context of International Arbitration

Julien Cantegreil

Almost fifteen years ago, in a conversation, Guillermo Aguilar Álvarez had the foresight to draw attention to the reasoning behind Arbitration in burgeoning contexts, particularly with regard to applicable standards. Back in these days, the substitution of 'international law' with 'customary international law' as the minimum standard of treatment in the North American Free Trade Agreement (NAFTA)-related *Mondev* case had decisive consequences in that regard.[1]

The meticulous attention paid to the nature and scope of applicable standards has proved essential with regard to arbitration in environmental matters,[2] particularly when it comes to Space, where ever-growing activities will likely lead to more arbitration proceedings at the very moment when customary international regulations on environmental matters are being patiently developed.

Needless to say commercial satellites' resiliency has been vastly improved since the launch of the very first commercial *Early Bird* communications satellite (Intelsat I) on 6 April 1965. In particular, operators will soon be able to provide the infrastructure for an ubiquitous and significantly faster Internet. Operators will have to assume an important liability the day they turn satellite constellations into the very critical

1. Mondev Int'l Ltd. v. United States, Final Award (Oct. 11, 2002) at para 12. On the interpretation of NAFTA Article 1105(1), See Julien Cantegreil, 'The Final Award in Mondev International v. United States of America', in Guillermo Alvarez and W.M. Reisman, *The Reasons Requirement in International Investment Arbitration* (Martinus Nijhoff, 2008), at 33-62.
2. Julien Cantegreil, 'Implementing Human Rights in the NAFTA Regime: The Potential of a Pending Case: Glamis Corp v. USA', in Pierre-Marie Dupuy et al., *Human Rights in International Investment Law and Arbitration* (Oxford Univ. Press, 2009) at 367–95.

component of global communication infrastructure. The current congestion at Low-Earth Orbit (LEO) due to these constellations and the risks of damage they represent for the space environment requires us to assess how international arbitration takes into account environmental issues during in-orbit lifetime. The chapter is designed to underscore the importance of ongoing *de lege ferenda* reflections on the 'space environment'.

I THE MANY REGULATORY CONSTRAINTS OF LAUNCHING A SATELLITE

First of all, it should be noted that the complexity of the rules governing the manufacturing, authorisation, launch and operation of a satellite network leads to very specific kinds of arbitral disputes.

Space players must comply with international norms. The *Outer Space Treaty* (OST, 1967)[3] and then the *Liability Convention* (LC, 1972)[4] authorise space activities. They make states the main subjects of international space law, ultimately liable for national activities, whether by national space agencies or by private entities (Article VI, OST) and, potentially liable for any damage caused by these space activities on Earth or on other aircraft (strict liability) or in space (fault-based liability). In practice, international space law regulates many issues such as the identity of the 'launching state' (e.g., the state that procures the launch, the state from whose territory an object is launched and the state from whose facility an object is launched) as well as all international rights associated with this characterisation. It promotes the registration of 'space objects' (Article I, LC).[5] Furthermore, it defines the activities of satellites, whether they are remote sensing systems for foreign states,[6] positioning systems in certain orbital regions, End-of-Life satellites, Space Debris Mitigation (passivation, de-orbit, re-orbit, and break-up).[7] All of the above, being now an industrial reality.

Satellites must then comply with national norms, whether they are specific to their launch state or national rules applicable to the partners of those launch states. Although not all states have yet developed a complete legislative framework[8], domestic law also applies in the vast majority of cases when characterising the launching state (e.g., when the notion of 'procurement' is involved), when characterising satellites as 'active' (otherwise, the launching state may withdraw from its supervisory role), when

3. *See, e.g.*, Treaty on Principles Governing the Activities of States in the Exploration and Use of Outer Space, including the Moon and Other Celestial Bodies, 27 January 1967, 18 U.S.T. 2410, T.I.A.S. No. 6347, 610 U.N.T.S. 205.
4. *See, e.g.*, Convention on International Liability for Damage Caused by Space Objects, 29 March 1972, 24 U.S.T. 2389, T.I.A.S. No. 7762, 961 U.N.T.S. 187.
5. *See, e.g.*, Convention on Registration of Objects Launched into Outer Space, 15 January 1975, 28 U.S.T. 695, T.I.A.S. No. 8480, 1023 U.N.T.S. 15.
6. *See, e.g.*, the Principles Relating to the Remote Sensing of the Earth from Outer Space (COPUOS, 1986), in part. Principles IV and XII.
7. *See, e.g.*, Article IX, OST as well as the Inter-Agency Debris Coordination Committee 2002 space mitigation guidelines (revised in 2007).
8. The UN Office for Outer Space Affairs keeps an online database of states with national space legislations (25 to this day).

it comes to launch and operation authorisations, or rules on compensation and waiver of claims in the event of an accident, or entry on their national register (to clarify jurisdiction), or in the framework of the import, export or use of advanced space technology.

Requirements are often mixed. For instance, radio frequencies are both managed internationally by the International Telecommunication Union[9] (launch, but also rules and guidelines for orderly allocation and use of radio frequencies), and allocated and coordinated by the national administrator, which uses the definitions and concepts of the International Telecommunication Union when it comes to implementing international rules.

II TURN A SATELLITE INTO A UNIQUE ITEM IN TERMS OF ARBITRATION

These introductory remarks, which are far too brief and should also include the industrial and commercial context of the satellite market, show the dual singularity of arbitration disputes regarding commercial satellite telecommunications, which are the subject of the following thoughts.

On the one hand, arbitration proceedings must deal effectively, correctly and consistently with a *large number of legal rules and a high degree of internationality*. The involvement of fundamentally different actors (states, interstate operators and private companies) often leads arbitration disputes to involve all or part of the fields of public international law, national administrative law, civil and sometimes even criminal law, as well as private international law and contract law. This type of litigation also has a strong international dimension. Equipment used on the territory of the states in question (ground stations, user communication terminals, etc.), software and protocols developed for these areas, and the waves 'crossing' multiple sovereign territories trigger a multitude of national laws and jurisdictions. The use of outer space and crossing of radio waves also imply that any limitation on a state's jurisdiction can only be based on international law.

The space community also needs *binding solutions*. Space activities are inherently risky. This broad kaleidoscope of applicable legal regimes, actors and stakeholders, and potentially contentious subjects multiplies the opportunities for conflict on substantial issues for which solutions must be found quickly and cannot be achieved through diplomacy or negotiation.

In the era of satellite constellations, the recent reform related to the arbitration of space issues (I) does not, by any means, cover all the necessary reforms to the current legal framework for space operations (II). Arbitrators will be among the first to take on the question of the 'space environment', for which their work to characterise customary international law will be absolutely essential.

9. 193 states have joined the ITU as Member States, and 192 states are party to the ITU Constitution and Convention.

III AN OPERATIONAL DISPUTE SETTLEMENT MECHANISM FOR SPACE LAW

A International Commercial Arbitration of Telecoms

The current NewSpace revolution has not transformed the overall organisation of the space industry (manufacturers, integrators, launchers, operators, insurers). The various players in this industry traditionally include arbitration clauses in commercial satellite contracts. In general, this matter is handled well at the commercial level.[10]

For the most part, space contracts raise six types of issues.

1 The Manufacturer and the Manufacturing Process

The performance of a satellite must be strictly compliant with the operator's service objectives. The fact that the operator is actively involved in the manufacturing process, as is often the case, should not exempt the manufacturer from the contractual obligations associated with its provision. In this regard, the design and integration of telecommunications satellites are subject to detailed contractual commitments. They provide for the manufacturer to deliver the satellites either on the ground for approval (and transfer) of the risk of loss (the manufacturer then contracts a launch supplier) or to orbit (in which case the manufacturer assumes this responsibility).

But whatever the solution chosen, the manufacturing contracts provide for two situations that can occur during the satellite's manufacturing phase. Since an *accident* can damage the satellite at any time, it is customary for manufacturing contracts to provide for the manufacturer (and their subcontractors) to take out insurance against risks of loss or damage to a satellite during the manufacturing phase. Because *delays* may also occur, satellite manufacturing contracts often state that 'time is of the essence' with, where appropriate, specific remedies in favour of the operator. In addition to these legal and factual assessments, arbitrations generally pertain to provisions relating to the 'waiver' / 'limitation of liability' (gross negligence, wilful conduct, damages due for delays in the manufacturer's execution, reimbursement of payments made).

Difficulties, which may lead to arbitrations, can arise once the satellite is placed into orbit. Satellite manufacturers, component suppliers (both for spacecraft and launchers) and launch service providers usually disclaim all warranties for their spacecraft from the time of launch. Warranty disclaimers and limited remedies for defects are commonplace. However, some satellite purchase contracts have broken new ground in introducing time-limited/ partial warranties (e.g., for specific components) in the event of orbital failure, and in implementing other contractual obligations

10. Pamela L. Meredith & Marshal M. Lammers, 'Commercial Satellite Contract Arbitration: Special Legal Consideration', *American Review of International Arbitration*, Vol. 24, No. 3, 2013. *See also* Raymond G. Bender, 'International Arbitration – Satellite Communications: Arbitrator Perspective', in Horacio A. Grigera Naón & Paul E. Mason, *International Commercial Arbitration Practice: 21st Century Perspectives* (Lexis-Nexis 2010), Chapter 39.

for the manufacturer. In some cases, the manufacturer provides an express warranty, which may cancel a waiver.

2 *The Launcher and Satellite Launch Agreements*

Launching a space object into space remains a risky activity, as illustrated by the recent failures of the European launcher Vega. An issue during launch can confront an operator with a large number of problems: in these cases, the loss of the Falcon Eye 1 satellite (1.2 ton) built by Airbus Defense and Space (prime contractor) and Thales Alenia Space on behalf of the United Arab Emirates Army, and then the loss of Space Weather European Space Agency (ESA) satellites. But it can also be a simple delay, damage to the satellite, suboptimal separation of the satellite from the launch vehicle or placement on a wrong orbit that can lead to sub-optimal telecommunication service.

In such cases, arbitration is frequent. Launch agreements provide that satellite operators require their insurers to waive any remedy against the launch provider, in return for which the latter generally agree to a *best efforts* requirement for launching and delivering the satellite in orbit. As with satellite manufacturing contracts, the parties often distribute the risks among launch stakeholders (e.g., a replacement launch, paid for by insurance, as sole and exclusive remedy in the event of a launch failure). A key issue in arbitration is the validity and enforceability of liability limitation provisions,[11] which protect the launch supplier in the event of a launch failure (similarly to satellite manufacturers in the event of a manufacturing defect).

3 *Unilateral Termination of Manufacturing or Launch Contracts*

Reassuring a client as to the reliability of the launch vehicle (with an 'opt-out' provision in the event of a launch failure for instance), or simply for convenience (providing *termination charges*) can often lead to planning for a termination for non-performance in the event of a material breach (non-payment or failure to meet a milestone that does not result from a client's action or omission, or from a case of *force majeure*). Arbitrators may have to rule on the client's right to retrieve the *work in progress* (hardware components, partially completed satellite structure) and the associated intellectual property rights.

4 *In-Orbit Satellite Operations*

Latent manufacturing defects, operational errors or external forces (e.g., satellite collisions with orbital debris or space weather) constitute technical anomalies that can

11. For example, *Martin Marietta Corporation v. INTELSAT* where Martin Marietta claimed that the Commercial Space Launch Act's inter-party waiver provisions overrode Maryland law and precluded INTELSAT's claim of gross negligence. The Fourth Circuit disagreed, finding that 'neither the language of [statute] nor [its] legislative history reflects a congressional intent to protect parties from liability for their own gross negligence'.

damage the satellite or impact its performance. Satellite manufacturers seek to limit their liability, under the assumption that satellite operators, if they have not secured an absolute contractual exemption, should assume all post-launch risks and insure against them.

In this respect, arbitrators may have to rule on two common practices. *Incentive payments* on the one hand, which allow a satellite operator to retain contractual incentives provided for the manufacturer (typically 10 to 20% of the total cost of the satellite) in the event of a serious malfunction or flagrant failure of the satellite. However, a *limitation of liability* often forms the foundation of *motions to dismiss*. This requires arbitrators to question whether, instead of complying with the terms of the contract which attribute liability to the manufacturer, the ruling should fall under the law applicable to the contract. This would thus invalidate a limitation of liability clause based on gross negligence from the manufacturer, intentional fault or other circumstances. Many arbitration rules, particularly in the United States, allow arbitrators to grant such requests by exercising their discretionary power when conducting the proceedings. Some of these provisions have been invalidated in France and validated in the United States.[12] The role of arbitrators in determining the lawfulness of these provisions is essential: as commented in doctrine already, some authors have gone as far as noting that a recurrent use of these limitation of liability provisions in satellite contracts (satellite launch and purchase contracts, as well as in related subcontracts) reflected a specific practice in the satellite industry that should entitle to disregard national laws overriding the limitation of liability provisions.[13]

5 *Operator's In-Orbit Insurance*

Satellite operators may be required to take out insurance to cover in-orbit anomalies, while simultaneously requiring their insurers to waive all rights of subrogation against the manufacturer. This transfer of manufacturer's risk of default to the operator results in a high duty of care on the satellite operator (on the nature and extent of the partial/total/implied total loss due for the claim and upon disclosure to the insurer of potential anomalies known to the manufacturer or operator before launch).

Arbitrators are often faced with reviewing satellite performance assessments from satellite manufacturers, operators or insurers.[14] Arbitrators must traditionally assess whether the satellite has suffered a 'constructive total loss' or a 'partial loss'; whether the operator has 'acted as if they were not insured'; whether they have

12. In the Arabsat / Aerospatiale case in connection with the malfunction of the Arabsat 1A satellite, in a decision dated 15 June 1988 the Paris Court of Appeals relied on applicable French law ('garantie des vices cachés' from section 1645 of the Civil Code) to invalidate a contract's limitation of liability clause. On the contrary, in *Appalachian Insurance Co. v. McDonnell Douglas Corp*, the California Court of Appeals held that the parties intended by their contract to limit the manufacturer's liability.
13. *See, e.g.,* Alexis Mourre's remarks on French, Belgian, English, Italian and German laws.
14. *See* the *Telesat Canada v. Boeing* case related to defective solar arrays on Telesat's Anik F1 satellite, where the claimants alleged that Boeing was guilty of gross negligence and wilful misconduct.

exercised due diligence and informed the insurers of any material change that may affect the insured risk; what are the rights of secured creditors of the satellite operator/the insured party in the event of satellite loss. If the insurer is required to pay lenders by virtue of an additional clause relating to an insurance policy in a situation where they are not liable under the underlying policy, the insurer will for instance, in some key American jurisdictions be subrogated to the lenders' claim against the insured party, to the extent of the insurance payment.

6 U.S. Space Technology Export Controls and the ITAR Regime

The majority of space objects are American. Arbitrators involved often have to exchange technical information about satellites/ launchers, their performance, anomalies and failure. When the arbitration includes a non-US party and when technical information reaches the threshold of 'technical data', these exchanges of information are strictly controlled by the International Traffic in Arms Regulations (ITAR) ('technical data', 'defense services', 'assistance', nationality at stake). Whether the exchange takes place in the United States or abroad, the US State Department oversees (subject to civil and criminal sanctions) the subsequent dissemination of technical data to third parties and the use of technical data beyond the purposes for which authorisation is sought.

These requirements will certainly impact the arbitration process. While the applicant (and the defendant) is allowed to initiate the plea for arbitration (respectively the defence statement) before obtaining a 'technical assistance agreement' (TAA), she/he will however have to wait to proceed to get this agreement to exchange technical data and defence services (interpretation, explanation, analysis and discussion of technical data) for the purpose of producing documents, depositions, statements by experts, briefs, testimony, arguments, exhibits. The TAA must be approved by the US State Department. Arbitrators are often well advised to retain the services of a special ITAR lawyer and to arrange for ad hoc logistical measures to facilitate the participation of the Defense Technology Security Administration (DTSA) controller during discovery and hearings.

B Ongoing Improvements

1 Benefits of International Arbitration

Arbitration clauses are included in almost all types of satellite manufacturing, launch and insurance contracts. For the space industry, international arbitration has a triple advantage over judicial arbitration.

a Usual Benefits: Consent, International, Locus, Execution

Arbitration traditionally offers three guarantees. As a voluntary scheme, it results only from the *consent* of all parties, which can be granted by simply including an arbitration clause into the legal instrument that defines the relationship between the parties. In a genuinely international industry involving ground and space equipment, communicating with each other via radio waves and controlled by software and protocols, with the involved parties possibly located in several countries international arbitration eliminates the bothering risk of appearing before a *foreign court* while being, advantageously, possibly conducted in a wide variety of locations and within various institutions.[15] Finally, international arbitration makes it possible to reach *definitive and binding decisions*, which are internationally recognised and enforceable in the 144 signatory states of the New York Convention.

b *A High Degree of Procedural Flexibility*

The main strength of international arbitration in satellite matters lies in the ability for parties to choose which law will govern the arbitration procedure (in most cases, the law of the country in which the arbitration takes place) and to adapt the procedural rules that are used. The preliminary conference's objective is to coordinate the effectiveness of the entire procedure by addressing a large number of issues from the outset, e.g., ***threshold questions*** (on jurisdiction, arbitrability of claims, summary provision, requests for interim relief), ***applicable law*** (procedural and substantive); the duration and timing of ***pre-hearing briefs and opening statements***; *hearing logistics*; lay and expert *witness testimony*; ***post-hearing briefs and oral argument*** and ***the award*** (reasoned award or summary decision).

There are two main issues. On the one hand, rules relating to *discovery* are key since the parties may have a very different relative knowledge of the relevant information (facts surrounding a launch failure, anomaly shown by a satellite in orbit). Discovery tools help curb issues before the hearing, which can prove very useful given the amount and complexity of evidence generally involved in satellite arbitrations. The nature and extent of pre-hearing are sometimes defined in the arbitration provision. Yet the judicial systems in some countries allow for very little discovery, and many international arbitrators are reluctant to approve certain types of discovery (e.g., depositions) on the grounds that it would undermine the effectiveness of arbitrations.

Ensuring *confidentiality* is also crucial in a context where satellite disputes raise significant reputation issues, and often involve highly technical data that may be considered proprietary commercial information or trade secrets. Non-disclosure agreements allow all the parties involved to protect confidential information from third parties, and limit its use by other parties. They also help governments protect technical data involving 'state secrets' or defence concerns. Arbitrators are required by ethical rules not to disclose confidential information they receive during an arbitration procedure, unless otherwise required by law.

15. Satellite arbitrations are administered by various arbitral institutions, including the International Center for Dispute Resolution of the American Arbitration Association, the International Chamber of Commerce, and the London Court of International Arbitration. Ad hoc satellite arbitrations are conducted under the UNCITRAL rules as well.

c Officiating by Specialised Arbitrators

Satellite contract arbitrations are for the most part consistent with commercial arbitrations involving expensive high-tech equipment. However, certain laws, regulations and contractual practices may impact the timing, discovery and/or outcome of the satellite industry arbitration (special export clearance requirements, pervasive use of liability waivers and warranty disclaimers, customary payment structures in purchase contracts and due diligence requirements under satellite insurance policies). When dealing with this type of contracts, arbitrators, before drawing conclusions, usually deal with counter-intuitive space physics, complex technical concepts and contradictory statements from aerospace engineers. They must also be able to recognise the customs and practices of the satellite industry and often interpret ambiguous contractual provisions pertaining to manufacturing, launch and insurance, in order to assess the intention of all parties to reach an agreement (satellite manufacturers can rely on liability limitation provisions to protect themselves from financial risk, while satellite operators often challenge the validity of such provisions). Ideally, satellite engineers serve as expert witnesses appointed by each party to resolve technical problems or explain applications of satellite contracts.

2 Ongoing Improvements: Attempt by the Permanent Court of Arbitration

The dispute settlement mechanism under international space law can be improved.[16] In this regard, a Permanent Court of Arbitration advisory group recently recalled that a 'relatively strong consensus in the academic world' had been calling for this development since the mid-1980s.

a Several Shortcomings Remained

i Limited to States

As international space law was initially intended as a branch of public international law, dispute settlement was only considered for litigations between states and is therefore traditionally not accessible to private parties. For the *Claims Commission* provided for by the LC, for instance, private entities can only assert their rights via their state of nationality, which is subsidiary to the state where the damage occurred.[17] The

16. Permanent Court of Arbitration, *Optional Rules for Arbitration of Disputes Relating to Outer Space Activities* (Effective, 6 December 2011). *See* F. Pocar, 'An introduction to the PCA's optional rules for arbitration of disputes relating to outer space activities', *Journal of Space Law*, Vol. 38, No. 1, 2012, 171-210; Frans G. von der Dunk, 'About the New PCA Rules and Their Application to Satellite Communication Disputes', *Space, Cyber and Telecommunications Law Program Faculty Publications* (2015).
17. In the case of privately suffered damage though, the waiver of the usual requirement under international law for 'exhaustion of local remedies' before state claims are admitted reflects a desire not to prevent private entities from obtaining compensation for the damage suffered.

same is true for other arbitral mechanisms. At the *ICJ*, private entities are even more dependent on the willingness of the state (usually their state of nationality) to undertake an action of 'diplomatic protection', and must necessarily meet the prior requirement of 'exhaustion of domestic remedies'. This is even true for the WTO and, unsurprisingly, the International Telecommunication Union (ITU), which as an intergovernmental organisation is composed of sovereign states.

ii Limited in Scope

Even the most elaborate inter-state dispute settlement procedures, such as those provided for in the *LC*, rely on a *material scope* that is too limited for the sheer diversity of situations encountered in space matters. The scope of the *Claims Commission* thus remains limited *ratione materiae* even if the LC's dispute settlement provisions deal broadly with damage caused by a 'space object': it only deals with damage caused by satellites and the resulting liability, whereas questions of accountability can sometimes exceed those of liability; and it does not apply to many potentially relevant cases, for instance, in the case of damage caused independently of satellites by other elements of satellite communication systems (e.g., ground stations or mobile devices). The situation is not much more satisfactory elsewhere. For the ESA, the ESA Convention provides for arbitration between two or more Member States, or between states and the agency, which only concerns disputes relating to its interpretation and implementation. The arbitration provided for by the ITU instruments is also limited to certain issues such as harmful interference to recorded radio frequencies.

iii Limited in Specialisation

International arbitration agreements relating to space law between private parties generally provide for arbitration under UNCITRAL Rules. These rules, while praised for their broad applicability, are not necessarily adapted to space-related disputes. Other international institutions mentioned above are not necessarily suited in terms of specialisation neither. For instance, the International Court of Justice (ICJ) - even disregarding the lack of expertise of its judges on satellite matters cannot implement national or contract law since the ICJ implements public international law as the 'law of nations' on which its judges are indeed experts. Conversely, the specific role of the ITU raises doubt about whether an arbitration established under Article 41 of the IUT Convention or the Optional Protocol would be sufficiently familiar with public international law, political and security aspects, as well as commercial notions raised by satellite issues, to comprehensively understand and address all possible angles of a dispute over satellite communications. By symmetry, these limitations would be similar in the WTO framework.

iv Limited in Their Constraining Power

The highly politicised environment surrounding space activities, including satellite communications, often makes it unlikely that both parties to a major dispute agree in advance to a binding arbitration. This is the case for the Claims Commission, whose decision is simply a 'final and recommendatory award, which the parties shall consider in good faith'. It is worth noting that the WTO could provide with a more interesting mechanism: while it does not (necessarily) lead to a binding solution imposed by a neutral third party, it does uphold the Dispute Settlement Body's recommendations and decisions when no consensus vote rejects them.

b *PCA Optional Rules (2011)*

Based on the analysis of these weaknesses, the PCA Optional Rules for Arbitration of Disputes Relating to Outer Space Activities were adopted on 6 December 2011 (although they have yet to be used). These rules are based on the 2010 UNCITRAL Arbitration Rules with amendments made to, among others things: reflect the specific characteristics of disputes involving the use of outer space by states, international organisations and private entities; reflect the relevant component of public international law and appropriate international practice; give parties the freedom to choose an arbitration court composed of one, three or five members; provide for the creation of a specialised list of arbitrators and a list of scientific and technical experts; and make suggestions for the implementation of procedures to ensure confidentiality.

i Fundamental Scope of the Rules

The authors of these optional rules put emphasis on a broad scope by avoiding discussions on whether a satellite communications dispute would only revolve around 'in space' aspects (necessary to trigger the LC dispute settlement mechanism for instance), or technical/operational aspects (to trigger the IUT dispute settlement mechanism) or trade-related aspects (necessary to trigger the WTO dispute settlement mechanism). The PCA rules leave it entirely to the parties to rely on the rules in question without having to justify the legal basis for the dispute. This incidentally helps bypass the issue of the nature of 'space activities' or where 'outer space' begins. As is customary in arbitration matters, a party's agreement to arbitration means that it expressly waives any immunity from jurisdiction that it might otherwise invoke.

ii Establishment and Operation of the Court

A high degree of flexibility was also sought when establishing the tribunal, even examining all possible sizes for the panel of arbitrators. The Secretary-General of the PCA must simply act as the appointing authority of the court, and allow the usual provisions to be applied, whether they refer to the mandatory disclosure by arbitrators of circumstances likely to affect their impartiality, the possibility for any party to challenge an arbitrator on this ground and, if necessary, a potential alternative procedure. A waiver of the liability of the arbitrators and, more broadly, of any person appointed by the arbitration court for any act or omission related to the arbitration is traditionally provided for.

iii Major Procedural Provisions

Arbitrators shall apply the rules of national and/or international law as they deem appropriate, in cases where the parties, who have the right to do so, have not decided on the law or rules of law applicable to the merits of the dispute. If the parties have expressly authorised it, the court may also decide the case as an '*amiable compositeur* or *ex aequo et bona*'. The broad discretionary powers given to arbitrators in procedural matters are well exemplified in four areas: (i) possibility for third parties to *join* the proceedings (subject only to the prerequisite that they are indeed a party to the arbitration agreement); (ii) possibility to resort to a *confidentiality adviser* in the context of sensitive commercial information; (iii) discretion left to arbitrators as to the admissibility, relevance, importance and probative value of the *evidence* presented, and the possibility of calling upon *experts* (possibly not included in the PCA's list of scientific, technical and/or operational experts) in scientific or technical matters after consultation with the parties; (iv) possibility of imposing *interim measures* at the request of one of the parties. Except a 'simple' mistake is subsequently detected and can be corrected, awards on these space disputes would be 'final and binding on the parties'.

IV SPECIFIC CHALLENGE OF A CRITICAL INFRASTRUCTURE

The previous reflection would be sufficient to exhaust the matter if the space dispute could be dealt with 'all other things being equal'. However, the emergence of the risks posed by satellite constellations requires reflection on international arbitration in space affairs to be taken to another level. The consequences of in-orbit collisions must shift attention from *ex post* to *ex ante*, from micro to macro, from the framework of the arbitral award to the ongoing maturation of applicable standards.

A The Benefits of Arbitration: A Hypothetical Case

Let us take the following example specifically rooted in a Swiss Re scenario.[18] A drifting satellite A hits satellite B1 of constellation B, destroying B1 completely, and causing a cloud of debris to pass through the daily orbit of the remaining operational satellites of constellation B. Let us imagine that JSpoC, the best indicator LEO risk to date was tracking A and B1 but that inaccurate collision risk information led to B1 not being relocated before the accident. For the sake of simplicity, let us finally suppose that B1 (now just drifting debris) was launched and operated in France, its 'launching state' while satellite A was launched from the United States, authorised by the Federal Communications Commission (FCC) and the National Oceanic and Atmospheric

18. The two use cases proposed by Swiss re in 2011 ('Space Debris, On collision course for insurers') and 2018 ('New space, new dimensions, new challenges, How satellite constellations impact space risk') are adapted here.

Administration (NOAA), and owned by an American company, which let us assume, is headquartered in California like many NewSpace companies.

Let us now suppose that A has neither taken out civil liability insurance for damage caused during in-orbit operations (which is currently not required under U.S. law or by the FCC) nor followed the plan for the disposal of end-of-life satellites presented by the FCC. Let us assume that no defects or malfunctions have been found, so it is unclear whether or not legal actions against A's manufacturer reasonably succeed. As for B, let us imagine that they have taken out a fully comprehensive ownership insurance (covering the replacement value of the satellite in the event of a launch failure, or malfunction due to an internal defect or external causes such as orbital debris) for the launch and the subsequent 24 months in orbit. However, B has not taken out 'revenue' insurance, their 'all risk' insurance has expired at the time of impact, and the risk of collision has been deemed acceptable by B1's operator: their insurance will not compensate for the damage.

Finally let us imagine that, at the time of the collision, only some of the satellites in constellation B had been deployed. Experts indicate that the incompleteness of the constellation will compromise the communication service provided by Constellation B to its customers, and therefore cause an additional loss of revenue for B. They also assess that the launch of the remaining satellites to form Constellation B could significantly increase the risk of a post-crash collision. Total losses for both A and B will therefore be significant.

1 Following in the Footstep of the National Legal Track

Without insurance coverage, B may wish to file a tort claim against A in a U.S. domestic court, as expressly permitted by the *LC*. Since A is headquartered in California, with the United States as their launching state, B could sue A in a California federal court[19] under the California state's tort law. California has a reputation to be a favourable jurisdiction for plaintiffs, and A will undoubtedly, but with great difficulty,[20] challenge the jurisdiction, adequacy of the court and applicability of California law to a collision in space.

In practice, if California law applies, B will have to prove that it was A's responsibility to avoid collision with B1, that A failed to meet the relevant required standards of conduct, that A's conduct was the 'proximate cause' of the collision and

19. The court has personal jurisdiction over A because it is headquartered there. The court has subject matter jurisdiction because of the international nature of the suit (the parties are in diversity) and the amount in question is over the requisite amount.
20. A would presumably oppose the use of the *LC* by a California court on the grounds that the treaty is not applicable law in the United States and that, even if a California court has jurisdiction, a court in France would be more suitable (Forum non conveniens, an argument that is unlikely to prevail). B1 would counter that: (1) the tortious act (A's decision-making and commanding of the satellite) was committed in California; (2) the res communis status of space is irrelevant since the US has jurisdiction over A under OST, Article 8; and (3) the LC expressly permits an aggrieved private party to use national courts.

that it resulted in substantial losses for B. Furthermore B will likely have to demonstrate negligence on the part of A, namely: a legal duty (an obligation to de-orbit their satellite, as indicated in their licence applications), a breach of legal duty by the defendant (by delaying the de-orbiting of A at the altitude of a satellite constellation such as B's), the fact that the offence constitutes the proximate or legal cause of the damage (i.e., presumption of negligence under California Negligence Law, or the fact that A's operator could have foreseen that their conduct could lead to collisions or alteration of other satellites and that the cause of collisions was a 'proximate' cause). If B makes a satisfactory damage mitigation effort,[21] the damages set in California tort law shall constitute 'the amount which will compensate for all the damage approximately caused thereby, whether it could have been anticipated or not', and may include earnings foregone, profits lost during repair, property replacement.

2 Following in the Footstep of the International Legal Track

B might also want to recoup its losses by asking France to exercise its right to a judicial remedy under existing treaties. This international strategy makes sense both for B because California (A's domicile) presents a victim-centred legal system, and for A because of the ambiguity surrounding Constellation insurance, especially since any attempt by B to sue the US government in a US court for failing to exercise adequate regulatory oversight over A would likely face a 'sovereign immunity' defence.[22] France may therefore wish to take action on behalf of B1 under the OST, the LC and the general principles of international law.

In this case, France would face the difficult task of showing that every provision of *LC*, Article 3, is met. The so-called Cosmos 954 case (1976) set a useful precedent in terms of damages:[23] the physical destruction of B1 falls under the 'loss of or damage to property of states or of persons, natural or juridical ...',[24] which justifies compensation damages under the *LC*. Since the damage occurred in space, France would have to prove a 'fault' on the part of A (*LC*, Article 3), knowing this term is in fact poorly defined in the *LC*: it most likely assumes a lower degree of guilt than that of 'gross negligence' (indeed this term is used elsewhere in the *LC*).[25] Finally France should

21. It is unlikely that A may prevail in urging the court to apply French law or the 'fault' standard of the LC, especially if these impose a greater burden on B1 and allow less damages. The court may revert to the default rule for the diversity cases and apply the substantive law of the forum state, here California tort law, and federal procedural law.
22. For example, *see* Swiss Re, 'New space, new dimensions, new challenges, How satellite constellations impact space risk' (July 2018).
23. In this case, the Soviet Union settled the claim with no admission of liability on its part.
24. Note that the debris impact and resulting impairment of other B satellites may also qualify as damage if B1 can establish that the damage was 'traceable directly' to the deorbiting manoeuvre of A and its collision with B1. The matter of indirect damage was only briefly considered by the drafters of the *LC*, with the majority, such as the United States, taking the position that indirect damage with only a hypothetical causal connection should not be covered as a general matter.
25. Is A's delayed deorbiting of the satellite compatible with the expected behaviour of a reasonable satellite operator under the same circumstances? Should the US government have exercised regulatory oversight over A? Today there are no mandatory international standards of conduct regarding debris mitigation to establish a standard of care against which fault can be assessed,

specify the compensation sought: if the *LC* does indeed provide for compensation damages in accordance with the 'condition, which would have existed if the damage had not occurred', to what extent should this 'condition, which would have existed' be restored if the damage had not been caused (loss of income and profits, other damage, under which legal system)? The Claim Commission provided for by the *LC* (which has only been formally invoked once and whose decision is only considered final and binding if the parties have agreed to be bound) shall make its decision whatever the ambiguity of terms such as 'fault' and 'damage'. Without compromise between France and the United States, this path would therefore be very uncertain.

As we can see, whether B opts for the treaty route or the American courts, they will have to prove that A was wrong. The particular legal standard (fault, negligence, culpa or any other standard) as well as the burden of proof varies according to the applicable law on conduct in space, whether national or international,[26] and it is not yet clear whether it would be enough to demonstrate liability.[27]

We can draw two provisional conclusions from this hypothetical (yet highly realistic) case. Both strategies are based on ambiguities regarding applicable terms and standards, a problem that remains even if the arbitration dispute is subject to the PCA. The risks posed by the space environment do not allow arbitration activities to undergo such uncertainty: legal reflection must move from *ex post* to *ex ante*, from micro to macro, and seek to further analyse applicable environmental standards. This research can be conducted in the following context.

B A New Context: 'New Space' in Perspective

Space is a relatively new resource, first explored in 1957 when the Soviet Union launched the first artificial satellite, Sputnik I, into space, followed shortly afterwards by the United States with their Explorer I satellite. Well over 100 countries now own or share ownership of a satellite in orbit.

From the start, the treaties' authors avoided the political question of national sovereignty in space[28] and defined space in the OST as the equivalent of a 'global common': '[o]uter space ... shall be free for exploration and used by all states without discrimination of any kind' and '[s]pace ... is not subject to national appropriation by

but only voluntary, non-binding standards and guidelines such as those of the Inter-Agency Space Debris Coordination Committee (IASDC), the UN, the International Organization for Standardization (ISO) and the International Telecommunication Union (ITU).

26. Aside from the OST and the LC, which concern the liability of states for damage caused by satellites in space, there is no treaty regulating space debris, only non-binding international guidelines (2007 COPUOS debris mitigation guidelines, 2010 ITU recommendations, etc.). B would argue that the obligation to move a satellite to a graveyard orbit has now reached the status of customary international law, which is binding. Such an opinion is questionable.
27. FCC regulations require companies applying for a satellite licence to describe the operational strategies they will implement to mitigate orbital debris. The FCC does not specify a post-mission disposal altitude.
28. *See* Articles I, II, III. Article I gives no definition for the term 'province of all mankind', and it differs from the terminology used in other global commons legal regimes, such as the high seas, deep seabed and Antarctica.

claim of sovereignty, by means of use or occupation, or by any other means'. Cooperation initially prevailed, as evidenced by the rapid emergence of an international legal regime to protect the collective interests of these global commons.

1 *LEO Is Currently Subject to Two Types of Risks*

LEO is currently subject to two types of risks. First, a military risk, for instance, with the American National Defence Authorization Act for Fiscal Year 2015, which calls for the development of 'offensive space control and active defensive strategies and capabilities'. Anti-satellite (ASAT) tests have taken place, and several 'space commandments' have been established in 2019 and 2020, with very sophisticated capabilities.

Second, a civil risk due to the convergence of several simultaneous phenomena. The first one is the multiplication of smallsats. Estimated at USD 2.69 billion in 2017, the global market for small satellites alone is expected to reach USD 6.91 billion by 2023. The miniaturisation of satellites entails risks of collisions,[29] in addition to the uncertainties posed by inaccurate trajectory measurements from the ground, high orbital speeds and many other unknowns, particularly in atmospheric density and failures models,[30] and the lack of experience/compliance of new players. Countries start to react to this risk, for instance, in the United States with the PROSWIFT ACT, signed into law on 21 October 2020 that works as a bipartisan and bicameral compromise to establish a federal level structure to deal with threats to critical infrastructure and national security that have becomes numerous in an era of smallsats.[31]

Moreover, the amount of debris (fragmentation debris, inactive payloads, operational debris and micro particles) has been increasing since 1957 because atmospheric drag at that altitude is not high enough to burn all flying derelict objects. This situation has become irreversible ('Kessler syndrome') and puts the most densely populated LEO orbits at even greater risk since only a small portion of this debris is catalogued (there are now nearly 19,000 objects over 10 cm, and debris between 10 cm and a few millimetres in low-earth orbit are in the hundreds of million).[32]

29. *See* the collision of two intact spacecrafts in outer space in 2009 (Iridium 33 / Cosmos 2251), the AUAR Satellite uncontrolled spiralling re-entry, Russia's Phobos-Grunt only estimated re-entry path, residual debris from Germany's ROSAT satellite into the Bay of Bengal as well as the 2013 collision of Ecuador's Pegasus with particles from the fuel tank of a Soviet rocket over the Indian Ocean.
30. Even in the GEO context. See the conclusions made by Altius Space Machines in 'Open Source Analysis of Iridium Failures and the implications for Big LEO Constellations', *Spacecraft Anomalies and Failures 2017 Workshop*, December 2017.
31. See the statement by Sen. Gary Peter (D-Michigan) at https://spacepolicyonline.com/news/president-signs-proswift-space-weather-bill-but-with-caveats.
32. *See* already in 2009, Brian Weeden, *The Numbers Game, The Space Review* (13 July 2009). Privately funded companies or organisations are collecting significant data on satellite orbits, which is dedicated to assisting in space safety and debris mitigation. See the Space Data Association, Exoanalytics, AGI, LeoLabs, NorthStar. In Space Data are key to provide assessment capabilities. See Robert Scott, 'Toward Microsatellite Based Space Situational Awareness' (2013) and Alex Herz et al., 'Utilizing Novel Non-traditional Sensor Tasking Approaches to

At the beginning of a new solar cycle, Space Weather also poses an increasingly accepted danger.[33] Radiation from coronal mass ejections is unpredictable and difficult to define, and can disrupt radio transmissions, affect satellites and, in extreme[34] cases, disrupt their functions[35] even to the point of failure.[36]

Finally, LEO satellites are still largely underinsured. Introduced as early as Intelsat 1, space insurance started off in the mid-1970s with initial policies covering all potential damage caused to a satellite until the end of its life. The market reached maturity in the 1990s and has since continued to grow, in line with the evolution of the space industry as a whole.[37] The insurance market is highly cyclical, focuses on geosynchronous equatorial orbit (GEO) and has long been facing a decline in premiums while it struggles to find a model that perfectly fits satellite constellations.[38] In 2018, the space insurance market as a whole posted a loss, with gross premiums of circa USD 458 million being overwhelmed by losses and claims of circa USD 597 million. In 2019, Swiss Re (with long-term post-launch cover ranging up to five years after launch, and a theoretical maximum capacity on a per-risk basis of circa USD 30-USD 40 million, representing about 5% of the entire market capacity) withdrew from space insurance, with an automatic rise in premium rates, and an effect on in-orbit space insurance premium rates. End of 2020, even with these rising premium rates, US insurer American International Group, Inc. (AIG) (with circa USD 20 million and USD 25 million in space business premium US dollar) has exited as well the space insurance market following an extended period of unprofitability. At the same time, most LEO Constellations are uninsured. Space insurance as we know is in need of change.

2 *Tragedy of the Commons*

These risks occur in a context of 'tragedy of the commons', which arises when many people benefit from a collective resource without anyone being compelled to bear the cost. The resource becomes overexploited and is generally destroyed.[39] This situation also occurs in Space: private and government actors are strongly compelled to launch

Enhance the Space Situational Awareness Picture Maintained by the Space Surveillance Network' (2016), and Bin Jia, 'Multiple Space Object tracking via a Space-Based Optical Sensor' (March 2016).

33. See ESA's Annual Space Environment Report (17 July 2019) and 'Space Weather Study Results', PwC, November 2016.
34. Seradata SpaceTrak.
35. On 13 March 1989, a solar flare tripped the circuit breakers for Quebec, Canada, which protect the electrical power grid, and caused a nine-hour blackout. About forty satellites are believed to have suffered critical or catastrophic mishaps as a direct result of a geomagnetic storm. *See* J. P. Eastwood, 'The Economic Impact of Space Weather: Where Do We Stand?', *Risk Analysis*, Vol. 37, No. 2, 2017.
36. Darren McKnight, 'Examination of Spacecraft Anomalies Provides Insight Into Complex Space Environment' (EUCASS, 2017).
37. In some countries such as France, third-party liability insurance has even become mandatory for all operators, in accordance with Statute No. 2008-518 (3 June 2008).
38. Cécile Gaubert, 'Insurance Involvement on New Space Activities Developments' (IAC Bremen, October 2018).
39. Herders using a shared pasture, according to Garrett Hardin's famous example (1968). This is generally the case when a rational actor using a common resource is encouraged to use as many

new satellites but much less to clean up potential debris, even though it poses a significant and lasting threat (repercussions could last thousands of years without specific intervention beyond 1,000 km in altitude). The deployment of smallsat constellations above 800 km will inevitably trigger an exponential growth in orbital debris and give rise to new accident risks, as illustrated by the near miss between Starlink and ESA satellites in September 2019.[40] This lack of incentives for space actors to remove and not add orbital debris creates a 'tragedy of the commons' on a spatial scale. This is the very specific challenge of the 'space environment'.

C Market to Find Technical Solutions

Solving this tragedy of the commons requires the implementation of a new legal framework that will impact the modalities of international satellite arbitration.

1 Solving the Past: The Case of Active Debris Removal

Numerous technical solutions have been suggested to limit the number of debris (laser, docking satellite to latch onto objects and force them into destructive re-entry, space tethers, Gossamer sails, etc.), notably through On-Orbit Servicing (OOS) solutions.[41] Some of the above are technically feasible as shown in March 2020, with one company refuelling an asset in GEO and, soon, in March 2021 another company deorbiting a Debris. It is common practice to transform these ideas into business through a tax approach (e.g., levy a tax on satellite launches to generate revenue to remove orbital debris or mitigate the creation of new debris by modifying the behaviour of private-sector space actors)[42] or an approach based on negotiable rights (which satellite operators would use to compensate for their debris pollution by removing others), indexed on the marginal cost of debris.[43]

As one of many examples, another suggestion consists in increasing the prospects of return on investment thanks to a blend of technological/insurance/regulation

resources as possible, as quickly as possible (reaping all the benefits while bearing fractional costs), even when done unsustainably.

40. Jon Brodkin, SpaceX Satellite was on 'collision course' until ESA satellite was re-routed, 3 September 2019, *Forbes*.
41. Numerous projects. See, for instance, Airbus DS, 'The Cycler, The affordable companion for Post Mission Disposal in massive constellations', *5th European Workshop on Space Debris Modelling and Remediation* (CNES, June 2018).
42. To avail itself of any tax credit for extracting orbital debris, a company must first obtain title to the space debris / owner's consent to harvest the debris. The Space Resource Act of 2015 allows the United States to license its citizens to engage in the commercial extraction of space resources (defined as an 'abiotic resource in situ in outer space'). Under the OST, the owner of a space object or part thereof located in space is not divested of title simply because the property or part thereof has become orbital debris. This title problem can be addressed by the United States exercising its sovereign power to take title to private property, either by the eminent domain power (taking, public purpose and just compensation) or by police power (Fifth Amendment's due process requirement usually satisfied by complying with the statutory procedures governing forfeiture of the targeted private property, see Space Act of 2015, Space Policy Directive).
43. Howard A. Baker, 'Space Debris: Legal and Policy Implications' 4 (1989).

solutions.[44] This proposal relies on the ownership of space objects' structural parts that were made of metal (and therefore reusable) and the fact that debris can be defined as an 'abiotic in situ space resource'. The introduction of *compulsory in-orbit civil liability insurance* (for the sake of argument, let us disregard some existing exceptions, for instance, gross negligence, intentionality, non-compliance), supplemented by the introduction of an *in extremis* rescue provision when a satellite is beyond repair or becomes useless,[45] also allows ownership and, as a last resort, ownership of the profits generated[46] to be transferred to insurers without this being the case for the spacecraft as such.[47]

Beyond these stopgap solutions, it is clear that Active Debris Removal (ADR) requires a profound legal reform.[48] International arbitrators should be part of this endeavour. As suggested in doctrine, they are in a prime position to build on the *Trail Smelter* decision ('cross-border rule') on the basis that the *OST* terms – apart from the 'register' condition were considered 'declaratory of general international law'.[49] The *Trail Smelter* case law recognises the ability of customary international law 'not to knowingly allow the territory of a state to be used for acts contrary to the rights of other states'. In its decision on the *Corfu channel case*, did not the ICJ declare Albania responsible for the minefields in its territorial waters? Did not the ICJ reaffirm the principle of prevention of the Corfu channel in the case of *Pulp Mills on the Uruguay River (Argentina v. Uruguay, 2009)*[50]? But it is difficult to see how to apply the *Trail Smelter* case law in the field of space, where the concept of 'jurisdiction' is so difficult

44. See Lucien Rapp, Maria Lucas-Rhimbassen, Cristiana Santos & George Antony Long, 'Conceptual Model for a Profitable Return on Investment from Space Debris as Abiotic Space Resource'.
45. UNIDROIT defines Salvage as 'a legal or contractual right or interest in, relating to or derived from a space asset that vests in the insurer upon payment of a loss relating to the space asset'. Private entities proceeding to such rescue might not, according to space law, obtain title (jurisdiction and control) since Registry States are responsible for 'their' space objects.
46. According to Article 1(d) LC, the 'space object' remains the property of the space object's owner at the time of launch or any lawful successor in the ownership interest. Note that Baker, while noting the United States position that 'space refuse' is potentially a 'space object' for purposes of the LC and OST, nevertheless considers the issue to be 'unclear'. (if however 'space object' is defined as an object 'designed *for use* in outer space', then inactive payloads would not be included).
47. The insurer might then outsource the 'debris' recycling to a third party and benefit from the benefits generated. Salvage has already been applied in 1984 when the Westar VI and the Palapa-B2, left stranded in LEO, were rescued by the Space Shuttle before being left in storage until being sold a few years later, respectively as Asiasat-1 and Palapa-B2R.
48. See, *e.g.*, Astroscale, 'Perspective from a Venture Space Company on Regulatory Framework for Addressing Space Debris', IAC Bremen, 2018.
49. Article III, OST which obliges states to pursue the exploration and use of outer space 'in accordance with international law', may also indicate that the rules of customary international law, as they apply between states, extend to space activities.
50. The ICJ has stated that this obligation 'is now part of the corpus of international environmental law'. In his study on space debris, Baker argued that 'the effect of Articles II and VI of the OST is to apply the *Corfu Channel* and *Trail Smelter* principles to governmental and non-governmental activity in outer space and to heighten a state's duty of due diligence. In the absence of any specific agreement to the contrary, there is a customary rule of international law, which provides that states, either individually or together with other states in international organizations, are liable for damages caused to other states through acts committed within their jurisdiction, particularly where those acts are committed with a high degree of state participation and supervision. Launching of space objects would appear to fall within that kind of category'.

to transpose to environments (and objects) that are not always subject to direct and real constraints. Legal developments would nevertheless remain particularly useful at two levels.

Customary international law applicable to military activities in outer space could be clarified. While Article III, OST, does indeed stipulate that all activities in outer space must comply with international law, how does this concretely apply to military activities? Several attempts have failed, such as the implementation of a non-binding international code of conduct for activities in outer space or, with no verification mechanism, the United Nations Conference on Disarmament's attempt at a treaty on the 'prevention of the placement of weapons in outer space' (PPWT). As mentioned, the project of a manual on 'international law applicable to military uses of outer space' (MILAMOS), led by *McGill University's Institute of Air and Space Law* in collaboration with Adelaide University, would impact the decision-making process and therefore, where appropriate, the formulation of customary law through state practice.

Clarifications must also be made at the civil level. ADR technologies assumes a state, or another private entity from a state, touches, interferes with or removes a space object without the consent of the launching state, and engages in risky activities. The initial launching state of the eliminated object, as well as the state that launched the spacecraft controlling the de-orbiting manoeuvre, could both be held liable for damage caused during de-orbiting. This is precisely why some clarifications are needed.[51] For example, launch states are liable, but to what extent[52]? There is uncertainty about the meaning of the term 'space object' / 'object launched into space' for the purposes of the *OST* and *LC*. 'Non-functional space objects' are still 'space objects', but is it the case for an exploded satellite? Are 'fragments of a space object' still a 'space object'? After all, states can renounce ownership of abandoned or disused objects, turning them into *res derelicta*. While space debris does originate from materials launched into space, it is essential to clarify whether all space debris is indeed 'objects [...] launched into space' and collisions involving such 'objects' trigger the provisions of Articles VI, OST (businesses) and Article VII, OST (states).[53] A similar argument could be made with regard to the *LC*, using fault liability for collisions in orbit. The way in which 'fault' can be attributed to space debris (assuming it is indeed a space 'object') is not without its own challenges.[54] It would be key to clear up whether debris can be described as a

51. Not just legal clarifications. In practice, these mechanisms could be used for surveillance activities or for more aggressive purposes mooring and removing debris could require detailed technical information on the space object or allow reverse engineering, which could have an impact on intellectual property, confidentiality and export control (ITAR). This operation therefore requires strict agreements between the 'mover' and the owner/operator of the space object, as well as export agreements for technical assistance and authorisations.
52. None of the space treaties contains a 'per se' ban on '[l]ittering the outer space environment' or specific rules about space debris. Arguments for state liability for space debris have often been based upon the more general statements contained in the OST, particularly Article VII.
53. See Article VII, Article VIII as well as Article VI (whose reference to responsibility is somewhat 'vague' though).
54. *See, e.g.*, the collision in orbit or a non-manoeuvrable small satellite (First Ecuadorian satellite NEE-01 Pegaso Launched 25 April 2013) with the particle cloud from an old Soviet-era rocket (launched in 1985). In this case, the satellite was insured and loss compensated by insurance, and there has been no claim under the LC.

'harmful contamination' under the *OST* Article.[55] Beyond *LC*, Article I (a), Article VIII (1), and Article XII,[56] it is not clear if the *LC* considers that 'damage' extends to the costs of environmental remediation or to any other damage that would not directly affect lives or economic property.[57] For the state (or international organisation) that controls the withdrawal from orbit to bear responsibility, an agreement between the two states would be necessary. The insurance market may need to take these risks into account.

2 *Caring for the Future: Have No In-Orbit Accidents*

The vast majority of commercial satellites providing telecommunications services operate in geostationary orbit. With mobile, 5G, ongoing developments in ground antennas and satellite constellations, etc., the low-earth orbit has progressively become a critical area for the future growth of a market aiming for both ubiquitous and faster internet[58] telecommunications. Only time will tell which parts of the LEO will be most used. Risks of collision have already become critical in these congested orbits,[59] where certain satellites are no longer manageable or even under control. In the meantime, understanding of the overall orbital situation remains limited, with regard to both debris and Space Weather, and the rise of satellite constellation only compounds existing risks.[60]

The international community is well aware of these risks and has taken several measures since the 1972 *LC* to curb space debris that could result from shocks, failures or erosions.[61] Various technologies have also been introduced to guarantee the

55. OST offers minimal guidance as to the mitigation of space debris at state level, with much interpretation left to lawyers. For example, Article IX of the OST (what constitutes 'harmful contamination' or what such 'appropriate measures' consist of + international consultation as to what would 'cause potentially harmful interference' with activities of other states) is hardly an 'absolute injunction' against risky activities and, in any event it only applies to 'future planned space activities', not 'activities already completed', meaning that Article IX, even if applicable, may be of little utility in dealing with space debris ('which usually is created through past activities'). Or Article V of the OST (what is a 'phenomenon' that may be 'a danger to the life or health of astronauts').
56. Article I (a) LC (definition), Article VIII (1) LC (damage) and Article XII LC (compensation).
57. This became obvious during the Kosmos 954 episode, for which the rather vague definition of damage in the LC posed a genuine challenge, and the main 'damage' claimed by Canadians was the cost of cleaning up environmental pollution on properties that were not used for agricultural or industrial purposes.
58. As a reflection on the companies' valuation, *see* Adam Jonas, 'SpaceX, Starlink and Tesla: Moving into Orbit' (Morgan Stanley, 17 September 2019).
59. See Brian Weeden, 'Congested and Contested: Current Trends in Space Security' (World Secure Foundation, 18 April 2016).
60. For example, Jonas Radtke, 'Interaction of the Space Debris Environment with Mega Constellations Using the Example of the OneWeb Constellation', 2016 and B. Bastida Virgili et al., 'Risk to Space Sustainability from Large Constellations of Satellites', *Acta Astronautica*, Vol. 126 (September-October 2016).
61. While applicable to situations in which space debris may cause damage to a functioning satellite ('fault', without defining the standard), the LC was yet primarily designed to address situations where de-orbiting satellites and space debris would cause damage in the Earth's atmosphere or on the Earth's surface (strict liability applies).

resilience of future satellites, using solutions such as avoidance, shock absorption, insulation (aluminium, Kapton or other polymers) or by adding external protection.

In its FCC application of September 2019, Amazon was not able to provide 'any casualty risk data to the FCC',[62] considering that 'the specific design and composition of certain satellite components remained outstanding'. In the future, the rise of LEO constellation programmes – as illustrated by the granting of numerous licences such as for OneWeb, by the launch of numerous satellites such as SpaceX's Starlink,[63] and by the 'verticalisation' of the entire value chain, like for Amazon and its Internet platform, Blue Origin launchers, Amazon Web Services Cloud solution and the Amazon Web Services ground stations antenna system – should contribute to significantly strengthen practices and standards regarding behaviour in space.[64]

Three major developments are expected.

a *Technical Assistance Missions to Drastically Limit In-Orbit Failures*

Satellites are certainly more fragile than they were originally meant to be.[65] Despite progresses made throughout the supply chain (as illustrated by OneWeb's breakthroughs), the establishment of nanosat constellations will only exacerbate this fragility. Furthermore, this will hardly be offset by the choice to operate at low altitude and reduce the programmed lifetime of satellites.[66] Indeed, the current volumes of constellations, and the fact that satellites are produced on a large scale, make it impossible to maintain failure ratios that have been tolerated until now (13 % of satellite failures, 8 % of anomalies inaccurately or not elucidated at all): the community must therefore drastically curb the amount of failures in orbit.

The On Orbit Servicers currently being developed are of limited interest in this respect. They are mainly geared towards GEO. They have led agencies to adopt strategies of either demonstration (NASA Restaure-L mission, and SPIDER project with Maxar) or future effective and regular operations in space (Defense Advanced Research Projects Agency's Robotic Servicing of Geosynchronous Satellites (RSGS) project, with

62. *See* Mark Harris, 'Amazon Reports Collision Risk for Mega-Constellation of Kuiper Internet Satellites' (IEEE spectrum, 16 October 2019).
63. For an estimate, *See* Dave Mosher, 'A Crushing Cost Estimate of SpaceX's Planned Mega-Fleet of 42,000 Starlink Internet Satellites Glosses over a Huge Detail' (Business Insider, 18 October 2019); Astronomer Jonathan McDowell tracks the constellation in: https://planet4589.org/space/con/star/stats.html.
64. The 1,000-1,500 km area is critical for debris. *See* Gian Luigi Somma et al., 'Sensitivity Analysis for a Space Debris Environment Model' (2017). This impacted OneWeb and SpaceX during their first five years of operation, see S. Le May et al., 'Space Debris Collision Probability Analysis for Proposed Global Broadband Constellations', *Acta Astronautica*, Vol. 151 (October 2018). Regulators are already making moves to address this concern, *see* Henry Caleb, 'FCC Moves Forward with Orbital Debris Reform Amid Soul-Searching about Its Responsibilities' (SpaceNews, 17 November 2018). Design thinking should go beyond mere technological improvement, *see* Dr Mark A. Skinner from *The Aerospace Corporation*, 'Conceptual Development of a Civil Space Traffic Management System Capability' (AMOS, 2018).
65. *See* Altius Space Machines in 'Open Source Analysis of Iridium Failures and the implications for Big LEO Constellations', *supra* n. 30.
66. Jeff Foust, 'Starlink Failures Highlight Space Sustainability Concerns' (SpaceNews, 1 July 2019).

a launch planned for 2022). The industry has developed various life extension options, some of which are now operational such as SpaceLogistics' MEV-1 (which approaches, captures, tilts and maintains the client satellite for five years before waiting for its next client in a graveyard orbit),[67] others that are allegedly soon to be operational, by the likes of Effective Space Solutions (space drones are much smaller and operate in a non-intrusive way), Aerospace Corporation or Airbus (with a wide range of solutions covering Automated Transfer Vehicle (ATV), European Service Module (ESM), Moon Cruiser for Gateway Logistics, Space Tugs and the DEOS/e.Deorbit project). New approaches have been developed, for example, by Novawucks (modularity in GEO) or Astroscale (able to collect disabled satellites in LEO by March 2021).

An inspection service dedicated to the complete – and near real-time understanding of all LEO satellites' failures and underperformance has yet to be implemented and would in time greatly contribute to avoid failures in orbit, better understand in situ space weather and remove the need to lower altitudes of Constellations or for redundant satellites. Many stakeholders are expecting such progress: consumers who want continuity of service, regulators who are determined to curb in-orbit risks, operators who need to be alerted as soon as possible of any damage to their satellite and the nature of any failure, and insurers who wish to better understand their exposure, and accurately set premiums.[68]

In practice, this low-earth orbit inspector would be highly beneficial in judicial or arbitration cases: they would provide, *with the agreement* of the operator and on behalf of an insurer (for instance, as part of an expert appraisal or amicable composition mission) authentic images. These images would have probative value in the context of an arbitration (or judicial) dispute, where proofs are paramount. As they are not artificial (unlike a derived image that involves human intervention), these images do not pose any privacy risk on Earth or go against image protection, as it may be the case with remote sensing. It is highly unlikely they would face any attempt at prohibition.[69]

At most, national laws defining satellite registration procedures and sometimes the authorisation of Non-Earth Imaging will require the operator of a near-space inspector to provide a description of their activities requiring them to take photographs in space. The state of registry would have no reason to oppose the registration of a space object on the sole ground that it would have the means to photograph defective satellites, given its objective would not be to photograph a satellite but to carry out a technical assistance mission corresponding to a commercial service, for which a contract has been concluded with the operator of the photographed satellite and for which all authorisations have been granted. This assistance mission would be perfectly in line with the obligations laid down by applicable Treaties, in particular pursuant to Article IX, OST. The ability to photograph a defective satellite should therefore provide a useful way of understanding, and therefore limiting, failures in space, and constitute

67. MEP and MRV first deployments are announced for the late 2023-2024.
68. As an introduction, see Victoria A. Samson, 'Can the Space Insurance Industry Help Incentivize the Responsible Use of Space?' (IAC Bremen, October 2018).
69. International treaties do not define it as such and it is difficult to outline in the OST a specific legal provision that would establish the state of registration of the photographed satellite object. This would be different from space imagery.

a decisive contribution to industrial disputes related to satellite defects. SpaceAble is about to provide the industry with such an inspection capacity.

b Implementing Relevant Behaviour Standards

This new kind of inspector, and more generally the securing and optimisation of manoeuvres in near space, requires low-orbit behaviour rules[70] to both be specified and developed as a whole. The preservation of the space environment depends on it. Behaviour standards in the low orbit are currently being defined, navigating between procedures that can at times be defective, and the implementation of best practices that are often only aspirational.[71]

Public institutions are tackling this issue: the most influential organisations for research and identification of guidelines and best practices for debris mitigation are NASA, Inter-Agency Space Debris Coordination Committee (IADC),[72] the UN Committee on the Peaceful Uses of Outer Space (COPUOS)[73] and, to a lesser extent, the ITU. The industry has also been strongly involved in promoting relevant international standards in International Organization for Standardization (ISO) format. Several organisations also play a decisive role in this matter, including the *Space Data Association* (controlled, reliable and efficient sharing of data to optimise space traffic coordination),[74] the Global VSAT Forum and the Global Sat Coalition (facilitate expanded access to satellite-based connectivity solutions globally), the Satellite Industry Association (promotion of the benefits and uses of commercial satellite technology), the Commercial Satellite Spectrum Management Association, the Satcoms Innovation Group (from reduction of Radio-Frequency incidents to the gain in efficiencies in other operational areas of satellites), and the Europe, Middle-East and Africa Satellite Operators Association (representing all satellite operators from the EMEA region).

For example, the Consortium for Execution of Rendezvous and Servicing Operations formed at the initiative of DARPA and now comprising thirty-five companies plays a key role in defining Guidelines principles for Commercial Rendezvous and Proximity Operations (RPO) and OOS to enhance operational safety and mission success.[75] They promote practices that are based on lessons learned from prior

70. *See* Sara A. Carioscia, 'Roundtable Proceedings: Ways Forward for On-Orbit Servicing, Assembly and Manufacturing of Spacecraft' (IDA, White House, July 2018).
71. On this matter, *see* Dan Oltrogge's action as US TAG Chair, ISO TC 14.
72. IADC Space Debris Mitigation Guidelines, IADC-02-01, Revision 1, September 2007, https://www.iadc-home.org.
73. Space Debris Mitigation Guidelines of the Committee on the Peaceful Uses of Outer Space, A/RES/62/217, 2007, available at http://www.unoosa.org/pdf/publications/st_space_49E.pdf. *See* the 21 guidelines adopted during the COPUOS' 62nd session. *See* http://www.unoosa.org/res/oosadoc/data/documents/2019/aac_105l/aac_105l_318add_6_0_html/AC105_L318Add06E.pdf. The IADC and COPUOS guidelines are not binding on any agency or entity, and agencies and entities may depart from the NASA guidelines when it is cost-effective to do so.
74. See P.J. Blount, 'Symposium on the New Space Race Traffic Management: Standardizing On-Orbit Behavior' (AJIL UNBOUND, 2019) at 120 et seq.
75. https://www.satelliteconfers.org/wp-content/uploads/2018/11/CONFERS-Guiding-Principles_7Nov18.pdf (November 2018) and its declination *CONFERS On-Orbit Servicing (OOS) Mission Phases* as well as *CONFERS Recommended Design and Operational Practices* (updated versions

servicing and RPO operations: they advocate focusing on the safety of satellites themselves as well as the risk they pose to their environment (the reflection here extends to the global commons). They cover a broad spectrum (in particular 'non-earth imaging', timely transparent licensing process, softening of control regulations, Space Situational Awareness (SSA) and Space Traffic Management (STM), etc.) and are intended to evolve as closely as possible to industry's experience, based on the know-how gained through future commercial and government servicing operations.

How can we create standards that are sometimes market relevant (ISO requirement) and sometimes correspond to aspirational best practices[76]? In May 2020, the FCC has updated its satellite rules on orbital debris mitigation for the first time in over fifteen years and also voted to seek further public comment on other proposals related to mitigating orbital debris.[77] Coalitions are being established between the Space Safety Coalition (with its publication of forty-two best practices in September 2019)[78] and the FCC/FAA (Federal Aviation Administration) to determine low/high-hanging fruits and see those that are ripe. Such activism is gradually being transposed at ISO level, in particular with the ISO-24113 standard on top-level satellite servicing standardised practices.[79] TC 20/SC13 (operated by the Consultative Committee for Space Data Systems (CCSDS), comprising eleven space agencies and with standards accessible as an ISO standard) develops communications and data-system standards for spaceflight to enhance government and commercial interoperability and cross-support, whilst reducing risk, development times and project costs.[80] Over nine hundred space missions have already chosen to fly with CCSDS-developed standards. With regard to STMs, TC20/SC14 builds space standards for best practices concerning CCSDS navigation data exchange message (orbit data message, conjunction data message, tracking data message, attitude data message, events data message, re-entry data message).

---

of 1 October 2019). For example, *see* CONFERS, 2019 Global Satellite Servicing Forum held in Washington DC on 1-2 October 2019.

76. Space Safety Coalition (60 organisations have signed).
77. https://docs.fcc.gov/public/attachments/DOC-363486A1.pdf. The Commission's orbital debris rules cover all Commission-licensed satellites and satellites granted access to the US market. Among other things, the new rules include requiring that satellite applicants assign numerical values to collision risk, probability of successful post-mission disposal, and casualty risk associated with those satellites that will re-enter earth's atmosphere. Satellite applicants will also have new disclosure requirements related to protecting inhabitable spacecraft, maneuverability, use of deployment devices, release of persistent liquids, proximity operations, trackability and identification, and information sharing for situational awareness. The Commission also adopted a Further Notice of Proposed Rulemaking, which invites additional comment on indemnification requirement, on orbital debris mitigation measures related to the probability of accidental explosions; collision risk and casualty risk for satellite constellations on a systemwide basis; and on requiring maneuverability for space stations located above a certain altitude in the low earth orbit region and limiting post-mission orbital lifetime.
78. *See* https://spacesafety.org/ and its Best Practices for the Sustainability of Space Operations at https://spacesafety.org/wp-content/uploads/2019/10/Endorsement-of-Best-Practices-for-Sustainability_v28.pdf (16 September 2019).
79. International Standards Organisation, Space Systems Space Debris Mitigation, ISO TC 20/SC 14 N 24113, 2011.
80. Standards available through ISA and also at https://public.ccsds.org. *See* https://public.ccsds.org/Publications/default.aspx.

c Providing Continuous Information on Space Operations

Fewer failures, safer behaviour rules, and better information on the state of assets and traffic are key for a more secure space environment.[81] Space data is the single best way to ensure space activity will prosper. For instance, Space Situational Awareness should allow for real-time risk assessment.[82] More generally, it should become both a commodity and a service.[83] Yet today, less than 7% of critical debris in the low earth orbit are under close scrutiny.

Beyond their work to implement standards, public agencies and private companies have been working to develop this market for a decade. Traditional technical solutions still hinder us from developing a satisfactory solution in terms of quality, speed, exhaustiveness, interoperability, certification and trust.[84] Too few actors have access to this data. The deployment of telecommunication constellations is making this situation simply unsustainable. Both the industry and public authorities have well understood that overcoming this challenge will require going beyond developing best practices: it will depend on the creation of technical solutions, made from more open architectures,[85] and platforms with much more functionalities[86] and better interfaces.

Thanks to the earth-observation industry and a few startups, this market for space data has evolved well. Today it is at the crossroads of numerous interests. For regulators, it is means of ensuring greater reliability of space infrastructure. For operators, it is an essential tool for optimising their constellations operation. For manufacturers of both nanosats and propulsion systems, it is a way of building even more rudimentary satellites, provided they rely on a good propulsion system, simply because they will rely on more relevant data. For insurers, it is a great solution to land an insurable risk and refine how they evaluate premiums. Finally, for investors, it is quite possibly the solution with the most potential for financial return. Times are good.[87] Several institutions and start-ups have taken the jump. It will ensure greater reliability of the low-orbit space environment.

81. Space Data is growing exponentially. See Jonathan Shieber, 'As Rocket Companies Proliferate, New Enabling Tech Emerges as the Next Wave in the Space Race' (Techcrunch, 5 May 2019). They have an important but not adequately quantified value, *see* Sandra Erwin, 'Military Sees Value in Commercial Data, but Needs to Figure out How to Buy It' (Space News, 28 September 2019).
82. Today's data is not sufficiently accurate. *See* B. Houlton, 'Orbit Determination Accuracy', 30th Space Symposium, Technical Track (Colorado Springs, Colorado, 2014).
83. Bhavya Lal et al., *Global Trends in Space Situation Awareness (SSA) and Space Traffic Management (STM)* (IDA, April 2018).
84. On a community approach, *see* Thomas J. Kubancik, 'A Broad Based Community Approach to Space Situational Awareness', ADS.
85. Open Architecture and Data need standards https://breakingdefense.com/2019/05/crider-ssa-data-library-will-open-to-allies.
86. See Emily S. Nightingale, 'Evaluating Options for Civil Space Situational Awareness (SSA)' (IDA, August 2016).
87. For example, Victoria Samson, 'Possible SSA Futures: A report of the 2017 Amos Dialogue', January 2018 and Dr Darren McKnight, 'Responsive SSA – Responsive to New Space and Old Problems', 34th Space Symposium (Colorado Springs, Colorado, April 2018).

It may well be that Space Law is being reshaped in a bottom-up way by the United States, which recently issued regulations on space mining extraction (2015, 2020),[88] on space exploration (2020),[89] on Lunar Protection (2020)[90] and on Space Weather (2020).[91] Time will tell. In any event, the future of low-earth orbit is contingent on fewer in-orbit failures, safer behaviour rules and better spatial data. The development of Space Safety standards and the implementation of technical and commercial information solutions (inspectors and space data) embody the practical implementation of customary international law of Space Environment. This will prevent – potentially catastrophic ('Kessler effect') accidents while gradually shaping the standard based on which many arbitration (and judicial) disputes shall be resolved. As an interpreter of the customary international law of Space Environment and guardian of the spirit of the founding Outer Space treaties, international arbitration of satellite disputes must exercise the full power conferred to it by the parties.

88. US Commercial Space Launch Competitiveness Act of 2015, and the Executive Order on Encouraging International Support for the Recovery and Use of Space Resources signed on 6 April 2020.
89. The Artemis Agreements were published by NASA on 15 May 2020.
90. Two new Interim directives have been issued by NASA on 9 July 2020.
91. PROSWIFT space weather bill was signed into law on 21 October 2020.

CHAPTER 20

Arbitration in the Public Interest: Closing the *Lacunae* of International Justice

Dirk Pulkowski[*]

I INTRODUCTION

The extraordinary success of arbitration as a method for settling disputes owes much to its adaptability. Commentators commonly highlight the use of arbitration as a neutral alternative method for settling cross-border commercial disputes when courts are perceived as unsuitable.[1] The potential role for arbitral tribunals, however, is much broader. In societies with weak or broken judicial institutions, arbitral justice on the basis of local custom has enabled communities to maintain the rule of law.[2] For example, to implement a peace agreement ending years of civil war, the government of Sudan and leaders of the opposing People's Liberation Movement chose arbitration to obtain an authoritative determination of a critical threshold issue.[3] This illustrates that when no forum for the satisfactory resolution of disputes exists, arbitral mechanisms can ensure that the maxim *ubi jus ibi remedium*[4] does not remain an empty promise.

The potential of arbitration to fill the *lacunae* of justice ensures it an enduring place in the architecture of twenty-first-century international dispute resolution.

---

* The views expressed are those of the author.

1. Toby Landau, 'Arbitral Lifelines: The Protection of Jurisdiction by Arbitrators', in Albert Jan van den Berg (ed.) *International Arbitration 2006: Back to Basics?* (2007), 282. Nigel Blackaby et al., *Redfern and Hunter on International Arbitration* (Sixth edition, 2015), 37-40.
2. Abdulqawi Ahmed Yusuf, 'The Contribution of Arbitration to the Rule of Law – The Experience of African Countries', in Andrea Menaker (ed.), *International Arbitration and the Rule of Law: Contribution and Conformity*, ICCA Congress Series, Volume 19 (ICCA & Kluwer Law International 2017), 27 at 28.
3. *Abyei Arbitration (The Government of Sudan / The Sudan People's Liberation Movement/Army)*, PCA Case No. 2008-07, Final Award, 22 July 2009.
4. Where there is a right, there is a remedy.

Transnational legal rules have grown exponentially, governing many aspects of international affairs. Such rules often take the form of treaties under public international law, but some rules have emanated from processes of informal lawmaking.[5] Many rules relate to what may be termed the 'public interest': they seek to impose international normative standards to further the common good.[6] As it is neither feasible nor desirable to establish a standing court under each normative arrangement, special arbitral mechanisms emerge as a preferred method for settling disputes arising from such rules or addressing instances of non-compliance.

This chapter sheds light on emerging trends towards the arbitral settlement of international disputes in several public interest areas: business and human rights, climate change, fisheries, and taxation. These trends illustrate that arbitration, its economic significance in supporting international business transactions notwithstanding, is fundamentally in the service of the public good. It is with this deep conviction that our esteemed professor at Yale Law School and dear colleague at the arbitration bar, Guillermo Aguilar Álvarez, approached his teaching and practice. This chapter is intended as a tribute to him and the legacy he has left within our field.

II BUSINESS AND HUMAN RIGHTS

On 16 June 2011, the United Nations Human Rights Council unanimously endorsed the Guiding Principles for Business and Human Rights, establishing an international soft-law framework for corporate responsibility for human rights violations.[7] Barely two years later, on 24 April 2013, an eight-story garment factory building named Rana Plaza in the Dhaka District of Bangladesh collapsed, leaving over one thousand dead. The building was structurally unsafe. Various global fashion companies had their garments produced at Rana Plaza through local subcontractors.[8]

In response to the disaster, and in the face of public pressure, fashion companies signed pledges to respect minimum safety conditions for workers. The Accord on Fire and Building Safety in Bangladesh, signed by now over 200 global clothing brands and trade unions, includes an arbitration clause:

---

5. *See* Joost Pauwelyn, Ramses Wessel & Jan Wouters (eds), *Informal International Lawmaking* (2012).
6. The precise definition of the concept of 'public interest' is contested in political theory, *see* Clarke E. Cochran, 'Political Science and "The Public Interest"', *The Journal of Politics* 36, no. 2 (May, 1974) 327-355.
7. Report of the Special Representative of the Secretary-General on the issue of human rights and transnational corporations and other business enterprises, John Ruggie – Guiding Principles on Business and Human Rights: Implementing the United Nations 'Protect, Respect and Remedy' Framework, 21 March 2011, A/HRC/17/31. Resolution adopted by the Human Rights Council 17/4, Human rights and transnational corporations and other business enterprises, A/HRC/RES/17/4.
8. International Labour Organization, 'The Rana Plaza Accident and Its Aftermath', available at https://www.ilo.org/global/topics/geip/WCMS_614394/lang--en/index.htm; Michael Safi, Dominic Rushe, 'Rana Plaza, Five Years On: Safety of Workers Hangs in Balance in Bangladesh', *The Guardian*, 24 April 2018, available at https://www.theguardian.com/global-development/2018/apr/24/bangladeshi-police-target-garment-workers-union-rana-plaza-five-years-on.

> Any dispute between the parties to, and arising under, the terms of this Agreement shall first be presented to and decided by the [Steering Committee], which shall decide the dispute by majority vote of the SC within a maximum of 21 days of a petition being filed by one of the parties. Upon request of either party, the decision of the SC may be appealed to a final and binding arbitration process. Any arbitration award shall be enforceable in a court of law of the domicile of the signatory against whom enforcement is sought and shall be subject to The Convention on the Recognition and Enforcement of Foreign Arbitral Awards (The New York Convention), where applicable.[9]

The arbitration mechanism was intended to close a structural gap in the judicial protection of workers; the ultimate beneficiaries of low prices for readymade garments from Bangladesh were international retailers, while the conditions of those working in factories fell within the responsibility of local subcontractors. Hence, workers had no prospect of holding international retailers accountable before local courts, let alone invoking transnational norms such as the Guiding Principles for Business and Human Rights.

The mechanism has proven to have teeth. On 8 July 2016 and 11 October 2016, IndustriALL Global Union and UNI Global Union, two non-governmental labour union federations based in Switzerland, submitted notices of arbitration against two global fashion brands (whose identity has remained confidential). In these first publicly known arbitrations pursuant to the Accord, administered by the Permanent Court of Arbitration (PCA), the claimants alleged that the fashion brands had failed to require their suppliers in Bangladesh to remediate deficiencies in their factory facilities and had failed to negotiate commercial terms that made it feasible for the supplier factories to cover the factory remediation costs.[10] The proceedings concluded in amicable settlements in July 2018.[11]

Concurrently with the arbitral proceedings, a Working Group on International Arbitration of Business and Human Rights considered the potential for a broader use of arbitration to address human rights concerns resulting from conduct of businesses. A report was published on 17 August 2017. The report recognizes that, in an ideal world, it might be possible to 'provide for universal, fair and impartial resolution of [business and human rights] [d]isputes in national courts'. However, given a lack of effective redress in many national courts, 'much [human rights] [a]buse will need to be addressed using alternative routes to access to justice – such as [business and human rights] [a]rbitration'.[12] On 12 December 2019, the Working Group officially launched a

9. Accord on Fire and Building Safety in Bangladesh, 13 May 2013, available at http://www.industriall-union.org/sites/default/files/uploads/documents/2013-05-13_-_accord_on_fire_and_building_safety_in_bangladesh_0.pdf.
10. Judith Levine, Ashwita Ambast, 'The Bangladesh Accord Arbitrations: Arbitrating Business and Human Rights Disputes', 1 *Transnational Commercial Law Review* 116-135 (2020); *see also* Judith Levine & Kashpee Wahid, 'Business and Human Rights: A "New Frontier" for International Arbitration?', 15(1) *Transnational Dispute Settlement* (January 2018) 1.
11. PCA Case No. 2016-36, Termination Order, Redacted Version for Publication, 17 July 2018; PCA Case No. 2016-37, Termination Order, Redacted Version for Publication, 17 July 2018, available at https://pca-cpa.org/en/cases/152/.
12. Claes Cronstedt, Jan Eijsbouts, Adrienne Margolis, Steven Ratner, Martijn Scheltema & Robert C. Thompson, 'International Arbitration of Business and Human Rights Disputes: Questions and

bespoke set of rules of procedure, based on the UNCITRAL Arbitration Rules, entitled the Hague Rules on Business and Human Rights Arbitration.[13]

The Hague Rules notably encourage the use of forms of 'collaborative settlement' of the dispute;[14] set out a strict code of conduct for arbitrators, compliance with which may be reviewed by a dedicated committee established or designated by the PCA;[15] and recommend the constitution of a diverse tribunal.[16] Moreover, the tribunal, in addition to conducting the proceedings in a manner that ensures that the parties are treated with equality and that each party is given a reasonable opportunity of presenting its case, must provide for a 'culturally appropriate and rights-compatible process for resolving the parties' dispute, including in particular by giving due regard to the urgency of addressing the alleged human rights impacts'.[17] The tribunal 'shall satisfy itself that the award is human rights-compatible'.[18]

Encouraging the arbitration of business and human rights disputes should be complementary to reinforcing the capacity of domestic courts to provide effective access to justice. In the current negotiations for a so-called Treaty on Business and Human Rights, the focus thus appears to be on effective national procedures.[19] That said, even where effective domestic institutions are available, there may be good reasons to rely on an international forum for enforcing human rights norms – for the same reasons that underlie the choice of arbitral jurisdiction in place of local courts in

---

Answers', 17 August 2017, p. 4 (available at http://www.l4bb.org/news/Q&A.pdf). *See also* Claes Cronstedt & Robert C. Thompson, 'A Proposal for an International Arbitration Tribunal on Business and Human Rights', 57 *Harvard International Law Journal* (2016) 66; Katerina Yiannibas, 'The Adaptability of International Arbitration: Reforming the Arbitration Mechanism to Provide Effective Remedy for Business-Related Human Rights Abuses', 36 *Netherlands Quarterly of Human Rights* (2018) 214.

13. The Hague Rules on Business and Human Rights Arbitration (2019), available at https://www.cilc.nl/cms/wp-content/uploads/2019/12/The-Hague-Rules-on-Business-and-Human-Rights-Arbitration_CILC-digital-version.pdf. For a discussion of 'salient features' of the Rules, *see* Brigitta John, 'The Hague Rules on Business and Human Rights Arbitration', Global Arbitration News, 21 April 2020, available at https://globalarbitrationnews.com/the-hague-rules-on-business-and-human-rights-arbitration/; Ylli Dautaj, 'Roll Out the Red Carpet: The Hague Rules on Business and Human Rights Arbitration are Finally Here!', Kluwer Arbitration Blog, 26 December 2019, available at: http://arbitrationblog.kluwerarbitration.com/2019/12/26/roll-out-the-red-carpet-the-hague-rules-on-business-and-human-rights-arbitration-are-finally-here/?doing_wp_cron=1592819779.3066930770874023437500.
14. The Hague Rules on Business and Human Rights Arbitration (2019), Preamble, para. 4, Article 1(6), Article 56, available at https://www.cilc.nl/cms/wp-content/uploads/2019/12/The-Hague-Rules-on-Business-and-Human-Rights-Arbitration_CILC-digital-version.pdf.
15. *Ibid.*, Code of Conduct.
16. *Ibid.*, Article 11(3).
17. *Ibid.*, Article 18(1).
18. *Ibid.*, Article 45(4).
19. The latest draft text provides, for example: 'State Parties shall ensure that effective national procedures are in place to ensure compliance with the obligations laid down under this Article, taking into consideration the potential impact on human rights resulting from the size, nature, context of and risk associated with the business activities, including those of transnational character, and that those procedures are available to all natural and legal persons having a legitimate interest, in accordance with domestic law.' Article 5(4) of the OEIGWG Chairmanship Revised Draft, 1 July 2019, available at https://www.ohchr.org/Documents/HRBodies/HRCouncil/WGTransCorp/OEIGWG_RevisedDraft_LBI.pdf.

international business contracts and, *a fortiori*, contracts with governments. International arbitration can provide a forum that is perceived to be neutral and thus more likely to produce mutually acceptable outcomes. Further, arbitral awards enjoy superior international enforceability by virtue of the 1958 New York Convention on the Recognition and Enforcement of Foreign Arbitral Awards. It may be in the interest of governments to explore the option of bringing human rights complaints against foreign companies operating on their territory to an international tribunal, as a complement to domestic enforcement.

Constructively, an interesting model of 'state-investor arbitration', with governments as potential claimants and corporations as potential respondents, is found in the Biodiversity Compact.[20] In the Compact, biotechnology companies are 'offering [s]tates a legally binding mechanism for seeking redress from a responsible party if the release of a Living Modified Organism (LMO) by that party causes damage to biological diversity'.[21] The mechanism combines the PCA's fact-finding, conciliation rules, and arbitration rules into a multistage dispute settlement mechanism.[22]

III CLIMATE CHANGE

The basic treaty for addressing climate change is the United Nations Framework Convention on Climate Change (UNFCCC), adopted on 9 May 1992.[23] Its objective is to achieve 'stabilization of greenhouse gas concentrations in the atmosphere at a level that would prevent dangerous anthropogenic interference with the climate system'.[24] Article 14 of the UNFCCC provides for an optional reference to the International Court of Justice or to interstate arbitration:

> 2. When ratifying, accepting, approving or acceding to the Convention, or at any time thereafter, a Party which is not a regional economic integration organization may declare in a written instrument submitted to the Depositary that, in respect of any dispute concerning the interpretation or application of the Convention, it recognizes as compulsory *ipso facto* and without special agreement, in relation to any Party accepting the same obligation:
> a. Submission of the dispute to the International Court of Justice, and/or
> b. Arbitration in accordance with procedures to be adopted by the Conference of the Parties as soon as practicable, in an annex on arbitration.

The Paris Agreement, in Article 24, provides that these provisions 'shall apply *mutatis mutandis* to this Agreement'.[25]

---

20. *See* http://www.biodiversitycompact.org.
21. *See* https://croplife.org/plant-biotechnology/stewardship-2/the-compact/.
22. Wen Xiang, 'International Liability and Redress for Genetically Modified Organisms and Challenges for China's Biosafety Regulation', in Vasilka Sancin, Masa Kovic Dine (eds), *International Environmental Law: Contemporary Concerns and Challenges* (2012), 581.
23. United Nations Framework Convention on Climate Change, 9 May 1992, 1771 UNTS 107.
24. *Ibid.*, Article 2.
25. Paris Agreement, 12 December 2015, as contained in the report of the Conference of the Parties on its twenty-first session, FCCC/CP/2015/10/Add.1.

At present, the interstate arbitration mechanism in the UNFCCC cannot be expected to close the *lacunae* of climate justice. Despite calls from civil society and the legal profession,[26] no 'annex on arbitration' has been adopted by the Parties to the Convention. Moreover, declarations pursuant to Article 14 have been made only by the Netherlands (accepting the jurisdiction of the International Court of Justice and arbitration), the Solomon Islands (accepting arbitration), and Tuvalu (accepting arbitration).[27]

Arbitral tribunals, however, have already dealt with aspects of the practical implementation of the UNFCCC. The PCA has handled nine contract cases arising from the 1997 Kyoto Protocol.[28] These cases involved so-called certified emission reduction credits, obtained by developed countries in exchange for funding a carbon-friendly project in a developing country (the Clean Development Mechanism), or emissions reduction units, generated from a carbon-friendly project in a developed country (the Joint Implementation scheme).[29] Moreover, it has been noted that treaty-based investor-state tribunals have had to deal with the allocation of the financial burden of transitioning to green energy – and may in the future have to examine measures specifically undertaken by states to meet their Paris Agreement commitments.[30] Finally, various forms of disputes arising from the operations of the primary finance body connected with the UNFCCC, the Green Climate Fund, may be settled by PCA arbitration.[31]

The stakes of climate justice are high – potentially very high. Professor David Estrin, Cochair of the International Bar Association's Presidential Task Force on Climate Change Justice and Human Rights, which is considering the legal challenges arising from 'climate disruption',[32] has predicted that 'litigation will be coming', with

26. An International Bar Association task force recommended that the 'UNFCCC COP Should Adopt the PCA as the UNFCCC's Preferred Arbitral Body', International Bar Association, 'Achieving Justice and Human Rights in an Era of Climate Disruption', Climate Change Justice and Human Rights Task Force Report (July 2014) 13, 28, 139-144.
27. *See:* https://unfccc.int/process/the-convention/status-of-ratification/declarations-by-parties.
28. Kyoto Protocol to the United Nations Framework Convention on Climate Change, 11 December 1997, 2303 UNTS 162.
29. Judith Levine, 'Climate Change Disputes: The PCA, The Paris Agreement and Prospects for Future Arbitrations', 14(1) *Transnational Dispute Management* (January 2017) 3.
30. C. Mark Baker, Holly Stebbing & Cara Dowling, 'Climate-Related Disputes: Adaptation and Innovation', October 2018, available at https://www.nortonrosefulbright.com/en-fr/knowledge/publications/cf5bb18c/climate-related-disputes---adaptation-and-innovation; Anatole Boute, 'Combating Climate Change Through Investment Arbitration', 35 *Fordham Int'l L.J.* (2012) 613. *But see* Daniel Behn & Malcolm Langford, 'Trumping the Environment? An Empirical Perspective on the Legitimacy of Investment Treaty Arbitration', 18 *The Journal of World Investment & Trade* (2017) 14.
31. Judith Levine, 'Adopting and Adapting Arbitration for Climate Change-Related Disputes: The Experience of the Permanent Court of Arbitration', in International Court of Arbitration (ed.) *Dispute Resolution and Climate Change: The Paris Agreement and Beyond* (2017) 28.
32. International Bar Association, 'Achieving Justice and Human Rights in an Era of Climate Disruption', Climate Change Justice and Human Rights Task Force Report (July 2014).

'billions of dollars on the table at some point'.[33] Yet, at this stage, climate justice appears to still be in search of its forum.

National courts are likely to have their role to play,[34] as is illustrated by a successful domestic lawsuit brought by the Urgenda Foundation against the government of the Netherlands aimed at compelling the government to reduce greenhouse gas emissions in fulfilment of its obligation to protect its citizens.[35] The Sabin Center at Columbia Law School has counted hundreds of climate change-related court cases brought against governments worldwide on a variety of legal grounds, including alleged breaches of obligations to adapt to climatic circumstances, human rights, laws for wildlife protection, laws for biodiversity protection, and clean air and water laws.[36]

The International Bar Association Task Force favoured the creation of an arbitration-based *ad hoc* International Tribunal for the Environment, which could eventually evolve into a permanent international court.[37] The attraction of that type of approach lies in the possibility of granting standing to all stakeholders (including states, corporations, and civil society organizations), the ability to select expert adjudicators, and the transnational nature of the mechanism.

IV FISHERIES

Another pressing question of environmental and economic significance concerns the sustainable management of fisheries. Regional fisheries management organizations have been set up in most parts of the world to facilitate intergovernmental cooperation in this area.[38] The management measures adopted in relation to particular fish stock by these organizations, including catch limits, may affect fishing fleets quite considerably.

33. Quoted in Judith Levine, 'Adopting and Adapting Arbitration for Climate Change-Related Disputes: The Experience of the Permanent Court of Arbitration', in International Court of Arbitration (ed.), *Dispute Resolution and Climate Change: The Paris Agreement and Beyond* (2017) 25.
34. For an overview, *see* Michael Gerrard, 'Overview of Climate Change Litigation', Kristin Casper (ed.), *Climate Justice: Holding Governments and Business Accountable for the Climate Crisis*, 113 Proceedings of the ASIL Annual Meeting 194-197 and 197-201 (2019). *See also* Judith Levine and Camilla Pondel, 'Updates on the Changing State of the Climate and International Arbitration', *The ACICA Review* (June 2019) 31 at 33 et seq.
35. *Urgenda Foundation v. The Netherlands* [2015] HAZA C/09/00456689, District Court of the Hague, 24 June 2015, The Hague Court of Appeal, 9 October 2018, available at https://uitspraken.rechtspraak.nl/inziendocument?id=ECLI:NL:GHDHA:2018:2591 (Dutch) and at https://uitspraken.rechtspraak.nl/inziendocument?id=ECLI:NL:GHDHA:2018:2610 (English, unofficial).
36. The Sabin Center for Climate Change Law, Columbia Law School, Climate Change Litigation Databases. *See* http://climatecasechart.com/us-climate-change-litigation/ for U.S. litigation and http://climatecasechart.com/non-us-case-category/suits-against-governments/ for non-U.S. litigation.
37. International Bar Association, 'Achieving Justice and Human Rights in an Era of Climate Disruption', Climate Change Justice and Human Rights Task Force Report (July 2014) 146-147.
38. According to the Food and Agriculture Organization of the United Nations, '[e]xisting RFMOs include: NAFO and NEAFC in the North Atlantic Ocean, SEAFO in the Southeast Atlantic Ocean, CCAMLR in the Southern Ocean, SPRFMO in the South Pacific Ocean, SIOFA in the Southern Indian Ocean and GFCM in the Mediterranean and the Black Sea'. Available at http://www.fao.org/fishery/topic/166304/en.

Yet, there is no international court to review such decisions, which are akin to 'global administrative law'.[39]

The Convention on the Conservation and Management of High Seas Fishery Resources in the South Pacific Ocean provides its Member States with the option of challenging decisions of the relevant regional organization before review panels, composed of 'three members appointed from the list of experts in the field of fisheries drawn up and maintained by the [Food and Agriculture Organization]'. The PCA has administered two such reviews to date, in response to 'objections' raised by the Russian Federation and Ecuador. The two states, in 2013 and 2018, each challenged a catch limit on a particular mackerel species on the basis that it 'unjustifiably discriminates in form or in fact' against them, contrary to the Convention and certain subsequent agreements.[40] The process before the review panels took the form of an accelerated multistate arbitration, following tailor-made rules of procedure. Despite various complexities, including hearings conducted in multiple languages, the disputes were resolved within only six weeks, at a cost far below that of many arbitrations (reportedly under €100,000).[41]

V TAXATION

The public power *par excellence,* foundational to the modern state, is the power of taxation. Taxation has been classically defined as:

> Une prestation de valeurs pécuniaires exigée des individus d'après des règles fixes, en vue de couvrir des dépenses d'intérêt général, et uniquement à raison du fait que les individus qui doivent les payer sont membres d'une communauté politique organisée.[42]

In the past decades, cross-border transactions have grown, multinational enterprises have become prevalent, and individual mobility has increased, with the consequence that one and the same taxpayer or transaction is potentially subject to taxation in multiple jurisdictions. While a network of over 3,000 double taxation treaties[43] is

39. *See* Benedict Kingsbury & Megan Donaldson, 'Global Administrative Law', Max Planck Encyclopedia of Public International Law (MPEPIL), last updated April 2011.
40. Review Panel established under the Convention on the Conservation and Management of High Seas Fishery Resources in the South Pacific Ocean, PCA Case No. 2013-41, Findings and Recommendations of the Review Panel, 5 July 2013, para. 53, available at https://pca-cpa.org/en/cases/33/; PCA Case No. 2018-13, Findings and Recommendations of the Review Panel, 5 June 2018, para. 42, available at https://pca-cpa.org/en/cases/156/.
41. Judith Levine, 'Adopting and Adapting Arbitration for Climate Change-Related Disputes: The Experience of the Permanent Court of Arbitration', in International Court of Arbitration (ed.), *Dispute Resolution and Climate Change: The Paris Agreement and Beyond* (2017) 30. Judith Levine & Camilla Pondel, 'There Are Not Plenty of Fish in the Sea: PCA Case No. 2018-13 On Ecuador's Objection to a Decision of the Commission of the South Pacific Regional Fisheries Management Organisation', 24 *Australian International Law Journal* (2018) 221.
42. Gaston Jèze, *Cours de finances publiques 1936-1937* (1937) p. 38.
43. UN Primer on Double Tax Treaties, https://www.un.org/esa/ffd/capacity-development-tax/primer-dtt.html.

intended to allocate jurisdiction among the signatory states, tax authorities may disagree as to the interpretation or application of such treaties.

In the event of such disagreement, the so-called mutual agreement procedure applies under the model tax treaties of the Organisation for Economic Co-operation and Development (OECD) and the United Nations (UN), which form the basis of the bulk of bilateral tax treaties in the world. Under that procedure, a competent authority must endeavour to resolve a case of alleged double taxation by mutual agreement with the competent authority of the other state.[44] However, under the older-generation treaties, there is no procedure for overcoming persistent disagreement between tax authorities. As a result, at the end of 2018, the OECD counted over 6,500 unresolved cases of alleged double taxation, of which many were classified as 'open'.[45]

Revisions to the OECD and UN models since 2008[46] have thus provided that, should the mutual agreement procedure not succeed, the dispute may be submitted to arbitration at the request of either the taxpayer concerned (OECD) or a competent authority (UN).[47] Despite those revised models, one may observe a '[r]ecurring [r]esistance to [t]ax [t]reaty [a]rbitration' in the treaty practice of states[48] – presumably out of concern to surrender fiscal sovereignty, as the public power *par excellence*, to an international tribunal.[49] Yet it is difficult to see any process other than arbitration that could effectively deal with the backlog built up, and enable taxpayers faced with contradictory decisions of tax authorities to obtain adequate legal protection.

The European Union (EU), in Council Directive 2017/1852 of 10 October 2017 'on tax dispute resolution mechanisms in the European Union',[50] has adopted an approach that is as pragmatic as it is promising. Rather than requiring Member States to subject themselves to interstate arbitration in traditional form, the Directive crafts a special 'advisory commission' mechanism, which reserves a privileged position to the tax authorities concerned while envisaging third-party rights of participation for the affected taxpayer.[51]

The advisory commission consists of one independent chair, two or four 'independent persons of standing', and two representatives of the competent authorities

44. Article 25, para. 2, United Nations Model Double Taxation Convention between Developed and Developing Countries (2017) / Organisation for Economic Co-operation and Development Model Tax Convention on Income and on Capital (2017).
45. OECD, Mutual Agreement Procedure Statistics for 2018, available at https://www.oecd.org/tax/dispute/mutual-agreement-procedure-statistics.htm.
46. Arno E. Gildemeister, 'Breakthrough at the OECD: Arbitration of Tax Treaty Disputes – The 2008 OECD Model for Income Tax Treaties Will Contain an Arbitration Clause', 5 *Transnational Dispute Management* (March 2007).
47. Article 25, para. 5.
48. Michelle Markham, 'Recurring Resistance to Tax Treaty Arbitration as a Dispute Resolution Mechanism', Austaxpolicy: Tax and Transfer Policy Blog, 23 October 2017, available at https://www.austaxpolicy.com/recurring-resistance-tax-treatyarbitration-dispute-resolution-mechanism/.
49. Michelle Markham, 'Mandatory Binding Tax Arbitration – Is This a Pathway to a More Efficient Mutual Agreement Procedure?', 35 *Arbitration International* (2019) 149 at 152. Hans Mooij, 'Tax Treaty Arbitration', 35 *Arbitration International* (2019) 195 at 205.
50. Council Directive (EU) 2017/1852 of 10 October 2017 on tax dispute resolution mechanisms in the European Union, Official Journal, L 265/1, 14.10.2017.
51. *Ibid.*, Article 11(2)(f).

concerned.[52] The process results in the advisory commission delivering an 'opinion to the competent authorities of the Member States concerned', which these authorities must then consider, while remaining free to deviate from it.[53] Crucially, however, if the competent authorities fail to reach agreement, the advisory procedure becomes constraining: in that case, the competent authorities 'shall be bound by that opinion'.[54] Since the advisory commission can result in a binding outcome, it may justly be considered a special arbitral mechanism.

In addition, the Directive empowers EU Member States who are willing to agree to arbitration not only in substance but also in form to set up an 'alternative dispute resolution commission'. That commission 'may differ regarding its composition and form from the [a]dvisory [c]omission'.[55] It may apply 'any dispute resolution processes or technique to solve the question in dispute in a binding manner', including 'the "final offer" arbitration process (otherwise known as "last best offer" arbitration)'.[56] Consultations between interested Member States with a view to establishing an alternative dispute resolution commission are currently underway.

VI CONCLUSION

The future of international arbitration as a method for resolving disputes in the public interest is bright – provided that full use is made of the adaptability that the system offers. In none of the examples provided was the boilerplate arbitral procedure followed. The example of business and human rights arbitration highlights the ability to cater to flexible party constellations, including by granting trade unions standing as claimants. The process for tax arbitration envisaged by the EU, in turn, guarantees the competent national authorities special powers throughout the proceedings. Moreover, individuals – the affected taxpayers – are accorded rights of participation that are unknown in most state-state proceedings. Finally, review proceedings in respect of fisheries management decisions demonstrate that even multistate arbitration involving written and oral argument may be completed within an expedited timeframe, at a drastically reduced cost.

Judge Gilbert Guillaume was doubtlessly correct when he observed, in a much-noted address delivered as president of the International Court of Justice, that 'new areas have been opened up to international law, whilst new players have entered the arena'.[57] Guillaume concluded that '[t]he proliferation of courts may be perceived as a process of adaptation to these fundamental changes'.[58] In the same vein, the creation

52. *Ibid.*, Article 8.
53. *Ibid.*, Article 15(1) and (2), first sentence.
54. *Ibid.*, Article 15(2), second sentence.
55. *Ibid.*, Article 10(2).
56. *Ibid.*, Article 10(2).
57. 'The proliferation of international judicial bodies: The outlook for the international legal order', Speech by His Excellency Judge Gilbert Guillaume, President of the International Court of Justice, to the Sixth Committee of the General Assembly of the United Nations, 27 October 2000, available at https://www.icj-cij.org/files/press-releases/1/3001.pdf.
58. *Ibid.*

of special arbitral mechanisms represents a response to the expansion of international law to new areas. Rather than leading to 'overlapping jurisdictions' and 'conflicting judgments', as Guillaume feared, such mechanisms have often enabled access to justice where otherwise no such access would have existed. Creative use of the procedural possibilities of arbitration can make a real contribution to closing the *lacunae* of international justice.

CHAPTER 21

The International Arbitrators' Responsibilities Regarding the Conduct of the Proceedings and the Applicable Law

Yves Derains

These are not thoughts about international arbitrators' liability. It is true that arbitrators' liability and arbitrators' responsibilities do overlap. But they should not be confused. Arbitrators' liability is more or less extensive according to the laws of the various jurisdictions. However, although few jurisdictions grant arbitrators an immunity comparable to that of judges, most admit that since arbitrators have a jurisdictional function, they require a certain level of immunity without which they would not enjoy the tranquillity of mind necessary to freely decide.[1] Yet, arbitrators remain liable in cases of gross negligence or wilful misconduct, let alone for criminal offences. But the arbitrators' responsibilities go beyond the duty to refrain from indulging in bad faith, recklessness and wilful misconduct, to echo the wording in Article 21.1 of the 2003 Spanish Law on arbitration.

International arbitrators enjoy considerable freedom in the conduct of proceedings and in the decisions they make on the merits of cases. With the limited exceptions mentioned above, they are not accountable for their decisions. But this does not mean that they may act arbitrarily and do whatever they like. Because of their wide powers, international arbitrators owe a responsibility to the parties that the absence of legal sanctions should not overshadow. Subject to few exceptions, their decisions are final. Although absence of jurisdiction, lack of independence, partiality, breach of due process, excess of power and violation of international public policy may lead to the setting aside of an award, incorrect procedural or substantive decisions may not, as such, be overruled. They are here to stay. This is particularly the case with regard to the

1. *See* on this subject 'The Arbitrator's liability', Report from the Club des Juristes, Ad Hoc Committee June 2017, Le Club de Juristes, www.leclubdesjuristes.com.

conduct of the proceedings (I) and the determination of the law applicable to the merits of the dispute and its practical application (II). In these two fields, international arbitrators have a considerable responsibility to the parties, which is proportional to the absence of effective control over their decisions.

I THE CONDUCT OF THE PROCEEDINGS

In order to assess the extent of the power granted to arbitrators with respect to the conduct of the proceedings, one must keep in mind that in most arbitration proceedings, no system of procedural rules is declared applicable in advance, and arbitrators are expected to make the appropriate decision each time this is necessary (A). Such decisions should not be taken arbitrarily, and arbitrators should pursue a number of main goals allowing them to discharge their responsibility to the parties as to the practical conduct of the proceedings (B).

A The Absence of Defined Rules Applicable to the Procedure

Arbitration laws throughout the world do not contain detailed provisions on the conduct of proceedings. Beyond very general principles, such as the respect of due process and the equality of the parties, they defer to the parties' agreement and, failing such agreement, to arbitrators' rulings.

Article 19 of the UNCITRAL Model Law, which is the inspiration for many modern laws on arbitration, authorizes arbitrators to conduct proceedings as they consider appropriate:

> (1) Subject to the provisions of this Law, the parties are free to agree on the procedure to be followed by the arbitral tribunal in conducting the proceedings.
> (2) Failing such agreement, the arbitral tribunal may, subject to the provisions of this Law, conduct the arbitration in such manner as it considers appropriate. The power conferred upon the arbitral tribunal includes the power to determine the admissibility, relevance, materiality and weight of any evidence.

Under the International Chamber of Commerce (ICC) Rules of Arbitration, arbitrators enjoy the same freedom since, in the absence of agreement between the parties, they may adopt any rule without being limited by the content of a national procedural law, whatever it may be. Article 19 reads:

> The proceedings before the Arbitral Tribunal shall be governed by the Rules, and, where the Rules are silent, by any rules which the parties or, failing them, the Arbitral Tribunal may settle on, whether or not reference is thereby made to the rules of procedure of a national law to be applied to the arbitration.

Article 17.1 of the UNCITRAL Rules does not hesitate to refer to the discretion of arbitrators, even if it reminds them that basic principles of procedural public policy should not be disregarded:

> Subject to these Rules, the arbitral tribunal may conduct the arbitration in such manner as it considers appropriate, provided that the parties are treated with equality and that at an appropriate stage of the proceedings each party is given a reasonable opportunity of presenting its case. The arbitral tribunal, in exercising its discretion, shall conduct the proceedings so as to avoid unnecessary delay and expense and to provide a fair and efficient process for resolving the parties' dispute.

Some arbitration clauses designate a specific national law to govern the arbitral proceedings, but such general agreements by the parties on the rules of procedure are rare. This is reasonable as domestic rules of procedure, which are designed for national courts, cannot easily be transposed to arbitration. Moreover, the mere indication in an arbitration clause that the law of a specific country will apply to the conduct of an arbitration is not very helpful since, in most countries, the law of arbitration gives arbitrators the power to conduct proceedings as they feel appropriate, regardless of the precise language used, with the result that the parties' agreement does not add anything substantial. At best, it is a useful indication that the parties are in favour of a certain type of procedure; for instance, they prefer the Civil Law tradition rather than the Common Law tradition or the reverse.

As a consequence, in the majority of cases, it falls to the arbitrators to determine the law that governs the proceedings, and they have the power to do so. However, they rarely do this and they are right to take this approach. If they tried to determine the governing law, they would face exactly the same difficulties as the parties since, with few exceptions, they would either have to choose procedural rules designed for state courts or refer to a national law on arbitration which empowers them to fix rules of procedure. But, more significantly, it is not part of their responsibilities. As indicated by the laws and the arbitration rules that have just been mentioned, arbitrators are expected to conduct the arbitration in the manner they consider appropriate. They do not have to define in advance a general procedural legal order applicable to this exercise, other than the *lex arbitri*, provided they respect the parties' agreement and the applicable arbitration rules. Even the ICC Rules of Arbitration that contemplate the possibility that the arbitrators make reference *to* the rules of procedure of a national law indicate in Article 22(1) that '[i]n order to ensure effective case management, the arbitral tribunal, after consulting the parties, may adopt such procedural measures as it considers appropriate, provided that they are not contrary to any agreement of the parties'. Likewise, Article 25(1) provides that '[t]he arbitral tribunal shall proceed within as short a time as possible to establish the facts of the case by all appropriate means'. Thus, the rules cannot be considered to be silent in that respect, for the purpose of Article 19[2] is that arbitrators may take any decision that they consider appropriate in order to efficiently manage the case and establish the facts of the case, regardless of the national law that they might have declared applicable to the procedure, provided they respect the parties' agreement. The main responsibility of the arbitrators to the parties with regard to the conduct of the proceedings is to take the appropriate decisions each time they are needed.

2. *See infra* note 6.

B The Main Goals to Be Pursued by International Arbitrators in the Conduct of Proceedings

An international arbitrator should have three main concerns when conducting proceedings: (1) to approach the proceedings with cultural neutrality; (2) to organize proceedings that are tailor-made for the case being conducted; and (3) to maintain at all times equality of treatment between the parties.

1 Cultural Neutrality

Arbitrators in charge of conducting proceedings in an international case should never forget that they are international arbitrators. Among the various factors that may explain the impressive success of international arbitration as a way of settling international disputes, its neutrality is probably the most significant. When parties have recourse to arbitration to settle disputes arising from international transactions, they do so because each of them is reluctant to accept the jurisdiction of the state courts of the other party's country. Rightly or wrongly, they feel that a State court in the other party's country will not be neutral. With the exception of countries where the judiciary is not independent from the government, it is not an issue of impartiality, although some laymen may think that this is the case. Impartiality is a subjective concept that requires that decisions are made on the basis of objective criteria, with no bias, prejudice or favour towards one of the parties, for any reason. The great majority of judges are impartial. On the contrary, neutrality is an objective situation. It does not refer to any prejudice towards one of the parties but to the distance which exists between the decision-maker and each of them. From that point of view, a State court of one of the parties cannot be neutral: its judges have too much in common with one of the parties, which allows them to easily understand that party's arguments and its procedural positions. They share the same cultural background, and the foreigner is an outsider.

Comparatists regroup the various legal systems into families with common features.[3] It is well known that the two main legal families are the Civil Law family and the Common Law family. To the Civil Law family belong those national legal systems with their roots in Roman law as codified by Justinian. During the nineteenth century in continental Europe, they codified their laws based on the model of the Napoleonic codes. Today, this family includes many countries outside Europe, in Africa, Asia and Latin America. The Common Law family contains national systems influenced by English law, which also has its roots in Roman law, but as it existed before the Justinian codification. Besides England, Ireland and Wales, this system is found in Africa, America, Asia and Oceania. It should be noted that national legal systems belonging to the same legal family are not identical and may differ considerably on various points.

International arbitration offers a legal framework within which the parties may directly or indirectly obtain the cultural neutrality they need. A first step on the path to

3. *See*, R. David, 'Les grands systèmes de droit contemporains,' n° 16, p. 21.

achieving it is to appoint as sole arbitrator, or as president of a three-person tribunal, someone with a nationality different to that of the parties. According to Article 11(5) of the UNCITRAL Model Law, a court or an appointing authority 'in the case of a sole or third arbitrator, shall take into account as well the advisability of appointing an arbitrator of a nationality other than those of the parties'.[4] Appointing sole arbitrators or presidents of a third nationality is a principle under the rules of the major arbitral institutions,[5] although some of them do not do this systematically[6] and others do not impose any nationality restriction concerning the appointment of arbitrators.[7] Yet, it is to be expected that in practice, even if not obliged to do so by their rules, leading arbitral institutions are likely to refrain from appointing a sole or presiding arbitrator with the same nationality as one of the parties. However, although a third nationality necessarily contributes to cultural neutrality, it is not a sufficient condition as far as international arbitration is concerned. There are more nationalities in the world than legal traditions, and it is more than probable that an arbitrator elected in a third country would belong to the same legal tradition as one of the parties: e.g., this would be the case if an English president was appointed in a dispute between a US company and a German company, or if there was a French president in a dispute between a Mexican company and an Indian company. As a matter of fact, cases where the president or the sole arbitrator does not belong to the same legal tradition as one of the parties are very rare. In order to avoid an inevitable situation jeopardizing their required neutrality, international arbitrators have a responsibility to the parties to do their best to conduct the proceedings with cultural neutrality.

With a view to carrying out this responsibility, an international arbitrator does not need to know all the procedural legal systems of the world but must be aware of the fundamental differences between them. Within a specific system, an international arbitrator must be able to distinguish what is fundamental from what is just historical or circumstantial. This is particularly necessary in order to understand the parties' respective procedural positions and assess whether they are defending concepts that are essential to them or just trying to complicate the proceedings for dilatory purposes. An international arbitrator must also be convinced that no national legal system amounts to natural law. In this regard, the well-known award rendered by Lord Asquith of Bishopstone in the case between Petroleum Development (Trucial Coast) and the Sheik of Abu Dhabi in 1951[8] is an example of what not to do. In this award, the

4. Article 6(7) of the UNCITRAL Rules of Arbitration includes a similar solution.
5. *See*, for instance, Article 13(5) of the ICC Rules: 'The sole arbitrator or the chairman of the arbitral tribunal shall be of a nationality other than those of the parties.' *See also* Article 6 of the London Court of International Arbitration (LCIA) rules or Article 17(6) of the 2017 Arbitration Institute of the Stockholm Chamber of Commerce's Arbitration Rules.
6. This is the case for the International Centre for Dispute Resolution (ICDR); Article 12(4) of its International Rules of Arbitration reads: 'At the request of any party or on its own initiative, the Administrator may appoint nationals of a country other than that of any of the parties.'
7. For example, the Swiss Rules of International Arbitration, the Arbitration Rules of the Singapore International Arbitration Centre (SIAC) and the China International Economic and Trade Arbitration Commission Rules.
8. 1 I.C.L.Q. 248 (1952). In this award, the arbitrator presented some rules of English law as part of a 'modern law of nature'.

arbitrator presented some rules of English law as part of a 'modern law of nature.' It was a matter of substantive law and not of procedural law, but the issue is the same in both cases. International arbitrators must approach the application of any rule, be it procedural or substantive, with the awareness that the solutions of their own national legal systems are just one of the many possible answers for a problem occurring in various human societies.

An international arbitrator's cultural neutrality also requires the knowledge that legal words reflect legal concepts which are not the same in the various legal systems. The word 'witness' provides a good example. As English is the language of most international arbitration procedures, it is part of the basic vocabulary of any counsel who happens to be involved in an international arbitration. For a French lawyer, it means '*témoin*'; it means '*testigo*' for a Spanish lawyer. However, a 'witness' and a '*témoin*' are not the same and the function of each of them in their respective legal system is different. In Civil Law countries, the '*témoin*', '*testigo*', '*testemunha*', etc., must be independent from the parties. It is their independence that gives their declaration any evidentiary value. The legal systems of the Common Law family have a completely different approach. A person under the control of a party, or who has an interest in the outcome of the dispute, even the party itself, may give testimony. There are historical reasons to explain this fundamental difference. In Common Law jurisdictions, the early and extensive use of the jury made it necessary for human beings to be present and to explain the documentary evidence to the laymen composing the jury. It was not the case in Civil Law countries where the only person to be convinced was the judge, who could read and interpret the documents. These historical differences have been progressively disappearing, but not completely. They are the source of misunderstandings in international arbitration when lawyers have limited international experience. They may understand that the word 'witness' is just the English translation of the word describing a person giving testimony in their own domestic legal system. International arbitrators are responsible for giving appropriate guidance to avoid misunderstandings between the parties. If they do not provide such guidance, a party from a Civil Law country may be convinced that it has very few witnesses to present, while the other, from a Common Law country, may feel that it cannot present its case properly without the witness evidence of all the persons who played a significant role in the genesis of the dispute. Likewise, Civil Law lawyers may understand that their case may be won on the basis of documents alone, while many Common Law lawyers may believe that they cannot properly use a document if a witness does not introduce it at the hearing.

The same misunderstandings are found with respect to the preparation of witnesses. Many Civil Law counsel, unfamiliar with the practice of international arbitration proceedings, are reluctant to the concept of witnesses' and experts' preparation. Some of them do not hesitate to declare that it is incompatible with their professional deontology.[9] This reaction is misconstrued, as the prohibition on preparing witnesses, when this exists in Civil Law jurisdictions, is a consequence of the

9. On 28 February 2008, the Paris Bar had to adopt a resolution authorizing Paris lawyers to prepare witnesses in international arbitration to put an end to legal actions against Parisian lawyers who

requirement of independence of the witness. It becomes meaningless when most witnesses are closely linked to the lawyer's client, and may have played a significant role in the preparation of the case. In Common Law countries, the preparation of the witnesses is a professional obligation of lawyers, although the extent of such preparation differs from country to country. A responsible international arbitrator must be aware of these differences and make sure that each side understands the rules of the game from the outset. These rules must be the same for everybody to avoid the situation where, during the hearing, one lawyer suddenly discovers that the witnesses were prepared by the other lawyer when he or she wrongly believed that rules applicable in court proceedings in his or her country were universally applicable.

Many other examples of procedural differences between the domestic procedural traditions could be presented, from the discovery of documents to the accepted methods for interrogating witnesses. Although the main differences are between the Civil Law and the Common Law traditions, some significant ones exist inside each of these families. In exceptional cases where witness testimonies are presented in French civil and commercial proceedings, the witnesses submit a written statement and are not interrogated at the hearing. In Italy, they are interrogated by the judge or the arbitrators in domestic cases, on the basis of a list of questions prepared in advance. These differences may also generate misunderstandings. What matters is that each party feels at home. For this goal to be reached, a party should not be surprised by an approach to the proceedings which comes directly, and without warning, from a culture which is different from that party's culture. This is obviously very difficult, but if each party comes from a different culture, and the arbitrator's legal system, as is usually the case, belongs to the same legal family as one of them, it is his or her responsibility to maintain a certain balance. To be able to do so, the arbitrator must show cultural neutrality.

2 *Tailor-Made Proceedings*

As a result of their cultural neutrality, experienced international arbitrators have developed, during the last four decades, procedures that borrow from both the Civil Law and the Common Law traditions. The result today is that almost all international arbitration proceedings are organized along the same pattern. The advantage is not only the neutrality which results from the combination of Civil Law and Common Law. Standardization provides predictability, which is indispensable in proceedings with parties from different legal traditions who need to know the rules of the game in advance. However, the danger is that arbitrators often lose sight of the specific characteristics of the case that they have to decide. What is gained in predictability is lost in flexibility.

Parties expect proceedings adapted to their dispute, the specificity of which must be assessed according to two main aspects: on the one hand, the nature of the claims

did not hesitate to do this, rightly considering that the traditional domestic prohibition was not applicable in these international proceedings.

and the evidence necessary to prove them; and on the other hand, the legal traditions of the parties. Why systematically contemplate a phase of disclosure of documents when none of the parties actually need it? Why present several witnesses to explain the content of documents that raise no problem of interpretation? Nobody knows the answer. It is just the procedural tradition in international arbitration, with all its consequences for the duration and the cost of the proceedings. The parties do not agree to international arbitration for its neutrality only. They also look for procedural freedom and flexibility, which allow the adoption of efficient and expeditious procedures. They rarely find them in international arbitration today and regularly complain about this state of affairs, and they expect that arbitrators will put an end to it. It is part of their responsibility.

To carry out this responsibility, arbitrators must enter into the substance of the case at the beginning of the proceedings and, unfortunately, many do not. They consider that the only thing they have to do when they receive the file is resort to the standardized pattern and discuss with the parties the time limits for the various steps of that pattern until the hearing. It is only some weeks before the hearing that they read the memorials and the attached documents which have been presented, in order to be well prepared for the hearing.

Having a good knowledge of the case as soon as possible and adapting the proceedings to its characteristics are part of international arbitrators' responsibility. However, it is not an easy task, in particular if they do not find counsels' support. Unfortunately, in too many cases, the irresponsible attitude of parties' counsel may frustrate even the most efficiency-minded arbitrators. The arbitrators may take the appropriate decisions to keep the proceedings on the rails when confronted with dilatory tactics by one of the parties. They are helpless where all counsel agree on a schedule that seems unreasonable. What can they do when they suggest to the parties a three-month period to submit their respective statement of claim and statement of defence if counsel agree that each of them will have six months? The arbitrators will certainly stress that, in light of the characteristics of the case, such long periods do not appear necessary, but if counsel insist, they are bound to accept. Not only because according to most rules and laws the parties have the last word in this respect but also because it remains possible that this attitude corresponds to the genuine need of the parties which, for instance, may have embarked on parallel negotiations unknown to the arbitrators. Arbitrators should never forget that their knowledge of the case is often only partial, and may be the tip of the iceberg of the dispute between the parties. For defining tailor-made proceedings, they need the cooperation of the parties who have some responsibility for managing their outside counsel when this is necessary. If they do not, they cannot just be astonished by the duration and the costs of a procedure that they did not control.

3 Equality of Treatment of the Parties

Maintaining equality among the parties is part of arbitrators' duties. For instance, Article 17(1) of the UNCITRAL Rules or Article 18 of the UNCITRAL Model Law provide that the parties are to be treated 'with equality.' It is the arbitrators' responsibility to apply the principle in practice, taking into consideration the characteristics of each case. It is not always easy and requires that the arbitrators have a full grasp of the issues at stake as soon as possible. In some cases, treating the parties in exactly the same manner may lead to unfair results, at least if '*equality*' is viewed in the abstract. As an example:[10] party A refuses to make a payment apparently due under a contract with party B, on the ground that it was discharged of its obligation by a letter from a representative of party B. Party B alleges that the letter was obtained through bribery. If there is prima facie evidence that party B's allegation might be true, fairness could require the arbitrator to treat the parties '*unequally*,' by giving party B more time to gather its evidence, since proving bribery is more time-consuming than presenting a letter of discharge. This does not mean that in some cases, the parties should not be treated equally, but that *equality* does not necessarily mean giving exactly the same amount of time to each party. Likewise, when there are twenty witnesses on one side and two on the other side, giving the same time to each party to cross-examine witnesses would not be equal treatment.

Equality of treatment also requires that the cultural environment of each party be taken into consideration. Article 9(5) of the International Bar Association (IBA) Rules on the Taking of Evidence in International Arbitration provides that 'If a Party fails without satisfactory explanation to produce any Document requested in a Request to Produce to which it has not objected in due time or fails to produce any Document ordered to be produced by the Arbitral Tribunal, the Arbitral Tribunal may infer that such document would be adverse to the interests of that Party.' Such adverse inferences may not be drawn without taking into account the specific situation of the party that did not produce documents as ordered by the arbitrator. It is the behaviour of that very party which must be assessed, and it should not be done without having in mind the usual practices in that party's country. Practices vary when it comes to drawing up and conserving documents. In Common Law countries, companies anticipate discovery procedures and go to great lengths to keep all kinds of documents. As there is a strong tradition of litigation, businessmen expect at some point to be called as witnesses in proceedings and, with this in mind, take detailed notes of meetings and telephone conversations, which they keep carefully. This is not necessarily the case in Civil Law countries, where there is no discovery, and the risk of being called as a witness in court proceedings is very remote. Moreover, whatever the legal traditions of the parties are, the practice of creation and conservation of documentary evidence is not the same in private and public companies or in small and big companies. Applying exactly the same criteria to all parties when drawing negative inferences from the fact that a party has declared that documents it was ordered to produce do not exist would not amount to equal treatment. Equality of treatment when drawing adverse inferences requires a personalized and *in concreto* assessment.

10. *See*, Y. Derains & E. Schwartz, *A Guide to the ICC Rules of Arbitration*, 2005, 2nd ed., p. 229.

II THE DETERMINATION OF THE LAW APPLICABLE TO THE MERITS AND ITS APPLICATION

National judges who have to decide an international case do so on the basis of the rules of private international law of the *lex fori*, i.e., the private international law of the State in which they sit. It is widely accepted that international arbitrators have no *lex fori* where they can find rules of private international law.[11] International conventions, modern laws on arbitration and the rules of international arbitration institutions have developed an internationally accepted solution, rooted in two basic principles: (1) international arbitrators must apply the law chosen by the parties as the law applicable to the merits of the dispute; and (2) when the parties fail to make such a choice, international arbitrators enjoy wide discretion when determining the law applicable to the merits of the dispute.

The origin of this solution is to be found in Article VII of the Geneva Convention of 21 April 1961 on international arbitration.[12] However, the reference made by the Convention to the application by arbitrators of the rule of conflict that they deem appropriate in case the parties have not determined the applicable law was progressively abandoned in the rules of arbitral institutions and by modern national laws of arbitration. It was replaced by the application by arbitrators of the law they consider appropriate, without being obliged to apply any rule of conflict. The ICC took the lead in this respect, as in many others, when revising its rules in 1998, specifying that, failing any agreement of the parties on the law applicable to the merits of the dispute, the arbitrators would apply the rules of law which they determine to be appropriate.[13] The UNCITRAL Arbitration Rules, in their 2010 version, provide for a similar solution in Article 35(1).[14] Under several national laws, in light of Article 28 of the UNCITRAL

---

11. *See Guide to the ICC Rules of Arbitration*, by Yves Derains & E. Schwartz, Kluwer Law International 2005, 2nd edn, p. 240; *see also* the Sapphire arbitration award: 'contrary to a State judge, who is bound to conform to the conflict law rules of the State in whose name he metes out justice, the arbitrator is not bound by such rules. He must look for the common intention of the parties and use the connecting factors generally used in doctrine and in case law and must disregard national peculiarities', cited in Nigel Blackaby et al., *Redfern and Hunter on International Arbitration*, Sixth Edition, Chapter 3 'Applicable Law,' paragraph 3.213, stating also at para. 3.212: 'The seat of the arbitration is invariably chosen for reasons that have nothing to do with the conflict rules of the law of the place of arbitration. This had led to the formulation of a doctrine that has found support in both the rules of arbitral institutions and the practice of international arbitration- namely that unlike the judge of a national court, an international arbitral tribunal is not bound to follow the conflict-of-law rules of the country in which it has its seat.'
12. 'The parties shall be free to determine, by agreement, the law to be applied by the arbitrators to the substance of the dispute. Failing any indication by the parties as to the applicable law, the arbitrators shall apply the proper law under the rules of conflict that the arbitrators deem applicable.'
13. Article 21(1) of the 2017 ICC Rules of Arbitration reads: 'The Parties shall be free to agree upon the rules of law to be applied by the arbitral tribunal to the merits of the dispute. In the absence of any such agreement, the arbitral tribunal shall apply the rules of law which it determines to be appropriate.'
14. The only significant difference between the ICC Rules and the UNCITRAL Rules in this respect is that, failing a choice by the parties, the arbitrators must apply a law and not rules of law, although the parties could have made that choice. Thus, the arbitrators are limited in finding out

Model Law,[15] adopted in 1985 and amended in 2006, arbitrators' freedom is limited to the application of the rules of conflict that they consider appropriate. They cannot determine the applicable law without indicating the rule of conflict supporting their decision. However, it does not make a great difference in practice. When arbitrators decide to apply the law that they consider appropriate, they must provide reasons for reaching that conclusion. To do so, they necessarily formulate a rule of conflict since a rule of conflict is nothing else than the expression of the justification for the application of a certain law to a certain legal relation or to a certain legal fact. As the arbitrators are not obliged to apply a national system of conflict of laws, they enjoy the same freedom in practice. The national laws, such as Swiss law,[16] that remain reluctant to grant arbitrators the power to apply the law that they determine to be appropriate in the absence of a choice of law by the parties are statistical exceptions.

It results from the above that international arbitrators find no serious limits to their freedom to determine the law or rules of law applicable to the merits of the dispute other than the will of the parties, including the applicable rules of arbitration (e.g., exclusion of the application of 'rules of laws'), or in exceptional cases the *lex arbitri*. Such freedom entails a huge responsibility for the arbitrators as the outcome of the dispute may differ due to the application of one law or another. International arbitrators must endeavour to meet the legitimate expectations of the parties. Due to the consequences of wrong decisions in this respect, the correct application of the law applicable to the merits, either chosen by the parties or determined by the arbitrators, is a huge responsibility for international arbitrators.

A The Legitimate Expectations of the Parties

International arbitrators must convince the parties that they do not determine the law applicable to the merits of the dispute at whim but that such determinations meet their legitimate expectations.[17]

It has been noted[18] that when international arbitrators look for the law applicable to the merits, they are implementing one of the three following methods: the cumulative application of the conflict of laws systems concerned with the dispute, the recourse to general principles of private international law or the '*voie directe*'.

---

what would have been an objectively reasonable choice of the parties, while this research is the implementation of a classical rule of conflict.

15. Article 28 of the 2010 UNCITRAL Model Law reads: 'The arbitral tribunal shall decide the dispute in accordance with such rules of law as are chosen by the parties as applicable to the substance of the dispute. Failing any designation by the parties, the arbitral tribunal shall apply the law determined by *the conflict of law rules* which it considers applicable' (emphasis added).
16. Article 187 of the Federal Statute on Private International Law states: 'The arbitral tribunal shall decide the case according to the rules of law chosen by the parties, or, in the absence thereof, according to the rules of law with which the case has the closest connection.'
17. *See* Y. Derains 'Attente Légitime des parties et droit applicable au fond en matière d'arbitrage commercial international', Travaux du Comité Français de Droit International Privé, 1984-1985, p. 81.
18. Ph. Lalive, 'Les Règles de conflit de lois appliquées au fond du litige par l'arbitre international siégeant en Suisse', Rev. Arb. 1976, 155.

Under the first method, arbitrators consider the conflict of laws rules of the various national legal systems connected to the disputes submitted to them, one by one. If these rules, although they may be substantially different, converge towards one single domestic law, the arbitrators declare that this is the applicable law. Let us take the example of a dispute between a party of country A and a party of country B. Each party requires the application of its own national law to the contract. The arbitrators may justify the application of the law of country B by noting that: (i) under the rule of conflict of country A, the applicable law is the law of the place where the contract was entered into; (ii) under the rule of conflict of country B, the governing law is that of the place of performance; and (iii) the contract was entered into and performed in country B.[19] The practical result of the method followed by the arbitrators meets the legitimate expectations of the parties since the rule of conflict of their respective country was applied. However, this method ceases to be available when the rules of conflict of the parties do not converge towards a single national law. Moreover, it has lost a large part of its interest now that most arbitration rules and national laws do not require that arbitrators refer to a rule of conflict to determine the applicable law.

The same can be said of recourse to general principles of private international law. When there is no obligation to apply a rule of conflict, arbitrators are entitled to directly decide that the contract must be subject to the law of a certain country in view of its nature and characteristics. It is what has been traditionally called '*voie directe*'. Yet, the arbitrators should not take the parties by surprise. There are two main reasons for this. One is simply procedural. When one party is requesting the application of the law of country A and the other, the law of country B, an arbitrator may not decide to apply the law of country C without hearing the parties' views on this solution. Otherwise, it would be a breach of the principle of the right to be heard.

The other reason for not taking the parties by surprise when determining the law applicable to the merits is that it is an a posteriori indication of the norm against which will be measured the past performance by the parties of their contractual obligations. It is unfortunate that the parties did not choose that norm before performing their respective contractual obligations. As pointed out by Arthur Von Mehren, 'Their approach [the arbitrators] can and should be more in terms of what the parties' expectations or understanding were or would have been, had they addressed the issue.'[20] This was what international arbitrators were endeavouring to achieve at the time when they were required to determine the rule of conflict which would determine the applicable law. This was clearly the case with the cumulative application of the conflict of laws systems connected with the dispute and the recourse to general principles of private international law. Under both methods, arbitrators were selecting a law that a community, to which the parties belong, agrees to recognize as applicable, whether this is a limited community as in the first case or the international community as in the second. When arbitrators have recourse to the '*voie directe*' as is generally the

19. For more details, *see* Y. Derains, 'L'application cumulative par l'arbitre des systèmes de conflit de lois intéressés au litige', Rev. Arb. 1972, p. 93.
20. A. Von Mehren 'To What Extent Is International Arbitration Autonomous' in Etudes Offertes à B. Goldman, p. 227.

case today, the outcome of their analysis must demonstrate to the parties that they could not legitimately expect the arbitrators to apply any law other than the one they have finally chosen.

B The Practical Application of the Applicable Law

Unless the parties have agreed to an appeal procedure, there are few jurisdictions where a superficial assessment of the facts or a misinterpretation of the contract are grounds for a reconsideration or an annulment of an award. The same applies to an inaccurate application of the law, with the exception of some Common Law countries where an award may be set aside for manifest disregard of the law, such as the United States or England, where a party to an arbitration may apply to the court for permission to appeal against an award on the grounds that it was based on an error of law.

In the practical application of the applicable law, international arbitrators may be confronted with three main problems: (1) the determination of the content of that law, (2) its possible lacunae, and (3) the need for its adaptation.

1 The Determination of the Content of the Applicable Law

In international commercial arbitration, it is exceptional for the three members of an arbitral tribunal to have more than a very superficial knowledge of the content of the law applicable to the merits of the case. It is one of the consequences of the cultural neutrality of the arbitrators that the parties expect to find in international arbitration. In most cases, it is of no practical effect since the solutions to the problems submitted to the arbitrators are more or less the same in the various legal systems, and often depend on the interpretation of the parties' agreement. Yet, similarity does not mean they are identical, and it may be very treacherous, in particular when laws pertaining to the same legal family are considered. What has been said above with regard to procedural law applies to substantive law. For instance, the approach to good faith is not the same in England and in the United States. Likewise, although they all belong to the Civil Law family, French, Italian, Portuguese and Spanish laws do not resolve in exactly the same way the problems that are caused by the effect of unforeseen circumstances on the performance of contracts. Moreover, when the solution of a specific national law is of the essence for resolving a dispute, even the parties and their experts are generally in disagreement as to its content.

Arbitration rules provide no guidance as to the determination by arbitrators of the content of the law applicable to the merits. The same may be said of national laws since few of them allow arbitrators to take advantage of the European Convention on Information on Foreign Law of 7 June 1968.[21] In practice, parties generally explain to

21. Article 1044 of the Dutch Code of Civil Procedure reads: 'Request for information on foreign law 1. The arbitral tribunal may, through the intervention of the Provisional Relief Judge of the District Court at The Hague, ask for information as mentioned in Article 3 of the European Convention on Information on Foreign Law, concluded at London, 7 June 1968 (Dutch Treaty Series 1968, 142). The Provisional Relief Judge shall, unless he considers the request to be

the arbitrators the content of the applicable law. They provide the legal texts and the relevant case law, often with the help of legal experts, although it is not always necessary as this can be efficiently done by the parties' lawyers. However, this is not always the case, and it happens that international arbitrators are confronted with no explanation by the parties as to the relevant content of the law applicable to the merits of the case. This creates a very complicated problem. In a few national legal systems, there is a presumption that the applicable law is identical to the law of the place of arbitration. According to an English case of 2000:[22]

> If there is no suggestion by the parties that there is an issue under the applicable system of law which is different from the law of England and Wales, or the tribunal does not itself raise a specific issue, then the tribunal is free to decide the matter on the basis of the presumption that the applicable system of law is the same as the law of England and Wales.

Yet, this archaic solution is not applied in most international arbitration cases. International arbitrators are not limited by the parties' submissions as far as the content of the applicable law is concerned and, contrary to national judges, they cannot introduce a different status between domestic law and foreign law. As a consequence of the absence of *lex fori*, there is no foreign law in international arbitration in the sense of a rule that is not part of the legal system of the authority responsible for resolving the dispute. All national laws have the same value, and none of them have privileged status. As national judges of some countries do, international arbitrators have the responsibility to carry out their own research to establish the content of the applicable law,[23] provided that they submit the result of such research to the parties for comments in order to respect due process. This point was perfectly expressed by Professor Gabrielle Kaufmann-Kohler:

> The parties shall establish the content of law applicable to the merits. The arbitral tribunal shall have the power, but not the obligation, to conduct its own research to establish such content. If it makes use of such power, the tribunal shall give the parties an opportunity to comment on the results of the tribunal research ... .[24]

Professor Gabrielle Kaufmann-Kohler also makes the suggestion that in case the content of the applicable law on a specific point is not established, the arbitral tribunal

without merit, send the request without delay to the agency mentioned in Article 2 of said Convention and notify the arbitral tribunal thereof. 2. The arbitral tribunal may suspend the proceedings until the day on which it has received the answer to its request for information.'

22. *Husman (Europe) v. Al Ameeen Dev. & Trade Co.* [2000] EWHC (Comm.), §42.
23. As is the case in Switzerland, pursuant to Art. 16(1) of the Swiss Private International Law Act, 1987; in France, the Cour de cassation has stressed in a decision of 24 June 2014 that '... the French judge who declares that a foreign law is applicable must research its content either ex officio or on the request of the party who relies on that law, with the help of all the parties and personally if necessary, and to give to the disputed issue a solution in accordance with the positive foreign law' (Cass. Com. 24 June 2014, free translation).
24. G. Kaufmann-Kohler, '*The Governing Law: Fact or Law?' – A Transnational Rule on Establishing its Contents*, Best Practices in International Arbitration, ASA Special Series n° 26, July 2006, p. 84.

might apply the law that it considers appropriate.[25] There is no reason not to deal with this issue with the *lacunae* of the applicable law.

2 *The* Lacunae *of the Applicable Law*

Because of the absence of *lex fori*, international arbitrators, unlike national judges, are deprived of an available legal system to find a subsidiary solution when there is none in the applicable law. When they are confronted with a *lacuna* in that law, they should refrain from referring to the law they are familiar with as a substitute. Sole arbitrators are particularly faced with this danger, as three-member tribunals are generally composed of persons with different legal cultures. International arbitrators should never forget that they are in charge of resolving an international dispute and that, in most cases, international disputes require international solutions. Most are fully aware of this and, traditionally, have filled the *lacunae* of the applicable law using international norms.[26] For instance, in 1988, the arbitral tribunal of the ICC Case No. 5314[27] decided to apply American law in general and in particular the law of Massachusetts, supplemented where necessary by the *lex mercatoria*. Another example may be found in an ICC award of 1989 in Case No. 5835,[28] with an Italian party opposing a party of Kuwait, where the arbitrators decided to apply the law of Kuwait and added:

> However, in accordance with a well-established practice in international commercial arbitration, the arbitrators shall take account also of the principles generally applicable in international commerce ... This proviso is particularly justified in view of the fact that the Parties refrained from choosing explicitly Kuwaiti law as the law on the merits ... The Arbitral Tribunal concludes that Kuwaiti law and, to the extent necessary, principles generally applicable in international commerce are applicable to the merits of the dispute.

Likewise, an award of 1992 in ICC Case No. 6500[29] decided to apply Lebanese law, supplemented by the *lex mercatoria* in case the former was silent. But nowadays, it is in the UNIDROIT Principles that many arbitrators find the elements that they need to fill the lacunae of the applicable law, as suggested by the Preamble of the Principles which points out that 'they may be used to interpret or supplement domestic law'. Paragraph 6 of the comment stresses that by referring to the Principles, the domestic law will be interpreted or supplemented in accordance with internationally accepted standards. This is exactly what international arbitrators have the responsibility to do when a lacuna of the applicable law needs to be filled.

25. *Ibid.*
26. E. Loquin: 'L'application des règles nationales dans l'arbitrage commercial international,' in *L'apport de la jurisprudence arbitrale,* Publication CCI no. 440-1, 1986 p. 67 et seq.
27. [ICC Case No. 5314 (1988)], Collection of ICC Arbitral Awards, 1991-1995, at 309, Jean-Jacques Arnaldez, Yves Derains & Dominique Hasher, eds. 1997.
28. ICC Award of 1989 in Case No. 5835, Bulletin of the ICC International Court of Arbitration, p. 33 (1999).
29. ICC Award of 1992, in Case No. 6500, JDI no. 1992, 1015, comments.

3 *The Need for Adaption of the Applicable Law*

It has been said that a national judge who applies a foreign law is more like a photographer than an architect.[30] This is understandable since the judge is outside the foreign legal system, some rules of which he or she has to apply. *Mutatis mutandis*, international arbitrators are in the same position. However, they should not stand as a photograph; they should not hesitate to adapt the applicable law to the needs of international relations.

An ICC award of 1996, in Case No. 8486,[31] provides an interesting example of the internationalization of applicable domestic law. Dutch law was applicable to the merits of the case. Article 3.12 of the Dutch Civil Code reads as follows: '[for] determining what the principle of "reasonableness and fairness" demands in a specific situation, one has to take into account the general accepted legal principles, the fundamental conceptions of law in the Netherlands and the relevant social and personal interests which are involved in the given situation'. The arbitral tribunal decided to adapt this rule to international commercial relations and considered 'the common opinion of international contractual law' instead of 'the fundamental conceptions of law in the Netherlands'. Referring to the works of Professor Klaus-Peter Berger,[32] it pointed out that 'this common opinion of law must also be taken into account for the application of national law to international relationships'.

This approach is to be commended. International arbitrators are given the responsibility to resolve international disputes, and this includes the duty to make the necessary adaptations to the applicable law, generally designed to resolve domestic issues. As underscored by Gary Born, '... an arbitral tribunal may properly conclude that a particular national judicial precedent was not intended to, or would not be applied to, international transactions, or a particular type of international transactions. There are frequently instances where domestic rules are not applied, or meant to apply, in transnational contexts, and arbitral tribunals would be free – and indeed obligated – not to give effect to domestic precedent in such circumstances'.[33] This shows that international arbitrators must not always act as mere photographers of the applicable domestic law. Should they go further by not giving effect to established solutions of the national domestic law? This would not be because the solutions were not conceived for international relations but rather because the arbitrators were convinced that this law did not have the ability to adapt to the evolutions of modern transactions. For instance, this was the case with French law which, before the revision of the Civil Code in 2016, did not accept the adaptation of contracts to unforeseen circumstances, with the exception of administrative contracts.

This is a difficult issue where international arbitrators should be very careful. Some particular rules of a national system of law are well known by international

30. *See* W. Goldschimdt, *Die philosophischen Grundlagen des internationalen Privatrechts*, Festschrift fur Martin Wolf, Tubingen, 1952, 217.
31. ICC Award of 1996 in Case No. 8486, JDI no. 1988, 1047-1052.
32. K.P. Berger, *Formalisierte oder 'schleichende' Kodifizierung des transnationalen Wirtschaftsrechts* (1996) pp. 174 et seq.
33. G. Born, *International Commercial Arbitration*, Vol. II, 2009, pp. 2964 et seq.

operators, and international arbitrators must refrain from not applying them just because they do not like them, in particular when that national system of law has been chosen by the parties to govern their contract. The parties are expected to have known them when they made that choice. The situation is different when specific case law is invoked. When it is a very old precedent of a supreme court, international arbitrators may wonder whether it is really representative of today's law. They are entitled to find that this is not the case in Civil Law countries, where the *stare decisis* doctrine does not apply when several lower courts have unanimously departed from the old Supreme Court's decision in recent judgments, and such judgments have not been tested by the Supreme Court. This indicates that the Supreme Court's decision is an old-fashioned one, and the arbitrators, after consultation with the parties, may assume that the Supreme Court would confirm the new case law if it were given the opportunity. If the law of a Common Law country is applicable, greater restraint and circumspection are required.

Those are just a few examples of the international arbitrators' responsibilities, with respect to important but limited issues. There are many others. But it is worth stressing that when arbitrators do not carry out their responsibility to the parties as they should do, the whole arbitration community is affected even if they are not in a position to sue them for damages to their reputation. Moreover, since they have a jurisdictional function, arbitrators also have a social responsibility that deserves another article. Guillermo Aguilar Álvarez was aware of such arbitrators' responsibilities. His many contributions to the international arbitration community, including teaching and mentoring young practitioners, illustrate that, for him, arbitration was not just a livelihood. In their famous book, *Dealing with virtue*, Y. Dezalay and B.G. Garth report that one of the pioneers of modern international arbitration told them that arbitration was a duty, not a career.[34] Guillermo shared that view.

34. Y. Dezalay & B.G. Garth, *Dealing in Virtue*, in *International Commercial Arbitration and the Construction of a Transnational Legal Order*, 1996, p. 34.

CHAPTER 22

Does an Annulled Award Constitute Legal Authority in Investment Arbitration?

Albert Jan van den Berg

Arbitration lawyers have been discussing the enforcement of annulled awards for some twenty-five years. Recently, another discussion regarding annulled awards is gaining traction: can an investment arbitrator rely on an annulled award?[1]

Reliance may concern two types of issues: factual findings and legal considerations. In this contribution, I will not address the first type. The factual findings in an annulled award are usually invoked in connected cases between the same or related parties. They involve matters of res judicata and, possibly, estoppel.[2]

The second type of issue is more problematic. At its core is the question of the legal status of an annulled investment award. If it is rendered in the context of an investment arbitration under the UNCITRAL Rules, the award has been annulled by a national court (of the place of arbitration). In that country, the annulled award legally no longer exists. Outside the country where the award was made, enforcement courts have to refuse enforcement under the New York Convention.[3] Such nonenforcement is

1. *See* Dimitris Kontogiannis, *Tribunal's Reference to Annulled Awards: Beyond a Question of Persuasiveness?*, Kluwer Arbitration Blog, May 15, 2019, http://arbitrationblog.kluwerarbitration.com/2019/05/15/tribunals-reference-to-annulled-awards-beyond-a-question-of-persuasiveness/.
2. *See* Procedural Order No. 1 of May 17, 2012 in *Fraport AG v Philippines*, ICSID Case No. ARB/11/12. The Tribunal considered that "the findings of fact and conclusions of law set forth in the original ICSID Award, having been annulled, can have no binding effect on the current proceeding" because the ad hoc Committee had annulled the award in its entirety (at ¶¶ 45-70). It also held that ICC awards in related International Bar Association (ICC) proceedings were not binding on the parties in the present proceeding "as there is no identity of (i) parties, (ii) *petitum*, and (iii) *causa petendi*" (at ¶¶ 79-84). *See also Amco Asia v. Indonesia II*, Decision on Jurisdiction of May 10, 1988, ¶¶ 10-15, 20-98, https://www.italaw.com/sites/default/files/case-documents/italaw6357_0.pdf.
3. Article V(1)(e) of the New York Convention provides as a ground for the refusal of enforcement that "the award ... has been ... set aside by the competent authority of the country in which ...

controversial as certain courts are of the view that they have a discretionary power to enforce an award under the Convention notwithstanding annulment in the country where it was made.[4] On the other hand, if the investment award is rendered in the context of the ICSID Convention, it is not questioned that an award annulled by an ad hoc Committee legally no longer exists and can no longer be enforced.[5]

Arbitrators (and parties) frequently refer to investment awards that have not been annulled. It is generally accepted that prior investment awards do not constitute binding precedent. Whether they constitute persuasive precedent is subject to debate. One school of thought believes investment arbitrators should pay due attention to earlier decisions of international tribunals and that, specifically, subject to compelling contrary grounds, they have a duty to adopt solutions established in a series of consistent cases (*jurisprudence constante*).[6] This school also believes that investment arbitrators have a duty to contribute to the harmonious development of investment law. Another school of thought is of the view that each case stands on its own and has its own legal and factual issues. This school does not believe in a duty to contribute to the development of investment law as arbitrators are chosen by parties for resolving the dispute between them only.[7]

For the first school of thought, prior arbitral awards are persuasive and even authoritative precedent. For the second school of thought, these awards are at best inspirational. Even so, when it comes to annulled investment awards, both schools will be confronted with the question of whether they can attribute any value to such awards, be it precedential or inspirational. In the arbitration context, that question becomes whether annulled awards constitute legal authority, with the related question of how the content of applicable law is to be ascertained.

Legal authority consists of statutes, case law, and doctrinal writings. In the case of investment arbitration, legal authority consists mostly of arbitral awards rendered by

that award was made." It may also be that the domestic law on enforcement of foreign or international awards (which can be applied by virtue of the more-favorable-right provision of Article VII(1) of the New York Convention) does not contain annulment in the country where the award was made as a ground for the refusal of enforcement. The latter is the case in France.

4. *See* my article *Should the Setting Aside of the Arbitral Award be Abolished?*, 29 ICSID Review—Foreign Investment Law Journal (2013) pp. 1-26.
5. *Quid* can an annulled ICSID award be enforced under the New York Convention in those courts that enforce awards under the New York Convention, notwithstanding their annulment in the country where made?
6. *See generally*, Gabrielle Kaufmann-Kohler, *Arbitral Precedent: Dream, Necessity or Excuse?*, 23 Arbitration International (2007) p. 327.
7. *See Burlington Resources Inc. v. Republic of Ecuador*, ICSID Case No. ARB/08/5 (Kaufmann-Kohler, Orrego Vicuña, Stern), Decision on Jurisdiction, June 2, 2010, ¶ 100: "The Tribunal considers that it is not bound by previous decisions.[footnote omitted] At the same time, it is of the opinion that it must pay due consideration to earlier decisions of international tribunals. The majority believes that, subject to compelling contrary grounds, it has a duty to adopt solutions established in a series of consistent cases. It also believes that, subject to the specifics of a given treaty and of the circumstances of the actual case, it has a duty to seek to contribute to the harmonious development of investment law, and thereby to meet the legitimate expectations of the community of States and investors towards the certainty of the rule of law. Arbitrator Stern does not analyze the arbitrator's role in the same manner, as she considers it her duty to decide each case on its own merits, independently of any apparent jurisprudential trend."

other investment tribunals. Parties refer to arbitral awards in support of their contentions regarding legal issues. Arbitrators refer to them in support of their findings regarding legal issues.

With respect to the related question, there is a divide as to how the content of applicable law is to be ascertained in investment arbitration. One group adheres to the rule that the content of the applicable law is to be proven by a party. Another group follows the rule that the content of the applicable law is to be determined by investment arbitrators upon submission of the parties (possibly assisted by legal experts).

Some believe that investment arbitrators may determine the content of the applicable law even without submission by the parties on the basis of the maxim *iura novit curia* (the court knows the law). That maxim exists in a number of national legal systems. It is controversial whether investment arbitrators are also allowed to apply this maxim. If they do so, it is advisable that they submit to the parties for comment their new thoughts on the applicable law. Otherwise, it can result in a surprise award that may be in jeopardy for violating due process.[8]

Against the foregoing background, the reference to annulled awards raises a number of questions that I will review below.

A *first question* is whether the aforementioned concept of enforcement of annulled awards under the New York Convention is relevant for the question whether investment arbitrators may rely on an annulled award. The answer to this question must be negative. The concept of enforcement of an annulled award requires a specific legal basis. In the context of the New York Convention, it is an interpretation of Article V(1) ("may"), and possibly VII(1) (more-favorable-right provision), of the Convention that is said to offer such legal basis. In the context of the ICSID Convention, there is no such legal basis. For that reason, it has never even been argued that an award annulled by the International Centre for Settlement of Investment Disputes (ICSID) ad hoc Committee can nonetheless be enforced.[9]

A *second question* is whether an annulled award constitutes legal authority at all. If the award has not been annulled, it would fall into the category of case law. An annulled award, on the other hand, does not fit into any of the categories (statutes, case law and doctrinal writing) within the concept of legal authority.

Once an award has been annulled, can the document be considered transformed into a doctrinal writing? I do not believe in such a "transformation." The nature of an arbitral award is fundamentally different from that of a doctrinal writing. An award is the result of an adjudicatory process and is written as the outcome of a deliberative procedure amongst the arbitrators in light of the rivalling positions of the parties. A doctrinal writing does not compare with such a process and result.

8. *Cf.* International Law Association, *Recommendations on Ascertaining the Contents of the Applicable Law in International Commercial Arbitration*, Rio de Janeiro, 2008. These Recommendations should, in my view, also be taken into account by investment arbitrators. Recommendation 6: "In general, and subject to Recommendation 13 [Public Policy], arbitrators should not introduce legal issues—propositions of law that may bear on the outcome of the dispute—that the parties have not raised."
9. *See also supra* n. 5.

For those reasons too, an annulled investment award would not qualify as "the teachings of the most highly qualified publicists of various nations," which is a subsidiary means for determination of rules of law under Article 38(1)(d) of the International Court of Justice (ICJ) Statute.[10] Moreover, it is open to debate whether all investment arbitrators can be considered "the most highly qualified publicists."[11]

A *third question* is whether investment arbitrators may rely on portions of an annulled award that were not the cause of its annulment. An example is an award that has been annulled for lack of a valid arbitration agreement. Can an investment arbitrator still rely on the portions in the annulled award that concern legal matters, such as interpreting the notion of fair and equitable treatment? If the award is annulled in part and the legal matter is considered in the part that was not annulled, an investment arbitrator may do so. If the award was annulled in its entirety (which is usually the case if the annulment occurred for lack of a valid arbitration agreement), it is difficult to conceive that any portion of the award can constitute legal authority. As mentioned, it does not fit into any category within the notion of legal authority (statutes, case law and doctrinal writing).

A *fourth question* concerns the abovementioned group that adheres to the rule that the content of the applicable law is to be proven by a party. As a matter of evidence, is the annulled award inadmissible evidence or does it go to weighing the evidence? Investment arbitrators who view an annulled award as legally nonexistent will probably declare an annulled award inadmissible evidence. Those who have a more generous view of an annulled award may consider it as going to weighing the evidence.[12]

A *fifth question* concerns the case where investment arbitrators have relied on an arbitral award as persuasive or authoritative precedent and where, after issuance of the award, the award relied upon is annulled. Could it be argued that the arbitrators have failed to state reasons? National courts and ad hoc ICSID Committees will not lightly accept that there is a failure to state reasons. However, if the reliance goes to the core of the reasoning, their attitude may be different.

A *sixth question* is whether investment arbitrators may refer to an annulled award on the basis of the doctrine of *iura novit curia*. Assuming that the doctrine applies in investment arbitration, which, as noted, is controversial, it is difficult to see how the doctrine of *iura novit curia* can be of any help in resolving the question of whether investment arbitrators may rely on an annulled award. The doctrine concerns "*iura*," which is law. An annulled award does not form part of "law" nor is it a source of law.

10. Assuming Article 38(1)(d) of the ICJ Statute would be applicable directly or by way of analogy. Nor can an annulled award be considered a "judicial decision" referred to in Article 38(1)(d) of the ICJ Statute.
11. Even if, in the case of ICSID arbitration, they are "persons of high moral character and recognized competence in the fields of law ... who may be relied upon to exercise independent judgment" (ICSID Convention, Article 14(1)).
12. A related question here is whether, instead of presenting an annulled award as legal authority, a party can present it as factual evidence. In addition to issues of relevance, if it is admissible as a factual matter, such presentation would seem unhelpful as it constitutes only proof of part of the factual matrix that the award has been annulled.

A *seventh question* is whether an annulled award can give guidance to investment arbitrators in another manner than as legal authority. Can it pertain to material sources which may assist in elucidating the content of the applicable law? I do not think so. It is difficult to see how an annulled award is legally capable of elucidating the content of the applicable law. This kind of free-for-all approach strays away from the legal analysis that is required to determine the content of the applicable law.

In conclusion, I submit that, in investment arbitration, an arbitral award, annulled by a national court in the UNCITRAL Rules context or by an ad hoc Committee in the ICSID context, does not constitute legal authority, nor can it give guidance on the content of the applicable law in another manner. Investment arbitration requires legal certainty and predictability. Reference to annulled awards does not serve these purposes.

CHAPTER 23

Can the Reasons for Reasons Rescue ICSID Annulment?

Scott Vesel[*]

I INTRODUCTION

A key feature of the ICSID arbitration system is that awards are meant to be final. An ICSID award 'shall be binding on the parties and shall not be subject to any appeal or to any other remedy except those provided in [the ICSID] Convention'.[1] The principal exception to finality contemplated in the Convention is the remedy of annulment, by which an award can be challenged before an ad hoc annulment committee on one of the enumerated grounds in the Convention.[2] Annulment committees, however, have struggled to define and respect the limitations of annulment review, which does not constitute an appeal and does not permit them to engage with the merits of the award. One ground for annulment that has posed particular difficulties for ad hoc committees is the ground that 'the award has failed to state the reasons on which it is based'.[3] Committees have tended to resort to vague metaphors rather than clear standards for assessing whether an award should be annulled for failure to state reasons, with the result that the line distinguishing annulment review from appeal has become blurred.

The challenge of respecting the boundaries of annulment review is rendered all the more difficult by the fact that awards are collaborative documents that are not always exemplars of clarity. In a 2008 book on *The Reasons Requirement in International Arbitration*, Guillermo Aguilar Álvarez and Michael Reisman, together with the participants in a seminar they led at the Yale Law School, examined how well investment awards are reasoned. The group's overall conclusion was that 'in almost all

* The views expressed herein are those of the author alone.
1. ICSID Convention, Article 53(1).
2. ICSID Convention, Article 52.
3. ICSID Convention, Article 52(e).

... instances, ... the right decision had probably been reached. But ... one could not reconstruct or 'reverse engineer' the reasoning of the tribunal'.[4] How is an ICSID annulment committee to approach a request to annul such an award without engaging in a full-blown appeal?

This chapter proposes an approach rooted in the recognition that a reasoned award is evidence that the procedure was a fair one. Accordingly, an annulment committee's role is not to critique the tribunal's drafting, reasoning, or its legal and factual analysis but rather to assess whether the reasoning in the award is so deficient as to establish a violation of the right to a fair hearing. Such an approach would impose clear limits on annulment review in a manner that is consistent with the drafting history and the approach of other international courts and tribunals to the reasons requirement.

II FINALITY VERSUS ANNULMENT FOR FAILURE TO STATE REASONS

International arbitration under the ICSID Convention is distinct from other forms of commercial and investor-state arbitration in that the arbitration proceedings are not 'seated' in any national jurisdiction and are not subject to any supervision by any domestic court system. The absence of such review is meant to be a strength of the ICSID system: an ICSID award, once rendered, is not subject to any kind of appeal or set aside in any court, but is final and directly enforceable in the courts of any ICSID member state, subject only to the limited post-award remedies available within the ICSID system itself.

The most powerful of these remedies, and the one most in tension with finality, is the remedy of annulment. The five grounds for annulment enumerated in Article 52 of the ICSID Convention are:

(a) the Tribunal was not properly constituted;
(b) the Tribunal manifestly exceeded its powers;
(c) corruption on the part of a member of the Tribunal;
(d) serious departure from a fundamental rule of procedure; and
(e) the award has failed to state the reasons on which it is based.[5]

Annulment for failure to state reasons under Article 52(e) must be understood in connection with Article 48 of the ICSID Convention, which requires each award to 'deal with every question submitted to it' and 'to state the reasons on which it is based'.[6] It is only a failure to satisfy the second of these requirements of Article 48 that can give rise to annulment.

4. Guillermo Aguilar Álvarez and W. Michael Reisman, eds, The Reasons Requirement in International Investment Arbitration: Critical Case Studies (2008), p. 1.
5. ICSID Convention, Article 52.
6. ICSID Convention, Article 48.

It is also useful to focus on the phrase included in both Article 48 and Article 52(e) that has been of great significance in the annulment context: 'on which it is based'.[7] Some committees, following the committee in *Klöckner v. Cameroon*, have interpreted this language as inviting an annulment committee to examine whether the reasons given by the tribunal provide a sufficient basis for the award. However, as illustrated by the *Klöckner v. Cameroon* decision and the backlash against it, such a reading risks transforming annulment into a full-blown merits review that is indistinguishable from appeal insofar as it invites the annulment committee to assess the adequacy of the reasons to support the result, rather than simply to ask whether reasons have been given.

III ANNULMENT'S ROCKY START IN *KLÖCKNER V. CAMEROON*

The annulment committee in *Klöckner v. Cameroon* focused on the phrase 'reasons on which it is based' from Article 52(e) and concluded that an annulment committee should be reviewing the award to determine whether the reasons are 'sufficiently relevant' in the sense of being 'reasonably capable of justifying the result reached by the Tribunal'.[8] The effect of this interpretation is to subject ICSID awards to extensive review of the quality of the tribunal's reasoning. And that is precisely what the *Klöckner* committee did. It found five instances in which the tribunal's reasoning failed to meet the standard. Accordingly, the committee annulled the award despite the committee's view that the tribunal's conclusions were 'perhaps ultimately perfectly justified and equitable'.[9] In other words, the committee's criticism was not about the result but rather the manner in which the tribunal had articulated its reasoning.

The reactions to the *Klöckner* annulment decision were overwhelmingly negative. Michael Reisman described the decision as 'arbitral review amok',[10] and Alan Redfern described it as creating an 'elaborate and expensive game of snakes and ladders' in which the decision of one panel of three eminent arbitrators wiped out the decision of another panel of three equally eminent arbitrators, with the result that proceedings would need to start over before yet another panel of three eminent arbitrators.[11] Given that many ICSID awards are issued after ten years or more of proceedings, requiring the parties to start over has enormous implications for time and costs, and even the credibility of the system as a whole.

7. *Ibid.*, Article 48 (3).
8. *Klöckner Industrie-Anlagen GmbH and others v. United Republic of Cameroon and Société Camerounaise des Engrais*, ICSID Case No. ARB/81/2, Decision on Annulment, 3 May 1985 (hereinafter '*Klöckner*'), para. 120.
9. *Klöckner*, para. 144.
10. W. Michael Reisman, 'The Breakdown of the Control Mechanism in ICSID Arbitration', *Duke Law Journal*, Vol. 1989, No. 4, pp. 739-807 at p. 755.
11. Alan Redfern, 'ICSID—Losing Its Appeal?', 3 *Arbitration International*, Vol. 3 (1987), Issue 2, pp. 98-118 at p. 99.

IV *MINE V. GUINEA*: REASONING ABOUT REASONS BY METAPHOR

Since *Klöckner*, annulment committees have generally sought to articulate a narrower scope for annulment under Article 52(e). The most often-quoted alternative formulation was provided a few years after *Klöckner* by the committee in *MINE v. Guinea*. The MINE committee declared that 'the requirement to state reasons is satisfied *as long as the award enables one to follow how the tribunal proceeded from Point A to Point B* (emphasis added)'.[12]

The *MINE* committee thus defined the requirement by reference to a metaphor about travelling. So long as a reader of an award can understand where the tribunal turned left or right, it does not matter where they ended up.

While many subsequent committees have quoted the 'Point A to Point B' language from *MINE*, this metaphor is not particularly helpful in deciding whether a tribunal has met its responsibility to state the reasons on which its award is based. There are a number of reasons why the metaphor does not quite work.

It is an oversimplification of the decision-making process involved in an award to suggest that it can be conveyed in something akin to a two-dimensional line. There is not always a clear starting 'Point A' or a single path to the final decision at 'Point B' but rather a multitude of points of decision that interact in complex ways. This complexity is compounded by the fact that the members of a tribunal may all agree that Point B is the right conclusion, but disagree about the path or paths to get there. Achieving consensus and unanimity within a tribunal may require fuzzy wording to paper over differences. Insistence upon clear, linear reasoning would militate against compromise within tribunals.

The metaphor also begs the question of the level of detail required in the articulation of the reasoning. Must the tribunal only explain their overall direction of travel, or must they explain each turning they have taken along the route (and why they did not take any of the other paths proposed by either party)? Any suggestion that a comprehensive map is required would be difficult to reconcile with the fact that a failure to meet the first requirement of Article 48 – that the tribunal deal with every question submitted to it – is not included within Article 52(e) as a basis for annulment.

Moreover, it is unclear how the metaphor about travelling from Point A to Point B fits with the idea that a tribunal will have failed to state reasons if the reasons it gives are contradictory. For example, could an award be annulled if the tribunal's reasoning performed the metaphorical equivalent of turning left by way of three right turns? If the result is correct, but the tribunal has not articulated its reasoning perfectly, what interest of justice would be served by requiring the parties to start over?

Consider a case in which the three arbitrators reach the same conclusion by three different paths of reasoning. Can such a tribunal craft an annulment-proof award? Some committees have recognized this problem, noting that 'annulment committees should not be quick to find contradiction when in fact what is evident from the award

---

12. *Maritime International Nominees Establishment (MINE) v. Republic of Guinea*, ICSID Case No. ARB/84/4, Decision on Annulment, 14 December 1989, para. 5.09.

is the compromise reached in an international collegiate adjudicative body'.[13] But warning of the danger is not the same as providing means of avoiding it: how is an annulment committee to know if opaque or vague reasoning reflects such a compromise? Suppose such a tribunal sought to avoid vagueness by issuing three separate concurring opinions, all reaching the same result but for different reasons. Would such an award be annullable for being based on contradictory reasons?

V THE ROAD NOT TAKEN: THE 'TIPSY COACHMAN'

ICSID annulment is not the only legal context in which metaphors about travelling have been used to describe a decision-maker's process of reasoning. For example, some common law jurisdictions have relied upon a different travelling metaphor about a 'tipsy coachman' in support of a doctrine under which an appellate court will uphold a lower court's decision where the reasoning is faulty, so long as the result is correct.

The metaphor comes from a passage in a 1774 poem *Retaliation* about a coachman who had too much to drink but nonetheless managed to find his way home. The first recorded legal appearance of the tipsy coachman as a metaphor for a certain approach to appellate practice is in the 1879 Georgia Supreme Court decision in *Lee v. Porter*. The court made the following observations and then quoted the poem:

> [M]any steps in the reasoning of the court below might be defective, and still its ultimate conclusion be correct. It not infrequently happens that a judgment is affirmed upon a theory of the case which did not occur to the court that rendered it, or which did occur and was expressly repudiated. The human mind is so constituted that in many instances it *finds the truth* when wholly unable to *find the way* that leads to it.
>
> The pupil of impulse it forc'd him along,
> His conduct still right, with his argument wrong;
> Still aiming at honour, yet fearing to roam;
> *The coachman was tipsy, the chariot drove home.*[14]

In ICSID practice, while annulment committees have been willing to infer reasons,[15] they have been reluctant to supply missing or alternative reasons for fear of exceeding their limited mandate. As the *Rumeli* committee put it: 'if reasons are not stated but are evident and a logical consequence of what is stated in an award, an ad

13. *Alapli v. Turkey*, ICSID Case No. ARB/08/13, Decision on Annulment, 10 July 2014, para. 200 (citing *Compañia de Aguas del Aconquija S.A. and Vivendi Universal v. Argentine Republic* (hereinafter '*Vivendi I*'), ICSID Case No. ARB/97/3, Decision on Annulment, 3 July 2002, para. 65).
14. *Lee v. Porter*, 63 Ga. 345, 346 (1879) (italics in original).
15. *See, e.g.*, *Continental Casualty v. Argentine Republic*, ICSID Case No. ARB/03/9, Decision on Annulment, 16 September 2011, para. 101 (citing previous decisions); *Tulip v. Turkey*, ICSID Case No. ARB/11/28, Decision on Annulment, 30 December 2015, para. 108 ('[A]n award is not subject to annulment if the reasons for a decision, though not stated explicitly, are readily apparent to the ad hoc committee. Implicit reasoning is sufficient as long as the committee can infer them reasonably from the terms and conclusions of the award as well as from the record before the tribunal. If the ad hoc committee can explain an award by clarifying reasons that may be only implicit, it may do so and need not annul').

hoc committee should be able to so hold', but 'if such reasons do not necessarily follow or flow from the award's reasoning, an ad hoc committee should not construct reasons in order to justify the decision of the tribunal'.[16]

The potentially paradoxical effect of annulment committees' restraint in supplying their own reasons is that ICSID awards will become *less final* than lower court judgments with substantively valid decisions being overturned for having poorly articulated reasoning. This is precisely what happened in *Klöckner*, where the award was annulled despite the committee's view that the award's conclusions were 'perhaps ultimately perfectly justified and equitable'.[17]

The danger exemplified by *Klöckner* cannot be avoided by annulment committees embracing the tipsy coachman doctrine and supplying their own reasons, as this would entail the conversion of annulment into full appellate review. Instead, the solution must be found by the application of an equivalent degree of restraint to the review of reasons. Parameters to define that restraint can be found in the drafting history of the ICSID Convention and practices of other courts and tribunals.

VI REASONS FOR REASONS: ICSID CONVENTION DRAFTING HISTORY

During the 1950s, the International Law Commission (ILC) had been tasked with the development of a 'Convention on Arbitral Procedure' for arbitrations between states, a draft of which was published with a commentary in 1955. Article 30(c) of the Draft Convention provided, in relevant part:

> The validity of an award may be challenged by either party on one or more of the following grounds:
>
> [...]
>
> (c) That there has been a serious departure from a fundamental rule of procedure, including failure to state the reasons for the award.[18]

The commentary on this provision observed that '[a]mong the fundamental procedural rights of parties to an international arbitration, denial of which will lead to the nullity of any award rendered therein are ... (1) Right to a judgment accompanied by a statement of reasons'.[19] Thus, for the ILC drafters, the right to reasons was considered a fundamental *procedural* right.

The 1963 preliminary draft of what would become the ICSID Convention incorporated the language from the ILC's Draft Convention on Arbitral Procedure verbatim. The relevant provision read as follows:

16. *Rumeli v. Kazakhstan*, ICSID Case No ARB/05/16, Decision on Annulment, 25 March 2010, para. 83.
17. *Klöckner*, para. 144.
18. Commentary on the Draft Convention on Arbitral Procedure Adopted by the International Law Commission at its Fifth Session, UNDOC A/CN.4/92, p. 105.
19. *Ibid.*, p. 110.

> (1) The validity of an award may be challenged by either party on one or more of the following grounds: [...]
> (c) that there has been a *serious departure from a fundamental rule of procedure, including failure to state the reasons for the award.*[20]

The commentary accompanying the 1963 preliminary draft further noted that the three then-enumerated grounds for annulment were intended to address situations in which 'there has been some violation of the fundamental principles of law governing the Tribunal's proceedings'.[21] In other words, the drafters understood the requirement to give reasons as a fundamental principle of procedure.

The 1964 draft made failure to state reasons a separate ground for annulment while providing for the possibility that the parties could agree to dispense with a reasoned award. The relevant passage read:

> (1) Either party may request annulment of the award by an application in writing addressed to the Secretary-General on one or more of the following grounds: [...]
> (e) failure to state the reasons for the award, unless the parties have agreed that reasons need not be stated.[22]

The 1964 draft was not accompanied by any explanatory comment as to the reason for separating out failure to state reasons, although it appears to be a consequence of the 1964 draft's inclusion of the following language in Article 51(3):

> (3) Except as the parties otherwise agree:
> (a) the award shall state the reasons upon which it is based; and
> (b) any arbitrator dissenting from the majority decision may attach his dissenting opinion or a bare statement of his dissent.[23]

Thus, it appears that the reason for separating out a failure to state reasons from other fundamental rules of procedure was to accommodate the possibility that the parties might opt out of compliance with this particular rule. The possibility of the parties waiving their right to a reasoned award, however, was removed from subsequent drafts,[24] but without reincorporating the failure to state reasons into the general

20. Preliminary Draft of a Convention on the Settlement of Investment Disputes between States and Nationals of Other States, 15 October 1963, Article VI, section 13, p. 26, *reprinted in* History of the ICSID Convention (1968), Vol. II-1, pp. 184-235.
21. Preliminary Draft of a Convention on the Settlement of Investment Disputes between States and Nationals of Other States, 15 October 1963, Comment 6, page 32, *reprinted in* History of the ICSID Convention (1968), Vol. II-1, p. 218.
22. Draft Convention on the Settlement of Investment Disputes between States and Nationals of Other States, 11 September 1964, Article 55(1)(e), p. 26, *reprinted in* History of the ICSID Convention (1968), Vol. II-1, p. 635.
23. Draft Convention on the Settlement of Investment Disputes between States and Nationals of Other States, 11 September 1964, Article 55(1)(e), p. 26, *reprinted in* History of the ICSID Convention (1968), Vol. II-1, p. 635.
24. A proposal to delete the option to waive reasons from Article 51(3) was approved in the Legal Committee by a vote of 28 to 3. *See* Summary Proceedings of the Legal Committee Meeting, 8 December 1964, p. 5, *reprinted in* History of the ICSID Convention (1968), Vol. II-2, p. 818. A proposal to delete the analogous language from Article 55(1) passed by a vote of 39 to 0. *See* Summary Proceedings of the Legal Committee Meeting, 9 December 1964, pp. 5, 7, *reprinted in*

provision concerning serious departures from a fundamental rule of procedure. It bears noting, however, that in response to a proposal from one delegation to delete subparagraph 55(1)(e) providing for annulment for failure to state reasons, the Deputy Secretary of the Legal Committee referred back to the ILC's 1955 commentary on the Draft Convention on Arbitral Procedure, in which 'failure to state the reasons for the award was considered as a serious departure from the fundamental rules of procedure',[25] and the proposal was not adopted. It thus appears that the drafters of the ICSID Convention continued to share the view reflected in the ILC Commentary and the preliminary 1963 draft that parties to an arbitration had a fundamental procedural right to a statement of reasons.[26]

The drafting history of the ICSID Convention was discussed before the *Tza Yap Shum* annulment committee, who quoted from Professor Michael Reisman's expert opinion, which explained that the Rapporteur, Professor Georges Scelle, 'understood 'a serious departure from a fundamental rule of procedure' implicitly to cover a tribunal's failure to state reasons, whereas the ICSID Convention makes that requirement express and installs it in a separate section, Article 52(1)(e)'.[27] Professor Reisman further described the movement of the reasons requirement into a separate sub-clause as having 'disaggregated the minimum procedure requirement'.[28]

The drafting history confirms that the movement of the reasons requirement into a separate provision was not intended to suggest that it was something other than a procedural requirement, but rather to allow for the possibility (later abandoned) that the parties might opt out of the requirement that the award contains reasons.

VII REASONS FOR REASONS: PRACTICES OF INTERNATIONAL COURTS

The practices of international courts reinforce the procedural nature of the requirement to give reasoned decisions.

In the case of *Suominen v. Finland*,[29] the European Court of Human Rights identified two rationales for why a reasoned decision was necessary: (i) in order to allow for appeal; and (ii) in order to 'demonstrate to the parties that they have been

History of the ICSID Convention (1968), Vol. II-2, pp. 854. There was little discussion of this point, although Turkey had objected to this waiver option in correspondence, noting that '[I]n the cases of judicial or arbitral decisions the reasons are of such importance to the interested parties that it would be hardly conceivable that parties might willingly waive their right of knowing such reasons.' Letter addressed to the Bank by the Ministry of Finance of Republic of Turkey, 27 October 1964, *reprinted in* History of the ICSID Convention (1968), Vol. II-2, p. 664.

25. Summary Proceedings of the Legal Committee Meeting, 9 December 1964, p. 7, *reprinted in* History of the ICSID Convention (1968), Vol. II-2, p. 851.
26. Curiously, in 1958 the ILC issued a set of Model Rules on Arbitral Procedure with a commentary, in which the relevant article provided for annulment in case of 'a failure to state the reasons for the award *or* a serious departure from a fundamental rule of procedure' (emphasis added).
27. Quoted in *Tza Yap Shum v. Peru*, ICSID Case No. ARB/07/6, Annulment Decision, 12 February 2015 (hereinafter '*Tza Yap Shum*'), para. 118.
28. *Ibid.*
29. *Suominen v. Finland* (App No 37801/97) ECHR 1 July 2003, paras 35-36.

heard'.[30] As no appeal exists in the ICSID context, reasons cannot be required in order to facilitate appeal.[31] However, the notion of demonstrating that the parties have been heard is an interesting one.

Article 56 of the Statute of the International Court of Justice (ICJ) provides that any judgment of the court 'shall state the reasons on which it is based'. Notably, this provision appears in Section III of the Statute that deals with procedure. As there is no reviewing court for the ICJ, we do not have any case law on the application of Article 56. However, there are some instances of the ICJ reviewing decisions of other tribunals. Two are worth considering.

The first is the ICJ's 1960 decision in *Honduras v. Nicaragua*. The dispute related to a 1906 arbitral award that fixed the boundary between the countries. Nicaragua sought to challenge the award fifty years later for an alleged inadequacy of reasons. The ICJ rejected the complaint in a single paragraph, which read as follows:

> The last ground of nullity raised by Nicaragua is the alleged lack or inadequacy of reasons in support of the conclusions arrived at by the arbitrator. However, an examination of the Award shows that it deals in logical order and in some detail with all relevant considerations and that it contains ample reasoning and explanations in support of the conclusions arrived at by the arbitrator. In the opinion of the Court, this ground is without foundation.[32]

It is difficult to draw much from this decision other than a general description of what a reasoned award looks like.

The ICJ issued a more interesting opinion in 1973 in its Judgment No. 158, reviewing a decision of the UN Administrative Tribunal.[33] The key paragraph reads, in relevant part:

> [A] judgment shall be supported by a stated process of reasoning. This statement must indicate in a general way the reasoning upon which the judgment is based; but it need not enter meticulously into every claim and contention on either side. [...] Nor are there any obligatory forms or techniques for drawing up judgments: a tribunal may employ direct or indirect reasoning, and state specific or merely implied conclusions, provided that the reasons on which the judgment is based are apparent. The question whether a judgment is so deficient in reasoning as to

30. The Court of Justice of the European Union has similarly emphasized the importance of giving reasons to allowing an effective right of appeal. *See, e.g.*, *Sison v. Council* (Case C-266/05) [2007] ECR I-01233, para. 80 ('[T]he statement of reasons required by Article 253 EC must be appropriate to the act at issue and must disclose in a clear and unequivocal fashion the reasoning followed by the institution which adopted the measure in question in such a way as to enable the persons concerned to ascertain the reasons for the measure and to enable the competent Community Court to exercise its power of review').
31. See *Tza Yap Shum*, para. 112 ('It is generally understood that one of the major purposes for giving reasons in a decision, apart from assuring the parties that the issues before the tribunal were considered and understood, is to serve as a basis for review of the decision. In the context of the ICSID Convention, the purpose of the review is, however, constrained by Article 52(1)(e) which only provides for a limited scope of review…').
32. Arbitral Award Made by the King of Spain on 23 December 1906 (Honduras/Nicaragua) [1960] ICJ Reports 216.
33. Application for Review of Judgment No. 158 of the United Nations Administrative Tribunal (Falsa), Advisory Opinion, 12 July 1973, [1973] ICJ Reports 166.

> amount to a denial of the right to a fair hearing and a failure of justice, is therefore one which necessarily has to be appreciated in the light both of the particular case and of the judgment as a whole.[34]

Four features of Judgment No. 158 could usefully be adopted by ICSID annulment committees:

> *First*, the ICJ articulated a usable standard, under which a reasoned decision is one that is 'supported by a stated process of reasoning' that 'indicates in a general way the reasoning upon which the judgment is based, but ... need not enter meticulously into every claim and contention'.[35] In this way, the ICJ drew a distinction similar to that drawn in the ICSID Convention between Article 48 and Article 52, which require a tribunal to consider all of the parties' submissions, but provide for the possibility of annulment only in case of a failure to state reasons, not for a failure to examine each argument in detail.[36]
>
> *Second*, the ICJ emphasized the lack of any formal requirements and the possibility of indirect or implied reasoning. As noted above, ICSID annulment committees have in the past shown some reluctance to consider implicit reasons, although the *Tulip* committee affirmed in 2015 that '[i]mplicit reasoning is sufficient as long as the committee can infer them reasonably from the terms and conclusions of the award as well as from the record before the tribunal'.[37]
>
> *Third*, and perhaps most usefully, the ICJ identified the ultimate question as 'whether a judgment is so deficient in reasoning as to amount to a denial of the right to a fair hearing and failure of justice'. This reinforces the idea that the reasons requirement is procedural in nature but also makes clear that the function of the reasoned opinion is as *evidence* about the fairness of the proceeding.
>
> *Fourth*, the ICJ made clear that the ultimate question is 'one which necessarily has to be appreciated in the light both of the particular case and of the judgment as a whole'.[38] In other words, rather than critiquing discrete aspects of reasoning in isolation, an annulment committee should be looking at the reasoning in the round and assessing whether deficiencies that it perceives in the reasoning are such as to call into question the fairness of the overall proceeding.

34. *Ibid.*
35. Application for Review of Judgment No. 158 of the United Nations Administrative Tribunal (Falsa), Advisory Opinion, 12 July 1973, [1973] ICJ Reports 166, para. 95.
36. See ICSID Convention, Article 48(3): 'The award shall deal with every question submitted to the Tribunal, and shall state the reasons upon which it is based'; ICSID Convention, Article 52(1)(e): 'Either party may request annulment of the award by an application in writing addressed to the Secretary-General on one or more of the following grounds: [...] that the award has failed to state the reasons on which it is based.'
37. *Tulip v. Turkey*, ICSID Case No. ARB/11/28, Decision on Annulment, 30 December 2015, para. 108.
38. Application for Review of Judgment No. 158 of the United Nations Administrative Tribunal (Falsa), Advisory Opinion, 12 July 1973 [1973] ICJ Reports 166, para. 95.

VIII RECENT ANNULMENT CASE LAW VALIDATES THE ICJ APPROACH

To test the utility of the ICJ's approach, it is useful to consider some recent annulment decisions against this standard. It bears noting that research identified only one annulment decision – the 1986 decision on annulment in *Amco v. Indonesia* – that referred to the ICJ decision on the Application for Review of Judgment No. 158. However, the *Amco* committee referred to the ICJ decision only for the proposition that a tribunal need not enter meticulously into every claim and contention by each side, but did not cite the ICJ's standards of determining when a failure to state reasons would justify annulment.[39]

A *Pey Casado v. Chile*

The 2008 *Pey Casado v. Chile* award was partially annulled in relation to damages for both a failure to state reasons and a serious violation of a fundamental rule of procedure; both annulment grounds arose out of the tribunal's award of damages. The annulment committee noted that the only submissions on damages before the tribunal had been in relation to expropriation.[40] Since the tribunal had found that the expropriation had occurred prior to the entry into force of the relevant treaty, the parties' submissions on damages for expropriation were not pertinent and could not be used to assess damages for the violations it did find to have occurred after the treaty entered into force, namely denial of justice or breach of fair and equitable treatment during domestic proceedings relating to the expropriation.[41] The tribunal nonetheless proceeded to award damages for these breaches without inviting the parties to make further submissions on the damages caused by these breaches and instead relying on damages submissions made in connection with the expropriation claim.

The annulment committee found that the tribunal had violated Chile's right to be heard by failing to allow it to make submissions on the assessment of damages for denial of justice and breach of fair and equitable treatment (FET); it also had failed to state reasons insofar as its calculation of damages on an expropriation basis contradicted its own statement a few paragraphs earlier that such a calculation was not pertinent to the breaches it had found.[42] In other words, the tribunal's inability to provide non-contradictory reasons for its calculation of damages was a direct consequence of its failure to give the parties an opportunity to make submissions. The defects in reasoning were thus confirmatory evidence of a defect in the procedure.

Following resubmission of the case to a new tribunal, a new award was issued in September 2016. The second tribunal characterized the decision of the first annulment

39. *Amco Asia Corporation and others v. Republic of Indonesia*, ICSID Case No. ARB/81/1, Decision on Annulment, 16 May 1986, para. 39.
40. *Pey Casado v. Chile*, ICSID Case No. ARB/98/2, Decision on Annulment, 18 December 2012 (hereinafter '*Pey Casado I*'), para. 261.
41. *Ibid.*
42. *Pey Casado I*, paras 269, 287.

committee rather differently than the committee had: it characterized the first committee's annulment for failure to give reasons as a 'substantial ground', distinguishing it from the 'procedural' ground of not affording the parties an opportunity to be heard on damages for breach of FET.[43] The second tribunal then 'levelled' some 'further criticism' at the annulled portions of the award, in particular for 'elid[ing] the distinction between injury (and the associated question of causation) and the assessment of the compensation due for that injury'.[44] Relying upon this distinction, the second tribunal proceeded to conclude that the Claimants had failed to establish any injury from the denial of justice that was distinct from the expropriation itself and were therefore entitled to no compensation.[45]

A second annulment committee was duly empanelled, and the key question was whether the second tribunal had manifestly exceeded its power by failing to give effect to the unannulled portion of the dispositive of the first award in which the First Tribunal concluded that the Claimants were entitled to 'compensation'. The second annulment committee found that the second tribunal had erred in giving the French word 'compensation' as used in the first award a different meaning than the French word 'indemnisation' as employed in Article 36 of the ILC Draft Articles, such that it did not necessarily imply *financial* damages, but declined to annul the second award because it concluded that the second tribunal's factual finding that the Claimants had failed to meet the burden to prove the amount of their financially assessable damage would still result in no damages being awarded.[46] The second committee 'hesitated as to how to qualify the Resubmission Tribunal's approach: as a non-annullable misapplication and misinterpretation of international law or as an annullable non-application of the applicable law'.[47] The second committee went on to reject an argument that the second tribunal's reasoning was contradictory by supplying a 'nuance' that it considered was 'implicit but certain' in the second tribunal's award.[48]

B *Tidewater v. Venezuela*

In *Tidewater v. Venezuela*, the committee described the requirement to give reasons as a 'procedural mandatory requirement' and emphasized the need to distinguish a 'procedural failure to state reasons' from an assessment of 'the substantive correctness of the award'.[49] It articulated the purpose of this procedural requirement as follows:

> An award is not a discretionary fiat but the result of the process of weighing evidence and applying and interpreting the law and subsuming the facts thus

43. *Pey Casado v. Chile*, ICSID Case No. ARB/98/2, Award, 13 December 2016 (hereinafter '*Pey Casado II Award*'), para. 215.
44. *Ibid.*
45. *Ibid.*, paras 234-235.
46. *Pey Casado v. Chile*, ICSID Case No. ARB/98/2, Decision on Annulment, 8 January 2020 (hereinafter '*Pey Casado II Annulment*'), paras 681, 698.
47. *Ibid.*, para. 682.
48. *Ibid.*, para. 713.
49. *Tidewater Investment SRL and Tidewater Caribe, C.A. v. Venezuela*, ICSID Case No. ARB/10/5, Decision on Annulment, 27 December 2016 (hereinafter '*Tidewater*'), paras 166, 171.

> established under the law as interpreted by the Tribunal. The legitimacy of the process depends on its intelligibility and transparency. The statement of reasons allows the Parties to understand the process through which the tribunal makes its findings.[50]

The *Tidewater* committee annulled an aspect of the damages portion of the award because the tribunal's estimate of the market value was based on calculation inputs that the tribunal had expressly rejected, with the result that the calculation was 'irreconcilable with the Tribunal's findings on the elements of the proper assessment of the market value'.[51] Unusually,[52] the committee annulled the award only insofar as the calculation of damages exceeded the amount that would have resulted from the application of the tribunal's findings on the elements for assessing market value, such that the effect of the decision was to correct the damages section of the award, rather than to annul it.

C *TECO v. Guatemala*

In *TECO v. Guatemala*, the committee annulled a damages finding ostensibly for failure to state reasons and therefore did not consider whether the same aspect of the decision was affected by a serious departure from a fundamental rule of procedure.[53] The committee's criticism focused on 'the complete absence of any discussion of the Parties' expert reports within the Tribunal's analysis of the loss of value claim',[54] and the committee was also troubled by the tribunal's statements that it lacked evidence on certain points when the committee was persuaded that such evidence was present on the record.[55]

The key passage is the following:

> The Committee wishes to point out that it cannot determine whether the evidence that was ignored by the Tribunal would have had an impact on the Award or not. What can be ascertained at the annulment stage is that *the Tribunal failed to observe evidence which at least had the potential to be relevant to the final outcome of the case.*[56]

The emphasized phrase indicates that the perceived deficiency in the reasoning was relevant insofar as it called into question the fairness of the process. The committee did not, however, assess this fairness concern against any articulated

50. *Ibid.*, para. 163.
51. *Ibid.*, para. 189.
52. The only other similar example in annulment practice was in *Occidental v. Ecuador,* where the committee annulled the damages calculation to the extent it was based on a 100% ownership rather than a 60% ownership and performed the arithmetic needed to determine the amount of damages to be annulled. *Occidental v. Ecuador,* ICSID Case No. ARB/06/11, Decision on Annulment, 2 November 2014, paras 296-299.
53. *TECO Guatemala Holdings LLC v. Guatemala*, ICSID Case No. ARB/10/23, Decision on Annulment, 5 April 2016 (hereinafter '*TECO*'), para. 150.
54. *TECO*, para. 131.
55. *TECO*, paras 133, 134.
56. *TECO*, para. 135 (emphasis added).

standard. It is not clear from the decision whether the annulment committee would have considered this deficiency to satisfy the ICJ's standard of amounting to a denial of the right to a fair hearing and failure of justice. Absent such a standard, the rationale of the emphasized passage above could be invoked as a basis to annul any award where a tribunal fails to specifically discuss a piece of evidence that a party considers important, in contradiction to the committee's invocation of the principle that 'a tribunal is not under an obligation to address every piece of evidence in the record or every single argument made by the parties'.[57]

D *Vivendi II*

The committee in *Vivendi II* confronted the potential risk of broad application of the *TECO* decision, and interpreted the *TECO* decision as finding annulment to be justified only if there was 'a total failure to address evidence that would have been "highly relevant" to the Tribunal's decision, i.e., evidence whose consideration could have had a significant impact on the Award'.[58]

This reading of *TECO* brings annulment for failure to state reasons back to where the drafters of the ICSID Convention had originally placed it: as a particular example of a serious departure ('total failure') from a fundamental rule of procedure (i.e., that a tribunal must consider the evidence).

E *Tza Yap Shum v. Peru*

The *Tza Yap Shum* annulment committee considered the drafting history described above and expressly held that 'examination by the arbitral tribunal of the evidence adduced by the parties is one of the fundamental rules of procedure protected by Article 52(1)(d) of the ICSID Convention to achieve a fair trial'.[59]

The committee went on to recognize that the reasons requirement is a fundamental rule of procedure within the meaning of Article 52(1)(d):

> The Committee is of the opinion that the right to a reasoned and final determination of the dispute by an arbitral tribunal is one of the aspects of the right of access to an arbitral forum. As such, it is also a fundamental rule of procedure protected by Article 52(1)(d) of the ICSID Convention. The existence of reasons ensures that there has been a minimum respect of the fundamental exigencies of justice by the tribunal, which would not square with an arbitrary decision, and is consonant with Article 52 of the ICSID Convention which serves as a safety valve against aberrant awards.[60]

57. *TECO*, para. 125.
58. Suez, Sociedad General de Aguas de Barcelona S.A. and Vivendi Universal S.A. v. Argentine Republic, ICSID Case No. ARB/03/19, Decision on Annulment, 5 May 2017 (hereinafter '*Vivendi II*') para. 163.
59. *Tza Yap Shum*, para. 116.
60. *Tza Yap Shum*, para. 119.

Somewhat at odds with this recognition, the committee took the view that a failure to state reasons under Article 52(1)(e), if established, would not per se constitute a serious departure from a fundamental rule of procedure under Article 52(1)(d).[61] It is doubtful whether this statement is correct. It seems to invite rather than to discourage the 'two bites at the apple' approach followed by Peru, of pursuing the same alleged failure to state reasons under both grounds for annulment in the hope that a different standard would be applied.

IX CONCLUSION

The drafters of the ICSID Convention recognized that a reasoned award was a procedural protection and initially identified a failure to state reasons as a particular example of a substantial departure from a fundamental rule of procedure. The separation of the requirement to give reasons into a separate sub-clause has had the (presumably unintended) consequence of opening the possibility that annulment committees would apply a lower threshold to annulment for failure to state reasons, as the phrase 'substantial departure' is not included within the sub-clause dealing with the reasons requirement. Case law from the last decade, including, in particular, the *Tza Yap Shum* annulment decision, has pointed the way to a restoration of an alignment of the standards for the two grounds of annulment.

The ICJ's Decision No. 158, meanwhile, articulates a standard for assessing an alleged failure to state reasons as *whether the award is so deficient in reasoning as to amount to a denial of the right to a fair hearing and failure of justice*. If applied in the ICSID context, such a standard will help annulment committees to focus their enquiry on the procedure and the fairness of the process and thus avoid the annulment process crossing the line and changing into a substantive appeal on the merits.

61. *Tza Yap Shum*, para. 120.

CHAPTER 24

Diversity and Inclusiveness in International Arbitration

Matteo M. Winkler & Mikaël Schinazi[*]

I INTRODUCTION

Although international arbitration has become the preferred method for resolving business disputes across multiple jurisdictions and is used in virtually all parts of the world in a wide range of economic, social, and cultural environments, the arbitration community itself has long suffered from a lack of diversity among its members. The typical arbitrator has been described as 'pale, male, and stale', meaning a white man of a certain age.[1] As one commentator has written, 'more women and more people of colour are active and in leadership positions than ever before [b]ut the alternative dispute resolution profession seems immune to these changes'.[2]

This chapter represents a humble attempt to build a framework for understanding diversity and inclusiveness in the field of international arbitration. Although during the past two decades the subject has given rise to scores of articles in specialized publications and countless conferences, training programs, and workshops, we feel that academic literature still lacks a holistic approach to understanding the multiplicity of issues and objectives inherent in this topic.[3] Such an approach should address four key questions: (i) what are the main aspects of diversity in international arbitration?,

---

* The authors wish to thank Sebastian Zamora-Muñoz and Romit Kohli for their research assistance, as well as the various colleagues with whom they exchanged views on this important topic. The usual caveats apply.

1. Michael Goldhaber, *Madame la Présidente: A Woman who Sits as President of a Major Arbitral Tribunal is a Rare Creature. Why?*, 3 Transnat'l Disp. Mgmt. 1 (2004).
2. Peter F. Phillips, *ADR Continental Drift: It Remains a White, Male Game*, Nat'l L.J. 1, 1 (2006).
3. *See*, however, the remarkable 2020 ICCA Report: International Council for Commercial Arbitration, *Report of the Cross-Institutional Task Force on Gender Diversity in Arbitral Appointments and Proceedings* (International Council for Commercial Arbitration 2020) (ICCA Report No. 8).

(ii) when did this become an important topic in the literature?, (iii) why should we engage in a serious conversation about diversity and inclusiveness in international arbitration?, and (iv) how can we make the international arbitration community more diverse and inclusive?

In trying to answer these questions, we draw on the insights of scholars in various fields and disciplines. The topic could be addressed from the perspective of the sociology of international arbitration[4] or that of empirical research.[5] Some scholars have shared their personal experience as a way of understanding some of the dynamics at play in the field.[6] In addition to these approaches, we draw on historical insights, as well as the rich business strategy literature on diversity and inclusiveness,[7] which has not yet been fully explored in international arbitration.[8] We attempt to combine these threads in order to sketch a minimal framework through which to understand diversity and pursue inclusiveness in the field of international arbitration.

The chapter is composed of four sections, each seeking to answer one of the questions raised above. Section II tries to understand how diversity became a focal point of research and discussion in international arbitration. Section III explores three aspects of diversity that are often discussed in this context, namely, gender, age, and geographic origin. Section IV examines and evaluates different rationales for inclusiveness, with a view to achieving a more balanced representation of all the constituencies in the international arbitration community that may claim a right of entry to the pool of potential arbitrators. Finally, section V discusses some measures that could be adopted to good effect by stakeholders in international arbitration.

II THE MOVE TO DIVERSITY IN INTERNATIONAL ARBITRATION SCHOLARSHIP

While early research on the 'invisible college' of international arbitration focused on the concentration of power in the arbitration community II.A, more recent scholarship has emphasized issues of diversity in international arbitration II.B.

4. *See*, e.g., Emmanuel Gaillard, *Sociology of International Arbitration*, 31 Arb. Int'l 1 (2015); Emmanuel Gaillard, *Nouvelles réflexions sur la sociologie de l'arbitrage*, 2 Procédures 35 (2020).
5. *See*, e.g., Susan D. Franck, *Empirically Evaluating Claims About Investment Treaty Arbitration*, 86 N.C. L. Rev. 1 (2008); Susan D. Franck, James Freda, Kellen Lavin, Tobias Lehmann & Anne van Aaken, *Diversity Challenge: Exploring the 'Invisible College' of International Arbitration*, 53 Colum. J. Transnat'l L. 429 (2015); Sergio Puig, *Social Capital in the Arbitration Market*, 25 Eur. J. Int'l L. 387 (2014).
6. *See*, e.g., Louise Barrington, *Arbitral Women: A Study of Women in International Commercial Arbitration*, *in The Commercial Way to Justice* (Geoffrey M. Beresford Hartwell ed., Kluwer Law International 1997); Benjamin G. Davis, *The Color Line in International Commercial Arbitration: An American Perspective*, 14 Am. Rev. Int'l Arb. 461 (2003); Mirèze Philippe, *When Did the Doors to Dispute Resolution Open for Women?*, 12 Transnat'l Disp. Mgmt. Spec. Issue Diversity 1 (2015).
7. *See*, e.g., Iris Bohnet, *What Works: Gender by Design* (Harvard University Press 2016).
8. *See*, however, Lucy Greenwood & Mark C. Baker, *Is the Balance Getting Better? An Update on the Issue of Gender Diversity in International Arbitration*, 31 Arb. Int'l 413 (2015), citing various business studies.

A The 'Invisible College' of International Arbitration: Myth or Reality?

Building on Schachter's 1977 seminal article on the 'invisible college of international lawyers',[9] several scholars have theorized the existence of an 'invisible college of international arbitration', comprising the entire galaxy of professionals inhabiting the arbitration ecosystem.[10]

Schachter's view was that international lawyers formed a community that, although globally dispersed, was 'dedicated to a common intellectual enterprise [and] engaged in a continuous process of communication and collaboration'.[11] As subsequent scholars have theorized, what marked this community was not so much the fact that it was formally organized, but rather that it considered itself 'a coherent professional group, seeing one another ... as fellow professionals in a common judicial enterprise that transcends national borders'[12] and developed a distinctive 'self-image'.[13] In Schachter's mind, this invisible college was 'made up almost entirely of upper-class, European, French-speaking, male lawyers who knew or were related to each other'.[14]

The invisible college of international arbitration soon became the target of demographic assessments and, needless to say, sharp criticism. Reflecting further on the issue of the concentration of power in the arbitration community, later scholars described the invisible college as 'an insular club of a few privileged elite'[15] and a 'class elite [that] structurally perpetuate[s itself]'.[16] Investment treaty arbitration, where statistical analysis was used to depict the arbitration community as in the hands of a few 'power-brokers' and 'elite arbitrators',[17] came in for particularly harsh criticism.

A related strand of research that focused on the 'invisible college' of international arbitration – twenty years after Schachter's article, and using different terminology – was initiated by the sociologists Yves Dezalay and Bryant Garth in their work *Dealing in Virtue*.[18] Dezalay and Garth undertook a demographic mapping of the arbitration community, which they viewed as 'relatively small and linked together pretty

9. Oscar Schachter, *The Invisible College of International Lawyers*, 72 Nw. U. L. Rev. 217 (1977).
10. *See*, e.g., Franck et al., *supra* n. 5, at 432-433; Catherine A. Rogers, *Ethics in International Arbitration* 17-18 (Oxford University Press 2014).
11. Schachter, *supra* n. 9, at 217.
12. Daniel Terris, Cesare P.R. Romano & Leigh Swigart, *Toward a Community of International Judges*, 30 Loy. L.A. Int'l & Comp. L. Rev. 419, 420 (2008).
13. Anne Orford, *Embodying Internationalism: The Making of International Lawyers*, 19 Aust. Y.B. Int'l L. 1, 5 (1998).
14. M.J. Clincy, *An Interview with Oscar Schachter*, 95 ASIL Proceedings 18, 18 (2001).
15. Douglas Pilawa, *Sifting Through the Arbitrators for the Woman, the Minority, the Newcomer*, 51 Case W. Res. J. Int'l L. 395, 397 (2019).
16. Won L. Kidane, *The Culture of International Arbitration* 245 (Oxford University Press 2017).
17. Puig, *supra* n. 5, at 419.
18. Yves Dezalay & Bryant G. Garth, *Dealing in Virtue: International Commercial Arbitration and the Construction of a Transnational Legal Order* (The University of Chicago Press 1996). There were, however, earlier texts on the sociology of arbitration by Oppetit (Bruno Oppetit, *Eléments pour une sociologie de l'arbitrage*, 27 L'Année sociologique 179 (1976)), and Glossner (Ottoarndt Glossner, *Sociological Aspects of International Commercial Arbitration*, *in The Art of Arbitration* 143 (Jan C. Schultsz and Albert Jan van den Berg eds., Kluwer Law and Taxation 1982)) (who noted that '[f]or better or worse, sociologists have not yet discovered arbitration').

closely'.[19] Relying on Bourdieu's analysis, they studied the relative positions of groups and individuals and highlighted a series of oppositions and complementarities that gave structure to the field of international commercial arbitration. The most important opposition – the 'key source of conflict, and also of transformation'[20] – was between 'grand old men' and 'young technocrats'. The 'grand old men' (which included no women) were part of the pioneering generation of arbitrators; they already had legitimacy and 'national aura' before taking up their activity as arbitrators and saw arbitration as a 'duty, not a career'.[21] Dezalay and Garth argued that, beginning in the late 1970s and accelerating in the 1980s, a new generation of 'young technocrats' contrasted their own technical expertise with the '"amateurism" or "idealism" of their predecessors'.[22]

Dezalay and Garth's research is increasingly called into question by researchers who point out that the 'founders' of the modern international arbitration system were not all 'grand old men', and that the crucial period of institutional transformation did not take place in the 1970s and 1980s, as Dezalay and Garth maintained, but in preceding decades.[23] However, it would be hard to deny that Dezalay and Garth's research, which they updated in a number of writings,[24] opened new perspectives. In particular, it led to further studies on the sociology of international arbitration,[25] including by some who identified a third generation of arbitrators, the 'Managers',[26] and others who spelled out the connection between concentration of power within a relatively small group of individuals and their lack of diversity. For example, Clay, while noting that part of Dezalay's research was 'excessive and seemed too imbued with ideological dogmatism',[27] used it to explore the lack of diversity in the field. He found that a typical arbitrator (at least in France) was a 'man, no longer young, fluent in many languages and working not far from Paris', and generally a lawyer by

19. Dezalay & Garth, *supra* n. 18, at 10.
20. *Ibid.*, 34.
21. *Ibid.*, 34-35.
22. *Ibid.*, 36-37.
23. Mikaël Schinazi, *The Three Ages of International Commercial Arbitration* (Cambridge University Press 2022), 9-13; Florian Grisel, *Competition and Cooperation in International Commercial Arbitration: The Birth of a Translational Legal Profession*, 51 L. & Soc. R. 790 (2017); Claire Lemercier & Jérôme Sgard, *Arbitrage privé international et globalisation(s), Mission de Recherche Droit et Justice* 143 (Sciences Po & CNRS 2015).
24. *See*, e.g., Bryan G. Garth, *Dealing in Virtue: A Perspective from Almost 25 Years Later, in The Cambridge Companion to International Arbitration* 38-58 (Chin L. Lim ed., Cambridge University Press 2021); Bryan G. Garth, *One Window into the State of Insiders' Arbitration Scholarship*, 19 J. World Invest. Trade 155 (2018).
25. *See*, e.g., Thomas Clay, *Qui sont les arbitres internationaux? Approche sociologique, in Les arbitres internationaux* 13 (José Rosell ed., Editions de la société de législation comparée 2005); Jean-Bapiste Racine, *Eléments pour une sociologie de l'arbitrage: Actes de la Journée d'étude du Groupe Sociologie de l'arbitrage du Comité français de l'arbitrage*, 4 Revue de l'arbitrage 709 (2012).
26. Thomas Schultz & Robert Kovacs, *The Rise of a Third Generation of Arbitrators? Fifteen Years after Dezalay and Garth*, 28 Arb. Int'l 161, 166-167 (2012).
27. Clay, *supra* n. 25, at 20 (translated by the authors).

profession.[28] Writing in 2005, Clay explained that international arbitration was still a 'very small world'.[29]

B The Debate on Diversity and Inclusiveness

In the last decade, the criticism expressed in the relevant academic literature has shifted from the problem of the concentration of power within the invisible college to its lack of inclusiveness. This shift occurred not only because diversity and inclusiveness have both become important topics in the public debate, and 'organization imperatives' in the corporate world,[30] but also, and more critically, because the arbitration community is now facing the emergence of a new generation of arbitration practitioners, professionals and academics who claim full access to arbitration appointments. Notably, the more diverse senior management in corporations and law firms becomes, the harder it is to contest the need for more inclusiveness in arbitrator appointment mechanisms, too. Instead of challenging the invisible college's elitism, newcomers now seek to hold it to account for its lack of diversity and to pressure the system into embracing greater inclusiveness.

Unlike previous research, which relied heavily on sociological frameworks such as those of Bourdieu or Weber,[31] scholars and commentators started using empirical data to buttress their arguments. Aggregating data or using statistics from arbitral institutions, various analyses were developed to show that the typical arbitrator profile was 'pale, male and stale'.[32] For example, in 2015, Franck and her co-authors surveyed attendees at the Congress of the International Council for Commercial Arbitration (ICCA) as a demographic representation of the invisible college of international arbitration. They found that the median arbitrator was 'male, fifty-three years of age, with some training from a common law jurisdiction, and from a developed state' and that 'less than eighteen percent of the arbitrators were women, twenty percent (or less) were from non-OECD or non-High Income states'.[33] Such a profile seemed to mirror that of the median arbitration counsel present at the ICCA Congress, even though the latter was six years younger and had fifteen years' experience in the sector.[34]

By contrast, at the other end of the spectrum, the Willem C. Vis Moot Competition, held annually in Vienna, is proof of the broad diversity that characterizes the young members of the international arbitration community.[35] The Vis Moot is a clear

28. *Ibid.*, 30.
29. *Ibid.*, 17.
30. Stephen Frost, *The Inclusion Imperative: How Real Inclusion Creates Better Business and Builds Better Societies* 1 (Kogan Page 2014).
31. *See*, e.g., Dezalay & Garth, *supra* n. 19; Catherine A. Rogers, *The Vocation of International Arbitrators*, 20 Am. U. Int'l L. Rev. 957 (2005).
32. Samaa Haridi, *Towards Greater Gender and Ethnic Diversity in International Arbitration*, 2 BCDR Int'l Arb R. 305, 307 (2015).
33. Franck et al., *supra* n. 5, at 469-470.
34. *Ibid.*, 466.
35. For example, the Twenty-Eight Annual Moot in 2021 drew 385 teams from 80 jurisdictions, totalling some 2,250 students, whose advocacy abilities were assessed by almost a thousand of professionals acting as arbitrators. These figures keep increasing each year.

example of the changing landscape of international arbitration, as it helps 'to level the playing field and encourage more diversity within the profession'.[36] The key question is whether participants in the Vis Moot will ever have the opportunity to build a career in an arbitration world that, for a long time, left little room for those who did not belong to the 'invisible college'.

III THREE ASPECTS OF DIVERSITY

There are, of course, different aspects to diversity, which reflect those traditionally embodied in non-discrimination laws: gender, national origin, age, ethnic origin, sexual orientation and gender identity, and religious beliefs.[37] In the international arbitration context, three of these have received particular attention – namely, gender III.A, age III.B, and geographic origin III.C – although other aspects – such as race[38] and religion[39]– are increasingly the focus of discussion as well.

36. Mark R. Shulman, *Making Progress: How Eric Bergsten and the Vis Moot Advance the Enterprise of Universal Peace*, 24 Pace Int'l L. Rev. 1, 11 (2012).
37. *See* Jacomijn van Haersolte-van Hof, *Diversity in Diversity, in Legitimacy: Myths, Realities, Challenges* 638, 639-40 (Albert Jan van den Berg ed., Kluwer Law International 2015).
38. With regard to race, Davis (Davis, *supra* n. 6, at 505) has written about a 'color line in international arbitration' and argued that, '[a]s contrasted with other arenas in the law and or in society as a whole in which minorities have made progress, the data suggest that U.S. minorities have made glacially slow progress in international commercial arbitration' (*see*, however, recent initiatives such as the launch of Racial Equality for Arbitration Lawyers (R.E.A.L.) in 2021). In the Queen Mary Survey (Queen Mary and White & Case, *2018 International Arbitration Survey: The Evolution of International Arbitration*, at 18), 37% of respondents disagreed that progress had been made in relation to ethnic diversity; as the survey noted, '[e]thnic diversity, in particular, emerged as an area where interviewees thought that there is a distinct need for improvement'. Racial diversity became the focus of increased attention in the field in 2018, after American rapper Jay-Z (whose legal name is Shawn Carter) won a temporary order staying arbitration for a dispute in New York. Carter alleged that a contract he had entered into contained an arbitration clause (submitting any disputes to arbitration administered by the American Arbitration Association) that violated New York law and was 'void as against public policy' because the AAA did not have enough African American arbitrators on its 'large and complex cases' roster. Jay-Z argued that this 'deprive[d] litigants of color of a meaningful opportunity to have their claims heard by a panel of arbitrators reflecting their backgrounds and life experience', and further stated that there was a risk of 'unconscious bias in decision-making' (*see Shawn C. Carter et. Al. v. Iconix Brand Group et. Al., Petitioners' Memorandum of Law in Support of the Order to Show Cause for a Temporary Restraining Order and Preliminary Injunction* (2018)). Jay-Z withdrew his motion to stay the arbitration after the AAA committed to identify and make available African American arbitrators for consideration.
39. Religious diversity in the field of international arbitration is also an area that merits close attention; for an example of a case with far-reaching implications, *see Jivraj v. Hashwani* [2011] UKSC 40, a decision by the UK Supreme Court, understood as establishing that parties may discriminate against the appointment of an arbitrator on the grounds of religion and nationality if such factors are sufficiently relevant in the case under consideration (*see* V.V. Veeder, *Arbitral Discrimination Under English and EU Law, in Is Arbitration Only as Good as the Arbitrator? Status, Powers and Role of the Arbitrator* 91 (Yves Derains & Laurent Lévy eds., ICC Institute of World Business Law 2011); V.V. Veeder, *Who Are the Arbitrators?, in Legitimacy: Myths, Realities, Challenges* 652, 656-60 (Albert Jan van den Berg ed., Kluwer Law International 2015)).

A Gender Diversity

The first aspect of diversity that is generally explored in the international arbitration context is gender, given its relevance to the representation of women on arbitral tribunals. It is clear that the field – and even some of its founding myths[40] – remained male-dominated throughout most of the nineteenth and twentieth centuries. Borrowing from Bourdieu,[41] one may even speak of a clear 'masculine domination' – or, as Bredin put it in 1987, a 'masculinity of arbitration'.[42]

When the modern system of international commercial arbitration was designed in the first half of the twentieth century, it was widely believed that this was a domain reserved for men. No women were involved in the establishment of the ICC Court of Arbitration in 1923, following the international trade conference in Atlantic City, New Jersey, in 1919 and the founding of the ICC in Paris the following year. The ICC owed its creation to a private business initiative, which sought to promote trade cooperation in the interwar years.[43] The 'merchants of peace', as the ICC's founders came to be known,[44] were all men – 'business men, practical men', as one participant at the Atlantic City conference noted.[45] There was not a single woman among the 120 plus initial members of the ICC Court of Arbitration in the early 1920s.[46] It took until 1982 for a woman (Tila Maria de Hancock) to be appointed Director of the Secretariat of the ICC Court of Arbitration; until 2001 for a woman (Anne-Marie Whitesell) to be appointed Secretary-General of the Court;[47] until 2017 for a woman (Karien van Gennip) to be appointed to a senior leadership position at the ICC, as Vice-Chair of the Executive Board;[48] and until 2021 for a woman (Claudia Salomon) to become the

40. *See*, for example, the famous anecdote about Peter Sanders (Peter Sanders, *The History of the New York Convention, in Improving the Efficiency of Arbitration Agreements and Awards: 40 Years of Application of the New York Convention* 11, 12-13 (Albert Jan van den Berg ed., Kluwer Law International 1999)), who came up with a new idea, known as the 'Dutch proposal' (part of which entailed the elimination of the so-called double *exequatur* requirement), at the 1958 United Nations Conference on International Commercial Arbitration: 'I spent the weekend at the house of my father-in-law in a suburb of New York. I can still see myself sitting in the garden with a small portable typewriter on my knees. It was there, sitting in the sun, that the "Dutch proposal" was conceived'. What matters is not whether this episode actually occurred, but the fact that such stories tend to reinforce the notion that a few 'grand old men' or 'founding fathers' have been responsible for creating the modern system of international arbitration.
41. Pierre Bourdieu, *La Domination masculine* (Seuil 1998).
42. Jean-Denis Bredin, *Intervention, in Colloque du 28 avril 1987 à la Chambre de commerce et d'industrie de Paris* 30, 33 (Association Française d'Arbitrage 1987) (translated by the authors).
43. *See* Schinazi, *supra* n. 23, at 98-115.
44. George L. Ridgeway, *Merchants of Peace: Twenty Years of Business Diplomacy Through the International Chamber of Commerce: 1919-1938* (Columbia University Press 1938).
45. Alfred Bedford, *Foreword, in International Trade Conference* 39 (Chamber of Commerce of the United States of America 1919).
46. International Chamber of Commerce, *Inauguration of the Court of Commercial Arbitration: Brochure No. 22* 6-12 (ICC International Headquarters 1923).
47. *See* Philippe, *supra* n. 6.
48. *See* International Chamber of Commerce, *Karien van Gennip elected ICC Vice-Chair*, https://iccwbo.org/media-wall/news-speeches/karien-van-gennip-elected-icc-vice-chair/ (accessed 17 Jan. 2022).

President of the ICC International Court of Arbitration.[49] No woman has yet been appointed Chair of the ICC or Chair of the ICC Institute of World Business Law.

These historical forces, as well as other factors (some of which are outlined below), have shaped the field of international arbitration in lasting ways. Empirical research in this area shows that, although progress has been made during the last five to ten years, men still outnumber women by far, in both international commercial arbitration and investment treaty arbitration.

In international commercial arbitration, Barrington reported that 'in 1990 the ICC Court named 517 arbitrators, of whom 4 were women. In 1995, out of a total of 766 arbitrators named by the ICC, 22 were women'.[50] In 2012, Greenwood and Baker found that a 'best estimate' of the proportion of women appointments to international commercial arbitration tribunals was around 6.5%.[51] In 2015, they revised this figure upward to around 10%,[52] and in 2017 to around 15%.[53] In 2015, when the International Chamber of Commerce first started releasing data on numbers of female arbitrators,[54] only 10.4% of arbitrators sitting on ICC tribunals were women.[55] In 2020, women arbitrators sitting on ICC tribunals represented 23.4% of all appointments and nominations.[56] Gaillard has found that 1,313 male appointments and 246 female appointments (16%) had been made in 658 ICC cases ongoing as of September 2019.[57] These figures suggest that, despite much progress, full gender parity in international commercial arbitration is still a long way off.

The situation is much more concerning in investment treaty arbitration. A 2006 study found only 'five women (3.5%) in the population of 145 investment treaty arbitrators' who were serving in international investment arbitration cases known to the public at the time.[58] Other scholars likewise noted 'an extreme gender imbalance', with 93% of appointments being men, and just two women – Gabrielle Kaufmann-Kohler and Brigitte Stern – accounting for three-quarters of all female appointments.[59]

In 2020, using publicly available data, Gaillard studied gender distribution in the 264 ICSID cases pending as of September 2019 (including 25 ad hoc committees). He

49. *See* International Chamber of Commerce, *Claudia Salomon becomes President of ICC Court*, https://iccwbo.org/media-wall/news-speeches/claudia-salomon-becomes-president-of-icc-court (accessed 17 Jan. 2022).
50. Barrington, *supra* n. 6, at 239.
51. Lucy Greenwood & C. Mark Baker, *Getting a Better Balance on International Arbitration Tribunals*, 28(4) Arb. Int'l 653, 656 (2012).
52. Greenwood & Baker, *supra* n. 8, at 418.
53. Lucy Greenwood, *Tipping the Balance – Diversity and Inclusion in International Arbitration*, 33(1) Arb. Int'l 99, 102 (2017).
54. In 2013, Philippe had already started sharing statistics about the representation of women in ICC arbitral tribunals; before that date, gender was not 'among the elements used to generate statistics' (*see* Philippe, *supra* n. 6, at 9).
55. International Chamber of Commerce, *ICC Dispute Resolution 2015 Statistics* 15 (International Chamber of Commerce 2016).
56. International Chamber of Commerce, *ICC Dispute Resolution 2020 Statistics* 12 (International Chamber of Commerce 2021).
57. Gaillard (2020), *supra* n. 4, at 37.
58. Franck, *supra* n. 5, at 81.
59. Puig, *supra* n. 5, at 404-405; *see also* Gus van Harten, *The (Lack of) Women Arbitrators in Investment Treaty Arbitration*, 59 Colum. FDI Persp. 1 (2012).

noted that the population of ICSID arbitrators was composed of 185 men and 37 women (17%). As far as numbers of appointments were concerned (a given arbitrator could be appointed in more than one case at any one time), male appointments in pending cases numbered 669 and female appointments 123 (16%). When it came to tribunal presidents, there were 228 male presidents and 36 female presidents (14%) serving in pending ICSID cases (at the time of his research), with two women being appointed ten times each as president.[60]

The current procedure for selecting and appointing tribunal members tends to hinder progress and hamper change. If the parties are unable to appoint all members of the tribunal within ninety days of the registration of the request for arbitration, either party may request that the Chairman of the ICSID Administrative Council appoint the arbitrator(s) not yet appointed.[61] When this request concerns a sole arbitrator or tribunal president, ICSID provides the parties with a ballot form containing the names of several candidates whom parties may select or reject. As Gaillard explained, because parties are understandably wary of the unknown, they are likely to reject new names put forth by the institution, which means that the current system merely 'reproduces what already exists'.[62] Gaillard argued that diversity in ICSID tribunals would be better promoted if ICSID were to appoint arbitrators without relying on the ballot procedure (while, of course, letting parties raise any circumstance showing that the person lacks the qualities required under the ICSID Convention).[63] In any event, the current situation in investment treaty arbitration is unsatisfactory and calls for immediate attention.

Various factors have been identified to explain the underrepresentation of women in international arbitration. As Greenwood and Baker have suggested in various articles,[64] a lack of transparency in the arbitrator appointment process, unconscious gender bias, and the lack of visibility of many potential female arbitrators would seem to be key reasons. The problem is exacerbated by the fact that international arbitrators tend to be selected from among law firm partners, academics, and former judges – professions in which there is already a gender gap – with the result that the pool of available female arbitrators inescapably remains narrow.[65]

Another key issue is the so-called pipeline leak or pipeline problem – the notion that the number of women decreases the higher they rise on the leadership ladder. This is all the more striking as in some countries, like the United States, statistics show that women now outnumber men in law schools. According to the American Bar Association, female law graduates make up almost half of the associates, but only 22% of partners, in law firms, and at partner level men are paid almost one-third more than

60. Gaillard (2020), *supra* n. 4, at 36.
61. Convention on the Settlement of Investment Disputes between States and Nationals of Other States art. 38, 14 Oct. 1966 (ICSID Convention).
62. Gaillard (2020), *supra* n. 4, at 36.
63. *Ibid.*
64. *See*, e.g., Greenwood & Baker, *supra* n. 51; Greenwood & Baker, *supra* n. 8.
65. *See* Greenwood & Baker, *supra* n. 51, at 654; Christophe Seraglini, *Who are the Arbitrators? Myths, Reality and Challenges, in Legitimacy: Myths, Realities, Challenges* 589, 592 (Albert Jan van den Berg ed., Kluwer Law International 2015).

their female colleagues.[66] Further, almost a third of the general counsel in Fortune 500 companies are women, but the proportion drops to 23% in Fortune 501-1,000 companies.[67]

The 'leak' appears to be caused by a number of factors, including a lack of female role models and mentoring opportunities, difficulties in managing dual careers, earnings differentials between spouses, gender stereotyping, no clear career path, and a perceived lack of skills/experience.[68] As Eagly and Carli have demonstrated in their book *Through the Labyrinth*, the gender promotion gap and the resulting 'glass ceiling', which prevent women from reaching leadership positions, are caused by enduring biases and stereotypical attitudes reproduced throughout the pipeline.[69] Researchers have shown that the gender gap is wider in countries where gender stereotypes are more pronounced.[70] Similar projections have been documented in international settings. For example, in a study of a dozen international courts, Grossman found that women occupy on average 20% of positions in such courts, with the International Criminal Court scoring best with 47% and the Court of Justice of the EU and the International Tribunal for the Law of the Sea performing worst (with 6% and 2%, respectively).[71] These examples serve as a reminder that, even though the situation in international arbitration appears to be moving in the right direction (in the commercial context at least), there is still a long way to go to reach full gender equality.

B Generational Diversity

In international arbitration, there are two main aspects to generational diversity: on the one hand, the representation of people of different ages in international arbitration; and on the other hand, and perhaps more counterintuitively, the need to avoid bias or prejudice based on age.

1 Balancing the Generations

Most commentators agree that the average age of international arbitrators is over 50.[72] In 2020, the average age of arbitrators confirmed or appointed in ICC cases was 56

66. American Bar Association, *A Current Glance at Women in the Law* (American Bar Association 2018).
67. *Ibid.*, 2-6.
68. *See* Greenwood & Baker, *supra* n. 51, at 657, citing a 2008 study entitled *The Leaking Pipeline: Where Are Our Female Leaders?* from *ICCA Report No. 8*, *supra* n. 3, at 43.
69. Alice H. Eagly & Linda L. Carli, *Through the Labyrinth: The Truth About How Women Become Leaders* (Harvard Business School Press 2007).
70. *See* Bohnet, *supra* n. 7, at 28-29.
71. Nienke Grossman, *Shattering the Glass Ceiling in International Adjudication*, 56 VA. J. Int'l L. 340 (2016).
72. Clay, *supra* n. 25, at 28; Franck et al., *supra* n. 5, at 430; Seraglini, *supra* n. 65, at 591. This average age has remained remarkably consistent over time. Lemercier & Sgard (Lemercier & Sgard, *supra* n. 23, at 51-53) have studied the profiles of the small group of 'core' members who dominated the ICC arbitration system in the 1920s and 1930s. In 1930, the age of these members varied greatly, from 26 years for a Swiss member, André Boissier, to 67 years for a Belgian member, Charles Neef. Most active members at the ICC appeared to be in their fifties; this

years.[73] Women arbitrators, many of whom have been established in the profession for less time than men, tend to be slightly younger than their male counterparts, averaging around 48-50 years.[74] The question of whether this can be considered 'old' is entirely subjective. There appears to be no clear consensus on what qualifies as 'old' in the international arbitration context. While some respondents of the Queen Mary and White & Case *2018 International Arbitration Survey* (Queen Mary Survey) considered a 'young' arbitrator to be under 40 years of age, others answered that anyone under 50 years of age was 'young', believing the average age of arbitrators to be well into their 60s.[75]

While no one would disagree that, as in other areas of the legal profession, there is a real need to train and educate younger lawyers, the question of whether age diversity is necessarily a good thing in international arbitration is a difficult one to answer. There is no doubt that some disputes involve highly complex factual and legal situations, which may call for arbitrators (and counsel) with considerable experience, acquired over many years. Yet, it can also be argued that 'younger' arbitrators are particularly diligent in performing their duties, maybe in the hope of attracting more appointments in the future.[76] Ultimately, the two views do not seem incompatible. What matters is not age but experience; there should be a clear effort to promote younger arbitrators for disputes involving less complex factual and/or legal situations, so that they may hone their skills and, sooner or later, join the ranks of the more experienced arbitrators.

2 *Avoiding Prejudice Based on Age*

A second aspect of generational diversity is the 'right of senior people not to be discriminated against'.[77] This issue may arise in international arbitration when parties, often for tactical reasons, seek to disqualify an arbitrator based on her or his age.

The issue became the focus of much commentary in an ICC case in 2018, following the respondent's attempt to disqualify the prominent Swedish arbitrator Sigvard Jarvin as president of the arbitral tribunal in a billion-dollar construction dispute. The respondent argued that Mr. Jarvin's age – 76 years at the time of the controversy – was incompatible with the proper conduct of a complex arbitration and that it would be too expensive to obtain insurance to cover the risks of such an appointment.[78]

---

included Charles Dolléans (52 years old in 1930), Albert Legrand (53 years old), René Duchemin (55 years old), and Nicolas Politis (58 years old).

73. International Chamber of Commerce, *supra* n. 56, at 15.
74. Mirèze Philippe, *How has Female Participation at ICC Evolved? ICC Arbitrators, Court Members and Court's Secretariat,* 3 ICC Disp. Resol. Bull. 37 (2017). *See also* International Chamber of Commerce, *supra* n. 56, at 15.
75. Queen Mary and White & Case, *supra* n. 38, at 17.
76. *Ibid.*, 17.
77. Van Haersolte-van Hof, *supra* n. 37, at 639.
78. *See* T. Jones, *ICC rejects challenge based on arbitrator's age,* https://globalarbitrationreview.com/article/1175658/icc-rejects-challenge-based-on-arbitrator%E2%80%99s-age (accessed 17 Jan. 2022).

The ICC International Court of Arbitration rejected the challenge against Mr. Jarvin and, in light of the importance of the policy issues at stake (and with the parties' approval), provided reasons for its decision. The ICC Court noted that '[t]he age of a prospective arbitrator is certainly an element that is and should be taken into account by the Court when appointing an arbitrator' but that 'it cannot be the sole consideration, and it cannot in and of itself be a discriminating circumstance'.[79]

The ICC Court explained that the respondent had expressed the view that the president of the arbitral tribunal should be 'a retired English High Court or Commonwealth equivalent Judge ... or a senior Queen's Counsel experienced in construction disputes'.[80] The ICC Court noted that this requirement of 'seniority' meant that the arbitrator would 'in all likelihood be at least 70 years of age' and that, moreover, there was 'no indication that [Mr. Jarvin's] health should be a source of concern'.[81] With regard to Mr. Jarvin's 'insurability', the Court found that '[t]here is in fact no requirement under the Rules [of Arbitration of the ICC] that an arbitrator's health conditions be "insurable"'.[82]

Finally, the Court explained that the respondent's reliance on public statements by the President of the ICC Court in favour of the promotion of a new generation of arbitrators and the need to promote young practitioners was 'misplaced in the context of the present challenge'.[83] This suggests that while the age of more senior arbitrators can, and sometimes does, lead to legitimate concerns over their ability to handle arbitration proceedings over an extended period of time, age should not be used for purely tactical reasons in international arbitration.

C Geographic Diversity

A third aspect of diversity that is increasingly discussed in the context of international arbitration relates to geographical origins, that is, parties' and arbitrators' nationalities. In the Queen Mary Survey, 29% of those consulted disagreed that progress had been made in relation to geographic diversity.[84] While it is certainly the case that little progress has been made with regard to the nationalities of arbitrators, the opposite is true of parties' nationalities, which reflects international arbitration's unprecedented expansion over the past century.

The full extent of this change can best be appreciated by studying the ICC's archives, which presently contain forty-seven arbitral awards from the 1920s and 1930s.[85] These awards show that the most common nationality of parties to ICC

79. ICC Case No. 23288/AYZ, *Decision of the ICC Court on Arbitrators Challenge*, paragraph 28 (12 Oct. 2018).
80. *Ibid.*, paragraph 29.
81. *Ibid.*, paragraph 31.
82. *Ibid.*, paragraph 37.
83. *Ibid.*, paragraph 27.
84. Queen Mary and White & Case, *supra* n. 38, at 18.
85. These are the awards from the 1920s and 1930s that are still available in the ICC archives, and they seem to represent a good sample of the awards that were rendered at the time. The 47 arbitral awards date from the period November 22, 1922 (ICC Case No. 6) to November 25, 1939

arbitration cases in those decades was French (thirty-four parties). Other parties were from Belgium (eleven parties), the Netherlands (seven parties), Germany (seven parties), the United Kingdom (five parties), and Spain (three parties), as well as the United States, the Czech Republic, Luxembourg, Greece, Austria, Sweden, Japan, and India (one party each).

If one considers only the available cases from the 1920s, it is clear that ICC arbitration mainly involved parties from France and nearby countries in Europe, such as England, Belgium, Spain, Italy, and Germany (an exception is ICC Case No. 163 (Oct. 26, 1927), where the claimant was from Japan). Much more geographical diversity can be found in the 1930s, with arbitrations between a Greek claimant and Italian respondent,[86] a Dutch claimant and a Tunisian respondent,[87] a Venezuelan claimant and a Belgian respondent,[88] and an Indian claimant and a German respondent.[89] This is a clear sign of both the ICC's growing influence - bolstered by its intensive 'propaganda' efforts, as they were called at the time - and the internationalization of the field as a whole.[90]

When it comes to the nationalities of arbitrators serving on tribunals in ICC cases, the available archives show that in the early years of ICC arbitration most arbitrators were French, with ten French arbitrators serving in cases from the 1920s and 1930s. Other arbitrators during that period were Belgian (eight arbitrators), Swiss (seven arbitrators), British, German, Dutch, Italian, or Austrian, but there were few arbitrators from other parts of the world.

Following the exponential growth of international commercial arbitration in the course of the twentieth century, parties from an extremely wide range of countries and legal backgrounds started using ICC arbitration. For instance, the parties in the ICC's 2020 filings came from as many as 145 countries and independent territories.[91] Parties from Northern and Western Europe represented 31.8% of the overall party population, with parties from Spain, France, Italy, Germany, the United Kingdom, and Switzerland being the most frequent in that region. Parties from the Americas accounted for roughly 25% of the overall party population, with the United States maintaining its top position (9% of all parties to ICC arbitration worldwide) and Brazil being the most frequent nationality among Latin American parties. Approximately 25% of parties came from Asia and the Pacific, while only 6.8% of the overall party population came from Africa.[92]

Although arbitrators come from a wide range of countries, with as many as ninety-two jurisdictions represented among arbitrators appointed and confirmed by the ICC Court in 2020,[93] they do not adequately match the diversity of the parties to ICC

(ICC Case No. 668); of these, 18 are from the 1920s and 29 from the 1930s. For a detailed analysis of these awards, *see* Schinazi, *supra* n. 23, at 172-188.

86. ICC Case No. 396 (Jan. 8, 1932).
87. ICC Case No. 477 (Mar. 21, 1932).
88. ICC Case No. 588 (Nov. 29, 1932).
89. ICC Case No. 598 (May 18, 1935).
90. *See* Schinazi, *supra* n. 23, at 173.
91. International Chamber of Commerce, *supra* n. 56, at 10.
92. *Ibid.*, 10-11.
93. *Ibid.*, 12.

arbitration. In 2020, 52.3% of arbitrators serving in ICC cases came from Northern and Western Europe (with arbitrators from the United Kingdom representing 14.5% of all arbitrators), and 28.8% of arbitrators came from the Americas. Meanwhile, only 11.7% of arbitrators came from Asia, 4.9% from Central and Eastern Europe, and 2.3% from the entire African continent.[94] Despite the fact that each year sees arbitrators from previously unrepresented countries appointed or confirmed in ICC cases, some parts of the world are still underrepresented. The ICC has made various attempts to remedy that problem, such as the launch of an Africa Commission to build 'capacity of African practitioners specialising in dispute resolution' and 'identify how ICC can expand its services to meet the needs of business in Africa'.[95] However, it remains to be seen whether such efforts will yield concrete results in the near future.

IV BUILDING THE CASE FOR INCLUSIVENESS

Given the diversity issues highlighted in the first section of this chapter, it comes as no surprise that inclusiveness in international arbitration has become the subject of intense and considered debate. As the literature on this topic continues to grow, a profound theoretical question arises: Why should the arbitration community engage in serious discussions on its own inclusiveness and implement effective measures to achieve greater inclusiveness? In this section, we provide a non-exhaustive list of four rationales for more inclusiveness – skill improvement and innovation IV.A, enlarging and enriching the arbitrator talent pool IV.B, better-quality decision-making IV.C, and representativeness and legitimacy IV.D – and point to future avenues for research.

A Skill Improvement and Innovation

One rationale for more inclusiveness in general is that it improves collective skills and fosters innovative products and ideas. The US Supreme Court acknowledged the added value of inclusiveness in a series of cases of positive discrimination in university settings.[96]

In those cases, a consortium of multinational corporations qualified as amici curiae argued that the government had a compelling interest in pursuing diversity in higher education. In particular, they developed a business case for diversity as a core component of their legal strategies by disclosing research stating that diverse teams contribute to innovation in products and ideas.[97] The Court agreed that the benefits of diversity 'are not theoretical but real, as … the skills needed in today's increasingly

94. *Ibid.*, 14.
95. *See* International Chamber of Commerce, *Africa Commission*, https://iccwbo.org/dispute-resolution-services/africa-commission/ (accessed 17 Jan. 2022).
96. *See Grutter v. Bollinger et al.*, 539 U.S. 306 (S. Ct. 2003); *Gratz et al. v. Bollinger et al.*, 539 U.S. 244 (S. Ct. 2003); *Fisher v. University of Texas at Austin*, 570 U.S. 297 (S. Ct. 2013).
97. *See* Jamillah Bowman Williams, *Breaking down Bias: Legal Mandates vs. Corporate Interests*, 92 Wash. L. Rev. 1473, 1487 (2017).

global marketplace can only be developed through exposure to widely diverse people, cultures, ideas, and viewpoints'.[98]

Research shows that heterogeneous groups generally outperform homogeneous ones[99] and that this difference constitutes a 'diversity dividend'[100] or a 'diversity bonus',[101] which results in 'a regular payout from inclusion'.[102] The furtherance of professional skills and the production of innovative ideas are part of such a diversity dividend or bonus. As the American Bar Association has noted, 'a diverse legal team is more just, productive and intelligent because diversity, both cognitive and cultural, often leads to better questions, analyses, solutions, and processes'.[103] These arguments can easily be extended to international arbitration.

B Enlarging and Enriching the Arbitrator Talent Pool

A powerful rationale for inclusiveness in international arbitration is that it enlarges the pool of potential arbitrators from which both parties and arbitral institutions may select candidates.[104] The argument underpinning this rationale is: the more diverse the arbitration community, the greater the number of skilled arbitrators available for appointment. In international arbitration, as in many other sectors and industries, the best talents do not all look alike and only an 'increasingly international and increasingly diverse [pool]' will ensure that the right talent is selected for the right position.[105]

Greater inclusiveness will in turn promote more diverse role models to which young arbitration professionals can look when planning their careers. People generally 'believe that their chances for promotion [diminish] the more people "like them" … [are] at their same level', so that '[i]f ten female associates see only one female partner, they could well make the inference that their chances of advancement to partner are quite limited'.[106] In other words, the scarcity of role models at the top of the career ladder – among partners in global law firms as well as within arbitral tribunals – reinforces the assumption that people belonging to the same demographic segment have to compete hard to reach the few positions that would appear to be open to them.

---

98. *Grutter*, *supra* n. 96, at 330.
99. *See* Vivian Hunt, Dennis Layton & Sara Prince, *Why Diversity Matters – McKinsey and Company Annual Report*, 3, https://www.mckinsey.com/~/media/mckinsey/business%20functions/people%20and%20organizational%20performance/our%20insights/why%20diversity%20matters/why%20diversity%20matters.pdf (accessed 17 Jan. 2022).
100. Mark Kaplan & Mason Donovan, *The Inclusion Dividend: Why Investing in Diversity & Inclusion Pays Off* 39 (Bibliomotion 2013).
101. Scott E. Page, *The Diversity Bonus: How Great Teams Pay Off in the Knowledge Economy* 37-51 (Princeton University Press 2017).
102. Darren Rosenblum, *When Does Sex Diversity on Boards Benefit Firms?*, 20 U. Pa. J. Bus. L. 429, 431 (2017).
103. American Bar Association, *Diversity in the Legal Profession: The Next Steps* 5 (American Bar Association 2010).
104. *See* Chiara Giorgetti, *Who Decides Who Decides in International Investment Arbitration?*, 35 U. Pa. J. Int'l L. 431, 480-81 (2014); Seraglini, *supra* n. 65, at 603-05.
105. Frost, *supra* n. 30, at 71.
106. Bohnet, *supra* n. 7, at 212.

Finally, more research needs to be carried out on the issue of repeat appointments, which can represent a clear impediment to the appointment of newcomers with different skill sets and from different backgrounds. To understand why the issue of repeat appointments might be a real problem, it is useful to consider the statistics released by arbitral institutions. For example, the 2019 annual report of the London Court of International Arbitration (LCIA) shows that in only 19% of appointments made in 2019 had the candidate not previously been appointed.[107] Moreover, of the arbitrators selected by the LCIA, only 15% were first-time arbitrators (up from 9% in 2018), compared to 21% of the arbitrators selected by the parties under the LCIA Rules (the LCIA explained this difference by stating that arbitrators selected by the Court tended to be sole arbitrators or chairs, roles for which prior experience of LCIA arbitration is generally required[108]). Such repeat appointments can prevent newcomers from gaining access to arbitral appointments and, therefore, hinder diversity.

C Better-Quality Decision-Making

Another rationale that needs to be explored in further detail is the connection (if any) between diversity and the quality of decision-making in international arbitration. There have been no thorough statistical analyses on this question. In the Queen Mary Survey, the idea that 'diversity leads to a significant improvement in quality' was not shared by the majority of respondents, some of whom were even unsure whether the enquiry was relevant.[109]

However, an argument could be made that 'a diverse tribunal will actually tend to be better prepared, more task-oriented, and more attentive to and receptive of the parties' arguments than a non-diverse tribunal'.[110] As authors in the business literature have acknowledged, 'having diverse teams can improve the quality of decision-making at all organizational levels, reduce groupthink and allow assumptions to be challenged more effectively'.[111]

There is indeed a case for arguing that greater inclusiveness leads to better-quality decision-making, as it improves the internal dynamics of the arbitral tribunal by preventing 'groupthink'. Research shows that some of the effects of non-diverse groups are uniformity and censorship, as well as replication of the 'cascade effect' (group members following the actions of those who act first), increased polarization, and a focus on shared information rather than novel ways of thinking.[112] Applied to international arbitration, these arguments suggest that there may be advantages in having the appointment of an arbitrator discussed by a diverse team of lawyers and

107. London Court of International Arbitration, *2019 Annual Casework Report* 16 (London Court of International Arbitration 2020).
108. *Ibid.*, 16.
109. Queen Mary and White & Case, *supra* n. 38, at 16.
110. Haridi, *supra* n. 32, at 311.
111. Frost, *supra* n. 30, at 79.
112. *See* Cass R. Sunstein & Reid Hastie, *Wiser: Getting Beyond Groupthink to Make Groups Smarter* 23-24 (Harvard Business Review Press 2015).

managers and in ensuring that the resulting arbitral tribunal reflects at least a certain level of diversity.

D Representativeness and Legitimacy

Finally, a rationale for more inclusiveness could be based on the notion of representativeness – the idea that arbitrators and practitioners should reflect the varied components of the corporate world. This could be described as a 'demographic' rationale. It has been observed in this respect that 'it is all the more important that parties view the tribunal as a cross section of the business world, or a cross section of an idealized business world that is modern, creative, and diverse'.[113]

Representativeness is essential to ensure that arbitral tribunals are perceived as legitimate by the corporate world.[114] As with any other adjudicative mechanism, arbitral tribunals that are more representative of society will attract greater trust and confidence and be considered more legitimate. If international arbitration is to continue being the favoured means of settling international business disputes, it must cultivate the trust of its users. Some authors have used the term 'demographic mirroring' to convey this idea,[115] although it should be borne in mind that 'mirroring' is a very controversial concept.[116]

V DESIGNING A MORE INCLUSIVE ARBITRATION COMMUNITY

To achieve greater inclusiveness, as V.V. Veeder posited, 'we do not need more laws, legal rules, and legal regulations', but to work 'primarily with major users and arbitral institutions'.[117] In this section, we wish to highlight a few innovative measures taken by stakeholders in the international arbitration community, in particular arbitral institutions V.A, clients and law firms V.B, and arbitral organizations and informal networks V.C.

A Arbitral Institutions

There is a widespread perception that arbitral institutions have a crucial role to play in promoting diversity in international arbitration. In the Queen Mary Survey, 45% of those consulted reported that arbitral institutions are 'best placed to ensure greater diversity across arbitral tribunals', followed by parties (including their in-house

113. Haridi, *supra* n. 32, at 308.
114. *See* Franck et al., *supra* n. 5, at 496.
115. *See*, e.g., Haridi, *supra* n. 32, at 308.
116. 'Mirroring' can in fact result in a 'pernicious practice' that pursues 'diversity without inclusion' (Marc Bendick Jr, Mary Lou Egan & Louis Lanier, *The Business Case for Diversity and the Pernicious Practice of Matching Employees with Customers*, 39 Pers. Rev. 468, 481 (2010)). What is particularly contested is the practice of 'race matching', which assumes that good business ideas for a certain customer segment can come exclusively from the employees who are members of the corresponding community.
117. Veeder (2015), *supra* n. 39, at 660.

counsel) and external counsel.[118] This view should be nuanced by observing that arbitral institutions are not responsible for the majority of arbitrator appointments. However, it is true that arbitral institutions play a key regulatory function in international arbitration and may set positive examples for others to follow.

Arbitral institutions seem to have taken this responsibility very seriously. For example, women represented 48% of all arbitrators selected by the LCIA Court in 2019 (up by 5% from 2018 and 16% from 2017), as opposed to 12% of those selected by the parties.[119] Meanwhile, the ICC has taken various initiatives in the recent past, such as promoting age and geographical diversity in arbitration through its ICC YAF (Young Arbitrators Forum) network, which, for the 2021-2023 term, comprises forty-eight women and forty-one men from fifty-nine countries. In 2018, the ICC signed a 'Gender Balance Pledge', committing the institution to increase gender diversity in panel discussions and conferences in which the ICC participates. That same year, under the impetus of its then-President Alexis Mourre, the ICC International Court of Arbitration achieved full gender parity, with eighty-eight men and eighty-eight women being appointed for the 2015-2018 term of the Court.[120] This was described as a 'giant step' in international arbitration.[121]

In addition, arbitral institutions can play an important role in promoting diversity when they are tasked with appointing arbitrators. Appointments by the institution represented 25% of all arbitrator appointments in ICC cases in 2020.[122] In such instances, the ICC Court makes the appointment upon proposal of a National Committee or Group of the ICC, or directly.[123] As stated in a recent 'Note to National Committees', when considering 'less complex cases or cases involving relatively low amounts in dispute', National Committees or Groups of the ICC are 'particularly encouraged to propose new and/or young arbitrators, as this may help the pool of potential arbitrators in that community to grow'.[124] Likewise, 'Committees and Groups are encouraged to favour gender diversity in their proposals.'[125]

Some National Committees have shown particular commitment to fulfilling this role; for instance, the French Committee on Selection and Nomination of Arbitrators (French Committee) has in recent years actively moved to include younger names in its database of potential arbitrators. Practitioners wishing to be included in this database - called '*vivier*' in French - must write to the French Committee and explain why they wish to be in the database (if the French Committee decides not to include a name in

118. Queen Mary and White & Case, *supra* n. 38, at 13.
119. London Court of International Arbitration, *supra* n. 107, at 16.
120. *See* International Chamber of Commerce, *ICC renews Alexis Mourre as President and nominates Court with full gender parity and unprecedented diversity*, https://iccwbo.org/media-wall/news-speeches/icc-renews-alexis-mourre-president-nominates-court-full-gender-parity-unprecedented-diversity/ (accessed 17 Jan. 2022).
121. Mirèze Philippe, *Achieving Gender Equality on the ICC International Court of Arbitration – A Giant Step*, 3 ICC Disp. Resol. Bull. 104 (2018).
122. International Chamber of Commerce, *supra* n. 56, at 12.
123. Rules of Arbitration of the ICC, art. 13(3) (2021).
124. International Chamber of Commerce, *Note to National Committees and Groups of the ICC on the Proposal of Arbitrators*, paragraph 38, https://iccwbo.org/publication/note-national-committees-groups-icc-proposal-arbitrators/ (accessed 17 Jan. 2022).
125. *Ibid.*, paragraph 39.

its database, it usually provides the reasons for its decision, so that applicants can improve their skills and profiles before reapplying). In 2020, arbitrators appointed by the ICC Court (either directly or following a proposal from a National Committee) were approximately six years younger (50.5 years) than the average age of ICC arbitrators (56 years).[126] When tasked with appointing arbitrators, arbitral institutions thus have an important role to play in ensuring that the pool of potential arbitrators becomes more open and diverse, and the ICC and its National Committees are already playing such a role.

B Clients and Law Firms

While arbitration institutions may have shown progressiveness in designing mechanisms to encourage the appointment of newcomers, it is often the parties who display conservatism and resist change.[127] Since parties ('essential actors' in sociological terms) work hand in hand with their counsel (who belong to the 'service providers'[128]) ahead of and throughout arbitration proceedings, all these actors play a crucial role in promoting diversity and ensuring access for newcomers.

As is well known, factors usually considered when selecting arbitrators for a given arbitration case include experience and previous appointments,[129] 'word of mouth, nationality and legal education',[130] and 'an arbitrator's way of thinking'.[131] Indeed, parties must make sure that the arbitrator they wish to appoint is 'not someone intellectually hostile to the anticipated arguments that will be advanced in the case'.[132] Parties and their counsel (whether in-house or external) should ensure that these factors, however important, do not lead to biased appointments.

Simple but effective measures could be taken to that end. Parties and counsel could start by acknowledging that it is their responsibility to ensure that the slate of potential arbitrators is diverse and represents the various components of the arbitration community and the wider business world. Parties and counsel could sign a pledge stating that no list of potential arbitrators will be complete unless it includes some names of women arbitrators, arbitration professionals from non-Western countries and, if appropriate, younger candidates. Such a pledge would also commit them to having a clear diversity and inclusion policy in place.

In addition, concrete steps could be taken to limit biases and create more inclusive designs. For instance, when considering potential candidates for an arbitrator

126. International Chamber of Commerce, *supra* n. 56, at 15.
127. *See* Gaillard (2015), *supra* n. 4, at 16.
128. *Ibid.*, 4-7.
129. Michael Waibel, *Arbitrator Selection: Towards Greater State Control, in Reassertion of Control over the Investment Treaty Regime* 333, 344 (A. Kulick ed., Cambridge University Press 2016).
130. Greenwood, *supra* n. 53, at 106.
131. Doak Bishop & Lucy Reed, *Practical Guidelines for Interviewing, Selecting and Challenging Party-Appointed Arbitrators in International Commercial Arbitration*, 14 Arb. Int'l 395, 401 (1998).
132. Emmanuel Gaillard & Philippe Pinsolle, *Advocacy in International Commercial Arbitration: France, in The Art of Advocacy in International Arbitration* 133, 144 (Doak Bishop ed., Juris 2004).

appointment, counsel would need to make sure that equal weight is given to all candidates with regard to their gender, age, and origin. One way of ensuring this would be to establish a *structured* procedural framework for selecting potential arbitrators, instead of relying on informal discussions and allowing decisions to be guided by 'gut reactions'. As Bohnet has shown in her influential work *What Works: Gender Equality by Design*, groups can reach better decisions only if they adopt more structured processes.[133] Among other measures, she recommends using predefined selection criteria in the form of a checklist and a scoring system allowing a comparative evaluation of candidates by decision-makers.[134] As Bohnet has shown, structured selection procedures contribute to the objectivity of the selection process itself.

While such methods would have to be fine-tuned for international arbitration, they provide useful examples of measures that could help 'de-biasing minds'.[135] It is indeed clear that choosing an arbitrator is not an unbiased exercise. An unconscious bias called 'culture fit' induces recruiters to prefer candidates who fit into the existing culture to the detriment of those who do not.[136] Because the profile of a typical arbitrator is that of a middle-aged man from a developed country, appointments tend to result in the selection of people who have similar characteristics. Adopting a more structured procedure for selecting and appointing arbitrators – and even, as Greenwood has suggested, a system of 'blind' appointments, whereby external counsel would remove identifying information from résumés before presenting clients with a list of potential arbitrators[137] – would likely contribute to having a more diverse pool of arbitrators.

C Arbitral Organizations and Informal Networks

In addition to arbitral institutions, clients, and law firms, various global organizations and informal networks have sought to make international arbitration more diverse and inclusive. These players act as 'value providers', offering 'guidance as to the way international arbitration should develop and social actors should behave'.[138] They play a key role in showing good practices and devising new solutions to address the diversity challenge in international arbitration.

To provide but a few examples,[139] ArbitralWomen is a well-known organization that has existed informally since 1993 and officially as a non-profit organization since

133. Bohnet, *supra* n. 7.
134. *Ibid.*, 139.
135. *Ibid.*, 44.
136. *Ibid.*, 128.
137. Lucy Greenwood, *Could 'Blind' Appointments Open Our Eyes to the Lack of Diversity in International Arbitration?*, 4 Transnat'l Disp. Mgmt. 1, 8 (2015).
138. Gaillard (2015), *supra* n. 4, at 7.
139. More gender diversity initiatives in international arbitration can be found in the ICCA Report No. 8, *supra* n. 3, on the ArbitralWomen website (https://www.arbitralwomen.org/gender-equality/) and on the Equal Representation in Arbitration Pledge website (http://www.arbitrationpledge.com/news). *See also* the Diversity Campaign promoted in 2021 by Arbitrator Intelligence, an organization aggregating arbitrators' track records to be made available to parties and their counsel.

2005.[140] It has organized awareness campaigns, events, and conferences, acting as 'one of many catalysts in the movement towards women's equality, by raising public consciousness, by positioning women in the foreground, and then by working along with others, both women and men, to bring about progress'.[141]

Another well-known initiative is the Equal Representation in Arbitration Pledge (Pledge), which seeks to 'increase, on an equal opportunity basis, the number of women appointed as arbitrators in order to achieve a fair representation as soon as practically possible, with the ultimate goal of full parity'.[142] In 2020, the Pledge had amassed more than 4,000 signatories from 113 countries.[143] This milestone suggests that the Pledge is a good way to effect change through collective impact.

Finally, other recent examples include the creation of: (i) an LGBTQIA network within the ICC International Court of Arbitration[144] and (ii) a Task Force on Disability Inclusion and International Arbitration, formed under the ICC Commission on Arbitration and ADR. The Task Force's mission is "to study and analyse the ways in which ICC can meet the needs of those in the international arbitration community who may need accommodations or changes for the way they work" and produce a set of guidelines to enable disability inclusion in international arbitration.[145]

VI CONCLUSION

This chapter has explored some of the major issues in the debate on diversity and inclusiveness in international arbitration. We raised four key questions concerning: the various aspects of diversity; their relevance in international arbitration scholarship; various rationales that can be used to build a case for more inclusiveness; and some of the measures that could be implemented across the board. The subsequent discussion

140. *See*, in particular, Barrington, *supra* n. 6; Louise Barrington, *Women Working for Change in Society: The Arbitral Women Example, in Women Pioneers in Dispute Resolution* (2nd ed., Deutsche Gesellschaft für Internationale Zusammenarbeit 2018); Philippe, *supra* n. 6.
141. Barrington, *supra* n. 140, at 14.
142. Equal Representation in Arbitration Pledge, *Commentary to the Pledge*, http://www.arbitrationpledge.com/about-the-pledge (accessed 17 Jan. 2022).
143. Ashley Jones & Stephanie Mbonu, The ERA Pledge surpasses 4,000 signatories, http://arbitrationblog.practicallaw.com/the-era-pledge-surpasses-4000-signatories (accessed 17 Jan. 2022).
144. The ICC Court LGBTQIA network was created in 2021 with an aim to "supporting personal development, enabling best practice sharing, building understanding, and ensuring accountability." While the LGBTQIA network is currently open to all members of the ICC Court, it is to be hoped that this network (or similar initiatives) will develop for other members of the international arbitration community as well. *See* International Chamber of Commerce, *ICC Court to build LGBTQIA network*, https://iccwbo.org/media-wall/news-speeches/icc-court-to-build-lgbtqia-network (accessed 17 Jan. 2022).
145. *See* International Chamber of Commerce, *ICC names new Disability and Inclusion Task Force leadership*, https://iccwbo.org/media-wall/news-speeches/icc-names-new-disability-and-inclusion-task-force-leadership/ (accessed 17 Jan. 2022). As a potent symbol to the international arbitration community, the creation of the Task Force was the first measure undertaken by Claudia Salomon, one week into her term as President of the ICC International Court of Arbitration.

has highlighted the fact that, even though the conversation on diversity and inclusiveness in international arbitration is now alive, much progress remains to be made. Future research will need to be carried out – in particular in sociology, history, and other disciplines – to heed the voices of those who have been consistently marginalized by the dominant discourse in international arbitration. At a time of deep contestation over the legitimacy and purpose of international arbitration, failure to do so would be a profound mistake.

CHAPTER 25

Against Stigma: How to Refute Negative Perception and Self-Reproach in Investment Treaty Arbitration and Fight Stigma in the Age of Global Arbitration*

*Karim A. Youssef***

I TRIBUTE

Guillermo Aguilar Álvarez was a true gentleman of international arbitration. I have had the pleasure of meeting him during his time teaching at Yale Law School and I counted him as a friend, who was very generous with his views and advice on arbitration in the developing world, and as a charismatic and cosmopolitan figure of international arbitration who inspired and continues to inspire all that this honorable field represents.

Very few people can claim to have achieved what Guillermo did through his immense contribution to international arbitration, and in particular, investment treaty arbitration. Guillermo was a key player in the negotiations and drafting of NAFTA, making history and marking a key milestone in the history of global arbitration, and in the history and dynamics of investment in the Americas.

What did Guillermo stand for? The answer is prolific and, to be comprehensive, would necessarily unfold in pages. But if one is asked to identify the greatest value or purpose that Guillermo stood for and represented through his work and remarkable

* This chapter is based on a keynote speech delivered at the Cairo Regional Centre (CRCICA) Sharm El Sheikh conference. The speech won the 2019 GAR Award for best global speech (https://globalarbitrationreview.com/article/1189726/paris-hosts-largest-ever-gar-awards).

** Thanks to Ms. Sarah El Saeed for assistance in the production of this chapter. The views expressed in this chapter are exclusively those of the author and do not necessarily reflect those of the institutions with which the author is affiliated.

contribution to international arbitration more than any other, my answer would be: fighting off stigma. Very few can claim to personify the cause of globalizing arbitration and fighting off various aspects of stigma more than or as much as Guillermo did. This chapter is a humble contribution to honor Guillermo's remarkable career, and his efforts in the enduring fight against stigma.

II THE IDEA

Literature on stigma is extremely scarce. That is to say, while it is an issue of profound importance, it has not been deliberated on or confronted directly, or in fact, as a self-standing issue. This is a problematic gap. The stigmatization of international arbitration is a perilous act, and so dealing with stigma is nothing short of a critical, if not existential, issue for international arbitration. Tackling the issue of stigma is as critical as other key issues and building blocks of the system of international arbitration such as issues with the independence of arbitrators, or with the sanctity of consent. The reason is that stigma, almost invariably, goes to core dynamics in the arbitration system, and the issues that it raises go, almost invariably, to the very essence of arbitration. In the words of Guillermo himself, "While there may be benefits from minor tinkering with this investment protection regime, general attacks on investment arbitration are likely to backfire, creating for all countries involved more problems than they solve."[1] Stigma is just that: it is an attack on the global system of international arbitration, as a whole.

This chapter aims to serve as a confrontation of the notion of stigma in international arbitration. It is an exercise both of refuting it and confirming how, and why, it fails. This chapter is a face-off with the notion of stigma in investment treaty arbitration, and aims to unroot stigma at its core. It is also a testimony that as citizens of the arbitration community, and as influencers and partakers in the shaping of what the field of arbitration is, and will become, we must fight stigma off at all costs.

III WHAT ARE WE DEALING WITH, AND WHY IS STIGMA A DANGEROUS THREAT TO THE INTERNATIONAL ARBITRATION SYSTEM?

The surge of investment treaty arbitration globally has also brought with it a plethora of criticisms and skepticisms of the system of international arbitration. Among the most dangerous is the notion of stigma surrounding investment arbitration. Like the galaxy far, far away in Star Wars, with its never-ending battle between the light and dark sides of the Force, the galaxy of international arbitration is confronted with its own dark side—stigma. Stigma is a serious and existential threat to the entire arbitration system for several reasons.

1. G.A. Álvarez & W.W. Park, *The New Face of Investment Arbitration: NAFTA Chapter 11*, Yale Journal of International Law, Volume 28 (2003), 365.

First, stigma is rampant. It manifests in attacking various aspects of the system of investment treaty arbitration, including its players and how they behave within it. Stigma surrounds states, when they are exposed to major investment treaty claims. Stigma also sometimes surrounds investors who activate bilateral investment treaty (BIT) protection and avail their arbitration rights, as well as other parties involved in investment treaty arbitrations, for example, legal counsel in specific cases. Stigma even attaches sometimes to specific types of behavior or patterns of behavior, for example, the systematic willingness or policy of a state to attempt to settle some of the investment claims it is exposed to. Stigma can also be directed at specific arbitration mechanisms, for example, by US opponents of NAFTA.[2] Stigma can even sometimes be self-inflicted. This occurs when certain state actors self-reproach the very fact that the state is designated as respondent in numerous arbitration cases. This mindset is self-defeating and dangerous because it promotes state attitudes that are counterproductive and hurtful to the state itself.

Second, stigma is dangerous because it is effectively an attack against the global arbitration system as a whole. If it is not dealt with properly and vanquished, it threatens to destabilize a vital global system put in place for the protection of investors and states alike.

Third, stigma is treacherous because, in our daily arbitral life, it is often passed under silence, as is often the case with preposterous things. They are sometimes easiest avoided or not discussed. In other cases, it is simply dismissed because it is deemed too outrageous to be seriously entertained, although its impact and danger runs deep.

IV STIGMATIZERS: THE VILLAINS OF THE GALAXY

"Stigmatizers"—those who inflict stigma on us—denigrate the system. They go about a dangerous and purposeless fault-finding exercise, indiscriminately placing blame on all parts of the system of international arbitration. Like the villains spread across the galaxy in Star Wars, stigmatizers walk among us and are spread across the galaxy of investment arbitration. This makes stigma a nasty, veiled weapon. Stigma often materializes in attacks perpetrated from within the system, by the very people who use it—its constituents, citizens, and players—and those who have come on board by having already consented to being part of the system and being bound by it. Stigma, the dark side of the Force, goes against the foundation of the system of arbitration: consent.

Even apparent proponents of the system can turn into stigmatizers sometimes. Consider a trade representative or investment minister who promotes the signature of investment treaties as a tool for promoting investments and foreign direct investment (FDI), but once the arbitration system is put in action, he or she becomes extremely

2. Among US opponents that are attacking NAFTA's arbitration mechanism are the New York Times in its article discrediting the credibility of the NAFTA arbitration mechanism as well as the Washington Post attacking investment arbitration. Additionally, NAFTA was described as a "sophisticated extortion racket" by the television host Bill Moyers. G.A. Álvarez & W.W. Park, *The New Face of Investment Arbitration: NAFTA Chapter 11*, Yale Journal of International Law, Volume 28 (2003), 365, pp. 30-32.

critical of investors who activate the protection afforded to them under BITs and resort to investment treaty arbitration. Consider an academic who discusses network and bandwagon effects of the BIT network, or a foreign investor who applauds a state for accepting to be bound by investment treaty arbitration but becomes critical of states who become respondents in investment treaty arbitration.

V THE DIFFERENT FACES OF STIGMA

Stigmatizers attach an arsenal of attacks to the investment treaty arbitration system. Five attacks are particularly striking and a clear testament to how disconnected stigma is from the reality of arbitral virtue and arbitral life.

A Stigma Against States Exposed to Investment Treaty Claims

In a problematic conflation of state responsibility and state fault, the main stigma against states involved in investment arbitrations simplistically holds that if states are exposed to an onslaught of arbitration claims, they are *necessarily* doing something wrong. Nonperformance by a state of its obligations under the relevant BIT or under international law is an indication of state responsibility, but separating state responsibility from a stigmatic depiction of state fault is essential. Many countries that have faced economic or political crises, and as a result major investment claims, have been indiscriminate victims of stigma. Particular examples include Argentina in the aftermath of the 2002-peso crisis and Egypt post-Arab Spring in 2011.

Stigmatizers necessarily begin at widely accepted and common ground statements, such as that states that enter into BITs accept to be bound by treaty obligations, including acceptance of the dispute resolution mechanism and the financial implications involved in the operation and enforcement of this mechanism. When put in the stigma blender, however, principles taken for granted are then warped into judgments and assumptions that have no connection to the *modus operandi* of international arbitration, and are not only wrong, but unfair.

Stigmatizers purport that once a state is found to have violated its treaty obligations, it will inescapably find its reputation with regard to respecting its international obligations tarnished. Critical arguments include that once an investment dispute emerges, and even after possible or full reparation by the state has been made, "there is still the harm to the state's reputation and standing in public opinion that comes with being the target of a dispute."[3] The argument essentially says that even full reparation does not remove the alleged stigma! These arguments involve stigmatic claims of a reflexive general impact on perception in the minds of investors in that state—namely that "Once an investment dispute arises investors will rethink their assessments of political risk in the 'defendant' country and be less likely to invest in a

3. T. Büthe & H.V. Milner, *Foreign Direct Investment and Institutional Diversity in Trade Agreements Credibility, Commitment, and Economic Flows in the Developing World, 1971–2007*, World Politics Volume 66, Issue 1, pp. 97-98.

country with a now questionable track record."[4] Stigma does not only strike states against whom an award is rendered. It goes as far as arguing that:

> [A] host country's appearance before [the International Centre for Settlement of Investment Disputes (ICSID)] already conveys a negative signal regarding its relationship with another foreign investor and its possible noncompliance with a BIT. We expect that when an investor initially registers a dispute at ICSID, even if the arbitration process is not concluded or no award has been issued, other firms should be more reluctant to invest in the respondent country.[5]

Arguments like these pose a very dangerous attack on the system because they paint a picture of an inescapably punitive system, which could easily deter various players from it.

In clouded parallel reasoning, negative perceptions include claims that exposure to investment arbitrations results in a loss of FDI.[6] The argument is that because the very existence of arbitral proceedings against a state, "regardless of the eventual outcome of the dispute, has a negative impact on the State's reputation in the eyes of foreign investors ...States are likely to receive less foreign direct investment following an investor's lodging of a BIT claim."[7] This stigma does not account for the various tools for reward the system affords or the relevant test for state behavior that the system sanctions. Empirical data and actual experiences, elaborated on below, show the exact opposite: that exposure to investment arbitration does not at all necessarily correlate to a loss of FDI.

Stigmatic assumptions against states can even extend to standard mechanisms of arbitral institutions. It has been suggested that one of the reasons ICSID awards are public is to signal high-risk countries to investors, and in turn attempt to induce deterrence in host states. Their reasoning follows that the existence of ICSID arbitrations against a host state acts as a warning sign that the host state is unreliable, hostile to investors, and incapable of keeping its commitments or its willingness to abide by them, making them "'cheaters' to the global community."[8] It is almost humorous that stigmatizers reverse the positive intention of the transparency of ICSID arbitrations aimed at ensuring the observability of the investment treaty arbitration system and find ways to permeate the dark force of stigma even into tools of light provided by the system.

4. T. Allee & C. Peinhardt, *Contingent Credibility: The Impact of Investment Treaty Violations on Foreign Direct Investment*, International Organization, Volume 65 (2011), p. 402.
5. *Ibid.*, p. 414.
6. K. Tienhaara, "Regulatory Chill and the Threat of Arbitration: A View from Political Science," in C. Brown & K. Miles (eds.) *Evolution in Investment Treaty Law and Arbitration*. Cambridge University Press, 2011, p. 613.
7. *Ibid.* Additionally, "Other possible negative impacts that could worry a host government faced with a dispute include strained relations with the government of the investor's home state (which may be an important trading partner or provider of financial aid) and/or with the World Bank." *Ibid.*
8. T. Allee & C. Peinhardt, *Contingent Credibility: The Reputational Effects of Investment Treaty Disputes on Foreign Direct Investment* (2008), p. 3.

B Stigma Attacking Settlement and Amicable Resolution of Investment Treaty Disputes

Because stigma is indiscriminate and senseless, it even surrounds states that walk the often prudent path of settlement. Those who stigmatize settlement are wrong. Negative perceptions about settlement, such as that states that settle investor disputes, offer settlement, or adopt a consistent policy in favor of settlement, do so due to an admission of fault, or a potential admission of fault, are not typically well placed, and are a form of the problematic conflation between state responsibility and state fault.[9] Perhaps more importantly, these views directly reverse and transpose the various obvious positive effects of settlement with misplaced negative stigma surrounding it. These criticisms once again attack a tool of light and peace that is settlement, with the dark side of the force, stigma.

C Stigma Against Investors Bringing Claims Against States

Negative perception also surrounds investors who activate BIT protection and bring investment claims against states. Criticism surrounding investors resorting to arbitration points to an alleged failure on their part to avoid disputes or to the possibility that they are benefiting from the disputes, or that they are even investing in the claims, as opposed to legitimately pursuing the remedies afforded by the system.[10] The mindset is "if you are suing, you are the bad guy" so to speak. This view of investor rights is oversimplistic, patronizing, and purports to overshadow the operation of a complex global system and replace it with an indiscriminate blame game. While this view could be seen as isolated, it is dangerous, and is often emitted by the state target of the investment claim. It is dangerous because it could adversely affect how the state continues to treat the investment, if it is an ongoing concern, and could reduce the chances of amicable resolution.

D Stigma Against Local Counsel Representing Investors in Investment Treaty Arbitrations

Stigma never tires. In its nonsensical attack against a range of players in the system, stigma has also been attached to local counsel representing foreign investors, in the

9. T. Allee & C. Peinhardt, *Contingent Credibility: The Impact of Investment Treaty Violations on Foreign Direct Investment*, International Organization, Volume 65, 2011, p. 416.
10. "If a businessman fails to prevent a difference in opinion from growing into a dispute or, at minimum, fails to find a solution once a dispute has arisen, thereby necessitating the intervention of a third party (whether such third party is a court or a conciliator or arbitration body) for settlement of such dispute, this is regarded as a gross failure by the businessman in the performance of his duties. In recent years this view seems to have gained some support in the United States and in Europe due to the enormous costs, both in terms of money and time, involved in the dispute resolution process. It goes without saying that this view is widely accepted in Japanese society, not only because of the monetary cost involved in dispute resolution, but also because of the strong Japanese social stigma attached to the failure to avoid disputes." S. Yanase, Bilateral Investment Treaties of Japan and Resolution of Disputes with Respect to Foreign Direct Investment. In Jan van den Berg, A. (ed.), *International Commercial Arbitration: Important Contemporary Questions*. ICCA Congress Series, Volume 11, p. 434.

form of a suggestion that foreign investors should not be entitled to representation by local counsel. Stigmatizers accuse local counsel representing foreign investors that by aiding foreign investors in investment claims against the counsel's own state, they are aiding in the assumed decline in the state's FDI and in causing the state reputational harm.

E Stigma Directed Against Specific Investment Treaty Mechanisms: The NAFTA

In some cases, the futility of stigma is shown in the fact that it goes beyond the critique of how the system operates to what the system is. An example of this is stigma that arose against NAFTA itself and against its dispute resolution mechanism, which initially provided the revolutionary ability for investors from Mexico, Canada, and the United States to bring claims protecting their investments in the host state. NAFTA has been generically criticized for diminishing the host nation's sovereignty by affording foreign investors added power in asserting investment claims in binding arbitrations.[11] NAFTA is a trade agreement, from which investment disputes will inevitably arise. While "minor tinkering,"[12] in the words of Guillermo, can be beneficial to various mechanisms of international arbitration, sweeping stigma against the very notion of investment arbitration mechanisms is senseless.

VI WHY STIGMA IS DOOMED TO FAIL?

Stigma is doomed to fail because it is deficient as a concept and is futile. Stigmatic arguments are simplistic and invariably inaccurate or wrong. Stigma fails because it is disengaged from reality and disconnected from any true understanding of global arbitration. Stigma and stigmatizers simply have no place in the age of global arbitration.

A States That Are Exposed to Investment Treaty Claims Are Not Necessarily Doing Something Wrong

The starting point is to ask the question: what does it really mean for a state to be exposed to an influx of investment treaty claims? It means, usually, that the state endured a political or economic event of a large magnitude, for example, like the economic crisis in Argentina in 2002 or the Arab Spring in Egypt in 2011. But, stigmatizers miss a silver lining. There are two critical (and evident) points here. First, a rise in investment claims necessarily means that there were major investments in the

11. R.C. Jones *NAFTA Chapter 11 Investor-to-State Dispute Resolution: A Shield to Be Embraced or a Sword to Be Feared?*, Brigham Young University Law Review Volume 2002, 527, 2002, pp. 542-546.
12. G.A. Álvarez & W.W. Park, *The New Face of Investment Arbitration: NAFTA Chapter 11*, Yale Journal of International Law Volume 28, 2003, p. 365.

period that preceded the rise in investment claims. A good example of this is Egypt in 2010, directly prior to the rise of the Arab Spring.[13] It goes without saying that if the Arab Spring had erupted in a country with very little FDI, there would have been no influx of investment treaty claims because there were no investments to start with. Second, a rise in investment claims also necessarily indicates that a state has a proper BIT network, without which there would obviously be no investment claims.[14]

B Stigma Fails Because It Applies the Wrong Test to State Conduct

Stigma focuses on the wrong test. The test is not whether a state is exposed to investment claims because it is an inevitability that complex factors in sociopolitical and economic systems will result in occasional breaches by states of their obligations under BITs or international law. Stigmatic mindsets often omit this evident inevitability. *The real test is how a state deals with those claims, and how it manages its reaction.* Placing less emphasis on the state conduct that triggered the specific claims and placing more emphasis on how the state dealt with the claims is the right lens to assess state conduct.

For a good example of a state effectively managing an influx of investment claims, our focus again turns to Egypt, in post-2011 Arab Spring. Egypt, like many other countries, including Argentina, Ecuador and Venezuela, which faced surges of economic or political crises, also faced a resulting influx of major investment claims. As of 2019, Egypt was the respondent to a total of twenty-two ICSID claims.[15] Since 2011, around a total of thirty-four were brought against Egypt.[16] On the range of good versus bad state reactions, however, Egypt seems to have aced the test of the Arab Spring by developing a track record of favorable dealing with, and management of, the investment treaty claims that have arisen since 2011. Egypt has maintained its international law obligations in relation to foreign investor protection. It did not withdraw from the ICSID convention, although other countries that faced a rise in investment claims chose that route, including, for example, Bolivia in 2007, Ecuador in 2010, and Venezuela in 2012.[17] Egypt also did not cancel or trigger any sunset periods under any of its BITs, including those under which claims were brought, recognizing the injudiciousness of doing so as a matter of international law. In fact, Egypt has signed new BITs since the

13. World Bank (IBRD IDA) data indicates that looking at the period from 2000 to 2010, FDI in Egypt started showing signs of growth as of 2004. It then significantly increased starting 2006 to 2010.
14. For example, Egypt has a very large BIT network, with 115 BITs signed, and 72 in force. Since 2011, three BITs were signed and entered into force. Argentina in 2002 had 58 BITs signed and 49 in force.
15. Retrieved from the official website of the International Centre for Settlement of Investment Disputes—World Bank Group. https://icsid.worldbank.org/en/Pages/cases/AdvancedSearch.aspx.
16. Retrieved from the official website of the International Centre for Settlement of Investment Disputes—World Bank Group. Retrieved from https://icsid.worldbank.org/cases/case-database.
17. V. Giraud, *Is Investment Arbitration in Latin American in Crisis?* (May 2014), Kluwer Arbitration Blog. http://arbitrationblog.kluwerarbitration.com/2014/05/19/is-investment-arbitration-in-latin-america-in-crisis/?_ga=2.84062364.485979495.1577876454-1089739443.1577876454.

2011 revolution.[18] In addition, Egypt created high-level dispute settlement mechanisms to deal systemically with investment claims, and effectively settled a number of major investment treaty (and also commercial) claims.[19]

Other states do not always handle the pressure of investment claims and the correlative stigma in the same way, as illustrated by the examples provided in the preceding paragraph. They engage in self-reproach and get drawn into counterproductive and hurtful attitudes and cycles. This is where states begin reneging on their international arbitration commitments. These situations illustrate how stigma can overreach and go beyond the fact that the state is exposed to numerous claims, to cover what stigmatizers are perceiving, in hindsight, as the "original sin": the state having consented to start with to binding arbitration.

Stigmatizing states for being exposed to claims (or for having consented to binding arbitration to start with) is completely disconnected from the reality of how the system itself operates and what it rewards. How states react to claims is the relevant test. As FDI impact figures show, states that act prudently and wisely when faced with investment claims are rewarded, notwithstanding the fact that they are exposed to those claims.[20]

C No Correlation Exists Between States Being Exposed to Investment Arbitration and Losing FDI

It is not true that states necessarily lose foreign investments because they are exposed to investment claims. Those who create this correlation are wrong. There is no de facto association and no direct link between exposure to arbitration and loss of FDI. In practical experience, states that are exposed to investment treaty claims do not, *per se*, lose foreign investments or witness a future decline in FDI. The real test for states, and the deciding factor for how FDI is affected, is how they manage the claims. The test, from start to finish, is verified in the case of Egypt,[21] and how its management of its investment cases was the more relevant factor in encouraging FDI, notwithstanding the influx of the claims. Egypt's FDI figures speak for themselves. In a longshot view of Egypt's FDI, a sharp decline in FDI occurred in 2011 immediately following the Arab Spring, and it is reasonable to assume that this relates directly to the economic and political context of the situation itself. However, starting in 2012 and onward, FDI

18. With Mauritius BIT in 2014, with Burundi in 2012 and with Switzerland in 2012.
19. "To avoid significant potential financial awards, Egypt successfully concluded 14 settlements during the period 1992-2020 (i.e. 56% of the total concluded cases)." Ahmed Bakry (Egyptian Ministry of Justice) (2020 March), "After 48 Years at ICSID (1972-2020): An Overview of the Status of Egypt in ICSID Arbitrations."
20. For example, in 2011 Egypt's FDI reached USD 0 million, in 2912 it reached USD 2,798 million and in 2016 it reached USD 8,107 million. Retrieved from the official website of the World Bank IBRD IDA. https://data.worldbank.org/indicator/BX.KLT.DINV.CD.WD?locations=EG.
21. *See supra* section VI.A.

figures consistently increased, more or less matching pre-Arab Spring figures as of 2014.[22]

D Stigma Against States Conflates State Responsibility and State Fault

Another reason stigma fails is because those who blame states for being exposed to investment claims confuse state responsibility and state fault. This is a critical misunderstanding of international law. Government conduct and state responsibility are two separate things.[23] Stigma is also blind: stigmatic mindsets involve simplistic judgments where right and wrong are assigned too lightly and in a reductionist fashion, without regard to circumstances or context, and without accounting for the complexity of global investment and the political and economic cycles that affect states.

First: In many cases, the basis for investment claims is not executive governmental conduct or regulatory acts. It could be, for example, a court decision. Egypt's privatization claims illustrate this exactly. These claims were triggered by judgments of the Council of State (Egypt's administrative courts), unwinding privatization transactions, and interestingly, the government (represented through its relevant ministries and the prime minister) was actually the one to challenge these decisions. Some of these decisions triggered investment treaty[24] and commercial claims.

Second: Similarly, the direct causes or trigger events for investment treaty claims are, not infrequently, events that cannot be attributed to a fault or misconduct by a state, for example, global economic crises and national economic or political events, such as the Arab Spring. Even when a state elects a certain course of action that potentially triggers state responsibility under an investment treaty or international law, for example, introducing regulatory changes or implementing reforms that affect certain existing rights, the state's choices should not be stigmatized as long as the state plays by the rules of the game: the BIT obligations and the arbitration procedures that may ensue.

Third: Alternatively, there are cases of perfectly lawful conduct, but conduct that opens a basis for compensation under international law, nonetheless. Cases of lawful expropriation are an example of this. Similarly, government agencies act with the belief they are right, but a tribunal may find a measure of liability notwithstanding the state's

22. "Egypt was the top destination in MENA for FDI last year: Egypt attracted USD 13.7 bn worth of foreign direct investments(FDI) in 2019, putting it atop the Middle East and North Africa region league table, according to a report from the Arab Investment and Export Credit Guarantee Corporation (Dhaman). FDI inflows to Egypt accounted for 23% of total netted by MENA countries and was up 7% from 2018. Egypt also topped the chart of average value per investment at USD 98 mn." Egypt was the top destination for FDI in MENA last year (July 2020), Enterprise. Retrieved from: https://enterprise.press/stories/2020/07/08/egypt-tops-mena-fdi-charts-in-2019-with-usd-13-7-bn-18483/.
23. "The State may engage its international liability and compensate for damage caused by its act, *regardless of the existence of a wrongful act. In more ways than one, a State's international liability constitutes proof of injurious consequences independent of a wrongful act attributable to that State*" [emphasis added]. S. Sucharitkul, *State Responsibility and International Liability under International Law*, Golden Gate University School of Law, p. 823.
24. *See, e.g., Indorama International Finance Limited v. Arab Republic of Egypt*, ICSID Case No. ARB/11/32.

good intentions. BITs typically "protect foreign investors against 'indirect,' 'de facto,' 'creeping' and 'constructive' expropriations, regardless of the state's intent."[25]

Fourth: In other cases, good faith government conduct is found, *post facto*, to fall short of the BIT standards because case law interpretation of the standards or their application had evolved *entre temps* on a specific point.

Finally, states sometimes directly assume liability vis-à-vis investors, and willingly assume the obligation to compensate them. The purpose is to make amends and indemnify investors, independently from any perception or admission of guilt. For example, in the famous steam boilers dispute,[26] the Egyptian Prime Minister issued decrees essentially providing that the Minister of Finance will make the necessary financial provisions for compensating the investor[27] Perceiving or judging such behavior in negative light is senseless and ill-conceived.

E Embracing Settlements Does Not Entail Guilt or Admission of Guilt

Stigmatizers who associate settlement with guilt or admission of guilt are wrong. In some cases, of course, the investor claims are simply wholly legitimate. In others, the investment is an ongoing concern that is important to the state economy, and therefore the investor is simply deemed to be entitled to compensation, and the state takes the decision to proceed with compensating him. But settlement proactivity is often a sign of sophisticated, unemotional, even detached reactions to investor claims. The negative perception of settlements omits that proper approaches to settlement unveil a governmental decision-making process that takes into consideration a more complex calculus that goes beyond black (the state is wrong) or white (the state is right). States often embrace settlement to limit their exposure to claims and to send positive signals to investors of investor-friendly states, thus inviting FDI growth. By showing willingness to settle, states also create a sort of "beneficial circle": good settlements bring about more good settlements and encourage investors to propose settlement themselves, without fear of negative perceptions, for example, being perceived that they have weak cases.

F Stigma Fails Because It Is Self-Defeating and Detached from the Reality of Global Arbitration and International Business

As long as there is international investment, and as long as there are investment treaties, states will always be exposed to investment claims. States will sometimes treat investors in ways they do not like or do not expect, and investors will always seek

25. K.M. Rooney, *ICSID and BIT Arbitrations and China*, Journal of International Arbitration, Volume 24 Issue 6, 2007, p. 693.
26. A. Ross *Egypt Sees Settlement of Post-revolution Claim*, Global Arbitration Review—Arbitration News, Features and Reviews, 2018, November, https://globalarbitrationreview.com/article/1176811/egypt-sees-settlement-of-post-revolution-claim.
27. Karim Abou Youssef, *Consent Ltd.: A Brief History of Egypt's Ministerial Approval Requirement for Arbitration of State Contracts and Why It Should Be Abolished*, BCDR International Arbitration Review, Volume 3 Issue 1, 2016, pp. 33-46.

remedies from real, perceived or even false prejudice to their investments. This is the reality of international life. Stigmatizers who blame states for being exposed to investment claims or blame investors for resorting to arbitration are detached from this reality. Their critique is effectively tantamount to telling investors "do not sue" and "do not exercise your BIT rights" which is pointless, and to telling states "guarantee that you avoid mistakes," which is futile, or "renege on your international arbitration commitment" which is catastrophic, and by and large impossible.

While one may have concerns about specific issues that may or may not exist in the operation of the arbitral system, what stigmatizers do is that they essentially criticize the system for being what it is. This is a damning aspect of stigma. Stigmatic arguments overreach, sometimes beyond criticizing how the system operates in specific cases to criticizing the existence of the arbitration system itself. Stigmatizing investors for bringing claims is not only irrational and a judgment disengaged from reality but also a criticism of the basic mechanisms of the system itself that enable the use of specifically afforded protections the moment they are needed. The ability to resort to arbitration is at the core of why investors rely on BITs: "A BIT without an adequate dispute resolution provision offers the investor about as much protection as a parachute without the silk: the harness and helmet give the illusion of protection, but once the skydiver in freefall pulls the ripcord to release nothing but a bundle of loose strings, a total failure of protection becomes painfully obvious."[28]

The same applies to stigmatizing foreign investors' access to local counsel. Those who propose limiting foreign investor access to local counsel are essentially endorsing a violation of the state's international law obligations under most BITs, including national treatment and potentially fair and equitable treatment.

In all cases, the question that stigmatizers would have no answer to is: why think in such punitive terms? Foreign investors are often shareholders in large local companies that contribute to the economy of the host state. The ultimate protection of the interests of the state does not involve placing undue limitations on investors' access to justice, but rather the exact opposite: allowing the system to operate fairly and be seen as operating fairly.

G Stigmatic Arguments Patronize the Arbitration System

Stigma is simplistic in that stigmatizers get easily drawn into patronizing the arbitration system. They rely on the inevitable fact that the operation of the investment arbitration system involves, at times, excesses or attempts to abuse the system. Stigmatizers use this to formulate general attacks on how the system works.

Fighting and refuting stigma does not, and should not entail, saying that the system does not contain excesses or attempts to abuse its operation. Those who advance these puritan arguments commit the same sin of the oversimplified views of complex systems that stigmatizers fall into.

28. J.O. Rodner & J.M. Estévez, *BITs in Pieces: The Effectiveness of ICSID Jurisdiction after the ICSID Convention Has Been Denounced*, Journal of International Arbitration, Volume 29 Issue 4, 2012, p. 437.

The fight against stigma should not overshadow the realities of investment and arbitral life. States sometimes commit straightforward and willful breaches of their treaty or international law obligations. Investors can have meritless claims or invest in claims. Jurisdiction is sometimes sought without basis, or the conditions for its establishment are secured through fraudulent means.

The flipside onus on us, those involved in fighting stigma, is that we should not develop the position against stigma into a general ban of any critique of the arbitration system. Fighting stigma involves the foundational realization that the system works, *notwithstanding* excesses, and the realization that the system does not need protection. The arbitration system works and has developed and continues to develop, through evolving case law, suitable mechanisms to deal with excesses. In that sense, investment tribunals are also protectors of the system against stigma. For example, investment treaty tribunals have allowed states to claim moral damages for the reputational harm they suffered as a consequence of investors bringing manifestly wrongful claims.[29]

VII STIGMA FAILS BECAUSE IT HAS NO PLACE IN THE AGE OF GLOBAL ARBITRATION

We are in the age of global arbitration. The New York Convention has more signatory states than the Genocide Convention.[30] The global BIT network encompasses more than 2,300 BITs. If we ask how stigma fits within our global arbitration system, the answer is simple: it does not. Stigmaonly aims at attacking a vital system without a clear or constructive purpose and, in fact, without any purpose at all.

Arbitration is the natural and default justice system for international business and investment. By attacking international arbitration, stigmatizers attack international rule of law, international business, and essentially, the international way of life. In the words of Gary Born, "Those who attack international arbitration attack cross-border trade and commerce and the rule of law in international life."[31] Arbitration for global business in today's world is as essential as the internet, or now social media, to daily life. We the citizens of this system cannot live without it, and none of the relevant parties would want to live without it, not states, and definitely not investors.

Stigma removes the essential and paramount notion of the democratization of arbitration. Stigma places undue limitations and emotional and psychological barriers

29. *See Europe Cement v. Turkey,* ICSID Case No. ARB(AF)/07/2, Final Award, s 128.
30. *See* the number of signatory parties to the New York Convention on the Recognition and Enforcement of Foreign Arbitral Awards is 161. *See also,* the Convention on the Prevention and Punishment of the Crime of Genocide, Approved and proposed for signature and ratification or accession by General Assembly resolution 260 A (III) of December 9, 1948, entry into force: January 12, 1951. The number of its signatory parties is 152 as of July 2019.
31. A. Ross (2018), *Born takes "Game of Thrones" Message to Freshfields,* GAR Arbitration Review.

> Gary Born has developed his famous "Winter is coming" message inspired by the hit Game of Thrones TV series in the latest Freshfields lecture—arguing that those who attack international arbitration attack cross-border trade and commerce and the rule of law in international life.

on what should be unfettered access to a global system. As such, stigma is a limitation on the true global nature of arbitration and threatens to bring down the entire system. The practical danger of stigma lies in that it can have the effect of deterring different players from the investment treaty system. It dilutes the reciprocal value the investment treaty regime affords all parties involved—the quid pro quo of investment treaty arbitration. Stigma paints a picture of a punitive system, when in fact the system is one that rewards those who play by the rules, and use the very tools afforded to them by the system itself. What is in it for states that consent to investment treaty protection by signing BITs, and go willingly through the process of arbitration if they end up being stigmatized for accepting to play by the rules? What is in it for investors who only accept to invest in the host state because it affords them effective investment protection through arbitration rights if they are stigmatized and reprimanded for using this protection when needed?[32]

VIII STIGMA VERSUS CONSENT: CONSENT AS THE ULTIMATE LIGHTSABER

International arbitration is a system founded on the consent of those who participate, and the global wave of consent to arbitration is what enables arbitration to be a truly global justice. The ultimate weakness of stigma is that it goes against and is inconsistent with the foundation of the system of international arbitration: consent. Stigmatizing players for using the system is diametrically opposed to the very notion of consenting to the system.

This makes it that consent is the ultimate lightsaber for fighting against the dark side of the force that is stigma. Understanding the deep ramifications of consent in investment treaty arbitration is the ultimate tool, conceptually and practically, for fighting stigma. Given that the inevitability of disputes is the very foundation of investment treaty arbitration to begin with, those who are part of the system, and have consented to it are estopped from stigmatizing states for having claims brought against them, or from stigmatizing investors for using the rights afforded to them. As a consenter to the system, one cannot stigmatize other players for using the tools you consented to give them. Stigma, therefore, causes an irreconcilable collision of forces: the light side of the force, consent, collides with the dark side of the force, stigma.

IX THE COLLECTIVE RESPONSIBILITY OF THE CITIZENS OF THE GLOBAL ARBITRATION COMMUNITY TO FIGHT IN THE WAR AGAINST STIGMA

It is essential that we be clearly and manifestly aware that stigma, in all its forms, has no place in international arbitration. We must see the danger it poses to the system.

32. In the same mindset, if local counsel are discouraged and foreign investors are deprived from the services of local counsel of the host state, rights of defense will be demeaned and investors will not be able to defend themselves on grounds of local law or national treatment.

This is the lens through which stigma must be seen. Stigma negates the system and what it stands for. Stigmatizers are spread across the galaxy of international arbitration, and they hurt the system. Our collective responsibility—like all those who hold the swords and lightsabers of arbitration—is to defeat them and fight off serious threats to the system as hard and as best as we can. The global arbitration system is composed of key players: states, investors, counsel, international law firms, regulators, arbitral judges, arbitral institutions, arbitral influencers and policy makers and trendsetters. These are the *Jedi* of international arbitration.

For stigma to be effectively fought, for it to become obsolete, it is necessary to recognize that the fight is a *collective* effort, and that fighting stigma is a continuous and ongoing battle. Stigma is not a villain that can be defeated once and for all.

Our responsibility, as protectors of the system, is that we rise to fight stigmatizers every day, that we do not get drawn into perpetrating stigma ourselves, and that we avoid the dangerous exercise of self-reproach and the infliction of stigma on ourselves. We must fight excesses and misuse of the system and not take part in them ourselves. Finally, our responsibility, above all, is to believe in the arbitration system and have the deep conviction that it works. "We must keep our faith in the Republic. The day we stop believing democracy can work is the day we lose it."—Queen Jamillia, *Star Wars: Episode II—Attack of the Clones* (2002).

www.ingramcontent.com/pod-product-compliance
Lightning Source LLC
Chambersburg PA
CBHW071235230926
51849CB00001B/112
9789403523804